Gold

Gold

How it Shaped History

Alan Ereira

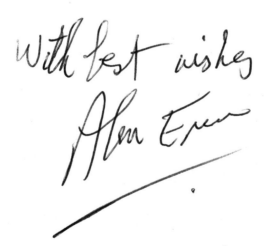

With best wishes
Alan Erer

PEN & SWORD
HISTORY

First published in Great Britain in 2024 by
Pen & Sword History
An imprint of Pen & Sword Books Limited
Yorkshire – Philadelphia

ISBN 978 1 03611 533 3

A CIP catalogue record for this book is
available from the British Library

Typeset by Mac Style
Printed in the UK by CPI Group (UK) Ltd, Croydon, CR0 4YY.

Pen & Sword Books Limited incorporates the imprints of After
the Battle, Atlas, Archaeology, Aviation, Discovery, Family History,
Fiction, History, Maritime, Military, Military Classics, Politics,
Select, Transport, True Crime, Air World, Frontline Publishing, Leo
Cooper, Remember When, Seaforth Publishing, The Praetorian Press,
Wharncliffe Local History, Wharncliffe Transport, Wharncliffe True
Crime and White Owl.

For a complete list of Pen & Sword titles please contact

PEN & SWORD BOOKS LIMITED
47 Church Street, Barnsley, South Yorkshire, S70 2AS, England
E-mail: enquiries@pen-and-sword.co.uk
Website: www.pen-and-sword.co.uk
or
PEN AND SWORD BOOKS
1950 Lawrence Rd, Havertown, PA 19083, USA
E-mail: uspen-and-sword@casematepublishers.com
Website: www.penandswordbooks.com

Contents

Plates

Maps

Acknowledgements

Trying to research and write this book, tracing a story that began nearly 7,000 years ago and involved almost every inhabited part of the world, is obviously an enterprise in inadequacy. To attempt it to even the limited degree I could, required the help, support and forbearance of a great number of people. The process has taken seven years, and I have imposed on a great number of very well informed authorities and wise critics, and on everyone who I thought might be able to give me guidance.

I am deeply in debt to my old friend and agent David Godwin, whose steadfast support and commitment have been fundamental to the book's creation. I also owe a huge debt to Rachel Kerr, who helped me edit my original text, and Professor Felipe Fernández-Armesto, who with great generosity read very carefully through everything, advising and correcting wherever his astonishing sweep of knowledge led him to think I needed support, redirection or a timely slap. I am extremely lucky to have such a friend. I should say that I know he will not agree with everything that is here, and of course I also take full responsibility for any errors. I have always maintained that a writer of history cannot lay claim to truth, only to truthfulness, but I also know that even truthfulness may be an unachievable ambition.

Other people who have devoted time and effort to helping me understand include Dr Joris van den Tol, Professor Nuno Palma, Professor Vassil Nikolov, Karmen Boyadziev, Vladimir Slavchev and Pravu Mazumdar. I am also very grateful to the patience and delightful company of Paul Craddock, who accompanied Sarah and myself on an astonishing journey through Mali, and took the time to explain his profound knowledge of early goldwork and try to correct my misunderstandings.

I mention my wife Sarah, who has uncomplainingly endured this long obsession, sustained me through it and ultimately created a truly marvellous index.

I would also like to thank the University of Wales, Trinity St David, for its support, and Professor Luci Attala for her thoughtful reading.

Without the driving force of the spiritual leaders of the Kogi people of Colombia I would never have embarked on this journey. They want me to understand and report the dangers of plundering the Earth, and in particular of stripping out its gold, which they perceive as fundamental to the life processes of the planet. We have no science to explain this, but we do have the capacity to connect actions and the events that follow, and see that the correlations are clear and their warnings have been prophetic. That may allow us to see the dangers of trying to harness and profit from the 'value' of gold.

Picture Credits
  1, 3, 12. Alan Ereira
  2. Yelkrokoyade via Wikimedia Commons
  4. www.sumerianshakespeare.com
  5, 8, 10. CNG Coins
  7, 13, 20, 21. Sarah Ereira
  9. Adobe Stock
  11. British Library, Cotton Vespasian A I. f 30v, 31r
  15. NASA
  18. Kunsthistorisches Museum, Wien via Wikimedia Commons
  22. Collection of Inner Mongolia Museum, Hohhot (China).

Preface

The Kogi of north Colombia, whose ancestors shaped the gold that Columbus hungered for, insist that we do not understand it. The little they have left has been carefully guarded. Infinitely malleable and ductile, shining like the sun and undimmed by time, they see it as essential to fertility. It is in the world but not of the world, so does not change or decay.

In 1990, still living hidden from modernity, they asked me to help them send a warning that by seizing and monetizing everything we are destroying all life. 'You need our help. We know what you have done. You have sold the clouds.' Part of their warning concerned gold, where they insist our plunder is more dangerous than we know. 'So from today stop digging into the earth and stealing the gold. If you go on the world will end. You are bringing the world to an end.' I had no idea why anyone should think that. But they asserted that it is the essence of life, comparing gold mining with extracting vitamins from a living body.

That was how they planted the seed of this book. I listened and studied. I learned that, in almost all societies, gold has been associated with life, fecundity, and some kind of value that transcends mortality.

In Central and South America, cities and empires developed without needing currency, though they understood gold as vital to their survival. Once Europeans imposed mastery those economies were destroyed. The very basis of their understanding was undermined and largely lost, and the place of gold was fundamentally altered. That process has dramatically accelerated since the Kogi issued their warning. By 1990 humans had used gold for 7,000 years and taken 100,000 tons. Just 35 years later we have torn twice as much from the ground.

We can see that we are now living through a mass extinction. Is this continuing plunder causing the changes afflicting all life on earth? At the same time, the nature of money has been transformed. It was fundamentally physical stuff, made from or representing bullion. Over the last few decades money has been increasingly regarded as an abstract set of numbers without concrete form. But the demand for gold has not diminished. It has grown vastly. This book is an attempt to trace what we have done with it, and what it has done with us.

It is true that we have sold the clouds for gold. What is its value? Can we stop? And what happens if we can't?

Introduction

Ours is the second civilization that shaped itself around the use of gold. The original gold users appeared around 7,500 years ago, dominating a small area on the west coast of the Black Sea. Their burial goods show that their power and presence reached out over great distances, but after about 500 years they vanished completely.

At one settlement, the inhabitants were destroyed in a mass slaughter. That is where archaeologists have identified what is called the 'skeleton horizon'. Those settlements that were not physically destroyed were all abandoned. Throughout the region, no trace survived of the people who had worked and used gold. Their culture and technology had been very different from any other. We know they had felt threatened because they surrounded their settlements with huge defensive walls. The evidence of methodical slaughter and incineration suggests that their removal was in some cases undertaken with righteous ferocity.

We can only speculate, but it is striking that the land here was not reused for a thousand years, and nor was gold. If the idea was to destroy its memory, that succeeded. The burials lay untouched for the next four-and-a-half millennia as though they were cursed.

The story of gold stopped here. It seems to have restarted 2,000km further south. Although a single strand of twisted gold from the Varna period has been found at Ur, in modern Iraq, and a few gold beads have been found from around 100 years later in other sites in Mesopotamia,[1] there is no evidence of its abundant use in the next thousand years. Then it started over again in a world which had no memory of the elaborate gold-work of Varna. Ancient stories were eventually turned into written tales of the beginning of trade, of cities, of kingship. But none recall what lay on the other side of the skeleton horizon, or its existence. Having found its way back, this undying, imperishable zombie substance would spend the rest of history being buried and re-emerging, and shaping the lives of the people who wanted it, without anyone knowing that it had once gone horribly wrong.

Ever since its discovery, gold has been associated with deathless and frightening power. It has been treated as immortal authority made visible. For that reason, sacred texts have been inscribed in gold or on it, and rulers have been encased in golden crowns, robes and sarcophagi. Its role linking earthly and heavenly authority was so fundamental that it is impossible to say which was invented first. Gold became the most precious gift handed out by sovereigns, acting as agents of the gods whose power they represented. That was how coins appeared. Four thousand years ago, Hammurabi, the ruler of Babylon, held a ceremony where he rewarded foreign soldiers with discs of gold. Two records of this extraordinary event have survived.[2] They mark the moment when gold became a deep force at the heart of our history. As soon as rulers needed gold to pay warriors, its availability became a driving force that controlled their own fates. Seizing it, finding it, spending it, losing it – these have been the often-unremarked and uncomprehended events that determined even the rise and fall of empires, including our own apparent rush to disaster. Tales of heroes and villains, of mighty battles, great discoveries and brilliant insights were, at a deeper level, inescapably shaped by the power of gold. Now, its role is being magnified.

Accumulating gold for 6,000 years, by the start of the First World War, humanity collected about 40,000 tons of it. But over the last thirty years, we have clawed out three times that quantity. In just the last ten, we have added as much gold as all the world possessed in 1914. Each year, a quarter of a trillion dollars' worth of the world's resources are spent on around 4,000 tons of gold.

The modern gold rush is created less by deliberate cunning than by a kind of osmosis, a huge unplanned flow which is barely reported. Its sheer scale, over $20 billion every month, means that the crisis of economics, politics and the environment which now grips the world is directly linked to this unprecedented conversion of other forms of wealth to gold. This is hard to explain in rational terms. There is something ancient and visceral happening, connected to the old magical power that makes us believe that gold is an unchanging store of value. As you cannot eat it, warm yourself with it, grow anything from it or wrap yourself in it, you might describe it as inherently worthless. Nations have no actual use for it, except as 'security' against the day when everything else loses its value. Possessing it is an act of faith, not of reason. A lump of gold has no more inherent value than a bitcoin or a painting – it is simply worth what someone will give for it, which is not fixed in any way. Its value is subjective, a dreamed bulwark against collapse. The size of a nation's gold reserve measures the darkness of its nightmares.

The production of this gold is an environmental horror story. The money spent buying it comes from accelerating the burning of fossil fuels, and the crime and corruption surrounding it destabilizes the rule of law on a global scale. Why is this happening? And why is it virtually unseen and unreported?

At first it, was a story set in Eurasia, but for the last six centuries, gold drove the desperate and ever-growing European-initiated plunder of the world for the illusion of wealth. That has now brought the entire planet to the brink of climate catastrophe.[3] To be able to talk about what has happened, and to stand any chance of taking control of our own destinies, we need a map of the past that traces the long flow of these largely unnoticed rivers of gold through the arteries of our societies; a re-envisioning of history, to avoid the next skeleton horizon.

That, and saving the world, defines the modest ambition of this work.

*   *   *

It took me a long time to realize that gold is important. I knew, of course – as we all do – that it is a precious measure of value, an indication of status and a way of saying 'the best' – gold stars, gold medals, golden age. I knew that, until fifty years ago, the 'gold standard' was the basis of money. But I did not think it was important, as things that keep us alive are important. All the gold in the world would make a cube of 22 metres.[4] Would it really matter if the whole lot vanished?

Then I met the Kogi.

It was 1988 and I was making a TV series about the Spanish Armada. Gold played a role in the story. Philip II of Spain was totally dependent on the gold and silver brought to Seville from his American colonies every year, and he decided that it was more practical to take over England than defend a fragile global network of ports and sea lanes from English 'pirates'. To illustrate the fabulous material that had made Spain rich, I went to the Gold Museum in Bogotá. It held 55,000 pieces of pre-Columbian gold work. Owned and run by the national bank, the heart of the museum was a time-locked bank vault. It was the most popular tourist attraction in the country, where indigenous and commercial understandings of gold collided.

Visitors waited for the vault to open at its scheduled time. Then the great wheel on the 2ft-thick steel door turned and we stepped into the dark interior. We were locked in. Slowly, the lights came up, revealing a huge display of gold objects – necklaces, bracelets, crowns, masks and strange images of people that are not people, animals that are not animals. Bogotá was, at that time, one of the most dangerous cities in the world. Its government was locked in battle with Marxist guerrilla armies and well-armed international drug cartels. This chamber felt extremely safe, but also extremely dangerous.

The gold was displayed as treasure, fabulous riches, with incomprehensible objects made and worn by the people who inhabited Colombia before Columbus. It invited awe because it was wealth, the wealth that had drawn conquistadores to America and which was plundered and sent in shiploads to Spain. The objects on display had been looted more recently by tomb robbers operating on an almost industrial scale. The bank had bought them from the robbers, most of them being acquired from a robber named Jose Cano.[5]

The finest objects in that vault were made by the Tairona people of northern Colombia. They have a baroque richness, a fullness of form and a fabulous delicacy of design and execution. Mysterious, sometimes intimidating, they were obviously products of a very sophisticated culture. Their meaning was not even hinted at. However, the BBC had asked me to visit that area to look at a recently discovered archaeological site being called 'the lost city' of the Tairona.

Their descendants, the Kogi, had been hiding from Cano's predecessors and the Spanish invasion for 400 years. I was not investigating their ancestral gold (I assumed that was long gone), but they still lived in similar cities and I wanted to see how these functioned. The Kogi were isolated and deeply suspicious. They had no roads, no wheel, no writing. Their home is the world's highest coastal mountain, an isolated, glaciated natural pyramid rising nearly 6km above the Caribbean. The secretive indigenous inhabitants consider it 'the heart of the world' and say it must be protected. They did not let me in for a year. When I was allowed in, it was a wide-eyed journey into another world. I had no knowledge of mountains, jungles or anthropology. One of the very few Kogi who spoke Spanish accompanied me up the mountain, and after dark led me into a large circular thatched space where some seventy white-robed, bare-footed men sat around four fires. His voice came from across the floor: 'You have come to speak to us. So, speak.' Judgement day!

I said that I had a machine which was an eye that remembers and an ear that remembers, so they could be seen and heard around the world. They rapidly grasped that they could make use of television and interrogated me about its truthfulness and the authenticity of an encounter with an image. I had never before felt so humbled. Their *raison d'être* is to maintain the balance of nature, but the scale of industrial damage was now global, and they had already decided to break cover to issue a stark warning of incipient environmental collapse.

The next year, they created a compelling film which demonstrated their continuity with their ancestors, their guardianship of detailed ecological knowledge and their clarity about the catastrophic damage done by deforestation and fossil fuel extraction. The impact was powerful and memorable. The BBC broadcast this ninety-minute statement from a lost civilization at 10.20 pm on its main channel, and the audience rose steadily as it went on, peaking just before midnight. It was quickly repeated.[6]

Viewers already knew something of the looming risks of deforestation and carbon emissions. I believed the Kogi were pushing on a wheel that had already started to turn. But they also spoke urgently and passionately about the need to stop plundering gold. What was that about? Gold, they said, is the menstrual blood of the Mother. It is, in some sense, fertility. I had no idea what they meant and worried that much of the audience would be unsympathetic. Why did they say that taking gold out of the Earth would produce new diseases for which there would be no cure? I could not understand, and they were unclear. What difference does it really make if we dig up gold? Consequently, I did not make much of that in the film, concentrating on the message that told me what I already understood. Over the following years, as we stayed in distant contact, they kept trying to get me to understand. Clearly, all those gold objects in the Bogotá museum had dangerous meaning, but I had no idea what.

It kept nagging at me. Over the decades that followed, encounters with indigenous and historical traditions around the world made me realize that the Kogis' certainty that gold is fundamental to life is not some local eccentricity. Cultures in Europe, Asia and Africa have also grown up with the certainty that gold is, in some sense, a sacred material that carries power and demands a respect accorded to no other substance. That, I eventually realized, is why gold became money, the fundamental store of our belief in value.

The Kogis' warning in 1990 about digging up gold was certainly prescient. Gold is not abundant – every 4,000 tons of the Earth's crust contains a single gram – but it is widespread, mined commercially in forty-three countries on every continent except, for the time being, Antarctica. And there is more available every year, so its high price is not a result of scarcity. Nor, outside electronics, is there any great need for it. 93 per cent of it is used for jewellery, glowing with the strange lustre of cold sunshine, or taken into darkness by governments and investors against the day when their money may lose its value.[7] As soft as chewing gum, useless for tools and weapons, impervious to time, it is perceived as solidified wealth.

Gold has shaped and underpinned civilization. The Kogi were trying to convey the importance of the objects I had seen in the gold museum, and I should have been less obtuse. Hard-headed people would not invest so much in it if they did not believe in its unique importance. Hoarding gold is an expensive business, because it earns no interest and has to be kept somewhere safe. But it is thought of as indestructible value, while currencies and investments can be destroyed. In November 1923, it took 300 billion German marks to buy an ounce of gold. It can get worse: in Yugoslavia, in the fifteen months from October 1993, the value of money fell by five quadrillion per cent. That means a number with fifteen zeros. Any currency, including the one you are using today, can become utterly worthless very fast. In Hungary in 1946, the value of savings halved every fifteen hours. Nothing like that has ever happened to gold. Gold mines only close when they run out; nobody closed one because it had too much.[8] Every ounce that appears has a buyer. Its price fluctuates, but the certain knowledge that gold has intrinsic value seems to be beyond question.

A hundred years ago, the economist John Maynard Keynes called that belief our barbarous superstition.[9] Ever since it was first discovered, around 7,000 years ago, gold has been widely understood to be utterly different from anything else on Earth – in fact, unearthly. Because it is indestructible, gold that has disappeared from prehistoric tombs and ancient plunder is still with us, refashioned untraceably into our wedding rings and gold decorations. It bears no link to its past and is not altered by beating, stretching, heating or being swallowed. Ancient peoples did not doubt its connection to eternity. It is not subject to earthly cycles of growth, change, imperfection, decay. It is in the living world, but not of it. Unborn, undying, soft but unchanging, pliant but incorruptible, it seems to sustain a connection between what is material and what is transcendent. That understanding was shared by much of humanity for millennia and gave gold power over people.

The Tairona were, of course, by no means the first to be convinced of its other-worldly qualities. That is obvious from the earliest stories about it. Around the Black Sea, people spoke of a Golden Fleece, from which came the constellation of the Ram and the birth of spring. Asian sages taught of the Brahmanda, the Sanskrit Golden Egg, from which emerged Heaven and Earth. The Temple of the Sun at the heart of the Inca Empire was the golden pivot between Earth and Heaven, where the Inca sat on a gold bench at the solstice and focussed the sun's rays to light a sacrifice fire; and in Africa, the Yoruba told European invaders of the gold chain that allowed the creator Obatala to descend from Heaven. All of these tales are, like gold itself, undatable, and all connect gold, fertility and the journey between earth and sky. They were not, so far as we know, derived from some common prehistoric root. They must be similar because they were responses summoned from human voices by the gold.

Modern science also believes that gold is literally other-worldly. Its presence is truly mysterious. Since it is almost twice as heavy as lead, all the gold that was in our young planet when it was soft and forming sank to the centre. It is now inaccessible, some 3,000km underground. The gold that we have gathered up must have come much later, after the planet solidified. It arrived from somewhere else.

There is a scientific consensus that even the gold at the centre of the Earth came from elsewhere. The process that formed the solar system did not have the power to make such a heavy element. The atoms of most other elements in the Earth were born in ferocious nuclear reactions that developed in stars, accelerating protons and neutrons to hundreds of millions of degrees. The heaviest and most plentiful of these elements is iron, which contains between fifty-six and fifty-eight protons and neutrons. But the giant nucleus of a gold atom requires 197 protons and neutrons to be forced together, and that needs a far more powerful process which could only happen much further away.

Science said that gold comes from the death of a star. At the end of its life, a certain type of star, one which is perhaps ten to twenty times as massive as the sun, explodes as a supernova. But the theory that this is where gold is made has been upset by examining the brightest supernova ever seen (BOAT – 'brightest of all time'), which was shown in 2024 to have apparently not made any heavy metals at all. At the moment, that just leaves a theory that is even more fantastic.

A supernova ends with the creation of an incredibly dense neutron star, the protons and neutrons of its atoms crushed together into a sphere about 10km in diameter. This city-sized ball has about the same mass as the sun. In 2013, astronomers saw a brief and inconceivably bright flash from another galaxy. They believe it was a collision between two neutron stars. A similar event was seen in 2017. We are told these super-dense balls accelerated towards each other at almost the speed of light and crashed in an inferno so prodigious that we have no way to imagine or describe it.[10] In two seconds, the total disruption of this immense mass of neutrons would have released as much energy as all the hundred billion stars in the Milky Way produce in a year. It is called a kilonova. The scale of the explosive violence is galactic. According to Caltech (the California Institute of Technology), the 2017 event, 'the greatest fireworks show in the Universe', produced gold, along with platinum and other heavy metals, equivalent to ten thousand times the mass of the Earth.[11] Gold, according to science, is the product of an inconceivable apocalypse.

That supposed event was, fortunately, 130 million light years away in another galaxy, so none of it will land here any time soon. It seems our gold came from other, much earlier kilonovae. But that does not explain how we have access to it. We find gold close to the surface. It is very evenly distributed in the Earth's crust.[12] Until people began collecting it, nuggets were just lying around. Most of them were gathered long ago, but the aboriginal inhabitants of Australia were not much interested in gold so in the 1850s it was still there for children to pick up, and they did.[13] In 1869, a nugget weighing 72kg was discovered just 5cm below the surface in Dunolly, Victoria, Australia. It is the weight of an adult.

The world seems to have been gifted with gold and other heavy elements when it was about half a billion years old, in a bombardment that left its mark in the craters of the moon. The theory was developed largely on the basis of samples taken from the moon in the 1970s, and is debatable in detail but seems likely in principle.[14]

The current best theory is that gold produced by kilonovae sprayed out across the universe. In the words of one leading researcher, 'most of the precious metals on which our economies and many key industrial processes are based have been added to our planet by lucky coincidence when the Earth was hit by about twenty billion billion tonnes of asteroidal material'.[15] So we seem to have won a cosmic lottery. The universe is incomprehensibly vast, the Earth is vanishingly tiny, and the odds against our planet being in the right place at the right time are so inconceivable that it has only happened once in the lifetime of the solar system. Our prize is thought to have arrived about 3.9 billion years ago when the planet was around 600 million years old. Its delivery is called the 'late heavy bombardment'.[16] So the scientific story is of crushed, cremated extra-terrestrial solar systems which perished billions of years ago, whose scattered shining dust fell from the firmament just when the Earth's surface had solidified and water had appeared on it.[17] That, give or take a few million years, seems also to be when life first appeared.[18] It is believed these phenomena may be connected, perhaps through the shock of the impacts, perhaps through the presence of new heavy metals.[19] It may indeed, as the Kogi story insists, have something to do with planetary fertility.

Even if you accept all that, it leaves more oddities unexplained. Gold was not the only heavy metal to arrive from outer space. The delivery also punched cobalt, nickel, copper, zinc, arsenic, tungsten, lead and mercury into the Earth's crust, which is about 35km thick. There was much less gold than any other heavy element in this bombardment – there is 20,000 times as much copper in the Earth's crust, 40,000 times more lead and over 300,000 times more nickel. This must be the residue of the largest meteors, which did not burn up as they fell through the atmosphere. Much of it, along with solid gold, was buried in the crust by the impact, then some of this heavy stuff was gradually lifted to the surface by slow flows in the rock. For example, tungsten, which has an almost identical density to gold, is generally found along the collision lines of tectonic plates, where one plate is being pushed up over another.[20] These heavy metals were brought up by convection in particular locations. But gold has an additional story, which is why it is much more evenly distributed. The gold from meteors that burned in the atmosphere drifted down as a molecular dust. Twenty million tons remain in the oceans (one gram in every hundred million tons of sea water). Much of the rest has been on the surface or has risen up inside the crust with magma, the molten rock of volcanoes. And then it was gathered up by the newly appearing 'extremophiles', bacteria which made the emergence of more complex life possible by cleansing toxic heavy metals from the environment. A by-product of this process just happens to be the bacterial construction of gold nuggets.[21]

All this sounds so bizarre that it is hard to believe, but the process was publicly demonstrated in 2012 in an art installation by Kazem Kashefi and Adam W.

Brown at Michigan State University, *The Great Work of the Metal Lover*. The title was a refence to the Magnum Opus Metallidurans, the alchemical process that was supposed to produce the Philosopher's Stone, and the installation allowed a live audience to watch 24 carat gold nano-nuggets being assembled by extremophile bacteria from a solution of gold chloride.[22]

Over the whole planet, in the ocean or inside sedimentary rock, molecular gold dust has been taken into solution by hot water[23] and gathered into rich veins waiting to be discovered, signalling its presence by releasing gold flakes into rivers.[24] If gold was buried like tungsten, we would probably never have found it. But gold presented itself.

And when, eventually, we began to take hold of it, it took hold of us.

Its desirability is somehow self-evident. Two-and-a-half thousand years ago, Herodotus reported that Europe's gold was said to come from far to the north, where it was guarded by fierce griffons, winged sphinx-like beasts with the bodies of lions and the heads of eagles. Desperate men in perpetual war with them snatched it from under their beaks.[25] He did not believe, as his source claimed, that the thieves were a race of one-eyed men. But he saw no reason to question the existence of gold-hungry griffons, or to ask why they valued this treasure. Persia's gold, he understood, had a different source, far to the east. It too was looted from beasts that valued it dearly, in this case giant killer ants that excavated it in the burning desert of India. Their hoards were seized by a particularly warlike tribe who tried to escape with their booty on racing camels.[26] In both accounts, gold is worth so much to man and beast as to be worth dying for. Herodotus lived over a thousand years after Hammurabi gave gold rewards to soldiers, and its value to humans, divinities and sentient creatures was beyond question.

The pursuit of gold is central to the oldest written stories we know, and those stories speak of its link to divinity. They date from a thousand years before Hammurabi. The epic of Gilgamesh, which survives inscribed on clay tablets from Sumer, was put together around 1800 BCE using materials written about 300 years earlier. It tells the adventures of the king of what became known as the world's first city, Uruk, a name that appears to survive now as Iraq. Gilgamesh lived somewhere between 2700 and 2500 BCE. In the tale, he is on a quest for cedar wood to construct a shrine, but when the goddess of love and war, Ishtar, wanted to seduce him, she did not offer him timber. A goddess's gift is gold. 'All that you touch will turn to gold,' Ishtar told him.[27] He turned it down, but gold was the most desirable stuff in the world, and two millennia later, the Greek king Midas was said to accept it from Dionysus. Of course, gold satisfies neither hunger nor thirst, and the embrace that, in Nathaniel Hawthorne's telling,[28] turned Midas's child into a lump of wealth is a catastrophic horror. Midas's touch, the universal monetizer, would have destroyed the world if it had not been stopped, either by Midas perishing (in Aristotle's version) or by Dionysus lifting the curse (in that of Ovid).[29]

At least, that was how it worked in the story. We know it well, but it is a very, very old story, one still being played out. We are just not sure that it really will end well.

Perhaps the oldest writing that speaks of gold and the hunger to obtain it is about an even earlier king of Uruk than Gilgamesh. A cuneiform clay tablet survives from about 2300 BCE telling of Enmerkar and the Lord of Aratta. Enmerkar was the mythic founder of Uruk around 2750 BCE. Aratta was a kingdom some 5,000km to the east in southern Afghanistan, near Kandahar. Gold's importance was understood to predate its commercial significance: the text begins by saying that the time of Enmerkar was 'before commerce was practised; before gold, silver, copper, tin, blocks of lapis lazuli, and mountain stones were brought down together from their mountains'.[30] Like Gilgamesh, Enmerkar wanted to source materials for a shrine, but he was not looking for cedar wood. Gold was pre-eminent. The journey of at least 2,500km went right across modern Iran and was almost inconceivably difficult, but the need was so strong that luxury goods really were brought to Sumer from Afghanistan. The text says: 'The lord of Aratta placed on his head the golden crown for Inanna.' Inanna is the goddess to whom a king was ritually wedded. A gold crown turned a human into the likeness of 'a purified shrine'. Modern coronation rituals echo that. Gold retained its lustre for the near-5,000 years that followed. Before the First World War, pretty well every country in the world apart from China was on the gold standard, using gold coins as their currency. It was the official measure of our values and the foundation of our finances until it was formally renounced by the US Treasury in 1971.

That was the year of the first microprocessor, whose circuits depend on gold contacts. If gold had disappeared from the world at the end of 1970, we would have continued our lives and might have thought that nothing significant had changed. When I started writing this book, there was no longer any currency whose value was fixed in gold. Switzerland was the last country to walk away from that, in 2000. The Bank of England will no longer exchange a £20 note for twenty sovereigns, and the Federal Reserve no longer swaps its bills for gold dollars. But belief in gold's value has not faltered; everywhere, wealth is proclaimed through gold. That is why visitors to the Federal Reserve Bank in New York are just shown one thing – a vault containing what may be more gold than any other place on earth. The Bank of England is more hands-on. Once visitors are past the doorkeepers, who wear pink tailcoats and top hats with gold hatbands, they are challenged to learn about money by lifting a gold bar about the size of a brick with one hand. It weighs more than six house-bricks and would buy half a million of them. The official line may be that gold does not matter in the modern world, but a gold bar will remain impressive and unchanged when its custodians have been long forgotten. These upstart banks did not make gold; gold made them, and they know it.

If gold disappeared from the world today, we would be much more conscious of the catastrophe. Our cities, transport, communications and sustenance would stop dead, and even our knowledge and memories would be annihilated. The old superstition is very far from dead: in July 2022, Zimbabwe, with 200 per cent inflation, decided to issue gold coins as a secure store of value for the wealthy.

The question at the heart of this book is not 'what have we done with gold?', but 'what has gold done with us?'. And what is it doing now?

Part I

The Gods Speak

Chapter 1

Golden Power: The First King

The Shock of the Old

Since gold does not decay, the evidence of how and why it started to be used should be plentiful. For millennia, some people felt obliged to bury gold with the illustrious dead. That would have made it straightforward for archaeologists to learn about if there had not been so many tomb robbers in the meantime. What the Lord (or priest) giveth, the thief taketh away. The early history of gold has had to be told on the frail basis of memory retained as myth rather than physical objects. In the twentieth century, a new breed of European professional archaeologists looked hardest for material evidence where their governments competed for empire. In 1922, Howard Carter discovered the tomb of Tutankhamun in Egypt, newly independent from Britain, while Leonard Woolley began excavating a great cemetery at Ur in the British Mandate territory of Iraq. Their discoveries revealed some of the oldest gold known at the time, but they were clearly by no means the start of the story. Tutankhamun was the earliest Egyptian king to be found with gold (and there was masses of it), but there had been over sixty-five Egyptian kings buried before him, with no trace left of their gold. The oldest Egyptian mummy wrapped in gold, a thousand years before Tutankhamun, was revealed in 2023 but is no older than the 'Royal' burials at Ur.[1] It is quite clear that gold work was already highly developed and very extensive by this time. But whatever had been made earlier had completely vanished.

So it was astonishing when, in 1972, a cemetery containing many burials of finely worked gold 2,000 years older than the discoveries at Ur was accidentally uncovered on the shores of the Black Sea. These unsuspected burials were brought to light when a young digger driver in Bulgaria's holiday resort of Varna spotted a shining yellow rectangle about 4 inches long in his trench. Raycho Marinov climbed down and found a number of yellow bracelets. He got them home and wondered what to do. Thinking they were antique copper or brass, he put them in a shoebox which he showed to his old teacher, who called the Varna museum.

Archaeologists gasped and took over the trench. They found gold from over a thousand years before people were believed to have worked any metal. The

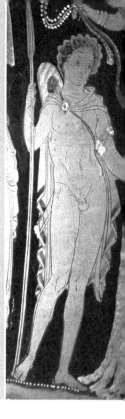

FLINT
SWORD

OBSIDIAN
BLADE

JADEITE
AXE HEAD

VARNA
·

Black Sea

MURSALEVO
·

YUNATSITE
·

COLCHIS

Varna.

population of the entire world in the mid-fifth millennium BCE was probably no larger than modern Tokyo and consisted mostly of scattered hunter-gatherers. Yet here there was an organized formal cemetery which contained the grave of a man from around 4,400 BCE bedecked with some 2kg of elaborately worked gold. This was a more advanced and complex society than seemed possible. The body had been carefully laid out as a performance of ceremonial authority, masculinity and military power, all manifested in his gold accoutrements, arranged to construct a new composite being of unique dominance.[2] He lay full length on his back. Both arms had gold arm-rings and his hands lay across his chest. He was buried in a gold diadem and gold-studded robes, holding a sceptre (a beautifully made stone axe-head on a gold-wrapped shaft) in his right hand.[3] He was well equipped with ceremonial weapons: a bow and quiver with gold fittings, a gold-wrapped copper spear, copper and flint points and an extraordinary flint blade, a sharp stone sword 45cm long. None of this made any sense. His regalia appeared as the central feature of a new status which no archaeologist thought yet existed. Staring up from a pit, after some six-and-a-half thousand years, was the Lord of Varna.

His burial was surrounded by hundreds of others, the oldest dating back to 4,600 BCE, and there were about 3,000 pieces of buried gold expertly crafted with a total weight of around 6kg, much of it in pits without bodies.[4] He alone was buried with a significant quantity of gold – one-third of all the gold in the cemetery. Fifteen hundred years before the semi-mythical Gilgamesh, a thousand years before the start of Egypt's First Dynasty of Kings, the Lord of Varna was buried in his golden pomp. In the egalitarian spirit of the local Communist bureaucracy, he was identified simply as the occupant of Grave 43.

Here was the beginning of humanity's relationship to gold. But why had there been no plunder here? And why did this culture leave no memory, no heritage? Why had they wanted gold at all, devoting a huge effort to finding a new substance, making completely new kinds of objects and then burying them? And then they simply vanished.

Some 250 years after starting to bury their dead with gold, their communities were all abandoned. The remains of sophisticated towns with paved streets and two-storey decorated houses are now being uncovered. At one, Yunatsite, the inhabitants were found sliced to pieces or with smashed skulls, the buildings carefully turned into charnel-houses and sealed over to eliminate all memory of what had been there. Varna's ceremonial cemetery was abandoned with its gold untouched and there was no reoccupation for a thousand years. The hunger for gold was evidently ended.

There was significant climate change in the fifth millennium, and the Black Sea, which had been a freshwater lake, was steadily rising and filling with salt seawater. It is possible that these changes undermined the region's economy so decisively that the link between gold and the realm of the gods was seen to be broken or discredited. Was gold itself held culpable, so that even its memory needed to be erased? It seems that we are not the heirs to the knowledge of the world's first goldsmiths, but of rediscoverers of the stuff fifty generations later, who lived thousands of kilometres further south. Knowing nothing of gold's previous use, they similarly decided that their most important people needed to carry it with them in death. The obliteration of Varna's civilization ensured that whatever lesson could have been learned was itself silenced. Far later, in ignorance of this past, gold was allowed to come back.

Gold and Divine Power

Why had it been used in the first place? There is no sign that anyone, anywhere was interested in gold until about 3,000 years after the first farming settlements. People have always liked decoration, and jewellery dates back tens of thousands of years, but across Europe and the Americas, early farmers preferred the shells of 'thorny oysters', spondylus.[5] Gold lying as nuggets and flakes in the bed of a stream is easier to retrieve, very soft, easily worked, welded and hammered, but no one seems to have made anything out of it until almost 7,000 years ago.

Fifty-six burials in this mysterious cemetery contained only goods, without human remains. They are spoken of as cenotaphs, 'empty tombs'. Half of the gold outside Grave 43 was found in three 'cenotaph' graves.[6] It included arm-rings, beads made into necklaces and bracelets, discs and pendants, gold plated tools and weapons, and gold images of horned bulls – their curved horns look like water buffalo. Each of these three cenotaphs contained a sceptre. The bodies in other graves are not from a single settlement; these were evidently important figures from settlements throughout the region, brought to this place of memory and ritual for the whole culture.[7] It is evidence of an unexpectedly sophisticated social organization, in which people over a wide area recognized some common allegiance.

Cemeteries, formal areas to bury a community's dead, were quite novel inventions in the Balkans in the time of the Lord of Varna. Before that, bodies were generally placed under house floors or in refuse pits.[8] Domestic burials were quite similar to each other, suggesting an egalitarian society, and include some bones from their grazing animals – presumably once bearing meat from the funeral feast or for the afterlife. The interments made no differentiation between sexes, age or status.[9] At the cemetery, though, things were quite different.

Sixty or so of these graves held gold, on average ten small pieces. These were not objects meant for use, but indications of status. The three cenotaph graves which contained accoutrements for a high-status burial were laid out as though the gold itself had been alive in the world and was now laid to eternal rest in a place where there was some connection to the eternity from which life springs and to which it returns. Perhaps people thought of this gold as still living in the underworld from which it had been taken, much as I have seen the Kogi sing to gold in museums. Their guardians of traditional knowledge are called 'Mamas', which comes from a word meaning the sun – suggesting a link to gold. (The female equivalent is a Saka, which means moon.) Mamas have escorted me around the small museum in Santa Marta to encounter what they see as the living entities whose material trace is in the gold, each with its own character, power and now profound loneliness, to be given sustenance in words and gentle song.

Close to Varna's gold-rich cenotaphs were three others that each contained a plaster head with gold foil on mouths and eyes, teeth and noses. These are taken to have been female figures as they had gold tiaras, earrings, lip ornaments and pendants shaped as women. Each was supplied, not with a sceptre, axe or bow, but with a copper pin, a flint knife and a whorl for spinning wool.[10] It seems that they are connected to the feminine, but not to a particular woman. Miniature figurines of women are commonplace in archaeological sites of this region around the time of these burials; it has been argued (and disputed) that they indicate a cult of a fertility mother goddess.[11] But these substantial figures with tools for spinning and cutting may be something quite different. They suggest the Homeric Greek Fates, the three Moirai who spun, measured and cut the thread of destiny.[12] I am reminded, too, of the Kogi belief that the world was created and structured in time and space by the thread spun at the beginning. These mysterious dolls, apparently connected to transcendence by seeing and breathing imperishable gold, may indeed be goddess-figures, perhaps linked to whatever was represented in the empty masculine 'royal' burials. These graves mark the entrance to the cemetery.[13]

The Meaning of Regalia

Grave 43, the only one containing a body with a significant quantity of gold, is very confusing. The bones' radiocarbon dates seem to indicate that it was the first grave, but the objects in there show it to be 200 years later, not the first grave but the final one. This 'first and last man' is physically adjacent to five of the cenotaph graves that were created at the end of the cemetery's use.

The gold itself is expertly worked, evidence of a long history of metallurgical expertise, but we have been introduced to the story after the earlier episodes have been lost, probably by drowning. The Varna burials are 500 metres from Bulgaria's deepest lake, which contains remains of a settlement of the period. Varna is also on the coast, and the Black Sea was at least 5 metres lower when these people lived.[14] The Bulgarian Centre for Underwater Archaeology has identified fifteen drowned sites along that section of coast. I spent some time with the Centre's director, Dr Kalim Dimitrov, who took the unequivocal view that the man in Grave 43 must be described – because of his gold crown and sceptre – as a king. Although earlier communities must have had commanding figures organizing communal projects, this is the first appearance of what we know as royal regalia. Perhaps that makes him the first king in the world. It was clear that gold identified one man as different from the rest; it is not so clear why.

The Lord of Varna left no memory, no stories and no trace of a heritage. Yet later cultures which gave their leaders gold regalia made use of the same symbols. Golden headdresses would reappear and dominate Europe and Asia. Gold regalia still appears at the coronation of every British sovereign. Of course, it differs in some details from his. He has a huge gold disc which may represent the circle of the world, or celestial power in the form of the sun. Could it be the prototype of today's golden coronation orb? Updating the accoutrements of royalty is a slow, deeply conservative process; the modern British orb is based on a medieval design, itself derived from ancient Greek and Roman symbols of power over the world.

There is something about these golden symbols that seems to be strangely fundamental to the power they signify. In 1987, a tomb was discovered in Sipán in northern Peru, which dates to around 300 CE.[15] The main figure in it, known as the Lord of Sipán, is surrounded by other spectacular burials. He shows signs of bone degeneration caused by the weight of gold that he wore. He wears gold on his head, has a sceptre of gold and silver, and was buried with war clubs, spears and shields. His body and its costume combine to create a performance reminiscent of Varna. His power was shown in depictions of slaves, captives and executions.[16]

The gulf between the Lords of Sipán and Varna is vast – they were 5,000 years and 12,000km apart.[17] But their relationship to gold appears strangely similar. In both societies, the gold itself was deliberately interred with the body, indicating similar beliefs about the passage from life to death and the nature of the afterworld. The gold that these men bore had evidently been essential to their place in this world and was thought to connect to a world beyond. In both burials, the corpse was crowned with gold, surrounded with weapons, adorned with heavy gold beads and ornaments and carried a gold sceptre in his right hand. This imagery and its significance in Peru were not learned from anywhere in Europe. Nor do these gold objects have any obvious practical explanation. But the significance of crown and sceptre do not, apparently, need to be learned. Some people seem to know that they represent transcendental power in mortal hands.

The ideas expressed in this regalia seem out of place in the Neolithic world where it was made. Our oldest direct insight into the meaning of a sceptre comes from a thousand years later, at the beginning of literary writing. The Sumerian epic about Enmerkar and the Lord of Aratta made it clear that a golden sceptre is not a product of human agency but a divinity in its own right which was bestowed upon the ruler by a god. The goldsmith may have worked in some kind of trance. The gods themselves were said to hold sceptres received from older deities, which represented life as well as heavenly authority and earthly supremacy. In Sumer, the sceptre's shaft was adorned with gold and lapis lazuli.[18]

It is startling to see the same object appear in much later, quite unconnected cultures. The people of pre-Columbian America had theocratic rulers with gold sceptres, and they did not learn the idea from the other side of the Atlantic. A Moche gold sceptre from Peru was recently auctioned for tens of thousands of dollars, and a Chimu gold sceptre from Colombia is kept in the Museo de América in Madrid.[19]

Of course, we do not know exactly what the Lord of Varna's regalia represented, but his burial was unique and he was clearly proclaimed by his gold as the prototype of a new kind of man, one elevated above the rest, possessing the product of a huge amount of other people's work and skill, and whose symbolic weapons commanded deference. He was unusually tall at about 1.75m. We do not know how he was addressed, but subsequent gold-adorned overlords would, in languages from ancient Egyptian and Sumerian to modern European tongues, be called 'Your Highness'.

Goldsmithing

The gold foil on the plaster heads was itself a new invention. It seems that all the complex mysteries of goldsmithing were understood and used here. For the first time, humans had a material as imperishable as stone, but which was so unresisting that it could be flattened to a flexible leaf. It was not easy work, as I was shown in the Japanese city of Kanazawa, where children walk the streets eating ice-cream cones wrapped in locally made gold foil ten-thousandths of a millimetre thick (being unchanged by time and biology, it does their bodies neither good nor harm).[20] It is made by interleaving small pieces of gold in a stack of pliant soft sheets – probably originally ox intestine. Unlike other metals, gold can be beaten to a thinness less than the wavelength of visible light without hardening and fracturing.[21] The stack is bound together, then beaten repetitively. Nowadays, a goldbeater might hammer for an hour, striking more than one blow a second on a stack placed on a wooden anvil sunk deep into the ground. Then the modern worker quarters the flattened pieces and assembles them into a new stack ten times as high and beaten for three times as long. If the rhythm is not steady and the blows are uneven, the sheets will split. At the end of the process, they can be gently lifted out, placed on skin coated with gypsum dust (so they do not stick to it) and straightened with a breath. The Varna goldsmiths wrapped the resulting gold skin on the plaster faces and around copper objects, making them incorruptible. Placing these objects in a grave connected it with the realm of the dead, the unseen space that surrounds the living. Tubular copper beads were gold-wrapped, and the handles of war hammers were wrapped in gold to make sceptres. A broken spondylus shell bracelet was 'healed' with a gold foil bandage. There were gold-covered objects never seen before, such as a spiral rod and a goldsmith's hammer.

The goldsmiths also invented a way to make moulds that could turn molten gold into objects rounded in three dimensions. They must have used the 'lost wax' method, which has been reinvented many times since. The desired form had first to be modelled in beeswax. This would be the mould's core; bone pins would be attached to hold it in place as it was encased in layers of plaster and clay. A wax funnel would give access to the core from the top of the mould, and it would have a drainage tube at the bottom. The mould was put in a furnace, along with a crucible containing precisely the same volume of gold as the wax. It probably also contained a pinch of lime (probably from roasted seashells). A modern goldsmith would describe the lime as a flux, needed to bind the gold particles together and expel impurities.

Every stage of this process required knowledge that must have been acquired from masters who had experienced a mysterious visionary process of insight and experiment. Blowing on the furnace fire through clay pipes could heat it to the temperature at which gold liquifies. Then some device (maybe sinew ropes, flexible withies or long bones?) would be needed to lift the crucible of gold and pour its blindingly bright, fiery contents into the waiting vent in the mould, vaporizing and expelling the wax within. This dramatic event needed to be swift – just a few seconds – and precise.

The injected gold had to be forced to flow swiftly through the mould so as not to solidify too soon or leave air bubbles. That might have been done with steam, using a wet pad immediately pressed down over the white-hot vent. The goldsmith would have needed protective clothing; probably soaking-wet animal skins. At the end of this terrifying performance of incandescent fire and the molten essence of sunlight, of hissing steam and boiling vapour, the clay mould would cool, be broken and the magical conclusion revealed.

Something new had been born, in a process that must have required the partnership of concentrated thought and non-human forces. An idea that had been shaped in the soft wax taken from insects had been made solid in a ritual that called on earth, air, fire and water. It was sealed in the darkness of an earthen womb from which a golden creation had emerged. Until these finds, it was believed that the oldest lost wax casting was a piece of copper shaped to furnish a temple at Ein Gedi, near the Dead Sea, around 3,700 BCE. The castings at Varna were made a thousand years before that.

Varna's artisans were also creating the first artificial alloys, mixing gold with silver and copper to achieve different colours and hardness. These objects are evidence of an established artisan workshop involving many people. The gold in these graves was worked by experts whose teachers had acquired their skills in a world that would disappear and be forgotten long before the making of Stonehenge or the Pyramids.

By the time of Homer, gold was the unquestioned mark of excellence. An apple of gold was said to have been the prize for the divine beauty contest that began the Trojan War. Yet that story from remote antiquity is set a mere 3,300 years ago. The people in Varna's golden graves lived twice as far back in time. The epic of Troy is encrusted with the memory of innumerable recitations about gods and heroes, but the vastly more ancient story of Varna is still untold and untellable, new and shiny, blinking in the light and still wet from the egg it hatched from. We see a chance collection of mute physical remains and try to decode them, but next year's new discoveries will undoubtedly change the questions as well as the answers.

The Antecedents of Lordship

There is now evidence that gold had been worked in Bulgaria 200 years before the Varna burials, and the appearance of that earlier gold was already directly linked to a new social differentiation. It was found forty-four years after Raycho's discovery, about 400km inland. In July 2016, Nanding Chen, a Chinese biochemistry student at Bryn Mawr College, Pennsylvania, was searching through a prehistoric mound called Tell Yunatsite, close to a river in southern Bulgaria. She was spending some of her vacation on this archaeological site, the remains of a village of some 150 early farmers from the fifth millennium BCE. The story of civilization was being rewritten here. The team had uncovered surfaced streets that were older than any in Egypt or Mesopotamia, and that were lined with two-storey houses. They had even seen evidence of what seemed to be symbolic markings, from a time which was long before writing. Nanding Chen had acquired a reputation for being lucky and sharp-eyed, and had found some small flat figurines. It was intensely, almost unbearably hot, and this was the last day of the dig. As part of the final clearing up, she was helping to check that nothing had been missed from the floor of a small house that dated from around 4,700 BCE. It was a tedious business, sorting through small pieces of soil and ash, separating them in a makeshift flotation tank.

The site director had tried to keep the volunteers alert by warning them that they might miss the gold by inattention. Everyone laughed politely; there was no such thing as worked gold in 4,700 BCE.

And then she saw a tiny shining fleck in the tank. She picked up a very small gold bead. Being gold, it was uncorroded. It looked new, but it was as far from new as it could possibly be. Almost 7,000 years ago, someone had made a gold bar about the length of a grain of wheat and bent it into a circle. Nanding Chen had found what is said to be the oldest piece of worked gold on Earth.[22]

A slightly older cemetery than the Lord of Varna's, now known as Varna II, has been uncovered right next to the original discoveries. It has a grave of roughly the same date as that bead. 'Grave 3' there holds a man in much the same posture as the Lord of Varna, along with thirty-one beads like this one.[23] He does not have a golden crown, but there is a special band around his head. He does not have gold ornaments, apart from those tiny beads, but he does have extravagant copper objects. Gold would subsequently be used to complete the process of displaying a man whose regalia connected him with transcendental power and, given the presence of weapons, the authority to command in battle.

Gold's appearance was the visible demonstration of a new social structure which had emerged from an immigrant population with a new way of life. South-east Europe was inhabited only by hunter-gatherers until the sixth millennium BCE. Then farmers moved in from the great steppes north of the Black Sea, after a long migration at a time of rising water levels. Whether their lands drowned in a mythologized flood is debated, but these farmers were able to ship their seeds and animals to northern Greece.[24] Around 5,500 BCE, they continued north-east to occupy fertile river valleys in the Balkans which had been avoided by the indigenous inhabitants. They established a new way of life, as domesticated as their herds, building well-ordered permanent villages.[25] New evidence of this 'Neolithic revolution' is discovered every year. The oldest migrant settlement that has been uncovered there at the time of writing was found in 2015 at Mursalevo in south-west Bulgaria. The settlement had cobbled streets with neatly aligned two-storey wattle and daub houses, their plastered walls painted red and white. It was founded about 1,200 years before the Varna burials and was a carefully designed colony for subsistence farmers. Some 200 communities from the fifth millennium BCE have been identified on the farmland south of the Danube in eastern Bulgaria. They are all quite similar, villages of a dozen or so houses, for perhaps 150 to at most 400 people. No one knows where the Lord of Varna lived (probably in a village now under water), but these small communities were where clear divisions between greater and lesser people appeared. The hierarchic social order that would dominate the world was first seen in this region and was eventually made powerfully visible by having a leader who needed to be adorned and enhanced with this new material: gold. The social changes that led to this have now been revealed by archaeology. What has been found is as surprising, in this Neolithic world, as the goldwork – and its necessary precursor. The changes began with the specialization of labour.

Where there had previously been similar self-sufficient households engaged in the common work of husbandry and cultivation, there emerged communities of specialist experts who served the wider society. This would have made their communities more productive and secure, but meant that power and authority must have been negotiated between and within them. The first specialized workers were producing something which all herders needed, but which could only be made in specific locations – salt. It was the need for salt that would eventually lead to gold.

Salt is essential for people and animals. In the wild, animals take it from plants, salt stones and salt licks – locations where they gather to find the mineral when they need it – and the meat that hunter-gatherers eat satisfies their own need for it. But farmers with herds had to keep them near the shore or one of the few salt springs, and relied on organizing small-scale evaporation pits. They also needed supplementary salt because they ate less meat and more cereals. Obtaining it from salt-making centres meant they could expand into new areas and salt their meat to preserve it, freeing them from dependence on freshly killed animals. Such a centre has been found some 50km due west of Varna at an extremely productive inland salt spring called Provadiya-Solnitsata ('the Provadiya salt-pit'), which the excavators believe was in production from 5500 BCE and was greatly expanded in the period of the Varna burials,[26] a time of significant population growth. It is believed that a specialized temperature-controlled furnace there was capable of producing 4–5 tons of salt at a time, in vessels which delivered it in standard-size blocks for delivery to other locations. This small proto-urban centre of about 350 people evidently came to need serious defensive walls.

Gold jewellery of the Varna grave period has been found there, which was not buried in a grave. It is perhaps an indication of the significance of gold as a mark of status, which can be linked to new forms of social structure that appear in burial practices. Bodies began to be placed in community cemeteries with individuals increasingly distinguished by grave goods such as fine pottery and luxury objects, especially spondylus bracelets and beads. Male, female and child burials became different. Animal bones were no longer placed with the dead, and women were often buried with rings on their front teeth and fingers, and what archaeologists call a 'sewing kit': a flint tool, a bone awl, a pebble polisher and a mussel shell in a standardized jar. Antler battle axes appeared, mostly in the burials of men. These are the first evidence of purposeful weapons specifically designed for fighting and herald the appearance of a new kind of man, the warrior, and his new activity, warfare.[27] Many of the graves at Provadiya-Solnitsata contain people killed with arrows or bludgeoned and speared to death, some of the burials being of bodies cut to pieces.[28]

Why had society changed so dramatically, and why did it need to invent gold artefacts? This can only be speculation. A cattle-using egalitarian community in which no one has the right to lay down rules can run into problems when it moves for the first time into permanent settlements. I happen to have seen this myself when staying in a Shipibo village on the Ucayali River, a tributary of the Amazon, in Peru in the 1990s. We were several days by canoe from the nearest road. Shipibo settlements used to be temporary, abandoned every few years when their small fields grew tired and their cattle needed to move away from the parasites there. Lately, however, they had been seduced into permanent settlement by a small group of Christian evangelical missionaries working to build a church-based community. I had been invited by some Shipibo traditional leaders, called '*curanderos*' (healers) because their work was essentially medical. It was based on the use of, and visions induced by, the plants around them (in their own tongue they are *morayos*, which refers to expertise in a hallucinogenic vine). No one had the authority to tell anyone else what to do, and the *morayos* were worried that this was becoming a problem. Individual cattle owners could not be prevented from letting their animals go where they liked, foul what they liked and infest the village. There were no rules for long-term waste disposal. This had not been a problem when the community could pack up and move on, but now it was making life unpleasant. The community had traditions but no legislation, and certainly had no one with the right to command. At the same time, the social structure was being refashioned by the development of a market economy among the women, who were travelling upriver to a town where they could sell their distinctive pottery and fabrics to adventurous tourists. As individual families acquired more wealth, the authority of the traditional leaders was seen by the young as less convincing. The community needed to discover a new kind of leadership that could legislate for this new way of living. The missionaries were ready to take up that responsibility, but I had been invited by Shipibo who wanted to find their own solution. Of course, there may be no parallel at all between that and the process that created the Lord of Varna, but it could provide a pointer to what was going on.

The new social structure that produced the road to gold must have appeared first at the salt works. It resulted from a novel invention, the controlled temperature furnace. This demanded a new kind of work in which an entire community of workers serviced it. There had to be co-ordinated teams collecting and delivering firewood, producing disposable pottery vessels, bringing and reducing brine and preparing and exporting the salt tablets that were being made, and an organized structure to support all these people. We can see the emergence of a form of society that we recognize, in which people work at their own jobs within a complex ordered society. This became even clearer with the development of additional thermal technologies in the mid-fifth millennium BCE, which allowed the manufacture of previously unknown high-status objects, apparently purely for display – beautiful, graceful coloured ceramics, and what may have been the world's first copper objects.

The objects had no practical use: this was purely aesthetic work. The Varna culture had a breathtaking aesthetic sensibility. Its wonderfully elegant, abstract painted ceramics are delicate and highly desirable. No one seeing this pottery for the first time would suppose it is nearly 7,000 years old: it looks utterly modern and luxuriously stylish. It makes a striking contrast with the late Neolithic pottery associated with Stonehenge, which is heavy and crude by comparison, yet that was made at least a thousand years later. These objects were made by elite craft workers and were clearly intended for elite users.

Metallurgy – from Copper to Gold

This led to another furnace-based process, metal casting, and more specialization. Experts must have taken firesticks into dark shafts to prospect for and extract beautiful green rock crystals of malachite. These were crushed, placed in a crucible and melted in a furnace which a blow-tube could bring to just under 1,100 degrees, hotter than required to fire pottery. The malachite melted and became liquid copper; the crucible was lifted (probably using green withies) and its contents poured into a stone mould that was also in the furnace. Pouring copper is unpredictable, even with modern facilities. To prevent bubbles, the temperature of the mould needs to be kept as close to melting point as possible, but within seconds of starting the pour the copper will start to solidify. The mould has to be perfectly evenly heated, and the pour must be smooth. These things are not entirely in the artisan's control. The whole process has a magical quality, and success might easily be seen as evidence of supernatural help.

They made castings shaped like stone axe-heads, using a mould of two halves. Some are called axe-hammers, metal imitations of stone tools that have a hole for a handle between the axe blade and the hammer head. There are not many copper axe-heads and axe-hammers, but in 2013, Europe's largest hoard – twenty-two of them – was found in north-east Bulgaria.[29]

There had to be a reason why so much skill and effort was devoted to this work. For many years, archaeologists argued that copper tools were a great leap forward in agricultural efficiency, but more recently it has become recognized that, since copper does not make a sharp edge and cannot be refashioned when damaged, stone was more useful. These show little evidence of use. Hammering them into their final perfect shape hardened them, and then they were burnished to a wondrous reflective red-brown glow. Their significance must lie in their beauty and visible symbolism: tools too magnificent to use, weapons too marvellous to wield. Possession of such a magically powerful object showed that a man had a degree of entitlement that made him recognizable and distinctive. Metallurgy may thus have had more to do with the construction of authority than improving farming.

It seems that copper objects stopped being made in the Balkans by the end of the fifth millennium BCE.[30] The Varna graves contain many copper objects, cast and beaten into shape, often as hammers and sharp points. But in the meantime, the furnaces were producing gold. It seems that the first gold was shaped in a coppersmith's workshop. This solidified sun-brilliance was linked to the mastery of a furnace.

It was evidently regarded with special awe. Like copper, it can be hammered and cast, and served a similar purpose in distinguishing special people, but it had more to offer. It is far softer, can be cold-welded by simple hammering and is much heavier than anything else known for the next 6,500 years.[31] It is dazzling and, unlike copper, incorruptible.

It must have been appreciated as an unearthly substance. Shining and incorruptible, the oldest piece of worked gold known, that tiny bead from Yunatsite, weighs just one-seventh of a gram. In theory, you could draw it out into a wire and just keep going until you have a gold thread 400m long and 400 times thinner than a hair. It would be long enough to surround the village rampart, encompassing 7,000 square metres. (In 2010, I filmed a group of Kogi Mamas symbolically laying a gold thread finer than hair for hundreds of kilometres around the base of their mountain.) Then you could roll it up and refashion the original tiny bead. The metal is not changed in any way. A master craftsman can hammer it flatter and flatter until it becomes a translucent leaf one-thousandth of the thickness of a sheet of newspaper, covering over 200 sq cm, and could then fold it over and over again and squash it back to the size it was, and turn it back into the same ageless bead.

The Birth of an Industry

The gold could have been from the chance discovery of nuggets, but is more likely to have been sifted from rivers, known as 'placer' gold.[32] The word comes from Spanish or Portuguese for an alluvial deposit. Tiny flakes were continually washed out of an underground vein by a mountain spring, and because of their exceptional density, they settled on the stream bed where the flow slows down. Their shining yellow brilliance is like nothing else on Earth; they catch your eye in the gravel and on rocks like drops that have fallen from the sun. Gold is a colour, in many languages the same as 'yellow', associated with dawn.

It is likely that a huge amount of work was involved in collecting it. We are used to placer gold being gathered by panning, swirling the silt in a perforated dish until only the grains of gold remain. They are far heavier than the grit and sink to the bottom while the other solids wash away. That was how it was done in modern gold rushes, but when I had the opportunity to try it, I realized how infinitely tedious is the back-breaking effort, how continuous the concentration required and how slight the reward – a few tiny flakes at a time.

In any case, this technique would not work with all the gold that was being collected. One of the masterpieces of Grave 43 is a large ceramic dish painted with abstract patterns of black and fine gold lines. The paint was made from the tiniest particles of gold dust, the kind that are so small that they do not sink in a panning dish but are held up by the surface tension of the water. They had to be trapped another way.

We know very little about life in this region before writing came into existence, but we do have one story which seems to contain a memory of the work of gold-gathering in the very distant past, which could explain how it was done. The story of Jason taking a golden fleece from Colchis, on the eastern side of the Black Sea, may be based on real fleeces that were used for collecting gold. The Jason story, told by the Greek poet Eumelos around 700 BCE, can be connected to considerable finds of gold objects in the region from succeeding centuries.[33] Villagers there have retained an ancient practice of washing the streams through fleeces pinned down in sluices to trap alluvial gold in their wool. It was first recorded by the first-century BCE geographer Strabo, who came from the region, and who suggested it was the origin of the Jason legend. These gold-laden fleeces are hung to dry and then burned. We have no way of knowing when this process was invented, but it could be very old indeed.

In the version of the story that survives, Jason had to sail to the distant land of Colchis on the Black Sea, in modern Georgia. From there, he had to fetch the golden fleece of a winged ram sent to Earth two generations earlier. The creature had been sacrificed there. That divine ram went into the sky, visible as the constellation Aries, first sign of the zodiac, the spring equinox signifier of energy and rebirth. But Aries's golden fleece remained on Earth, where it was hung on an oak in a sacred grove. It was a link between Earth and the heavens, and its owner was entitled to 'the sceptre of single rule and the throne'. The fabulous fleece was defended by fire-breathing bulls and an unsleeping dragon. Jason's success was ensured by divine assistance and by the king of Colchis's daughter, the enchantress Medea, who fell in love with him. The golden fleece he captured was not wealth but the physical presence of transcendent purity. It did not make Jason rich, but it was central to his link to the gods. It became the wedding bed for the hero and his enchantress.

The tale bears traces of great antiquity. It may be that 6,500 years ago, the gold-hunters of Varna learned to dig down into the silt of a stream bed, through the barren surface gravel to the heavier pay dirt, and lift out handfuls of silt laden with gold that had been washed down, sunk and accumulated over millions of years. To separate the gold, they would have needed to clear out the top gravel and push tons of the silt into a sluice with a fleece in the bottom. Then they could burn the fleece and be left with shining, brilliant, undamaged and undamageable gold. To collect the fine gold dust that was held up by the surface tension, they just had to skim a dish over the top of the water. But it is equally possible that they used nothing more than their own bodies, like the native gold-collectors on the Gulf Coast of Mexico in 1517. The Spanish found that they panned the gold with their bare hands, keeping the grains in their mouths and melting them in a crucible on the spot.[34]

Amassing this quantity was a huge effort. If the gold was taken from a spectacularly rich stream, as seems likely, it still took a lot of work. A prospector's dream is to stumble on a 'bonanza' deposit created by a hot spring. The most astonishing example known is the Sleeper deposit in Nevada, which upon discovery yielded 200 grams per metric ton of soil.[35] That would be enough to capture someone's attention. The richest burials at Varna – the Lord of Varna and the accompanying symbolic graves – contain about 5kg of gold. Altogether, there is 6kg of it in the necropolis. Even if they had found the biggest bonanza in the world, gathering the gold for Varna's burials from streams would have required shifting 30 tons of silt and gravel by hand, without even the benefit of a wheelbarrow.[36] This was substantial production by a very small population.

Whoever did the work must have been dependent on others to supply the food for themselves and their families. The acquisition of the gold was a larger-scale operation than any other except the building of the new and elaborate defence walls that were going up pretty well all the communities of this region. It had to be organized by a new layer of society, an elite group that must have been in the service of the warlord, and it demonstrated his supernatural authority. But why was such extraordinary work needed?

There is no evidence that gold was being used for exchange for other valued objects: it only turns up in tiny pieces in village sites. It was needed for the graves. Long after they had been forgotten, that became the significance of gold in cultures around the world. We see it, for example, among the Scythian nomads of Siberia and Kazakhstan thousands of years later, around 600 BCE. They had wonderfully worked ornamental gold which appears to have been made solely for the embellishment and burial of their leaders. Accumulated through their lives from craftsmen in, or influenced by, the cultures that bordered their vast range from Greece to China, they seem to have devoted themselves to preparing their own burial costumes. The most stunning example is a 'royal' burial site in Tuva Republic, Siberia. A joint German-Russian expedition from 2000–2003 found a wooden chamber dated to the seventh century BCE, contemporary with the earliest known depiction of Jason's golden fleece, containing a man and a woman who had been committed to the afterlife completely covered with gold.[37] Between the gold-covered hat-crowns on their heads and their gold-bearing boots, they wore a mighty weight of gold torcs, necklaces, ear ornaments, pendants and pins, and were wrapped in capes covered with thousands of small gold panthers. They had gold objects – a miniature cup, a quiver and its carrying belt, and a wooden bowl with its handle covered with gold. And there were iron weapons decorated with gold and silver inlay, such as daggers, knives, arrowheads and a gold-wrapped battle-axe (sceptre). Altogether, they needed over 20kg of gold to take them from this world to the next. Some of it shows signs of wear, indicating that it was worn before death, but some was clearly made especially for the tomb. Tens or hundreds of thousands of microscopic gold beads were stitched to the leggings of the dead, which could not have lasted half an hour being worn by these energetic riders when alive.[38]

It is from the Scythians that we derive the term 'shaman', and the shaman's role is to cross, or appear to cross, the space between this world and another reality. Brilliant, unchanging, infinitely malleable gold seems to bridge the gap. There was, arguably, an historical path from Varna to Siberia. A new DNA study of Scythian remains has shown a direct connection with the late Bronze Age population of the northern Black Sea region, living on the coast of what is now Romania, perhaps 100 miles north of the Varna necropolis.[39] A Varna grave contains DNA linked to people from the steppes. But the Scythian shamans lived 4,000 years after the Lord of Varna perished. It is just as likely that the Scythians created their shamanic vision of gold for royal burials without learning it from anyone else.

The catalogue of the world's funerary gold suggests that this mysterious substance summoned the same response from widely disparate communities. It is the reason why, around 1000 CE, a formal-faced golden death mask was placed on a 17-year-old Mongolian princess of the Liao imperial family,[40] and on the other side of the world the entranced expression of a young Quimbaya man was preserved for ever in Colombia in his gold death mask, complete with decorative hangings. A confident bearded Mycenaean was buried with his face modelled in gold around 1600 BCE, with such force that his modern discoverer is said to have announced that he had gazed upon the face of Agamemnon,[41] and about 200 years later, Tutankhamun was entombed with a mask containing over 10kg of gold, which has become the icon of Pharaonic Egypt. The Mycenaean grave predates any known contact with Egypt,[42] and there was no communication a thousand years ago between Mongolia and South America. Once human beings embraced gold, they found it very natural to embody their most important dead in it.

Gold and Power

Associating Varna's graves with gold was part of their linkage with rare exotica. The power that was privileged by its use could be seen to span huge distances. Grave 41, rich in gold, had an obsidian blade that had come 1,000km from

Cjekov, in the Serbian Carpathian Mountains.[43] The sword buried with the Lord of Varna was made from a 40cm flint blade, an astonishing object apparently brought 2,000km from somewhere near Turin. Varna was part of a network that stretched across the whole of the Balkans and far beyond, and had this gold at its hub. Some gold pieces are pendants with one large central perforation and two smaller suspension holes. An exactly similar piece, but carved in red sandstone, was found in a passage-grave in Brittany of the same date. Nothing else like it is known in Brittany.[44] It is not incredible to deduce that what was going on in Varna may have had reverberations up to 3,000km away; after all, the transport of Mediterranean spondylus shells reached from Bulgaria to the Bristol Channel.[45]

The mechanical skills seen in some of these objects beggar belief. A three-holed gold piece seems to have had a cord through the top two holes, on which were strung dark red carnelian beads. Carnelian is an exceptionally hard substance, but these beads have been very precisely cut with thirty-two facets, and the hole of one is still lined with a tiny gold cylinder. Our understanding of the technology of the period cannot make sense of it. This bead suggests the existence of a rotary grinding wheel in the Stone Age.[46] I am constantly reminded of how little we know of ancient skills and pre-modern mechanical sophistication. In February 2020, I arrived at a meeting of Kogi traditional authorities and was required to begin with a meditation to be 'remembered' by a pre-Colombian object I was given to hold. To my surprise and confusion, it was a small sixteen-sided bead, apparently of jet, with a tiny hole lined with what appeared to be a sleeve of gold. It seems impossible. We need to accept with humility that we cannot understand how such things were made, just as we cannot know how the Varna gems appear to have been treated to obtain uniform colouring, and how they come to be of precise weights, linked to the weight of the gold pieces. In fact, archaeologists have begun cataloguing the gold there according to its weight in 'vans', the name they have given to Varna gold-workers' unit of weight.[47]

These farmers had created a new way of living, and gold was now central to it – or at least to its public presentation. The cemetery was a huge ritual site serving a deep hinterland,[48] and the centrality of the Lord of Varna was fundamental to it.

The Skeleton Horizon

It seems that the people of the Balkans deliberately put an end to the golden society that had appeared there. The history that began with neat farming villages and the growth of specialized work, and that was represented to the afterlife by the creation and burial of gold, did not just collapse: it was ruthlessly stamped on.

After the growth in population that led up to the development of the salt works, something seems to have gone badly wrong. The development of new technologies in ceramics and metallurgy may have been responses to stress rather than what we think of as 'progress'.

The cemetery was abandoned in 4250 BCE, about 450 years after its creation. By the time of its end, the population of the south-east Balkans had fallen by about a third. The majority of the villages were destroyed by violence. The first to be eliminated was Mursalevo, the earliest farming settlement known in the region. Its inhabitants seem to have fled. Masses of firewood were brought and the houses, stocked with possessions, were incinerated at furnace temperatures.[49] This may not have been a hostile act; it could have been a deliberate destruction by the inhabitants. Something had gone wrong. Later villages would have defences – ditches and embankments. And there would be weapons, with some kind of commander.

Slaughter was certainly happening. An archaeological 'horizon' is a layer of similar deposits over a large area, defined by what is in it. Here the reports speak of a 'skeleton horizon'. It appears at Yunatsite, the source of that original gold bead. One forensic analysis says: 'The brutality of the attackers is noticeable. We can almost see their murderous frenzy. It seems like they wanted to annihilate the population.'[50] At least seventy people were slaughtered, many of them infants. The fighting men of the village were absent – or were the executioners. Almost all the dead were old men, children and women. Their heads were ferociously smashed, and the excavators report that many people were apparently multiple victims of the same killer. Once the frenzy ended, with the dead unburied, Yunatsite was turned into a charnel-house. The close-packed wooden houses of the dead became fuel for their incineration. Finally, and slowly, the entire site was thoroughly covered with 'a loose grey layer ... of artificial origin' over half a metre deep, sealing its fate.[51] We do not know whether the aggressors were from other villages, their own menfolk or an invasion of the indigenous hunter-gatherers. But whatever was represented here was being ended with pathological determination. Something here was perceived as so unspeakable that it must be removed for all time to a place from which it could never return: beyond the skeleton horizon.

The site was not occupied again for 1,000 years.

But a thousand years later, gold-work did return from the dead and resumed the slow process of shaping humanity, spreading steadily across the landscape. With our hindsight, the Lord of Varna appears to be the archetype of the military theocrats that would rule so much of humanity. His life and death had clearly been manifestations of a new social order, required by specialized technology and production, that brought together an entire region under the ritual power of a unique figure who could command resources from hundreds or even thousands of kilometres away, and had gold made for him so that he could bridge the space between this world and the one beyond. It may be that this was the first time when weapons intended solely for war – maces, battle-axes, war hammers, spears and arrows with specialized tips – made an appearance.[52] He was well-equipped with symbolic weapons, and his gold mace and gold-sheathed bow evidently bestowed the authority to slay his enemies. The sceptre is a battle-axe, and there are spears and a sword-like long flint.

Is that why his people had to be destroyed? But destroying the memory meant there was no warning against its reanimation.

So Varna's social order based on hierarchy and specialized labour, under the rule of a warrior overlord whose reach extended over huge distances and whose cosmic power was manifest through gold, eventually did reappear, and endure, and has now completed its conquest of all humanity. Which is why we may be advancing towards a new skeleton horizon.

The Owner of the Golden Calendar

There was a mystic relationship to gold which, once having begun, would remain at the heart of culture for millennia. It was taken from the earth or river gravel, shaped with thought and skill, and used for display, for ritual use and costume, for prestige gifts, in formal exchanges and as jewellery for marriage and inheritance. But all this was preparation for the gold to be sent back to where it had come from. At its journey's end, its significance to the living was made clear in the meaning and drama of funerary gold. It was evidently understood as present in the mundane world but belonging to eternity. Sharing in the undimmed perfection of the golden sun-disc that oversees the cycle of seasons, it could be – and was – melded with powerful interventions by human consciousness, at enormous cost in labour and care, to communicate with and convey issues of life and death into the afterlife. It served an esoteric purpose.

So, for example, we see gold being pressed into use in England around the middle of the third millennium BCE. Gold objects were being placed in burials in Wiltshire, Dorset and Norfolk.[53] The earliest appear to have been attached to garments, and to show signs of wear, which indicates perhaps ritual use by some shamanic specialist connected to the world beyond. The most remarkable gold from this culture comes from about 500 years later, when a tall, sturdy man was given an exceptionally lavish interment under a mound near Stonehenge. At the time that monument was being remade, putting the bluestones in an outer circle and an inner oval, and the central altar stone probably given its final position. He was laid out with a number of gold objects which had been created with an astonishing degree of effort and precision. On his chest there was a large gold foil lozenge, inscribed with a complex and very carefully measured geometric pattern. It has been demonstrated to be capable of functioning as a solar calendar, showing the start of each solar month at sunrise. It was too delicate to be frequently used and may be a ceremonial replica of a more robust working instrument.[54]

This calendrical expert was also buried with weapons, including a bronze dagger of such fine workmanship that it would be impossible to replicate today. The wooden handle was covered with about 140,000 tiny gold studs, each made from wire thinner than a human hair and measuring 1 x 0.2mm. Five of them would fit across the head of a small pin. Each was individually manipulated and glued to a microscopically tiny hole precisely placed in the wooden handle to create a herringbone pattern. There were over 1,000 gold studs embedded in each square centimetre. It is suggested that only small children have fine-enough eyesight for such work, though a water drop can magnify a tiny item by four or five times. The gold may have come from Ireland; the work may have been done in Brittany. It must have taken at least 2,500 hours.

The ideas that inspired this way of using gold must have seemed self-evident to people in many unconnected parts of the world. It remained alive in the Americas when the Spanish arrived in the sixteenth century, and long continued among the Tairona people who inspired this book. There is still an atavistic urge among people visiting a well or fountain to offer it a coin; Minnesota's Mall of America is reported to collect about $24,000 of coins a year from its fountains and ponds,[55] and Rome's Trevi Fountain received $1.5 million in 2016.[56]

Gold-rich burials were also being made in Mesopotamia and Egypt. That is where the terrible, unprecedented violence that accompanied the first gold-making civilization reappeared, and gradually extended its influence through the world, fundamentally driving our history, usually without us knowing much of what was going on.

Chapter 2

Gods of the Cities

Tomb Robbers

In the fourth millennium BCE, people in Egypt and Mesopotamia began once more to bury their leaders in gold regalia. Only hints and bare traces of those graves survive, but the reasons for their disappearance are more mercenary than at Varna. Here, states had developed which depended on long-distance trade for survival. They were ruled by priest-kings who used immortal gold to establish their connection with eternity and the gods, but also came to use it as the fundamental guarantee of value in trade. It was not currency – indeed, in Egypt it was regarded as the flesh of the gods, not to be possessed by any mortal except the divine ruler – but it was the ultimate reference for value in exchanges with other rulers, so everything from grain to copper and other commodities eventually acquired a value that could be expressed in gold. And people regarded gold as worth having.

So, unlike the situation at Varna, after going into the ground with the dead, it was not usually left there to speak to gods and archaeologists. In fact, gold now created not one but two new kinds of person: kings and tomb robbers. By around 3000 BCE, efforts to frustrate the thieves in Egypt were causing tombs to be designed defensively. It may have been needed for another burial, as not only Pharaohs were shrouded in it. The robberies were unstoppable, so our understanding of the link between gold and kings is based on the evidence of written symbols rather than the missing metal. The hieroglyph for gold appeared in the fourth millennium BCE. It was a gold collar, and the word is *nub* or *nubu*. Gold was found from the Nile delta to the region south of Aswan called Nubia. The king was represented by a falcon, the sky-god Horus, perched on the collar, and immortal gold evidently transformed him into a transcendental figure. Deep mining for gold went on in the Eastern Desert from at least 3,500 BCE, crushing the ore with huge stone hammers,[1] but evidently everything that went into burial sites was comprehensively looted.[2]

In the same way, the evidence of royal burials in Mesopotamia, which must have used gold from Turkey or Iran, was wiped away. Archaeologists have found Sumerian cities that started life in the fifth millennium BCE and came to vastly outstrip the small settlements where gold had first appeared: Uruk had tens of thousands of inhabitants by 3,500 BCE, and certainly had rulers and gold work, but nothing survives except reliefs, statues and cylinder seals showing what look like unnamed king-priests who organized warfare with slingshot artillery.[3]

The Golden Helmet of Ur

Until the Varna finds were made, because so much was looted, the oldest golden burial known was from 2800 BCE. In the 1920s, Leonard Woolley found what he called the Royal Burials of Ur. They had escaped plunder and created a sensation. The oldest contained a gold sceptre. As with the Lord of Varna nearly two millennia before, the sense that gold can connect a human to the gods and grant a place above others remained. In another tomb, Woolley found a body with gold accoutrements bearing the name Meskalamdug.

Here lay the Lord of Varna colossally magnified. His burial was marked by the astonishing scale of his golden military accoutrements and of his elevation over the rest of humanity. He bore the title 'Lu-gal', 'biggest man' ('gal' is the root of Goliath). It could be translated as 'His Highness', king. People in this cemetery ruled not villages or towns, but the great city of Ur. 'Uru' meant 'the city', in the same way that Rome later considered itself the mother-city (and the Pope still annually blesses 'The city and the world'). Gold was clearly the visible demonstration of these rulers' righteous authority, in this life and the next, to judge, as well as their power to smite and of the benediction they bestowed on the city and its land. They required the service of others in their next lives, so they were accompanied by large numbers of human sacrifices. Meskalamdug means 'hero of the good land'. One significant difference with Varna was that there were women with rich decorations among the burials, and a fabulously dressed queen.

Ur was the first and greatest of the cities of Sumer, and Sumer was the first civilization to develop cities as the model for human society. It was a coastal city on the Persian Gulf and was already 1,200 years old by the time of this cemetery. It would not just fall once, like the towns around Varna, but many times until, after being inhabited for more than 3,000 years, the sea and rivers moved in the sixth century BCE and left it deserted. But even after that, it was revisited by battle many times, right down to the Iraq War of 2003. Matthew Bogdanos trained as a lawyer, classicist and soldier. A US Marine, he was appointed head of the counter-terrorist task force in southern Iraq in 2003. He established and led a small team to investigate the widely reported looting of the Iraq Museum. He found that many of its display cases were empty not because they had been looted, but because the contents had been moved into safe keeping. In particular, the museum staff had moved all the jewellery and ivories on display to a secret location known to five museum officials. They had sworn on the Koran to remain silent until US forces left the country.[4]

Colonel Bogdanos, who tells the story, is evidently a persuasive man. Having established the identities of the five guardians, 'after weeks of building trust we were finally given access to that secret area'. He was looking for the most celebrated treasures of the museum, including what is called the Treasure of Nimrud, more than 1,000 pieces of gold jewellery and precious stones from the eighth and ninth centuries BCE discovered in 1988–89. He also wanted to find that celebrated collection of gold objects discovered by Woolley at Ur, 340km south of Baghdad. Bogdanos was told it had all been safely locked away, and the Ur treasure was in a flooded basement vault of the Central Bank. A National Geographic film crew following him arranged for the basement to be pumped out. After three weeks, he was able to get in and discovered that he was not the first to make the attempt. An Iraqi had fired a rocket-propelled grenade at one of the vault doors, damaging it but blasting himself to bits. The manager unlocked the vault and found five boxes. They were allowed to dry for four days before being opened.

The largest box was saved until last. As it was slowly opened, what Bogdanos calls 'the entire treasure' lay before him. His eye was immediately drawn to a massive gold helmet. He knew the meaning of a helmet; that was why he did not wear one or allow members of his team to do so. A helmet separates its wearer from other people and forms a barrier that would hobble any investigator. Of course, that is normally a secondary effect of its protective function, but this helmet had no other purpose than to separate its owner from the rest of humanity. It was made from a single sheet of gold. Weighing over a kilogram, with holes to bind a padded lining, it had cheek pieces either side of a sculpted cap of wavy gold hair shaped in a bun at the back.

It had been found in the tomb of Meskalamdug, with an equally symbolic gold dagger, gold bowls, a gold lamp and many other treasures.[5] The tombs here date from around the time when the first ring of Stonehenge was erected, and they predate Tutankhamun by more than a thousand years.

Meskalamdug's bones are those of a robust man about 1.67m (5ft 6in) tall who died before he was 30. His rule came too early to be included in the Sumerian King-List, the first Mesopotamian history text.[6] According to the King-List, compiled within a few centuries of his death, the first king of Ur was Mesannepada. An inscribed lapis lazuli bead given to the ruler of the trade centre of Mari 700km to the north-west says it was a gift from Mesannepada, who identified himself as Meskalamdug's son.[7] The written historical record of Sumer, and so of the world, begins with Mesannepada.[8] Meskalamdug belonged to the last prehistoric generation, in an age before any written records.

The Birth of History

Until the nineteenth century, European scholars understood the pre-Christian past through surviving Latin, Greek and Hebrew accounts. History had been recorded much earlier in carved stone inscriptions from Egypt and incised clay tablets from Mesopotamia, but both had long been incomprehensible.

The texts were eventually persuaded to speak by scholarly codebreakers. The only clue to the meaning of Egyptian hieroglyphs ('sacred carvings') was a garbled ancient Greek text, but the discovery of a hieroglyph inscription also written in Greek enabled Jean-François Champollion to begin to solve that riddle in 1822. The cuneiform ('wedge shaped') characters on ancient Mesopotamian clay tablets were almost as baffling until, between 1838 and 1843, Henry Rawlinson was able to apply a similar approach to a rock-carved inscription at Behistun in western Iran, which repeated its text in old Persian. As more and more cuneiform tablets and hieroglyph inscriptions were discovered, a vast lost world was revealed, dating back into the fourth millennium BCE. References appeared to names and places that people thought they knew from the Old Testament, the world in which Pharaohs sent out armies and the great city of Babylon had been born. But the existence of a vast complex of giant cities with tens of thousands of inhabitants throughout the Tigris and Euphrates valleys thousands of years before the biblical patriarchs was unknown.

Meskalamdug's gold helmet is in the form of a distinctive hairstyle which is shown in portraits to be the form of the crown of the King of Kish.[9] Kish is said in the King-List to have been where kingship first began after the Flood. It has never been found and was probably some 80km south of Baghdad. Meskalamdug's crown identified him as the ruler of both Kish and Sumer, with the right to what was said to be the most ancient kingship in the world. Cuneiform texts state that Ur had, on a number of occasions, ruled over all Sumer. Woolley had been hired to excavate it by the British Museum and the University of Pennsylvania, and he helped to raise finance by emphasizing the links to the Book of Genesis. Ur was not only the source of the Flood story; it was also probably the place named in Genesis as Abraham's birthplace and potential funders were told that its ziggurat, the high stepped platform temple that was the city's core, might even be Jacob's ladder.[10]

After five years of digging, and uncovering hundreds of graves from the ancient city, Woolley struck gold in the most literal sense. Some of the burials were of later members of Meskalamdug's family and included claims to the Kingship of Kish. He also found the oldest known inscription in Akkadian, the language of Kish, on a bowl. In the third millennium BCE, Sargon of Akkad in northern Mesopotamia conquered Sumer and Akkadian came to replace

Sumerian. Known to us now as the language of Babylon, its literature absorbed and enhanced the achievements of Sumerian civilization to such an extent that most of what we know of Sumer comes to us through Akkadian.

Gold and Value

Here, gold was the link between the ruler and his city's resident god. The god was understood to be a powerful living presence, and in partnership with the king, owned the city and its land. The king's administrators organized the city's economic life, while the priesthood ran its rituals. By the end of the third millennium BCE, it is estimated that 90 per cent of the population of southern Mesopotamia were city-dwellers. We live in a time of rapid urbanization, yet according to the World Bank, only 82 per cent of the population of the USA and the UK now live in urban areas.[11] These great cities were created by trade; it enabled them to live. They had no material resources beyond agriculture: they had little stone and no timber or copper. These had to be obtained by exchange over huge distances, so they developed large-scale trade. To make that possible, they turned to materials that would be accepted as units of exchange. They were creating the idea of money.

We have no record of how this happened. The currency was related to things useful in daily life, such as barleycorns, wool and cattle, and they gave them relative values: a gur was about 300 litres of barleycorn and was worth an ox in good health. But these were represented by pieces of a novel substance that, like gold, was malleable, ductile, shining and useless except as decoration – silver. Sheet silver was being made and used in the Levant in the fourth millennium BCE.[12] It was actually harder to access than gold, because it reacts with almost every other element. In Egypt, silver was probably being extracted (with some difficulty) from a natural silver-rich gold ore likely coming from the same mines that provided Egypt with the majority of its gold. For this reason, silver was valued in Egypt at close to or sometimes more than gold. In Sumer, it was probably acquired alloyed with lead rather than gold, and the ore had to be mined and refined.[13] It was valued for decorative use and for high-status objects (four large silver lyres were found by Woolley in a grotesque excavation of human sacrifices at Ur which he called the Death Pit). A gur of silver was eventually called a shekel, meaning a bushel of wheat.[14]

So, the Akkadian word for silver came to mean money. That would be permanently embedded in tongues that trace their ancestry to the Levant, including Hebrew, French, Spanish and Romanian. The first evidence of this comes from around 2500 BCE, the time of Meskalamdug, in a tablet that refers to silver being worth 180 times its weight in copper. There were no set units such as coins, but silver could be used as rings, wire or bars because it is not burdensomely heavy, can be worn decoratively and only decays very slowly – tarnish can be easily removed. Weights of silver, the shekel and the mina, were effectively units of money. A shekel was the weight of 200 grains of barley; a mina was sixty shekels. They were widely accepted as payment. Sumerian merchants were pricing transactions in silver, and that was made possible by defining a fixed anchor in the incorruptible golden material that transcended the mortal world.[15] Kings set the value of silver in their decrees. It varied according to supply but was generally stated to be 'worth' one-tenth of its weight in gold, the immutable store of value.

All this was understood not as economic activity but as religious obligation. That was what the gods were there for. The core of the temple was gold, the physical link between the worlds.[16] The city was an extension of the temple, which was understood to be the residence of the city's god and its king.

So, the currency that appears in Sumerian texts is weights of silver and barley,[17] which were measured against gold, the bearer of value and adornment of the great.[18] Sacks of barley were carried to temple granaries. Life in Ur around 2500 BCE is wonderfully illustrated on a luxuriously inlaid box found in the 'Royal Burials' there and known as the 'Royal Standard'. Its lowest panel shows a series of figures dressed differently from the wealthy folk above, carrying well-stuffed shoulder bags or backpacks, probably of barley, which was used for daily purchases and taxes.[19] It was low in value, heavy, deteriorated, needed careful storage and did not travel well; it was often represented by clay tokens. Distant transactions and larger payments by rich folk were better made in silver. This was too expensive for labourers to use; a shekel-weight (about 8.3g/3oz) would buy an ox and was about a month's barley-pay for a worker,[20] but it became the basic currency in official accounts.

The oldest law-code known, composed by the Sumerian king Ur-Nammu around 2100 BCE, was intended for a palace-temple society whose families had significant levels of personal wealth and whose lives seem to have been pretty violent. It set gold at the heart of law, monetizing what people did to and with each other. The cost of knocking out a man's eye was thirty shekels, a foot cost ten shekels, a broken limb cost a mina. The reparation for cutting off a man's nose was forty shekels, knocking out a tooth, two shekels. To divorce a woman, her husband had to pay her a mina, sixty shekels of silver, though if he had married a widow, compensation was halved A kidnapper was imprisoned and fined fifteen shekels, the rapist of a man's virgin slave had to pay five shekels, and the reward for returning an escaped slave was two shekels. Perjury cost fifteen shekels.

The Trade Economy

We know about Mesopotamian trade and the value system because they inscribed their letters on clay tablets. Palaces and temples were from time to time destroyed by fire, meaning records kept on organic material would have vanished, but the clay documents in their libraries were baked and preserved. Attacks intended to blot out the memory of the defeated thus sometimes preserved them for ever. From these, we can see how gold became the validator of money at least 1,500 years before the idea of coins emerged.

Its value was recognized over huge distances by societies with different languages and gods. It enabled the exchange of resources necessary for the great Mesopotamian cities to obtain timber, metals, stone and jewels. Very little stone was available; it had to be imported, and the main building material was brick. A significant surplus of barley and wool had to be produced for this trade. Caravans of pack-animals went out carrying 70kg of cloth each, covering 25km a day, returning with 90kg of metal – some of it tin from Afghanistan for hardening copper into bronze.[21] Sumerians acquired exotic goods from very distant places, as Varna had done. Tombs at the small town of Tepe Gawra, close to Nineveh, around 3900 BCE, contain lapis from 3,500km away in northern Afghanistan, turquoise from Iran and obsidian from Anatolia.[22] But the nature of the exchange conducted by large cities was quite unlike that for small communities. Traders sent out from the palace-temple ziggurats of Mesopotamia were engaged in huge contracts to sustain tens of thousands of people and their rulers.

These traders were understood to be agents of their cities' gods. Gold here was not only the bridge to the world of the dead, but also the connection to individual divinities who took up active residence among humans. People here believed that they were ruled by divine apparitions who lived at the heart of each city, nurturing and protecting it. These Earth-dwelling divinities needed gold to anchor them to the world of men and underwrite the values that allowed the cities to trade, survive and prosper. According to Herodotus, the Babylonian Ziggurat of Etemenanki, the temple of the foundation of heaven and earth, was topped with a shrine in which was 'a fine large couch, richly covered, and a golden table beside it'. It contained no image. Herodotus continues: 'The Chaldeans also say – though I do not believe them – that the god enters the temple in person and takes his rest upon the bed.'[23] He had been told that a human woman would be chosen for a kind of ritual marriage to Marduk, the god who built the city, and spoke of a very similar ritual in the temple in Thebes in Egypt. He also said that the ziggurat contained a large gold image of its god, sitting at a large gold table with a gold footstool and chair; 'the gold of the whole was said by the Chaldeans to be of eight hundred talents' weight'. That is almost 21 tons.

Herodotus was writing in the fifth century BCE and had never actually visited Babylon, but the basic idea of such a city had clearly not changed much since the third millennium BCE, when Uruk had public buildings of a kind never seen before, immense and lavishly decorated, housing many priests, those specialized administrators of the material and transcendental world. Their city revolved entirely around the ziggurat of the sky-god An and the temple of the bride-goddess Inanna, whose festivals filled it with song, dance and beautiful women. The magical, transcendent power of gold was fundamental to the binding together of divine and human authority through which a city functioned. At the heart of the city, gold allowed human leaders and the gods to occupy the same mythologized space.

Organizing agriculture and trade, temples managed and sustained large numbers of servants and record-keepers, who did not produce much if any of their own food. The temples organized their education, emphasizing the necessary literacy and advanced calculation skills that were needed for the system to function. The cities' craftsmen, who produced sophisticated metalwork, fabrics and luxury handicrafts, were trained under the eyes of the priests and directed by them, as were the merchants sent on missions to obtain the resources they required. The word for merchant, *damgar*, is found in some of the earliest tablets.[24]

Hammurabi, who ruled Babylon around 1725 BCE, stated that silver was 'worth' one-sixth of its weight in gold.[25] Hard to find, directly associated with divinity, gold was generally too rarefied, and for a long time too sacred to be considered as a means of payment. In fact, it rarely changed hands. A document would suffice. It was the substance that validated and endorsed rulers, who exchanged it as gifts, tribute and recognition. Gold's physical role was not secular, but it was fundamental to underwriting long-distance trade transactions in records made using ceramic IOUs. That became big business.

Gold for Soldiers

The city of Mari, in what is now Syria, seems to have been constructed to facilitate this kind of trade. Built across an important trade-route intersection, Mari was the world's first pre-planned city, a copper and bronze-smelting centre laid out at the beginning of the third millennium BCE as a circular structure with a complex drainage and irrigation system. It was a city for business, and here we see evidence of gold being used as a form of private reward.

On one occasion, Hammurabi held a documented reception in his palace gardens for soldiers sent from Mari to serve him under treaty. His object was clearly to create a memorable event; he gave them gold in the form of 'sun disks' and rings, and silver tokens stamped with a value in shekels. The document explained that the stamps stated values higher than the tokens were worth by weight. 1 shekel pieces were a third underweight, and tokens of two and three shekels were light by 20 per cent.[26] This looks like a move towards silver coinage. The tokens were not meant to be used as circulating currency, but perhaps as a form of medal which would also be accepted by the temple as credit for more than their weight. The gold sun-discs and rings appear to be the first known evidence of gold being used, not in a sacred context, but as military pay. Of course, Hammurabi was understood to be a divinity himself, so this was not entirely secular, but it does look like an early step towards paying mercenaries in gold. It was an idea that took hold and would eventually transform the world.

This gleaming, incorruptible substance so deeply associated with divinity and eternity had become the ultimate repository of worth and guarantor of the value of money. The connection between the religious idea of worthiness and the commercial idea of monetary worth survives, even in our own language. The ambivalence in meaning may have been originally expressed in *worth*'s proto-Indo-European root, *wer-*, meaning to bend, turn or transform. The transformation of gold's divine value, worthy of absolute respect, into commercial value, worth acquiring, was the most fundamental step on humanity's journey to where we are now. It was the basis of commerce.

In 1958, the economist John Maynard Keynes speculated that the Sumerian cities could not have succeeded without gold. He argued that long before coinage, this indestructible, portable and recognizable material was used by traders to make deals and build the commercial network that sustained the city.[27] Around the time of Hammurabi, the newly dominant city of Babylon was indeed developing a new economic model which allowed merchants to make profits and build capital. The temple and the king no longer owned everyone and everything. They were still the ideological heart of the city, but Babylon was sustained with privately held land and privately conducted trade. That was how it became so successful.

Gold in Egypt

Commerce was fundamental to Mesopotamia, but it meant little to Egypt, where the god in the temple-palace was represented not by a gold statue but by the living body of the ruler. Egypt's cities were also huge – in 3000 BCE, when Uruk had around 40,000 inhabitants, Memphis was not much smaller – but Egypt's resources were far more varied, trade was not so essential to survival and currency was not significant. In the third millennium BCE, when Mesopotamian rulers were defining the relative values of silver and gold, there was no Egyptian word for silver, and it was virtually unknown there. They spoke of it as 'white

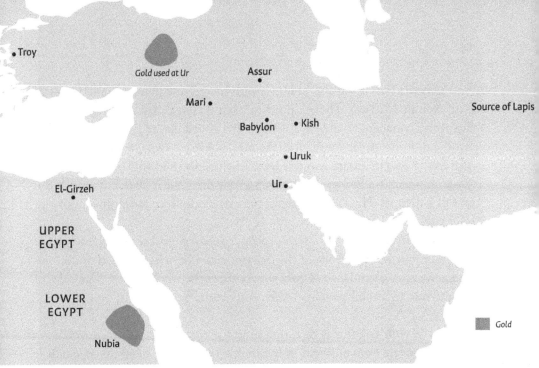

Troy

Gold used at Ur

Assur

Mari

Source of Lapis

Babylon • Kish

• Uruk

El-Girzeh

Ur

UPPER
EGYPT

LOWER
EGYPT

Gold

Nubia

Ancient Mesopotamia.

gold', and it did not acquire significance as currency there until the time of Ramesses II, in the thirteenth century BCE. Commerce was conducted in Egypt by establishing all values against the Egyptian equivalent of a gold shekel, a weight of gold called a shat (7.5 grams). The weight of twelve shats was called a deben.[28] So even though gold was utterly sacred and the flesh of the gods, it became worth stealing.

Egypt's tomb robbers did a more thorough job than Sumer's. We do not know about gold in Egyptian funerary rites until the early second millennium BCE, and then only from a text. A literary work survives from about 1875 BCE, a narrative in the form of the autobiography of a senior Egyptian warrior-diplomat called Sinuhe, who does not dare to return from a venture abroad when the king suddenly dies. He then has a successful career among Syrians, but in old age he desperately longs to return. He cannot bear the thought of dying in Syria, buried in a sheepskin shroud, his spirit wandering the Earth for ever. He fantasizes about returning to 'the Residence' and being granted the funerary rites of a ruler:

'A procession of passing is made for you, on the day of re-joining the earth.
A case of gold, a mask of lapis lazuli, the sky over you, placed in the bier.
The oxen drawing you, chanters in front of you.
Dances are made by the sacred dancers at the door of your tomb.
Offerings are pronounced for you, meat is butchered at the door of your chapel.'[29]

No Pharaoh's burial was found intact with its treasure before Tutankhamun's, from around 1323 BCE. He belonged to what is now called the 18th Dynasty. Egypt had conquered Nubia in 1500 BCE; the availability of gold then increased greatly, and one of the results was the new, gold-rich dynasty. The staggering quantity of gold in Tutankhamun's burial included a solid gold coffin and death mask, in which he had evidently been given the golden skin and lapis lazuli hair of a divinity. His inner sarcophagus was made from more than 100kg of solid gold.

He was short-lived and unremarkable; it seems probable that the tombs of the other fourteen pharaohs of the dynasty could have held a total of 20 tons. The new super-abundance of gold would affect the whole region. The ruler of Assur wrote to Tutankhamun's father, Akhenaton:

'Gold in your country is dirt; one simply gathers it up. Why are you so sparing of it? I am engaged in building a new palace. Send me as much gold as is needed for its adornment. When Ashur-nadin-ahhe, my ancestor, wrote to Egypt, twenty talents of gold were sent to him. When the king of Hanigalbat wrote to your father in Egypt, he sent twenty talents of gold to him. Now, I am the equal of the king of Hanigalbat, but you sent me ... of gold, and it is not enough for the pay of my messengers on the journey and back. If your purpose is graciously one of friendship, send me much gold.'[30]

Electrum

In Mesopotamia, the goldsmith's work was in the service of the death-ritual of the leading servants of the city's gods. Similar thinking was at work in Egypt, where the capstones of third-millennium BCE pyramids were covered in 'white gold', a naturally occurring gold-silver blend which we call electrum.[31] Alloying gold with other metals produced red, white and green gold for ritual spaces. Harder than unalloyed gold, electrum was used where brilliant display was needed or as a gold base for a throne or the grandest of votive statues. When the hero of the 'Tale of Sinuhe' returned to Egypt as an old man, in fulfilment of his wish, he saw his king enthroned on a platform of electrum. An obelisk dedicated by Queen Hatshepsut to the god Amun in the temple at Karnak around 1450 BCE was inscribed, 'then my heart incited me to fashion for him two obelisks from electrum'.[32]

But now it was becoming more available, and able to finance a great increase in trade, people began to appear in Mesopotamia who did not think of gold in this mystical way, and who could exploit the value placed on it by everyone else. Around 1530 BCE, Babylon was taken over by people with a completely different worldview, known as Kassites.[33] They were not Sumerians but nomads who appeared from the Zagros mountains to the north-east of Mesopotamia, and were regarded as primitive savages by the urban metropolitan elite. They did not see gold as having any important otherworldly role in human affairs. Our knowledge of ancient Mesopotamia is built on sand and cuneiform, and since we have found no comprehensible Kassite writing beyond a mass of fragmentary administrative and legal material, mostly from the city of Nippur, all we are left with is what is in the sand.[34] It looks as if they deliberately suppressed literacy, while carefully maintaining Babylon's physical traditions and trade network. They built and added very brief inscriptions to Babylonian temples but worshipped different gods: horses (which they introduced to the region) and mountain-deities. They ruled Babylon for 400 years, leaving not a single literary text. But they used the value others placed on gold. They evidently preferred it to silver for accounting, and put Babylon, in effect, on a gold standard. 'Red gold' was stated to be worth eight times its weight in silver, and 'white gold' half of that.[35] They established a great trading empire,[36] and in its later years they were using gold from Egypt as money (traded by weight). In the first millennium BCE, after Kassite rule had ended, we find sealed packages of lumps of gold and silver pieces which have been made up as a kind of money for specific deals. The lumps have been snapped off ingots made for this purpose. Archaeologists call them chocolate bars, because of their form. Intact 'chocolate' bars of electrum were found at Troy.[37] Troy and Ur were trade partners, and gold had become the currency of international commerce.[38] It brought divine substance into the mundane through the agency of priests and merchants.

From Assur to Babylon

The priests of the great Mesopotamian temple-cities were entitled to believe that they had a very good understanding of the functioning of people and gods, because their greatest cities flourished for 2,000 years. Gold was essential for their gods, their temples and to give worth to their contracts. Consequently, they and their gods fought for it. Gold and war were connected. When a city was conquered, its gods and their living, divine gold were seized from the fallen temple and carried to do obeisance to the victorious deity. Assur's kings, who established their capital early in the second millennium BCE, controlled a well-trained standing army which relied on terror and cruelty. Assur was a deity and the incarnation of a rocky crag towering over the Tigris, the place of the temple of the deity whose city and army this was. Its people, the Assyrians, conquered a huge empire, sacking its greatest rival, Babylon, around 1225 BCE and building up Nineveh as a centre of royal splendour. The Assyrian Empire ensured by its grotesque cruelty (flaying alive huge numbers) that it would constantly provoke rebellion. Assur and Babylon competed, aggressively and ruthlessly, for total dominance in the names of their golden gods. These were the cities that made the most effective use of new technology and methods of warfare. By 1000 BCE, when the Kassites had lost control of Babylon, horses had reduced distances, and new, sharper, more readily produced iron weapons were replacing bronze.

By this time, new forms of city had been established by the Greeks and Phoenicians. This kind of city was not the extension and instrument of the temple and its priests. Unlike Mesopotamian cities, they did have wood, stone and some metal: trade for them was not the basis of survival but was important for luxury goods, to source tin for bronze-making and for profit. Phoenicians traded as far afield as Britain and imported gold from Nubia, from which they fashioned high-value gifts for export such as the finely worked rings, earrings, pendants and bracelets from the eighth–seventh century BCE uncovered in Cyprus in 1998.[39] Greeks developed their own trade networks also based on shipping, founding colonies around the Mediterranean, and this seems to be the period when they were aware of a particularly wealthy Anatolian subject-ruler of Assyria named Midas. The Greek myth that denigrates him is connected to anxiety about the sacred metal that underpinned trade being touched by the hands of greed.[40]

There was, of course, competition between Mesopotamian cities for the rich trade of Greece and Phoenicia. Assur faced endless rebellions, and in 612 BCE, Babylon, in alliance with Medean nomads from the Iranian steppes, completely destroyed Nineveh and comprehensively razed Assur. Nineveh ceased to exist and was depopulated for centuries afterwards. Its memory was obliterated.

Two hundred years after the fall of Assur and Nineveh, the Greek historian Xenophon visited the sites of two great Assyrian cities whose names were unknown; he found mute stone with no memory and believed they had been cities of the Medes – who had actually annihilated them.[41]

But the idea of civilization sustained by gods, gold and battles was now too fundamental to be rethought. There had been a powerful desire to wipe out Assyria, but not to remove the idea of the city as a way of life. Mass slaughter did not, as it had done at Varna, result in the disappearance of the whole civilization. Babylon was left unchallenged, and its hugely valuable trade links to the resources of Greece flowed untrammelled through Anatolia.

Yet having now secured control of all the gold of Mesopotamia did not make Babylon as prosperous as it might have expected. Its people may have believed that gold enabled its jealous god Marduk, through his king and temple, to overthrow all rivals and shower wealth on the city's traders, but the mechanics of finance can change the value of money and reshape everything.

They duly did. The problem was made worse by the fact that hardly anyone could be quite sure what they really meant by 'gold'.

Chapter 3

The Birth of Money

The Invention of Trade Tokens

The greatest transformation wrought by gold on the life of humanity was its metamorphosis into coins. These precious little tokens would spread through the world like an infection, fundamentally changing every community that came in contact with them. The process by which they came to be invented, and the reason, have been deeply puzzling.

The idea that an authority could produce officially marked standardized metal tokens to facilitate trade seems to have appeared in the seventh century BCE, at the same time in Anatolia and China. This followed a long period of agricultural prosperity from the Mediterranean to the Pacific, when population growth was apparently driven by a benevolent climate and the availability of new iron tools. The seventh century BCE, though, seems to have been a time of significant climate change and major political upheavals, which evidently provoked a huge increase in commerce in both regions.[1] Traders in a dangerous world needed some simple way of managing a growing number of exchanges over long distances, and portable tokens guaranteed by a powerful ruler were an idea whose time had evidently come.

The idea was taken up in the Chinese kingdom of Chu, in the Yangtze River valley, and seems to have been used in a trade network extending well beyond Chu, spanning about 1,500km. Where there had been a gift-giving economy, commerce now appeared. Cast bronze tokens were increasingly used to facilitate this, initially shaped like the cowrie shells that had been gift tokens. They were inscribed with the mark of the issuing authority (whether a merchant or a ruler is unknown). They then began to be made in the form of knives and axes.[2] Chu also started producing small gold blocks of variable sizes stamped with the name of a city and the word '*yuan*', which were broken into sections appropriate for the purchase.[3] This was presumably because bronze tokens, having little intrinsic value, were only recognized relatively locally, but gold was accepted as valuable even where there was no basis for trust.

A similar process seems to have occurred around the sixth century in India, where stamped pieces of copper, silver and gold, called *karshapana*, *Purana* and *Suvarna*, were minted by bankers and merchants.

But dating these tokens is difficult. In Anatolia, however, the record is a little clearer.

Gold in Sardis

In Mesopotamia in the late seventh century BCE, the Assyrian Empire collapsed, a situation linked to political disintegration and an acceleration of trade. The Lydian city of Sardis, about 100km inland of modern Izmir and 325km south-east of Troy, sat astride fast-growing trade routes that stretched for more than 3,000km. Sardis had become the entrepôt between the Greek and Mesopotamian worlds. The cities on the west coast of Anatolia were occupied by Ionian Greeks who had established hundreds of colonies extending to France, Spain and the Black Sea. Sea routes to the south of Lydia led to Phoenicia, Assyria and Egypt, and eastward lay Afghanistan, Babylon and Persia. The Greek city-states were extended assembly spaces, while the cities of the East were extended temples. Sardis, the crossroad between their worlds, was an extended market stall.

According to Herodotus, writing 200 years later (and who knew nothing of China), 'the first of men, so far as we know, who struck and used coin of gold or silver' were here.[4] In the nineteenth century, French archaeologists brought long-buried Sardis back to the surface. There was a great palace and suburban slums, all dominated by a bazaar with narrow winding streets, large, two-storey caravanserais (hostels for merchants with space for their goods and animals), masses of permanent shops as well as bathhouses and public spaces for ritual performances. The streets would have been clogged with merchants and animals, as well as food and drink sellers and hustlers. It must have been very similar to the great bazaars of the Middle East ever since, teeming with every kind of trade and spice, rich in scents and perfumes, displaying exotic fabrics, medicines, jewels and weapons, and offering entertainments and contests to induce visiting customers to stay for longer.[5] Herodotus regarded it as the prototype of all such entrepôts.[6] This bazaar was the financial and political engine of Sardis.

Here, long before coinage, gold was the currency between strangers with different gods, different languages, appearances, habits, manners and needs, and it was at this city's heart. Its river, the Pactolus, was yellow with the gold it carried. In almost every other gold-bearing river, the element came naturally blended with silver, but the flakes in these sands were virtually pure gold.[7] The Greeks gave the river a legend to itself, the story of King Midas. When the god of wine eventually allowed him to wash the curse away, he left the river filled with gold.[8] That was why Sardis was the place to buy and sell with gold and celebrate Dionysus. Midas had left his successors uniquely and phenomenally rich, but according to the Greeks, the desirability of gold endangered them.

Using naturally occurring gold for making bargains was a specialist and highly personal business. The peculiar nature of this strange substance, which does not share in the universal processes of decay and corruption, made it the basis of value throughout Mesopotamia and the Mediterranean, but most of the gold brought to Sardis by foreign merchants was far from pure. It was very difficult to compare the value of the different gold objects they carried.

The ancient world knew gold in many forms, all of which played different roles. The word covered a wide range of alloys. The Mesopotamians called it 'sun metal', but green, amber, red, fine gold and superfine gold were all recognized. These were alloys of different hardness, containing different quantities of silver (making it paler) and copper (making it redder). Wonderfully skilled goldsmiths created artefacts with the qualities appropriate to their purpose, with surfaces often treated after completion, so their gold-ness was hard to compare.

The ingots and metal scraps used as currency by merchants were not 'money', as they had no defined value. The value of their gold might vary on the same day between six and seventeen times that of silver, depending on its supposed degree of refinement.[9] The commonest high-value substance long-distance traders offered for large purchases was electrum, which might contain anything between 65 and 90 per cent gold, the rest of it being mostly silver. 'Electrum' was also the word for amber: the alloy was a similar colour, pale yellow. Its variability made the use of 'gold' in trade extremely complicated. The metal that merchants brought to Sardis had to be assessed on the spot.

A king might apparently have its purity checked 'in the fire' (though we don't know how), but that was not normally practical. Experts used needles of different purity to compare the colour of streaks made by the metal on a hard black stone, known as a touchstone. The word became a metaphor for judging quality and reminds us of the tension of the moment of testing. The gold merchant was a technical specialist and a man of known character who brought his reputation to the touchstone. This kind of trade had always been a special event. In Mesopotamia, the use of physical gold for commerce was rare and involved high values. But by the middle of the seventh century BCE, as populations and their productivity grew, Sardis was seeing a huge increase in traders arriving to make high-value exchanges. Each piece of gold used in the market would need to be examined by an expert every time it changed hands to check its weight and purity, and this was impractical, especially with tiny pieces. A fragment smaller than 4mm weighing an eighth of a gram might be worth enough to feed a Babylonian labourer for a week,[10] but that depended on being sure how much gold it contained.

The ruler of Sardis was well placed to solve the problem and wanted to do so. One of Lydia's unusual features was that, unlike Greece and Persia, its leaders did not regard trade as beneath their contempt. Ancient Greek literature shows no interest in gold for trade. Homer's story of the Trojan War, possibly recorded in the eighth century BCE, began with a golden apple supplied by the Goddess of Discord as the prize in a divinely ordained beauty contest – desirable, coveted, but like all the gold he mentioned, outside the world of commerce. As Homer depicted it, gold generally appeared in artefacts belonging to the gods, coming from the gods, used in rituals or associated with immortality.[11] Divinity is unbounded, and the identification of gold with the divine makes it hard to quantify and commodify its value. Homer's gods and heroes wore golden armour, had golden shields and helmets and wielded golden weapons. Such things have existed and had neither utility nor economic value. Homer's Agamemnon proffered gifts to Achilles that included ten 'talents' of gold, but this was not the low currency of trade.[12] A talent, roughly the weight of a human, is never mentioned as anything but gold, and here was offered by a king to a semi-divine hero.[13] Gold in Homer is a substance belonging to their transcendent world. It is immortal and ageless; its incorruptibility separates it from the mundane.[14] There is no mention of the traders' gold, and when merchants do appear in the *Odyssey*, they are regarded as shifty and contemptible.[15]

Lydia had a more business-orientated perspective. The Lydian language was unrelated to Greek or, as far as can be discovered, any other known tongue. No temple remains have been found there from this time and it seems unlikely that their culture saw gold as having much of a divine connection. Perhaps they were linked to the Kassites, those horsemen who took over Babylon for four centuries, who did not think of gold as connected to gods but were instead interested in using it as currency.

The Gold Glut

It certainly seems that Lydians were prepared to handle gold taken from the homes of gods and the hands of priests, which perhaps made them unusual. There was plenty of sacred golden plunder in the seventh century BCE. The Assyrian Empire was in upheaval, with palaces and temples being ransacked. When the availability of gold increased, its value fell, so silver bought more gold and more goods. There is evidence that this was happening in Babylon in the last decades of the seventh century BCE.

We read that in Babylonian financial records. In recent years, a surprisingly clear picture of the Babylonian economy has appeared, thanks to the ongoing translation of a continuous dataset of prices maintained by scribes from the late seventh century BCE for about 550 years. Along with monthly records of six commodities, they also record information on the weather and the level of the Euphrates. They also note the position of the moon and planets, so are now called 'Astronomical Diaries'. The movement of prices was understood to be either a reflection of, or reflected in, the movement of the heavens. Tens of thousands of cuneiform tablets were stored to identify patterns that could help predict market movements. A great number of these ancient economic forecasting tools, damaged but often readable, are now in the British Museum. We may have more reliable very long-term economic data about ancient Babylon than about modern Europe or the USA.[16]

The evident fall in the value of gold was probably caused by major upheavals in the Assyrian Empire flooding markets with electrum stripped from palaces, temples and great houses. This was monetized as 'spoil'.[17] Some of it would be used to finance trade.

White Gold Coins

Valuing this spoil was cumbersome and uncertain. There was a standard trade-weight of about 7 grams called a 'stater' (a Greek word simply meaning a weight), but until you could establish the purity of its metal, that meant nothing. The ruler of Sardis, Alyattes, solved the merchants' problem by taking in the highly variable electrum brought to Sardis. Its gold content could be officially assessed and instead of ever needing to do that again, it was exchanged for the appropriate quantity of an artificial alloy which was guaranteed to be 60 per cent silver and 40 per cent gold.[18] Merchants received discs with precise weights of different fractions of a stater. Ungilded, they looked more like silver, and this must be the metal Herodotus spoke of as 'white gold'. But they were made to look golden by surface gilding, which made them appear more valuable and also had the practical effect of preventing touchstone analysis to check the actual metal value.[19] It is clear that mined silver was deliberately added to make the metal consistent, because that increased the amount of lead, and some of the coins had more mined silver added than others to produce the white gold.[20] They were stamped with elements of the royal device, a sunburst on a lion's head, and are spoken of as the world's first coins.

Their value was not dependent on the metal they contained, instead coming from that royal guarantee visibly stamped on them. This was fiduciary currency, meaning its value was based on trust.[21] The image on a stater was a royal guarantee of value, and it must have meant it was convertible to gold.[22]

Alyattes could have exchanged merchants' electrum for pure gold from the Pactolus River, but evidently thought it made more sense to make 'white gold' coins. There could have been two reasons for that. Firstly, the value of gold fluctuated, whereas he fixed the value of coins. In addition, he set their price at more than the metal content, which made their issue profitable.[23] Merchants bringing electrum 'spoil' of uncertain consistency who may have come huge distances to make great contracts would have been attracted by the opportunity to have it securely converted into coins with a clear value, and were evidently willing to pay for certainty.

Lydian coinage was a new metal in a new form. In order to make people accept it, King Alyattes probably insisted on using it himself and on taxes being paid with it.

A one-third stater coin was worth about two months' wages, perhaps equivalent to around $10,000, which obviously rendered it useless for small purchases. As a result, tiny fractional tokens were minted, going down to the incredible size of 1/192nd of a stater weighing seven-hundredths of a gram. In an extraordinary feat of precision minting, this 2mm pinhead token carried the image of a lion's paw.[24] To us it seems a ridiculous object, but it had a value equivalent to $150 today. The physical evidence of wear shows that these coins did circulate, and the smaller ones circulated most.[25] The ancient world became quite happy with tiny coins: when Athens later produced silver drachmas, they were minted in 48ths, 4mm across.

This innovation was initially a huge success and minting white gold coins became a competitive business. Some 400 mints sprang up in Ionia selling coins, probably competing on price, with each mint guaranteeing their redemption value backed by their own stamp. There were certainly more mints than cities. Money had arrived. Enough of the coins and dies survive to suggest that there were more than 50,000kg minted, perhaps far more, so millions of staters appeared.[26] Trade evidently prospered, and prices seem to have stabilized.

But white gold currency did not last long. The world's first minted money, an alloy of silver and gold, collapsed and was soon replaced by coins made instead from discs of solid gold or silver.[27] By the fifth century BCE, when Herodotus wrote about Lydians and their invention of money, electrum coinage had pretty much vanished. All he knew was that Lydians had created the coins he used, made of pure bullion. Over the following 2,500 years, the spread of gold and silver coins would transform every aspect of life on Earth. Everyone would become a customer.

What had gone wrong with white gold, and why was pure gold the solution?

The problem appears to have been a result of gold and silver being packaged together. We can see from the 'Astronomical Diaries' that for the first fifteen years of Nebuchadnezzar's rule in Babylon, from 605 BCE, the cost of a pound of barley in silver remained steady. Then it began to fall, so that by his death in 562 BCE it had halved.

That meant that the value of the metal in a stater coin was significantly less than one stater, and people began demanding gold instead. Croesus, who succeeded Alyattes as ruler of Lydia around 560 BCE, was evidently obliged to redeem the white gold coins with pure gold taken out of the Pactolus River.

The economic earthquake that ended white gold coinage can, in a sense, be ascribed to the hand of God, probably as a direct result of Nebuchadnezzar's destruction of Jerusalem. The fall of the Jerusalem Temple may very well be the event that precipitated the launch of golden money.

Until 721 BCE, there had been two neighbouring Israelite kingdoms: Israel and Judah. Then Assyrian forces overran Israel, carrying off a great swathe of its population, while thousands fled south to Judah and its capital city, Jerusalem.[28] Sennacherib of Assyria tried and failed to eliminate Jerusalem, and then, as Assyria crumbled, Jerusalem grew in size and prosperity.[29] It became a flourishing part of the regional trade network, dealing in the gold of Egypt, spices of Arabia, treasures of Phoenicia and much else.[30] By the time Nebuchadnezzar came to power in neighbouring Babylon, the Jerusalem temple was more than a golden sanctuary: it was the treasure-chest where merchants stored their physical wealth.

Nebuchadnezzar replaced the Assyrian Empire with his own, reaching from the Mediterranean to the Persian Gulf and from southern Anatolia to the Arabian Desert. In 597 BCE, he succeeded where Sennacherib had failed and quite literally wiped Jerusalem off the map. He took everything. He removed a large number of Israelites to Babylon, their catastrophe being remembered in the Psalms and so carried through Christian tradition into the poetic rhythms of enslaved Africans, kept compellingly alive in music and story right down to Boney M's recording 2,595 years later:

'By the rivers of Babylon, there we sat down.
'Yeah, we wept, when we remembered Zion.'

What was remembered of Zion was the demolished sanctuary.

Gold from Jerusalem

The sanctuary at Jerusalem was said to hold about 40 tons of gold. It would have included a great deal of electrum. Ezekiel's spectacular delirious Hebrew religious visions, composed in Babylon soon after its destruction, describe God seated on an electrum throne.[31]

The building is described in the *First Book of Kings*, whose core may date from before the destruction. Its inner sanctum (the 'Holy of Holies') contained the Ark of the Covenant, a gold-covered box containing divine laws, with a gold seat and a gold table. The description seems to be drawn from the same divine architectural playbook as the ziggurat of Babylon, with its golden table and seat for Marduk, but without a golden figure of a deity. Instead, the table was sheltered under the extended wings of two gold-covered figures called 'cherubs'. No one is sure what these were: probably a form of griffon, the creatures Herodotus says guarded gold. They were said to be 3 metres (10 cubits) high, and their outstretched wings spanned the chamber. The author(s) of the *Book of Exodus* believed that versions of these had been specifically commissioned by the God that took the Israelites out of Egypt, in instructions that he gave to Moses.[32] Those instructions were the justification for costuming the High Priest in beaten and woven gold, with a gold crown inscribed 'Holy to the Lord'.[33] His priesthood was innate in what he wore.[34] It recalls the third-millennium cuneiform text in which the Lord of Aratta put on the golden crown for the goddess Inanna and became the manifestation of a shrine.[35]

But by the time of its destruction, Israelite gold seems to have become unusually detached from any divine presence. In the mid-seventh century BCE, when Assyria was in decline, Josiah, King of Judah, brutally purged his country of all foreign divinities, destroying their images and priests, and dedicating the Jerusalem temple to a single god who had no physical representation at all.[36] After that, the Temple gold was a manifestation of splendour, not divinity. This is thought to be when the *Book of Deuteronomy* was written. It opens by listing the places where Moses is said to have spoken, one of which seems to have been invented as a warning against attaching gold to gods. The place is named as Di-Zahav, 'Quite Enough/Too Much Gold'.[37] An entirely novel concept.

Too much gold is what was in the Temple, and would cause havoc. It has been a source of fascinated speculation ever since. Nebuchadnezzar's vandalism, by an extraordinary irony, preserved it as a cultural icon. Neither Babylon's temple of Marduk nor any other temple of the ancient world survives in anybody's memory, only this one. Every year on the ninth day of the month of Av, the anniversary in the Jewish/Babylonian calendar of its destruction, observant Jews the world over still fast and sing a lamentation. The space which is said to have been occupied by that Temple became the most potent religious focus on Earth, the spiritual nuclear reactor at the heart of modern geopolitical conflict.

The sacred vessels and golden décor were removed to Babylon[38] as homage supposedly paid by the conquered Israelite god to Marduk. But privately owned gold that could be rescued evidently went into hiding and then circulation. Most Israelites were forced into servitude,[39] but substantial merchants who had managed to escape the disaster with access to their gold had existing connections outside Judah and began putting them to work. It seems that they had lost any sense of gold's transcendental significance (no gold has been found in pre-

Roman Jewish burials),[40] and that made them useful. For example, the temple of Ebbabar in Sippur, where the Tigris and Euphrates are closest together, now used a Hebrew family of specialist merchants to supply their gold.[41] The temple got a good price, paying just 8 shekels of silver for each of gold.

So gold was on the move on an unprecedented scale. Pharaohs had gifted gold to kings for shrines and had filled tombs with it, but this was mercantile gold, set in constant motion to lubricate exchanges made in distant cities. As it flowed from Jerusalem, its value fell, and prices rose in Babylon and Lydia. Each white gold coin lost nearly half its buying power. As for the stamp guaranteeing a redemption value, that depended on confidence in the mint, and most of the mints in Ionia were in territory which was suddenly conquered. Croesus seized nearly all the Greek colonies on the Anatolian coast, which must have undermined the stamped guarantee of value on the electrum coins they had minted.

Monetizing Divinity

Around the time when Croesus became ruler of Lydia, there was a widespread shift away from the notion that gold was intimately linked with worship. The connection between gold and divinity had been central in Mesopotamia and Egypt. The urban centres that grew in Mesopotamia were each based around a pyramid sanctuary, a palace-temple ziggurat that was the earthly residence of the city's god. Divine personalities were thought of as physically present in these buildings. Incorruptible gold filled them, allowing specially empowered humans to occupy the same physical space as divinities. Ancient Egyptians too believed their gods were physically present in their temples, inhabiting the statues that represented them – and there the Pharaoh became a human vessel for divinity. Gold was understood to be divine flesh, and the intimate association of gold and special humans necessitated large quantities of it.

But by Croesus's day, belief in the literal reality of this great community of rival gods was evidently waning. The 'bronze age' of the old priesthoods had begun to vanish as society had changed. Agricultural production had been transformed by the introduction of iron tools, from hoes and rakes in Italy to complete ploughs in China, and by the development of new rice-growing systems in India. The result was a huge increase in population and urbanization, and the growth of more complex states with new elites and well-educated bureaucrats and administrators. This meant that a new class of public educators was emerging, from the Mediterranean to China, who did not think of divinity in the old way. Zoroastrianism was being taught in Persia, with a divinity, Ahuramazda, that had no interest in gold, did not inhabit the same space as humans but had a moral and political programme that they must subscribe to. The ideas of the Talmud were being debated in Babylon. Pythagoras, Lao Tzu and Confucius were all alive when Croesus invented golden coins, as was Thales, the man regarded as the first Greek philosopher. He lived in Asia Minor, not far from Sardis, and died in 546 BCE. He argued that the cosmos was bound together by a single substance, and that substance was water. He did not think of water as purely material, but equated it with divine spirit; Aristotle quoted him as saying: 'What is the Divine? That which has no beginning nor end.'

It seems gold no longer shared that boundless quality, and could now be valued like any other commodity.

Pure Gold Coinage

Croesus had to redeem Sardis's white gold coins with pure gold, but it was still in the form of coins. He obviously had to take back a huge quantity of white gold, which may well explain his donation to Delphi of a pyramid of the stuff weighing over 6 tons, produced from a vast store of it that he had lying around.[42] The new pure gold staters he issued were more bean-shaped, and showed the royal lion roaring at the head of a bull. This was not a fiduciary currency given value by a royal guarantee, but commodity money, literally worth its weight in gold. The design conveyed that it was pure gold not connected with any temple, and it showed Croesus powerfully facing down divinity. The bull was associated with gods throughout Croesus's world. The same design was used on similar silver coins of one-tenth the value.

Some people, perhaps unable to access the redemption process or maybe holding white gold from other mints, began physically disassembling their old coins. A refinery was excavated in Sardis in the 1980s which turns out to have been a private enterprise separating the metals.[43] The process was like a form of magic.[44] They would hammer the electrum to a thin foil, mix it with salt and baked clay dust, seal it in an earthenware pot with urine and cook it gently for a few days. Breaking the pot open required a careful ritual. There was no salt or urine left in there but highly astringent iron chloride and a poisonous vapour (chlorine), unknown in nature. And there was pure soft gold, shining like the sun. The pot had now been impregnated with silver oxides or chlorides, which could be turned into pure silver.

The value of Croesus's gold coins was accepted everywhere, and the value of gold recovered. His gold and silver staters were first issued weighing 10.7 grams, with ten silver ones supposedly worth one gold – the old ratio of one:ten. But soon the value of gold rose by a third, so Croesus shrank the gold staters to 8.1 grams, to ensure that ten silver were still worth one gold. The Babylonian

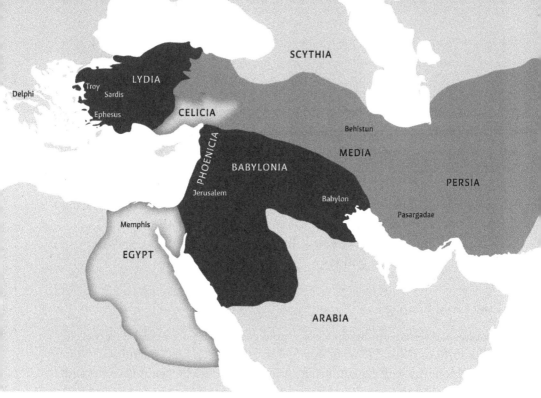

Croesus's world.

records show that the fall in commodity prices ended. Buying and selling became easy, which is why Herodotus believed that Lydia had been able to invent shops.

Now gold began a dual existence, as the transcendental representation of divinity in temples and as a commodity in the market. Babylon did not list it as a commodity in the 'Astronomical Diaries', but its exchange value underpinned everything that was listed there. Lydia was not very engaged with gold's mystic power. The evidence of Lydian burials, a few of which were not disturbed until quite recently, is that gold only made its way into the tombs as small decorative objects and appliqué on clothing, not as a special link to anything other-worldly.[45] Lydian interest in gods seems to have been mainly concerned with fertility rather than the afterlife. It is far easier to find evidence of goddesses than gods there, and their kings' tombs seem to have been topped with monumental stone penises.[46]

It is true that when Croesus did build a temple, he did it on a grand scale. The Temple of Artemis was one of the Seven Wonders of the World, the first temple built entirely of marble. It is said to have taken ten years and been the largest building in the ancient world.[47] Recent excavation revealed a huge quantity of golden objects, more than has been found in any other sanctuary of the period.[48] But Croesus did not build it in Sardis. Instead, it was created in the Greek city of Ephesus on the Ionian coast, which Croesus conquered at the start of his reign. This building was not put up out of piety but as the propaganda of power, designed through its sheer magnificence to overwhelm

Greek resistance to their new Asian overlord. It was clearly branded with his authority: his name remains inscribed on its columns.

About 440 BCE, Herodotus described Sardis as a debased, corrupt society which put its daughters up for sale. He saw the evidence of this on Croesus's father's tomb, the great tumulus still standing north of the long-vanished city. Instead of referencing a deity or a dynasty, five stones on top recorded the Lydians who subscribed to this monument to Alyattes. It was a list of market stallholders and craftsmen, including women; he was struck by the fact that these 'prostitutes' made the largest contribution to the tomb-monument.

Herodotus's view of the Lydians was interesting, but is perhaps an unreliable result of the Greek and aristocratic Persian distaste for traders. Sardis's faith in divinely managed fertility may have once been expressed in sacred prostitution, as in many eastern cities, but according to Herodotus its young women had now become commodities and their parents sold their daughters' bodies to build up a dowry. This was evidently what he believed happened when power was in the hands of men who treated divine gold as personal cash. The virtue, honour and dignity of Sardis's daughters had been monetized.

Croesus had made the mystery of gold into a commodity available to anyone, creating a break with the past. The nature of that break is of course debatable. In Herodotus's view, the effect of de-sacralising gold was the collapse of social order as men were debased from heroes into emasculated dealers who could not control 'their' women. He seems to have ascribed Lydia's growing military weakness under Croesus to this socio-economic upheaval. Sardis's merchants used to be defended by horse-mounted archers raised in an archaic heroic culture. Their kings needed them to secure the dominance of their merchants over trade between Greeks, Phoenicians and Babylonians, and that is how Croesus and his predecessors conquered Ionia. According to Herodotus, Croesus discovered that raising boys as merchants removed their fighting spirit: 'You will soon see that they have been turned from men into women.'[49] It seems unlikely that Herodotus would have known that Croesus said or thought any such thing, but he did know that after his initial conquests and vast increase in trade, Croesus had come to depend on foreign mercenaries and then been humiliated.

It is very unlikely that gold staters crossed the counters of shops and taverns. They were symbols of luxury and could only be used for extravagance or as tokens of finance. Their primary function was to underwrite large transactions and reassert confidence in the value of gold. The likelihood is that they enabled the market to function. They were probably used by stallholders to pay their rent, and so provided an incontestable basis for calculating prices and commercial value.

In the Grand Bazaar in Istanbul, I have seen traders take their earnings at the end of the day and convert them at gold exchanges to pay their rent in bullion. The stallholders wield great economic power, represented by rents of $2,000 and more per square metre.[50] It made sense that Sardis's stallholders needed to convert the payments they received in copper, fragments of silver and small packets of electrum dust into gold and silver coins of defined purity and value. It would also have been a way for Croesus to establish his authority over the self-sufficient world of the bazaar, and for the market's prices to be benchmarked against a secure standard. Successful commerce depends on trust, and this was a way of providing it.

I spent a short time in Shiraz in the 1990s, an Iranian city where the bazaar was sufficiently self-contained to ignore the country's use of summertime. Its clocks never changed, and government found it hard to penetrate. Merchants told me that the Shah had tried to modernize it by driving new roads through the narrow alleys; they had no doubt that this was an effort to impose his authority there. If Croesus obliged the merchants of Sardis to convert their takings into his coins, and use some of them to pay their rent, he would have taken a huge stride towards exerting royal authority over this self-governing economic dynamo. And if the gold standard increased customer confidence in the market, the traders would embrace that willingly. It was all about belief in value. Pure gold coinage magnified wealth for Croesus and kept the market functioning smoothly.

Gold for Mercenaries

It was all going so well until the middle of the sixth century BCE, when a renegade Persian grandson of the king of the Medes, Cyrus, won the support of leading nobles and swept to power. The Medes, since the destruction of Assyria, were masters of a vast area including much of modern Iran and northern Mesopotamia, as well as Armenia and Cappadocia, in eastern Anatolia. Cyrus now created a new imperial structure that absorbed their kingdom. He became, in Herodotus's words, 'master of Asia' and controlled a sprawling empire with a huge population of fighting men. The trade route between this new Persian Empire and Ionia went through Lydia. Lydia had been allied to the defeated Medes and Croesus controlled the key mountain passes. Cyrus had demonstrated his ability to mobilize and use overwhelming force, and evidently felt that he needed to take pre-emptive action to retain control of his trade route. Besides, he needed to stop the gold from helping Babylon.

To confront the massive power at Cyrus's disposal, Croesus needed to recruit mercenaries. They would come from Greece. There had been professional soldiers throughout the Middle East for many generations, but they were not paid wages: they were warriors who received sustenance and plunder.[51] In the seventh century BCE, Greek mercenaries began offering themselves for hire in Egypt, seeking not just plunder but also payment in land. The Egyptians, who seem never before to have encountered warriors with bronze armour, were keen to use them.[52] Croesus was keen too, and he could offer gold.

He may not have placed much store by the transcendent mystery of gold, but Greek mercenaries did. Men who fight for a living need to believe that they will be on the winning side, and that their paymaster will flourish. Croesus needed to ensure that his recruits believed that the gods foresaw his triumph. He could not buy the gods, but he could certainly buy their oracles. Herodotus speaks a good deal about Croesus's gold, which is of such legendary status that we still speak of modern billionaires being 'as rich as Croesus'. But to Herodotus, as to the whole Greek world, what was important was the size of the gold offerings Croesus made to the gods at Delphi. His fate, they thought, depended on the power of gold to connect him to the realm of the gods. As a consequence, his hiring arrangements involved trips to Delphi, and he needed to publicize the results of his heavily subsidized oracular guarantees of success.

He gave Delphi a gold bowl weighing over 250kg and a 270kg solid gold lion. The lion was his own royal emblem, and it stood on four gold half-bricks of the same weight, all on top of a pyramid of what Herodotus called white gold, weighing over 6 tons. This was presumably where the redeemed white gold staters ended up. Herodotus saw the remains of the lion after it had been damaged in a fire – an event which seems to have occurred soon after Croesus presented it and would have been deemed a very bad omen.[53]

As the huge armies gathered, the gods of Babylon, of Persia and of Greece would be understood to be deciding what happened next to markets, temples and kings. Was this a conflict between the gods, or the opening battle in the war between gods and Mammon?

Chapter 4

Fall of the Gods

The Defeat of Croesus

Cyrus had no power centre at all. The lands of the Medes and Persians, stretching over 3,500km from central Anatolia to the Indus valley, contained no great city. Its people were mostly nomadic pastoralists without temples, statues or cultic centres. The Medes traded in horses and agricultural produce, and imported gold for decoration and drinking vessels, but they did not think that divine personalities had homes on Earth and did not seek to connect with otherworldly powers through gold. When Cyrus had taken over the throne of the ruler of the Medes, it was not in a great hall but in a tent.[1] He acquired a certain amount of treasure, but to confront Babylon he needed huge quantities of gold to put a large army on the move with gifts to commanders and to undermine the great city's walls with bribery. He would take the gold from Croesus.

Croesus was ready. The message he brought back from the oracle at Delphi was that he would destroy a great empire. He assumed this was a prophecy of doom for Cyrus; just what his troops needed to hear. But Delphi was guarding its reputation with ambiguity, and it turned out that the great empire he would destroy was his own.

The use of gold to pay soldiers was well established and would now play a crucial role. If Sardis had not been so rich in gold, it seems unlikely that Cyrus would have been drawn to attack it. He knew that Croesus proposed to mobilize his own and Babylon's defence with golden cash, and consequently seems to have engineered one of the most notorious acts of treachery in all history. According to the first-century BCE Greek historian Diodorus Siculus, Croesus had sent a trusted lieutenant, Eurybates, from Ephesus to Greece to hire mercenaries.[2] The cover story for Eurybates's load of gold was that it was being taken to the oracle at Delphi, which meant that it was sacred and untouchable. It is conceivable that Eurybates himself was uncomfortable with the misuse of sacred gold; in any case, it seems he changed sides and revealed the plan to Cyrus. And it was the king of the Medes, not the waiting Greeks, who received the gold. Plato, in his *Protagoras*, written about a century after the event, tells the story as one with which every Greek is familiar, and uses

Eurybates's name as a byword for treachery – treachery which was believed to have changed the history of the world.

Croesus still had enough money for his own defence, but perhaps not to help spendthrift Babylon. His own army was immense – perhaps 100,000 hired mercenaries. Cyrus did not rely on hired men; he had established more of a permanent, professional force sustained by a network of personal and tribal obligation and great gifts. It was a carefully conceived mixture of heavy cavalry of Persian nobility supported by light cavalry of horse-archers under Persian commanders, with Egyptian infantrymen and Indian intelligence operatives. He also had newly designed chariots with scythes on their wheels, heavy siege-engines and a complex logistics operation with military engineers to strengthen roads and enable the whole force to cross rivers.[3] It was impressive, but only half the size of the mercenary force of Sardis. Cyrus had to negate the power of Croesus's remaining coins. He simply waited for the end of the campaigning season, when Croesus stopped paying. Winter began and the mercenaries were being sent home. Wars were not fought in winter – up until now. Cyrus's midwinter attack was so unexpected that even when Croesus was told it was coming, he did not believe it.

Cyrus was still greatly outnumbered, but he fought in a completely novel way. Croesus's battle line of half-disbanded Egyptian and Greek mercenaries, hurriedly supplemented by local levies, found themselves facing a huge advancing square of archers. The Lydian battle line tried to surround the sides of the square, but was stretched too thin and was reduced to chaos as it was blanketed with swarms of arrows. The coup de grace came when Cyrus ordered the camels of his baggage train to charge against the Lydian cavalry. The smell of thousands of bewildered stampeding camels terrified the horses. Sardis, Croesus and all the gold fell into Cyrus's hands.[4]

As Sardis fell, Croesus climbed onto his own funeral pyre. There are moments when the world is seen to have changed in an instant, and afterwards, for a generation or two, people find a sense of commonality by asking: 'Where were you when …?' The assassination of Kennedy was one such moment; so was 9/11. The first of these waypoints was the fall of Croesus:[5] 'Where were you when Cyrus came?' The actual date is uncertain, with chronology simply calculated from the length of rulers' lives, and Croesus's destruction has now faded from memory, but his name has certainly not.[6]

His offerings to the oracle were proved to be entirely futile, but that did not diminish people's confidence in the authenticity of otherworldly communications. It was just that he was not the kind of man who could understand them. His gold offerings were not powerful enough to monetize and monopolize power. But gold's role in human affairs had hardly got started.

Sardis had been a great hub of trade, and gold currency became the basis of the trade network that allowed cities to flourish, but there is no evidence that his coins were used in daily life beyond its territory.[7] Greek city-states were quick to imitate the production of coinage, but in silver rather than gold, and Mesopotamia did not display the same interest at all. That may be because its people were not subsistence farmers, did much more shopping and made more use of small change in the form of cheap materials like shekels of barley – or clay tokens representing them. The expense of minting very low-value coins was ridiculous.[8]

The Writing on the Wall

In Babylon, the equation between gods, gold, trade and might was wrapped up into a single package that would have ruled the world. But its currency, silver, began to collapse when Cyrus moved on to his next target. Having been steadied by the new gold and silver coinage, so that silver stopped rising and gold falling, everything should have kept on a level footing even after Cyrus took over Sardis. But far greater shifts were about to come.

We know what a financial collapse looks like. On 28 September 2008, the US stock market crashed, the Dow Jones index showing the largest drop in points that had ever happened. This was just the beginning: 85 per cent of the fall was still to come, as panicked investors frantically sold stocks to buy gold, which after 4,000 years still seemed the only true form of value. Five years later, the Dow Jones had not recovered, but the price of gold had doubled.

The 2008 crash was made manifest on the screens of the exchanges. The brokers of London and New York were notorious for their lavish competitive extravagance and gross luxury: now the alarming writing on their wall displays appeared to be beyond human control or even comprehension. These were scenes oddly reminiscent of Rembrandt's painting of Belshazzar's Feast presaging the fall of Babylon.

The painting is based on a story in Chapter Five of the biblical *Book of Daniel*, according to which, immediately before the city fell, writing appeared to tell revellers that their world was about to end. It shows the horror-struck ruler Belshazzar watching a disembodied hand writing golden Hebrew letters on his banqueting house wall. The message was very similar to a trader's screen.

Babylon was a centre of luxury and indulgence, not just for its merchants and traders, but for its nobles, priests and rulers. It had magnificent public buildings, palaces and temples. Nebuchadnezzar, who died sixteen years before Belshazzar's Feast, had turned the city into a work of art, centre of arts and learning and the core of a powerful empire.

The fall of Lydia had been a great battle that shook the world from Greece to India. Lydia, though, was a recent upstart. The fall of Babylon was more fundamental, ending 3,000 years of Mesopotamian dominance, bringing Persia to the Mediterranean and setting the stage for what would be seen as Asia's existential confrontation with Europe. It should have been a big deal, yet it happened without any battle at all. Indeed, at first Babylon did not even notice that it had fallen. Herodotus reported that there was a festival in progress, and the revellers knew nothing of the attack until they had been captured.[9]

We have a multiplicity of written sources for what happened in 539 BCE. This alarming graffiti only appears in one of them. There are four different cuneiform accounts, including one attributed to Cyrus himself;[10] we also have a number of Greek texts. And we have the *Book of Daniel*, which is a collection of prophetic and apocalyptic texts in Hebrew and court stories written in Aramaic, the common language of the Persian Empire, possibly in the third century BCE and evidently drawing on older material.[11] Its fifth chapter includes what appear to be references to real events.

The first lesson of these histories turns out, unsurprisingly, to be that written accounts tell different stories, have different agendas, incompatible chronologies and are based on different beliefs about reality – and are then understood through the prism of the reader's beliefs. For a long time, this chapter of the *Book of Daniel* was regarded as fantastical. The feast-giver, Belshazzar, is not mentioned in any of the Greek texts and was taken to be an invention. The king was Nabonidus. But during excavations at Ur in 1854, evidence appeared that Belshazzar was not only real, but was Nabonidus's son and regent.[12] The story of the writing on the wall may after all have some authenticity.

This story of an exiled Hebrew prophet in Babylon is the only account that links money and the defeat. There were three units of value used for trade in Babylon: at this time, sixty shekels made a mina, and sixty minas were a talent.[13] Their value was measured against gold, 13.5 grams of silver representing 1 gram of gold.[14] The ancient world was used to prophetic signs and wonders, but this was quite different. The words written on the wall said, very simply, 'Mina: mina, shekel – halved'.[15] It meant that the value of Babylon's silver money was crashing.

The panic created by a screen in the twenty-first century showing a plummet in asset-values and its disastrous consequences was being played out here in 539 BCE, eight or nine years after the death of Croesus. Belshazzar is described as trembling and involuntarily soiling himself.[16]

Babylon is Taken

Belshazzar evidently had seen no threat that his city could fall, although clearly the financing of Babylon's defence should have been rethought after the fall of Sardis. Instead, he relied on walls and gates, and did not guard the water-gates into and out of the city. The fateful day was the sixteenth of the seventh month, Tašrîtu, in 539 BCE, in the middle of a new year party. This was the great feast that Herodotus said blinded the inhabitants to Cyrus's seizure of their city for three days.

New Year in Babylon was a time when the frailty of the human-divine link was acknowledged.[17] Over a period of days, the ruler considered his faults, made atonement and at the culmination was given a renewed mandate by the city's god.[18] The figures of gods of subject cities were brought with gold chariots and gold ritual vessels. It was not normal to completely erase the temple of a conquered people. In a civilization where every city was an extension of its temple, the home of its god, wars between cities were understood to be wars between their gods. When a city fell, its god was humbled and defeated, and the god-statue had to be brought to pay homage. But the Jerusalem temple held no statue. Its god was disembodied. There was only the wealth with which it was lavished. The *Book of Daniel* says that gold vessels seized from the Jerusalem Temple were used at the feast.

The destruction of the Jerusalem Temple and the seizure of its treasures in 586 BCE was, of course, the reason why Hebrews like Daniel were in Babylon in the first place.

Nebuchadnezzar had taken the temple vessels from Jerusalem as the entitlement of, and Judah's homage to, Marduk. But it was not Marduk who was being honoured at this feast in 539 BCE. Babylonian texts and the Cyrus Cylinder agree that Belshazzar had replaced that deity with the moon-god, Sin, the god of Uruk. This was the night of the moon god,[19] and Belshazzar seems to have been relying on this divinity to protect his city. The symbolism was stark and is visible in the 'writing on the wall'. Marduk's name appears to mean 'bull-calf of the sun',[20] and his sanctuary and statue were gold. The association of the moon-god with silver is self-evident: Belshazzar's father had reconstructed a famous ancient sanctuary of Sin, which had been lavished with silver.[21]

Cyrus said that he advanced on Babylon as Marduk's hero and defender – the agent of a divinity of gold against silver. When it fell, he formally accepted the rulership from its gold figure of Marduk in the ziggurat. Gold triumphed; silver collapsed.

Value Vanishes

This event sealed the establishment of Cyrus's empire as the greatest in the ancient world. He became King of the Four Corners of the World. The fall of Babylon was the start of the most fundamental struggle in the ancient world, the thousand-year war between the civilizations of Persia and Greece. The Persian War would be the spine of history until the rise of Christianity and Islam, and

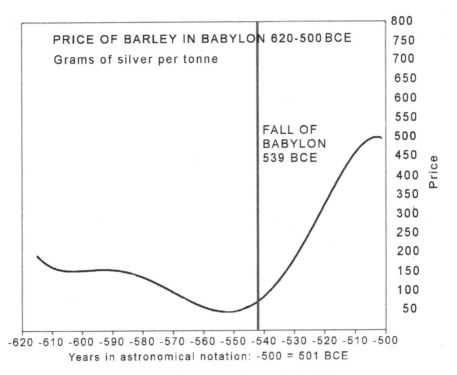

The price of barley in Babylon 610–500 BCE. From Van der Spek (2014)

then bestow a terrible legacy right down to our own time. Herodotus invented the writing of narrative history in order to trace the emergence of the conflict, which he rightly saw as world-shaping.

The message of the supernatural hand as the Persian army approached had been that the currency of Babylon would collapse. The *Astronomical Diaries* show that the cost of living did soar after the fall of the city and continued to rise hugely for around fifty years. In other words, the value of money fell, and kept falling.

The price of barley is the best measure to use, as it was a fundamental staple and the price records are less damaged than others. The evidence in the chart is clear and reflects real-world political changes. Since the authors of the *Astronomical Diaries* were professional forecasters, perhaps one of them had been the source for the writing on the wall, with some whistleblower putting it up there. If it happened at all.[22]

Gods without Gold

Cyrus had presented himself as loyal to Marduk, who had been usurped by Sin. But this was a theology that Cyrus had learned for political reasons. He came from a very different culture, where the idea of gods living and competing among human communities made no sense at all. Persian belief was centred on the notion of a divine presence perceived in light, in fire, in air. It was associated with a deity called Mithra, who was then identified with Ahuramazda, representing settled civilization, locked in conflict with darkness and the gold-adoring nomads of the great steppe. His prophet was Zoroaster or Zarathustra. His sacred books, the *Avesta*, contain very ancient material.[23] Gold did not have any sacred place in these beliefs.

Cyrus had captured a vast golden treasure, but he did not need it for tombs or temples. Nor did he need it for trade. As Herodotus explained, the Persians were not traders, and 'the market is completely non-existent in their country'.[24] Cyrus had contempt for merchants: 'I have never yet feared such men, for whom there is a place appointed in the middle of the city for them to come together and deceive each other on oath.'[25] Goods in his empire were exchanged without currency, and bargaining meant nothing to him.

The lands of the Medes and Persians, as we have seen, had no urban centre. Cyrus built a capital for himself, but it was a palace-city, Pasargadae, with a landscaped garden (a 'paradise') where his isolated stone shed of a tomb still stands among evidence of vanished buildings.[26] He was laid to rest in a gold coffin with a divan standing on gold feet, but these were not there to ease his journey to an afterlife. No evidence survives of his own beliefs beyond the inscription there; it addressed the visitor, saying: 'I am Cyrus, who founded the Persian Empire. Do not begrudge me my tomb.'[27] The intermediary power of gold was non-existent and irrelevant.

Gold and Jerusalem

To the astonishment of the Hebrews in Babylon, Cyrus announced their restoration to their original homeland and gave them back what gold still survived from their temple. As he did for all his conquered peoples, he issued decrees respecting their form of worship. He appears to have seen them as potentially useful allies in defending that part of his newly won territory, who could serve with gratitude in his armies. He did not put much faith in hired mercenaries; the gold was not for spending. Nor did he see it as empowering the Hebrews' god. It was given to be treasured, as a sign of royal approval. Cyrus understood that so far as the Hebrews were concerned, the purpose of their return to Zion was to rebuild it. They considered themselves the people of 'the covenant', that set of commands stored in the now-vanished ark, and they had to restore worship on the temple site. Cyrus's successor, Darius, followed through, sending more back to the empty site of Jerusalem to rebuild its temple and wall, and to farm the land.

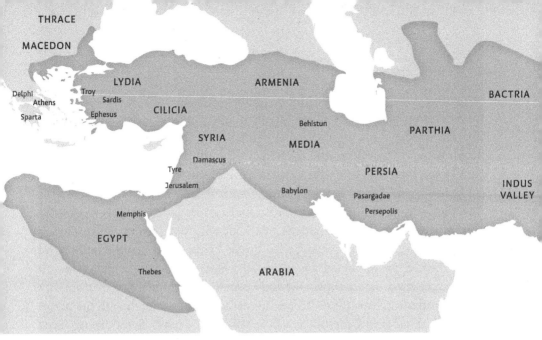

The Persian Empire.

Only seventy years separated the destruction of the first Jerusalem Temple from the building of its replacement. But the Hebrews who built the second temple no longer assumed a necessary connection between their god and gold. They did have a use for gold in the service of religion, but in a rather different way. Its connection was as much to the King of Persia as to God. To revalidate the temple, successive Persian kings restored much of the gold that Babylon had seized from it – not the cherubs, which seem to have flown away, but candlesticks, vessels and thirty bowls of gold. This was handed over by the man in charge of the Persian Treasury, Mithredath, a name which expresses the core of the earliest Persian religion.[28] It means 'gift of Mithra', the ancient Indo-European god of light. The function of the gold was not to establish a link to God's authority, but to serve as a physical representation of the king's will, a guarantee that it was he who was establishing the people we now call Jews in Jerusalem.

Gold was building more of a connection between the Jerusalem Temple and the King of Persia than with a god. The Jews called Cyrus a new Moses, *Mashiah*, 'messiah'. The word had originally meant someone divinely anointed but now meant an apocalyptic saviour, divinely supplied. The idea of a messiah became so powerful for the Jews that it would eventually produce Christianity and strongly influence Islam. The gold sent to Jerusalem achieved far more than mere money could ever do.

Gold and Secular Power

The huge store of gold Cyrus had seized was not circulated, and the commercial reality said to have been spelt out on the wall in Babylon, that gold was now expensive – and scarce – must have remained a basic truth. A certain amount of Sardis's own coinage continued to be minted, presumably for use by its own market-traders. That did not mean that coins were necessarily acceptable in polite society. They were, after all, associated with the sordid world of markets. In Greece, there was an enthusiastic take-up of the idea of coinage, but not of monetizing gold. Silver coins were minted as a way for every city-state to promote itself as a brand and a political entity, and for the political class to exercise control over dealers and merchants, but gold coins were seen as presumptuous.

In 515 BCE, Cyrus's successor, the usurper Darius, initiated the building of what the Greeks would call Persepolis, the Persian city.[29] Like Pasargadae, it was not centred on a temple and had no marketplace. It was a treasure-city, and the offerings brought to it were not dedicated to a god, though the palace itself was. Four gold Croesus staters, and two Greek silver staters, were placed in each of two boxes under the foundation tablets of the audience hall, in two boxes inscribed with the limits of his kingdom and requesting the protection of Ahuramazda, 'the greatest of the gods'.[30] But although the walls of Persepolis are covered with wonderful reliefs showing the great variety of men making offerings from around the Persian Empire, there are no images of priests or gods. The Persian ruler was not the representative of otherworldly power. He simply served Ahuramazda by taking in vast quantities of gold and so increasing its scarcity. The relative value of silver fell so far that prices in Babylon were ten times higher in 500 BCE than they had been at Nebuchadnezzar's death.

Darius introduced new coins of his own, with each gold coin costing ten times as much as the silver ones. But these coins did not circulate much at all. The Persian kings' coinage was the most commanding evidence of royal authority. The gold ones were called darics by classical authors. In place of Croesus's bean-shaped coins stamped with a bull and a lion, the daric was a circular disc showing the king himself, in battle posture with a spear and a bow. The gold daric was not used to pay soldiers, traders or suppliers: his fine silver coinage was produced for that. These coins were ideological statements of Darius's unique place in human history.[31] The Persian king's power was associated with the incorruptible splendour of gold, and anyone else who dared produce coins was executed.

His kingdom became the creator of symbolic gold currency, with its gold coins possessing eternal value but now secularized. The darics were fixed units of purity and weight, with a value which allowed them to be understood as the guarantee standing behind lesser tokens made of silver and bronze. The coins were also Darius's way of imposing his presence and vision throughout his huge empire, as though he was ruler of a continent-spanning city and master of its money. The daric was completely novel, in that it carried not the badge of a city or a god, but the figure of Darius himself. For the first time, an identifiable human being was stamped onto pure gold.

The multilingual inscription at Darius's rock-carved monument at Behistun, which became the key to reading cuneiform, was written to proclaim that it was Darius's mission to bring about the triumph of Ahuramazda, God of Light, over the forces of darkness: 'Ahuramazda has granted me this empire. Ahuramazda brought me help, until I gained this empire; I hold this empire by the grace of Ahuramazda.'

He towers over his defeated prisoners, while the god floats above them. A new kind of religion was on the march, in which there was said to be just one god, demanding justice and morality, and gold was not the way to connect with him.

The link between gold and the foundations of society appeared to be over.

Chapter 5

Golden Alexander

Macedonia – Gold's Refuge

In Greek eyes, the fact that Persian kings used gold coins was evidence that they were enemies, not saviours. To many Greeks, gold was the money of tyrants, men who saw themselves as claiming to rule with divine sanction or to exercise divine absolute power. There were some Greeks who placed gold in graves. So far, about forty inscribed gold tablets have been found in burials throughout the Mediterranean, dating back to the fifth century BCE, which seem to be intended as passports to paradise. But Greeks had no enthusiasm for golden money.

Coining did spread through the Greek world: fifty years after Croesus's death, coins were produced by more than a hundred mints and were circulating in the city-states of Greece, Italy, Sicily and Anatolia. But they were not gold. The summoning of divine authority to validate personal rule was, to the Greeks, anathema. Their coins were only silver. They were stamped with the symbol and authority of the city, and it was that, rather than the mystical power of the metal, that comforted merchants. The city itself was the guarantee of its silver coins, and Athens's silver quickly predominated. Between 550 and 350 BCE, Athens, which led the resistance to Persian expansion, minted only silver coins, famously pure and trustworthy, stamped with the owl of Athena. There was a happy coincidence between Athens's disapproval of golden money and its abundant supply of silver.

Lydians were not Greek and minted both gold and silver coins, giving its silver a fixed value in gold. Greek silver coins had no fixed value in gold and were not meant to be convertible. Silver was earthly and appropriate for use by modest mortals. Gold was not. This perspective would shape the Greek response to power and history and would infect the cultures that inherited it. Others, as the Greeks saw things, lusted after tyranny.

North of Greece, on the north-west coast of the Aegean, the king of Macedon felt no discomfort in associating himself with the works of the gods and did lust after tyranny. In 338 BCE, Philip II, who had built a powerful personal military machine and ruled as untrammelled master of his land, defeated the combined forces of Athens and Thebes. Athenian 'democracy' (the public participation of free adult men in politics) was snuffed out, and Philip became the sole ruler

– the hegemon – of Greece. The Athenian silver owl would disappear, as the hegemon minted his own splendid silver coins. But he also had gold – masses of gold – from mines on Mount Pangaeus in northern Greece and minted magnificent gold medallions that signified his divinely authorized power. Philip thought of himself as living in a world filled with interactions between humans and gods. He did not use gold to connect with gods but as a way to channel his own power with their backing, and issued gold currency to display that.

Philip's 'staters' showed him racing an Olympic chariot on one side and the head of Apollo with a victory wreath on the other. Their intrinsic value was underwritten by their otherworldly incorruptibility, but their use was perfectly secular. They were pay and he felt entitled to bestow it. They were designed to be compatible with the daric, which meant they could be used easily in Persian territory, including Thrace and Tyre. His coins circulated far beyond Macedonia and transformed economic relations between rulers and their followers from the Danube to the Thames. First-century BCE Celtic gold coins found in Henley in 2005 had designs that imitated the coins with which Philip had paid his mercenaries some 200 years before.

Here, gold still had the double meaning of wealth and mystic power. In 2015, a skeleton buried in Macedon was finally identified as being Philip. He and his queen were interred in massive pure gold boxes. These were certainly not to impress humans: the reason why the bones took so long to identify is that the world was told the couple had been cremated and had no tomb. The bones in the tomb had indeed been cremated, but were then buried in a ceremony apparently imitating the one described by Homer when Achilles interred Patroclus, allowing

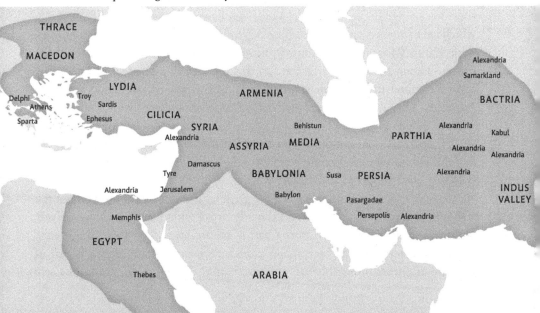

Alexander's conquests. Eight of the many 'cities' he named Alexandria are shown.

the hero to properly begin his journey to Hades.[1] In the Macedonian cosmos, gold still had a role in connecting the ruler to another world.

Alexander the God

Philip's son, Alexander, actually thought of himself as belonging to the other world, and that he was not Philip's child at all, but Zeus's. He was crowned in Egypt as the son of Zeus-Amun. The Greeks had regarded Philip as a northern barbarian, but Alexander was identifying himself as Greek, the offspring of a Greek god. He internalized the great war of civilizations between the Greek and Persian worlds as one in which he played a transcendent role as the defender and avenger of his god-father. Macedonian military power was not entirely based on gold; it was driven by shrewd planning, but without the cash it would not have existed. In more traditional Greek eyes, this was a war between gold-empowered tyrants. To Alexander, it was self-evident that he had a filial duty to crack open the strongbox of Persepolis and disperse its contents, transforming the world.

The accumulation of treasure he captured there was staggering. Tribute had flowed into Persepolis from an area including Thrace, Libya, Nubia and far beyond, even to the borders of Punjab. India alone, which Darius took around 518 BCE, had to pay 11 tons of gold a year, a talent a day for 360 days. Whether it ever succeeded in paying is unknown. This tribute (or taxation, or gift-collecting) was used to spread largesse in the form of luxurious gifts (including coins), to bribe useful foreigners and to pay armies, but a very large part was retained as a royal gold mountain, staggering evidence of the infinite gulf between the Great King and the rest of humanity. Greek accounts of the Persian Empire all agree, rather smugly, that it was undermined by this accumulation of wealth. For them, this was shown in a moral decay, a growing enjoyment of luxury at the expense of manliness, which led to an increasing and perilous dependence on the robust energy of Greek mercenaries. More recent historians, using more modern assumptions about the causes of change, have stressed the fact that a policy of gathering and hoarding capital resulted in economic stagnation and overstressed, overtaxed, resentful provinces. The latest analyses work hard to undermine these Greek-centred and Marxist-informed perspectives, but it is hard to avoid recognizing that Alexander was generally welcomed as he advanced on Persia, and the Great King, Darius III, had difficulty mobilizing enough effective forces to resist him. The mountain of gold was not a support for the Persian Empire: it was a dead weight.

Alexander's determination to loot the great treasury of Persepolis was not the sole reason for his invasion, but it certainly drove what he did once he arrived. In breaking open that gargantuan and ever-swelling moneybox in 330 BCE, he transformed the Mediterranean world. Persepolis contained a hoard of treasure eighteen times the size of Persia's annual tributes. In Iran, they still remember the invader as Alexander the Terrible. Once he had stripped it, he turned Persepolis into the pyre of the Persian Empire. According to Alireza Shahbazi, the archaeologist and one-time director of the site, stone slabs from the treasury were used to build a grandstand for Alexander and his men to watch this apocalypse. They saw a world die. Another would be born, not from its ashes, but from its gold.

Diodorus Siculus, writing around 50 BCE, said that reckoning gold in terms of silver, 120,000 talents were found there. Alexander sent for mules from Babylon, Mesopotamia and Susa, as well as 3,000 dromedaries, to remove all the treasure. According to Plutarch, about 150 years later, there were 20,000 mules and 5,000 camels. If that was true, the caravan would have been more than 70 miles (113km) long. This seems unlikely, as it would take five days to pass and the beasts at the end of the line would be left nothing to eat. But the point is clear: Persia's treasure was beyond calculation, the greatest seizure of wealth known in the world until the Spanish took America. And with the same results; as gold flowed into the money supply, its value fell.

Although the quantity sounds, as it was, enormous, this was only a fraction of the gold gathered by Persia's Great Kings. Even if all the 120,000 talents of Persepolis treasure were gold, 'reckoning gold in terms of silver' at the ration of ten-to-one there would 'only' have been 300 tons of gold. One important caveat is that numbers in ancient sources very rarely reflect any measurable truth: whether they refer to armies, deaths or treasure, they are essentially poetic, conjured for effect. There are modern historians who argue that the whole of humanity's stock of gold remained below 300 tons until 1492.[2]

The bulk of the tribute that flowed in had been distributed through the Persian Empire, not as cash but as treasure bestowed, or waiting to be bestowed, on servants, aristocrats, emissaries, administrators – whoever the Great King wanted to bind. From the treasury at Susa, the most opulent court in the world, Alexander took 50,000 talents in gold and silver. This was a system that dealt not in money but in luxury, and which defined the aesthetic of personal significance in terms of gold accoutrements. Everyone of rank and ambition knew what they should aspire to, and showing off gold to illustrate the importance of its wearer would long outlast Persia. It educated Alexander in what it meant to be royal, and that vision transferred to the Greek world with huge success.

Alexander's gold, which financed a vast expansion of power and city-building, clearly granted him earthly immortality, at least in stories. It was also, of course, supposed to be evidence of his transcendental immortality as the son of Zeus, which is why his corpse was placed in a gold sarcophagus inside a gold coffin.

Dispersal of the Treasury

What was not in any way immortal was his empire, which died with him in 323 BCE, just seven years after he destroyed Persepolis. According to one numismatist's arithmetic, if every human on Earth at the time owned one drachma, Alexander would have been eleven times richer than the lot of them; assuming, of course, that we knew how many people there were in the world. And assuming we know how much Alexander actually had. Nevertheless, monetary wealth is not anything tangible. It is a story, a belief, credit, inspired – however distantly – by a sense of otherworldly significance. The Persian treasure was worth what people believed it was worth, measured by what they thought it could buy in an infinitely accommodating market. Since people invested fantasies of fortune in gold, that was its value. So, the break-up of the Persian treasury, its conversion into coin and dispersal to Alexander's generals changed the balance of power between Europe and Asia. The gold coins they made were just small yellow counters, but they could be exchanged for whatever people wanted. Everyone had their own gods, but everyone believed in gold. Seventeen years after Alexander's death, one of his generals, Ptolemy, took the title Basileus (King) of Egypt and became the first man who dared to mint gold coins bearing a human face – his own. The only faces on coins up to then had been mythological or divine beings.

Coinage was little used in Egypt until Basileus Ptolemy and his successors started monetizing the country to make a space for state power and taxation.[3] It also made him the first ruler who was perpetually visible throughout his lands. He forbade the presence of any foreign coins, all of which had to be recast to bear his own image, and so the process began in which coin-portraits of rulers would monetize the world. Ptolemy was not actually deified until he died, but the message of his coins was quite clear: he exercised divine authority and his portrait did not just endorse the value of gold – it endowed it. That was such an intolerable concept to the Jews that their community in Palestine had to be allowed to use different coins although under Ptolemy's rule.

As gold flowed through the lands held by Alexander's successors, an enlarged Hellenic world emerged as a connected economy from the coast of the Ionian Sea to the eastern borders of Persia, and from the Balkans to the North African coast, Egypt and the Persian Gulf. Its courts now had the wealth to spend on exotic luxuries, and the Eastern Mediterranean became home to a new, rich civilization which could afford and enjoy trade with the distant East. This was now a money economy, tied together with an extensive sea trade. The currency was silver for daily use and gold for long-distance trade and the contracts of the great.

The Greeks had once claimed to disapprove of Persian luxury. Alexander wanted to create a syncretic amalgamation of the two worlds. That did not happen, but his successors were keen to live in oriental luxury and they had the gold to buy it. So, having been carried away and coined, much of the gold of Persia began flowing back there again.

After Alexander's death, Persia was ruled by one of his generals, Seleucus, and under his descendants' rule the Seleucid Empire became host to an orientalized Greek urban culture that traded eastern goods for Egyptian and Greek gold. In 200 BCE, the Seleucids defeated the Ptolemies of Egypt, and in the process acquired control of Jerusalem. More precisely, they acquired the Temple. This great religious centre, the core institution of the Jews, which had been created under the benevolent eyes of the Great Kings of Persia, was now the national bank of Judea. It was, of course, full of gold.

Gold of the Temple

There was a very remarkable description of the gold that had supposedly been in Solomon's Temple, and so was carried off to Babylon. This would certainly have interested the Seleucid rulers. It seems to have been produced by the temple priesthood, at some time in the long period while the Ptolemies and Seleucids were fighting each other. The text is now part of the Bible, called the *Books of Chronicles*. It is a thorough summary of the whole of history, from Adam to Cyrus, from the perspective of the priests who governed Jerusalem. It devotes special and loving attention to the contents of Solomon's Temple. It could well have been written in the time of Ptolemy III (245–222 BCE), who is said to have personally visited the temple and made a sacrifice there. He was conducting a hugely successful campaign against the Seleucids which appeared to be on the point of reassembling Alexander's empire under his rule (and which was cut short by natural disasters in Egypt). It was just the moment for the temple priests to present a sympathetic world-dominator with an account of what Cyrus should have restored to put the temple back where it was before Babylon destroyed it. Like any good negotiators, they pitched high.

According to *Chronicles I (2)*, Solomon had used 8,000 talents of gold in building his temple. That is more than 270 tons. There was a lot of gold in the first temple, but nothing like that much. The text says that Solomon got it from a place called Parvaim, which is never mentioned anywhere else. The name may be related to the Sanskrit 'purva', meaning 'East', and seems to be a word suggesting Paradise.

It is clear that the author of *Chronicles* was used to gold being used as cash in commercial transactions. He says that when David bought land, he paid its owner 600 gold shekels. The only other reference in the Bible to gold being wealth (rather than jewellery) for ordinary people is in the *Book of Joshua*, where a character confesses to stealing and hiding a gold bar. The *Book of Joshua*, like *Chronicles*, is regarded as being written well after the time of Cyrus.

Once the Seleucids acquired Jerusalem, a predatory eye turned towards this holy bank deposit. A few years later, Antiochus IV, who had inherited the throne, adopted the identity 'Epiphanes' ('God manifest') and launched a ferocious assault on Judaism and its temple. In 167 BCE, he stripped its gold. At first, he had seen it as a useful pot to draw on to supplement his income, but then he took the lot. According to one account, he took away 1,800 talents, 55 tons. He used some of it to mint coins proclaiming his divinity.

Darius's royal imprint on his darics had said that he operated with divine unquestionable authority. His coins were certainly money, and the eternal value of these gold tokens had been guaranteed by the image stamped on them. Now Antiochus had taken a final step on the journey meant to demonstrate that a human tyrant was a god. He forbade the practice of Judaism, which of course rejected his worship, and massacred Jews. This provoked what is described as the first recorded uprising in the name of freedom of religion; it included rural Jews making war on Hellenized Jews in Jerusalem who had accepted Greek forms of worship. The long and bitter guerrilla war that followed, known as the Maccabean Revolt, resulted in Seleucid power over Judea being broken and the restoration of the temple.[4] Had the Maccabean Revolt failed, that would possibly have been the end of the Jerusalem temple and Judaism. History would have taken a different course. Without a Jewish Jerusalem, there could have been no Christianity, and Islam would not have developed as it did. In a sense, the modern world was born out of the victory of the Maccabees.

As the Seleucids lost their power, a new indigenous Persian Empire emerged out of north-eastern Iran. Under the rule of kings of Parthia, who took on the old Persian title of 'King of Kings', their territory came to control the trade routes between the East (India and China) and the Mediterranean.

The Flow to Parthia

The new power that emerged had its heartland in Sistan, that part of Iran which borders Pakistan and Afghanistan. It sucked back gold that Alexander had dispersed. From Syria, caravans travelled on Parthian roads carrying fine glass, expensive fabrics, wine and other valued goods to India and China. There is little hard information about the value of this trade to the Parthian treasury, but in one year the tax on the import and export of balsam from Judea is recorded as representing 64kg of gold. Even more profitable was the trade on Parthian roads into the Mediterranean world, carrying Chinese silk and Indian precious stones, perfumes, opium, pepper and other spices, as well as enslaved eunuchs. And just like their Persian predecessors, the Parthians had a desire to gather gold and little desire to spend it. They did not regard gold as sacred but did use it as a statement of their power and wealth. They encouraged it to flow to them, and then they hoarded it. They did not turn any of their gold into coins. The equation between gold and personal wealth seemed to have been broken.

Part II

Gold Makes Rome

Chapter 6

Celts And Carthage

Rejecting Gold

I have explained that the inspiration behind this book is the way the leaders of the Kogi people talked to me of gold, and why we want it. I have listened for years to their bitter and profoundly worried complaints about what they perceive as the terrible harm done to the living earth by mining. When I first arrived among this remote South American people – linguistically, culturally and physically isolated on a mountain – it was hard for them to make me understand. Yet I had read the same complaint in a Roman document by Pliny the Elder, writing in 79 CE. The original scrolls are long gone, but his work was extensively and lovingly copied through the Middle Ages with the care normally devoted to religious texts. Pliny, like the Kogi, knew gold as a substance carried in rivers for humans to collect and work into very special objects that have a sacred purpose. The Kogis' concern at mining for gold, plundering the Mother Earth, is powerfully expressed by Pliny in one of the final chapters of his great encyclopaedia, *Natural History*. He insists that everything we really need is provided by Mother Earth, 'our sacred parent', on her surface. He argues that what is sunk far beneath her surface, materials that have been slowly formed over very long periods, urge us to our ruin and drive us to the depths. It is not just us, but our parent the Earth that is being ruined. These digging operations, he observes, continue endlessly. He demands that we should consider where this will end, when we finally exhaust the Earth, and to what point greed will finally penetrate.[1]

Rereading him, I am reminded of sitting in a large dark hut with four fires, and dozens of barefoot, serious men in white robes. They are speaking to a camera that will carry their message into our world, the world run by the dangerous children they call their 'younger brother', from whom they have been hiding for centuries:

'The Mother gave us what we needed to live. But now they are taking out the Mother's heart. They are digging up the ground and cutting out her liver and her guts. The Mother is being cut to pieces and stripped of everything.

'We work to take care of the world. But they are ending it.

'So, from today stop digging into the earth and stealing the gold. If you go on the world will end. You are bringing the world to an end.

'I want to give some advice, to tell the real truth to the Younger Brother, if they go on like this, and they don't change their ways at once they'll see what will happen. They'll see what will happen.'

The Romans and Athenians had tried to step away from gold. Thirty years after Cyrus captured Babylon, there was a successful democratic uprising in Rome against tyranny. It was perhaps connected with the great fall in the value of silver money in the Persian Empire, and with the weakening belief that absolute political power was bestowed by gods through ever-more-expensive gold. Roman histories later explained that King Tarquin 'the haughty' (*superbus*) was a tyrant whose outrageous enrichment and entitlement was represented by his gold crown and golden robe. As we have seen, new ideas about political ethics had emerged. The Roman Republic traced its origin to the revolution in 509 BCE, the first ever recorded, which ended Tarquin's rule. Four hundred years later, Cicero wrote of what happened as 'revolution' (*convertere*), using the metaphor of planetary movements just as it would be used in modern times.[2] The new state was ruled by elected consuls and by an atavistic horror of gold as an expression of status. The notion of a man who partook of divinity, and whose status allowed him to possess and distribute this sacral material, did not sit happily with declarations of Republican morals. Even Pliny, writing 100 years after the Republic had been abandoned, when emperors were installed by the army and were deified, still clung to those values, and saw the mundane exploitation of gold as corruption. Gold seal-rings were a mark of rank, but nobles who wanted to show their love of traditional values pointedly preferred iron ones.

Pliny the Elder died when he went to study the strange cloud that was coming out of Vesuvius and causing terror in Pompeii. He never quite finished his great work. But his voice can still be heard coming from the Kogi. Pliny was emphatic that the hunt for gold was the supreme example of unsustainable plunder: 'The worst crime against mankind was committed by the first person to put a gold ring upon his fingers.'[3] That led inexorably to the next crime committed against humanity, 'by whoever was first to make a gold coin'.[4] His peroration is the condemnation of Mark Antony for debasing gold in the most extreme way – having it made into a chamber pot. Pliny was not simply railing against greed and luxury. For him, it was clear that gold should be left in the Earth because it has a sacred role, and what he was describing was sacrilege.

Plundering Rome and Delphi

A hundred years after its anti-monarchic revolution, Rome had a store of gold totalling rather less than a cubic foot[5] – most of it presumably left by the old kings. It was not to be coined, and except for family heirlooms, was not to be privately owned; it was the property of the Republic, the transcendental link between the city and its gods, and stored in temples. In a sense, the gold that had been the manifestation of Rome's king was now Rome itself.

The Republic was a rather frail arrangement, and around 400 BCE it was confronted by a very large tribal migration from Gaul. These were people with an enthusiasm for gold. It seems that great social changes, perhaps resulting from a population increase, had been transforming their female-dominated social system and producing a much more warrior-based society. They were aggressively migrating, and were increasingly regarded by the settled people of South-East Europe and North Africa as having an alarmingly violent culture.[6] One group, the Senones, conquered and sacked the city of Rome in 387 BCE. A dramatically detailed account was given by the great storyteller, Livy, over 300 years later. We may not really know what happened, but that story would sit at the heart of Rome's attitude to power and to gold.

Having occupied the city, the leader of the Senones, Brennus, demanded a gold ransom weighing 1,000lb. That, according to Livy, was more than was held in the temples, and the senators had to call on the city's matrons to surrender their jewellery. As the payment was measured out, Brennus became irritated and weighed down the scales with his sword, declaiming: 'Woe to the vanquished!' The woe he imposed was not physical suffering, the destruction of buildings or enslavement. Nor was it impoverishment. It was the surrender of their entire store of a useless substance that embodied transcendental value. The foundation that physically connected social order with the gods had been stripped away.

The echo of Brennus's humiliating boast, *Vae Victis*, would resound through Roman consciousness. They considered abandoning their city, but decided to rebuild it with added paranoia. In a land of competing hill tribes, they set out never to be losers again, and to teach the lesson of *Vae Victis* to anyone who might threaten them – which meant anyone within reach. Rome would either extirpate its enemies or turn them into imitation Romans. The Republic became unlike any other conqueror; more ruthless, more implacable, more certain of its own mission to remake the world in its own image. The vanquished would simply vanish.[7] As it won new territories, it grew in resources and power like an ever-growing snowball. Rome did not need physical gold to grow, but it was driven by the memory of what had been done to it. Gold was buried deep in the roots of its identity.

Brennus did not want gold as wealth. As a warrior leader, he gave it as a sign of his favour and generosity, but most would be hoarded and dedicated to the gods who had so favoured him. What actually happened to it is unclear. As Livy tells the tale, the Gauls were never actually given the ransom because just as its transfer was being completed, their morale collapsed, the noble Romans rallied and the rough Gallic brutes were not simply ejected but actually slaughtered to the last man.[8] A more likely scenario was recorded by Suetonius around the end of the first century CE; he specifically denied the truth of that part of Livy's story, and said that the Senones carried off the gold and simply deposited it (in the ground? In a lake?). The Roman determination to reverse the humiliation took time: the Senones were finally defeated around 283 BCE, when Rome recovered the gold and returned it to the city's temples.[9] That was the end of the Senones. But shortly after, in 280 BCE, another Gallic expedition was aimed at the softer target of Greece.

Their mass migration, including women and children,[10] had become a continuous upheaval, and one group of warriors led by a new Brennus (or Brennos), chief of the Galatians from central Anatolia, attacked Attica through Thermopylae, the narrow pass where the Spartans had famously laid down their lives to hold back the Persians in 480 BCE. The Persians originally got through having been shown a hidden route. Now, 200 years later, a Greek coalition tried to block the Gauls at the same spot and were apparently circumvented by the invaders finding the same secret path. Two successive Macedonian relief armies were destroyed. Brennos succeeded in getting part of his force to the gold-rich sanctuary of Delphi, which Cassius Dio says they attacked and plundered.[11]

Brennos was then killed, and as with the plunder of Rome, there are two versions of what followed. According to the Greek tradition, Delphi's god, Apollo, struck down the Gauls with thunderstorms and earthquakes, and then the Greeks finished them off. The Roman version of events is somewhat different, insisting that the retreating Gauls carried their booty to Toulouse, where in proper Gallic fashion they dedicated it to their gods, depositing it in a lake – from which it was recovered centuries later by a Roman general.

Once more, it is clear that the Gauls were desperate for gold not as wealth but as a central feature of their culture, to be offered up to their gods and to provide status-offerings to their warriors. In the extreme social upheavals that produced these large migrations, it seems that more and more gold was needed. A 'Dying Galatian' is immortalized in a statue in Rome's Capitoline Museums which movingly portrays a wounded, fallen, naked warrior with typical Gallic hair and moustache, wearing the symbol of his status and identity: a gold torc around his neck. It is a Roman copy of a Greek original, probably created to commemorate the final defeat of the Galatians around 228 BCE.

Gold for Mercenaries

After the sack of Delphi there was a struggle for the throne of Macedonia, and both sides hired Celts to fight for them. Payment of hired mercenaries had begun in the eighth century BCE, or before, and had become commonplace in the Greek world; we have seen its importance to Lydia. A conceptual link was forged between Greek and Persian tyrants and mercenaries rewarded with gold coin. Men who offered their services on the killing fields of battle had wanted to be rewarded in gold for a very long time, and the invention of gold coin by Croesus systematized the business. We think of coins as tokens that have no meaning beyond their purchasing power, but they carried a greater weight in the ancient world. The soldier's coin identified his paymaster and the paymaster's deity. It was a golden receipt for the service supplied and a recognition of loyalty. When Philip II of Macedonia defeated the Phoenicians, he punished anyone holding a coin identified as Phoenician pay.[12]

This payment originally had a sacred character, at least to the extent of representing a sacred obligation. So, at least from the early fourth century BCE, it was common for the coins to be stored in temples, under the eyes of a god, before they were distributed to generals for payment. From the fourth century BCE, Celtic mercenaries began to replace Greeks. They were in great demand in Greece, the Levant and North Africa, where Ptolemy II employed 4,000 of them, because the Celtic warrior culture that had emerged gave them a reputation for courage to the point of insanity. They wanted to be rewarded with gold.

Macedonian rulers tried to persuade them to accept silver, and official Macedonian mints even produced fake coins for them, covering the silver with gold foil.[13] This seems to have led to the Celts minting their own coins from the gold they were given, imitating and altering the Macedonian designs as a sign of authenticity.

The Celts hired to fight for the throne of Macedonia were paid not as individuals but as tribes, the payment being communal.[14] So long as Romans fought their own battles and did not hire mercenaries, they could avoid what they saw as the moral pitfalls of minting gold. It is said that they originally measured wealth by sheep (the Latin *pecunia*, meaning money, comes from *pecus*, sheep and cattle) and pay was in measures of salt (the root of 'salary'). These are meaningful measures of value; they are life-sustaining. Rome's citizen soldiers were rewarded for their service with a share of booty but also with a daily rate of pay, originally in bronze, translatable to animals and salt. Gold, to Romans, was tainted with the history and propaganda of tyrants and was the pay of barbarians hired by opulent cowards.

Gold and Carthage

That, in the eyes of Roman republicans, was their difference from their great enemy, Carthage. To them, Carthage represented luxury and degeneracy. Carthage had been created in what is now Tunisia in the ninth century BCE, tradition dating its foundation to the flight from Tyre of a princess, Dido, seventy-two years before Rome began. It was a Phoenician trading outpost and developed rapidly when a large number of wealthy Phoenicians settled there to escape Alexander's destruction of Tyre. Within 100 years of the influx, it was a phenomenally rich agricultural and trade centre, with over 200 docks and elegant palatial homes. As Rome extended its authority over most of Italy, and south towards Sicily, Carthage extended itself over the North African coast, also towards Sicily. That was the flash point.

Carthage was not ruled by a tyrant; in 308 BCE, fifteen years after the death of Alexander, it became a republic with a very similar constitution to Rome. Instead of consuls it had two annually elected 'Judges', and in place of a senate there was a council drawn from its leading families. It came reluctantly to gold – in fact it came reluctantly to coinage at all. For centuries its gold was simply stored up as sacred treasure. But it did not have the manpower to defend its growing interests around the Mediterranean and set about recruiting a mercenary army, or rather paying communities in Spain and Africa to supply paid allies, which was much the same. Carthage adjusted its understanding of religion and began making fine gold staters in enormous quantities.[15] It was also making a range of other coinage and became a full-blooded money economy. Inheriting its values from Phoenician culture, Carthage now had an entirely pragmatic view of gold, as a tool to get what it wanted from others. Without a word written on them, its gold staters bore the head of the goddess of fertility with wheat stalks in her hair on one side, and a splendid standing horse on the other. The nearest they came to using gold to connect to the afterlife was a habit of placing twelve or thirteen coins in a burial, presumably as a fee for passage.[16] This was a common gesture which even turns up in early Christian burials in England and does not rely on the coins being gold.[17]

Carthage was gold-rich. It probably acquired it from Spain, Nubia, Sardinia and the Atlas Mountains in North Africa. Herodotus describes its traders' negotiations with the gold producers on African beaches beyond the Strait of Gibraltar.[18] There was no communication at all, just dumb barter:

> 'They unload their goods, arrange them tidily along the beach, and then, returning to their boats, raise a smoke. Seeing the smoke, the natives come down to the beach, place on the ground a certain quantity of gold in

exchange for the goods and go off again to a distance ... the Carthaginians never touch the gold until it equals in value what they have offered for sale, and the natives never touch the goods until the gold has been taken away.'[19]

Carthage Must Be Destroyed

Gold was symbolically placed at the heart of the epic existential war between Rome and Carthage. Stern Roman senators feared and detested the culture of gold-loving luxury, and what they saw as the ethical vacuum that went with it. Carthage's deities required human sacrifices, particularly children, as recompense for failures in religious ritual.[20] According to the Roman historian Diodorus Siculus, when the city of Carthage was threatened in 310 BCE by Agathocles, the tyrant of Syracuse, its rulers sacrificed hundreds of children from leading families.[21] Romans equated these horrors with the love of gold and believed the key to their struggle must be to strip it from Carthage. A grimly moralistic politician, Cato, campaigned in the early second century BCE as the incorruptible upholder of Roman tradition. He spoke of a time when 'all the gold in the world was spurned over a bowl of honest broth',[22] and warned: 'We have crossed into Greece and Asia (regions full of all kinds of sensual allurements) and are even laying hands on the treasures of kings – I am the more alarmed lest these things should capture us instead of our capturing them.' His version of morality led him to call for the total destruction of Carthage and its people. So it was logical that when Rome's first war against Carthage ended in 241 BCE, it should seize all Carthage's gold. It was not for enrichment of Rome, but to remove its terrible corrupting power.

Instead of being buried, Carthage's gold, weighing over 78 tons, was taken to Rome and sealed in the Temple of Saturn.[23] That was when Carthage's mercenaries asked for their pay.

It was a scene that confirmed the Romans in their memory of Brennus, but on an epic scale. The Graeco-Roman historian Polybius, writing about sixty years later, described a situation we might recognize from *Mad Max*. Carthage became host to more than 20,000 heavily armed North Africans, armoured Greeks, lightly armed Iberians, ferocious Celts, Ligurian spearmen, sling-shot fighters from the Balearic islands as well as a rabble of blade-wielding, half-Greek deserters and slaves.[24] Some had their wives and slaves, some had their booty in carts or on pack animals, and after twenty-three years of war they were not only seriously battle-hardened but some were bolstered by their own mercenary dynasties born and raised in their camps. These were not people you wanted to annoy. The Carthaginians did not even have the languages to deal with the situation, and as Polybius says, 'to address them through several interpreters, repeating the same thing four or five times, was, if anything, more impracticable'. The first stage was to persuade them to move to another location some way off, which required gold – one gold stater for every man, for immediate expenses.

This was never going to end well. The mercenaries believed they were entitled to their pay. The waiting horde became increasingly dangerous as it was reinforced by thousands of escaped slaves and ruined Libyan farmers. Eventually, as chaos reigned, Rome stepped in and assisted in their wholesale massacre. They were slaughtered and trampled with elephants. Rome had already removed the gold with which Carthage was supposed to pay them.

Carthage's subsequent need to replace its currency drove it to move into Spain, hoping to seize areas that produced gold and silver (an invasion that stopped when its general was killed). It also made an alliance with Macedonia, and then the Carthaginian general Hannibal became chief military adviser to the Seleucid emperor – the inheritor of Alexander's Persian conquest, who had now recovered almost all that land and its gold. Carthage's restored access to gold gave it financial credit for supplies, weapons and mercenaries. Rome feared that, fuelled by all this wealth for fighting men, Carthage and the Seleucid Empire were going to launch a new full-scale assault to conquer both Greece and Rome. A second Punic War was looming.[25]

That is when Rome did a mighty U-turn on the subject of gold. As the Republic's buying power lost credibility, its senators were forced to hold their fine Roman noses and make coins from the Carthaginian gold they had tried to remove from human use. The image Rome put on its new golden staters[26] was of the mythical twins Castor and Pollux going into battle – the battle in question being one in which, according to the story, they helped Rome to prevent the return of Tarquin Superbus, the symbolic gold-loving king they had expelled.[27] It was perhaps designed to make citizens of the Republic feel uncomfortable about possessing it, but it allowed them to buy the supplies they needed as a temporary measure.

Rome launched a pre-emptive attack to knock the Seleucids out of the war and leave Rome mistress of Greece. The Second Punic War erupted in 218 BCE, and Hannibal made his celebrated crossing of the Alps in a failed effort to extinguish his enemy. By 212 BCE, Rome had recovered enough strength to have 200,000 men under arms and could stop minting gold. It returned as fast as possible to its posture of moral propagandizing superiority over Carthage and its alien, corrupting currency.

By the time of the Third Punic War, the Temple of Saturn held 17,410lb of uncoined gold – what the Greeks would call twenty-two talents.[28] Rome's goal now became not just to remove Carthage's gold but to eliminate it, a key part of the process of destroying them and all they stood for. Other peoples

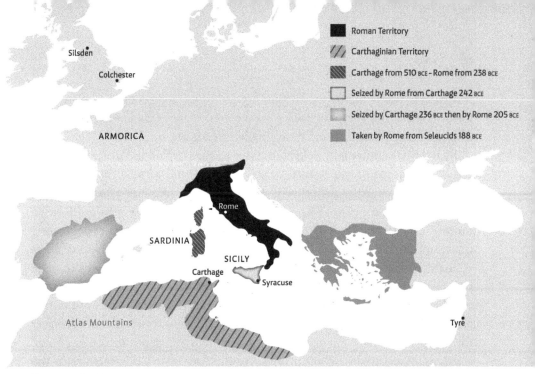

Rome vs Carthage.

conquered by Roman armies and placed under the Republic's rule were allowed to keep their own coinage, but when Carthage was finally defeated in 146 BCE, its currency was completely eliminated, along with the city, which was wiped from the face of the Earth in a savage slaughter. Polybius, who participated in the campaign, confirmed that they were 'utterly exterminated', in what has been called the first campaign of genocide.[29] Was this a repeat of the slaughter around Varna some 2,000 years before, the elimination once more of gold and the people who used it?

Monetary Gold Vanishes

By 60 BCE, it did seem that gold money had gone out of fashion. Much international trade was valued in gold, but gold coins were increasingly difficult to find. The normal small change of daily life was bronze, and the equivalent of our banknote was the Greek (or Greek-imitating) silver stater, worth roughly a shekel. After 90 BCE, however, silver coinage was being debased by the addition of copper. It was bewildering that the value of money could change; Cicero describes people not knowing the value of their land.[30] There was still also a gold stater, twice as heavy and worth twenty times as much, which was the unit of account for large transactions, but it was disappearing as people had no enthusiasm to spend valuable gold. It made more sense to spend silver before its value fell further. Gold coins were also vanishing because the Seleucid Greeks had minted the flood of gold from Persia to buy luxury goods, so transferring it back east, where it stopped circulating, and to pay mercenaries coming from Celtic lands to the west, who took a good part of it out of circulation by offering it to the deities they believed it originally came from.

By the first century BCE, gold coins were so hard to find in Greece that when some were needed for a festival near Thebes around 85 BCE, they had to be bought at fifteen times the price of silver, far above their face value.[31]

Northern European Celts had once buried their leaders in gold-laden tombs,[32] but they had stopped doing that. They had taken instead to depositing unaccompanied offerings in the ground or in lakes. Buried assemblages of coins – 'hoards' – used to be considered secret and forgotten deposits of wealth to be retrieved later. Thanks to the discoveries of detectorists, they are turning up in ever larger numbers and it is becoming clear that they were usually not buried for safekeeping, but as deliberate offerings to hidden powers, evidence of respect for the supernatural.[33] For example, a group of fourteen deposits totalling 5,292 coins was excavated in 2000 from a site in south-east Leicestershire in the English Midlands.[34] Their placing, in the entrance way to a settlement, clearly showed the ritual intent. They were buried in the first century BCE, when there was a shift in the Celtic world from burying gold weapons and accoutrements with a leader's corpse to burying the profits of the community's work in a gateway to that community and to the world beyond. The Celts seem to have developed a new confidence in the power of their communities to connect with the afterlife for themselves, and so, no longer relying on a leader travelling with gold to the afterlife, they were using gold to make a communal connection with the world beyond.

They were also minting their own coins, which generally still carried imitations of the horse designs of old Macedonian staters. But they were strangely altered: the horses on coins of Armorica in western France sprout human heads, while in south-west Britain they dissolve into dots.

These redesigns have generally been blamed on artistic incompetence. Given the spectacular level of craftmanship and precision in Celtic goldwork, that seems unlikely. These are purposeful transformations, which may be deliberate invocations of shamanic trance-images, and which indicate the presence of human mindfulness in the finished work. Such powerful, shape-shifting pieces of gold could hardly be regarded as spending money.[35] They were meant to do their work as offerings, to keep the world in a healthy balance. The Gaelic word *iocodh* means 'a rendering of payment', and also 'a curing' or 'a healing'. It takes a special coin to do that.

Perhaps Celts felt obliged to strike a balance between the gold they placed in the ground and what they took out. They replenished their supply from hundreds of mines: almost 250 pre-Roman mines dating from the fifth to the first century BCE have been identified in Limousin alone, in central France. To begin with, they took what was readily available at the surface, but as conflicts grew with Rome after 200 BCE, these autonomous tribal societies needed to mint more coins to reward their neighbours for military support. They could only do that by deep mining, up to 100ft down, with fully lined galleries. They used Archimedes screw pumps, wide rotating vertical drums with spiral grooves that turned inside a cylinder, lifting water out of the mine. Rome used the same technology. Béatrice Cauuet, who has excavated these, estimates that over five or six centuries, the Gauls in Limousin must have produced nearly 70 tons of gold.[36] Only in the end-game of the conflict with Rome were large quantities of Celtic gold coined. Some of it must have been used, as the Greeks used it, to buy oriental luxuries. But until the second century BCE, the Celts were almost as reluctant as the Persians to spend their gold once they had it. It had a higher purpose.[37]

We see this in a deposit of twenty-seven Celtic gold staters dating from the first century CE found in 1998 at Silsden, on the southern edge of the Yorkshire Dales. Most of them were minted at Colchester, 400km to the south-east. Many of the rest were made by a tribe whose capital was at Leicester, between Colchester and Silsden. The Romans were moving in, and ominously, the find included a Roman's iron ring. This is evidence of a retreat as the Romans advanced north.[38] The coins had been accumulated over many years, were worn with handling but never dispersed. They were probably kept because of their connection to the issuers and the gods, rather than their material value. The final deposit was almost certainly made as a religious offering, rather than to hide a fund to be recovered later. The owner's retreat seems to have ended here.

Rome, too, hoarded gold rather than spend it. In 60 BCE, no Roman gold coins were being minted at all. Rome was now ruler of colonies outside Italy, including all Greek lands as well as the territory that had been Carthage and its Spanish conquests. It no longer needed to tax its own people: direct tax on Roman citizens in Italy had been abolished in 167 BCE. According to Pliny,[39] in 91 BCE, the Temple of Saturn was hosting 1,620,831lb of gold – over 530 tons of dead weight,[40] over a hundred times the 400,000 bars stored today in the Bank of England. This does indicate that, to the autocrats of the Senate, Rome now seemed financially secure. It was not: its astonishing growth in wealth and power had created huge internal tensions, and without the pressure of the war with Carthage it quickly imploded. Over the course of the first century BCE, the Roman Republic that had so despised Carthage for its dependence on gold, swallowed itself in tumultuous civil wars and was replaced by a military tyranny that turned to that terrible, indestructible pile of corrupting yellow metal and demanded ever-growing quantities of it to stay in business.

Chapter 7

Gold Conquers

Gold for Rome's Dictatorship

The Republic had started to become unsustainable when there was no longer any Carthage to fight. The citizen soldiers had come home, if they bothered to return at all, to small farms in ruins or unaffordably mortgaged. Many moved to the city, abandoning their land to be absorbed into the large estates of the rich, and the city's population swelled to around 600,000.[1]

Soon Rome was overwhelmed by internal armed struggle, at the heart of which was a ferocious fight over how to sustain the army. The history of the late Roman Republic is the chronology of military men taking power to reform the army. The popular solution was seen as land reform, giving landless men the property that would enable them to once more be part of a citizen army, paying their own way and supplying their families' needs. But that meant taking land away from the new super-rich. Instead, Rome turned into a welfare state for its citizens with food handouts, offering a paid military career to poor men. Within a few years, the treasury was empty.

In 88 BCE, an army had to be sent to crush a challenge from a ruler on the Black Sea coast. Mithridates of Pontus had raised a popular revolt against years of corrupt Roman rule, culminating in his order that every Roman in the province of Asia should be killed. It is said that 80,000 were butchered in a single day. Rome needed to act, but it seems that after the previous three years of chaos there was no money to supply an army. A Roman general, Sulla, marched on Rome with his troops to impose his takeover of the war. This was a dramatic breach of the convention that no general may bring an army inside the city boundary, and some senators holding positions of command under him refused to go, but the legionaries' oath was to him, not to Rome – a fact that would transform power in the Republic. Sulla forced the Senate to find some cash by selling off lands believed to have been dedicated to the gods 500 years before, and which financed the priestly colleges. That only provided 9,000lb of gold.[2] Gold was what was needed. Apart from anything else, silver was simply too bulky to cart around to pay tens of thousands of men. Once he arrived in Greece, Sulla began stripping temples of their gold and coining it to pay his forces.[3] He behaved as though he believed in the power of gods – he consulted the oracle at Delphi and made offerings as instructed, and insisted that the Greek gods were simply lending their gold to their chosen warrior – but he was also a pragmatist. Gold was what soldiers wanted, and it needed to be coined. The fact that it had been consecrated was now no bar to cashing it in. It was still understood as value incarnate, and it made the individual who received it, in some strange way, worth more in himself.

But the coins were struck using local dies: they did not speak of Sulla, or of Rome. When someone used a coin, there was no way to tell who had paid it to him. Sulla was paying his way with the same currency as other people.

When he returned to Rome, the Senate appointed him as 'Dictator for the Reconstitution of the Republic'. He closed the Republic down and minted the gold he had seized in Asia to pay his troops. Sulla's new coins carried all the implications of kingly sacred authority, but now in his name. They declared him to be '*imperator*' and showed his head. They represented a bond between the dictator and his soldiers.

The title '*imperator*' – the source, of course, of our word 'emperor' – meant 'victorious and acclaimed commander' and had regal implications. It was first used by the Roman general Scipio, after he defeated the Carthaginians in Iberia in 206 BCE. When the Iberians saluted him as king, Scipio experienced the shudder that every Roman felt at that word. He told them that he did not want anyone to call him that, ordering them instead to call him *imperator*,[4] a word that would cast a long shadow. Sulla was hailed *imperator* by his troops and defeated his rival Marius in a war for power. Marius had already reformed the army by changing it from a body of affluent citizens loyal to the Republic into a career path for the poor, paid for their service and bound to their general.

After a few years, Sulla did restore the Republic, at least notionally, and gold stopped being coined in 79 BCE at the end of his dictatorship. But the direction was clear. To have control of Rome, you needed an army, and that army would need to be paid in gold. If there was not enough in the Temple of Saturn, it would have to be taken from somewhere else.

Sulla's solution had been totalitarian. In a reign of terror, he executed some 520 rich people and confiscated their property.[5] Names of those he considered, or was told were, enemies of the state were written on a list in the Forum. All were automatically proscribed – stripped of all rights and property. Any person who killed a proscribed man was entitled to keep part of his estate. The rest went to the state. The Forum was decorated with their heads. Anyone might be called on at night by a group of Sulla's ex-slaves, all named 'Lucius Cornelius', and disappear. Negative consequences arose for anyone who chose to assist those on the list, despite not being listed on the proscribed lists themselves. Anyone who was found guilty of assisting the condemned was capitally punished. All the possessions of the proscribed were auctioned off, often to the people who killed them, and the Temple of Saturn was refilled.

The New Oligarchs

After the dictatorship, Rome had new oligarchs who saw the answer to military finance in the privatization of military force. Its great exponent was a commander called Crassus, who had helped Sulla's rise to power. He saw that as his filial duty: his father had been defeated by Marius and committed suicide, and must be revenged. The family had lost everything. Young Crassus fled to Spain and spent eight months living in a cave.[6] He came back with an implacable determination to destroy Marius and become as rich as humanly possible. He achieved both. The victims of Sulla's proscription were largely people associated with Marius.

Crassus's definition of wealth was frightening. He said that a rich man was one who could maintain a legion out of his income. His forte was offering privatized services. To that end, he set up Rome's fire service, which had 500 men ready to turn out as soon as the cry went up. They often knew just when that would be, as he also employed arsonists. When the firefighters arrived, Crassus would demand a massive fee for their services. If the shocked owner refused, he let the fire run its course and then bought the ruins. Meantime, he would move to the house next door and offer to buy that before it too went up in flames. He soon became Rome's biggest landlord, with lands worth 200 million sestertii. Plutarch, who said that his wealth was based on fire and rape, valued his estate at the mind-boggling sum of 7,100 talents.

Julius Caesar's Campaigns for Gold

The future of Rome, as Crassus understood, would belong to men who could finance armies. Status and power were constructed on visible wealth, which was publicly displayed in extravagance, for example in luxurious banquets. Expensive spices and perfumes, luxurious exotic furnishings and goblets and public acts of generosity were all necessary to hold your place on the greasy social ladder of plutocratic power, and all of these had to be imported from the East in exchange for gold.

Marius's nephew, Julius Caesar, set himself the task of building up as much wealth as possible, and in 60 BCE became governor of south-eastern Spain with the aim of exploiting the silver mines that had been created there by Carthage. His political career had been enabled by massive borrowing, such that he needed 25 million sestertii to clear his debts.[7] That was just over 6 million denarii, enough to pay a legion's wages for ten years. There were rich men in Rome who had a lot invested in Caesar. The richest of them was Crassus, who acted as surety for this man he saw as a money-making tool: he ensured that Caesar became governor of Spain, where the silver mines excavated Rome's money.

The mines produced vast sums using slaves who worked brutally enforced twenty-four-hour shifts. Reports speak of a huge death toll, with the observation that 'although some of them have the strength and will to stay alive, they suffer so much and for so long that they would rather be dead'.[8] But Caesar could not wring what Crassus needed out of Spain. That required gold, twelve times as valuable, and there was none left in southern Spain. (It would be found in northern Spain after the Roman conquest there thirty-five years later.[9]) Caesar attacked towns in western Iberia, and when they opened their gates in surrender, he sacked them. He was said to sack towns simply for the plunder they offered. On his return, when he was elected consul, he stole 3,000lb of gold from the Capitoline Hill, replacing it with the same weight of gilded bronze.[10] It would have looked twice as good as the gold, as there had to be twice as much of it to make up the weight.

We see Julius Caesar through the lens that he shaped for us, writing his own hagiography in the form of *The Gallic Wars*, carefully preserved long after his assassination. His name straddles the ages more effectively even than Alexander's. Sulla may have been *imperator*, but it was Caesar's *imperium* that became permanent, the Roman Empire. He was later glorified as the ancestor of Western civilization; the British, German and Russian Empires taught their children about the glory of his legacy, Imperial Rome. When I was 18, it was a condition of my university admission that I uncritically study Caesar's text. This education was designed to blind me to who Julius Caesar actually was, and what he was doing.

We have one very thorough account, by Suetonius – historian, biographer of no fewer than twelve Roman rulers and the best-informed gossip of antiquity. Until recently, commentators have shied away from what he says, because it is not what we have been told, both by Caesar and those who wanted us to admire him. But we have no reason to disbelieve Suetonius. And there were other contemporary voices that regarded Caesar in the same way. He was motivated by nothing, they said, except glory and gold.

Gold would pay for an army. An army would provide military victory and acclaim him as *imperator*, so he went hunting gold. It happened to be outside Rome's territory, but that was a problem Caesar was ready to solve. That solution gave birth to the Roman Empire.

His first idea was to plunder Dacia, a Celtic kingdom newly formed on the Danube which was quite fabulously gold-rich. He had been given military authority over Rome's territories in Cisalpine Gaul (south-east France) and Illyricum (Croatia). He was assembling his forces to use Illyricum as a springboard for attacking Dacia, but had not yet found the excuse. Instead, he was offered an opportunity to deal with what might be a threat to Cisalpine Gaul. A tribe from Switzerland was moving into Gaul to escape pressure from migrating Germans. It turned out that Gauls would, in his opinion, benefit hugely from having Caesar protect them. Some Gauls might be dubious, but he persuaded the Senate and in 58 BCE he began what turned into an historic project of slaughter, annexation and, above all, robbery.

Stealing From the Gods

The Romans knew that the Celts buried gold in the ground and in deep lakes. They had no real idea why, but they knew there was plenty of it. Gallic warriors wore gold collars and gold bracelets, and they paid their gods and their allies with golden coin. Even remote Britain, Ultima Thule, which Rome knew as the island at the end of the Earth inhabited by half-human animals, minted golden coins. The Celts deposited coins in the ground, but most of the gold was offered up in sacred lakes.

This is one of the ways in which gold seems to inform human behaviour at different times and in different places in similar ways without any possible communication between the people concerned. The Chibcha people of the Andes, from whom the Kogi are descended, deposited gold in special lakes in rituals which we describe as 'offerings'. The Kogi themselves use the expression 'payments', as though these were a form of tribute demanded by a higher authority. But the gold concerned is not raw bullion: it has been prepared and worked. In itself, the gold has no evidence of its own history, but in its worked form it embodies the concentrated thought that shaped it, and once placed in the water it is believed to be engaged in an act of communication to help sustain life. The Chibchas' principal deposit lake was a caldera near Bogotá, Lake Guatavita. In 1545, Spanish adventurers took a huge chunk out of the side, like taking a slice out of a Pavlova cake, to drain it and lay their hands on some of the contents.

The cut they made lowered the lake by 60ft and revealed some treasures, but the centre was untouched. In the early years of the twentieth century, modern technology was used to undermine the lake and drain the water off, but golden equatorial sun shone down on the offerings and baked the lake bottom as hard as concrete. The sluices jammed with mud and the lake filled up again.

Caesar plundered the lakes of Gaul for their golden offerings 1,600 years before the robbery of Lake Guatavita. He was evidently inspired by his predecessor as the proconsul of Cisalpine Gaul, Quintus Servilius Caepio, who in 105 BCE reported that he had found the gold taken from Delphi 175 years before by Brennos. He was said to have found over 50,000 15lb bars of gold and 10,000 15lb bars of silver at Tolosa (Toulouse), much of it deposited in lakes. The entire treasure was seized by robbers on its way back to the Senate. It was never found; people supposed that Caepio himself had staged the robbery. It has been said that the treasure ended up with his great-grandson, Brutus, who would eventually assassinate Caesar.

The sixteenth-century Spanish did not understand why the Chibcha deposited gold in sacred lakes. Similarly, Caesar and his contemporaries had little idea why the Celts did it, supposing that they were simply dumping it because they wanted to hide it.[11] Caesar's contemporary, Diodorus Siculus, was mystified why the Celts made gold offerings.[12] There is abundant evidence of Celtic offerings of weapons, bullion and wood carvings at water sites – lakes, wells and springs – which were clearly used as portals to the world beyond.[13] But most Romans' view of gold was simply that it was wealth, which could represent the authority of a supreme earthly ruler, if there was one, but it made you rich – or, perhaps more importantly, made you look rich.

Caesar had the Senate appoint him Protector of the Gauls, a grimly ironic title. His army invaded their land and set about looting the sacred sites where their golden offerings and hoards were secreted. With the advantage of a full-time army, he could fight through all the seasons of the year and not stop for planting or harvest. The Gauls tried to protect the golden links they had forged between the mortal and immortal worlds and were professionally dispatched into whatever afterlife they thought was waiting. Caesar killed around a million of them, and some tribes with the largest gold accumulation were simply wiped out.[14] According to Suetonius, he pillaged shrines and temples filled with offerings.

Gold Advertises its Master

Caesar also understood, as Sulla had done, that gold coins needed to identify their source. It now seems that was the primary tool in his takeover of southern Britain – not a military victory, but a military visit followed by an invasion of specially created currency to be issued by rulers who swore allegiance. This insight is not based on any written source but on the coins themselves. There was a sudden change in coin colour. British gold coins were without inscription and were yellow-gold. Suddenly, rulers in south-east Britain who had made agreements with Caesar began issuing red-gold coins inscribed with their names. All of the new coins are made from refined gold alloy and have the same copper and silver content; the bullion was evidently being supplied from the continent on a very large scale. One of these kings, Cunobelin, minted 4.4

tons of refined gold; another, Verica, half as much again. It seems that after Caesar's visit there was a complete recoining subsidized by Rome.[15] He had bought southern Britain, and everyone who saw, for example, a coin with 'VER' on one side and 'REX' on the other knew that Verica was Rome's local king. The Celtic royal title on coins was 'RIG'.

Rome Turns Gold into a Commodity

Up to this time, although gold was without question a store of value, it also carried a sacred charge. There was always the suggestion of a link to the divine, or to a supreme earthly ruler. Alexander's looting of Persepolis certainly created a gold coinage that transformed Greece and the Middle East, but it retained a magical quality by association with Alexander himself. But by the time Caesar had pillaged Gaul and flooded Rome with gold, there was a fundamental change. Gold was now a commodity. As Suetonius said, Caesar had more gold than he knew what to do with; at his triumph in 46 BCE, he paraded 20,000lb of gold and offered it for sale throughout Italy and the provinces at a 25 per cent discount. Though some Roman commentators criticized the savage slaughter of the Celts from whom he took it, they did not see what he did as sacrilege. In fact, the sacred lakes of Gaul were auctioned off to Roman treasure-hunters.

In the meantime, Caesar's backer, Crassus, struck out in 53 BCE to take Persia's gold. Being able to finance a single legion out of your income was no longer

Rome and the Persian Empire at the death of Julius Caesar.

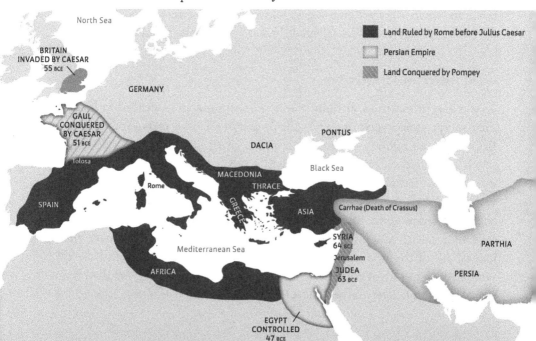

good enough: Caesar had twenty-two. Crassus needed a Gaul of his own, for the gold and the victories. He decided it should be Persia.

Persia was now ruled by Parthians, who were far more formidable than the Gauls. His military venture was a catastrophe; only a quarter of his army survived. Crassus did not. It was said in Rome, according to Cassius Dio, that the Parthians poured liquid gold down the throat of Crassus's corpse. But the theatrical punishment could be performed without needing the ancient myth: we have a parallel in Central America, where the body of an exceptionally gold-hungry Spanish governor of Ecuador was treated the same way by the Jivaro tribe in 1599. In this case, the victim was not yet dead. An experiment in 2003 using a bovine larynx demonstrated, for the benefit of the morbidly curious, that the steam produced would have burst him open. Crassus too.[16]

Crassus's attack on Persia had begun the longest war in history, longer even than Rome's war with Carthage. In fact, that war has never ended. It would be waged through the whole of Rome's history and be revived in the Middle Ages as the Crusades. It would then be reinvented as a European colonial adventure and proceed remorselessly through the creation and disruption of modern Iran. Crassus's pursuit of the wealth of Persia is still continuing – today in the form of sanctions against Iran, which are in effect a confiscation of much of the country's assets.

But Rome now had gold and used it as the symbol of power and significance. Caesar paid his legions with it, which used up about two-thirds of his cash. He was buying power with the gold of their pay. In 61 BCE, Pompey had celebrated a Triumph in Rome and had given each legionary a 'donative' of 1,500 silver denarii weighing nearly 18lb, representing over thirteen years' pay. When Caesar celebrated his great triumphal procession fifteen years later, his 'donative' only weighed a third of that, but it was in gold, worth 6,000 denarii for each man. Even after his doubling of army pay, that was forty-eight years' pay! In silver it would have weighed more than all the armour, weapons and survival kit they carried.[17] The coins were made in the Temple of Juno Moneta on top of the Capitoline Hill – Moneta gave us the words 'mint' and 'money', and the flow that poured from the door became 'currency'.

He was minting gold. This was not an emergency coinage, to be abandoned, like that of the Second Punic War or Sulla. To put it another way, this was a permanent emergency. Caesar had taken his army into Rome and he took over. The Republic was ended.

Rome would never be the same again; nor would gold. Caesar's exuberance and ruthlessness had transformed it. Mystical stamped discs that had empowered the rulers of Lydia, Carthage and the Celtic tribes had now become the tokens that carried the essence of Rome. Instead of the gold creating a transcendental link between the ruler and the world beyond, it was given value by bearing the ruler's stamp. Caesar was the supernatural authority. A statue of him was placed in a temple inscribed 'To the invincible God', and he stood behind the gold. Gold was eternal, and so was Caesar.

Julius was mortal, of course, as was clearly demonstrated when he was assassinated for his presumption. But Caesar was not mortal. His assassination, on the Ides of March, 44 BCE, triggered a civil war that finally destroyed the Republic. His adopted son, Octavian, declared himself to be 'Imperator Caesar', and Caesar in his many incarnations would remain Emperor of Rome for many centuries. The title continued in Byzantium, and after the fall of Byzantium to the Turks, the title Caesar fell onto the Turkish Emperor. Down through history, rulers with a connection to Rome would call themselves Caesar, Tsar/Czar, Kaiser.

Caesar after Caesar, the role had set in motion an irresistible need. Without the link between immortal Caesar and immortal wealth, the Empire in any of its forms would collapse. The soldiers must be paid, and from the beginning, each Caesar needed to sustain his Empire by winning and distributing ever more gold.

Chapter 8

The Empire's Golden Fetters

The Price of Succeeding Caesar

The need to find gold, to find people to take it from, drove the creation of Rome's world-empire, which at its peak controlled perhaps a quarter of all humanity (another quarter was ruled by its great economic competitor, Han Dynasty China). The key to its success was establishing the world's first money-based economy, making everything dependent on the pay of its permanent army. But that meant that it had to struggle with an interesting set of economic problems. Most obviously, it had to cope with the fact that its golden money did not really have any constant value. Other alarming problems flowed from that, which drove Rome's actions and eventually destroyed its power in Europe. Because gold was now fundamental to Imperial power, it mattered more than ever before. There was a problem with money which would haunt, and eventually destroy, the city that dominated Europe and the Mediterranean.

The struggle for power between Caesar's assassins and his heir, Octavian, had obliged the rival warlords to mint vast quantities of currency. Cassius and Brutus gathered 54.6 tons of gold to mint 7 million coins which they paid out as military bonuses, 'donatives',[1] to enable them to confront the forces of Mark Antony and Octavian in 42 BCE. The Battle of Philippi was a catastrophic mess. Octavian's troops were routed, and it is reported that 18,000 were killed; 9,000 were said to have died on the other side. The struggle is impossible to imagine; there was a death toll apparently half that of the first day on the Somme in 1916, but all the butchery was face-to-face, close up and personal. The battle was invisible, because it created a vast dust cloud. Cassius became convinced that he had lost and committed suicide, which meant that Octavian and Mark Antony were made victorious by default, and Brutus too killed himself.

What had driven two huge armies to such a terrible slaughter? There were certainly some who were not there simply for the cash reward. The poet Horace was one of the Roman students in Athens who made a choice to join Brutus in what they saw as the defence of the Republic and were given junior commands. In the adrenaline-charged moment of seeing the face of an enemy, an inexperienced soldier may kill in a frenzy of shock and terror. Later, Horace would write the words that helped draw idealistic English public schoolboys to the slaughter of the trenches in the 1914–18 war: '*Dulce et decorum est pro patria mori*' ('It is sweet and proper to die for your country'). But that was not what he had felt at the time. Wilfred Owen called it 'the old lie'; Horace had thrown down his shield and fled in terror as the battle unfolded. His motivation had switched from political idealism to sheer survival, and he soon became a functionary of the other side.

Horace and his friends were rich young men. Most of the common soldiers were there for the gold. Many died for it, and many changed sides as offers and counter-offers were made in leaflets distributed during the course of the battle.[2] The money-motive became even clearer in the next phase of the struggle, when Octavian and Mark Antony fought each other.

This struggle was resolved by money changing sides. Mark Antony was dependent on the great wealth of Egypt, supplied by Cleopatra. On 1 August 30 BCE, the opposing forces were moving to their final conflict near Alexandria. It was to begin as a naval battle. But as Antony's ships rowed rhythmically towards Octavian's, the oarsmen suddenly stopped pulling. Then they raised their oars in salute, cheered, and his fleet glided into place as part of Octavian's force. The cavalry too changed sides. Antony did not know that Cleopatra had withdrawn into her mausoleum with her treasure, but the troops did. Their pay had been cut off: Antony was finished.[3]

The troops who had given Octavian his victory were lavishly rewarded. If they had been fighting for an ideal, it was quite clear that getting very rich was an important part of that ideal. They had, it seemed, looted most of the known world. Three days of lavish and spectacular processions through Rome began on 13 August 29 BCE. The Triumph of an *imperator* was the greatest war ritual Rome ever practised, and a fabulous display of treasure.

The doors of the Temple of Janus were closed, signifying that Rome was at last at peace, and Octavian was recognized as 'conqueror of the known world'.[4] Triumphal arches were erected, adorned with decoration to explain and commemorate this historic moment. One still stands, the Arch of Actium in the Forum. The great procession would include 120,000 legionaries and 700 senators. Over 115 tons of gold were given to the legionaries; each received a handout of 120 aurei, 960 grams of 24-carat gold.[5] That would be worth over $50,000 today.

Octavian rode in a four-horse chariot dressed as the god Jupiter, with a laurel crown and a gold-trimmed purple toga. He had achieved what would be his definitive role in the history of the world as the ruler not just of Rome, but of what Rome knew as civilization itself, from the Atlantic to Mesopotamia, from Anatolia to Libya and Alexandria. He would be hailed over the next few years as Augustus, the first of the first men, the original *Princeps*. Prince, Caesar, Emperor.

Rome had achieved its definitive nature as a city, its geography centred on a Forum embellished with the images of Augustus's transcendent excellence. And the army had achieved its definitive status as Augustus established it, for the first time, as a permanent body. The Roman Army was now the organization which sustained and underwrote the Roman state. For gold; only, and always, for gold.

Gold was the supreme measure, the arbiter and enabler of power. Augustus had re-formed Rome's currency, issuing virtually pure gold and silver coins, 'denarii', of beautiful and precise design, both being of equal significance. The gold version was worth twenty-five of the silver, and was generally simply called 'aureus', 'a gold'. This was the deal that would make each future emperor. The Roman *Imperium* was built on handing out tons of precious metal to armed men. Cato's warning that captured gold would itself capture Rome would turn out to be prescient.

The Price of a Payroll

The Empire now had to grow to satisfy the unending demand that it had created, proving its right to exist by pouring out coins onto its soldiers. Apart from a small core of salaried officials, the Republic had been a subsistence economy outside Rome and a gig economy in the city, where most people were either slaves or plebeians, traders or earning by the job. But by the time of Augustus, there were around 300,000 people on the military payroll, having to be paid a basic wage amounting to around 65 million silver denarii a year. That was over a quarter of a million tons of silver. This great weight of precious metal was carted and shipped to the troops, and that was obviously a massive inconvenience. It was easier in gold. The whole annual military payroll was equivalent to just 20 tons of gold. A legionary earned 225 denarii a year. Day-to-day purchases were made with bronze, but he would not have wanted to change his denarii for a sack of 3,600 bronze coins. Silver was bad enough: each soldier went away from the pay parade hefting almost a kilogram of metal. A gold aureus was worth twenty-five times the denarius but only weighed twice as much. A legionary was entitled to nine aurei a year, a cavalryman to one a month.

The Contest for Luxury

The flood of gold that had poured into Rome from the days of Julius Caesar to Augustus had a transformative impact on the Roman senatorial and governing class. Latin writers complain at great length that in place of a Republican morality of personal austerity, there was now a competitive glee in flaunting luxury. Tacitus said that a century of extravagance had ruined many senatorial families. Some of this wealth was displayed in new buildings and lavish gladiatorial shows, which involved huge costs, including importing exotic beasts. Domestic conspicuous consumption was necessary in the late Republic and early Empire to achieve social and political status, and led to being sucked into the vast expense of living near the heart of power. The luxuries that demonstrated status were acquired through long-distance trade: they included ivory, precious stones, amber, pearls, silk, cups, vases and furniture made of rare materials, as well as perfumes, incense, pepper and other spices.[6]

The sense of gold's value was international and trans-cultural. It was the reason for the value of gold as currency. Wealthy Romans were served by merchants who took their money to import luxuries from the East.[7] Silk in particular was a spectacular novelty. The first time Romans saw it seems to have been when Crassus's army had been destroyed by the Parthians in 53 BCE. They were confronted by horsemen in full armour, a sight that would not appear in Europe for over 1,000 years, and the banners the riders carried were not like the heavy linen Roman standards. They were shimmering, almost weightless sheets of rippling silk. Crassus, of course, was in pursuit of gold – within a few years, Romans would be giving up gold for silk. Julius Caesar showed off Parthian banners at his Triumph in 46 BCE, and then, to popular delight and amazement, draped the Forum with silk awnings.[8] It was soon adopted as the most glamorous way to dress, and was a drain on coinage. From the time of Augustus, attempts were made to stop Romans buying it. It was also a threat to the male ownership of women's bodies. Seneca complained: 'The adulteress may be visible through her thin dress, so that her husband has no more acquaintance than any outsider or foreigner with his wife's body.'[9] Augustus tried to restrain excessive luxury, and forbade men to wear silk, but luxury was what the rich wanted, to show their wealth, so it was a hopeless struggle. Two hundred years later, the Emperor Elagabalus dressed in nothing else.

When Augustus died, in 14 CE, his will gave 300 sestertii to every legionary, four months' pay. His heir, Tiberius, doubled it.[10] It was absolutely clear that without the backing of the Army, there was no emperor. Tiberius also appears to have doubled the pay of the Praetorian Guard, his personal force of 4,500 elite troops.[11]

He tried to withdraw from power and from Rome, and to allow the Empire to run itself as a bureaucratic machine. He left Sejanus, the commander of the Praetorian Guard, in charge of business. Sejanus began taking over the centres of power in a properly Roman way, with a combination of greed and brutal ruthlessness. The power of gold to drive the display of luxury was magnified – 'leveraged' in modern parlance – by cheery moneylenders. Sejanus encouraged a huge growth in financial speculation by his friends, slackening controls. The

Senate used to make decrees restricting credit and rates of interest, limiting what moneylenders could demand from borrowers. But the flood of money that had created the Empire had also reduced the Senate and its consuls to cyphers, leaving almost all power in the emperor's hands. Augustus had been very hands-on; Tiberius had become a much more distant figure, quite literally, as he avoided Rome and lived a life of indulgence on the island of Capri while he left things to Sejanus. Sejanus believed in self-regulation.

The Debt Crash

Gold was now creating a new kind of crisis: one of consumption. The unrestrained enthusiasm of the Roman elite for making themselves as rich as possible caused the entire financial system to come crashing down. A vast money-market had been created, people were borrowing to buy land and, with land rising in value, they could borrow more, for luxury living. They did not need to worry about repayment because so many potential buyers had access to loans that the value of land would apparently rise for ever. It was an effect now known as the 'greater fool' principle. Buyers knew that they might seem fools to pay high prices, but they could see there was always a greater fool waiting to buy for even more. Land was excellent security, so they could borrow more and buy more. The moneylenders were raking in huge profits lending money they did not have. According to Tacitus, almost every senator was making loans which were theoretically illegal. This may not have been the first bubble in the history of the world, but it is the first we know about.

When Rome's supply of money had been extravagant, it had been hard to prevent food prices from rising dangerously, so Augustus had established a permanent dole of free corn for 200,000 people. But now there was rampant inflation. Speculation in corn – easily stored by those with warehouses – became profitable. Tiberius tried to bring prices down by arranging for a massive increase in grain imports from Sicily, Egypt and North Africa and offering subsidies to sellers,[12] but the money was available to soak it all up before it reached the public. Even price controls were ineffective. Violent rioting began. Rome's theatres became stages for popular protest against the establishment, including the emperor. Tiberius was seriously annoyed – Rome was being hijacked by moneylenders. And they had a candidate to take over from him, the head of his own Praetorian Guard, whom he had left in charge, Sejanus.

Tiberius had to make himself emperor again, and the only way to do that was by separating the Praetorian Guard from their commander with huge quantities of money. In 31 CE, they were given 1,000 sestertii each to allow Sejanus to become dead meat.

Tiberius took drastic action against Sejanus and his supporters and seized their assets. But then the bubble collapsed as the property market suddenly ran out of fools. Everyone to whom these speculators had given mortgages had to make immediate repayment. This created huge problems, one of which was that the loans exceeded the available supply of coins. Repayment was physically impossible. There was a swathe of lawsuits against the moneylenders claiming that the loans were illegal and could not be called in. In the words of the legendary modern speculator Warren Buffett, 'You only find out who is swimming naked when the tide goes out.' Those who had been lending money they did not have were suddenly exposed, and many others found their swimsuits had been confiscated. They were uncovered; the word for 'uncovering' was *'apokalypsis'*. It was frightening.

The consuls, impotent and terrified figures, asked Tiberius what to do. He told them to be decisive, so they imposed limits to interest rates. When that did not solve the problems or satisfy popular rage, they were forced to close their eyes, cross their fingers and outlaw mortgages.[13] They also tried to bolster collapsing land values by demanding that moneylenders must invest two-thirds of their wealth in land in Italy. Since they themselves were the moneylenders, they gave themselves eighteen months' grace to do this, but that made things worse, as that meant they could simply withdraw money from the market and hide it for a year and a half. Rome's coinage vanished.[14] Credit disappeared.

Recreating Value

This was a new kind of crisis, a liquidity crisis. First-century Romans had never heard of anything like it. They regarded economics as a practical, domestic concern extrapolated from household management, with no place in the political arena. Of course, there was a bridge from the domestic to the public sphere because a Roman's social position was rooted in the size of his family's land holding, which was the source of political dignity and the reason why Augustus set the minimum wealth for senators at a million sestertii.[15] But most Senators regarded their finances as matters of entitlement, with the managing of budgets being a matter for women and slaves, and the question of whether sestertii actually existed would not have made sense to them. Money could be represented by written commitments in the form of loans and promises, but for Romans it was as real as any other physical object, and there was obviously enough gold to keep commerce flowing and domestic life afloat while the millionaire senators performed their symbolic political rituals. But now there wasn't enough. All the money in the world, in the richest civilization imaginable, had suddenly stopped. Roman historical commentators who normally analysed events in terms of personal, political and military struggles felt obliged, for the first time, to try to describe economic upheaval, and had to descend into the unfamiliar world of cash flow and bookkeeping. It is the only time that Tacitus provides us with real economic information, and not surprisingly his account takes a bit of unpicking. But he knew, as did everyone else concerned with Rome's survival, that the crash of 33 CE was seriously important. Gold had come, done its thing, and somehow gone. Rome might not survive.

The story was very sharply paralleled in the traumatic financial crash of 2007–08, which caused the global financial system to run out of money. That was similarly unthinkable, in an economy that was rich enough to support every indulgence imaginable. The rules controlling bank lending had been relaxed so as to be completely ineffectual, and people were borrowing money which they could never possibly repay while land prices soared. There had been an unprecedented increase in American wealth; gross domestic income grew by 40 per cent between 2000 and 2007,[16] but personal savings fell by half in the same period.[17] Americans were spending all the money they could lay their hands on; inflation more than doubled between 2002 and 2007. Above all, they were spending on property; and then the property bubble burst. The banks discovered that they were holding worthless security for their loans and quite simply collapsed. Americans lost a quarter of their wealth in eighteen months, and food prices rose sharply.

Of course, Rome in 33 CE and the USA in 2008 had completely different financial systems. The American collapse was not triggered by a failed coup but by the automatic tripping of spreadsheet alarms. They also had different crowd management systems. Popular protest about the outrageous greed that caused the 2008 crash did not erupt until the Occupy Wall Street movement of 2011, and that was pushed aside. In Rome, popular protest came sooner, and it seemed more dangerous.

In both cases there had to be some accounting for what had happened, and in both cases that was bodged. In the USA, despite the clear evidence of massive fraud that plunged the whole world into recession, only one banker was ever convicted – a relatively minor Credit Suisse Egyptian-born investment banker called Kareem Serageldin. He was given a thirty-month sentence for his small role, because he pleaded guilty. Every other banker charged fought back and found the system had no teeth with which to bite.

Tiberius took a simpler line: it was obvious that the richest bankers must be moral lepers and also obvious that they must hand their wealth back to the emperor. But it could not be a Roman insider who publicly carried the can, just as in the twenty-first century the Wall Street insiders must all go free. Consequently, an outsider, the richest man in Spain, Sextus Marius, was convicted of incest and thrown off the Tarpeian Rock, a cliff overlooking the Forum.

The most important thing, in both situations, was to avoid the entire collapse of the financial system. The credit system had to be rebooted, and the moneylenders put back on their feet. In the USA and Europe, the danger was that with all credit frozen, the most basic systems for paying for food and fuel would cease working. In America, the Federal Reserve ordered the printing of bonds and securities to the value of 2 trillion dollars, which were used to allow financial institutions to re-engage with the payments system. In London, the banks were handed £50 billion of suddenly invented cash. This was called 'quantitative easing'. Tiberius rescued Rome's bankers the same way, giving them an interest-free loan of 25 million denarii. The difference – a key difference – was that he had to give them coins from his own treasury.

The twenty-first-century rescue was simply a matter of political will. The mechanics of printing money were essentially the production of a fiction which the financial world needed to say it believed in. Rome had a bigger problem. No one would have believed in paper money. The money had to be gold coins, and it was extremely fortunate that Tiberius had enough of them to skate across this very thin ice. Rome could not survive without physical gold; its Army would vanish and its elite would be ruined. Such was the nature of the Empire which had been created by Augustus. Now it looked into the abyss. Great banking houses were collapsing; a major Corinthian bank, Leucippus' Sons, closed, quickly followed by an important banking house in Carthage; all the surviving banks on Rome's Via Sacra suspended payment to their depositors, as well as two in Lyon and another in Byzantium.[18] As panic and fear of revolt washed across the Empire, it may not be surprising that Pontius Pilate, the governor of Judea, decided, according to Luke's gospel, to appease a demanding mob and crucify a harmless heretical Jew, Jesus of Nazareth, rather than trigger more unrest.[19] There was a real fear that the ties that held the Empire together might be undone as its money disappeared. The pre-Imperial world of Gauls and Carthaginians, of Egyptians and Iberians, might rise like ghosts and the city could fall to its own starving masses. More solid than Rome's old stone wall was the new metaphorical wall of golden aurei. The whole world needed to believe in it and know the coins were there in abundance.

It is reckoned that within a few years of its appearance, the gold aureus represented a quarter of the currency in circulation in the Empire. During the excavation of Pompeii, that time capsule of 79 CE, two-thirds of the cash found was gold.[20] Since an aureus could only be used for very large purchases (it can be thought of as a $500 banknote for practical purposes), people would stash their gold somewhere safe and change it a coin at a time. It made them feel secure.

Tiberius had grasped that to survive as emperor, he had to feed his troops cash; especially the Praetorian Guard. Ten years after his bribe of 1,000 sestertii a man to them, they killed his successor, Caligula, and dragged his uncle, Claudius, to the throne. Claudius paid each of them 3,750 denarii a year (1.2kg of gold aurei) to stay alive. Businessmen might accept letters of credit, but soldiers were not interested. And since money always flowed out in a torrent and came back in dribbles, a new source had to be plundered.

Plundering Britain

Julius Caesar had set Rome on the road to Empire, seizing Gaul. But that was no longer enough. The silver mines of Spain were running out, and it was understood that there were significant deposits of silver and gold in Britain. The geographer Strabo, writing after Julius Caesar had made two expeditions there, stated firmly that there was no financial sense in making Britain Roman. There was considerable trade across the Channel, with Britain exporting luxury woollen garments, hunting dogs, basketry and mined minerals, and importing fruit and vegetables. If occupied by force, the island would need the permanent presence of at least one legion and some cavalry, and their cost would be greater than the tribute that could be raised – especially as Britain would then become part of the Roman Common Market and customs duties would have to be reduced.[21] But in 43 CE, Claudius did set out to conquer and occupy Britain.

Modern interpretations tend to mirror the Roman sources, which explain this in terms of Claudius's character. But even if this frightened, cautious, scholarly man had been the kind of person to gamble his precarious position for the prestige of conquering a semi-mythical island, that would not explain the colossal investment of men and treasure involved in permanently holding on to the place. Rome took over southern Britain because Strabo's assessment was out of date. Once Rome ruled Cleopatra's Egypt, it took over Egypt's trade through the Red Sea and the Indian Ocean. This connected its traders to a highly developed commodity market which reached via India to places of which Rome knew nothing – China, Vietnam, Indonesia, East Africa – but which delivered new and delightful products which quickly became marks of status for rich Europeans. Trade was growing much faster than the money supply.[22] Traders did not have access to enough coin to keep business flowing, but Britain appeared to be an untapped source of silver and gold. The cost of occupation was to be met by the value of its precious metals.

It took 40,000 men to occupy the island, rising to 55,000 by the middle of the second century. By then, it was obvious that Strabo's calculation was right after all: Britain was unprofitable.[23] But within six years of the invasion, the lead mines in the Mendip Hills near Bath were in full production, and silver was being extracted from them.[24] By 70 CE, Britain was the largest supplier of silver in the Empire. There was also the gold. There is no concrete evidence for pre-Roman gold production in Wales, but it is hard to see why the Romans fought so hard for, and invested so heavily in, the remote hills of mid-Wales unless they knew about it already. The target was the River Cothi. The Britons put up a ferocious resistance to the Roman advance. Eventually, a general who had suppressed a huge revolt in the Rhineland, then served as one of Rome's consuls, and also happened to be the Empire's leading hydraulic engineer, was appointed governor of Britain with the dual goals of militarily crushing resistance and hydraulically crushing rocks. The Britons must have taken gold from the gravel of riverbeds, but it became evident that there was a deep seam near the Cothi that would have to be excavated by using water at high-pressure. The technique was well established in Rome's notorious Spanish mines. Frontinus, who would go on to restore Rome's water supply and write the definitive work on the subject, built a set of aqueducts through the Welsh mountains, one of them over 10km long, to provide the high-pressure jets that would scour away the hillside and mill the rock to extract as much as they possibly could. Yet it was nowhere near enough.

It took Rome fifty years to empty the mine, but having decided to take over unprofitable Britain, they could not withdraw. The Roman Imperial enterprise was not just a raid by marauders. The troops had been offered land as well as gold, and retired soldiers became colonists. The object was to promote the Romanization of the natives, which clearly did happen, but it also meant that Rome had to show that it would stand by its soldiers and their descendants. This was a particular issue in Britain, where Boudicca's rebellion killed some 70,000 Roman citizens and allies.[25] So Rome found itself, in Britain and elsewhere, committed to the continual defence of frontiers which moved further and further from the city. The Empire became self-justifying, an enterprise in promoting and protecting Roman-ness. Its great engineering projects, its roads and aqueducts, were necessary to sustain the state and its military effectiveness. The Roman elite saw their city as the shining heart of civilization, enjoying a brilliant literature around the Imperial court. But the real shine came from its gold, which financed the luxury of sophisticated culture, and which would eventually bring the city, and the Empire in Europe, to ruin.

Plundering Jerusalem

The price extracted by soldiers for the Imperial crown kept growing. After Claudius's death, Nero paid the Praetorian Guard as much as Claudius had done to sit safely on the throne. That did not stop them taking a huge sum for his removal and the installation of his two (very brief) successors. The amount of money being spent by the Empire grew, but the supply of precious metal was shrinking. In Nero's last four years, the number of mints in Rome halved. A statue of Alexander was first gilded, then the gold had to be stripped off (Nero said it was not as attractive as he expected).[26] As the cash to pay troops disappeared, open rebellion broke out. The Batavian soldiers who had been used to crush Druid resistance in Wales and defeat Boudicca now abandoned their allegiance, took over the Low Countries, destroyed two unenthusiastic legions and were in control of the whole area as far as Cologne.

After Nero's assassination, faction fighting around the Empire became civil war. It ended during 69 CE, the 'Year of the Four Emperors', when the legions of Egypt and Judea hailed their commander, Vespasian, and he led them in the conquest of Rome. The city and its economy had been wrecked. Vespasian made it perfectly clear that his authority came from the Army, not from the Senate or any constitutional arrangement. He told the Senate that the Empire would be unable to pay its troops and restore Rome without an extra 400 million gold pieces in cash.[27] The senators recognized the need for the city and its provinces to pay up.

Austerity was now at the heart of the Empire, and Vespasian was an austere man. One major physical task confronting him was to restore the devastated sacred centre of the city. That involved quarrying great columns of stone and carrying them up to the top of the Capitoline Hill. A Greek engineer, possibly Heron of Alexandria, offered him a mechanical device to do this. We don't know what it was, but it was clearly a machine that replaced human power with mechanical power, and was capable of shifting tons at a time, vertically. It could have been a static steam engine. There were such devices in Alexandria, being used to operate temple doors and theatrical automata. Vespasian bought the machine and scrapped it, believing it would lead to slaves being dumped onto the streets. He could not afford to replace unpaid work with welfare.[28] The Industrial Revolution, and its attendant social crisis, was postponed for about 1,500 years.

Gold's double life, spiritual and material, was a contest between its two valuations – a contest between spending it on the next life or this one. The sacred significance of gold did not vanish once it was used to buy soldiers. In 70 CE, the year after Vespasian made his unprecedented demand for millions to pay the Army, his son, Titus, destroyed and sacked the Temple in Jerusalem. He took the great treasure stacked up in it; perhaps 50 tons of gold. That was enough to make more than 6 million of the gold coins Vespasian needed. The Temple had served as the Judean national treasury. Its golden table, giant gold candelabra and trumpets, which had been well-known tourist attractions, were paraded in Titus's triumph through Rome and are depicted there on his arch. But despite his father's desperate need, the massive ritual gold objects of the sanctuary were not added to Rome's treasury. They were transferred to a new temple in Rome itself, a 'Temple of Peace', which was financed with the profit of the looting. There was no legal protection for non-Roman sacred places,[29] but the magic of this gold, which could not be confused with luxury adornment, was felt to be overwhelming.

The question of where the Temple of Jerusalem's gold finally ended up has been a subject of fantasy and misconceived treasure hunting ever since. Lately, it was recycled into a fable for the credulous involving the Goth leader, Alaric, getting hold of it during the sack of Rome hundreds of years later, its carriage into France and ending up hidden in the Visigoths' last redoubt, Rennes-le-Château. This magical tale involved a nineteenth-century parish priest who uncovered the secret, the Knights Templar (who had access to the Temple's hidden vaults during the Crusades) and Freemasons (who had the secrets of the temple-builders). The story was given credence by the priest's very real transformation from a poor man to a very rich one, spending lavishly on his community and on himself.

Sadly, but unsurprisingly, the truth was that he had spun this cover story to explain the large profits he was making from illegally exploiting his religious office.[30] But the boost to the story of Temple treasure, which spawned a whole genre of narratives about Freemasons, was a massive demonstration of the connection in modern minds between gold and divine mystery. The treasures of the Temple included silver, precious stones and rich hangings, but they do not carry the mystical charge of its gold.

The irony is that Temple gold would not have that powerful attraction if it was still sacred, accessible only to a god and that god's chosen or appointed servant. The Romans saw it as exotic treasure. As now, it retained some of the magic but it was also secularized, understood as wealth. The priest at Rennes-le-Château was not thought of as the guardian of God's sacred gold. He was thought to have used the treasure to become stinking rich, and the treasure-hunters wanted to be part of that. They still do.

Plundering Dacia

After Titus died in 81 CE, his brother, Domitian, took over and found himself trying to balance the budget while fighting defensive frontier wars. He also felt obliged to increase soldiers' pay by a third, which was unsustainable. His brief-lived successor, Nerva, turned Domitian's gold statues into coins.[31] One of Domitian's wars was with the Celts of Dacia, the region on the banks of the Danube that Julius Caesar had intended to loot before he was distracted by Gaul. When Trajan took power in 98 CE, he saw Dacia as the solution to the gold problem.

Vespasian had seen the sacred treasure of the Jews, which was well known in Rome, as exotic, but no one had any feelings about the sacred treasures of barbarian Celts. Dacia was ruthlessly crushed. The resulting loot was so massive that Rome's income was augmented by 28 million aurei a year (about 225 tons of gold), putting the Army on a more secure footing for a few years and financing the rebuilding of the city into the monumental capital we now recognize. A hill was removed to build a new Forum flanked by libraries, and at its centre was placed what is now called Trajan's Column. It reaches the lost summit of the annihilated hill, and it records the epic story of the plunder of the gold that was the new foundation of the city.

Trajan and his wife were interred in gold urns in its base – not because these connected the couple to the afterlife but because this gold was Rome itself.

A hundred thousand Dacian men were dragged off to become Roman slaves, and an entirely new population of slaves was imported to Dacia to be worked to death in its mines. Nobody bothered with steam engines. The Roman Empire had reached its limit, but Rome did not know that. Not yet.

The money continued to drain away and soldiers (now legions as well as Praetorian Guards) continued to sell the Empire to the highest bidders. 'Donativae' to the whole Roman Army became the price of accession in the second and third centuries. Apart from money that was spent on expensive imports, a considerable part of the gold distributed by emperors to hold the loyalty of their troops vanished as it was turned into buried treasure, presumably being secreted by the recipients, who survived more by barter than shopping. A recent study of 230 uncovered coin hoards with a face value of around 2 million sestertii, buried between 31 BCE and 235 CE, indicates that they were part of these Imperial handouts. This covers a long period during which the composition of the legions was changing, including many recruits from far beyond Italy. It may well be that they had a less commodified understanding of gold and were more inclined to think of it as having a strong transcendental connection. Certainly, gold was the dominant material to be buried. As at Pompeii, 70 per cent of the coins, by value, were gold.[32]

The year 193 CE became known as the 'Year of the Five Emperors'. The first, Pertinax, was a decent man, the son of a slave, who was forced by the Praetorian Guard to sell off his predecessor's property, including his concubines and catamites, and give them the proceeds. He then tried to reform the currency and discipline them; they raised his severed head on a lance and held an auction for

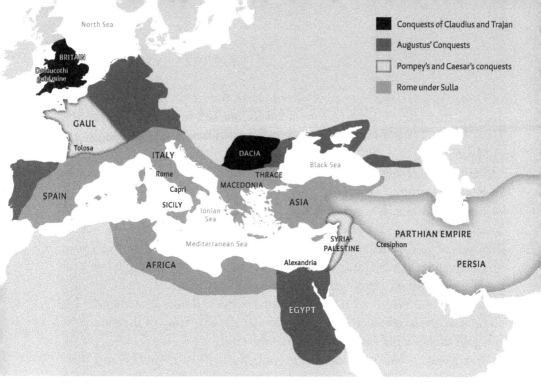

The Roman Empire at its limits.

his throne. He had lasted three months. The winner of the auction, a politician called Didius Julianus, offered the soldiers 25,000 sestertii each, and actually paid 30,000. His wife and daughter felt he had made a serious mistake.[33] They were right. He lasted nine weeks, as the legions of Pannonia, on the Danube near Dacia, ignored the auction and took their own governor, Septimius Severus, to Rome to seize power. After disposing of Rome's new buyer and the next two claimants, he responded in the obvious way, raising the troops' pay from 300 to 500 denarii a year. The silver denarius was gold's small change. Under Augustus it had contained almost 4 grams of silver, but under Septimius it contained less than 1.5 grams. So what could he do but follow tradition and swallow a gold-rich neighbour? The trouble was, the only one left was Persia.

Plundering Persia

Septimius Severus's contemporary, the historian Cassius Dio, described the need for the Empire to seize ever-more gold as the driving force that had turned the Army into a mass of armed brigands for whom the whole world was prey: 'From what source, then, is the money to be provided for these soldiers … For we cannot survive without soldiers and soldiers will not serve without pay.'[34] In 198 CE, Septimius Severus managed to sack Persia's capital, Ctesiphon, a city more than twice the size of Rome. The gold he took was enough to pay Rome's armies for decades. But Persia was not to be swallowed by Rome, nor would it accept what had happened. Nevertheless, about ten years later, Severus's son, Caracalla, raised military pay by 50 per cent and declared: 'Nobody should have any money but I, so that I may bestow it on the soldiers.'[35]

The balance of trade did not change, and over the following fifty years Rome lost some 80 per cent of its gold to the East. Rome's gold starvation kept driving its war on Persia. Gold is a very inert metal in physical terms, but its gravitational pull upon minds and purses is strong, and the centre of gravity of the Roman Empire was being pulled eastwards.

Plundering Rome

The military payroll in Europe was destroying the currency, and with it, political authority. In the third century, breakaway self-proclaimed emperors in Gaul and Britain were able to establish their power on the basis of locally minted gold coins from sources no longer accessible to Rome. Confidence in Rome's debased silver currency collapsed completely, inflation hit 1,000 per cent and Rome was forced to stop pretending that its 'silver' coins held any value. The financial system was bust, and evidence for banks disappears between 260 and 330 CE.[36] The Empire had been made for gold and was now starved of it. Its military weakness and overextended frontiers needed to be seriously addressed. In the late third century, Diocletian reduced army pay, giving them debased coinage, and created a new basis for military service in place of gold. He forced citizens to enlist by conscription and made military service hereditary. Most of their pay was in food and equipment. These were not likely to be enthusiastic warriors. The only troops who could be paid in gold were non-Roman mercenaries, who would not serve without it, so Diocletian bolstered the frontier forces with gold-paid recruits from Germanic tribes. Since about a quarter of the Army was recruited from, and officered by, Germanic or Sarmatian tribesmen, the word 'barbarian' would come to mean a Roman auxiliary soldier.[37] Many had entered the Empire as migrant workers to enlist.

Diocletian introduced a reformed currency based on a new gold coin, the gold denarius, now known as a solidus. But he could not find the gold to make it work, and inflation destroyed it. He tried to stop the rot with an edict fixing maximum prices. His successors continued to debase what currency they had, to increase the coins they could mint to pay soldiers and officials and stave off the collapse of the frontiers.[38] The currency continued to lose its value, with average annual inflation of about 17 per cent.[39] Trade collapsed, city life became intolerable for many and increasing numbers of Romans entered a form of hereditary serfdom to survive in a society where money had lost much of its value.

The Army, and therefore the Empire, was in serious trouble: there were huge movements of population across the frontiers of the East. Rome's forced disruption of the Balkans and North Africa in its pursuit of gold stirred up great movements of people, and also of disease carriers. On the human level, tribal peoples – Alamanni, Sarmatians and Goths – sought new homes in Gaul, the Alpine regions, Italy and the Balkans. Inevitably, there was also an upheaval of other life forms, some bearing pathogens. New pandemics swept the Empire, perhaps killing one person in three. The first was the 'Antonine Plague' of 165–180 CE – carefully described by the great doctor Galen, it was probably smallpox.[40] At its peak, some 2,000 were said to be dying daily in Rome, and the total mortality may have been 10 per cent of the Empire's population. Then in 249 CE, the 'Plague of Cyprian' appeared, named after the writer who described it, the Bishop of Carthage. He painted a terrifying picture of gruesome suffering, with elements of viral haemorrhagic fever (Lassa fever? Ebola?) transmitted by skin contact, violent diarrhoea and vomiting, fever and fatigue, haemorrhaging from the eyes and the mouth, putrefaction of limbs, deafness and blindness.[41] It was an incomprehensible disaster. With a drastic shortfall in the size of the Army, and a need for forces to suppress military secessions and hold the frontiers, huge numbers of 'barbarians' were recruited. The need for coin was greater than ever.

The new recruits were armed and trained, organized to use force. But they were serving only for the promise of golden pay; which would be fine, until payday.

Chapter 9

Gold Going East

Indian Temples

The incessant flow of gold away from Europe has been a theme of history for 2,000 years, and its cause has not been an oriental love of wealth – at least, not entirely. The role of gold as a link to divinity is still a tremendous force in the world, though many Europeans and Americans suppose that idea belongs to the distant past. But they are generally not aware that India consumes more than twice as much gold each year as all other countries combined, nor are they aware why. In the first quarter of 2017, India was the main support of the global gold market.[1] It is used to buy blessings: blessings bestowed on family and friends in the form of jewellery and dowries, and blessings sought by making massive donations of gold to the Hindu gods in their temples. The state of Andhra Pradesh alone has 45,000 temples. Just one of them, in Tirupati, receives around a ton of gold a year, worth over $60 million, from devotees. In 2016, it deposited 2,780kg of gold with the Indian State Bank.[2] That is a tiny fraction of India's 22,000 tons, most of which has been dedicated to temples.[3] Much of the world's gold has its value measured not in the market, but in its sacred purpose. That has always underpinned the certainty that there is value inherent in gold.

Do civilizations that once relied on gold, sink without it? Some people in Europe and America feel that is a reason for slight anxiety now. It looks as if the Chinese government also feels worried, which is presumably why it has collected nearly as much gold as India.[4]

About half of India's gold – over 400 tons a year – goes to a single state, Kerala. Kerala has been absorbing gold for millennia, and that is where much of Rome's gold seems to have gone. On 30 June 2011, a small group of selected observers descended a narrow stairway hidden under a stone slab into an airless underground chamber below the Sree Padmanabhaswamy Temple in the state capital, Thiruvananthapuram. Oxygen was pumped in for them. They were there at the command of the Indian Supreme Court. The dress code of the temple required them to be barefoot, wearing dhotis. In the dark of the subterranean vault, they were astonished to be confronted by millions of twinkling reflections from the largest treasure ever known.[5] The vast mass of jewels and gold include golden chains and gemstones, precious objects and coins dating from antiquity down to the time of Napoleon. Among them are hundreds of thousands of Roman gold coins, which arrived in trade and were deposited over centuries. There is no inventory. It is all the property of the god Vishnu, preserver and protector of the universe.

The temple's executive had said that the treasure in the vaults consisted of nothing but cobwebs and dust. The current estimate of its value is around 14 billion pounds sterling, perhaps $19 billion.

The Sree Padmanabhaswamy Temple visible today is believed to have been built in the ninth century, but it has clearly served as a kind of divine sinkhole for immense quantities of gold dedicated to the gods from 200 BCE until now. Kerala, on the southern tip of India, was the entrepot for goods brought by sea from further east. Its traders sold sesame seeds and gems, indigo and parrots, hides and ivory, tortoiseshell, pepper and spices to ships that traded to Roman Egypt, and they gathered up gold. Some of it covered their costs, some was for gifts and benedictions of jewellery, but much was for the temples. The imperial portraits on coins given as temple offerings were slashed across the face, to make them unacceptable ever again to Rome. The sums involved were extraordinary. One second-century papyrus records a contract between an Alexandrian merchant importer and a financier dealing with a shipment from Kerala, valuing that single cargo at 7 million sestertii.[6] When the fictional first-century merchant Trimalchio, in Petronius's *Satyricon*, lost five ships in a storm, he valued the loss at 30 million sestertii.[7] That would have seemed very credible.

Luxuries to Rome, Gold to the East

Diocletian's Edict on Maximum Prices shows just how much gold the Roman super-rich elite were spending on luxuries, even at the end of the third century when the Empire was in desperate financial trouble. For example, it set the price of one pound of raw white silk at 12,000 denarii, which meant thirty gold aurei a kilo – the equivalent of two years' pay for a legionary. A kilo is enough to make one dress. Purple silk, which could only be used with Imperial permission, cost twelve-and-a-half times more. It was manufactured exclusively in Tyre, which was a key transmission point for oriental luxury goods into Rome. 'Phoenicia' was probably the word for purple.

The Romans had always known that their gold was draining East, but they did not know exactly where it was going. They just knew that it was not serving a spiritual purpose, at least as far as they were concerned. Around 78 CE, Pliny had complained: 'India, the Seres and the Arabian Peninsula take one hundred million sestertii from our empire per annum at a conservative estimate: that

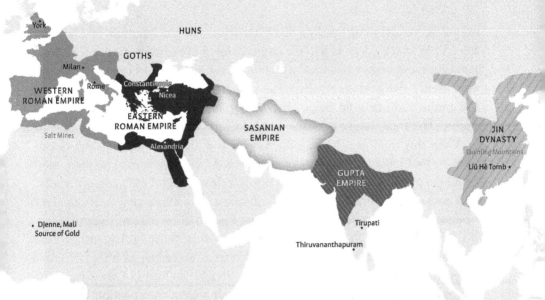

Eurasia in 320 BCE.

is what our luxuries and women cost us. For what fraction of these imports is intended for sacrifices to the gods or the spirits of the dead?'

He would have been interested, though perhaps not consoled, to learn that a significant part of the gold itself was being dedicated to Vishnu and many other deities. In fact, it was wanted precisely for its divine and transcendental purposes, for the splendour of gods and the immortality of humans. From that perspective, the Roman Empire was taking over the world for gold which it then enthusiastically exchanged for exotic fancy goods which were, in the great scheme of things, quite worthless.

The sea-route to India was also the main avenue for trade with the Seres, beyond the edge of the world known to Rome. No-one was quite certain who they were. In fact, they were the Chinese, and along with Indians they had a serious hunger for gold. The Roman Empire was being driven to expand to the point of collapse by civilizations that were so far away that it knew absolutely nothing about them. But the impact on Rome's immediate neighbours, and ultimately on the Empire itself, would be devastating. The Empire was being sucked dry by people concerned with gold's connection to divinity and immortality, including Daoist alchemists of the Han Dynasty.

Chinese Alchemy

In November 2015, the Chinese press reported the discovery of a tomb believed to be that of the deposed Han Emperor Liú Hè.[8] He was deposed after only twenty-seven days but lived on for fifteen years as the Marquis of Haihun, dying in 59 BCE. Under a bed in the main chamber of the tomb were three boxes containing the largest batch of gold items ever found in a Han tomb. There were twenty-five gold ingots shaped as animal hoofs, weighing between 40 and 250 grams, and fifty gold 'coins', disc-shaped ingots, each weighing about 250 grams.[9] The total weight of gold was 115kg.

When this tomb was built, Julius Caesar was about to start his assault on Gaul, to loot its sacred deposits of gold as a source of finance. The Han, too, wanted to gather up as much gold as possible. It was useful for trade, especially with nomads – for bribes, royal gifts, tribute and as an emergency cash reserve – but above all for achieving immortality. Pliny had no idea of the existence of the Han Chinese. Strabo's geography of the globe finished Asia just east of the Ganges, and the 'Seres' who lived there were, according to him, tall, fair-haired, blue-eyed folk. Whoever it was that Strabo had heard of, they were not the Han Chinese, who would suck up as much gold as they possibly could. A chronicle of the dynasty from 206 BCE to 23 CE, by coincidence the year Strabo published his *Geography*, appears to list Han Imperial grants totalling 225 tons of gold.[10] The final emperor in the chronicle, Wang Mang, had no interest at all in money and commandeered all the gold in his Empire, abolishing gold coinage and creating financial havoc. What he wanted was the stuff of immortality, and when he fell, he was found to have stored up more than 150 tons of it in his palace, enough to pay the entire budget of the Roman Empire.[11] Tiberius soon after complained of foreign luxuries causing a critical shortage of currency.[12] In the entire century after 1492, Spain recorded the import of just 20 tons more than Wang Mang had in his palace.

Gold in China was filled with magical connotations: 'yellow' and 'shining' were terms associated with Imperial splendour and authority. It was seen as being very useful to anyone interested in its most significant property: immortality. In China, as in Mesoamerica,[13] jade was valued as promising an extension of life. It is found in burials dating back to the late Neolithic, and by the time of the Han was being placed on the dead as masks or entire body coverings which were supposed to protect the body from decay and so allow entry into the world of immortals. The earliest examples known are the jade suits of Liu Sheng and his wife, from around 150 BCE.[14] Until they were revealed in 1968, such fantastic objects were thought to be legendary. But apart from Queen Hsi Wang Mu, a female spirit from the beginning of time who drank powdered jade, the stone was not used as an elixir of life. That role was given to gold; the jade suit panels were held together with gold wire, and gold acupuncture needles were next to them. The medical use of gold to extend life could date back in China to 2,500 BCE.[15] In *On Salt and Iron* (81 BCE), Huan Kuan of the Western Han Dynasty said that 'immortals swallow gold', a proposition explained by Wei Boyang of the Eastern Han Dynasty in the less snappily titled *Token for the agreement of the Three according to the Book of Changes*. He said: 'Gold is the most valuable thing in all the world because it is immortal and never gets rotten. Alchemists eat it, and they enjoy longevity.' He was the alchemist who explained how to make gunpowder in 142 CE. In the early fourth century, another alchemist, Ge Hong, wrote an entire treatise on cooking for immortality, explaining that because gold is unchanged by smelting or burial, eating it 'will therefore so strengthen one's body that he will not grow old and die'.[16]

The pre-Imperial Chinese were not really interested in gold as currency, and they produced very little. Some gold coins appeared somewhere around the fifth or sixth century BCE, in the Warring States period. The state of Chu, south of the Yellow River, was stamping characters onto various sized sheets of gold 3–5mm thick known as Ying Yuan. One of the characters is often yuan, which remains the name of the modern unit of currency. But the Ying Yuan were for keeping, not spending. Nevertheless, by the fourth century BCE, it would appear that it was sufficiently desirable for the kingdom of Shu to dismantle its defences in the hope of receiving gold-producing cattle. Or so the story goes.

In an echo of Odysseus ending the siege of Troy by the ruse of a wooden horse back in 1184 BCE, some 870 years later a Chinese 'Odysseus', King Huiwen of Qin, came up with a similar plan to get his army into the Kingdom of Shu, which was only accessible by very narrow unstable tracks through the Qinling Mountains. He had five realistic life-sized stone cows carved, with traces of gold excrement and large golden cowpats, placed where they could be seen only from a distance. The King of Shu was delighted by his neighbour offering to send him some of these unusual beasts and agreed to the construction of a road sturdy enough for substantial bovines. The mountain defences were broken through and the road was built, large enough for five useless stone cattle and one very useful army. The King of Shu had hoped the gold would bring him immortality, and in a way it did, but not in a good way. The Stone Cattle road is still there; the Kingdom of Shu is not.

This was a precursor to the unification of China in 221 BCE. In the following century, southern Chinese aristocrats became obsessed with alchemical ideas from India and took to swallowing gold in quantities to achieve immortality.[17] Since little gold was produced inside the Chinese Empire, there was a great interest in acquiring it from outside. It was all excreted, of course.

Wang Mang's fall had been followed by total chaos; his destruction of money led to the death of perhaps half China's population, but that did not slow the flow of gold east from Rome. China was not the only drain on Rome's gold: Indian trade was massive too, and far more Roman gold coins are found there than in China. That is probably because the Chinese had no direct trade with Rome, and Roman gold that flowed that far east may well have been recast into ingots on the journey. Persia, too, was a waystation for Chinese trade with the West, and when it was not necessary for the Persians to pay Chinese merchants in gold, they used other currency and kept the gold themselves. The Persian Empire did not value the gold it collected as currency – it did not make any golden coins – but preserved it as a store of transcendental wealth.[18] So instead of circulating back again, it was imprisoned there.

The Emperor Plunders Constantinople

Rome had to use gold for trade because there was nothing of significance that the East was interested in buying from Romans. That is why Rome found it harder and harder to pay its soldiers. In effect, gold had become what Rome was made of, and it was vanishing.

Rome's Empire was in serious difficulties as it tried to cope with mass immigration pressure in the east and currency and social collapse in the west. The ancient system of shoring up the Army by new conquests of gold had come to a complete stop. Rome had been forced in 275 CE to abandon Dacia to migrating Goths; the province had in any case been worked dry.[19] The Empire was now divided between regional warlords who were trying to fund their vast forces and following the money where they could find it. Constantine, an Illyrian Greek, was serving as a military commander in York in 306 CE when his troops hailed him as emperor. He took them out of Britain and after six years conquered Rome, but Rome was lacking resources. He ruled in the West while his brother-in-law, Licinius, had taken the East, ruling from Byzantium, where there was still great wealth. The inevitable war between them ended with Constantine's victory in 324 CE, and he moved his capital far to the east, to Licinius's city. Byzantium was New Rome and became Constantine's city, Constantinople. The Empire's gold now began its final move out of Europe, and the Eastern, Greek-speaking provinces became separated from the West.

The most fundamental problem Constantine faced was the lack of coins. He reduced the weight of the gold solidus by a quarter and set about the serious business of plundering all the gold he could from Licinius's domains. There were fabulous stores of treasure in the Eastern Empire that had not been available to emperors because it was locked away in temples, protected by being dedicated to the gods. Suddenly, the gods were abandoned in favour of Christianity and this protection was stripped away. Constantine may never have subjected himself to the Christian Church, but his mother was a practising Christian and he adored his mother. His hagiographer, Eusebius, said that the emperor was converted by seeing a cross above the sun while he was marching with his army and an inscription in Greek in the sky saying, 'in this [sign], conquer'. He certainly recognized Christianity and ended the authority of the old Roman gods.

In 313 CE, on the occasion of his sister's wedding, he had already joined with Licinius in issuing the Edict of Milan, a proclamation of general religious toleration which gave Christianity legal status. The Edict was a weapon against another regional warlord, Maximinus, who was persecuting Christians as enemies of the Empire's ancestral pantheon. Constantine then went much further than the Edict. He believed that his military success was a sign that he was empowered by a higher divine mind and found that entirely compatible with the Christian God.[20] So in 325 CE, he convened the bishops in Nicaea, put Christianity under his patronage and made himself the political authority behind their declarations. Religious orthodoxy would now be bound irrevocably to loyalty to the emperor. At the same time, he was the *Pontifex Maximus*, the high priest, which was of course a pagan office, and he identified himself with the Invincible Sun, *Sol Invictus*. The gold of the eastern temples was his for the taking. He forbade the use of the temples for sacrifices, and they were open to official plunder.

The Church made great efforts to claim Constantine as a Christian, but they are unconvincing. He set his Empire on the path to Christianization without ever becoming a member of the Church himself. His panegyric biographer, Bishop Eusebius of Caesarea, was reduced to claiming that Constantine was baptized on his deathbed. Another writer, who wrote a continuation of Eusebius's work, said Eusebius had been more interested in praising the emperor than in accuracy, but then came up with an account of his baptism that is even less credible.[21] The Church would for centuries base its authority on false claims about the 'first Christian Emperor', culminating 400 years after his death in the appearance of a 'donation' by which Constantine had supposedly transferred authority over Rome and the western part of the Roman Empire to the Pope. In 1440, it was proved a forgery by a Catholic priest. Constantine projected himself as a being of overpowering dominance and did not seem to feel any need to persuade the Christian God to save his soul. But he was interested in saving his Empire. By making Christianity respectable and paganism disreputable, he unlocked the golden treasures that would make his solidus a strong permanent currency and the financial backbone of his power: 'When the gold and silver and the huge quantity of precious stones which had been long ago stored away in the temples reached the public, they enkindled all men's possessive and spendthrift instincts … This store of gold meant that the houses of the powerful were crammed full.'[22]

In May 330 CE, Constantine dedicated a column 25 metres high topped with a gold statue of himself as the sun-god, with rays emanating from his head.

He was *Deus Sol Invictus*, the Invincible Sun God, holding a figure of Tyche, the goddess of fortune, in his hand. The dedication began with Tyche being invited to live in the city and the emperor's statue being lifted into position.[23] The Church, submitting to his radiance with a clear eye to its own advancement, accepted the rule of a man whose identity was embodied in gold. It gave him an authority that pagan religion did not, and it was transformed. As *Pontifex Maximus*, he created a new calendar which would convert Christianity to him. He declared the Day of the Sun, *dies solis*, Sunday, to be the Empire's day of rest. And he confirmed the birthday of the Invincible Sun as the winter solstice, 25 December, which in the thirtieth year of his rule the Church recognized as Christ's birthday.

The Golden Emperor coined most of the gold that had been stored in temples and could still then afford to pour 1½ tons of it over churches. As Byzantium was transformed into Constantinople, a new church was erected at its heart. Visitors today are awestruck by Hagia Sophia, originally constructed by Justinian in the sixth century, but the great original church of the city, the Church of the Holy Apostles, was built 200 years earlier, on the new main street, on top of the highest hill. It was later rebuilt several times, eventually to be demolished and replaced by a mosque, but for 700 years it was the busiest church in Constantinople, the mausoleum of its emperors and a vivid statement of the centrality of Christ and his Apostles to the Imperial claim to power. The high ceiling was entirely overlaid with gold, and the brass roof was so heavily gilded that it 'reflected the sun's rays with a brilliancy which dazzled the distant beholder'.[24]

Constantinople, probably the richest city in the world, was a palace-dominated economy in which most aspects of life, trade and industry were governed by the religious and administrative authorities. This was more like old Babylon than Augustus's Rome. The language here was Greek, and the emperor's title was 'Autokrator', meaning absolute ruler. He was not quite a king-priest, but not far off. He was not a subject of the Church but its master, enforcing the 'correct' form of its developing religion. His palace rose to less than half the height of the great ziggurat of Marduk at Babylon, but it sprawled over more than twice the area.[25] The Autokrator Constantine did not share his home with the golden figure of a god who gave him power, but he built a mausoleum for himself where he would be installed as the Thirteenth Apostle, at Christ's right hand, in a space laden with gold. There were two rows of six coffins, representing the apostles, his own tomb standing in the centre.[26] New Rome's theologians described gold as condensed light and the sun, the essence of incorruptibility, truth and glory. Gold was used as a metaphor for light, above all for the Divine Light.

The Middle Eastern and Egyptian tradition of using gold in temples as an indication of divine presence was absorbed wholesale into Constantinople's

Christianity. Eastern theologians such as St Basil and Pseudo-Dionysius used gold as a sign of light and divinity.[27]

By 340 CE, the Empire was coining a third more gold than in 310, and 80 per cent of it was being minted in Byzantium.[28] By then, Constantine was dead and had divided the Empire between East and West. The West would have to solve its own problems.

The Collapse of the West

Constantine's Empire was in theory briefly politically reunited by Constantius in 353 CE, but ten years later the final attempt to use legions to win new gold collapsed when an army almost 100,000 strong attacked Persia and was humiliated. The Emperor Julian, the last emperor who tried to protect and restore paganism, was killed. Valentinian, who took over, re-divided the Empire into East and West, took control of the West (handing the East to his brother, Valens) and did a most impressive job of holding the line. But the Empire was now dependent on its gold reserves.

The private ownership of gold was stopped. A new official, the Count of the Sacred Largesses, was responsible for the production, supply and distribution of imperial wealth, particularly the solidus, now made of 99 per cent pure gold. This was evidently essential to buy the loyalty of solders and nobility. With no new source, the coins were mostly made using recycled gold. The idea was to take it back as taxes, but this supposedly closed system was very leaky. Some coins were hoarded, others were melted down for jewellery, plate and tableware, and quantities were sent to barbarians beyond the frontiers to buy relief from plunder.[29]

Just at this point, Rome was thrown a very surprising lifeline – a new kind of army, which did not need to be paid in the old way. Hundreds of thousands of Western Goth farmers, Visigoths, in desperate flight from aggressive and terrifying nomads who were being called Huns, began piling up on the banks of the Danube, seeking succour inside the Empire. The river was in flood, uncrossable. Valens agreed to allow them entry and promised that they would be fed, on condition that they disarmed and provided troops for his army, and that the pagans among them become Christians. The Visigoths were grouped into companies, and then over several days and nights were ferried across 'in boats, rafts and in hollowed tree-trunks'. The officials in charge often tried to reckon their number but gave up their attempt: 'Who wishes to know this would wish to know the number of grains of sand on the Libyan plain.'[30]

Valens's motives were not humanitarian. He had committed huge resources to fighting Persia and had been persuaded that the influx of 'so many young recruits from the ends of the earth' would expand his legions into an invincible army. It was hoped that the annual levy of soldiers from each province could be suspended, and that the resulting savings would swell the coffers of the treasury. It did not work out quite as intended.

Instead, it led to what is remembered as the final catastrophe. The Goths became part of the Roman Army, but a resentful part. They were kept short of supplies, were not rewarded and had every reason to mistrust their Roman masters. They became Christians, but chose a different brand of Christianity, they spoke their own language and they felt permanently cheated. They were right. The final blow to the West was, in the eyes of people at the time, the event now known as the 'sack of Rome', which is generally thought of as a barbarian invasion under a Goth chieftain called Alaric. In reality, these were Rome's Gothic soldiers. Alaric was the commanding officer of a Roman army of Christian auxiliaries, who came to Rome in a desperate attempt to persuade the city to release their pay. There was no rape, no pillage. They demanded that the citizens hand over their wealth, and they stripped bronze tiles off a roof by mistake. That was the famous barbarian invasion.

The Finale

Rome had run out of money, and then so did the East. There is an account of Attila the Hun's capture of Milan in 452 CE, where he saw a painting of Roman emperors sitting upon golden thrones with what he took to be Huns lying dead at their feet. He wanted to make it clear that was a world that had vanished, so he ordered a painter to change the fresco to show himself on the throne and the Roman emperors pouring out sacks of gold before his feet.[31] Constantinople was at his mercy, and he demanded tribute of up to 2,100lb of gold a year. This was not for spending but, like the remade painting, to demonstrate the new world order. Much of it probably became tableware.

Either there had to be a new source of gold, or the Empire would need a new theology, and a new economy, in which survival and salvation could be managed without having any gold.

Unlike the destruction of Varna or Carthage, this was not a deliberate choice. There would be different answers on each side of the divided *Imperium*.

Part III

The Summons to Europe

Chapter 10

Life Without Gold

Desperate Gold Hunters

People will put themselves through incredible ordeals when they stand a chance of digging up gold. The coldest places in the United States are Barrow, on the northern tip of Alaska, and the old gold rush town of Bodie, California. Bodie sits 2,600 metres high on a bare windswept plateau of the Sierra Mountains and has never known an entire month without frost. There is no wood for fuel. But gold was found here in 1859, so desperate prospectors struggled up the mountains with timber and supplies and built themselves cabins. In 1879, when its population peaked at around 8,000, the local newspaper reported that two double blankets and three in a bed was not enough to keep warm. People were freezing to death. They may not all have been in bed. The main street, a mile long, had sixty-five saloons. It was littered with drunks and the relics of brawls. Bodie had become, famously, the wildest town in the Wild West. In another twenty years, the town was virtually empty. The accessible gold had been torn out; there was nothing left to die for.

In April 1988, I visited what remained. I knew that the final section of road was not yet open, so I rented cross-country skis. I was impressed that the rental shop let me have them: I had never tried using cross-country skis before.

I drove up the mountain until I buried the fender in a snowdrift, got out the skis and headed off on a compass bearing. Utterly alone in the quiet of the snow, I had one of the most memorable days of my life. And then I found Bodie: a small community of completely abandoned buildings, decaying and collapsing, some leaning at drunken angles; shops with their goods still on display, broken crockery on the ground, a Marie Celeste town.

The behaviour of the gold seekers has been seen many times before. In 1982, two archaeologists stumbled on the Roman Empire's 'Bodie', not by crossing snowdrifts but sand dunes about 40 miles east of Luxor. They were travelling across Egypt's central western desert, from Luxor to their dig on the Red Sea, and stopped for tea at a desert settlement. Knowing they were interested in ancient ruins, a local led them to a hidden wadi containing the remains of a forgotten gold-mining settlement, where people had once laboured in the searing heat. As with Bodie, the buildings are tumbledown but intact. Most are two or three rooms and two or three storeys, with seats and ovens. Personal possessions too burdensome to carry were left behind when it was abandoned, and the traces of ordinary working lives were preserved by inaccessibility and dry air. Their cooking utensils, wine jars and even personal jewellery remain. The houses were not Pharaonic or classical Roman. Ten years of excavation, from 1991 onwards, revealed that this was a mining town that had sprung up in the fifth century CE and was abandoned about 150 years later. Like Bodie, it appears to have been worked by gold-hungry prospectors, prepared to endure the harshest conditions until, after around 100 years, there was nothing left.

The support needed to sustain this town, where over 1,000 people worked, was massive. There were wells, but everything else needed to be carried across the desert, to a community with virtually no vegetation that had to endure temperatures up to 50 degrees Celsius. That was not the only problem. The ore had to be extracted from rocks which were very hard and difficult to smelt, so the process of purifying it was extremely laborious and sophisticated. There was no civic building and no surrounding wall; these workers were not prisoners, slaves or working under officials. They were treasure hunters, and they had probably been led there by an ancient treasure map which still exists.

The site is now called Bir Umm Fawakhir. It has now been recognized on the oldest treasure map ever found, the Turin Papyrus drawn about 1150 BCE, where it appears as a gold-working settlement with four houses.[1] The settlement found in 1982 was built on top of it by desperate gold-hunters 1,600 years later, when the division of the Roman Empire was firmly established. The Eastern emperors, in Constantinople, ruled Greece and the Balkans, Egypt and the whole Roman world east of the Bosphorus. They would continue to call themselves 'Roman', but in the sixteenth century – 150 years after it fell to Suleiman the Magnificent – a German historian dubbed this the Byzantine Empire, and the name has stuck.

Egypt was ruled from Constantinople, and fifth-century Constantinople was desperate for gold. So was Europe, but it had nowhere to dig. Perhaps these adventurers had found the map and so rediscovered a mine abandoned a thousand years before, when it was better watered (the map shows three trees there). The fact that no one subsequently thought this was a profitable place to work shows just how determined they must have been to secure that gold.[2]

Life in a Plundered Empire

There were three great differences between the Eastern and Western Roman Empires. One was that the administrative language of the East was Greek, while in the West it was Latin. The second was that in the East there were gold mines, and in the West there were none. The Egyptian mine was not alone: there was gold in Nubia and other mines were scattered through the Balkans, as well as near modern Adana in south-east Turkey. There was also gold in Sicily and in Armenia, which Constantinople was determined to control.[3] Which brings us to the third great difference between the Eastern and Western Roman Empires: the East lasted a thousand years; the West disappeared. The last Western emperor, Romulus Augustulus, was deposed in 476 CE. He was given the throne by his father, who had once been a secretary for Attila the Hun. His empire had no influence beyond Italy and parts of what are now Austria and Croatia. It was a dreadful warning to the Eastern Empire. For Constantinople, gold was the sign of light and divinity, but it also offered institutional immortality. No one in New Rome seems to have thought that gold would help them live for ever, but they understood very well what had happened to Old Rome when it ran out of gold. The Byzantine Empire would only endure if it had the gold.

There was still some gold in Europe, but it was not available to church or government, or circulating as currency. It had been gathered in by military leaders as tribute and was held as treasure. In 1963, a hoard of 1,437 gold solidi of Theodosius II turned up in Hungary. It seems to be a payment of 10 Roman pounds of gold given as 'tribute' to Attila the Hun (three coins having been removed). Theodosius is reported to have paid Attila 4,000 times that much in twenty years from 430,[4] and of course there was plenty more loot hidden away. But it was not for spending, so markets had pretty well vanished. The absence of gold currency from the Western Empire meant an absence of professional soldiers, and the result was a very profound change in the way people lived. In the past, soldiers had received pay and spent it. Markets grew, trade flourished and cities thrived. When the flow of currency evaporated, markets emptied, trade diminished and cities starved. Seven-eighths of Rome's population in 400 CE is reckoned to have vanished in the next hundred years – the evidence is insecure, but if that is true, a great world-city of 800,000 now had just about 100,000 souls. That's smaller than South Bend, Indiana, or Worcester in the UK. It is hard to estimate what happened in other European cities, but it looks as if London's population might have fallen from 60,000 to 10,000 between 200 and 800 CE, and that of Paris to 20,000. Germany's oldest city, Trier, which had once been an Imperial capital, is believed to have lost some 85 per cent of its inhabitants and may have been reduced to about 15,000 people. The absence of records is itself telling. There were no thriving commercial centres left in Western Europe, and by the mid-seventh century, gold had been abandoned as currency in much of the West.[5]

The survival of what remained of the Empire depended on the gold solidus.

Gold and Camels

In the time of Carthage, a trans-Saharan trade exchanging gold and salt had been made possible by a people known as the Garamantes, who exploited underground fossil water, but that had run out and the flow of gold north had stopped. In the sixth century, however, Constantinople had found a way to restore it.[6] Camels had opened up trade routes across the Sahara, allowing the gold-rich inland delta of the Niger to buy desperately needed salt from North Africa.[7] Salt worth its weight in gold was mined in Libya: Pliny describes houses there built of salt blocks.[8] Slabs weighing 200lb were strapped to the sides of camels and taken south for sale. They still are; I have seen them arriving in Mali, and I met the son of one of the Libyan traders there. He showed me photographs of the mine and miners, who he said were slaves. Nothing much seemed to have changed in 1,600 years, except that the camels were gradually being displaced by trucks.

Constantinople minted gold to pay mercenaries, pay off possible invaders and maintain its prestige and income. Its traders needed gold to establish their credit in distant ports. A sixth-century Alexandrian traveller gives the example of an Egyptian merchant called Sopatrus whose ship arrived in Sri Lanka at the same time as a Persian one. They were given an audience by the king, who asked which had the more powerful monarch. After hearing the venerable Persian's boasts, the Roman invited the king to compare their rulers by looking at their heads on coins. But of course, this was not about the portraits:

'The Roman coin had a right good ring, was of bright metal and finely shaped, for pieces of this kind are picked for export to the island. But the dirham, to put it bluntly, was of silver, and not to be compared with the gold coin. So, the king after he had turned them this way and that, and had attentively examined both, highly commended the solidus saying that the Romans were certainly a splendid, powerful, and sagacious people. So he ordered great honour to be paid to Sopatrus, causing him to be mounted on an elephant, and conducted round the city with drums beating and high state. These circumstances were told us by Sopatrus himself and his companions, and as they told the story, the Persian was deeply chagrined at what had occurred.'[9]

Without its gold coins, the Empire could not have challenged the new kingdoms of Visigoths and Vandals, Burgundians, Franks and other Germanic peoples in the West. It did challenge them. In 532, Justinian had an annual income of 5 million sestertii, but it was not enough. He bought peace with the Persians for

11,000lb of gold, and set out on the recovery of North Africa, followed by Italy and southern Spain. As a result, his income grew by 20 per cent.

Golden Light

Under Justinian, gold became ever more firmly entrenched as the fundamental projection of Imperial power and religion, as well as currency. The Middle Eastern and Egyptian traditions of using gold as an indication of the presence of a god had been absorbed wholesale into Byzantine Christianity. Now Justinian shifted its emphasis from golden substance to golden light.

At the same time as launching his campaign to retake the West, he began building the great church of Hagia Sophia at the side of his palace. It cost 320,000lb of gold.[10] There had never been a building like it; a gigantic domed basilica filled with golden light, reflected not by gilding but by a new kind of surface, walls covered with millions of gold tesserae, tiny squares of gold leaf embedded in glass. Ten thousand square metres of them were put in place without grouting, so that they channelled light from lamps and windows above into the inside of the wall surface. They were set at slight angles to each other, so that the light inside them reflected off the gold to shine with what seemed to be their own heavenly illumination. Contemporary historian Procopius exclaimed: 'You would declare that the place is not lighted by the sun from without, but that the rays are produced within itself, such an abundance of light is poured into this church.'[11] Nothing like this had been seen before. Justinian declared that he had out-done Solomon. In Solomon's Temple, as in pagan temples, gold was lavishly used as a solid material that properly belonged to divinity. But theologians were troubled that this was too base a way of portraying heavenly images.[12] Hagia Sophia was a great theatre of heaven, where nothing was tangible and yet all was real, an incorruptible vision.

Here, and in subsequent Byzantine churches, gold mosaic was the source of an emanation that filled holy space, space that was both divine and imperial. This was not about gold as money. The cost of the material was relatively slight, less than a thousandth of the church's construction cost,[13] but the impact was astounding. Outside the church, in the secular world, the solidus was universally understood as a manifestation of both Imperial and divine authority, and any challenge to it was virtually heresy.

In Mainz, Frankish ruler Theudebert was taught that lesson when he minted golden solidi carrying his own image and his own name. He used solidi from Justinian, who had paid for his (unreliable) allegiance. According to Procopius, he claimed that he was using his own gold mine, which seems extremely unlikely; perhaps he thought that would make the minting less offensive. It made no difference at all. Procopius asserted (mistakenly) that no barbarians, not even

Europe 530 CE.

the Persians, had ever claimed the right to put their own images on a gold coin, even if it was gold from their own land – and when they had dared to do it, the coin could not be used 'even though the barbarians themselves should be the traffickers'.[14] Theudebert's head on a gold coin thus supposedly rendered it worthless. This goes to the heart of the question of why gold has been considered to have value. The notion which had been established by Julius Caesar, that gold coinage was given its authority by the divine dictator, had crumbled to dust and devaluation. It was then immortal gold that gave authority to emperors, such as they were. It seems that in Justinian's Empire, the union of Christian and political authority was so complete that a gold coin without the Imperial head was said to be empty of value of any kind.

Gifts, Not Cash

The situation was made more desperate by a new pandemic, the Justinian Plague, which swept the whole Roman world in the sixth century, perhaps propelled by the massive migrations. It was thought to have come from infected rats on grain ships. This was probably the first appearance of bubonic plague. Constantinople lost about 20 per cent of its people. Justinian caught it and recovered, and Procopius recorded that it wiped out most of the farming community. Justinian had already committed a huge outlay on wars and church building, and so tried to insist that taxes were paid by ruined survivors. His great project was the reconquest of the West. That attempt collapsed.

The whole of the Roman world was left in a rather moribund state. In the East, where the Imperial household virtually *was* the state, professional legionary soldiers were replaced by an unpaid militia. This militia was drawn from the occupants of state-owned land, and the state was by far the greatest landholder. These men were supplemented by paid 'barbarian' mercenaries. Few others received gold cash except for state officials, so there was a very localized subsistence economy, virtually cashless, in the countryside, and a high-end luxury economy in the cities, sustained by the state employing merchants as its agents.[15].

The new kingdoms of the West also had little use for cash. They were essentially peasant societies, as self-sufficient as possible, with long-distance trade only in luxury items. The money for that trade was paid from booty, or in gold retrieved from hoards or coming from Constantinople for goods or military assistance. Many communities here were descended from warrior cultures of the great westward migration. Whether pagan or Christian, Germanic and Nordic peoples saw golden treasure not as a source of trade wealth (which of course it was) but as a validation of heroic stature.[16] It was not so much earned as bestowed.

An Old English poem known as *The Wanderer*, probably from the ninth or tenth century, was written as the voice of the sole survivor of his community, massacred many years before. His ties to his lord were not of wages but of love, materially expressed to him in gold and repaid not just in loyalty but in profound affection:

> 'He remembers hall-warriors
> and the giving of treasure
> How in youth his lord (gold-friend)
> accustomed him
> to the feasting.
> All the joy has died!
> …
> He thinks in his mind
> that he embraces and kisses
> his lord,
> and on the lord's knees lays
> his hands and his head,
> Just as, sometimes, before,
> in days gone by,
> he enjoyed the gift-seat (*throne*).'

The death of his lord and companions could not be unexpected in the heroic warband. Leaders were called 'ring-givers' and bound their followers with gifts of gold, not as currency to be used, but as recognition to be worn and, literally, treasured. From the time of Attila in the fifth century and before, the gold gifted from a ring-giver's hoard was originally acquired by him as plunder. *The Wanderer* inhabits a post-apocalyptic world of empty cities that were built, he supposes, by forgotten giants. Their only meaning is that they have all been laid waste, a divine punishment expressed in slaughter. Perhaps this is how the aftermath of Varna would have once been understood. The poem continues:

> 'Walls stand,
> blown by the wind,
> covered with frost,
> storm-swept the buildings.
> The halls decay,
> their lords lie
> deprived of joy,
> the whole troop has fallen,
> …
> And so He destroyed this city,
> He, the Creator of Mcn,
> until deprived of the noise
> of the citizens,
> the ancient work of giants
> stood empty.'[17]

Another Old English poem, *Beowulf*, written down around 1000 CE, speaks of its hero as a gold-giver and ring-giver, and describes gold as the decoration of weapons, helmets and feasting halls. Just as in the theology of Constantinople, its gleam is described in symbolic terms and is linked with the sun.[18] One of the most startling examples of the role of the ring-giver in Christian Europe is in a ninth-century version of the gospels called *Heliand* ('Saviour'). This was adapted from a second-century Syrian Christian digest of the gospels. The gospel story was incomprehensible to these Northern fighting men. What sense could they make of rabbis and the Sanhedrin, of facing evil by turning the other cheek and a virtue of submissiveness? This alien scripture was astonishingly reinvented as an Old Saxon alliterative epic, the story of a cosmic struggle in the last days of the old Norse gods. The story opens with the introduction of 'might-wielding Christ'. In mead halls and monastery refectories, newly converted Germanic warriors and novice monks enjoyed the recitation of the Christian story in a form that made sense to them. Rabbis become chieftains; John the Baptist is a warrior-companion of the King of Heaven. Christ is a supreme leader, rising as the successor to Odin and Wotan. He never mentions turning the other cheek. His disciples are his thanes, battle companions to whom he reveals the Runic spell of the Lord's Prayer. His work is to defeat Satan, saving men from being carried to Hell instead of Valhalla. Herod is a powerful ring-giver in his hillfort, and what binds the disciples to Christ is their love of and loyalty to their 'treasure-giver' and the gifts of gold that evidence his love for them. There is no value placed on poverty here; Christ makes his followers rich, but the value of his gifts comes from the treasure-giver, not from the treasure.

The value of gold is its provenance, not its weight. Just as in Procopius's assertion that the value of a solidus derives from the person whose face it bears, so in the heroic world the value of gold is entirely dependent on where – and who – it comes from. At Beowulf's burial, 'the gold-proud warrior' is interred with gold he won from killing the dragon. But Beowulf is not the Lord of Varna; this gold does not connect him to the afterlife for the benefit of the community. That first golden civilization perished in massacres, and any glorious innocence gold treasure may have originally held had by now been steeped in blood for millennia. Beowulf's gold is tainted with the necessity of slaughter, and his mourners 'let the earth keep the earl's treasure, gold in the ground, where it now is still, as useless to men as it ever was'.

The gold-work of the seventh-century Sutton Hoo burial, which is clearly reflected in *Beowulf*, would have impressed Fabergé. After Rome's legions vanished, there was still some gold to be used in the world of heroes and slaves, but not as money.

The Post-gold Economy

In 1000 CE, it did seem as though Europe north of the Alps had developed a social and economic structure that functioned without any dependence on gold, and which was ruled by sovereigns whose authority was bestowed by the Pope and his bishops. This was a fragmented agricultural society with not much use for money. It also did not have much use for literacy or offer much in the way of urbanity. The contrast with lands where gold still circulated was quite startling. Constantinople had around a half a million inhabitants – more than the total urban population of the entire Roman Catholic world. Baghdad probably had twice that. Palermo, the capital of Muslim Sicily, had about 350,000. In the Arab world, secular literate readers bought poems and stories written on paper. The bezant and the dinar enabled large urban infrastructures and comfortable secular lives. The Khmer Empire, Armenia, Gujarat, Persia, Egypt, Spain, southern Italy, China and Japan all had cities with more than 100,000 people, where the privileged lived in sophisticated elegance. But in Europe, over a vast territory from Scandinavia to the Alps and Pyrenees, and from the Atlantic to modern Turkey, once-great towns and cities had shrunk to the size of large villages. Christian literacy was generally confined to trained experts in religious houses and to expensive parchment documents. The records that survive are so inadequate that we can only guess at the size of the largest communities there, but it is unlikely that any had more than 10,000 people. Even south of the Alps, where Florence was still trading with Arab and Byzantine merchants and may have had 50,000 people, Rome's population had fallen by about 95 per cent. Most Europeans depended on a subsistence economy. Little was bought and sold; gift exchange was far more important and created its own social bonds.

Gold was still spoken of as currency, but this was a polite fiction. Most people exchanged goods by barter, unrecorded payments in kind. Some transactions between distinguished people are recorded. Pennies were fine for the *hoi polloi*, but great men did not descend to that grubby level. Norman documents record payments being due in bezants, the gold coins of Byzantium, but there were none and the payments were actually made in silver. They said they were paying in bezants to elevate the transaction to a more dignified level.[19] In a similar way, when I was writing scripts for the BBC in the 1960s, my contracts specified my fee in guineas. The guinea was a gold coin that had not been minted since 1814, and the days of gold currency were over, but my supposed social status as a gentleman scribbler apparently meant that it would be demeaning to specify my fee in the base metal of pounds, shillings and pence.

By 1000 CE, Norse raiders had really finished off economic activity in Northern Europe. England had managed to produce millions of silver coins in the late tenth century, but these were to cope with the demands of Vikings, not for trade.[20] Aethelred II handed over nearly 40 million silver pennies. By 1016, English kings had paid them more than 100 tons of silver.[21] Cnut then conquered the country and gave his troops another 20 million pennies to take home to Scandinavia. More Anglo-Saxon pennies of the period have been found in Denmark than in England.[22] These raids were stripping out money from Frankish territory too; perhaps 50 tons of coin and most of the silver vessels held in religious houses.[23]

By the time William the Bastard assembled a force to seize England, it had become normal for Frankish and Norman nobles to have to fight without pay. They had to assemble a company of fighting men when called on by their overlord as a condition of their tenancy.[24] But if that had been the only way of putting together an army, the Norman Conquest would have been impossible.

It is true that after the Conquest, William imposed the most systematic feudal system possible on his new kingdom. His tenants-in-chief, and their tenants, held land in return for unpaid military service. But this was not the way he had achieved his historic victory. Rather ironically, William was making a significant contribution to the slow return of economic life, to the use of coins and, eventually, of gold, to pay soldiers. The Norman Conquest was a key moment in a commercial revolution that gradually reopened Europe's atrophied trade arteries and saw its urban life slowly reborn.

The Conquest had been put in motion with cash. William was doing all he could to attract it. He had battled his way to supremacy in the chaotic violence of Normandy, and by 1060 established a stable and relatively peaceful regime. In 1047, the Church Council of Caen supported him by establishing 'The Truce of God', by which anyone except William who waged private war between Wednesday evening and Monday morning was excommunicated[25] (it was apparently hopeless to expect Normans to live at peace on Tuesdays). In the tenth century, a new port had been created at Caen, and now William developed it as the commercial and administrative heart of his duchy. He built a castle there to ensure its safety and stretched a chain across the port entrance to compel trading ships to pay a tax. The Duchy's main centre, Rouen, a short distance down the Seine from Paris, already attracted merchants from Italy. The new market at Caen was designed to attract coastal trade, especially from England and the North Sea.[26]

William's own estates were huge and profitable, but he was spending money on a scale which must have exceeded his income. As well as the castle at Caen, for example, he and his wife erected large religious houses there. The Church in Normandy was being well supplied with funds and William was obviously getting the money from somewhere; this was not a subsistence cashless economy just ticking over.

Their ability to produce cash was the key to the invasion, which was on a different scale from anything attempted since the Roman Empire. Norse invaders of England had been foot warriors who brought a few small horses in their longboats. This was different: an amphibious cavalry assault, with thousands of knights on horseback as well as crossbowmen and infantry. Feudal land-tenure did not require knights to serve overseas, or to leave their homes for more than forty days, so William could not oblige them to join his invasion army. It was true that they had sworn oaths of fealty and he was able to persuade thousands to join him, but this was on their terms, and they wanted to know that William had raised large additional forces to guarantee victory. He needed men from further afield, 'stipendiaries', who swore fealty because they were offered money. He also needed cash to fund the construction of hundreds of ships, including horse transports that were quite unlike any North European vessels, and to hire experts in the management of the fleet. This must have needed Byzantine or Norman specialists from southern Italy.[27] Again, money was essential.

And then there was the food. One historian has calculated that if they were fed nothing but porridge (and they had to be better fed than that), the troops would have consumed 28 tons of grain every day they were waiting to embark. Under normal circumstances, that might have cost over 55,000 pennies, or over 80 tons of silver every day.[28] On top of that, the horses would have got through 12–18 tons of grain, 13–20 tons of hay and 4–5 tons of straw every day.[29] William had not just to pay for the provisions, but also hire something like 120 ox carts a day just to sustain the men and horses until they sailed.

So where did the money come from? Who provided him with the credit and the cash? The explanation seems to have been brought to light in the last few years by the discovery, from a cache of previously ignored Hebrew documents and new excavations, of a very wealthy and sophisticated Jewish community in Rouen, with smaller Jewish settlements all over the Duchy.[30] Twenty-five streets in various parts of Normandy have been identified as Jewish. Jews were the permitted moneylenders; Christians were forbidden to charge interest, and in any case did not have the networks of connections of successful Jewish families. The Jews of Gaul maintained good connections with their co-religionists in Spain, and so with the economic life of the Islamic world. The Rouen Jewish community, with substantial buildings, an education system and a network of international trade and rabbinical scholarship, were inevitably financiers to the duke and probably to the Norman Church. Its members certainly had the confidence to travel to Rome and appeal directly to the Pope when they needed legal support. Their role as his financial backers also explains why, after being crowned in Westminster Abbey, William insisted on bringing members of the Rouen Jewish community to London. He needed the credit network they could provide, and installed them as wards of the king, with freedom of the king's highways, exemption from tolls and the ability to hold land directly from the monarch. They could provide credit for his huge castle-building programme, and he granted them shelter there. Of course, once the Conquest succeeded, the loan repayments were pretty well guaranteed. England was exceptionally wealthy, more urbanized than most of Europe, and was still rich in silver currency.[31] William made England a feudal land, but it was fully monetized. That was the point of the Domesday Book, which contained a precise valuation in cash terms of much of the land and livestock under William's rule in 1086.

The campaign also involved a revolution in the relationship between the Church and secular power. William was a duke, determined to overthrow and replace a king. What kind of authority could he possibly establish that would give him the magical aura of kingship? Harold Godwinson had been consecrated, crowned and anointed King of England.

But the Church decided that Harold's coronation was a fraud. The Roman Church taught that Jesus gave the Keys of Heaven to the apostle Peter in Rome, and that each Pope succeeded to his apostolic power. That power was now being exercised by a series of radical Popes, determined to assert their authority over kings and the Holy Roman Emperor. Their starting point was to take control of appointments to ecclesiastical positions throughout Christendom. Every ruler depended on his bishops, and they were no longer his to appoint at will or for a fee. They were now supposed to be put there by the Pope. England was a particular target, where one man, Stigand, had become an ecclesiastical oligarch. He had never been a monk but had been useful to King Edward the Confessor's wife and to Earl Godwin, and so had been made Archbishop of Winchester. Then Edward appointed him Archbishop of Canterbury. The existing archbishop was not happy about that, so four Popes in succession excommunicated Stigand. He held the two richest Church positions in the country and the backing of Godwin, the most powerful nobleman. By the time of the coronation of Godwin's son, Harold Godwinson, Stigand was head of the Church in England, running the royal administration and appointing his own men as bishops, and was phenomenally rich, holding land in ten counties. In some he held more than the king.

The Pope was very clear that Harold's coronation was invalid, and that the English Church needed to be purged. This was an early move in the Papal programme to establish Church authority over kings and emperors. William was not just a duke. His authority came from a banner supplied by the outraged Pope. Divine authority was now embodied in the Pope, not in gold.

The Papal banner was a claim that the authority of the Church was greater than that of a crowned king. The Pope alone controlled the keys of heaven. His demands were being supported by upstart Normans who were also keen to weaken crowned heads as they carved out their own territories. Norman nobles were fighting against Muslims in Southern Europe and were given Papal banners that were seen as connecting them directly with heaven. Harold was a king, and his golden crown and sceptre made him into something more than a mortal man, but the power of his regalia was less than the Pope's. William was preceded by his Papal banner, and his was a Holy War.

That was how it was possible for William to assemble the largest force seen in Northern Europe for centuries. He was eventually crowned, but more crucially anointed. Once installed, he declared the whole of England was his own personal possession and gave his men tenancies with obligations to match. Power in William's England came not from gold but from the tenancy of land.

Feudalism as we understand it, the creation of the cavalryman's military obligation in exchange for land tenancy, was being pragmatically invented on the hoof. For the time being at least, the military life of Europe was becoming self-sufficient and building a social order on the basis of the obligation to go to war. It would not be long before those with money could pay to get out of that obligation of military service; it would be commuted for silver pennies. But the payment simply allowed the king to hire professional fighting men, without having to find the money from his own resources.

Throughout Europe, the population was generally growing as agricultural production grew, and trade grew with it. Silver pennies were locally made and locally used: they were not trusted in areas where they were not made, and in fact often not even trusted where they were made. A primary function of money became to pay royal taxes, especially in England. Draconian efforts to control the quality of pennies, such as Henry I's castration of cheating coiners,[32] did not help. Without trusted currency, trade was obviously hamstrung. In England in the twelfth century, William of Malmesbury said the population was too lazy to be bothered to trade. European pennies were the currency of a rural subsistence economy where power was encased in castles, literacy was confined to cloisters and trade was mostly conducted in markets in towns which would be reckoned today to be hamlets. Everyone was engaged in the service of another. The land was worked by serfs tied to their lords' estates. The only exception, slowly emerging, was that those living in the small towns were free. By the twelfth century, it was recognized that bonded men who had escaped and survived in a town for a year and a day shared that freedom.

There was still some gold in Europe, but it was mostly recycled. Goldsmiths used ancient coins, jewellery or other gold objects as their raw material. In Europe, gold was fully identified with divine splendour – there was too little of it for real live human beings. Its place was in art, as one element in the stylized and symbolic world of religious objects. Even when it was available in quantity, it had no spending power in this subsistence economy. Around 983, the cathedral of Mainz commissioned a larger-than-life statue of the crucifixion made from 600lb of solid gold and gold plate. The gold had come from a Lombard king's treasure taken as tribute by the Frankish king Pepin in 756. It is likely to have been Byzantine, taken when the Lombards seized Ravenna in 751. Once it had left Byzantium, no one – Lombards, Franks or the Church – wanted the gold as spending money. Its value was in its prestige and mystical power, ending up manifested in this remarkable form. The crucified Christ was normally labelled over his head 'INRI', the acronym for the title that criminalized him – '*Iesus Nazarenus, Rex Iudaeorum*' ('Jesus of Nazareth, King of the Jews'). But the label over this one declared: 'This golden cross contains 600 pounds of gold.'

It proclaimed a value in rarity and incorruptibility, and so signified how highly the image was valued in spiritual terms. Europeans' interest in gold as money seemed over. By the end of the thirteenth century, they may have only owned about 40 tons of gold – enough to just about overflow a bath tub.[33]

So far as Europe was concerned, it seemed that the tremendous impulse given to civilization by this extraordinary substance had petered out. But this was a pause, not a full stop. Gold would not leave Europe in peace, and Mainz Cathedral turned out to have inadvertently created a visible indicator of the changing relationship between its spiritual and economic value. The statue was only displayed on special occasions and was made in fourteen sections, so that it could be packed away in its case. After about 160 years, the spending power of gold began to rise and flow into the case. That showed in 1142, when one of Christ's feet was missing. It had been melted down. Presumably from then on, public displays of the statue must have been quite extraordinary. The other foot and both legs disappeared in 1157, and an arm was used in 1160 to pay for the archbishop's trip to Rome. The remainder of the crucifix then sank beneath the tide of economic history and disappeared into the furnace in the following year.[34] The gold was vanishing because gold was coming back.

A New Role for Gold

Perhaps a new Christian society could develop without any link to gold. Rulers had always been understood to have a direct connection to power outside the material world, and the channel to that power had once been gold. It was expressed in their golden crowns. But the significance of gold in coronations was now very different from its place in the ancient world. Emperors were still crowned in Constantinople, but a crown was no longer a divine gift endorsing a mortal. Emperors gave their own superhuman endorsement to the golden coins they minted. In the West, the rulers of the new 'barbarian' kingdoms also had coronations, but there the transformation of men into kings was being effected by the Church, not by gold. Their crowns carried a new Christian meaning and devalued gold.

The Iron Crown of Lombardy, perhaps the first of these crowns, can still be seen in the cathedral at Monza. Analysis indicates that the crown may date back, at least in part, to the fourth or fifth century.[35] The gold and jewelled hinged panels were originally surmounted by iron, probably a hoop, which gave the crown its name and is attested by a twelfth-century document. That hoop was supposedly made from a holy relic, one of the iron nails that crucified Jesus. It was said that Constantine's mother discovered a number of crucifixion nails while excavating for remains of the Christian story in Jerusalem, and this one was given to a barbarian ruler by her son. It was used to crown kings, but its mystic power came from the sacred relic, not from any gold. Sadly, the iron hoop disappeared, along with a couple of the gold and jewelled panels. With the hinges damaged, the circlet was repaired in the fourteenth century by inserting a silver ring. That ring is now spoken of as the original iron nail, miraculously transformed. The grant of legitimacy and the elevation of a king was no longer performed through golden regalia but through a holy relic that directly communicated with Christ. The Iron Crown may have been used for the first Christian king of the Lombards, Aripert, in the 650s. He was a man of peace, very committed to the religion, and was the founder of a significant number of churches.

Royal authority was now bestowed by a direct connection with God, and the Church began offering that in a form which could not be as easily stolen as an iron nail. When Charles Martel's son, Pepin, had himself proclaimed King of the Franks in 751, he was crowned by an archbishop, but more significantly he was anointed with 'holy oil' in a newly invented ceremony that was meant to evoke the biblical coronations of Saul and David, and to create a direct link to David's descendant, Jesus. The Greek for an anointed person is '*Christos*', and this ceremony became and remains the essence of European royal coronations.

A solidus contained gold to the modern value of about £180. It was hard to spend in this subsistence economy. A new coin of one-third its value, the triens or tremiss, was minted between the fifth and eighth centuries in Europe's new kingdoms, but the quantity fell to a trickle, and though some solidi were struck in Frisia, beyond the old Roman frontier, they had runes on them and seem to have been amulets, gifts from a ring-giver.[36]

Things were very different to the south of the Christian world, where there was plenty of gold, coined as dinars, and plenty of trade.

Gold of the Caliphate

The dinar was the product of an entirely new empire, the Caliphate. The Caliphs were successors to Muhammad, who died in 632, and the Islamic conquests were so rapid and overwhelming that in its first 100 years this became the largest empire to have ever existed. By 750 CE, it had conquered Persia and Arabia, as well as all the Byzantine territory east of Anatolia, the whole of North Africa and all but the very north of Iberia. More than 5 million square miles were subject to the Caliphate, and its wealth was prodigious. Before the end of the seventh century, Arabic copies of the solidus were being minted, gold coins that were meant as an alternative currency to that of Constantinople and whose name was derived from 'denarius': dinars.

The Caliphate was an empire that had been created, in the first instance, by people whose lives were spent with camels, using them on trade networks that bridged and connected the Roman and Persian worlds. The poetry of pre-Islamic Arabia is embedded in a landscape of camels and trade:

'Look how many good times I've spent with beautiful girls;
I especially remember the day at the oasis of Darat-i-Juljul.
    ... That was the day I entered the camel's howdah, Unaizah's howdah!
But she objected, saying, "Shame on you, now I'll have to go by foot."
    She pushed me away, while the howdah was swaying with the motion;
She said, "You're wearing my camel out, Oh Imru-ul-Quais, so get off."
    Then I said, "Drive him on! Let his reins loose, while you turn to me.
Don't think of the camel and how we weigh him down; let's be happy."
    ... The clouds poured their gift on Ghabeet desert till it blossomed
as if a Yemeni merchant spread out all the rich clothes from his trunks,
as if the little birds of the valley of Jiwaa all woke in the morning
And burst forth in song after a morning sip of old, pure, spiced wine.
    As if all the beasts had been rolled in sand and mud like onion bulbs
drowned and lost in the depths of the desert at evening.'[37]

This poem, perhaps the most celebrated of all Arabic poems, is known as *Let us stop and weep*, and was written shortly before the time of Muhammad by Imru'u al-Qais, a prince disinherited for his debauchery. He is said to have been put in charge of a camel train, with disastrous results. He spent the latter part of his life trying to avenge his father's assassination.

The trade caravans that used to carry silk, cotton, spices, pepper, incense and leather became victims of increasing friction between the collapsing Roman and Persian empires, which fought five wars from 500–630. The camel trains were armed against plunder and rivalry, and increasingly tied into commercial alliances with their violently competing customers.

The essence of merchant life is trade, and trade requires trust (especially where law does not function). For the caravan traders to operate, they needed a safe space where they could trust each other. Islamic tradition attributes that function to a shrine at Mecca, on an Arabian trade route in territory disputed between the Byzantine and Persian empires. The shrine, a stone structure (the Kaaba, 'cube'), was based on a meteorite (the black stone) and was seen as the junction point of heaven and Earth, of the sacred and profane worlds. It was pre-eminently dedicated to a deity called Hubal, whose statue had a golden hand.[38]

It is said that around the time when the last Western Emperor was being deposed, Mecca was being taken over by a forceful and innovative clan leader,

Hashim, who organized agreements for safe passage for caravans and instigated merchant partnerships to build much larger caravans and spread the risk. He was Muhammad's great grandfather.

The greatest problem with sustaining long-distance trade is one of confidence between agents. For that reason, tribal and family connections were of vital importance to merchants operating internationally.[39] By the time of Muhammad, it appears that there was also a reputational connection that allowed for the creation of very large inter-tribal camel trains that could travel in safety over long distances. What they really needed, though, was an ethical law that was internalized, enforced and shared throughout the Arab world. Their prosperity would depend on the spread of Islam; the faster the better.

The new religion was superficially similar to Judaism and Christianity, but its social values were utterly different. Muhammad did not receive his calling until he was a 40-year-old widower, a mature and successful merchant who had been managing the significant trading business of the woman he had married. A *hadith*, a reported saying of Muhammad, proclaims: 'A trustworthy and truthful merchant will be raised up with the prophets, the truthful and martyrs on the day of resurrection.' In the classical and Christian world, merchants had been people of little account; the social hierarchy there was defined by land ownership, and trade was demeaning. The rapid and overwhelming advance of the new faith was achieved not just by military determination, but by the power of business to undermine opposition and win support,[40] and the existence of an extensive network of traders with many connections who committed to Islamic values and had a strong vested interest in spreading the faith. The recent development of network theory seems to illuminate the way in which merchants enabled Islam to go viral.[41] Credit was built on trust; trust was built on belief. Islam had no priestly standard-bearers. Its missionaries were not just warriors but also merchants, giving the message of the *Qur'an* with every transaction. But those who were outside the territory of the faith were subject to a different rule – the rule of plunder: 'The spoils of war belong to God and his Messengers.'[42]

Once it had control of the great hoards of stored-up gold in Persia and the gold treasures of the Pharaohs, the conquering Caliphate had a moral duty to spend them, which was done with vigorous enthusiasm. The *Qur'an* firmly declared hoarding to be a sin: 'There are those who bury gold and silver and spend it not in the way of Allah: announce unto them a most grievous penalty.' The way of Allah was honest dealing and community-based charity, enforced by an extensive legal code which was regarded as coming directly from God, and therefore not to be unpicked.[43] Gold began to circulate on an entirely new scale. The declining, gold-starved economy of Europe was now surrounded to the south and east by an energized enthusiasm for doing business which would, eventually, change everything.

In 696 and 697, when Syria, Egypt, Mesopotamia and Persia had all been seized, the ninth Caliph, Abd al-Malik, took control of the money supply of the state he was creating and ruling from Damascus. He introduced a gold coin equivalent to the solidus, but whereas the Byzantine coin depicted the bland bearded face of Emperor Tiberius III Aspimarus holding a spear, this had no image. It carried instead the new Arabic script created to convey the words of scripture. The words are the oldest *Qur'anic* text to have survived. Gold was now given a new role, not just as a connector to divinity, but as the messenger of God. Trade was now to be conducted with a missionary purpose. Every time a person accepted a dinar, they were receiving the written message, 'There is no God but Allah, The One, Without Equal, and Muhammad is his Messenger, Muhammad is the Messenger of Allah, Who sent him with the doctrine and the true faith to prevail over every other religion.'

The Islamic tide flowed into southern France. Gibraltar was crossed early in 711, whereafter the Visigoth kingdom of Hispania crumbled. Seven years later, Islamic forces crossed the Pyrenees, and the new province of Al-Andalus had Aquitaine in its sights. An attack on Toulouse was repelled in 721. The advance was too fast, the Islamic forces too makeshift, and it failed. But in 732, the Umayyad commander Abd al-Rahman al-Ghafiqi invaded Aquitaine with a well-organized army and advanced on the Loire and what is now the city of Tours. This was very possibly the beginning of the end for the ruined Christian West.

Gold Confronts Feudalism

Al-Ghafiqi expected to meet an improvised force of peasants and landowners who had no power to resist. After all, Europe's rulers had no money to pay soldiers, and his own force was composed of professional troops, paid in gold, spearheaded by cavalry. The terrifying Persian vision of armoured cavalry that had destroyed Crassus in the last days of the Roman Republic had been adopted by the Caliph's soldiers after they absorbed the Sassanian Empire and transferred across North Africa to Spain with its excellent horses. But to al-Ghafiqi's surprise, the Frankish prince Charles Martel ('The Hammer') had organized a new kind of military enterprise to meet his attack. The old problem of how to pay for soldiers and bind their loyalty without an unending stream of gold had a new solution. The Hammer could keep a permanent force of full-time mounted warriors and the social system to sustain them without needing any money at all.

Charles Martel had established himself as master of a unified kingdom reaching from the Low Countries to the Loire. He needed cavalry to face down the invaders, which was very expensive. Of course, he did not have the gold to summon a paid force. But instead of paying with coin, he could pay with land tenure.

This used to be described as 'the birth of feudalism', which is jumping the gun a bit. There was no coherent plan to restructure society in the eighth century, and what did happen was piecemeal and unclear. Contemporary documents are few and far between, but Martel got hold of land to reward his leading followers by borrowing it from the Church. After all, it was the Church that was under threat from the invaders. The land was not returned as quickly as the Church had hoped. In 743, Martel's son explained at a Church council that 'Because of the wars which threaten, and on account of the hostility of the rest of the peoples who surround us', they would not return it quite yet.[44] Nobles who had been given tenure in exchange for military service were also supposed to pay a very high rent to the Church – one solidus a year for each household on the lands, and there could be hundreds of households in an estate. There were no solidus coins; it was a unit of account, to be paid in produce. The land was, of course, never returned, and years later Charles's grandson, Charlemagne, slashed the rent due to the Church by 80 per cent.

The tenure granted was not the equivalent of pay for military service. It had more in common with the ring-giver relationship, creating a bond of

The Umayyad Caliphate and Europe, 750 CE.

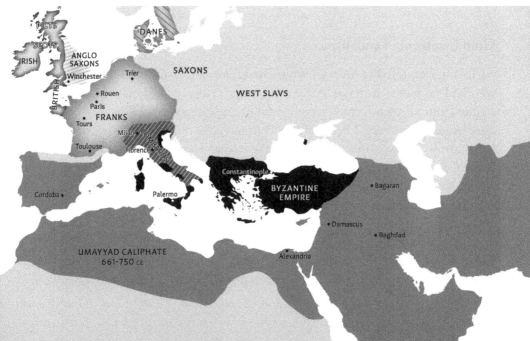

'fealty', sworn loyalty. In this world without gold, there was no longer a ring-giver handing out gold to create virtually unbreakable bonds of loyalty and affection. But land tenure created an even stronger dependency, because the warriors' families and livelihoods were now rooted in their estates, and the obligations of fealty and manor left them little choice but to fight for their lord when summoned.

The Islamic army was fighting for the glory of God, and for gold, but not necessarily in that order. They were paid in dinars, merchant coins, not carrying the name of the giver but the message of the Prophet. The coins demanded loyalty to Islam, and in the first days of Islamic expansion that zeal was the driving force behind the conquests. But by the time Andalusian forces were in France, their purpose was plunder. They seem to have put a lot of energy into looting. The dinar was a small part of the soldiers' reward, and not really a symbol of religious duty.

It has been argued that the collision of these forces on 25 October 732 was one of the most important battles in the history of the world. To Christians it is known as the Battle of Tours, or of Poitiers. In Arabic it is the Battle of the Highway of Martyrs, which contains the essence of the story. It was so important that evidence of what happened, and why, has been fractured, manufactured, falsified and mythologized by European writers down to the present day to suit grand propaganda perspectives. Consequently, a degree of scepticism is in order. The determination of the highly experienced and well-drilled Christian infantry, who were able to withstand cavalry attacks, was a novelty, but was their victory, and the battlefield death of Abd al-Rahman al-Ghafiqi, really the moment when the Islamic advance was stopped and Christendom born? When you unpick the detail, nothing is ever that cut and dried, but it does seem clear that the old equation of gold and armies was here confronted with something new. The advance of Islam out of Spain would indeed stop. Europe could fight wars and build a future without golden money. Had history really turned a corner?

Gold on the Page, Silver in the Purse

Sometime in the eighth century, monks working in south-east England created the most beautiful *Book of Psalms* they possibly could. Only one of the full-page illustrations survives: it shows King David on a throne, playing a harp, with musicians performing around him. Academically, it is celebrated because a scribe made notes between the elegant lines of the hymn on the facing page, and these are the first known words of the Bible written in Old English. But it is the illumination that is brilliant and memorable. Illumination means literally that; the text is lit by the brilliance of gold. The colours are rich and vibrant, and on the columns and arch that frame the performance, gold lozenges, flower petals and swirls are carefully placed in the composition. These are delicate pieces of gold leaf, stuck to the vellum page. David's throne is carefully delineated in gold, and he has a gold halo. In a world from which gold has almost vanished, this proclaims the separation of the holy book from the mortal world. Gold here is not for heroes, not even for God; it is for the words that religion is made of.

Finding the gold to do this was a major challenge. There was a little sifting of gold flakes from rivers, but the primary source for illumination must have been the melting down of a few coins or some treasure fragment. The place of gold in Europe was mostly limited to decoration: the writing of sacred text, the embellishment of holy relics and personal adornment (though Charles Martel's grandson, Charlemagne, did have a gold-plated desk).

Charlemagne captured a very large 'barbarian' treasure, but it did not become money.[45] His currency was the silver penny, a tiny coin less than 1cm across; 240 denarii or pennies were made from a pound of silver. There were in theory twelve pennies to the solidus, or gold shilling. In Britain, where this standard was quickly adopted, there would be twelve pennies to the shilling and 240 pennies to the pound until 1971, over a thousand years later, when the coinage was finally decimalized. The pound emerged as a disc of base metal worth a hundred 'pence'. (1971 was also the year the USA abandoned the gold dollar). Charlemagne forbade the use of gold coin in 781,[46] and produced few silver pennies in his own name. In 2008, a silver penny was found in an archaeological excavation of Charlemagne's chapel in Aachen, the city where he was crowned. It had been placed under the floor, and is the only coin minted by him discovered in the city, although he had a mint there. It has been argued that because there were so many mints, millions, perhaps tens of millions, of coins must have been minted and that they were widely used.[47] At the moment, that seems to be a triumph of logic over evidence. Although some coins travelled significant distances, suggesting long-distance trade, most were minted in small numbers for very local use. The few Charlemagne silver pennies that exist appear generally unused, and most come from hoards squirrelled away.[48] The gold solidus of his contemporary in the East, Empress Irene, is regarded as a very rare coin, but it sells at auction for around the same price as one of Charlemagne's silver pennies, which are even rarer.

Charlemagne's English contemporary, Offa, King of Mercia, seems to have been a more enthusiastic moneyer; his silver pennies were plentiful enough to be much less valuable than Charlemagne's in today's market, though more beautifully made. Offa also had the distinction of minting a few gold coins. Three are known, and they do not seem to have been meant as money. They were probably gifts to the Pope. The most intriguing, the only one with Offa's name on, was probably minted to fulfil his offer of 365 gold coins a year to Rome in exchange for being granted an archbishop in Lichfield. It is rather startlingly inscribed 'There is no God but Allah, The One, Without Equal, and Muhammad is his Messenger' and 'Muhammad is the Messenger of Allah, Who sent him with the doctrine and the true faith to prevail over every other religion'. It also carries the Islamic date 157, which was 754–55 CE – about forty years before the coin was minted. The writing was Arabic; Offa, a Christian Anglo-Saxon, could not read it and probably had no idea that the inscription was anything except a pretty pattern. His own name and title were stamped on upside down. The coin is a replica of an Islamic dinar struck for the Abbasid caliph, al-Mansur, who ruled from Baghdad. It bore an Islamic missionary proclamation that neither Offa nor the Pope were likely to understand. Dinars circulated in Europe, and it seems likely that Offa was given one as a model for what he was to produce. It might have been preferred to one of Irene's solidi, as it had no portrait on it for Offa to imitate.

Chapter 11

The Making of Bankers

The Problem with Local Money

For trade to flourish, there had to be gold. No one in thirteenth-century Europe deliberately set out to create a trade network by seeding the continent with gold, but of course it would not need a conscious will for that to happen. Populations and productivity grew, markets recovered their vitality and the reach of traders was extended. Gold would seep in through the cracks, and people would turn towards it with curiosity and desire. Gold coins might be very unfamiliar, and carry messages in strange alphabets, but gold speaks its own language and can be understood anywhere. That would help Europe to rediscover commerce.

People do not trust unfamiliar currency. That was the problem with silver pennies. They varied from place to place, so people refused them. Early medieval laws made it illegal not to accept them, and the harsh penalties show that this was exactly what was happening. In Frankfurt at the end of the eighth century, and then in Normandy and Burgundy, laws were passed trying to force people to take the things. In Anglo-Saxon England, refusing one penny resulted in a fine of 1,440 of them. That's about £30,000 to us. There were mints operating in different cities – Winchester, Hertford, London, Lincoln, Shaftesbury, York, Chichester – all using different designs, and the object of this draconian law was presumably to persuade people being paid by local officials that their pay had value.

There were not enough of these coins, and they were not terribly useful in any case: worth about £20 in our money, they were too big for small purchases and not big enough for large ones. People would chop them into half-pennies or into four-things (farthings), but then you had a tiny scrap of silver that was still three times the value of a loaf of bread. For a large payment, such as a year's rent on a piece of land, it would be difficult and inconvenient to gather sufficient pennies. Payment might involve just a few pennies accompanied by a quantity of corn and wine. That had the advantage that the landlord could live on his income. It is hard to eat silver.

Gold money, which was flowing freely in the Islamic world, had disappeared from Europe. So long as Europeans rarely used large sums of cash, they did not miss it. But the Church did.

Church Power

The Norman Conquest of England had been the start of what became a Papal programme in which secular power would acknowledge its submission to Christ and his representative on Earth. Pope Alexander II had been installed after dark, in a coup. The cardinal bishops had the help of Norman troops to get into Rome, and for the first time since Charlemagne had installed a Pope without reference to the Holy Roman Emperor. Alexander's successor, Gregory VII, fought for control with revolutionary fervour, and a ferocious power struggle developed between him and the Holy Roman Emperor Henry IV. The Pope excommunicated the emperor for refusing to respond to his summons. Henry's enemies supported the Pope as a useful tool against him, and now the emperor's judiciary, chancellery, secretary and even his cooks were risking their immortal souls by continuing to obey him. To avoid the collapse of his empire, Henry humiliated himself by walking barefoot in a hair shirt in the snow to the Pope's Alpine stronghold at Canossa, standing at the locked gate and begging the Pope to lift his excommunication.

The core institution driving this revolutionary new Papacy was the great Benedictine monastery of Cluny, then the largest habitable building in the world, where Gregory was educated. It closely supervised its daughter monasteries, building a power structure of like-minded educated administrators. In a continent of mostly illiterate and innumerate warrior nobility, monasteries supplied the skills that every king needed. This is how gold began to penetrate Europe once again. The Church was not only seeking to take up the overarching authority that had once been enjoyed by the Western Empire, it was also resuming the plunder of the wider world. Cluny was heavily backing the Christian conquest of 'infidel' territories, building monasteries south of the Pyrenees in the tenth century.[1] It was not converting Muslims, but was taking charge of Christian expansion and collecting gold. It needed gold to finance its huge administrative structure, ambitious building projects and pilgrimage management – all of which were investments that further enriched the Church and magnified its power.

Even before the Norman Conquest, Ferdinand of Castile was exacting tribute from defeated Spanish emirs and making an annual tribute to Cluny of a thousand gold dinars. His son, Alfonso VI, doubled that in about 1077.[2] By then, the operation of holy war was well under way, with the papacy giving banners to Norman warriors who acknowledged the Pope's supremacy rather than the emperor's. Norman adventurers had already seized much of southern Italy from the Byzantine Empire, and in 1081 they invaded the Islamic Emirate of Sicily. Pope Nicholas II had given Robert Guiscard the title 'Duke of Sicily'. By 1072, he had taken the great and rich city of Palermo. By the time their conquest was completed, the Normans of southern Italy were considered to be the richest rulers in the West.[3]

In 1094, Moorish Valencia fell to the Castilian Christian warrior known as El Cid, and the poet who told the story was enthralled by the wealth that flowed: 'All were now rich, everyone there. Thirty thousand marks fell to my Cid, and the other wealth, who could count it?'

But although the gold was clearly being used in Europe for elite transactions between rulers and the Church, the only Christian region where it was having any wider circulation was Languedoc. Christians in Barcelona were using Muslim coins in the early years of the eleventh century; these would have been part of the funds sent to Cluny, along with coins minted in exact imitation of Islamic ones, designed to be used in trade with Muslims. The Christian who minted them from 1026–1028 added his name and the date in Arabic.[4] Cluny probably melted down the ones it received, obliterating their message. Eventually, the quotes from the *Qur'an* were replaced with Christian abbreviations, but still in Arabic script. It was evidently not enough for a gold coin to be made of gold: it needed to look as if it came from the world of Islam to be acceptable. No one was comfortable with Latin on a gold coin.

The Value of Crusades

The language of gold, and all it represented, would have to change. In 1095, the Pope, who regarded all Europe's Christians as the Church's own to command, launched a military campaign to supplant Muslim power over the 'Holy Land'. In particular, it set its sights on Jerusalem, and so began a process that reversed everything. The Islamic conquest of the Levant through *jihad* was replaced by Christian conquest through Crusade. Catholic Europe began handling money on a scale that was new to it. Gradually, the East, which had been short of silver and rich in gold, found its gold flowing west. Christian Europe would become golden, while the Islamic world found it had less gold and much more silver. From the late 1100s, silver displaced gold as the basis of many Islamic currencies.[5]

The First Crusade was launched by mistake within thirty years of the Norman Conquest of England, in November 1095. The emperor in Constantinople, Alexios Komnenos, had sent a plea for the assistance of European knights to push back a wave of Seljuk Turks who had invaded his lands. The emperor dominated the Eastern Church, and Alexios would probably have sent his request to his opposite number, Holy Roman Emperor Henry IV, had Henry been in a position of strength. But Henry was still at war with the Pope, and the Pope was winning. In 1082, Alexios had sent Henry 144,000 gold pieces, and promised him 216,000 more, to finance his effort to occupy Rome and help

Constantinople fend off an attack from Pope Gregory's Norman backer. It was money down the drain, and by 1095 the Holy Roman Emperor was trapped in north-east Italy. So Alexios's plea went to the Pope, and he provided what he thought Gregory VII's successor, Urban II, would find a compelling narrative. He stressed the Turks' aggressive religious agenda and their threat to the viability of pilgrimage, which was an important source of Church revenue and influence. The Hospitallers had been looking after sick pilgrims to Jerusalem for about twenty years.[6] Alexios seems to have hoped for a couple of thousand mercenaries.

This Pope was the first to take the name Urban for over 800 years. Previously the Prior of Cluny, he took on the persona of the city of Rome and was clearly inspired by the idea of extending its authority over the world. He saw a great opportunity to spread his church's mantle over all Christendom and raise an army that served the Papacy. What's more, the warriors would fund themselves and he would reward them with the abrogation of penance for all their sins. He could, and did, sanctify war.

The Pope went on the stump for eight months around France. Evangelical preachers took up the cause in north-east France and Germany, and soon Urban found that he had not only enlisted a significant body of knights but also a vast throng of labourers who simply took up the offer of what they understood to be a free ticket to heaven. These enthusiasts set off as a huge mob of militarized and ungoverned pilgrims with the intention of seizing the Holy Land for Christ, the Pope and themselves; perhaps not in that order. They sustained themselves by pillage and slaughter, and their venture did not end well. To some extent, the example they set presaged everything to follow.

Many of the knightly enthusiasts who then set out on what is now called the First Crusade were engaged in a huge investment opportunity as well as in a religious duty. This meant converting immovable assets into portable cash on a huge scale, thus inadvertently giving a tremendous boost to the economy of Europe. We get an idea of what was going on from some of the richest participants: Godfrey of Bouillon sold his county of Verdun, among other lands, to a bishop to fund his campaign. There were no letters of credit, and the Templars' system of crusade assistance did not yet exist. The leaders needed bags and chests of coins. It was a good investment. Three years after setting out, Godfrey was the ruler of Jerusalem. Other crusaders had become rich on the way there from the spoils of defeated armies and ransomed nobles, or, spectacularly, from the seizure of Antioch. Stephen of Blois wrote home from there that he was already in profit. In 1101, Caesarea and Arsuf, on the coast, were taken with the help of a commercial partnership of Genoese business crusaders, who were backed by subscribers. They divided up the profits at that point and dissolved their crusade.[7]

Crusading, 1100 CE.

The newly transformed and spectacularly enriched Church establishment began to take over the landscape; the buildings it began to erect in the mid-twelfth century were nothing like the old thick-walled secure assembly spaces under barrel roofs. Communities living in small squat houses that huddled in the shadows of windowless castle donjons were now drafted to help in constructing fabulous heaven-piercing airy fantasies of spires and sculptures. They were soon building vast soaring groves of stone whose tall trunks extended their fronds in a canopy 35 metres (100ft) or more above the congregation. The slight walls would have fallen outward under the weight of that deceptively heavy stone canopy if they were not balanced by flying buttresses, elegant props that connected to high and stable pillars surrounding the building. The lands of kings and nobles were now glorified by these incredible poetic visions, which were vivid demonstrations of the arrival of gold.

The first of these 'gothic' structures, the choir of St Denis just north of Paris, completed in 1144, was as notable for its lavish display of gold as for its architectural originality. Abbot Suger recorded that he used around 90lb of gold on the altar, the cross and a chalice.[8]

About twenty-five years after the First Crusade, Fulcher of Chartres, the chaplain to one of its leaders, said: 'We, who were Occidentals, have now become Orientals ... Those who had few coins, here possess countless bezants.'[9] The use of money, and especially gold coin, was the fundamental difference between Europe and the Orient.

Europe now had some of the gold that was needed for large transactions, but there was not enough for it to appear much outside the treasuries of courts and cathedrals. It would stay there until the tide of value flowed back. The crusaders, overwhelmingly Franks, had established their own Kingdom of Jerusalem. It roughly corresponded to present-day Israel including the occupied territories, plus a bulge of land on the east side of the Jordan. Little of the gold they won ever left this Latin Kingdom, where the running costs of its luxuriating inhabitants were huge. They had also taken power in Tripoli, Antioch and Edessa (roughly Lebanon, Syria and south-east Turkey). When you live among the wealthy, your own outgoings inevitably rise to match. In these new kingdoms on the far side of the Mediterranean, known as *Outremer* ('Overseas'), castles needed to be built to the highest standard, armour and weapons of the finest quality had to be commissioned, and nobles, prelates and ladies felt obliged to be dressed in styles and fabrics that were being learned from the Arab nobility, using silk and gold embroidery, embellished with jewels and the very richest decoration. New styles of tailoring and dressmaking appeared, which took advantage of buttons, unknown in Europe. There was not much that this kingdom wanted to buy from Germany or France, and it may be that the amount of tribute to Rome was going down rather than up. In 1077, the gold sent from Spain to Cluny had been used for grain to feed its great army of monks, but the abbey's food bill of over 20,000 shillings a year outstripped its income in the next century and it began to depend on moneylenders.[10]

Incredibly large sums of gold were needed to defend and sustain the crusader states. There were set tariffs for ransom, from a thousand gold bezants for a knight rising to 100,000 for a king, the sum which Baldwin, Count of Edessa, had to pay after his capture in 1104. Another crusade leader, Bohemond, who had captured Antioch, had been ransomed the year before for possibly even more.[11] In 1123, Baldwin, now installed as King Baldwin II of Jerusalem, was captured again. It became evident that he could not, and the Latin nobility would not, pay the going rate for his release, and he seems to have agreed on 80,000 dinars and a bunch of fortresses. Only a quarter of his ransom was actually paid.

These vast sums indicate the difference between Fulcher's Orientals and Occidentals. When King Richard I ('the Lionheart') was taken captive in 1192 by the Duke of Austria, the Holy Roman Emperor demanded 100,000lb of silver for his ransom. Because that was silver, not gold, it was only one-twelfth of Baldwin's ransom in 1104, but it was far too much for England to readily pay, two to three times the total income of the crown. The old land tax had to be replaced with a 25 per cent charge on lay and Church lands, and there were heavy exactions from the landless. There was a mass protest in London in 1196, and the Archbishop of Canterbury ordered his men to attack the protesters, who barricaded themselves in the church of St Mary Le Bow. The archbishop's men set fire to the church and the protest's spokesman was forced out onto the street, captured and executed. An oriental ransom would have been unthinkable.

Revival

But the financial gulf between 'Orient' and 'Occident' was closing fast. The stimulus of crusade-financing in Europe, with huge quantities of silver being raised, was supplemented by the exploitation of a silver-rich mountain at Rammelsberg, in Lower Saxony. Other silver resources were also being plundered. The demand for it was so great that the Islamic world was being drained of it. The English were minting 4 million silver pennies a year in the 1220s, rising to ten times that number by 1280. The money was needed because crusading was now supported by a steady increase in agricultural productivity and population, stimulating the rebirth of urbanization. An improving climate meant, for instance, that from 1220–1315, there was no famine in England. This coincided with improvements in agricultural technology (primarily faster ploughing as horse teams replaced oxen in favourable areas) and the growth of markets and towns. The result was a golden age for the peasant, and a spectacular rise in population, from about 2½ to perhaps 5 million people in England by 1315. Around Europe, waste land was taken into cultivation, marginal land was converted into farms and the standard of living rose. This meant a considerable movement of people and inevitably resulted in a large number of peasant families having relatives in newly growing towns. In England alone, 132 new planned urban settlements were established in the twelfth and thirteenth centuries.[12]

The Emergence of Venice

Whereas in 1000 the population of Constantinople had exceeded the total urban population of Roman Catholic Europe, by 1200, Europe's towns and cities had grown explosively. There were at least twenty towns and cities with over 10,000 inhabitants and their total population was now more than three times that of the Byzantine capital. Paris had grown from perhaps 20,000 to well over 100,000. Its growth was driven by the wealth of the Kings of France, who made it their principal residence from the start of the twelfth century. This was closely linked to an ever-growing religious presence, with the great Cathedral of Nôtre-Dame, the Abbeys of St Germaine-des-Prés and St Geneviève, and the religious houses on the left bank that became a great university. Paris's trade was based on the river and was closely tied to the court. Royal finance was prodigious, and royal wealth was kept in very visible strongholds whose vastly rich keepers were occasionally condemned by royal whim. Paris was becoming the largest city in the West.

In northern Italy, under the impetus of growing commerce with Byzantium and the Arab world, urban communes had developed which operated as capitalist money and credit-based economies. The new urban populations had moved from the countryside, seeking opportunity by escape or agreement and being released from feudal servitude. Genoa, for example, became a hub of Mediterranean commerce, with an immigrant workforce from Lombardy, Tuscany, Provence and Flanders. Thirteenth-century proverbial wisdom declared that 'Genoese' was synonymous with 'merchant'. The whole population of the city was in trade – 'men and women, rich and poor, young and old, nobles and commoners'.[13]

But the city that would play the pivotal role in bridging the gulf between Orient and Occident was the one situated on the hinge between them: Venice. In the years between the Conquest of England and the First Crusade, the Byzantine Emperor Alexios was at least as worried about the assaults of Normans from the west as Turks from the east. He had no navy of any size and was desperately vulnerable to the Normans, who were now launching effective amphibious attacks. Venice was an oddity: a republic acknowledged by Charlemagne as Byzantine territory (so outside the Holy Roman Empire), but with no real foothold on dry land and no way to live except by trading on the sea. Although by the time of Gregory VII it was nominally Roman Catholic, it was as uneasy about the Pope's Norman supporters, as was Alexios. Venice's existence was based on an effective and powerful fleet of galleys, and around 1090, the city had signed a treaty which committed its ships to defend Alexios's empire. In exchange, he gave this strange city control of most of the port of Constantinople and tax-free trade.

Shortly afterwards, he conjured the crusades into existence and inadvertently gave the Normans a much more rewarding proposition. The Venetians never did have to defend Constantinople. But they had been given a commercial hinterland that extended through the whole Byzantine world and on to central Asia. Exotic materials and decorative treasures flowed west, into Venice and on to the markets of the new, growing cities.

The First Crusade offered other northern Italian traders the chance to break into this lucrative market. Genoa was first off the mark, running supplies and equipment to the siege of Antioch, and they were granted their own market there as soon as the town was captured in August 1098. In the process of gaining remission of their sins, Genoese merchants had won direct access to the silks and spices of Asia and were now handling gold bezants and dinars. Suddenly, the potential became obvious; the Pisans quickly sent their own ships to get a slice of the action. The Venetians then decided that this was serious, and they could not stand idly by. In spring 1099, they sent some 200 warships with about 9,000 of their own crusaders under the command of the head of state, the Doge. This was the largest single contingent to join the crusade, and it would operate decisively. They made straight for the Pisan fleet and sank it, taking 4,000 prisoners. In subsequent crusades, Venice won the right to its own market in Acre and a third of the city of Tyre. Genoa, Pisa and Venice became heavily dependent on their income from the new Latin Kingdom of Jerusalem, which was economically their fief. They had their own quarters in the major ports, with the rights to run their own markets and use their own weights and measures, and they had complete control of all transport between Christendom and Syria. Acre was especially important; the old oriental trade route through Egypt had changed direction and now ran through Acre instead.

A new financial order was emerging in Europe, as the growth of large cities and the wealth of Italian merchant city-states shifted the balance of political and military power away from the old feudal nobility and their estates. The dispute between Pope and Holy Roman Emperor over who should have supremacy, the religious or secular power, was to be settled by the decisive defeat of Emperor Frederick Barbarossa, who had come to power in 1155, by the combined power of the north Italian cities. These cities were determined to retain their independence, and so supported the Pope against him. In 1177, Barbarossa submitted to the Pope, much as Henry IV had submitted at Canossa, but this time his obeisance was performed at Venice.

It was Ascension Day, and the city was filled with pilgrims who were expecting to observe an annual ceremony in which the Doge was rowed out to sea to offer a prayer for maritime safety. The ceremony of 1177 was unforgettable. The Pope and the Holy Roman Emperor were brought to the Church of San Nicolò on the Lido, where the emperor kissed the Pope's feet. The story goes that the Pope gave the Doge a golden ring. The Doge was rowed out in a gold-painted barge to the junction of the lagoon and the Adriatic, and cast the ring into the sea, under religious supervision, for a sacramental wedding between the government of the Most Serene Republic and the sea. The ceremony was then performed every year until Napoleon extinguished the Republic. Painted on the walls of the ducal palace, it marked Venice's belief in its own gilded ascendancy.[14]

The Plunder of Constantinople

That ascendancy was confirmed a few years later, in 1204, when Venice took control of 11,000 European knights who had arrived to crusade against the Turks, and manipulated them into making an overwhelmingly successful military assault on Constantinople. This was very much in line with the ideas of a new Pope,

Innocent III, a man determined to complete the revolution of Gregory VII and establish himself as supreme over all Christian monarchs. His programme called for the submission of kings, the subjection of the Eastern Church to Rome, the elimination of all but his own interpretation of the Christian message and the reconquest of Jerusalem under his own command. He gave crusade-preaching full papal authority and sent letters to the clergy and nobility throughout France and northern Italy urging them to take up the Cross. The Latin Kingdom had been destroyed by Saladin, and Jerusalem was lost. The knights were to be the Pope's own army to recover the Holy Land, and their leaders assembled their forces under a Papal banner just as William of Normandy had done. The Fourth Crusade had been declared in 1199 by three Frankish counts at a tournament in Champagne, and six envoys were given full powers to contract an Italian city to supply and transport the troops.[15] The envoys selected were feudal nobles who understood military risk, but not commercial risk.

These envoys told their chosen city, Venice, that the total number of crusaders would be 33,500 men, and they would guarantee payment for their residence and transport. This was an absurd number. Venice's businessmen, who were good at this, assembled in the Church of San Marco. The envoys said they had been commanded to kneel at their feet and not to rise until those noble people agreed 'to take pity on the Holy Land over the sea', whereupon they threw themselves on their knees in tears. The Doge, who was well over 80 and virtually blind, but still in full command of all his faculties, wept. So did all the Venetians gathered there, and with one accord they all raised their hands to heaven and shouted out: 'We consent! We consent!' In the uproar that followed, you would have thought the whole world was crumbling to pieces, according to one of the envoys, Geoffroi de Villehardouin.

Each crusader would pay a share of the total. But when only a third of the expected number arrived, the crusade was immediately bankrupt. Or it would have been, if that sweet old blind Doge had not offered to lead them and forgive the debt if they just carried out a few useful tasks, by attacking a couple of Christian targets first. So the Fourth Crusade was taken on a significant diversion which involved storming Constantinople, the greatest Christian city in the world, on 6 April 1203. A week later, their commander, the blind Doge, and the crusading barons moved into the Great Palace.

The soldiers were told they had three days to pillage the city. Every house was open to rape and murder. In Hagia Sophia, drunken soldiers tore down the silk hangings and pulled the silver iconostasis to pieces. A prostitute sat on the Patriarch's throne and sang ribald songs. Nuns were ravished in their convents. Children and women were left to die in the streets. The bloodshed went on and on. Even the Saracens would have been more merciful, cried the historian

Nicetas Choniates.[16] Venice had taken full possession of the fabulous wealth of Byzantium. Innocent III had tried to pay for an army under his authority by offering a guaranteed place in heaven to each crusader. Doge Dandolo offered them instead the golden spoils of Venice, and the Pope's army had been hijacked. That was the end of Innocent III's ambition to establish Papal supremacy over the rulers of Christendom. Cluny's gold had initiated this magnification of Church power under Gregory VII, and now it had drained away.

The New Venice

The transfer of property and power from the world's greatest Christian city to the ambitious seaport was so massive that it created the Venice we now recognize. I made a film about this in 1990, inventing a Doge's Ball in the Venice Carnival to tell the story. It resonated so powerfully in the city that it immediately became, and still remains, the most celebrated event of the Carnival. Venice was created out of Constantinople, and it became the nest from which the fire-and-gold phoenix of Europe's civilization was reborn.

The most valuable loot, in European eyes, was the phenomenal store of holy relics, which itself became a huge economic asset. The relic venerated in Constantinople as the Crown of Thorns was bought by Louis IX from a Venetian banker, who was holding it as security for a loan to Baldwin II, and he built the fabulous Sainte Chapelle to house it in Paris. This spectacular building is a glamorous multicoloured glass reliquary 42.5 metres (140ft) high, whose stone vaulted roof is supported on the slenderest stalks. Here there are no flying buttresses; the walls are kept from outward collapse by iron bars, straps and ties. Completed in 1248, this was a new architecture, which did not belong to the Church but the king, guardian now of the most sacred relic in Christendom.[17]

Louis IX, who was declared a saint in 1297, was now a more elevated spiritual authority than the Pope, who was embroiled in a destructive crusade against the Holy Roman Emperor. Royal wealth, and its power to possess the holy relics that offered salvation, now clearly trumped the authority of St Peter. King Louis would depend on the banking power of the Knights Templar rather than the authority of any Pope.

Venice too had little concern for the Pope, who had excommunicated the city when it diverted the crusaders to its own agenda. St Mark's Square in Venice was rebuilt with architectural structures shipped from Constantinople, and the Basilica of St Mark claims to have acquired, among much else, a vial of Christ's blood, the gold cross that Constantine had taken into battle and a part of the head of John the Baptist.[18] Relics drew pilgrims, and so stimulated trade. But the most enduring wealth that came to Venice was a massive increase in its trading power. Northern Europe's trade had the potential for growth, especially as it had developed a substantial wool surplus and the skill to make highly desirable luxury fabrics. Gold now flowed into Italy, and money enabled trade. In a few years, Venice, Florence and Genoa were minting their own gold coins, and these ducats, florins and genovinos were happily accepted wherever commerce flourished; at least, happily accepted by money-changers. The first of these coins, in 1252, was probably the Florentine 'florin', valued at a lira, 240 pennies or denarii. Florence had already begun minting a new silver soldo worth twelve denarii, so the notional currency of l.s.d. (librae, solidi, denarii – pounds, shillings and pence) introduced by Charlemagne had now moved into real, physical existence.

Each city insisted that only its own coin could be used in its markets, and the profession of money-changer became fundamental to trade. The value of holy relics was dependent on a fickle market; authentication might easily be undermined, and sometimes relics were downgraded (and even punished) for failing to deliver miracle cures. The supernatural was no longer regarded in Europe as a guarantor of value, especially now that it was mediated through a Church that was in constant conflict with secular rulers. The guarantee that gave Italian gold coins their value, and that was seen as being as everlasting as the gold itself, was civic authority. And that civic authority was assured by the coins themselves. Italian cities, run by merchants, imposed a compulsory duty of honesty on the money-changers, who worked at benches (*bancas*) under public scrutiny. At Lucca, they were in the shadow of the cathedral, below a plaque that set out their duty of honesty in a form comparable to the doctors' Hippocratic Oath. Those who failed had their benches publicly smashed (*banca rupta*). The supposed incorruptibility of the bank and the incorruptibility of gold were now one and the same.

Minting Gold in Europe

Gold had come back into Europe as the currency of great lords of Church and state, but not as the currency of daily life. Merchants in Italy were willing to use their own city's new gold pieces because they trusted in, and were invested in, their own cities, but Northern European merchants preferred to use thin strips of uncoined gold, supplemented by Byzantine and Arabic coins that were in effect treated as bullion.[19]

This created a problem for Northern Europe's kings. Their business was now in gold, but it was still in very short supply so they could not produce coins themselves. Gold had always been the ghost currency behind Europe's silver, the currency of account by which debts were measured even though it did not exist there as coin. Now it had begun to flow again they were paying for wars, crusades and their sumptuous courts and buildings in currency which they were short of and did not control. They were thrown into the welcoming arms of Italian bankers, who combined access to coinage with the ability to keep (and adjust) the books.[20]

The problem was made very clear when Henry III of England scraped together enough gold to produce his own magnificent gold penny, with himself enthroned on it. This splendid status symbol was issued in August 1257, just five years after the florin, the first European gold coin. Henry's coin was priced, quite correctly, at ten times its weight in silver. He was making a statement of his magnificence, and probably hoped that he could charge others for coining their gold strips. By November, the plan had unravelled. There was so little gold in his kingdom that he had swamped the market, and gold in England lost up to 20 per cent of its value.[21] The complaints were so forceful that he was forced to proclaim the coin was not legal tender. Consequently, it disappeared. Nine years later, Louis IX of France tried exactly the same trick, issuing a gold *écu d'or* with the royal coat of arms on it, again with a face value of ten times its weight in silver. Once more, the coins had to be withdrawn or melted down.

Europe needed an increase in trade to deliver additional gold. The required stimulus came from a ruler on the other side of the world, one who is understood in European mythology to be the personification of ruthless, mindless tyranny.

Marco Polo

The sight of the Mongolian parliament building in Ulan Bator comes as a bit of a shock to any European steeped in the regional stereotypes of history. At the top of a mighty stairway rising to the central portico, blocking what appears to be the main entrance, sits the massive statue of the enthroned, man-spreading figure of Genghis Khan, creator of the largest empire the world has ever seen. It is currently estimated that he was responsible for the slaughter of around 21.3 million people, which may have been 5 per cent of the total world population.[22] In modern terms, with a global population now fifteen times larger, it is the equivalent of killing everyone alive today in the USA and Canada. I visited the remains of Merv, and found it hard to grasp the industriousness required to physically carry out what Rashid al-Din (1247–1318) described, the slaughter of over 1,300,000 inhabitants. The evidence for killing tens of millions is debatable, but there was obviously a huge demographic change across Asia. At its greatest extent, the Mongol Khanate stretched from the Mediterranean and the Black Sea to the Pacific, ruling almost 30 per cent of the known world.[23]

Genghis Khan is spoken of by Mongolians as their national hero, the bringer of civilization, the creator of literacy, wise judge and pacifier.

On a global scale, the jury may well still be out on some of that. But it is abundantly clear that he was an enthusiastic facilitator of trade across his entire empire and beyond. As the Mongol conquest rolled on, it mobilized the resources of the civilizations it was swallowing – northern China, central Asia, Russia, the Caucuses, Iran and the Caliphate.[24] It was like seizing a great treasure chest. Genghis and his successors knew that as nomads with no infrastructure, they were completely dependent on trade for every aspect of military and domestic supply. Merchants were now carefully privileged and protected, and caravan routes were developed linking the eastern Mediterranean to the Pacific, with a network of rest stations en route available to these privileged travellers free of charge. Islamic, Byzantine and Chinese rulers had blocked foreigners from travelling in their territories. Now the Mongols opened every door, and trade from Constantinople right across the 7,000km to the Khan capital (modern Beijing) became far easier than ever before or ever again. They knew that travelling merchants kept their rule from collapsing, and a new age of long-distance trade was suddenly created. The entire land mass was opened for business, with no taxes or restrictions on the movement of goods. The result was a blossoming of commercial life, in which the Genoese and Venetians were particularly well placed to participate.

Marco Polo's father and uncle travelled from Venice through Asia in the mid-thirteenth century and met Kublai Khan. They were among thousands of Europeans who made their way to China looking for commercial profit, military assistance against the Muslims or to seek out the supposed Christian Asian kingdom of Prester John. Tales had been told about his fabled lost kingdom for over a hundred years, and some people hoped that he might engage with Europe in a pincer movement against Islam. Marco Polo started out in 1271, and the account he wrote became a permanent inspiration to travellers in search of exotic wealth. But of perhaps even greater moment was the prodigious flow of profit being brought into Europe by these traders through Venice and Genoa. One detailed document enumerates the costs and risks of a journey to China from Tanais, an Italian trading station at the northern tip of the Black Sea, with goods worth 25,000 gold florins. The total expenses of the journey are little more than 1,000 florins. Their currency was silver, and they were travelling into a world which had a completely different idea of the nature and function of money.

China's Understanding of Money

The fundamental question at the heart of this book is why people believe that gold has intrinsic value, and why that became the basis of money. In ancient

Imperial China, people did not share that belief. The Mongol Empire paid no attention to any magical link between gold, gods and eternal value. The Venetians were adventuring in a vast centralized state where absolute power was said to be bestowed on the emperor by the Mandate of Heaven, a mandate which gave him the power of life and death over everyone. The empire had been established in 221 BCE, and although it had gone through long periods of fracture it was now firmly restored under Mongol rule and still relied on its old Imperial philosophies and texts. Its understanding of money was set out in a fundamental collection of writings on economics and political philosophy, the *Guanzi*. This probably originated in the seventh century BCE, when coinage had been invented but before there was an emperor. Named after Guan Zhong, a minister of state who died in 645 BCE, the original text was subsumed in a 'modern' re-edit by Liu Xiang about 26 BCE, during the Han Dynasty, when the state was managed by a centralized and scholarly Confucian bureaucracy. It was still the standard text on money when Marco Polo arrived.

The *Guanzi* teaches economics at a level which was unknown in Europe until the sixteenth century. One chapter, 'Light and Heavy', sets out the way imbalances between supply and demand affect market behaviour so that official intervention is unnecessary. If there is a shortage of grain in one state, its price becomes 'heavy', and a surplus elsewhere, where the price is 'light', will spontaneously flow to the 'heavy' market.

The function of currency is to enable this market smoothing to operate efficiently, and a chapter on 'State Savings' sets out how this can be achieved. Centuries before sixteenth-century Europeans discovered the idea, the *Guanzi* taught what is known today as 'the quantity theory of money'. The basic proposition was that money does not contain value, but its availability establishes the value of everything else. It explained that the state has to provide symbolic tokens in the correct quantity to keep the supply of goods and services flowing without throttling or overstimulating demand. These tokens had very little intrinsic value, but their exchange value was guaranteed by the life-and-death authority of the holder of the Mandate of Heaven.[25] Everything depended on the ruler's control of the supply of this money, which by the eleventh century took the form of blade-shaped bronze coins, forty of which were valued at a *jin* of gold (about 250g). When the state found it was unable to produce enough bronze, it turned to the ritual creation of tokens printed on rectangles of mulberry bark. This paper currency was itself called *Guanzi*. It was backed by silk and gold and guaranteed by the empire. This meant that China could insist that foreign merchants bought paper money, which could be redeemed when they left.[26]

Although he liked its convenience, Marco Polo inevitably saw paper money as a trick by which the emperor enriched himself at a negligible cost in mulberry bark. To a European mind, this conceptual money was nothing more than a charade enforced by absolute power. Florence and Genoa had introduced gold coins in the twenty years before Marco Polo set out, and Venice began coining virtually pure gold ducats in 1284, while Polo was still in China. That was real money. The difference was obvious from the fact that refusing paper money risked a death sentence. That did not happen with gold.

Italian Bankers

Europe had lived without gold, but there was commercial pressure for the old ways to return. There was a need for a new, larger denomination currency in Europe as trade was growing, and the medieval world of local exchange and silver pennies was being burst apart. Kings and bankers were using Islamic gold coins: they could never have got away with paper currency, even if the idea occurred to them. Italian merchants now had access to enough gold to mint useful quantities of coin advertising their own civic identity. They stored it with goldsmiths who became their bankers. The bankers holding the coins gave the depositors bills of exchange. These were not the equivalent of Chinese paper money: they could only be used in trusted networks of associates, usually their own relatives in distant cities, and the wider that network reached, the better placed they were to attract deposits. From the depositors' point of view, the attraction was that their bank's bill of exchange could be redeemed wherever the bank had another branch. From the bank's point of view, the more deposits they attracted, the more they could earn by lending those deposits at interest. Of course, they could not call it interest – that would be usury. But they could persuasively request a voluntary gift from the borrower, or a reward for the risk they were taking in making the loan.

North Italian bankers, known as Lombards, now financed Europe's Church and kings, who began borrowing from them on far too large a scale. They made loans to both sides in a war between Edward I of England and Philip IV of France which neither king could afford. Much of the moneylending was supplemented by Jews, who were untroubled by the Church's ban on charging interest, and in 1290 King Edward had tried to stave off his creditors by seizing the Jews' property in England and expelling them.[27] There were only about 2,000 Jews in the country, so that was not enough, and in 1294 both he and Philip defaulted. The bankers of Lucca, Florence and Siena were ruined.[28] Many of their wealthy depositors suffered, and some bankers were imprisoned. In England, Edward was driven to increase taxes and over-issue government

IOUs, leading to a constitutional crisis in 1297. In France, one part of Philip's solution was to massively debase his 'silver' currency, which probably caused even more economic harm. More dramatic was what he did to the Church. His Siena bankers were also bankers to the Papacy. When the Church tried to protect its funds from his default, Philip took over the Papacy, moved the Church to France and installed a French Pope. The importance of gold swept away any theological issues about Papal power and the legacy of Gregory VII.

Meanwhile, the surviving Frankish Crusader outposts of Outremer were steadily crushed by the remorseless advance of the Egyptian Mameluk leader, Baibars, until all that was left was the city of Acre. That was smashed to pieces in 1291; it was said that a thousand Muslim engineers were assigned to the destruction of each of the city's towers. The same ruthlessness that had empowered the creation of the Latin Kingdom of Jerusalem was now mirrored in its elimination, and the remaining wealth that could be rescued was removed by the Knights Templar to Cyprus. Now King Philip had his own Pope, who served him by proclaiming, in 1307, that the Knights Templar were violating God's laws and their assets should be seized.[29] Philip's torture and killing of the Knights Templar has left a fantasy of hidden gold that resonates with mystically inclined treasure hunters to this day. In 1306, Philip also expelled his very large Jewish population, around 100,000, cancelling his debts and confiscating their property.[30]

Bankers who dared to lend to kings were taking a huge risk, but that risk offered huge rewards. A bigger problem was that the credit they could extend was limited by the deposits they held, and so by the supply of bullion. Silver was an unsatisfactory substitute: it was less dense and less valuable, so a trade in Venice requiring one bag of gold would need twenty-six bags of silver.[31] New gold mines were opened in Hungary, controlled by the Italians.[32] Italians felt they were reclaiming their old heritage; the cultural shift we call the Renaissance was beginning.

In Siena, in 1311, Duccio completed his *Maestà*, the greatest work of his life – perhaps the greatest in the world. His studio was covered with wooden panels, painted front and back, which when assembled made a masterpiece occupying some 250 square feet.[33] It is the whole story of the New Testament, from the Annunciation to the Resurrection. It was painted as never before – the figures are life-like, rounded, moving as human beings really move, with their robes hanging in soft folds. These were not the stiff, symbolic creatures of other men's art. Even the Saviour himself was painted the same size as everyone else, not twice the size because he is more important.

The metal for the final pigment was so precious that it was brought under guard, and his studio was guarded day and night until he finished. There was great surprise that he needed so much of it. He ground the gold to dust, mixed it with oil and began to paint. Each saint needed a golden halo. Then each halo was outlined in a subtly different pattern of gold. When this illusion of mystical reality was almost complete, he ground down all the rest of the gold and mixed more paint than he had used of any other colour.

When he finished, a huge crowd gathered outside the studio and bore the vast, epic painting through the streets to the cathedral. The procession was led by musicians, and behind them priests swinging censers. Everyone was amazed at the veracity with which the Gospels had been brought to life. Painting would never be the same. This was hyperrealism, the way the world should be perceived. Even the sky in the Holy Land is revealed as entirely gold. The story was biblical, but the realistic, sculptural figures were determinedly classical. Art, faith and hard cash had been forged into a new reality. Everyone could see the glory of the work, its beauty and the value displayed. It cost 3,000 florins, over 3.5kg of gold.

As gold was once more flowing through Italian cities, it was seen to connect them to their classical heritage, to the heritage of the Church and to heaven itself. But their coins, which carried civic and saintly emblems, not the faces of men,[34] represented neither sacred nor imperial power. They were underwritten by a new kind of trader, who lived and died by the power of reputation. The banker had to be more trustworthy than any lord of sacred or secular power. So when a Barcelona banker, Francesh Castello, failed to settle his debts in 1360, he was beheaded in front of his bench.[35]

Chapter 12

Out of Africa

Gold of Ghana

B y the early fourteenth century, bankers and traders in Europe were held back by a shortage of coin. Just as the Roman Empire depended on finding ever more gold for its armies, the new commercial world needed ever more gold for commerce. Just as the old Empire had been run from Italy but embraced all Europe, so now banking was run from Italy and stretched its fingers over the continent. Wool from England, textiles from France and the Low Countries, timber from Scandinavia, all depended on merchants handling gold coins, and there simply were not enough. But Christian Europe, having exhausted its own supplies, really did not know where new gold came from.

It arrived from Egypt and North Africa, for example as payment for grain from Sicily, but its journey started much further south. Europe had been cut off from its flow when Egypt was taken over by Saladin and caught up in the Islamic response to the Crusades. That response achieved its goal in 1291 when Egypt's Mamluk soldiers destroyed Acre, the last citadel of Outremer, and wiped out the legal fiction of the Latin Kingdom of Jerusalem. The Mamluks, who had seized power in 1250, introduced a period of massive upheaval that did not offer any security for the ancient gold mines of Nubia. The impressive gold dinars of the overthrown Ayyubid Dynasty that Saladin had founded were replaced with badly made coins with no standard weight and often stamped from a piece of gold too small for the die.[1] The mines of Iraq and Persia were also defunct. Indeed, at the end of the thirteenth century, the only significant source of new gold for the Arab world was dust arriving by secretive camel trains from the territory which was now embraced by Mali, and had been part of the collapsed kingdom of Ghana.[2]

*   *   *

'Would you like to see my wife's gold?' It was 2009, and I was in a small and desperately poor town deep in the Niger's inland delta, about 350km south-west of Timbuktu. I was travelling with my wife and two friends looking for evidence of the fourteenth-century source of Europe's and Arabia's gold. The journey has seldom been easy: no European is known to have made it there and back alive until René Caillié successfully passed himself off as an Arab in 1828. Modern travellers have needed to be cautious. But when an amnesty was signed with Tuareg rebels, it became easier than usual. By then, the very word 'Timbuktu' meant the ends of the Earth. You grab these chances when you can. Thanks to ISIS and Islamic Jihad, there is no going back now.

I had not expected anyone to volunteer to show me the legendary, vanished gold. Especially not in this small mud-built community, which has no road across the flat waste and is cut off by flooding for half the year. I was hunting stories, not objects. But the beautiful young Fulani woman who came out of her house was wearing gold circlets in her ears and nose and a huge pair of traditional earrings, suspended from stout red silk ropes to protect her ears.

The other gold treasures I was shown, in other communities, were fakes made of brass or – wonderfully – of straw. But this village, which was so impoverished that it could not afford a clean room for women to give birth, still clung proudly to its treasure. This was not wealth. It was the gold that connected to spirits that provided it and to ancestry that shaped it.

Gold in West Africa was as magical as it had been in Europe and Asia, and for the same reason – it was the link to eternity. Ancient Ghana, which spread over what is now south-eastern Mauritania, Senegal and western Mali, had been associated by Arab geographers since the ninth and tenth centuries with rich gold mines, 'the richest on earth'.[3] (This was well to the north of the modern coastal state of Ghana.[4]) There was a well-developed trans-Sahara trade between Ghana and Muslim North Africa, exchanging gold for salt, copper and sea shells on huge camel trains. That trade brought Islam to sub-Saharan Africa, but the local religion continued. In Ghana, it revolved around sorcery and death, and gold was the nobility's connection to immortality, being worn plaited into the hair of the sons of vassal kings.[5] Golden stools, comparable to the golden crowns of Sumeria, were the mark of kingship.[6] Today, one such stool said to have been sent from the gods to the first Asante king in the seventeenth century is the throne of the current ruler.[7] It is the seat of the king's soul and must never touch the ground; instead it is placed on a blanket. In old Ghana, gold connected divine authority, ancestor worship and land management.

The places where it was extracted were well hidden, though they may have involved a huge population. It has been speculatively calculated that up to half a million shafts may have been worked, each yielding less than 5 grams of gold a year.[8] The community laboured very privately, outside the control of kings and merchants. The old system of silent exchange for gold reported by Herodotus with Carthaginians seems to have been replicated here.[9]

Mali

The empire of Ghana collapsed around the year 1000 CE and was eventually taken over by the growing state of Mali. Its ruler in 1325, Mansa Musa, had, by a combination of circumstances and conquest, established an empire of half a million square miles and cornered the market in gold. He was by far the richest man in the world. Having grown from the earlier gold empire, Mali managed to balance Islamic belief, which saw gold as the basis of commerce, with the traditional gold-magic that allowed its people to produce the metal. It was understood to be imbued with supernatural power. This magic was redolent with curses and dangers; gold production was enmeshed in a system of beliefs that has not yet been extinguished.[10] Some of the witchcraft stalls I saw in Bamoko market were quite scary, and local reports of ongoing human sacrifice were chilling. The gold was valued in the Islamic world not for its magical power but its buying power, but when efforts were made to convert its producers to Islam they simply stopped working. Gold was too dangerous without the right rituals and sacrifices.[11] Mansa Musa backed off from trying to convert the miners, and while remaining committed to his Islamic faith, was seen to perform the traditional rites and ceremonies and preside over courts of indigenous faiths, including witchcraft trials.

So this gold that ended up in Mamluk coins was laden with traditions of spells and dangerous powers. Though the people who used them knew nothing of that, the gold certainly conveyed something that demanded respect.

Rabbinic documents show that Jewish merchants from Andalusia were trading in Mali's main city, Timbuktu.[12] Some relocated there in the fourteenth century to escape Spanish pressure for Christian conversion. Linked by trade and family to the Talmudic centres of Andalusia, Egypt and Baghdad, they provided a flow of information to Mansa Musa that would have expanded his understanding and cultural ambition. His empire was larger than any other except the Mongol. Its intellectual core was the 'university' organized in three great mosques in Timbuktu. A quarter of the 100,000 inhabitants of the city were counted as students in its madrassahs, and classes given in teachers' homes, far more than in any European university. But he was very conscious that although his court was rich in music, pottery, poetry and scholarship, his status was unknown in Arab lands, and he wanted to bring his sub-Saharan empire into the brilliant intellectual heartland of Islamic culture. In 1324, Mansa Musa set out on a pilgrimage to Mecca.

The Golden Haj

His journey became the greatest spectacle ever mounted as he rode in splendour over 7,000km, with an entourage that started out 60,000 strong walking the trade path across the Sahara and east through the Maghreb. According to a member of the expedition, 12,000 slaves chosen for their beauty were dressed in silk or brocade tunics. Five hundred of them went ahead, each carrying a staff of pure gold. Gold was the theme of this performance, which was meant to be unforgettable. Where once a steady tide of gold dust had quietly flowed towards Egypt, Mansa Musa had conjured a tsunami of the stuff, and was happily surfing it as it swept away the cities it swamped; 9 tons of gold dust, carried on eighty camels, was brought crashing down on them.

At that time, Genoa was minting over 800kg of African gold a year.[13] Each camel was carrying Genoa's entire production for 18 months. With the best of intentions, he was about to make money worthless.

Once in Cairo, he gave 20,000 gold pieces in alms. Anyone who has been to Cairo can imagine how that might have gone. He did the same in Mecca and Medina. He spent lavishly on souvenirs and hospitality. His huge retinue was spending gold dust as if it was sand, and he paid whatever prices were demanded. Traders in these cities were convinced this was the best thing that had ever happened to them; they eventually realized that this was a mistake.

Cairo was the market where the price of gold was established. When Mansa Musa left the city, the market had been wrecked. When he moved on to Mecca and Medina, money also lost its value there. The poor whom he tried to charitably help found that the price of basic necessities soared. They would have to eat gold.

Musa concentrated on meeting the leading talents and enticing some to return with him. By the time of his journey home, it seems he had run out of gold. There was plenty of it washing around, of course, and he borrowed huge sums, at exorbitant rates of interest. Gold recovered its value as fast as he borrowed it. Moneylenders, having seen their wealth annihilated by massive inflation, saw reasons to be cheerful. Everything suddenly became cheaper than ever before, compared to gold. But when Mansa Musa finally got home, he repaid his entire debt in a single huge transfer of the dust. The value of money plunged again. His spectacular entry into the Arabian world had devastated it. The price of gold fluctuated for many other reasons, but the Egyptian historian al-Maqrizi, writing about a century later, said that it took twelve years for it to recover from this pilgrimage.[14]

But Mansa Musa had certainly succeeded in introducing his golden riches to the wider world. That may have been the second biggest mistake on record, beaten only by eating the forbidden fruit of paradise. According to the myth, Adam and Eve kick-started the Neolithic farming revolution and the punishments of physical labour and labour in childbirth. The rather better-documented haj of Mansa Musa kick-started the European plunder of the planet.

The Irresistible Lure

He had put Mali on the map. European understanding of the world was derived from classical authors and the Bible. About twenty years before the golden haj, Christian knowledge of the continents was painted on the huge *mappa mundi* in Hereford Cathedral. It is filled with biblical locations, myths and legends surrounded by a skinny encircling ocean. Africa was shown rich in fantastical creatures, not gold. Geographical knowledge was also shown on 'portolans', remarkably accurate Italian sea-charts of the Mediterranean and Black Sea, extending to the North Sea and the west coast of Africa. These displayed carefully plotted coastlines with virtually empty land. Now the very nature of the world needed to be reimagined.

In 1339, fifteen years after Mansa Musa's haj (and about two years after his death), a new kind of map appeared, drawn by an Italian-Majorcan, Angelino Dulcert, in the city of Palma. Now in the Bilbiothèque Nationale in Paris, it was a portolan which showed the interior of continents, but with very different information from a *mappa mundi*. Its largest feature, near the southern limit of the map, was a giant African potentate called Rex Melly sitting on a golden throne, described in Latin as a Saracen who ruled over a land of sands and had gold mines in great abundance. Dulcert was very well informed: he placed the Mali emperor in his correct location.

This was a turning point in the history of the world. It would open the door to a new kind of European conqueror who had a ship instead of an army. Dulcert's map referred to a River of Gold on Africa's west coast. In 1346, a Majorcan seaman, Jaume Ferrer, set off in search of it. Now forgotten (despite a statue and a street name in Palma), his was once a famous voyage, one of the precursors of the Iberian expeditions that found their way round the bulge of Africa and colonized most of the world. At the time, Ferrer's expedition attracted international interest.

For Arabs, knowledge of Mansa Musa had been more an alarming curiosity than a revelation; they had access to Mali's gold through trade routes that were centuries old. But the actual source of the gold was still a mystery. The wealth of Mali seemed unreachable. The great Moroccan travel writer, Ibn Battuta, learned as much as he could about Mansa Musa in Cairo in 1326, when the city was still reeling from the collapse of its currency. In 1350, four years after Ferrer headed for the great king's capital by ship, Ibn Battuta set out to discover it overland, attaching himself to a sequence of camel trains. It was an endurance test, travelling twenty-five days across the desert to a town made of salt, then crossing 500 miles of trackless dunes haunted by thirst, the fear of losing sight of his companions and the danger of demons. Finally, he continued south through the semi-desert of the Sahel for two weeks, eventually arriving at the royal palace. Mansa Musa was long dead, and the ruler was his brother, in a glamorous palace constructed by an Andalusian architect.

Around 1380, Ferrer appeared on an updated version of Dulcert's map drawn by two Jewish mapmakers also based in Majorca. They were employed by the King of Aragon and commissioned by Charles V of France. Dulcert's inscriptions had been in Latin for scholars, but this was written in Catalan and is known as the Catalan Atlas. It showed the long-dead Mansa Musa with a golden crown as still being alive, inspecting a disc or ball of gold and being approached by an Arab trader. It depicts only one ship in the Atlantic, and that is Ferrer's galley aiming directly towards him. A note in the secret archives of the Republic of Genoa[15] says that he had heard that the river was a collection point for gold, that the people on the shores were all engaged in that work and that it was navigable. The secret archive note said the vessel was never heard of again.

The voyage had been one of desperation, because the flow of gold out of Mali to Cairo had stopped. After Mansa Musa's death, his kingdom lost control of Timbuktu and the Niger's inland delta. The Tuareg took it over for forty years, and gold dust stopped making its traditional journey.[16] That is why economic historians now speak of The Great Bullion Famine that began in the late fourteenth century.[17]

Mali and Portugal.

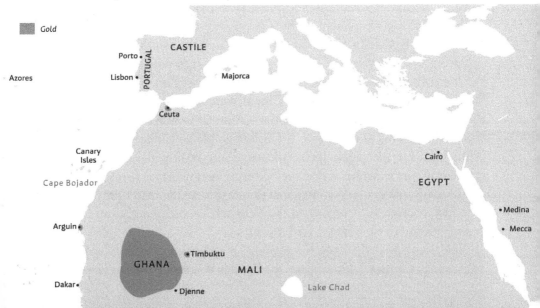

Gold or Pepper

With a desperate shortage of money, Europeans began to use other commodities instead of coin: spices imported overland from the Indies, especially dried pepper, became valued not for cooking but as currency. Foreign traders in the north German towns of the Hanseatic League were called 'peppermen'.[18]

Gold coin production in north-west Europe collapsed; gold was worth more than the coins made from it. The existing stock was flowing out to the Islamic world through Venice to buy spices, silk and other oriental goods that Europeans wanted but had little to sell in return. The small gold production of Europe, around a million gold ducats a year, flowed into the city, and of course some of it stuck: between 1428 and 1430, one of its longest established families built 'the golden house', a completely gilded palace, on the Grand Canal. But at least a quarter of the gold went east. Once the European coins arrived there, they were reminted by the Mamluks and did not return. Whoever had gold – whether they were churchmen, nobles, officials or merchants – preferred hoarding.[19] In 1450, the only functioning mint in the whole of north-west Europe was the Tower of London.

In previous eras, when gold had become scarce, the only recourse had been to either attempt a war of conquest over somewhere that had it (the Roman way) or simply to let markets decay (the early feudal way). But this time there was no possibility of sending an army to seize gold, and no enthusiasm for reverting to a world of subsistence feudalism. There were bigger problems.

Had Ferrer made it back to Majorca in 1346, his chances of survival would not have been good. In 1348, it became one of the first places in Spain to be afflicted by the Black Death. Nineteen per cent of the island's population died in the first few months, and the disease progressed to wipe out at least a third of Europe's population. By a peculiar irony, the catastrophe seems to have been triggered by the marmots that Herodotus identified as the original gold-diggers (they seem to be his 'giant ants'). It is now believed that they, or rather their fleas, living on the so-called Tibetan Plateau (a vast area from the western Himalayas to eastern China), were the original incubators of the 'yersinia pestis' bacillus – the Black Death. Animals from the easterly section are currently fingered as the source.[20] The benign global climate change that had stimulated Europe's agriculture had swung into reverse and may have driven these marmots and other rodents to flee dried out grasslands to more populated areas on the 'silk road'. Nestorian graves dating to 1338–39 in Kyrgyzstan have the first inscriptions referring to the outbreak,[21] which had begun its steady march towards a catastrophe for humanity.

The fleas travelled on new hosts, probably rats, from Central Asia down the silk road to Crimea.[22] From there, the bacillus boarded merchant ships.

Europe was very vulnerable. When its population had grown with prosperity, agriculture expanded into the most marginal lands, and was at increased risk. The climate shift now undermined it, worsened by a massive eruption at Tarawera in New Zealand. There was a terrible famine in Europe from 1315–17, in which millions starved, and draught animals and seed corn were consumed by a famished population. After years of suffering and rampant disease, the world was visited by this catastrophic epidemic. The Black Death is reckoned to have killed over 100 million Europeans. It struck in England in 1348–49. A survivor scratched on a church wall in Ashwell, Hertfordshire, '1350 – pitiful, fierce, violent'. Towns were particularly hard hit. The combination of bank failures, famine and disease meant that the financial clock stopped. England, which has good records and was reminting foreign coin, virtually minted nothing at all in the 100 years from 1363.[23] In England and Germany, silver mines stopped production.

Without new bullion, and with Arab prices rising steeply,[24] Europe's scarce gold stock was needed to fill the trade gap with the east. As trade collapsed, Northern Europe blamed the Italians for draining all their gold away. There was some justice to this: the Black Death effectively left luxuries and treasure concentrated in fewer, richer hands, and Italians understood trade better than northerners and so profited more. But fear of the plague also encouraged sinners (every Christian) to make bigger donations to the Church, renewing the ancient deal by which gold bought access to the afterlife. In the twenty years from 1378, a third of France's annual gold coinage flowed to the French Pope residing at Avignon.[25] Piety and fear drained away bullion, creating a recession.[26]

The dramatic collapse of population, and the resulting difficulty in sustaining agriculture, had a surprising effect on the south-west seaboard of Europe. The Portuguese became determined to recover by seizing wealth from Africa. The Black Death devastated the small population of this agrarian kingdom, leaving very few people to record its effect, especially as it seems to have killed about two-thirds of public notaries.[27] The population of England may have been around 4 million, and the effect of the disease there was to wipe out about half of them by 1377.[28] In Portugal it is believed, with subsequent eruptions of war and disease over the next few decades, to have killed a similar proportion. But what happened next was very different in these two ocean-facing lands. The English population did not fully recover until around 1760. The Portuguese surpassed their pre-plague population by 1530. That seems to be because they were getting rich and could afford babies.

Portugal's kings had taken on board the message of the new maps and had sent their subjects to find gold in Africa.

Portugal Breaks out of Europe

Portugal was cut off from the rest of Europe by poor inland communications which ended at the mountainous frontier with the generally hostile kingdom of Castile. It faced westwards into the endless unknown ocean, and sent its small agricultural surplus in slow, fat, high-castled ships ('cogs') to northern lands.[29] But after the Black Death there was no surplus. There was a dearth of corn from 1350.[30] Lisbon and Porto expanded rapidly and became dependent on supplies arriving by ship. When Pedro the Cruel's illegitimate son, João, was declared King of Portugal in 1385, he immediately supervised the expulsion of occupying Castilian forces, married the English noble John of Gaunt's daughter and concentrated on finding ways to make his kingdom economically and territorially secure. According to the chronicler, João's treasurer urged his master to seize the Moroccan city of Ceuta, 'a very notable city ready to be taken; and this I know principally from one of my employees that I sent there. He related to me what a large city it is, rich and beautiful.'[31] He was right. It was a terminus for the gold coming across the Sahara and spices from the Indies.

In 1415, João led an expedition across the Strait of Gibraltar to capture it in a single day's fighting. Europeans had up until then failed to establish any firm footholds on other continents. The running had been made by Norsemen, Europe's most restless inhabitants. Vikings had taken over uninhabited lands of Iceland and Greenland, but when they had tried to colonise Newfoundland around 1000 CE, they had been driven out by the indigenous people. Later in the eleventh century, Normans stormed Islamic lands in the Levant as crusaders and eventually the resulting Frankish-Norman kingdom of Outremer was also ejected by the inhabitants. Now southern Europeans who had pushed the Arabs out of Iberia were beginning their own adventure of seizure on other continents. They captured spices, gold and slaves. The Church made it difficult to enslave Christians, and Africa provided a solution to that.[32] The pursuit of gold had started a process that would eat deep into African society and allow Europeans to develop their wealth on the backs of people visibly identified as enslavable. Ceuta became a dead-end; the Islamic trade routes simply moved elsewhere, but Portugal would not let it go. King João's four sons took part in its conquest and were especially interested to find where the gold came from. One of them, the Duke Henrique of Viseu (nicknamed 'Henry the Navigator' by nineteenth-century English historians), was substantially responsible for initiating a major effort of ocean exploration.

Portugal's rulers set themselves to find a way to the source of these riches. On the way they supposed they might meet up with the legendary Prester John, who was now being said not to be in Asia but king of the Christian Nubians in Ethiopia. That way they hoped they would not only grow rich but complete the rout of Islam.[33] Year after year, Duke Henrique funded sailors to attempt to round Cape Bojador, a Saharan headland just south of the Canaries called in Arabic 'Abu Khaṭar' ('Father of Danger'). The 10-mile stretch approaching it was the shallow and tempestuous Sea of Terror, whose shore was reported to be utterly barren and lifeless, where many European ships perished, probably including Ferrer in 1346. An even bigger problem was the journey home, against the prevailing winds and currents.

For twelve years, Henrique's sailors kept returning without ever reaching Cape Bojador. He kept ploughing money into these fruitless voyages, rewarding the captains and sending them back for another go. Prospects improved in 1427 with finding the Azores, 1,500km west of Portugal, where the winds were variable.

Eventually, in 1434, after having cautiously returned from another failed voyage, his squire[34] Gil Eanes was fired up sufficiently to get past the Cape and home again. The secret was to dare to go much further from the coast, and Europeans would now launch themselves on tremendous journeys of discovery in pursuit of what they believed to be wealth. They were better equipped in their heads than in their ships. The only European ships that had ever made long ocean voyages were open Scandinavian longboats sailing for a few days to Iceland. This was a far longer voyage requiring ships offering cover and storage, but Portugal's lumbering coastal cargo vessels could not probe shallow inlets or struggle against headwinds. Ferrer's vessel had been better, but it was essentially a sailing galley.

The duke's determination was unwavering. He arranged the building of a new kind of ship, a low-profile ocean-going vessel with no forecastle and a smaller draft, carrying both a European square sail and an Arab lateen sail, able to tack and manoeuvre. It carried less cargo than a cog, was not as fast as a galley, but was seaworthy and manoeuvrable, and could enter shallow rivers. It was a ship for exploration.[35]

This 'caravel' would utterly change the world. At first it did not strike gold; instead, the ships came home laden with slaves. But in 1443, Portuguese sailors built a fortress on the island of Arguin, on the far side of Cape Bojador. They traded wheat and cloth for gold and slaves. Two years later, Portugal received the first gold to reach Europe from sub-Saharan Africa without Muslim mediation.

Now the profit of exploration was demonstrated, it was time to send out more ships. The hunt for gold that had turned Rome into an empire was now rebooted, and just as that empire had worked to turn its new subjects into Latin-speaking Romans, Europeans would work to convert the people they would subject, training them in a different religion, the languages of their new masters and the customs and values of the conquerors' 'civilization'. This time they would commandeer the whole planet.

Chapter 13

Opening the Oceans

The World's New Shape

In 2005, NASA released a stunning high-definition picture of the Earth, which it described as a blue marble. It created a great impact because of the perfection and familiarity of the image, now confirmed as the reality of our achievement in space. It was the image of our home that we wanted and expected, to cherish and protect.

Around 1450, a strikingly similar image was created by a Venetian monk, Fra Mauro. The importance of Mauro's image was its complete unfamiliarity. This was the Earth as it had never been seen or imagined. The journey that Europeans would make from Fra Mauro's drawing to NASA's photo would transform their civilization, and everyone else's.

The drawing was acquired by Afonso V of Portugal in order to guide Portugal in its quest for riches – above all, gold. It was a huge, glamorous image, shining with gold leaf, nearly 8ft in diameter (2.4 metres). It was hung in Lisbon's castle to inform and inspire explorers. But setting out to follow these coastlines was a desperate act of faith.

A fierce wind had arisen and filled Portuguese sails for over fifty years, driving them past the edges of their known world. It blew them towards gold; nature, they say, abhors a vacuum, and Europe's treasuries had been emptying since the middle of the fourteenth century. As gold became scarcer, its purchasing power roughly doubled.[1] That made the effort and expense of exploring Africa seem very worthwhile to Italian merchants and the desperately poor kings of Portugal. Since Portugal was the obvious departure coast, but lacked the financial resources to send out expeditions, Italian merchants and Portuguese kings became partners.

The voyages of Portugal's caravels down the African coast were, by 1445, approaching what seemed to be the limits of the world. They had just reached the westernmost point of Africa's bulge, modern Dakar. The Catalan Atlas only went as far south as Mali; Ferrer's attempt to find the Rio del Oro had evidently taken him to the edge of reality. No living European had sailed to within 2,000 km of the Equator.

The hunt for gold had led to a transformation in the way Europeans thought about the world and their place upon it. They had been cut off from the wider world by the collapse of the Mongol Empire, which extinguished the trade routes travelled by Marco Polo, and by the success of the Ottomans in closing Christian access to the Levant and Egypt. Most reliable geographical expertise was now in the hands of the sailors of northern Italy, who had been in the forefront of navigational knowledge since the twelfth century, and whose portolan charts showed the Mediterranean coast with a degree of accuracy that is quite astonishing – so astonishing that no one can explain how these charts were drawn.[2] The first portolan chart had probably appeared in Genoa, and the Italians had been very active in creating newly accurate images of coastlines ever since. But these did not have much impact on the way most Europeans thought about the world.

That changed quite seriously when Dulcert transfigured the portolan chart by taking an informed interest in what lay inland, and above all by including a big picture of an African potentate on his gold throne. Portugal's determined efforts to navigate towards Africa's gold revealed the scale of European ignorance. Africa needed a new shape based on empirical knowledge, and people would be sent out to obtain it. A new mindset had developed, in which modern men had to put aside biblical and Aristotelian authorities. Fra Mauro worked at a crossroads of trade and information between Europe and the Orient.

The geography that Fra Mauro rejected was shown in a version of Ptolemy's second-century *Cosmographia* produced in 1467 by Nicolaus Germanus, a monk at the Reichenbach Priory in Germany. In the world that he depicted, based on Ptolemy, nobody would ever sail around Africa to India. He showed Africa as a land mass which joins up, in the Far East, with eastern Asia. The Indian Ocean is entirely enclosed and can only be reached from Europe by travelling overland to Egypt or Arabia.

But some fifteen years earlier, Fra Mauro had given a very different picture. He was extraordinarily well informed. At a time when Portugal's navigators had still not discovered what lay south of Cape Bojador, 2,800km north of the Equator, Fra Mauro gave a good idea of the whole world that lay open to them to the south and east. His map is densely covered in writing, some of which explicitly rejects the information given in ancient and venerated texts. It was in the form of a circular *mappa mundi*, a circle of land surrounded by sea, but *mappae mundi* were illustrations of biblical geography with added fantasy. Fra Mauro could not place, as they did, Jerusalem at the centre of the Earth (for which he apologized), or find a location for the Garden of Eden (he put it in a circle beyond the world). Nor did he show the customary assemblies of exotic African inhabitants: he had no place for people without noses or mouths, for giants and people with four eyes or those whose upper lips are so huge that they can pull them up over their heads to serve as sunshades. The old world of mysteries, where troglodytes rode on stags, Artabatitae fell on their faces as they walked along and Africa was occupied by men with four feet and the heads of dogs, was abolished. He had investigated a wide range of sources, and said these things were not true (though sea monsters survived). Even if they were true, they were not interesting. What was true, and was interesting, is spelt out in 3,000 inscriptions. These are not in Latin, the language of book learning, but in his own tongue. Among the dense mass of information is the attested certainty that there was gold to be found in the 'gold gulf' that stretched from the Senegal River to the inland delta of the Niger and its gold-bearing sands, as well as in the West African rivers, in the kingdom of 'Museneli' and in 'Tombatu' (Mali and Timbuktu), and in Mauretania (north-west Africa), the Sahara and south-west Africa. The really substantial gold wealth of the world is further east, according to this map – in the rivers of Yunnan, in Quanziou, in Java and Sumatra, in the Mekong delta and in India. And he shows how to get there.

The knowledge of these places had once been carried back by travellers over land. Fra Mauro showed that it was possible to reach them in ships. He showed Africa as being triangular and gave evidence that a junk had sailed west round the Cape of Good Hope around 1420. That ship was said to have come from the Indian Ocean, which Ptolemy had said was closed off, but which was here shown as connected to the rest of the sea and extensively navigated: 'Without any doubt … this southern and southwestern part is navigable, and that the Sea of India is an ocean and not an inland sea. This is what is said by all those who sail this sea and live in those islands.' Forget the old authorities; new knowledge had arrived. The map shows the rivers of India and the cities of China, with Java and Japan. It lays out what was known from Marco Polo and more recent Italian merchant-explorers.[3] It has at the top neither East (as *mappae mundi* did) nor North (as the Catalan Atlas did). The picture of it here is inverted to make it recognizable. The top of the map is actually south, like a sea chart. That made plain its purpose.

The First Ocean Navigations

This huge and fabulous image in Lisbon castle displayed in vast detail an encyclopaedic vision that was designed to replace biblical and classical authority, the very basis of European knowledge. It demanded that the king's navigators must leave behind that certainty and ride their frail craft through tempests and hurricanes on voyages of unknown length to reach unguessable prizes. They would do it and go far beyond even Fra Mauro's understanding. Iberians launched themselves on an epic adventure that opened up worlds that were completely new to them. The great heroes of Europe's ancestral memory such as Caesar and Alexander were suddenly seen to have walked in very restricted paths, knowing nothing of the worlds beyond the oceans. It was as though Europeans had been living out their lives, fighting their epic battles and creating their stories about gods and heroes on a beautiful, curtained stage, from which the drapes now fell away, revealing a vast terrain of strange landscapes gleaming with the promise of gold and infinite wealth.

Columbus's discovery of the lands of the Caribbean in 1492, and Vasco da Gama's discovery of the sea route to India five years later, began a sequence of catastrophes for the discovered and the discoverers. The desperate pursuit of gold across the world's oceans created colonial enterprises that destroyed the civilizations of the plundered and the economies of the plunderers. For the latter, it created economic disaster, first splendidly enhancing and then wrecking the economies of Portugal and Spain. It was also a human and cultural catastrophe, as the colonizers developed an appetite for racial enslavement which led to the destruction of entire societies. For the people who were robbed, their experience of being conquered has still not run its course. They had seen themselves as part of the landscape, in societies guided by deeply embedded authorities. The land was now removed from them, their authorities were cast down and they were subjected to an alien system of belief and law, conducted in alien tongues. They have had to invent new identities in a 'post-colonial' world that normally offers them lives of poverty, violence and powerlessness.

It all flowed from the hunt for gold.

Europe's First African Gold Mine

By 1460, it was known that the coast of Africa turned east after completing its great westward bulge, but the progress of exploratory voyages was painfully slow and unprofitable until they arrived on the so-called 'Gold Coast', modern Ghana, in 1471. The small fishing villages they found were happy to trade ivory, food and gold, and in 1482 the Portuguese built a castle, São Jorge da Mina, the first major European outpost in tropical Africa.[4] Its name, 'St George of the Mine', was designed to suggest that there was some serious mining enterprise here, but in fact it was less effort than that. The gold was being brought to the settlers from the inland forest where people extracted it from sands and shafts in huge quantities. Mali's western forests had been home, since before the eighth century, to an extensive gold-producing farming society whose settlements were protected with large earthworks, and which were part of an Islamic trade network. The gold was taken by Muslim traders, the Wangara from the upper

Niger, who had until recently been sending it by camel across the Sahara. Their trade route had stretched south-west to this coast, where they acquired slaves. But by the time the Portuguese arrived, Mali's empire had collapsed. The forest settlements had been abandoned in what was probably a population collapse associated with the Black Death.[5] That may well have played a significant part in Europe's fourteenth and fifteenth-century gold famine. The gold was still there, but the Islamic trade route, which had probably carried the disease, was not much more than a memory.

The forest dwellers were now induced to deal with the Portuguese.[6] It was not a comfortable place for Europeans, as temperatures remain around 27 degrees centigrade day and night all year long, but life expectancy on land, despite diseases such as malaria and smallpox, may well have been higher than on board Portuguese ships.

The Portuguese built their fortress with the objective of enrichment by trade. They sent home a shipload of gold a month, much of which was acquired in exchange for slaves purchased inexpensively from traders further down the coast. The slaves exchanged for the gold were probably used as a labour force for the regeneration of the local gold coast economy. The Portuguese had finally arrived in a region where gold was well known and plentiful. It was the mark of status, power and divine connection in the communities they encountered. It was also so plentiful that it could be bought more cheaply than silver.

Europe's gold famine was over. A few decades later, this settlement would supply Portugal with around 170,000 fine gold doubloons a year. But there was more to be had if the ships could just go further. A century earlier, Marco Polo had written about the Malay Peninsula, where 'gold is so plentiful that no one who did not see it could believe it'. Fra Mauro's map, following the celebrated traveller, describes Colombo as rich in gold, as well as Sumatra (where there was also pepper).

Sailing East

Europeans had now been given an approximate physical geography of Asia, but no human geography. They understood the world to be occupied by Christians, Jews, Muslims and pagans; they had no concept of the people of South-East Asia or what gold meant there.[7] For Hindus it was wealth, but above all it was a sacramental treasure, spiritual wealth, worn on sacred occasions, gifted to temples, stored as heirlooms and presented as a blessing to family and loved ones. Indian literature describes offerings of vast quantities of the metal. Marco Polo visited what he said was the largest island in the world, Java.[8] So did the fourteenth-century Arab ethnographic traveller Ibn Battuta.[9] They were both drawn by its reputation for golden wealth. The great Indian epic *Ramayana*, written down around 300 BCE, says: 'Explore Java Dwipa carefully, it is adorned by seven kingdoms, a gold and silver island, rich in gold mines.' Java Dwipa was a whole archipelago: early Sanskrit inscriptions were more explicit. They referred to Suwarna Dwipa, which means 'Island of Gold'; Sumatra.[10]

How could Europeans actually lay hands on this gold? The flow of gold was normally overland from Europe towards Asia. But now there was the sea, the caravel and a map. Could the flow be reversed?

A new king of Portugal, João II, had come to the throne in 1481, the year before the castle at São Jorge da Mina was built, and he was determined not to let the project rest there. His noble families had younger sons who needed to find chivalric adventures to pay their way. His working population were living in poverty. His seamen were the boldest and most capable in the world. And his kingdom had been created by crusades against Islam. He offered a campaign to satisfy them all: extend their sea-power to surround the Muslims, join forces with the fabled East African Christian kingdom of Prester John to finish them off, and lay hands on all the gold of Africa. In pursuit of this goal, he gave rich rewards to seamen to go out year after year on fruitless efforts to find the route Fra Mauro offered. They planted stone pillars, *padrãos*, to mark their progress: in 1483, one was placed at the mouth of the Congo River, and another further south on the coast of Angola. That one has survived. An inscription on it reads: 'In the era of 6681 years from the creation of the world, 1482 years since the birth of Our Lord Jesus, the most High and Excellent and Mighty Prince, King D. João II of Portugal, sent Diogo Cão squire of his house to discover this land and plant these pillars.'[11]

Seaborne Artillery

To ensure their success at plunder, they carried brand new military power, guns of a kind previously unknown. Hand-held gunpowder weapons had been used in China since the thirteenth century; a 'hand-cannon' made before 1288 was excavated in the far north-east of China in the 1970s. The Mongols were using the same kind of weapons and carried this technology to India and the Arab world as well as Korea and Japan.[12] But when Fra Mauro made his map, gunpowder weapons were being transformed in a literally shattering way. In 1449, the Portuguese king had invented the post of 'Superintendent of the Artillery', with the specific intention of ensuring that his forces, on land and at sea, would have the very latest in heavy cannon. The technology's power was demonstrated in 1453, when Orban, a Transylvanian iron founder, provided a supergun to the Ottoman sultan for use in his attack on Constantinople. He had already offered to build it for the Byzantine emperor to use for defence, but had been turned down. It took three months to build the giant weapon, deep in Anatolia, and it was then dragged by sixty oxen, together with smaller cannon, the 250km to Constantinople. After a barrage of forty days, the mighty walls of the Byzantine capital were smashed.[13] The gun founder and his crew were killed by a gun exploding, but that is a footnote in a different story. The history of the world was changed.

For the time being, there was no longer such a thing as an impregnable stronghold. European, and especially Portuguese, genius was urgently applied to making this power portable. Cannon could be, and were, carried on ships. It did not take long for the people of the Indian Ocean to learn what that meant. Once Portuguese explorer Bartolomeu Dias finally succeeded in sailing round the southern tip of Africa in 1488, the way was open. Ptolemy's picture of the world was soon proved wrong; the whole world's seas were regions of a single ocean. In 1497, four Portuguese vessels under Vasco da Gama carried these weapons from Portugal into the Indian Ocean.

The Great Trade Ocean

In 1492, Columbus had unknowingly stumbled upon the threshold of an unimagined world that blocked his journey, reaching almost from pole to pole in the western ocean. Five years later, da Gama expanded Portugal's reach into the vast magnificence of the Orient. Suddenly, the people of Western Europe had extraordinary access to the treasure of the whole globe. Both Columbus and da Gama shared the general European belief that their lives could be transformed by gold. The public justifications spoke of extending Christianity; the sovereigns of Spain and Portugal were, in their own eyes, crusaders. But these voyages were powered by the dream and expectation of gold.

The Portuguese understanding was made plain in *The Lusiads*, the great literary creation of a treasure-fleet sailor. The author, Luís Vaz de Camões, believed he had to make up for the bare literacy of Vasco da Gama, Portugal's home-grown Alexander. Camões had sailed for India in 1553 on the great new adventure that had transformed his tiny country into a world-spanning enterprise; transformed it, and by the time of his voyage, already broken it. There were four ships in Camões's fleet, but his was the only one to survive. He recounts, unreliably, that as da Gama set out from Portugal, an old man on the shore foretold in a clear voice where he was taking his crew and his nation.

'What visions of kingdoms and gold-mines
Will you guide them to infallibly? ...
Already in this vainglorious business
Delusions are possessing you,
Already ferocity and brute force
Are labelled heroism and valour ...
The devil take the man who first put
Dry wood on the waves with a sail.'[14]

Gold was not, after all, there for the taking, and though Camões's object was to celebrate his country's heroic adventure, he could not be blind to the dark side of the hunger that drove it. The existing Pacific trade network spanned thousands of miles of ocean, from the East African coast to India, Malaysia and the 'Spice Islands'. Its great wealth owed much to the gold mines of Zimbabwe, which were quite unknown to Europeans; the ruins of Great Zimbabwe, which once may have had 17,000 inhabitants, have yielded artefacts from Syria and China.[15] The way that trade functioned is barely understood: the archaeology and history of pre-European Africa–India trade is in its infancy. It has been suggested that more than 20 million ounces of gold were extracted from Zimbabwe over some 2,000 years, firstly from shallow deposits across the Zimbabwean plateau and placer gold from the tributaries of the Zambezi River, and then from shafts up to 30 metres deep.[16] This gold was used as uncoined currency, along with ivory, copper, iron and salt. But around the time Vasco da Gama arrived on the Swahili coast, Great Zimbabwe seems to have been collapsing, its gold mines probably exhausted.

The official Portuguese object was to connect with Prester John and conquer the whole Islamic world. (Prester John was now understood to be the ruler of Ethiopia, as an Ethiopian priest had appeared in Rome; the Pope sent him on to Lisbon). This conquest was to be effected by a new kind of crusader. Like human crusaders, they bore a cross on their fronts, but these cruzados were gold coins. They were equivalent to ducats, except for the image on them, but the image was the point. Venice's ducats showed the Doge and said 'Venice'. It was important that the King of Portugal's representatives used coins displaying his name and arms. Some have been found in the wreck of a ship from da Gama's second voyage.[17] These crusaders were intended to conquer Islam and Venice simultaneously, filling the ships with spices, cutting out the Arab and Italian middlemen and being replaced with much more gold from Northern Europe.

The Portuguese were quite correct in assuming that they would be dealing with people who understood gold as having trade value. They had entered the world's greatest trade network, thirty times larger than the Mediterranean, which had for millennia connected Egypt with China, the East Indies with the Persian Gulf. Malacca was larger than Venice. Half of the world's trade passed peacefully across these seas. After tricky and baffling first encounters, da Gama reached the Sheikh of Mozambique, and received this wealthy potentate and his attendants with all due civility on board his vessel. He told the Sheikh they wanted to trade for pepper, cinnamon and ginger; he said they could pay with gold and silver, but since they had very little, he lied that it was in other, non-existent ships. According to Gaspar Correia, who arrived in India around 1512 and became an historian, the Sheikh said that 'with gold and silver they would obtain what they sought all over the world'.[18] They were taken to be Moslems from Turkey, and when that was obviously not so, the Sheikh distanced himself. They sailed on to their historic goal, India, but when they reached Calicut in gold-rich Kerala, they were greeted by a familiar tongue, with two Tunisian merchants who spoke Castilian and Genoese.[19] The Portuguese had no idea of where they were and had brought trade gifts of no interest. They gave the ruler a few cloaks and hats, some sugar and honey and so on – that might have been satisfactory in Africa, but not here. The ruler sent a message asking for better payment: 'Vasco da Gama, a gentleman of your household, came to my country, whereat I was much pleased. My country is rich in cinnamon, cloves, ginger, pepper and precious stones. That which I ask of you in exchange is gold, silver, corals and scarlet cloth.'[20] Da Gama ended up kidnapping some locals out of anger and set off with what spices he could buy, arriving home in 1498 after a grim voyage against the wind, having lost one ship and about 115 of the 170 men who set out.

It was regarded as a triumph. They were carrying 6 tons of pepper and a fair quantity of cinnamon and ginger, and they did not spend much gold and silver for it. Their profit was officially computed in Lisbon as some 6,000 per cent of the expedition's cost.

Spices

Spices such as pepper, cinnamon and ginger could only be grown in the region of the Indian Ocean and were the key ingredients of the ready-mixed blends sold in Europe for cooking. They were used to give status to the table.[21] They were considered essential to a good and healthy diet, and in an age when epidemic disease was a constant threat, no one with money dared ignore advice about a healthy diet. Better-off people were thus accustomed to far spicier cooking than we have today. The Earl of Oxford's accounts for 1431–32 show that a pound of pepper cost as much as a whole pig, and a family in Shropshire spent as much on spices as they did on beef and pork combined.[22] It was the same all over Europe, which was how Venice had become so rich. But now Venice had been elbowed aside. A Portuguese apothecary went to Malacca in 1512 because 'Whoever is Lord of Malacca has his hand on the throat of Venice'.[23]

So began Portugal's trade for spices, in which human lives were simply not counted as part of the cost. In 1500, 1,200 men were dispatched on thirteen heavily armed ships led by Pedro Àlvares Cabral. Four ships were lost on the way. Once in Calicut, more than fifty Portuguese were massacred in a surprise attack, to which Cabral responded by seizing the cargoes of ten anchored Arab merchant ships, burning the vessels and killing the 600 or so aboard. Cabral used his cannon to demand that the ruler of Calicut stop trading with Muslims.

Only six of Cabral's ships returned, and two of them were empty; the Portuguese lives lost were never assessed, but were at least 500. But the spices they collected were gathered so cheaply that there was still a profit, and the Crown made over 800 per cent on the voyage. Cabral's demonstration of ruthless firepower and lack of concern for human life set the tone for everything that followed over the next four centuries.

Vasco da Gama's second voyage, in 1502, was a military expedition with a much bigger and better-armed fleet. The object was to seize control of the trading ports. The lesson of Ceuta, that seizing a trading post simply meant the trade flowed somewhere else, had not been understood. The Indian Ocean spice trade dealt in huge volumes, and Europe bought perhaps 25 per cent or less of it, but Europeans did not appreciate that fact. All the Portuguese understood was that Calicut was hostile and the wealth of its spice trade flowed through many hands to Venice: their object was to capture it at source and cut Venice out.

In 1502, the Portuguese fleet of twenty ships arrived at Kilva (Quiloa), an island off the coast of modern Tanzania whose sultan controlled the wealthy and highly organized trade of the Swahili coast, including what we know as Kenya, Tanzania, northern Mozambique and Zanzibar. The sultan's people had small firearms, but da Gama gave an immediate demonstration of the power of his artillery and made it plain that he could, and if displeased would, 'in one single hour reduce your city to ashes, and if I chose to kill your people, they would all be burned in the fire'.[24]

Da Gama did not tell the sultan that before setting out he had been titled 'Admiral of the Seas of Arabia, Persia, India and all the Orient' or that he had gone there to turn this great ruler into a vassal. His mission had been explained by King Manuel as he dispatched him to find the sea route to India in 1497: 'We will wrest new kingdoms, states and wealth by force of arms from the hands of the infidels.' So the sultan was told that 'he should become the vassal of the King of Portugal so as to remain in friendship with him, and under his protection, paying a tribute of five hundred mithqals of gold'. The mithqal is an Islamic unit of weight, and the demand was for over 2kg. It was made clear that this was simply a down payment. To establish clearly the arrival of this new supreme kingship, the admiral sent the sultan a standard of the Portuguese royal arms. Correia records:

> 'This standard was raised upon a spear and carried in a boat accompanied by others containing many people in gay clothing, with trumpets; and the King came to receive it on the beach, saluting it as though he recognised in it a sign of his protection. He took it in his own hands, and carried it for a good space, and then delivered it to a chief man of the Moors, who went round all the city, and the people behind him, shouting Portugal! Portugal! At last, it was placed in sight of our ships on a tower of the King's houses. When this solemnity was ended the admiral took leave of the King.'[25]

The sultan's gold tribute was given a cash value, but it was not turned into spending money. The Portuguese valued gold for its spiritual meaning as much as its buying power, and once back in Portugal it was turned into a monstrance for the new Jeronimós monastery at Belém, which was being built from a 5 per cent tax on the profits of private trade by officers of da Gama's fleet. The sailors could go there and venerate the consecrated host in its fabulous case, which blends the brilliant skill of the goldsmith with the indestructible metal plundered from East Africa. It is, inadvertently, a memorial to the rich culture of the cities of Swaziland and to the vaulting ambition of the Portuguese Christian king.

The Role of Slaughter

The savagery with which da Gama tried to establish his will in India was breathtaking. It was meant as a demonstration of the Christian European impunity of armed supremacy. Having heavily bombarded Calicut, da Gama seized a newly arrived Moorish trade fleet, stole the fabric and rice it carried, and cut off the hands, ears and noses of all their crews. He put these all into one boat along with the ruler's emissary, whose ears, nose and hands were cut off and strung round his neck. He then ordered all the mutilated sailors to have their feet tied together. They had no hands, but they might gnaw the ropes, so he had their teeth knocked down their throats. These wretched men were then 'heaped up in a vessel, mixed up with the blood which streamed from them; and he ordered mats and dry leaves to be spread over them, and the sails to be set for the shore, and the vessel set on fire: and there were more than eight hundred

Moors; and the small vessel with all the hands and ears, was also sent on shore under sail, without being fired'.[26] He won trade at the mouths of his cannon.

Less than twenty years after da Gama's first arrival, Portugal had seized control of all the sea routes of East Africa, the Indian Ocean, the South China Sea and the Persian Gulf.

The Profit

Portugal had everything, but it had nothing.

In 2008, a geologist working for the diamond mining company De Beers came across the wreck of a heavily armed Portuguese ship, the *Bom Jesus*, buried in the sands of Namibia on a forbidden diamond-mining shore.[27] It is the oldest and richest wreck found in sub-Saharan Africa, and it was laden with thousands of gold coins and hundreds of copper ingots. Many coins were newly minted gold Portugueses, but there was also a fortune in Spanish gold. None of this was the profit of the voyage: the *Bom Jesus* was on its outward trip. The gold was never supposed to come back. The Spanish coins were part of a loan from Spanish investors, while the copper ingots were an investment from the German bankers, the house of Fugger. It was all to buy spices.

In September 2018, another wreck turned up, at Cascais, the entrance to Lisbon's river. This was the counterpart to the *Bom Jesus*, a ship that was arriving home with whatever it had managed to win from its expedition. It had taken gold, and returned with its massive artillery protecting a cargo of peppercorns, cowrie shells and ceramics.[28]

This was a trade that had gone badly wrong, even from the point of view of the aggressors. Profits and people were swallowed up in guarding the 15,000 miles of sea lanes between Goa and Lisbon. In one year alone, Portugal lost 300 ships. Many of the sailors were criminals, and the voyage was their punishment. They slept like slaves on crowded decks, without bunks or hammocks. They drank dirty water and ate salted meat and hardtack biscuits infested with weevils and the droppings of rodents, supplemented with some fish, oil, cheese and beans. Thousands died from dysentery, typhoid and shipwreck, but even more from scurvy. Half the men in a fleet to India would be unlikely to survive. The voice of Portugal's women was ultimately to be preserved and celebrated in *fado*, the songs of love, longing and loss to the sea, and in a unique national culture of *saudade*, nostalgia and melancholic longing.[29] The supplies needed for the ships were themselves a national sacrifice; it is commonly said that all available beef was salted for the sailors and only offal was left in the port. The people of Porto are still referred to as '*tripeiros*', tripe eaters, and it is still served in many ordinary restaurants.[30]

At first it had all seemed to go very well. Vasco da Gama's first cargo of spices sold at an extraordinary profit, creating serious alarm in Venice and encouraging the Portuguese king to believe that his fortune was assured. But it became clear that to convert spices into gold required an international trading hub with good market access and experienced merchants. Portugal had none of this, so the trade centre was established in Antwerp, where it was hard to control what happened. Da Gama's second fleet took its cargo there, but Antwerp dealers were reluctant to surrender gold for what the Portuguese said was pepper, and the price collapsed dramatically.[31] Things did improve, and it is said that by 1510 the Portuguese throne was pocketing a million cruzados yearly, 3½ tons of gold, from the spice trade. Venice's cargoes of pepper and spices in the first few years of the century had fallen by almost 80 per cent, and by 1510 it had stopped selling pepper at all.[32] By the middle of the century, pepper contributed about half of all Portugal's earnings from the Low Countries. Gold was used to buy copper from Central Europe, which was worth almost three times as much when traded on the Malabar coast, and the pepper and other spices it bought tripled in value when they came back to Europe. A ship that started out with copper, silver and gold costing 24,000 cruzados brought home spices that sold for over 190,000.[33] But Portugal did not have the expertise to run an international market servicing all of Europe, so the Antwerp enterprise went awry and its earnings somehow managed to fall dramatically by mid-century. It was bankrupted in 1549.

Nor did Portugal have control of the source, and England and the Netherlands eventually moved in. Portugal did not prosper in the sixteenth century. Farms and industries decayed for want of manpower, so the government was forced to buy food and other necessities abroad. In the first fifty years of Portugal's spice trade, the value of wages there (an indication of national prosperity) fell by around two-thirds.[34] Meanwhile, Italian cities used their mercantile skills to build new European markets for other luxury goods from the Orient, and wages in Italy did not fall at all in the sixteenth century.[35]

Spices became a shrinking market. The European assumption that they were in such demand that they compared with gold soon turned out to be a mistake. For reasons which are much debated, from around the middle of the sixteenth century, Europeans simply lost the passion to buy pepper and other spices at luxury prices.[36]

Today, Vasco da Gama, unlike Columbus, is far from a household name outside Portugal. The cultures of the Indian Ocean were resilient and are largely still there. It was reported in 1992 that, although the largest city in Goa carries his name, working people in Calcutta suppose Vasco da Gama was an American businessman or an Indian king.[37] That report came on the 500th anniversary of one other great effort to seize the gold of the East, and the voyager who made that trip is far more extensively remembered, even though he never arrived at his objective.

The Alternative Route

He did not need to arrive there. Cristóbal Colón (Columbus) knew, as everyone else knew, that the Earth is round. It was therefore possible, in theory, to sail west to Asia instead of bothering with going round Africa. He set out to do that, with one overriding purpose in mind: the discovery and acquisition of gold. In the journal of his first voyage, he uses the word 137 times. That is nearly twice as often as 'God', 'Jesus', 'Our Lord' and 'the Church' combined, and gives a clear idea of his priorities. On 4 March 1493, having arrived back at the Tagus River, he was finally able to send a report of what he had found and stressed the importance of gold over anything else – though of course he gave the gold a higher purpose. He said that his aim had been to enable the monarchy to finance a new crusade, and that he had done.[38] After his final voyage, he wrote: 'Gold is most excellent. Whoever has it may do what he wishes in this world.'[39] And that was the reason that he was allowed to venture on a potentially suicidal voyage into the unknown, with (so far as we know) no previous experience of commanding a ship.

The first-century geographer Strabo said that he knew of people who had tried to sail west to Asia, but they had failed through want of resolution and supplies. The Florentine physician Toscanelli provided a calculation to the King of Portugal in 1474 that the Chinese city of Quinsay (Hangzhou) was about 5,000 nautical miles west of Lisbon.[40] Some three years later, the young Genoese Columbus joined his younger brother, a chart-maker, in Lisbon. He worked selling books and charts and learning the science of them. He went to sea, travelling to the new fort at São Jorge da Mina, which delivered gold to Lisbon. And he wrote to Toscanelli to clarify what could be achieved by sailing west.

The great question, of course, was how great a percentage of the Earth's globe was shown on Fra Mauro's map? How wide was the ocean that completed the sphere? Ptolemy's geography said the land mass covered half the Earth; the ocean stretched for 180 degrees on the other side. But Toscanelli agreed with Fra Mauro that Ptolemy had been proved wrong by Marco Polo. That meant, in his view, that the easternmost point of China was 30 degrees closer to Europe than Ptolemy had allowed. And 1,500 miles yet further east, said Marco Polo, lay Cipangu (Japan). Marco Polo had evidently heard tales from Chinese merchants: 'People on the Island of Zipangu [Japan] have tremendous quantities of gold. The King's palace is roofed with pure gold, and his floors are paved in gold two fingers thick.' This might have given a misleading impression – in reality, it looks as if it would have taken nearly twenty years for Japan to produce the 5,500kg of gold used in the Bangkok Buddha,[41] while Portugal was importing over 400kg a year from its Gold Coast base at São Jorge da Mina alone, twice as much as Japan produced.[42]

Marinus of Tyre, who had done the mathematics on which Ptolemy drew, thought Europe and Asia covered 225 degrees of the globe, which Columbus believed was more credible than Ptolemy's 180 degrees. The eastward crossing thus shrank to 135 degrees. Of course, fifteenth-century sailors also had the advantage of starting from the Canaries, which were unknown to the ancients and 25 degrees closer to Asia. That left just 105 degrees of ocean to manage. Extending Asia further to the east on the basis of Marco Polo's evidence, and recognizing that Japan was closer than China, Columbus reckoned there were only 68 degrees between the Canaries and Japan. On further reflection, he thought Marinus of Tyre had miscalculated the size of degrees and the ocean crossing was really only 60 degrees. It is generally said today that Columbus was a great navigator, but he evidently believed that a degree of longitude at the Canaries was 45 nautical miles; it is more like 53.

There are not actually 68 degrees of longitude between the Canaries and Tokyo; there are 205. Columbus told his crew they only had to cover 750 leagues, 2,400 nautical miles, to strike land. The distance west to Japan was actually about 11,000 nautical miles.

We all make mistakes. Had he understood the scale of his error he would never have set out. But of course, having sailed rather further than he expected, he made landfall 3,000 nautical miles from the Canaries. And there, just as he had anticipated, he found gold. No European yet knew about America, but that gold was enough to launch an invasion and refashion the world.

Chapter 14

A New World to Plunder

The Gold of the Taino

The fierce wind that had filled the sails of Portuguese caravels and pushed them south around Africa into the unfamiliar seas of Asia became an easterly hurricane at the backs of Spanish galleons from Seville once Columbus reported that he had found gold on the island of Haiti, which means 'high and mountainous'. He renamed it The Spanish Island (La Isla Española/Hispaniola). Colonization by changing the name and identity of locations is one of the fundamental ways in which Europeans have taken possession of the world. It serves to obliterate ancestral memory and create new realities. The great discoverer never had any idea of where Hispaniola was on the surface of the globe, but that hardly mattered. As late as 1504, he worked out, using a fortuitous eclipse, that at noon in Jamaica, the time in Cadiz was 7.15 pm. In fact, it is 5.50 pm,[1] and he had made an error in longitude of over 1,200 nautical miles. Historians have puzzled over how he could have made such a huge mistake. Perhaps it was due to misreading his tables,[2] but it fitted neatly with his belief that he had found his way to the Orient. He remained convinced for the rest of his life that Cuba was part of Asia.[3] Setting out on his final voyage in 1502, he expected to meet Vasco da Gama, closing a circle in which there was no continent between Cathay and the Canaries. It is entirely due to Columbus's confusion that for centuries we have called the indigenous people of America 'Indians'.

From Columbus's point of view, what mattered was that he did find gold. That was the purpose of his voyage. But the meaning of gold here was utterly incomprehensible to the Spanish. They had found islands on the edge of what they would eventually realize was a globe-spanning wall between them and Asia. Here there were great ancient civilizations, empires and huge cities which had grown and were flourishing without using money and where exchange was conducted over huge distances without currency, traders or prices. It was an alternative reality in which gold could be of great cultural importance but had no intrinsic exchange value. The Spanish tried very hard to interpret what they saw in terms they could understand, but that could never be possible.

The cultures of South America and Mesoamerica (roughly what we now call Central America) inhabited conceptual worlds that had no connection to

Eurasia. Some of these lands were controlled by organized states – the Aztecs, Incas, Mayas – and each had its own distinctive material culture, but there was a shared pattern of exchange without money and a shared understanding of the central importance of gold to the proper functioning of the world.

In that understanding, all matter – animal, vegetable, mineral, solid and liquid – participates in an immaterial living consciousness. Gold is the trace of connection between this material world and the totality of the cosmos. One metaphor for it was the sweat or excrement of the sun; another was the menstrual blood of the Mother. It is a conduit for the energy of life, and it connects the dead to the place of ancestors. Specially trained people could connect their own consciousness to the totality of consciousness, and work human thought into the gold. The pieces that resulted, which we call offerings, talismans or marks of status, were ways of pinning humans and nature together in their shared life. Every community in the whole of this territory would be found to have such golden objects. In the case of great lords, there would be many of them. That is not very different from the very first European idea of gold and is why the tomb of the Lord of Sipán in Peru looks so similar, in its use of gold, to the tomb of the Lord of Varna in Bulgaria.

But between the times of Varna and Columbus, Europeans had changed rather a lot. Since the days of Sumer, goods had been exchanged through traders for profit. They negotiated prices described with gold. Gold now had no transcendental meaning to Christians until it passed into the hands of the Church. It could be, and often was, made sacred, but that was a transformation performed by Christian magic.

In December 1492, having already seen that the native Taino people[4] had some golden objects, Columbus was entertained by a local 'king', Guacanagari. '*Guaca*' was a word signifying a powerful object of copper-gold alloy, *guanín*. These came from the Tairona, and '*Guachero*' is now the word in Colombia for a robber of indigenous tombs. Columbus was given feasts and gold – he mentions jewellery, a gold-decorated mask and a golden crown.[5]

The Elimination of Haiti

Columbus returned to Spain to declare his astonishing finds and claim his status as the Admiral of the Ocean Sea. Having lost a ship by grounding, and cannibalized it to build a fort, he left behind about thirty-eight men with instructions to trade for gold. They had no women and little to exchange. Ten months later, he arrived back to find that his colonists had been killed. The local chief blamed his neighbours and joined Columbus on a punitive expedition. The Taino of Haiti had no effective protection (no iron, no steel) and only volcanic glass blades. They were not able to offer much resistance.[6] But the most effective weapon that the Admiral of the Ocean Sea brought against them was one he did not even know he carried – pathogens. He had imported some animals, including eight hogs, and 1,500 settlers. They landed in December. It is impossible to know what they carried (whether smallpox, swine fever, typhus or malaria). Whatever the cause, many colonists, including Columbus himself, became seriously sick. He spent several weeks unable to function.[7] The effect on the Taino was devastating; 'all through the land the Indians lay dead everywhere. The stench was very great and pestiferous.'[8]

Columbus blamed the sickness and death of his colonists on Haiti itself:[9] the trees and grasses, the animals and insects of Haiti were different from those in Christian Europe, and evidently bad for their health. The old Roman Imperial programme had been to transform conquered peoples into a new population modelled on and by their conquerors. Columbus now determined on a more radical programme of cultural cleansing while terraforming the occupied territory, converting not just the inhabitants but their habitat.[10] Goodbye Haiti; hello Hispaniola. If Spaniards were to succeed in their mission of extracting the gold, they had to survive, and to do that, they believed, they needed to produce European food.[11] Christianity demanded bread and wine for communion (only wheat flour was permitted for the purpose), so wheat and vines were swiftly planted, along with olives and many other crops. It was also believed that the physical differences between Europeans and Amerindians were a result of their different diets. Without European food, it was feared Spaniards would become as beardless as the natives, which would make it impossible to stay there.

The Taino had known their lands and sea as 'the world', 'the earth' and 'the mother'. That was now to be replaced with a replica of a landscape which they had never seen, of which they were not part and where they would not survive. Within a few years, sheep and goats, pigs, cattle and horses, as well as European vegetables and other plants, were changing the 'New World'. Their arrival was accompanied by unplanned invasions of ships' cats and rats and malaria-carrying mosquitoes[12] breeding in water barrels. They disembarked and began to reform the island and, with remarkable speed, the continent, colonizing far faster than humans. New breeds of dogs arrived and indigenous ones, bonded to indigenous households, disappeared.[13] It was even believed that settlement was making the climate more bearable to colonists.[14]

By a grotesque irony, known today as 'the Columbus exchange', the Taino may have inadvertently and unwittingly brought about the deaths of perhaps 5 million Europeans through a pathogen of their own. Columbus had taken men and women to display at the royal court, and sexual encounters followed. The mixing of relatively harmless variations of the spirochete *Treponema pallidum* present in Europeans and Native Americans appears to have produced an aggressive new form, syphilis. It seems likely that its presence in Europe was multiplied by the entry of some of Columbus's men into the Spanish army at the siege of Naples in 1495, and it spread through Europe in a terrifying form that killed within a few months.[15]

From 1494, when Columbus moved on to Cuba, the Spanish in Hispaniola stopped treating the Taino as human. One modern historian has suggested that all the gold that the natives had accumulated in the previous millennium was seized in two or three years.[16] Parasites living entirely in the moment, the Spanish destroyed the human resources on which they depended. In the next few years, a campaign of subjugation and enslavement in pursuit of gold effectively exterminated the islanders.

A new way of living was introduced for the colonists. Architecture and the layout of communal structures is a representation of the community's fundamental cosmological space, and the colonial town founded in 1496 in Hispaniola, Santo Domingo, laid out a physical three-dimensional structure of power and purpose from the other side of the ocean. It was designed on a grid pattern: regular parallel streets and a central plaza with buildings with meanings the Taino would have to learn: cathedral, town hall, governor's palace and official buildings. The gridiron would be the fundamental structure of the Spanish Empire and eventually the ground-plan of Spain's imperial palace, the Escorial. The supposed instrument of torture of St Lawrence, the actual instrument of torture for the Taino, the gridiron was also the basis of urban planning. This would become the archetype of Spanish colonial cities. The idea was to live in a military camp. Columbus and some of his men had been in just such a camp in 1491, Santa Fé, which had been the temporary base for the capture of Granada from the Moors.[17] A fortified rectangle with two main axes and four gates, it set out precisely and clearly how the Spanish viewed their place here. This would eventually be the archetype city for much of America.

Slavery

In 1499, the settlers had found gold deposits in the central mountains of Hispaniola, and small mining towns sprang up where Taino labourers were worked to death. As the available workforce perished, slaves were imported. The trans-Atlantic slave trade, which ultimately left such an indelible and continuing legacy of suffering and shaped the contours of the modern world, was inaugurated in 1501 in Hispaniola with the considered consent of the Catholic monarchs of Spain. They gave the new governor, Nicolas Ovando, permission to import black slaves of African descent. To avoid undermining the royal programme of conversion, they had to have been raised as Christians, so were born in Spain as children of African slaves.[18] They proved less docile than expected. When they arrived, almost all of them escaped into the mountains and began launching raids against Spanish settlements. Ovando feared they might incite the surviving Taino to rebellion, and in 1503 persuaded the Crown to prohibit more being shipped. But by 1505, the indigenous population was so reduced that the work would cease unless the ban was lifted, and Ovando asked for seventeen more. The king decided to send 100, ordering that all those already in Hispaniola must be put to work in the gold mines.[19]

That, of course, was why they were there. It has been (unreliably) estimated that by 1506, three-quarters of a million Taino had died on Hispaniola at the hands and the breath of the invaders.[20] Two years later, sixteen years after first greeting Europeans with amazement and grace, it is said that just 60,000 Taino were left alive. The island was full of recent burials, killed by European diseases, but also by battle, enslavement, rape and forced labour in the pursuit of gold. Children were taken as slaves and women as sex slaves. This was illegal, and Columbus was put on trial in Spain in 1501 for enslaving the Crown's new subjects. Evidence was given of slave auctions, mutilations and unbearable cruelty.[21] He was soon released.

Nominal conversion and profits overrode any other consideration. What was happening here would soak into the structure of the New World that would now grow. Each year from 1503–1510, Seville recorded that, on average, gold to the value of 9,325 pesos arrived and went to the Crown.[22] But by then, the indigenous population was so small that the work would cease unless new slaves were imported from the neighbouring island of Trinidad. On 6 June 1511, King Ferdinand II wrote to express his mild concern for their fate. On reflection, he decided to encourage the operation and was sufficiently optimistic about increasing his gold revenues that he gave up the Crown's tax on the slaves' transfer value: 'Do what may seem best to you; and so that more Indians may be brought, proclaim a licence for doing so without paying us the fifth of their value: that is our gift to the inhabitants of Hispaniola and San Juan.' Of course, he went on, the main purpose of 'the conquest' was to convert them, so he would prefer it if they survived rather than 'diminish as in Hispaniola'.[23] In essence, the king was saying to try to keep them alive, but get the gold.

The Black Legend

Settlers arrived from Spain in the hope of making a fortune. Thus was born a completely new kind of community. Concepción de la Vega was the world's first gold rush town, a model for the ruthless exploitation of land and people by desperate adventurers in the pursuit of imperishable wealth.[24] By 1514, by some calculations, 12,000 Taino, about half of all who were left, were forced labourers in the mines.[25] Four years later, the arrival of smallpox killed 8,000 of them in one month.[26]

When a number of inhabitants rose up in a desperate attempt to repel the colonists, they were massacred:

> 'When the Spaniards saw what was happening, they, mounted on fine steeds, well equipped with lances and swords, begin to exercise their bloody butcheries and stratagems, and overrunning their cities and towns, spared no age, or sex, not even pregnant women, but ripping up their bellies, tore them alive in pieces. They placed bets on who could cut a man in two with a single sword cut, or which of them could behead a man, with the greatest dexterity, and even who could sheath his sword fastest in a man's bowels.'

This report is from *A Short Account of the Destruction of the Indies* written by Bartolomé de las Casas. Las Casas had arrived aged 18 with his father in 1502, and was himself a slave owner until he changed his perspective.[27] Eventually he became a Dominican, was appointed 'Protector of the Indians' and wrote accounts of what he claimed to have seen. His work became the basis of English propaganda against Spanish colonialism, the so-called 'Black Legend' of Spanish cruelty, but the overall picture is no legend. One form of entertainment was to roast humans alive on gridirons:

> 'I once saw four or five of their most powerful lords laid on these gridirons and roasted, and not far off, two or three more spread with the same commodity, human flesh; but the shrill clamours which were heard there being offensive to the Captain, by disturbing his rest, he commanded them to be strangled. The Executioner (whose name and parents at Seville are not unknown to me) prohibited that, but stuffed gags into their mouths to keep down the noise (he himself making the fire) until they died, when they had been roasted as long as he thought convenient. I was an eye-witness of these and innumerable other cruelties.'

Profit and Loss

To capture the gold, Spain had physically devastated the people of the New World and corrupted European society in a way not seen since antiquity. There was nothing novel about European rulers acting with brutality and savagery, and the cruel treatment of Jews and Muslims by Ferdinand and Isabella in the name of Christianity predated the settlement of the Americas. But you have to look on Trajan's Column in Rome to see the celebration of a similar kind of slaughtering colonization to extract gold from a subject people. In the second century, the Dacians had been replaced by imported slave labour. So it was with the Taino. Most who survived their forced labour and the epidemics escaped by drinking poison, inhaling deadly fumes, killing their babies, destroying their own food supply and taking to boats.[28] In 1542, it was reported that only 200 Taino were still alive on Hispaniola.

Indelible Memory

It has been a puzzle that centuries after the Taino had perished, their black African replacements knew about them, identified with them and declared this to be their land. The gold had gone, and the western third of the island had been taken over by France in 1697. The French colony, renamed Saint-Domingue, now extracted great wealth by forcing its slaves to grow sugar. The French maintained their predecessors' tradition of extreme brutality and continued with slavery even after the French Revolution. In 1791, the slaves rebelled and seized power, liberating themselves. In 1804, Napoleon tried to recapture the colony and restore slavery: the French were driven off and the revolution now became genocidal. The ex-slaves set about exterminating the white population as completely as the original inhabitants had been exterminated. The price of gold, and all that had followed, would now be paid on a bill drawn up, its author declared, using 'the skin of a white man for parchment, his skull for an inkwell, his blood for ink and a bayonet for a pen'.[29] By apparently universal consent, the revolutionaries now restored the name Haiti, bringing back the land of the Taino from the dead.

Colonizing the world in the pursuit of gold involved remaking peoples, landscapes, languages and memory. Undoing that process called for the resurrection of all that had died, including, in 1804, the excavation of the Taino from whatever traces of memory lingered. Those traces still existed; there is clear evidence that the identity of Haiti was being reclaimed by black outlaws in the eighteenth century. The Taino were dead, but indigenous identity still survived from 1519, when African slaves had escaped into the mountains and established a renegade settlement with Taino rebels.[30] A French historian reported around 1730 that a community some 40 miles north of the city of Santo Domingo was descended from them, and that their leader called himself 'Cacique [chieftain] of the Island of Haiti'.[31]

The memory of the suffering that was imposed to secure the gold and which brought black enslavement to America was powerful enough to shape everything that followed. In Haiti, the legacy of ruthless exploitation, slavery and a combination of African and Catholic religion eventually produced the impoverished Voodoo republic there, which fell with American help into the grim hands of 'Papa Doc' Duvalier. He ruled as the incarnation of a dark god, Baron Samedi, and his militia, the Tonton Macoutes, were believed to be zombies. They and their successors chose their recollections carefully. In 1989, I included the Haitian story in a documentary about the French Revolution. When I asked to see the recently discovered site of Columbus's original settlement, I was told it had been bulldozed and covered to make it presentable to important visitors. It was evidently Hispaniola, not Haiti, and came from a past that needed to be buried.

But great financial interests will not let that past lie, and the determination to hunt for Columbus's gold still continues. It is believed that modern methods could extract $20 billion from this desperately impoverished land, and illiterate farmers are being swindled one by one out of their rights to any of it, while great corporations wait for the chance to resume the sixteenth-century plunder and bring back Hispaniola.[32] The island's best defence is, horribly, its current descent into violence and gang rule.

Chapter 15

Discovering America

The New Shape of Realty

Voyages of discovery were investments and the information learned was secret. Charts revealing them were tightly controlled. Gold was the lure that drew Europeans across the Atlantic. Their voyages of discovery were not pursuing knowledge for its own sake, or the conversion of unprofitable souls. Since there was little interest in colonizing trans-Atlantic land without gold, such expeditions were dismissed as failures.

The discovery of gold was so important that the shape of the world itself became a state secret. The first known map to show both sides of the Atlantic was not rediscovered until the early nineteenth century.[1] Dated 1500, it was signed by Juan de la Cosa, who had sailed on a number of the earliest voyages. The secretive community of Europe's kings, merchants and navigators had become certain about five years before that the circumference of the world was almost 50 per cent greater than Ptolemy had said. Beyond the western sea were unknown lands with resources ripe for the taking, and they needed to privately reimagine global geography. This was the most up-to-date vision of the result, displaying the New World in green as a colourful counterbalance to the pallid old one. The huge document, painted on two ox-hides, was probably created for the Spanish monarchs.

At this startlingly early date, it maps the North American seaboard. Five English flags are shown offshore, from Newfoundland to somewhere around Martha's Vineyard, with the inscription 'Sea discovered by the English'.[2] La Cosa was revealing undocumented voyages authorized by Henry VII.

These fifteenth-century explorations, made by John Cabot, William Weston and perhaps others, were officially forgotten. Their purpose was to find gold or a passage to the riches of China: they failed, and claiming this useless land would simply have created pointless conflict with Spain. The discovery of this map was so starling that it was argued for many years that it actually belongs to a later date.[3] But in 1987, the Prado analysed the pigments and showed that it does indeed date from 1500.[4] The English had been uninterested in their discoveries. It was a similar story with the Portuguese voyages further south. If trans-Atlantic exploration had been about more than finding gold, Europeans would have colonized the continent far sooner.

The Forgotten Discovery of Brazil

The established story is that Brazil was discovered in 1500, the same year as la Cosa's map. The discovery is credited to Pedro Álvares Cabral,[5] who was conducting the second Portuguese voyage round Africa to India, and the King of Portugal decreed that anyone who revealed a map of his voyage was liable to the death penalty.[6]

The secret to getting to the southern tip of Africa, as Dias had discovered, was not to fight the opposing coastal winds and currents but to make a wide swing out into the southern Atlantic. There was plenty of room, after all. Or was there? For reasons which have never been quite clear, his westerly loop out before heading south-east for the Cape of Good Hope just happened to take Cabral straight to a brand-new landfall in quite the opposite direction. At least, that is how the story was told. But he then only investigated the easternmost tip, around modern Recife, and sailed away towards Africa. La Cosa's map shows about 2,000km of the 'undiscovered' coast of Brazil extending further south. Perhaps Cabral had made a conscious detour to investigate this headland as the follow-up to an earlier, unrevealed voyage which la Cosa also knew about, but was destined to be ignored when it failed to lead to gold.

Cabral's trans-Atlantic voyage then makes sense, as being very deliberate. A rather remarkable treaty between Spain and Portugal had divided up the Atlantic world.

The Treaty of Tordesillas of 1494 drew a north–south line through the ocean about halfway between the Cape Verde islands (which had been discovered by Portugal) and the islands found by Columbus on his first voyage (claimed for Castile and León). Columbus's islands were named as Japan (Cipangu) and

Division of the world between Spain and Portugal.

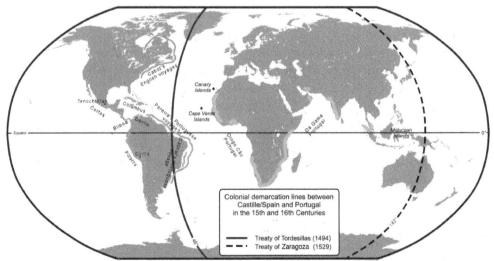

Hispaniola (Antilia). Everything east of the line, up to the European coast, was now Portuguese, everything west of it, including 'Japan', was Spanish. How the Emperor of Japan might feel about the treaty was of no concern. He was known to have gold; that's what Columbus had gone for. His time was up.

Portugal had been discovering and claiming Atlantic islands in a haphazard programme of exploration: Madeira and the Azores were settled as useful agricultural opportunities. Portugal went to Africa for gold, but now that Spain had shown treasure to be accessible a little further west, Portugal was bound to launch its own expeditions in that direction. There were a number,[7] and la Casa's map could suggest that one of them had identified the large land mass south of the Caribbean, heavily populated and extending far towards the South Pole.[8] But perhaps it was partly, in truth, on Portugal's side of the line? Identifying longitude accurately was beyond anyone's capability at this time; the only way to know how far west of Lisbon this land was, would be to compare the local time of a lunar eclipse with the known time of the eclipse in Lisbon. This may be why Cabral needed to go there.[9] He claimed the land for Portugal. Did its longitude make it Portuguese by the treaty? There was an eclipse due on 13 May 1500, and he landed on 22 April. Perhaps he could make a definitive measurement. But if this was normal weather, as people now experience it in the region, he would have discovered that the sky was overcast, with over 0.5cm of rain a day, and the friendly naked native 'warriors' would have conveyed, after a few days of gift-giving, that the moon was unlikely to be seen for many weeks. So Cabral sent a ship back to report what he had found, left a couple of criminals behind (who seem to have bonded very successfully with the indigenous people) and set off again for India. Having found no gold, his discovery was of no interest and he was never employed again. The problem of finding longitude would bedevil land claims for a long time: the Treaty of Zaragoza drew a Pacific line between Spain and Portugal in 1529, after both claimed the Moluccas, but no one could accurately say where it went.

Gold and Guanín

Had there been gold on the coasts of North America and Brazil, England and Portugal would have sent settlers. But that work was now entirely in the hands of the Spanish. There was obviously a significant source of gold somewhere in the region they were ripping up. The islanders had enough to prove that, and they tried to distract the Spanish with accounts of it being somewhere else, over the sea. In 1511, an expedition set out from western Hispaniola to seize Cuba. It was commanded by the deputy governor, Diego Velázquez. His secretary was the 26-year-old Hernán Cortés, who had crossed the Atlantic in 1504 and established himself as a properly ruthless estate-owner. The conquest of Cuba was achieved immediately, once the customary butchery had been demonstrated. And there was gold; Cortés soon made a fortune. But he wanted far more. There was also a confusing difference between the Spanish and indigenous understanding of what was meant by 'gold'.

At the heart of this book is the problem of why gold is understood to be a store of value. The Spanish in the Americas were face-to-face with the paradox of that idea. According to Columbus's journal of his first voyage, 'some of the Indians brought pieces of gold hanging from their noses which they readily changed for a hawk's bell suitable for a sparrow-hawk, and for little glass beads'.[10] The Spanish could see that the Taino placed no significant exchange value on it. Yet they obviously treated it as a very special material to be approached with trepidation. Columbus was surprised to learn that Taino men had to fast and spend twenty days separated from their wives before they could search for gold. The sacramental value attached to it by the Taino made perfect sense to him, so he insisted that his own men take the sacrament and undertake penances before seeking it themselves.[11] But even at a time when Europeans still remembered some divine connection to gold, they understood it in a very different way.

The most obvious difference is that the Taino valued objects made from copper-gold alloy (which they called *guanín*) far more highly than pure gold: la Casa recorded that they would give the Spanish gold weighing 100 'castellanos' – a staggering half-kilo – for *guanín* earrings.[12] The indigenous people had no concept of expressing value as a price. The Spanish knew the price of everything and the value of nothing: for the Taino, it was the other way round. *Guanín* objects were worn by high-status individuals and placed in burials. There is clear evidence that the Taino of eastern Cuba used imported Tairona gold-copper alloys (now called *tumbaga*[13]) formed into objects in the Sierra Nevada de Santa Marta, Colombia.[14] This alloy was manufactured by humans, but the Taino regarded their *guanín* as having supernatural origins.[15] I was surprised when a very senior Kogi Mama, Shibulata, said the same about the *guanín* (*tumbaga*) objects of his Tairona ancestors. Today's Kogi Mamas, like the Taino, appear to have no knowledge of copper and Mama Shibulata assures me that the different colours are to be understood as different forms of gold. Although we know very little about Taino cosmology, which has been studied from fragmentary colonial sources,[16] we know something about Tairona cosmology as preserved by the people of the Sierra Nevada,[17] and the cultural linkage is immediately evident.[18] One purpose of using the alloy (apart from a saving in gold, of course) was that it rendered the metal far harder. Gold was unreal, transcendental and also soft. The *tumbaga* object was hard. The process of making it was also highly significant. The object itself had a part to play in shaping the living world. It appeared as a beautiful, three-dimensional work of art, filled with meaning, and it was not really the product of a human maker. Made using the 'lost wax' process, it was the end result of a concealed ritual in which profound human thought and ancestral memory became physically manifested through intimate interaction with materials granted by the Great Mother.

But for the Spanish, it simply meant that the gold had been seriously degraded, and must now be melted down.

Who Could Work With Gold

The Kogi demonstrated for me the process of making domestic pottery, which requires a man to go to a river and plunge his hands into the mud to lift out the clay that he will need. This is a direct physical engagement between a mortal man and the stuff of the Earth, and it requires great caution. The process must be supervised by a cultural guardian, a Mama. A man had asked for help dealing with sickness in his family, and part of the cure involved replacing all his storage and cooking pots. The Mama first had to examine his character, to ensure that he was a morally 'proper' person. He then had to live apart from his wife for a month and spend a while fasting.

This is the traditional requirement before daring to undertake work of cosmological significance and would probably have been a requirement for gold working. For the indigenous people, immortal gold, coming from the world beyond, enabled specially endowed humans to connect with that world in life and in death. *Tumbaga* was also their place-holder in human, mortal society. It identified who they were, to themselves and their community.

The Panamanian who led the Spanish across Panama to the Pacific watched with bewilderment as they melted down *tumbaga* treasures for the gold, reportedly telling Balboa: 'We place no more value on rough gold before it has been transformed by the workman's hand than on a lump of clay.'[19] This destruction continued for centuries; thousands of pounds worth of Central American indigenous gold pieces were being sold to the Bank of England each year to be turned into bullion until 1859,[20] and it was only in 1939 that the Banco de la República in Bogotá stopped doing the same with tomb robbers' finds and put them in its new Gold Museum. No indigenous person from Colombia now knows how to produce the *tumbaga* lost-wax objects made by their ancestors. Everyone with that knowledge perished, while their conquerors assiduously got on with rendering down every piece they could get hold of. All that remains are the few pieces retrieved from burials. In February 2021, Héctor García-Botero, curator of archaeology and ethnography at the Gold Museum, told me that they had run workshops with professional goldsmiths, none of whom could successfully recreate them. The technical secrets disappeared with the craftsmen.

The Spanish were left with what we consider to be gold, the raw material extracted from the living treasure. No ledger of profit and loss has been compiled, obviously.

Chapter 16

The End of Pre-Colombian History

Seizing Mesoamerica

On 13 March 1981, Francisco Bautista, a construction worker in Mexico City, had a lucky find. About 5 metres below street level, in a hole dug for the Bank of Mexico's new office block, he pulled out a strangely shaped bar of pure gold. It had a concave curve, and although it was 26.4cm long and 5cm wide, it was just 1cm thick. Mexico City sits on top of the old Aztec capital of Tenochtitlan, and archaeology students were on site in case any pre-Hispanic artefacts were unearthed. The bar was handed over to them, and then to the National Institute of Anthropology.[1]

It is now said to be the only surviving fragment of Moctezuma's treasure, the fabled gold taken by Cortés from the ruler of the Mexica, the people with the largest kingdom ever seen in Mesoamerica.

The invaders were making assaults on the Caribbean coast of Venezuela and Colombia from 1500, but I am told that the Taino had already sent out a warning. The Kogi who told me their history, Mama Valencio, said that before any Spanish ships appeared off the mainland, a woman had travelled through the region carrying an oar as a sign of her island and describing the danger. Unfortunately, the Mama spoke no Spanish and the warning was preserved in the ancient priestly Tairona language which no one else could or would translate for me, only summarize. Spanish sources say that a succession of attempted assaults by individual ships were driven off using poison arrows. The settlement of the mainland did not begin until 1509, at the location of modern Cartagena. That was when Vasco Núñez de Balboa persuaded his companions to abandon the endangered camp they made and begin hunting for gold in the isthmus further north. It turned out to be a neck of mountains. He reported that his new colony of Darien, present-day Panama, had vast quantities of gold, that the chiefs had it by the basket-full, all the rivers had gold and there were 'big nuggets on a large scale'.[2] Killing and robbing as he went, he and 190 companions cut a swathe right through it, melting down the treasures they seized. They rode on their strange, swift and powerful beasts, were protected with shining clothing and head coverings harder than stone, wielded blades that could slice though any known weapon or shield, and summoned lightning, thunder and death from heavy tubes – and would then unleash their wolfish, man-tearing carnivorous hounds.

This was the expedition that robbed and slaughtered its way to the Pacific, and so finally opened up the route, if anyone still wanted it, to Japan. But with rivers of gold under their feet, they had rather forgotten about Japan. Columbus had been dead for seven years. As for the inhabitants, the so-called Indians, farmers who lived in rich stockaded towns of 1,500 or so people, they were very ready to give 'presents' of whatever the aliens wanted, especially gold. After all, it was not like giving away food or clothing.

Balboa's report of rivers of gold had a galvanizing effect on the Spanish monarchy. The Crown now launched an official expedition on a massive scale; twenty-three ships lavishly equipped and led by an elderly senior military commander, Pedro Arias Dávila, with instructions to take possession of the lands, people and wealth of what was now to be known as 'Golden Castile'. This was when the Spanish first encountered the Tairona.

Colombia

The peaks of the Sierra Nevada de Santa Marta rise 5,200 metres out of the Caribbean, the world's highest coastal mountain and a navigation marker. At its foot, Dávila found, in 1514, the most complex and sophisticated society Spain had yet encountered,

The Tairona were waiting, having covered themselves in red juice. It was customary in Central America for the high-status dead to be painted red.[3] Dávila sent a small party to land, but the natives ran up to the landing boats 'and with their bows and arrows and with a courteous manner, showed us that they would have to resist our landing'. A lengthy document had been prepared to launch the official seizure of Golden Castile. It began by explaining that God created the world, all humans are descended from the original pair, and that their descendants spread over the Earth. It went on to explain the fundamental doctrines of Christianity, including the Trinity and the position of the Pope, which led in a natural and interesting way to the information that political structures had been empowered by Papal authority. The logical and obvious conclusion was that the listeners were now to consider themselves subjects of the Spanish Crown and should begin taking instruction for baptism. As a treatise in Renaissance political theory and theology, it was a well-considered speech. In case the audience could not understand Spanish, it was repeated in Carib, the language of some natives of the Caribbean. It was a thoughtful touch, even though the native people of this shore understood it no more than Spanish.

That hardly mattered to either side. When the Spaniards' scribe protested that the indigenous people had not understood a word that had been said to them, the soldiers laughed at him. After all, it did not really mean anything. In fact, they would have understood the real meaning whatever language was used. It was obvious, and indigenous people here pay less attention to spoken language than to everything else the speaker presents to them. When I am summoned to give an account of myself to the Kogi Mamas, on a serious occasion, I am required to describe the process by which I have come, my experiences on the way, and what most drives and motivates me. I used, at first, to ask what language they wanted. I was told it did not matter, as they can see what I am talking about and why.

Having heard the declaration and understood it well enough, the natives fired some arrows harmlessly towards the landing craft, an indication that the visitors should leave. This was interpreted as an act of rebellion against their new rulers, and the Spanish fired at them. The Tairona disappeared, leaving nothing, so Dávila's fleet sailed on.

One among the many bizarre features of this moment is that before refusing them permission to land, the Tairona also tried to explain something to the Spanish. It is even possible that both sides had been saying something rather similar. The Tairona had an exchange system that extended throughout the Caribbean and Central America and knew what had been happening. Certainly, they are saying something along the same lines today. One of the speeches made to me by a Mama seems like an answering echo to the Spanish argument, that humanity was divided geographically after being shaped, and the way the world and humanity were created leads to political duty. The people of the Sierra, though, believe they were created before their 'younger brothers' elsewhere, and have special duties. The Mama told me:

'The world was made in the beginning, and we were made afterwards.

'Then Serankua looked at the Earth which we have. He said to the humans, "You are beings created to protect it, to maintain the balance, to care for the world, the universe. Concentrate and take care of it."

'Our history, the history of the Mama, says that in this land all people held the same beliefs as one another. We were all Elder Brothers. When we collect firewood, it is paid for, bought. We pay Serankua for firewood, for water, for the air we breathe, for what we need to live, for every little animal. We have always known that there is a payment to be made for everything.

'Then a Younger Brother was given knowledge of mechanical things. And because this land was very sacred, if Younger Brother stayed here, he would do harm to Mother Earth. He would not have respected Mother Earth, he would only ever tear out the eyes of the Mother, he would only ever tear out the guts of the Mother, without compassion, without feeling pain.

'Thus, the Younger Brother had less understanding. Then Serankua said, "Let us send them away to the other side and, so that they respect us and so that they shall not pass, I make a division – the sea."

'But the Mamas say the Younger Brother came back across to this side, thinking he had learned, had studied, and was wise. They came and started to tear out the blood of the Mother Earth, started to tear out the eyes of the Mother Earth without respect.

'Serankua said very clearly, "Elder Brother must respect Younger Brother and Younger Brother must respect Elder Brother. Do not come here, I have created a division." But Younger Brother did not respect it, he came and violated the law, the original spiritual law of Serankua, and today the people here, the Mamas, say that Younger Brother must listen to us, that he must learn to respect us. Thus speak the Mamas.'

The Spanish proclamation ended more fearsomely. If the native people did not submit, they would be deliberately destroyed:

'I assure you that with the help of God I will enter powerfully against you, and I will make war on you in every place and in every way that I can, and I will subject you to the yoke and obedience of the church and their highnesses, and I will take your persons and your women and your children, and I will make them slaves, and as such I will sell them, and dispose of them as their highnesses command: I will take your goods, and I will do you all the evils and harms which I can, just as to vassals who do not obey and do not want to receive their lord, resist him and contradict him. And I declare that the deaths and harms which arise from this will be your fault, and not that of their highnesses, nor mine, nor of the gentlemen who have come with me here.'

But in reality, Dávila simply sailed away to Darien and the Tairona were left alone.

Dávila's arrival in Darien did not reveal any rivers of gold, and the new settlers he brought, dying of hunger and disease, ravaged the land around with extreme savagery in a ferocious hunt for slaves (who they often killed) and gold (which was absent). He took command of the colony and had Balboa murdered, founding Panama City in 1519.[4] Pedrarias the Cruel, as he became known, retained power until he was over 90. Hundreds of Spaniards and thousands of natives perished. Most of the indigenous fled. The Spanish had no idea of the great civilization flourishing 1,000km further north.

The Aztec Empire

About 1,800km west of Cuba, separated from it by 1,500km of sea, there was a city so fabulous that the Spanish settlers could not have ever imagined it. It was more fantastic, and more alien, than anything described by Marco Polo. Tenochtitlan was a planned city-state of perhaps over 100,000 people, at least four times larger than Seville and regarded with astonishment by the Spanish who eventually arrived.[5] It had broad avenues with central canals and great numbers of brick buildings – domestic compounds, with courtyards and gardens – around a centre with huge, impressive ceremonial structures. This was built on a grid plan with a central plaza. It shared this structure with Spanish colonial cities, but for quite different reasons. It was not based on a military camp, but on the supposed structure of the cosmos. At its heart was the Great Temple, the city's first building, a platform with stairways climbing up four or five stepped levels to the sanctuaries of two transcendental authorities, the rulers of war and of the rain. Like Venice, the city was built on islands connected by bridges, and it was fabulously rich. But unlike Venice, its wealth came not from commerce but conquest. Eventually, an encyclopaedia of the Aztec Empire was created for Charles V. It is known today as the *Codex Mendoza*. It cites in Aztec glyphic writing the tribute that used to be paid by conquered cities and tabulates the huge income of the Aztec Empire. Also unlike Venice, its cathedral-equivalent was the stage for huge human sacrifices.[6] Once the Spanish found the place, that fact would give them all the moral authority they wanted to annihilate it.

There was gold here, though not on the scale that the Spanish dreamed of. Mexico had little gold: the country's gold archaeological collection amounts to 500 or so tiny pieces.[7] The annual golden tribute taken by Tenochtitlan from its whole empire was ten large gold bars, twenty 1cm-thick discs of fine gold the size of dinner plates and twenty 15cm diameter bowls of gold dust; not a lot, compared to Portugal's profits from Africa.

Cortés

In 1518, Hernán Cortés was appointed to lead an expedition to Yucatan on the mainland to gather information and capture slaves to use for gold prospecting in Cuba. He was not sent to conquer or colonize, but he knew that gold had been acquired there, following contact with very sophisticated natives, and there had been stories of something remarkable called *Mexica*. These stories, and the gold given in barter, were the result of Aztec emissaries flagging down a Spanish ship to get more information. They were glamorously and exotically costumed, and feasted the Spaniards royally, but of course the Spanish had not understood who they were or what they wanted.

At the last minute, the Cuban governor, Velázquez, tried to block Cortés's departure, but it was too late. The call of gold was too strong. Cortés had 530 European men, hundreds of Indians and Africans, thirteen horses, mastiffs and artillery. He soon acquired local allies and a native woman interpreter. Bringing back slaves for Cuba was not on his personal agenda. He saw himself as a modern Julius Caesar, with this land as the Gaul he would conquer and so make himself rich in gold and politically powerful. An educated man, he wrote long and detailed letters demonstrating what he did and celebrating himself in the simple, Caesar-like language of a trustworthy military leader. He had decided to ignore his master in Cuba and communicate directly with the Holy Roman Emperor, his king, in Spain.

Moctezuma sent rich emissaries to Cortés, with gifts (giving gold, of course) and an invitation to his capital.[8] He was the new ruler of this huge and powerful empire, which had an army of tens of thousands, was in the later stages of a great campaign of expansion and had invited the independent Tlaxcala people and other city-states to attend his forthcoming coronation. The Tlaxcala, together with another community, the Otomis, now confronted Cortés. The battle became desperate but acted as a showpiece demonstration of the power of Cortés's small armoured force, with firearms, crossbows, dogs, horses, pikes, swords and discipline, to overcome much larger numbers of copper-age heroic warrior-farmers whose battles were fought with clubs studded with volcanic glass.[9] The defeated Tlaxcala decided that it made sense to engage with these aliens, and Cortés accompanied their officials and warriors to Moctezuma's capital. The Aztecs did not yet understand much about the invaders, but they were aware that they were being used as the spearhead of their enemies and commanded novel forms of deadly force.

Cortés ignored orders to return to Cuba and instead set out to win a new province in the name of the Crown. He intended to take the Aztec Empire under his own authority.

The indigenous people of Central America, from Mexico to Colombia, understand the world as a cosmically ordered space, with preordained narratives played out in the starry sky and on Earth. Everything that happens is connected to everything else, much as in Europe at this time people believed that prophecies and the movement of the heavens were sources of information that needed to be taken seriously. This often involves the reconsideration of existing histories to find the precedents that amount to a prophecy concerning current events. This information is needed to know how to proceed. When I first encountered the Kogi and discussed making a film with them, I proposed that they and I needed to spend time thinking about each other before beginning. I suspected that one process that would take place would be that they would ransack their history to find presaging traces of the work we would do, and so it proved. By the time I returned for the filming, a year later, I already had two conflicting prophesied identities spoken of in their society – one benevolent, in which I served as the link for which they had been preparing for many years, the other malevolent, in which I was virtually a reincarnated conquistador, come to continue the work of enslavement and land appropriation (and cannibalism) in the name of the political authority that sent me, the BBC.

I mention this to give a possible perspective on how Cortés was received. The Mexica (Aztecs) needed to find an explanation of him in their past, and there were competing, and opposed, explanations on offer. He was not to be confronted with war as though his people were just another indigenous group. Moctezuma was responsible to his subjects, their ancestors and their descendants, for negotiating with strangers with incomprehensible knowledge who represented something beyond themselves.[10] There were many different ways for the Mexica to understand who had arrived, but all of them were based on the certainty that nothing happens by chance, or without the engagement of forces outside the material world.

The strangers wanted gifts: the gifts Moctezuma gave included many 'gold' objects, though it is likely that, except for perhaps personal decoration such as necklaces, these were generally gold-copper alloy.[11] In July 1519, Cortés sent the new Spanish sovereign, Charles V, the obligatory 20 per cent of his booty. These treasures went to Charles's court at Brussels, where they were seen by Albrecht Dürer, who recognized their cash value and their artistry. Dürer had come to engraving through being trained as a goldsmith by his father:

'I saw the things which have been brought to the King from the new land of gold, a sun all of gold a whole fathom broad, and a moon all of silver of the same size, also two rooms full of armour of the people there, and all manner of wondrous weapons of theirs … These things were all so precious that they are valued at 100,000 florins. All the days of my life I have seen nothing that rejoiced my heart so much as these things, for I saw amongst them wonderful works of art, and I marvelled at the subtle natural ability of men in foreign lands.'[12]

What he did not grasp, of course, was their meaning; the golden sun was covered in symbolic images which were as meaningless to him as his own apocalyptic woodcuts, such as *The Opening of the Fifth and Sixth Seals* (which includes the sun and moon), would have been to the Aztecs. But at least Dürer's work remains visible today. Every piece of Aztec craft that Dürer saw has been destroyed, the precious metal melted down.

The European obsession with gold was not shared by the Aztecs, though they certainly regarded it as vital to nature. They associated it with the gods, and saw it as decorative and eternal, but their word for it was 'god-shit'. They saw it emerging from the Earth as nature's own excrement and seem to have believed they could manage perfectly well without it. It was not money to them, nor did they trade.

Only one Aztec burial has been discovered with a significant quantity of gold in it. At the end of 2017, an excavation on the site of the great temple of Tenochtitlan found the stone coffin of a young wolf with its heart removed. It was dressed with gold ear and nose ornaments and a gold breastplate.[13] The burial dates from the reign of Moctezuma's predecessor, who took his name from a mythical water-dog that was said to feast on human flesh. All the Aztec gold surviving in Mexico until the discovery of that wolf burial would fit into your cupped hands.

The Aztecs were cultural outsiders in Central America. They had only appeared in the fourteenth century, a large group of impoverished nomads from the north-east who had a supernatural prophet who would lead them to a promised land, assuring them that the god of sun and war, Huitzilopochtli, was guiding them to a new home from which they would dominate all the world and receive tribute in the form of precious stones, gold, quetzal feathers, emeralds, coral and amethysts. They had an origin myth that told of their arrival in their promised land in our year 1325 CE, being allowed to settle in a swamp where they created a floating foundation for their great temple, then made more for their planned city – living, according to their own account, on snakes and reptiles until they had created floating platforms for soil and could grow food. From there, they set about the conquest of Central America.

Now their nemesis had come, with the unfathomable aim of robbing them of stuff they did not significantly value. According to Cortés, an unreliable narrator, Moctezuma said that what little gold he had was all to be given to the Spanish if they wanted it.[14] Cortés and his men were nervously installed in Moctezuma's father's palace, where they found a sealed door concealing a chamber of gold and feathers. Moctezuma apparently said they could keep the gold, but not the feathers.

Installed in his capital, which Cortés described as 'the most beautiful thing in the world', they were vulnerable and seized Moctezuma as their hostage. They now used their time in the palace to melt down all the gold they had been given and make bars that could be transported out. As tension grew, Cortés had to confront an expedition sent from Cuba to bring him back under control.

His flouting of Velazquez's authority was clear and intolerable; he was making himself the independent conqueror of a supposed newfound land of gold. He immediately left Tenochtitlan and launched a surprise attack on the force sent from Cuba to arrest him. The officer in charge was nearly killed and most of the newly arrived soldiers decided to change sides. Among them were the first men to carry smallpox onto the American continent. They had brought it from the islands. The incubation period is about two weeks.

Meanwhile, Cortés's deputy in Tenochtitlan, who may have feared that they were preparing to sacrifice the Spanish, launched a surprise attack on a huge number of Aztec lords and their people gathered for a major ritual. In a three-hour massacre, they cut down first the musicians, then the singers, then the spectators and everyone in the temple. The day after Cortés returned, the city erupted in insurrection, resulting in the death of Moctezuma. Cortés launched a ferocious attack on the great temple, seizing and destroying the shrines. The object was clearly to rip the heart out of the city as the city ripped the hearts out of its captives. He succeeded, but his position was militarily untenable. That night, the Spanish made a desperate secret flight over a makeshift canal bridge, trying to carry as much loot as possible. They were spotted and their column was stormed. Many died under the weight of gold, while others simply shed what they had as they struggled to cross the canal. At least 600 Spanish perished. That is where Francisco Bauhista found his thin curved bar of gold. It had been shaped to be hidden inside armour. This gold bar seems to be the sole surviving trace of the event and might have been a relic of the destruction of the conquistadors in America. But that is not how it turned out.

The fleeing Spanish left behind victims of their most potent weapon, virulent infection.[15] Did they understand that? The Aztecs had driven out Cortés but were finished.

Cortés was in a far stronger position. True, he had lost many hundreds of men and all his artillery, but he had destroyed Tenochtitlan's political structure as well as infecting the city. With the help of an indigenous woman who was his advisor and consort, he now gathered an alliance of the Aztecs' defeated enemies and began organizing them, importing supplies from Cuba, building a canal and using a workforce of 8,000 to construct a fleet of armed brigantines to float to Tenochtitlan. Meanwhile, disease, widely supposed to be smallpox but possibly typhus, raged in the city. An indigenous account says:

'It began to spread ... striking everywhere in the city and killing a vast number of our people. Sores erupted on our faces, our breasts, our bellies; we were covered with agonizing sores from head to foot. The illness was so dreadful that no one could walk or move. The sick were so utterly helpless that they could only lie on their beds like corpses, unable to move their limbs or even their heads. They could not lie face down or roll from one side to the other. If they did move their bodies, they screamed with pain. A great many died from this plague, and many others died of hunger. They could not get up to search for food, and everyone else was too sick to care for them, so they starved to death in their beds.'[16]

The battle for the city went on for days, with Cortés now having a huge force of native enemies of the Aztecs.

Upon entering the defeated city, he was confronted with piles of bodies, starved, poisoned from drinking saline water or dead from disease. On 13 August 1521, he effectively put an end to the city and its civilization's entire existence. Stepping over the heaps, he estimated the number of dead at 50,000.[17] Cortés had the city and whatever gold it possessed; gold that he had originally been offered freely but had been driven by fear to fight and kill for. The surviving ruler was baptized, imprisoned and his feet were burned to make him reveal gold he did not have.

Cortés personally governed Mexico in the name of the Crown, and Tenochtitlan was renamed Mexico City. The Aztec world was over.

The Elimination of the Aztecs

What was the reckoning, the price of the great Mexican Empire of perhaps 5 million or more people? Cortés wrote: 'Having collected the gold and other things, we had them melted, with the approbation of Your Majesty's officials, and what was melted amounted to one hundred and thirty thousand castellanos.'[18] That is 534.3kg of gold. To get the measure of that, you might want to visit Seville Cathedral. The guides will tell you that its shimmering interior is gilded with what they believe to be 40,000kg of gold, and that the altar alone was made with 2,500kg. If true, that altar has nearly five times all the gold Cortés took from Tenochtitlan.

Not much of the cathedral's gold is from Mexico, and Cortés was not remembered as a new Caesar. He found himself surrounded by enemies and distrusted by Charles V, who regarded him as a dangerous loose cannon who had not delivered the royal share of the fabulous wealth he had apparently seized. Charles had bought the title of Holy Roman Emperor in 1519 by bribing the electors. He used a loan of 850,000 florins from the banking houses of Fugger and Welser, which fell due after the election. That loan had enabled him to see off the competition of Francis I of France. But he had borrowed on the security of gold flowing from the Caribbean. Cortés's spectacular demonstration of Aztec gold, which so impressed Dürer, had arrived in a most timely manner just a few weeks after his coronation. Unfortunately for Charles, the collapse of the indigenous population of the Caribbean halved his income from this encouraging source over the years 1521 1530, even when Cortés's rather small contribution was included.[19] In 1528, Cortés was summoned to account for himself in Spain.

He put on a great show, as close as he could get to mounting a Roman triumph, with two shiploads of treasure, native crafts and animals unknown in Europe such as jaguars, opossums, pumas and armadillos, along with indigenous albinos and dwarfs. The extent to which he consciously thought of himself as a modern Caesar is debatable,[20] but in 1529, a hostile witness reported him as quoting the conqueror of Gaul and declaring: 'Caesar or nothing!'[21] His effort at winning Imperial renown failed, and he died in debt and relative obscurity. But he had done enough to inspire his cousin, Francisco Pizarro, to conquer an empire of his own further south, and that, at last, would end Europe's desperate need for gold. In fact, it would bury it. That is what is on show in Seville's cathedral.

Obliterating the Past

The hunt for gold, of course, needed to be intensified. When Dávila had made his threats at the foot of the Sierra Nevada, he ended with the release of dogs and a volley. The shots missed, the dogs attacked each other, and in the general mêlée the Indians vanished. The troops pursued them and picked up 7,000 pesos of gold before returning to their ships. It must be worth a return visit.

Eleven years later, in 1525, having scoured the Caribbean for fifty families who would come with him on this great adventure, Don Rodrigo de Bastidas began to construct a town at Santa Marta. As in Mexico, the invaders did all they could to extinguish the past of the inhabitants, replacing their authorities with new masters, written laws and a new god. Where towns were allowed to survive, they were refashioned under the rule of a church and monarch whose commands came from the other side of the world. The languages that described an interconnected living cosmos with its own inherent rules were displaced. Power now expressed itself in Castilian and Latin, the languages of a fundamentally different cosmology which punished 'sin' and commanded humans to conquer and rule all life on Earth.[22]

Indigenous cultures survived, but when the pressure on their land and resources drove them to rebel, the response was utterly ruthless.

In some cases, indigenous leaders were incorporated into the colonial power structure to enable it to function, much as the Romans did. In these situations, native elites could adapt but the past could of course not be resurrected. The suppression of the past can be seen even where Spanish efforts to maintain a colonial presence failed. Santa Marta is the oldest colonial city in America, but it could not eliminate the surrounding Tairona culture, living in the folds of the Sierra Nevada, a steep and difficult massif. By 1599, the determination to extract gold from them led to an uprising that was suppressed by a three-month campaign of genocide. One community after another was burned and looted, destroying crops and houses and taking prisoner all the leading inhabitants with their families. Warriors were, of course, condemned to death, their commander being dragged by two horses and then quartered, the parts of his body and his head being distributed on public display. The whole population were officially dispossessed and forbidden under pain of death to retire into the Sierra Nevada. Their towns were turned over whole to the soldiers for them to sack as they wanted for their services, and 'those Indians who they wish to live' were condemned in addition to pay a fine of 'pacification' amounting to 1,500lb of gold.

The shattered remnants of this society – the lowest-ranking people, the unnoticed survivors – fled through the jungle and up the mountain. The Kogi memory is of a great mass of refugees from all the many families of the Sierra, desperate for food and succour. For the next 500 years, the indigenous people higher up, including the Kogi, evaded conversion and retained their languages, dress and way of life. Community authorities are still trained in the dark from infancy to adulthood in traditional oral learning and retain their power. But the Kogi carefully avoid making any images. There are no pictures, no faces on their pottery, no toys. The savage campaign launched against them from Santa Marta is remembered as a deadly iconoclastic assault on images and supposed devil worship. Spiritual leaders were drawn and quartered, while prisoners were crucified or hung from metal hooks through the ribs. Women were garrotted, children enslaved. Every village that could be reached was destroyed. At one settlement, the noses, ears and lips of every adult were sliced off.[23] Memory ascribes a single motive to the holocaust:

> 'They took away the things that were ours.
> They took away our gold.
> They took away all our sacred gold.
> … They took our soul.
> They took everything.
> … Before then, everyone knew how to dance, all of them, all of them, all of them. Every Indian knew how to dance.'[24]

The Secret of Success

This destruction was achieved by a tiny number of adventurers. The ships that brought them only carried an average of seventeen passengers. They were in general very frightening people making desperate gambles. In five years from 1510, less than 2,000 passengers were listed as licenced to make the journey from Seville.[25] There were certainly other, unrecorded adventurers, but it does illustrate the apocalyptic impact of a tiny group of aliens. How did they do it? Horses, gunpowder and iron made a difference, but did not make the Spanish impregnable. Cortés lost about half his force. Overwhelming determination and immeasurable ambition, plus the indigenous culture of hospitality and openness, made it easy for the invaders to acquire large numbers of effective allies who wanted to bring down powerful local enemies. The invaders did not need to negotiate for gold. They could simply wipe away the people in charge here and force the survivors to deliver it. The indigenous Americans' failure to think of gold as money was used as evidence of their primitive status and as the justification for the Spanish takeover of their land and property.[26]

Yet they had been able to sustain empires and great cities, exchanging and distributing resources and products without needing currency or banks. We may need to understand how that can be done.

Chapter 17

Gold at Last

Pizarro's Quest

Unlike Cortés, Pizarro had no visions of himself as one of the great conquerors; he was an illiterate thug out for whatever wealth he could find, and with an unquenchable determination to get it for himself. In 1522, when Cortés had just overthrown the Aztec Empire, Pizarro was in Panama with Dávila and received a report that there was a gold-rich territory far to the south on a river called the Pirú (later corrupted to Perú).[1] Pizarro had no doubt that this was his do-or-die opportunity.

Just as Spaniards knew nothing of the Aztecs in 1518, in 1522 there were only rumours of the far richer empire to the south. It had been created over the previous hundred years by conquest and peaceful expansion. Tradition says that it was ruled by the twelfth Inca (Inca was the imperial title), who was master of perhaps 12 million people in the Andes and down a wide strip of the Pacific coast, from Ecuador to southern Chile. It was twice the size of Portugal and

Europe's view of the Atlantic in the sixteenth century.

perhaps six times as densely populated. The Inca ruled a military state far larger than the Aztecs, who the Inca had never heard of. Quechua was the equivalent of Latin, an official language that united the various peoples that had lost their independence. The Inca Empire had a professional military command, a huge army and an efficient military road system. But like the Aztecs, they had no iron, no horses, and no gunpowder.

Logistics defeated Pizarro in 1524 and 1526, but when the nervous governor of Panama sent two ships to bring him back from his bolthole on the southern part of the Colombian Pacific coast, he and thirteen gaunt and desperate followers refused to obey. They clung on for seven months, then in 1528 a rescue ship arrived to take them further south.

On the northern limits of the Inca Empire, they were met with generosity and kindness in a kind of fairyland. Here were fine streets, beautiful women and gold on temple walls. Having explored a little further south and seen clear evidence of an elaborate and stunningly rich civilization, Pizarro took the material evidence and made his laborious way back to Seville to get the backing of Charles V. The Holy Roman Emperor was in serious financial trouble. His unpaid troops had sacked Rome in 1527, and in 1528 he had transferred any profits of Venezuela to a German banker, who renamed the territory Klein-Venedig. He desperately needed gold. Pizarro was thus licenced 'to discover and conquer Peru'.

In the meantime, the germs the Spanish carried seem to have gone on ahead of them. By 1527, the 12th Inca and his intended successor had died of what was probably smallpox. The empire was then divided between his two sons; Atahualpa ruled the north from Quito, Huáscar from Cuzco in the south. They immediately plunged into a devastating civil war, which was in full swing by the time Pizarro landed back on the Ecuador coast in 1531. It was an internal struggle in which tens of thousands were killed; the northern capital of Tumebamba was destroyed and its population massacred. Pizarro was connecting two empires 9,000km apart, the Spanish and the Inca, which were both in deep trouble, were about to go to war with each other but knew nothing of each other's existence.

The secret of his survival was paranoia; Pizarro arrived at an island where he concluded that the local chiefs, who behaved with great kindness, were secretly hostile. He launched a pre-emptive strike on them, looting their households, including their gold objects. He was immediately attacked by thousands of hostile warriors. He had just 100 men and sixty horses, but cavalry and swords presented an impregnable wall of death, and their arquebus volleys created a terrifying sound with incomprehensible slaughter. His chronicler, who of course glorifies him, describes how a cavalry charge on beasts that were as terrifying and fantastic as dragons finished off his hosts. The inhabitants fled.[2]

Finding the Inca

Pizarro immediately took his men deep into Inca territory, hunting for gold. His force was almost ridiculously debilitated by hunger and infections.[3] There were indigenous towns which welcomed these strange and powerful warriors as potential allies, and in one of these he heard about the wealth and power of the Inca and saw how terrified local lords were of Atahualpa's army, which had killed thousands of their people. Upon being told by their chief that it was 50,000 strong, Pizarro did not believe it until they taught him how to count in powers of ten.[4] He was told that Atahualpa was looking for him. That made him careful, but evading indigenous enemies was Pizarro's skill. So far as he was concerned, their military strength was irrelevant. The difficult mountain terrain was very tough for 150 Europeans, but even more so for an army of 50,000. So long as he was well informed by local helpers and translators, and remained sharp-witted, the prize was his for the taking. His secretary, Francisco Xerez, was with him on the expedition and published a detailed account as soon as he returned to Seville in 1534. It was, of course, shaped for the Christian king. He described Pizarro's speech to his tiny force before they climbed the Andes to stalk Atahualpa: 'He exhorted all his men to make up their minds to act as he hoped they would, and to have no fear of the great number of soldiers in the army of Atahualpa, for though the Christians might be few, yet the help of our Lord would be sufficient to confound their enemies.'[5]

In reality, his men's resolve in the face of terrible odds came from confidence in their external and internal steel and the wits of their leader. He probably did not point to a miracle until after they pulled off the victory.

As the story is told, it was a great, world-shaking drama. Atahualpa was in the heart of his own territory, three weeks' journey from its southern limit. He was close to the impressive city of Cajamarca, about 1,300km south of his city of Quito and almost 2,000km north of Cuzco, a city of palaces reserved for the aristocracy. He knew that the Spanish were for some reason eager for gold, but he had no grasp of Spanish weaponry or ferocity. By the time Pizarro reached him, the entire invasion force consisted of only 110 infantry, sixty-seven cavalry and a few firearms. Atahualpa was accompanied by tens of thousands of skilled warriors. He had deliberately invited Pizarro into what he may have believed was a trap, baited with gold. He agreed to meet in a town square with 'five or six thousand' unarmed attendants.[6]

Pizarro had prepared carefully. His soldiers were hidden and silent. They had already decided to take the emperor hostage, replicating the approach taken by Cortés. Pizarro's younger brother, Pedro, reported seeing many concealed Spaniards unconsciously wetting themselves with terror. According to Xerez, their leader had told them they were outnumbered 500 to one, 'and they must trust that God would fight on their side. He told them that, at the moment of attacking, they must come out with desperate fury and break through the enemy.'[7] He needed them to be at maximum tension, ready to go berserk at the signal. They must only avoid getting their horses in each other's way.

Atahualpa arrived, carried on a golden litter by thirty men, surrounded by an impressive ceremonial procession. They came into an apparently empty square. A Spanish priest appeared with an interpreter and declaimed a version of the document that Dávila had read to the Tairona. Atahualpa replied, 'I will be no man's tributary', and rejected the proffered Bible. This was the pretext for the ambush to kidnap him. The sudden eruption from concealment of gunfire and cavalry terrified the Inca guards, who had never seen such things. The litter-bearers had their arms sliced off but continued to hold up the Inca until they fell and were replaced by others. The massacre that followed is known as the Battle of Cajamarca. The Inca army fled.

The business with the priest was deadly theatre: Pizarro was not there to convert anyone. When asked later by a priest to do more to convert the Peruvians, he said: 'I have not come for any such reason. I have come to take away their gold.'[8] Atahualpa's huge empire simply faded, while chieftains came to Pizarro to offer allegiance.[9] The defeated Inca then made his celebrated offer to fill an entire room with gold, and two more with silver, in exchange for his life. Spanish gold hunger had made a ghost of the Inca, as it had of the Aztec. A new history was being born.

Tracking the Source of Gold

Atahualpa's ransom (he was killed anyway) was a room packed with 8 tons of golden objects. Unlike the people of the Caribbean coast, the inhabitants of Peru evidently had no cultural problem with digging gold out of the ground, and there were small mines in what is now southern Peru. But these were evidently not the main source of supply, and the hunt began for the chimera of a legendary land associated with a supposed river of gold. Atahualpa's ransom was equivalent to a quarter of all the gold in Europe, so it was assumed there must be some prodigious source. It was said by 1541 to be the land of El Dorado, a king dusted with gold every morning.[10] The natives spoke of it being far to the north in the mountains, in a place the Spanish believed to be near the Equator. The indigenous people related gold to the sun; Spaniards understood that connection. It would surely be found at the headwaters of a great river near equatorial heat, in a remote location. According to Jesuit naturalist José de Acosta, 'God placed the greatest abundance of mines ... [in remote places] so that this would invite men to seek those lands and hold them.'[11]

The magnetism of the idea was so compelling that hundreds of men lost their lives in the struggle to discover El Dorado, spending years on desperate hunts through dense jungle, up and across thunderous rivers and over forbidding and freezing mountains. They attacked, murdered and raped the inhabitants, torturing them for information, demonstrating that, as Cortés had told Moctezuma's emissary, they suffered from sickness in their hearts that could only be cured by gold.

One of Pizarro's men, Sebastian Benalcázar, went off on his own private gold hunt in 1535 to conquer the Inca city of Quito. By the time he got there, all its gold had been hidden. Enraged, when he found a village whose men were all away fighting, he butchered the women and children to inspire terror. By now the story of El Dorado had somehow morphed into a tale about a territory, called Meta. He then marched over 1,000km north-east and climbed the Andes to find Meta. He trekked for eight months through bitter snow and ice, and after a long and circuitous struggle eventually found a perfectly circular lake with high raised sides, sitting in a plain in the high mountains. He also found a jungle-ravaged party of about 160 men from Santa Marta on the Caribbean coast, survivors of a group of 800 settlers who had set out two years earlier in pursuit of this legend, through the unyielding Colombian jungle and up the other side of the Andes. They were led by Gonzalo Jiménez de Quesada on what had become a war of conquest of the Muisca. Then another exhausted adventurer arrived. Nikolaus Federmann had set out from the Orinoco, from Venezuela, which had been transferred to a German banker by Charles V. He had ended by spending twenty-two days crossing the high paramo, the bare moorland of the cordillera. Sixteen of his horses froze there.

El Dorado means 'the Golden Man'. There was a truth here, but it did not lead to a gold mine. To inaugurate a new *cacique* of the Chibcha people (the group that includes the Tairona and the Muisca), the chosen one was entirely covered in gold. Carrying gold and emeralds, he was taken on a ceremonial raft into the water of a lake and was immersed, completing the link between human and the spirit-world, just as the Celts had done, renewing life itself.

The lake was Guatavita; it was the lake where the three conquistadors had met to lay claim to Meta, knowing nothing at all about the ceremony or the place. Three desperate looters of the world, each wanting to be the sole claimant to what must be the infinite wealth of the indigenous people there, the Muisca. They reached an extraordinary agreement, to travel together back to Spain to put their rival claims to Charles V. They descended to the Magdalena River, built boats and reached Cartagena. From there, they took ship together.

It is hard to imagine life on board. None of them were granted the land.[12]

The Place of Gold in the Land

Most indigenous gold in America was filtered from rivers. There are descriptions in colonial sources of shallow mines, but no evidence that these existed before the Spanish arrived. The Kogi insist that gold can be taken from rivers but should not be mined because they believe it is a component of the quasi-biological living earth connected to fertility. Throughout South America, the land was laced with a network of golden figures in which gold and thought, nature and mind, were blended to guarantee the fertility of living things and their human guardianship. The Kogi understand them to be living documents carrying the laws of nature, the spiritual equivalent of the genetic code of species of plants and animals, and their removal can extinguish that.[13]

All that the Spanish could find was seized and melted down. Most was shipped to Spain, where much of it was used to furnish a network of gold-covered churches in a different ritual of connection to divinity. Even to the conquerors, gold was not just money.

Columbus's tomb is in Seville Cathedral, the largest Gothic cathedral ever built. Converted from a mosque, it displays the conversion of one religion's understanding to another, and places Columbus in the crusading heritage from which he sprang. But far more dramatically, it displays the conversion of a very different system of belief to the service of Columbus's god. The 20-metre-high reredos that dominates the great nave is covered with hundreds of wooden carvings coated with what is said to be over a ton of gold from the Americas. The display represents the victory of one theology over another, the removal of gold from the Mother and its presentation to the Father and Son.

A large part of the Inca gold was taken from Coricancha, the temple of the sun in the central city, Cuzco. Inca temples, like those of the ancient Middle East, were houses for gods, not assembly places for people. The only people who could enter were the ruler, certain nobles, and priests and virgins serving the gods.[14] Coricancha means 'golden enclosure'. Here were sanctuaries of the major deities, including Viracocha (law-giver), Inti (the sun), Mamaquilla (the moon) and Illapa (thunder). The chapel of Inti had walls and ceiling of sheet gold. The whole complex of some 200 square metres was surrounded by a wall on which was a band of gold three fingers thick and 30cm wide. There was a ceremonial garden with earth made from lumps of gold growing cornstalks made of gold. There were more than twenty life-size gold llamas, with gold shepherds carrying gold staffs and slings. The thatch was interwoven with gold wire.

Coricancha was not by any means the only golden temple because, as in ancient Mesopotamia, gold served throughout the empire as the link between the mortal world and the immortal realm of the gods. Suddenly, the problems of the Holy Roman Emperor appeared to be solved. The gold had a new divine linkage to celebrate. Atahualpa was killed. The entire Inca civilization was stripped and gradually demolished. The troublesome Pizarro was murdered as the Spanish fought for control of Atahualpa's capital. And Charles V's import of gold quadrupled.

There were some Spaniards who had a clearer understanding. Cristóbal de Mena, one of Pizarro's cavalry captains, said: 'Their sole concern was to grab the gold and silver and become rich … without thinking that they were causing harm, spoiling and destroying things. And what they were destroying was more perfect than anything they ever owned.'[15] His words appeared in Seville in 1534, in the first published chronicle of the conquest. He had been demoted once the Inca was destroyed, and returned, a sad man, to Spain.

A World Without Money

The Spanish were now in control of the Inca territories and of the high plateau around Bogotá and Guatavita, the lands of the Muisca. Anyone who minted gold in the new Spanish province was required to pay 20 per cent of its value, the 'royal fifth', to the Crown. Naturally, officials soon began to request the right to act as tax collectors. But there was a fundamental problem; the entire indigenous world had no understanding of money and no use for it.[16]

Understanding gold as having value as 'money' is a cultural choice, not an historical inevitability. It requires people to understand their responsibilities in a very different way from pre-Columbian Americans. Every transaction is monetized, assigned a number to record the winner, the loser and the profit. The process privileges greed and competition over community and mutual support.

The Muisca certainly shared the general human need to look after their own and their families' interests, but exchanges of goods and services were conducted within a powerful social and cosmological framework that insisted on reciprocity between people, and between humans and the natural world. There was no demand for profit, and individual enrichment was suspicious. They carried out exchanges 'in silence and without speaking',[17] with markets in every town, and travellers would travel for many days to exchange goods. Our knowledge is based on the reports of the Spanish colonial officials who were required to investigate and report (and tax) what was going on, and it is clear that both they and modern historians had difficulty understanding what happened. A simple example of the problem is their assumption that goods handed by producers to *caciques* (lords) were 'tribute', obligatory gifts demanded to enrich the elite. But the Muisca did not call these transfers gifts or tribute. In reality they were surplus production given to specialist storekeepers for eventual distribution when needed, a practical example of reciprocal obligation.

The fact that the markets operated in silence does not sit easily with the notion of negotiation and a variable 'market price'. A system of dumb trade between communities, allowing them to exchange necessities on set days and in designated places, integrated economic and social arrangements between communities.[18] One example still survives in Colombia, where the U'wa, whose territory includes the headwaters of the Orinoco River, exchange goods this way. They have clans producing products such as beeswax, woven bags, medicinal plants, dried fish, coca, cotton fabrics and salt, which are deposited on fixed dates at exchange sites marked with tall carved stones. When the sites are revisited by the depositors, other goods have appeared to be collected in their place. Goods can be exchanged without debate if their relative values are well known, especially when there are storehouses to iron out shortages, and it seems that exchange values were well understood.

The Value of Gold Coins

Value in a money-based market is normally established by the balance of supply and demand, which is unpredictable. Value in the indigenous market was fixed, made up of the material in an object, the distance it had travelled and the work that had gone into it. There were clearly times when this broke down; archaeological evidence of hardship and starvation, for example among the Maya, seems to be connected with climate change or over-population. But when the climate was more regular, the economy seems to have been very stable. This was most unsatisfactory for the Spanish. Here were millions of people participating in a complex economy with no specialized traders and there was no space in the transaction for outside authority. It excluded the king and his tax collectors. The colonial solution was for Muisca communities to monetize exchange and for Spain to insist on their use of gold 'coins'. These were *tenjuelos*, 'pimples', small domed circles of gold left in the bottoms of moulds after casting. The Muisca accepted them, but did not comprehend that they were supposed to have a negotiable value linked to their size. They usually weighed 4 grams, the same as the later British half-sovereign, but some might be 50 per cent thicker and the Muisca attached no significance to that. They treated them all as the same value. What counted was not thickness or weight but diameter (one finger-joint) and circumference, approximately 6cm. The Muisca did not like using large numbers of *tenjuelos* (or found them too scarce), and since the gold had no value to them, being nothing but unworked raw material, they used 6cm lengths of cotton, matching their circumference, as coin equivalents. They thereby immediately invented symbolic currency. That was less intellectually challenging for them than for the Spanish, as the Muisca did not attach more intrinsic value to gold *tenjuelos* than to cotton threads. It may not be a coincidence that every person arriving in Kogi territory today is instructed by a Mama, in what could be seen as a solemn pastiche of an official colonial interview, to report on the process that brought them and is given approximately 6cm of cotton thread to hold while speaking. It must then be returned and is kept as a record of the interview.

The value of a piece of gold lay in what had been done to it; the indigenous people valued the effort that went into fabrication far more than the raw material. One sign of the indigenous value system is that when officials stamped a mark on the gold *tenjuelos*, their value rose by 50 per cent.

To the Spanish, it was obvious that the value of a gold coin was in the weight of gold, not in how it looked. So it was not at all clear to them why their coins lost value as they flowed in ever greater quantities. But they did, so much that twenty-three years after the gold of Peru began to be delivered to Spain, the King of Spain defaulted on his loans.[19] It happened again eighteen years later.[20] The next default took eleven years, then ten, then twenty, another ten, then just four years. Altogether, between 1557 and 1666, the rulers of Spain went bust nine times. Gold wasn't all it was cracked up to be.

Part IV

The Making of States

Chapter 18

The Disintegration of Christendom

The Paradox of Plenty

Spain's hunt for gold would become a central enterprise, supposedly enriching it vastly. Yet bullion contains no inherent value. It is one of the greatest and most satisfying paradoxes in all history that the success of the ferocious search for gold by Spain and Portugal led to their exclusion from the surging prosperity of Europe that followed. Their whole attention and strength had been committed to physically seizing it from people and places that were at the very limit of their grasp, and when they had it, its value faded away. They wanted it so much, and as the old English saying has it, 'want shall be your master'. They had been among the most affluent regions in the world in 1500, but over the following centuries fell behind all the main European powers.[1] The rest of Europe watched with envy and then puzzlement as Spain amassed piles of treasure and became relatively poorer. American gold was sent first to Andalusia, which was the richest region of continental Spain in 1530. By 1591, it was one of the poorest and remained mired in poverty for centuries.[2] The gold vanished as soon as it arrived, used to pay off vast and profitless borrowing for war. The Spanish became used to seeing the gold disappear to foreign creditors as soon as it arrived. The latest analyses endorse the observation of David Hume in the eighteenth century that the effect of the huge inflow of bullion was not to increase wealth but prices, 'obliging everyone to pay a greater number of these little yellow or white pieces for every thing he purchases', and so cripple exports.[3] Modern research is unequivocal that the immediate benefits to Spain were undermined by the steady inflow of precious metals. Instead of growing richer and more secure, inflation, depopulation and lack of commercial energy diminished exports and paralyzed domestic political institutions.[4] Spain was left far behind by the Netherlands, England and France, which benefited much more from economic growth.

By 1700, the average inhabitant of England had an income 50 per cent higher than the average Iberian. Spain and Portugal had the lowest incomes per capita in Western Europe, and that remained true right down to the end of the twentieth century. That was the reward for launching Europe's gold-hungry conquest of the world.

We should not suppose that our age is any cleverer. In 1960, five countries with large oil reserves – Iran, Iraq, Kuwait, Saudi Arabia and Venezuela – formed OPEC, a cartel of governments to protect the value of their oil. More oil-producing states joined. Its operation was very effective, and the price of oil quadrupled between 1972 and 1975. OPEC countries were suddenly extraordinarily wealthy and delighted in the power that flowed to them. In 1976, OPEC's founder, the Venezuelan politician Juan Pablo Pérez Alfonzo, who knew all about the story of Spanish gold, warned: 'Ten years from now, twenty years from now, you will see, oil will bring us ruin … It is the devil's excrement.' No one believed him. Venezuela, Libya, Algeria, Indonesia and Nigeria all looked forward to a new age in which they would be the prosperous arbiters of the global economy. However, by the dawn of the twenty-first century, they were all in desperate and deepening poverty. Even Kuwait and Saudi Arabia saw their real incomes per head fall dramatically. Bewildered observers began talking about 'The Paradox of Plenty'.[5]

The modern disaster was caused by enthusiastic borrowing and spending on spectacular luxuries, a complete lack of investment in productive enterprise or infrastructure, a spectacular degree of corruption, contempt for the idea of paying taxes and, of course, total dependence on one single source of income, while the rest of the world figured out ways to turn all this to their advantage. To that may be added, in many cases, oil wealth supporting the stifling power of severe religious orthodoxy and ferocious suppression of dissent.

That is very similar to what happened to Spain 400 years earlier, except that what the Aztecs called 'god-shit' was bright and shining and completely odourless. Unlike oil, bullion was used as money, so this was an even more fundamental upheaval, but the journey through the paradox was very similar. The sudden initial offer of unlimited power and wealth took Spain – by way of extravagance, corruption, indolence and religious intolerance – up the infernal creek without a paddle. By the end of the sixteenth century, the Cortes (parliament) of Castile was complaining that the more gold that came in, the poorer the kingdom became; instead of being the richest in the world, the Spanish kingdoms became the poorest, because everything flowed straight out again 'to the Kingdoms of our enemies'.[6] By then, a Spanish theologian, Martín de Azpilcueta, and a French political analyst, Jean Bodin, had both set out the underlying explanation of the fall in the value of gold in Spanish markets. Known today as the 'Quantity Theory of Money', in its simplest form it says that if the supply of money increases faster than anything else, its value falls.[7] That upsets the balance between different forms of wealth and power. As the ground shifts, society changes.

Charles V, Universal Monarch

Europe's practical education in the Quantity Theory of Money began with a bizarre stroke of fate in 1520. That year, the gold of Moctezuma arrived, and it flowed to a young man who had just acquired sovereignty over more of the world than any European since the fall of Rome. Sooner or later, the great families of Christendom, who chose their marriages from a tiny pool of their equals, were bound to produce an inbred scion who inherited from almost all of them. Fortune had fallen on Charles. This was the closest any man has come to holding formal titles over all the lands on Earth. Charles was readily persuaded, in his younger years, that destiny had called him to be the Universal Monarch of Christendom.

The idea that there was a Christian *imperium*, a commonwealth of Christendom descended from the Western Roman Empire, was a powerful force throughout the Middle Ages, but Charles V became the first Holy Roman Emperor since Charlemagne who could be spoken of as the leader of a re-emerging Universal Christian Commonwealth.[8]

The Cost of Imperium

He had inherited lordship over perhaps a thousand different subject territories across Europe, each with its own language or dialect, its own traditions and often a charter of rights and 'privileges' (literally 'private laws'), which entitled it to resist taxation, insist on consultation, control trade and oppose the appointment of outsiders to their government. Every step to gather absolute power in the ruler's hands was experienced as a challenge to the ancient pride and hard-won rights of some community somewhere. Resistance would begin immediately after his accession, in the heart of his empire, and it would introduce 'communities', *Comunidades*, as political actors for the first time. Without the promise of gold, Charles would not have been able to try to reshape Christendom.

He was king of the whole Iberian Peninsula apart from Portugal and had probably more power over Castile than anywhere else in Europe, but he came from Flanders and spoke hardly any Spanish. In 1520, the urban communes of Castile felt disempowered, complaining that they were being made to pay for foreign adventures and their kingdom subsumed into Aragon. He was confronted by his first uprising. It was truly revolutionary, a forerunner of uprisings across Europe a century later, and it was expensive to suppress. The final destruction of Castile's radical revolt on 23 April 1521 is commemorated today as Castile and León Day in a celebration of nationalism.

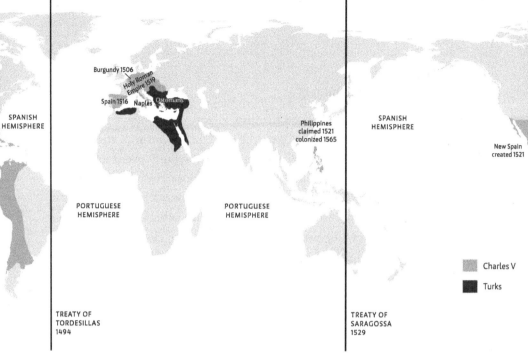

Burgundy 1506

Holy Roman
Empire 1519

Spain 1516   Naples   Ottomans

SPANISH
HEMISPHERE

SPANISH
HEMISPHERE

Philippines
claimed 1521
colonized 1565

New Spain
created 1521

PORTUGUESE
HEMISPHERE

PORTUGUESE
HEMISPHERE

Charles V

Turks

TREATY OF
TORDESILLAS
1494

TREATY OF
SARAGOSSA
1529

The world of Charles V.

Enforcing his authority in Castile had consumed a great deal of time and treasure: ruling the whole world would be costly beyond calculation, but the gold was on its way from his Kingdom of the Islands and Mainland of the Ocean Sea. As soon as the first tranche was unloaded in 1519, he had been able to begin the exploitation of this spectacular acquisition. He could afford to pay off the seven German princes who had the power to elect him as Holy Roman Emperor.[9] However high the price, it was preferable to allowing the King of France to outbid him. The Holy Roman Empire meant suzerainty over all of Central Europe: it embraced the whole of the northern coastline from the Low Counties to Poland, only excluding Denmark, and took in Central Europe and Italy, bordered by Venice and the Ottoman Empire. Included within it were the 150 or so separate dukedoms, countships, free cities and electorates that were called Germany. Charles had the nominal title 'King of the Romans', which meant 'Emperor in waiting', but when the chips were down that meant nothing. Whoever became emperor, ruling by divine right, would have the power to challenge everyone up to and including the Pope. If Francis of France had more chips on the table, Charles's positions as Archduke of Austria, Count of Tyrol, Duke of Carinthia and Landgrave of Alsace would all be vulnerable. Francis would be seen to have authority over him. The belief in gold from America put paid to that challenge. A consortium of German and Italian bankers lent him 850,000 florins, a little over 3 metric tons of gold. Gold was coming, they were sure of it.

Handling Gold Currency

While he was waiting for that to happen, though, Charles was handing over huge quantities of gold coins. When his forces captured the King of France after the Battle of Pavia in 1526, he realized that he had found a way to extract from France what he was not receiving from America. He held Francis's children hostage and demanded ransom in the form of 2 million gold *écus*. This was a cash transaction, with the money crossing the border on a boat going one way and the princes on a boat going the other. It was supposed to happen on 1 April 1529, but everyone had to wait while 6½ tons of gold coins were checked and counted. They were individually handmade; 40,000 were rejected as substandard. The King of France ran out of his own currency, so foreign coins of uncertain composition were rounded up and reminted.[10] The exchange finally took place on 1 July.

It was a clear demonstration of the huge problem of using gold coins; the Muisca seem to have been very sensible in preferring pieces of cotton thread. It also turned into a demonstration of how little grasp Europeans had of finance. Charles had correctly realized that the French nobility and clergy would be impoverished by having to hand over their treasure, but he did not understand that acquiring his own ability to spend huge amounts of gold in Spain would create a wave of inflation. Since rents were fixed, their relative value fell sharply, impoverishing his own nobility. Nor did he expect the lack of gold in France to create deflation there, reducing prices. Spaniards began buying cheap French goods with their newfound gold, which quite quickly drained back to France. Charles's expectation that the ransom would solve his debt problems was dashed and he began degrading his own currency.

Gold to Support the Emperor

Five years later, the plunder from Peru began to pour into Seville. It overwhelmed the senses, the imagination and the fantasies of the city. When Pizarro's first shipload arrived, on 9 January 1534, crowds rushed to the wharves to watch the ingots and treasures pile up in more than a hundred carts. Some of the treasures were still intact, such as a gold 'idol' the size of a 4-year-old child. It all came ashore at the Torre del Oro, once the 'gold' watchtower of the Almohad Caliphs. Its name derived from the golden glow of its stones. Gold here was now no longer just an illusory glow; the Torre del Oro was literally a place of gold. Masses were sung to give thanks. One 14-year-old, Pedro Cieza de León, would write years later about the life-changing effect of seeing Atahualpa's treasure being carried off to the House of Trade to be weighed.[11] Charles V gave urgent orders for the whole lot to be turned into coin immediately. He was entitled to one-fifth of the conquistadors' treasure, but he confiscated another 800,000 ducats in exchange for bonds on which he promised to pay 3 per cent. Surrounded by the unconquered worlds of England, France, Portugal and the Turks, he was making a start on the Empire of Islam. He needed to pay and equip an army to capture Tunis,[12] so he had to have more gold, as fast as possible. The following year, young Cieza de León shipped out to the northern Colombian coast and became a tomb robber.[13] Meanwhile, Holy Roman Emperor Charles V took Tunis, flexing a continent-spanning power that had not been seen in Europe for 1,500 years.

American gold held his empire together by allowing him to conjure up overwhelming shows of his infinite might and limitless wealth. This Holy Roman Empire became a game of smoke and mirrors that depended on spectacular, highly focussed displays of the power to crush dissent to pulp. Charles did not understand economics, but read and understood Machiavelli and the science of power. When his home city of Ghent violently rebelled in 1539, he destroyed it without any military force. The city's merchants had thought they were rich and powerful; they were about to discover the full meaning of those terms. Charles had left in 1517 as the young Duke of Burgundy, to become a king in Spain. Now he returned as the head of a behemoth stamping the Earth, rich beyond calculation, with power that enveloped the globe. His supplies began arriving in a continuous stream of wagons over several days, and then his procession walked through the city gates. It was a pantomime with the power to freeze blood, taking more than six hours.

There were about 4,000 Netherlands cavalry, including 800 archers and men-at-arms, lances at the ready. They were accompanied by 4,000 German infantry: pike men, halberdiers and arquebusiers with the weapons that had so dramatically unnerved the Aztecs and the Inca. The empire was an overwhelming military machine, but it had also now become a great gold-powered cathedral on wheels, with wagonloads of sacred equipment to open the gates of heaven, to be managed by a chilling horde of cardinals, archbishops, bishops 'and other great ecclesiastical lords and princes'. Then came the greatest perambulating court ever seen:

'... many great princes, dukes, marquesses, counts, barons grandmasters, and lords, as well as most of the knights of his Order of the Golden Fleece and others, and a very great number of noblemen from every quarter and country, Spain, Naples, Sicily, Italy, Germany, as well as the Netherlands and other lands where His Majesty held sway, along with various ambassadors from our Holy Father the Pope, the kings of France, England, Portugal, and Poland, as well as from many princes of the Empire and Italy, and from the republic of Venice and other countries, provinces and potentates.'[14]

Tairona gold work.

The Lord of Varna.

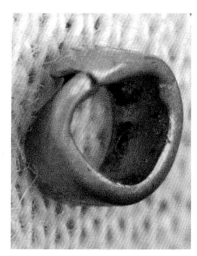

The oldest gold object. Diameter approximately 4mm.

Meskalamdug's helmet.

Croesus's gold stater.

Rembrandt, *Belshazzar's Feast.*

The rock carving at Behistun, Iran.

Gold coin of Philip of Macedon. Gold coin from Henley-on-Thames, Britain.

Interior of the Hagia Sophia, Constantinople.

The Iron Crown of Lombardy.

Vespasian Psalter.

Sainte Chapelle, Paris.

Fulani gold.

The Catalan Atlas: Ferrer's ship and Mansa Musa.

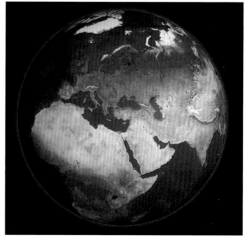

Fra Mauro's map rotated and NASA image with clouds removed.

Juan de la Cosa's world map.

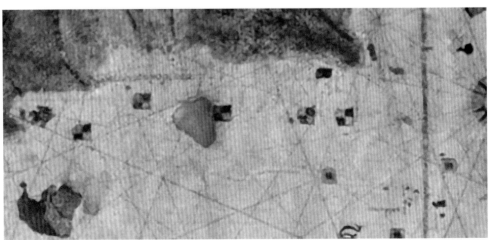

English flags on Juan de la Cosa's map of America.

Cellini salt cellar, Kunsthistorisches Museum, Wien.

Philip II medal: The World is Not Enough.

A modern replica of the roller press in Hall.

Church of São Francisco, Porto.

Gold mask of Princess of Chen, 1018 CE.

Europe in 1520.

Of course, Charles also brought his household and his domestic officers, as well as his personal bodyguard.

Ghent trembled as thousands of feet, hooves and wheels moved through it. And then they stopped. The entire military, religious and royal establishment of the empire required lodging; and food. The emperor's behemoth had come to eat Ghent. The city crumbled, its supposed privileges willingly surrendered in the hope that Charles would leave. Twenty-five people were executed. Hundreds of nobles, civic leaders, officials, guildsmen and workers had to beg for mercy. Only then did the monster move off.

To maintain this power was anything but cheap. It had a golden appetite. It was obviously expensive to suppress local autonomy and shut down resentment at taking money from one territory to deal with problems in another. But Charles also faced endless wars, against European rivals and beyond. In 1520, Suleiman the Magnificent had begun to advance up the Danube, then the Ottoman army moved close to Vienna, threatening the very existence of Christendom.

The Mystery of Income

Meanwhile, gold was not making Charles rich; it was just fuelling his belief that he must be able to afford whatever he wanted. It was belief rather than fact, because Charles had no idea how much gold was actually coming to him.

In 1522, he had set up the Consejo de la Hacienda to give him some idea, but it failed.[15] No one knew the figures then, and no one knows them now. As we move from the obscurity of sporadic medieval records to the intense recordkeeping of Spanish bureaucracy, there is no improvement in reliability. Records are not the truth. From 1503–30, 20,000kg of gold was recorded as being landed at Seville.[16] In the 1550s, apparently nine times as much came in, and over a period of 70 years, it has been said that Spain took 625 tons of gold from Peru. It is nice to circumscribe the past with serried ranks of numbers, but the only certainty is that they are mistaken. The records were designed to conceal the ignorance and duplicity of assessors and tax collectors, who carefully ignored the 'black economy' and whose interest was in survival, profit and what they could get away with. These records started off being incomplete, only to become more incomplete as wars, fires and floods tossed them around. They were then repaired by historians using their own guesswork and that of the occasional elevated contemporary commentator. This is how the population of Hispaniola in 1492 can be said to be either 60,000 or 8 million; the population of Mexico was anything from 3 million to 52 million; there could have been anything from 11 to 150 million people living in the whole of the Americas; and 90 per cent of them either did or did not die because of European diseases.[17] The amount of precious metal that poured into Europe from America is similarly unquantifiable. The leading historians that have published the figures disagree by a margin of 100 per cent. The only thing we can be sure of is that however much gold was put in the record, and so was liable to royal tax, was a huge understatement.

Charles could manage without knowing because he had bankers in Germany, the Fuggers, who were happy to advance funds on the belief that bullion would come. He started off borrowing over half a million guilders a year (just under 2 tons of gold), for which he was charged fees of up to 40 per cent, and the sum went up from there.[18] Charles was more concerned with his entitlement than his actual wealth, so Europe's money supply was to some extent fictional.

The Silver Mountain

As the flow of gold drove spending, the whole economic structure of Europe began to change, and with it the structure of trade in America and Asia. One of the biggest changes was the sudden availability of gold's small change, silver, in quantities that beggared belief and, inevitably, populations.

In 1550, Jesuit priest Domingo de Santo Tomás wrote from Lima to the Council of the Indies in Seville to warn his sovereign about the reality in Peru of '*el infierno*' (hell):

'It was four years ago, to conclude the perdition of this land, that a mouth of hell was discovered through which every year a great many people are immolated, which the greed of the Spaniards sacrifice to their god that is gold, and it is a mine of silver that is named Potosí.'[19]

Peruvians had used silver as a partner to gold in the jewellery of the elite and property of gods. The golden temple of Coricancha had silver between its stones instead of mortar. It is said that while they spoke of gold as the sweat of the sun, silver was the tears of the moon. To the Spanish it has a different meaning: silver, *plata*, is literally 'money'. Potosí rises some 600 metres to a perfectly symmetrical dark red conical peak 4,200 metres high. This hill was made of 50,000 tons of *plata*, showing an outcrop of ore that was 50 per cent pure silver, 100 metres long and 4 metres wide. In Spanish, Potosí became known as 'the rich hill'; in Quechua, it was 'the mountain that eats men'. The huge city that sprang up there became a primitive man-heap of violence and squalor. In its first fifty years, no European child born in Potosí lived for more than a fortnight.[20] Working conditions were deadly. In the early years, much of the mining was managed by indigenous entrepreneurs,[21] but a census in 1570 made 1.68 million Peruvian men aged between 15 and 50 liable for forced labour; one in seven of them was to be chosen by each village to serve for 121 days every seven years. The summons was regarded as a death warrant. For 200 years, half the world's silver came from Potosí. The Department of Potosí is now one of the poorest places in all the Americas.

When production peaked in 1560, the silver recorded coming into Seville was worth about nine times as much as the gold. Spain was awash with *plata*. And the *plata* was measured in gold. Gold was the king of metals and defined the value of the whole exercise. Today, it is easy enough to find Iberian churches and cathedrals lathered with American gold; never silver. As the Jesuit priest said, those who perished in the silver mines of Potosí were sacrificed at the mouth of hell to the Spanish god, gold.

The Extravagance of Gold and Salt

Everyone understood that the wealth of Peru was changing the world, and there was a strong feeling in Spain that the arrival of the gold and silver was evidence of a special divine blessing. The Church did not exactly switch to the worship of gold, but it was certainly closely bound up with it. The new availability of gold was also used to demonstrate the transcendent status of every other great lord of Europe. Nobility, royalty and powerful men all over Europe spent increasingly lavishly on competitive display, imposing architecture and the creation of masterpieces. The late Renaissance vision of how really important humans should appear in an age of excess was dressed with gold, with gold-threaded clothing and tapestry, massive chains and tableware designed to demonstrate the power, wealth and superhuman magnificence of the mighty. According to one historian, three times as much gold was 'hoarded' – which included being turned into objects and materials for extravagant display – as was coined.[22] A new kind of human being was now spoken of, born out of the humble artisan: the brilliant 'artist' who could turn wealth into fabulous masterpieces. That was certainly how the goldsmith Benvenuto Cellini wanted the world to see him, and he achieved his purpose.[23]

In the indigenous communities of South America, a mysterious power of transcendental connection was understood to be required for a metallurgist to alloy and transform gold into an object with the power to affect and sustain life. The Kogi speak of this lost knowledge, which they believe is contained in the surviving ancestral pieces now in museums. It is almost as though that mystical power was carried in the stolen gold. That showed in Cellini's autobiography, where he established himself as using a power beyond the reach of ordinary mortals when he created his salt cellar for Francis I of France.

Cellini's design was approximately 10 inches in height and 13 inches in width, 'wrought of solid gold, and worked entirely with the chisel',[24] resting on a base of ebony with ivory bearings to move it around. It was an allegory of the world:

'I made two figures sitting cross-legged against each other. The sea, formed as a man, held a richly crafted ship, which could hold salt enough, under which I had attached four seahorses and put the trident in the right hand; the earth I had formed a female, of such beautiful shape and graceful, as only I could; I had placed next to her a rich, ornate temple on the ground. The arms of the sea are seen running into the earth which should contain the pepper.'

In the base of the pedestal, the figures of the four main winds, the times of the day and the emblems of human activities complete this allegory. The King of France was stunned by the design and agreed to pay for the work.[25]

Cellini, who never doubted his brilliance in life as in art, single-handedly fought off four armed bandits on his way home with the gold. When he presented the finished piece, in 1543, he claims the king 'uttered a loud outcry of astonishment and could not sate his eyes with gazing at it'. Its point was to convey the power and discernment of the great king, who by moving the salt and pepper around his table was demonstrating mastery of the riches of the Earth and the sea and the power to bend genius to his service. Francis of France, like

Henry VIII of England and the potentates of the Church, had his gold from Spain. In Spain, its coining was known as the minting of golden raindrops, which immediately evaporated on the hot ground to condense again in foreign purses.

Some of the gold wrought into such stunning metaphors of Earth and sea may even have come from the treasure looted from indigenous tombs and have once represented similar mythologized beings there. Those, though, were made by anonymous craftsmen who believed they were working to hold the world in balance. Cellini was celebrating his own brilliance and the arrogance of the king who employed him. Both were determined to hold the world in thrall.

The Great Price Rise

The Mansa Musa effect, the paradox of plenty in which lavish spending undermines the purchasing power of what is thought to be valuable, was working its seismic magic. The more bullion that arrived, the less it was worth. It is now called the 'Great Price Rise', and of course there were winners as well as losers. It took wealth from those who lived on fixed incomes and enriched those with things to sell. Parts of Europe were quite transformed as farmers, merchants and traders prospered. In the sixteenth century, real wages in Valencia more than doubled, as did the wages of builders in Antwerp, Madrid, Paris and Gdansk.[26] In France, by the end of the century, butter was ten times the price it had been 100 years earlier. Wine was nine times as expensive, olive oil eight times.[27] This was very good for wine and olive growers, but less wonderful for great lords with big kitchens and feasting halls. In southern England, where wages and wool profits rose with inflation, thousands of farmhouses had their low thatched roofs raised, stairs and new floors inserted, open hearths replaced by chimneys and windows glazed, together with a significant increase in furnishings.[28] In England and the Netherlands, workers had more freedom to negotiate their wages than the peasants of Spain and France, and their wages rose with inflation.[29] The flow of money began to change the nature of large-scale land ownership, as agriculture became a capitalist enterprise. The wool trade dominated much of it, and those with access to finance became a new kind of aristocracy.

The losers were often semi-regal nobles who felt that raising rents to keep up with inflation was beneath them, even dishonourable. One recent historian studying the affairs of the Earl of Shrewsbury felt prompted to comment on the oddity that 'before the 1590s many, perhaps most large landowners seem to have done little effective to preserve their financial stability'.[30] He suggests that like their medieval forbears, they found estate management dirty and demeaning. The magisterial Earl of Westmoreland and the great Northern baron Lord Darcy preferred to boast that they lived as their fathers had done, off the old rents of their lands. Inflation would obviously make them poorer, and the people who paid their rents, on their land and in their towns, would become relatively better off. In fact, some would become better off than the great lords. Inflation stimulated the emergence of an entirely new society in Europe.

The New Warfare

The rising price of butter was not a problem for great princes, but the rising cost of military victory certainly was. As medieval Europe became a money economy, armies of mercenaries had been recruited and the old Roman problem of paying huge numbers of soldiers reappeared. An influx of gold changed the scale of what was militarily possible. It had been associated with a social revolution when it was first used, 6,000 years earlier, when it empowered new forms of society with the first weapons for war, under the power of warlords and supreme leaders who had the authority of gods. Military power had become the basis of civilization. Now, as gold poured into Europe on an unprecedented scale, it paid for a magnification and transformation of war: bigger armies, better equipment, more powerful weapons.

Once-secure walls could not stand against modern artillery. The response was the invention of a new kind of military architecture, in which fortresses were protected not by crenelated walls but by huge sloping ramparts, with projecting triangular bastions as artillery emplacements. To build such places cost a fortune; to attack them was even more expensive. Europe's sovereigns were ready to spend their gold not just on display but on military architecture and huge numbers of troops.

The effect of American gold was not to make Charles V rich – his expenditure ballooned far faster than he swallowed treasure – but to encourage him to borrow more to wage war on a greater scale. Of course, that meant that every other ruler in Europe also had to borrow, to protect themselves. They were passing their present and future fortunes through the hands of bankers. In place of sinful interest, bankers could and did impose a handling charge which fluctuated according to the risk. When Charles won a great victory, the charge might be 14.5 per cent; when he lost, it could be 80 or even 100 per cent. In total, he borrowed nearly 29 million ducats. The charges added another 9 million, 31.5 tons of gold.[31]

That is not a huge sum by our own standards. In 2018, the UK paid over fifteen times as much to service its loans, but we live in a very different kind of economy. This was Charles's own money, making lowly common bankers richer and more powerful than princes.

Inflation was also at work in the Arab world. It was effectively imported from Europe, to some extent as a result of Europe's enhanced capacity to spend money on warfare. As the Ottoman Empire advanced to take on the new military forces of Europe, it had to spend at the same level. Large armies were paid in coin, accelerating the development of market economies and speeding up the circulation of money. Prices in Istanbul rose 500 per cent between 1500 and 1700. One debasement of the currency in 1586 meant that prices doubled in three years.[32] In other words, gold was getting cheaper here too. To stay wedded to it, the entire basis of taxation and administration had to change. As in most of Europe, urban workers saw their real incomes decline, but medium-size landholders and estate owners producing goods for market did very well. Traders rode the inflationary wave and got rich. The Grand Bazaar in Istanbul massively expanded in the sixteenth century under Suleiman the Magnificent. Even today, the bazaar includes a number of gold exchanges, where traders buy the bullion to pay their monthly rent. No one is much interested in trusting a cheque or counting stacks of banknotes, when a 20 square metre stall in the main street may cost over half a million pounds a year;[33] 1.5kg of gold a month is easier to manage and far more certain.

The Price of Forgiveness

The Christian Church, too, needed to keep up with princes. In the new age of flamboyance, where power was made visible by extravagant luxury, the Church needed to show that it was not going to disappear from view. Pope Leo X spent beyond his income simply on his own personal life of pomp and display, but he proposed to turn St Peter's into the greatest church in the world and a magnet for profitable pilgrimage. His budget for this work, according to his architect, Raphael, was a million ducats, and Raphael was allocated 60,000 a year.[34] Not that the Pope had the money. It was to be raised by the sale of indulgences. There had once been a subtle theological justification for the Church recognizing an act that could secure personal 'remission before God of the temporal punishment due to sins whose guilt has already been forgiven', but by now this was a simple cash bargain.[35] The Church taught that indulgences could be bought for friends and family who were already dead.[36] In 1517, a Dominican friar called Johann Tetzel was made commissioner of indulgences for Archbishop Albrecht von Brandenburg and saw this as a spectacular sales opportunity: 'Do you not hear the voices of your dead parents and other people, screaming and saying: "Have pity on me, have pity on me ... We are suffering severe punishments and pain, from which you could rescue us with a few alms, if only you would."'[37] He is said to have marketed his products with the slogan 'As soon as the coin in the coffer rings, the soul from purgatory springs'.[38]

Kings, princes and prelates paid twenty-five gold guilders to wipe out their sins, and those of their dead relatives. They had quite a lot of sins in the family. There followed a sliding scale of charges, down to burgers and merchants making 200 guilders a year, who were charged three guilders, and those on smaller incomes had to pay one guilder, or just a half guilder. The Church was inviting people to put their faith in gold.

The eruption against monetizing God's forgiveness would be volcanic. In 1517, a theology teacher at Wittenberg University is said to have fixed his now legendary list of ninety-five single-sentence Latin criticisms ('theses') to a church door. Martin Luther hoped to provoke the intellectual debate that might eventually reform matters. As we all know, he succeeded on a scale that shook and fractured the foundations of Christendom. The echo of the golden guilders that fell into the coffer would ring louder than all the church bells together.

For the first time, a Church critic was able to communicate as though he had a pulpit in the home of anyone who wanted to hear him. The printing press had been invented and developed eighty years before by two goldsmiths in Strasbourg, Johann Fust and Johannes Gutenberg, as a device, in effect, to print money. Luther duly turned the presses of Strasbourg, Wittenberg, Augsburg and Nuremburg into wonderful money-spinners. In the early 1520s, some 6 million argumentative pamphlets were published for a German population of about 12 million. Cheap pamphlets were a completely new phenomenon. Only about one person in ten was literate, and hardly anyone could afford a book, but these pamphlets cost about the same as a hen,[39] and were read aloud. They were spoken (or even sung), and quite often included pictures to make their points. When Tetzel tried to rebut Luther in a pamphlet of his own, Luther's response was vitriolic, accusing Tetzel of treating scripture the way a sow treated a feed sack.

Luther emerged as a protectionist populist leader,[40] raging both about the Church's monetization of salvation and trade's monetization of society:

> 'We have to throw our gold and silver into foreign lands and make the whole world rich while we ourselves remain beggars. England would have less gold if Germany let it keep its cloth, and the king of Portugal, too, would have less if we let him keep his spices. Count up how much gold is taken out of Germany, without need or reason, from a single Frankfurt fair, and you will wonder how it happens that there is a heller [coin] left in German lands. Frankfurt is the golden and silver hole through which everything that springs and grows, is minted or coined here, flows out of Germany. If that hole were stopped up, we should not now have to listen

to the complaint that there are debts everywhere and no money; that all lands and cities are burdened with taxes and payments.'[41]

It was obvious that Charles's golden empire and the Pope's golden Church were bound up in each other, so Charles decided to personally sit in judgement on Martin Luther in 1521. His pronouncement was the condemnation of Luther and a declaration of war on Protestantism. Not surprisingly, many German princes and the King of England saw this as an opportunity to weaken the authorities that weighed on them, Pope and emperor. Frederick III of Saxony spirited Luther away to sanctuary in his castle at Wartburg. It was less a theological issue than a matter of power.

The result was endless strife, and some 2,000 executions for heresy.[42] By 1553, Charles was in such trouble with suppressing heresy that, having failed to smash the Protestant bastion of Metz, he had to flee to Innsbruck and be rescued. He was only 55, but was prematurely aged, sclerotic and toothless, suffering from painful gout and despairing. He could not reconcile himself to the obvious fact that he would, as Holy Roman Emperor, have to accept that his subjects would include Protestants. The next year, he began to withdraw from power. He wanted to abdicate in favour of his son, Philip, but it was not practical for any single man to cope with his sprawling lands. He handed the Holy Roman Empire to his brother, Ferdinand, and then Spain, Italy and the Netherlands to Philip. The dream of a single Christendom under Pope and emperor disappeared. Charles retired to a monastery and died two years later while the Reformation raged on.

Chapter 19

Ruin of the Spanish Crown

No Such Thing as Enough

In 1583, Charles's son, Philip II of Spain, issued a gold-plated medal showing the whole globe surmounted by a leaping horse (his symbol: *Philippus* means 'horse-lover'). His head was surrounded by 'PHILIPP II HISP ET NOVI ORBIS REX' ('Philip II King of Spain and the New World'). The other side bore the astonishing slogan 'NON SUFFICIT ORBIS' ('The world is not enough').

Dated 1580, it sounds like a cry of bottomless pain, but that is not what was meant. He had become, in Spanish law, master of the whole world's oceans and non-Christian lands. In his father's time, Papally-agreed treaties had recognized most of the trans-Atlantic world as Spain's, while Brazil, along with the Pacific Ocean, Asia and Africa, was officially decreed to be Portugal's exclusive sphere of influence.[1] That did not leave Philip with enough sources of gold and silver to sustain his boundless ambition, and by 1580 he had defaulted three times. So that year he took advantage of a dynastic crisis to seize Portugal, and Portugal's half of the planet. The whole world, he proclaimed, was not enough.

The terrible irony was that it was true – being the legitimate ruler of much of the world (at least in his own eyes) did not give him mastery over it. The year before seizing Portugal, he had been confronted by the secession of the Protestant provinces of northern Flanders, and in 1581 the States-General of these United Provinces declared independence. He had to crush what seemed to be an indestructible Protestant threat in the north. And then there were the Turks.

He committed himself and his empire unstintingly to battling the enemies that surrounded him. The whole world did not have enough gold to pay his armies, and in 1596 he defaulted for a fourth time. Some of my ancestors became involved in managing Spain's financial arrangements through Amsterdam, and the family memory is that the Spanish Crown's defaults were painful.[2] Many families evidently learned a bitter understanding that the world really wasn't enough for great kings. I was very puzzled as a small child when my impoverished grandmother sternly warned me, 'Never lend money to princes'.[3]

The direct costs of war took 60 per cent of his income.[4] Bullion and the loans raised on it allowed Philip to be at war every year of his reign. The injection of unprecedented wealth into his war machine would reshape the balance of power in the Mediterranean and totally transform both the nature of war and the societies that waged it in Northern Europe.

War Against the Ottoman Empire

When Philip came to the throne in 1556, Spain was engaged in an existential struggle against the Ottoman Empire, whose long advance threatened to reverse the expulsion of the Moors.[5] They had seized the whole eastern Mediterranean, including Egypt, and almost all of North Africa, including Tunis. It was down to Philip to turn the tide. That, he believed – as his father had done – was a primary reason why God had given him the wealth of America. But the Turks, who had the finest land-cannon in the world, were widely thought to be invincible. In 1558, they raided Minorca, just 250km from Barcelona, sailing victoriously back to Istanbul with Spanish ships stuffed with prisoners and loot. The Habsburg ambassador was taunted by crowds asking if any of his staff had relatives among the captives.[6]

Philip's titles included King of not just Spain, Flanders, Milan and Naples but also King of Jerusalem and sovereign of the Western and Eastern Indies, including 'the Islands and Mainland of the Ocean Sea'. But these claims were slight compared to the titles proclaimed for the Ottoman Sultan, Suleiman

Philip and Suleiman, 1595.

the Magnificent, in Istanbul. From his conquest of Constantinople, the Sultan inherited the title Emperor of Rome and of all the lands of Byzantium; he called himself Caesar. He believed the whole world had been granted him as a divine gift and that he was the universal Caliph. These two great empires were in a competition without limits. Obviously, the world was not enough.

The fundamental difference between their powers was that, at least on a superficial level, Philip was receiving a huge flow of money from America, and the Sultan was not. The Islamic Empire's wealth had grown by conquest, and unless Turkish conquests continued, the only income to be expected was from taxing agricultural production and trade. Turkish currency had been silver, but that began to be seriously debased after the conquest of Constantinople and a new gold coin was produced, the sultani.[7] As a prince, Suleiman was trained as a goldsmith, like his father,[8] and he regarded gold as the symbol of ultimate value on Earth; his palace dazzled with it, and visitors were astounded. The Divan room where the Grand Vizier held audience was embellished with gold and jewels under a gold dome. His personal gold adornments, including the most incredible tall pointed solid gold crown-helmet, were not even made in his own empire; he bought them from Venice. Gold only came to Istanbul if it was captured or by way of trade. After 1560, gold and silver from America was being used by Europeans to buy Ottoman luxuries, but the effect was to create inflation there and the old Islamic currency lost its value, eventually collapsing completely.[9] The spice trade through Venice had been an important source of gold, but with Europeans now in the Indian Ocean, that was disappearing. The English estimated that the Ottoman treasury was on track to lose customs revenue of over 300,000 sovereigns a year.[10]

The Cost of Muskets

Philip laid out the gold for new technology in the form of a new killing machine, the musket. There is some debate among specialists about exactly what was meant by 'musket',[11] but it is clear that a new heavy personal firearm was produced which was far more potent than the arquebus. Philip had the wealth and the will to develop 'a specialist infantry weapon, awesome in its power',[12] which would be able to safely kill an armoured knight at significant range, and so give his forces a tremendous advantage. Weapons manufacturing became a royal industry. In 1565, when Philip's only active military effort was supporting the relief of Malta, he nevertheless spent nearly 2 million ducats on his forces.[13] Elizabeth I of England's military budget totalled about a sixth of that.[14] The new hand-held super-weapon bent the wealth of America to transform warfare by bringing together metallurgical skill, mechanical inventiveness and alchemical cunning. Inventors came, and experiments led to production under the control of a court official, the *veedor*. This was a kind of Manhattan Project to spend whatever was needed to transform warfare. An even bigger expense was the gunpowder. The production of saltpetre was an alchemical mystery best understood in Bohemia and northern Germany; it was said, at least rhetorically, to be worth its weight in gold.[15]

Its effect was first seen in 1565. In May of that year, an Ottoman fleet of nearly 200 vessels attacked Malta. It was said to have been the largest seaborne force assembled since antiquity. The defenders suffered massive losses but managed to hold out until Philip's relief force eventually arrived on 7 September. The new muskets, handled by men without armour, seem to have totally destroyed the besiegers' will to fight.[16] Within a few years, plate armour would be discarded to display as heirlooms.

New Weapons at Sea

Gold also financed a transformation of war at sea to put a stop to the Turkish conquest of the Mediterranean. In 1568, Philip paid Venice to build a dozen or more entirely novel giant oar-powered battleships, called galleasses. Mediterranean galleys had been floating platforms for fighting men, supplemented by a few rather ineffective gunpowder weapons. Now the Venetians had invented a way of putting far more heavy artillery on board. It was an investment that paid off spectacularly, when the Spanish and Venetian fleets did battle with the Ottomans at Lepanto in 1571. Some 400 Ottoman and Christian warships clashed in 'the most noble and memorable event that past centuries have seen, or future generations can ever hope to witness'. That was the judgement of Cervantes, who was a professional soldier at the battle (and proudly showed off his damaged left hand, struck by an Ottoman arquebus shot). The Ottomans' judgement was equally dramatic; they said it was the worst blow in 170 years, since Timur (Tamerlane) smashed the Ottoman state and captured the Sultan in 1402.[17] Almost half of the 80,000 Turkish soldiers and sailors perished, and only forty-eight of their 278 ships returned home. The total death toll on that afternoon, around 40,000, was about a third higher than the slaughter on the first day of the Battle of the Somme. The Christian fleet lost only thirteen galleys. Apart from having the devastating new galleasses, they had almost three times as many guns and vastly more ammunition than their adversaries. Afterwards, it was decided to melt down the captured Ottoman guns as they were too badly made to be useful. The scale of Christian investment was also revealed in the manning of the fleets; the Ottomans were seriously undermanned, and relied mostly on bowmen, whereas men like Cervantes were given at least 25 ducats when they signed on, plus annual pay of 12 ducats (the pay of an unskilled worker) as well as food and clothing.[18]

Calvinism and Finance

Philip's focus was split between the war against Islam and the battle to destroy heretics in his own lands. Philip shared his father's firm determination to oppose Protestant theology as an existential threat to a world order that God had given him the resources to defend.

This bloodshed was explained in terms of Catholics and Protestants, but the Protestant 'heresy' was closely connected with the needs of commerce. John Calvin's version of Protestantism had spread from his city of Geneva into France and Flanders because, unlike Luther (who wanted to stop international trade), it offered a Church that was sympathetic to trade and finance, and was built with the efforts of 'godly merchants'.[19] He was preaching in an environment where the flow of money was vital, and lending on interest was an essential part of urban life. The Geneva fairs had been international clearing houses since the fourteenth century, and the Medici banking family had a branch there long before the Reformation. In Geneva, usury was now being given a new definition. According to Calvin, only 'biting' loans are forbidden, and you can lend at interest to businesspeople who would make a profit using the money. Reasonable interest was fine, and the pastors of Geneva were moneylenders themselves.[20] Calvinist Christianity was shaped by golden money.

This became very clear in France, where a vicious civil war erupted between Catholics and Huguenots (French Calvinists) in 1562. Only about 7 per cent of the mid-sixteenth-century French were Protestants, but they were mostly to be found in very commercial places, such as the artisan workshops and merchant houses of Rouen, Sénlis, Orléans and Tours.[21] Over the whole of northern Europe, the more commercially connected an artisan was (reflected in his status), the more likely he was to prefer the new version of religion. In Paris, merchants and financiers, as well as factional nobles, would be likely to be Protestant and end up having to fight for survival.[22]

Revolt of the Netherlands

Competitive Calvinist bankers even appeared in the Italian city of Lucca, though they were soon driven out to the safety of Northern Europe.[23] The synergy between business, war and Protestantism was even evident in the revolt of the Netherlands. Antwerp, Europe's pre-eminent trading city, depended on providing a safe and open marketplace for merchants of all religious convictions. The city was run by magistrates and aldermen who were themselves largely Calvinist. A king who believed that he ruled by divine authority, and that the flood of gold that came to him was simply God's endorsement of his role on Earth, found himself up against merchants whom he obviously viewed as lesser beings who must obey or be crushed.

Philip's primary weapon against Protestantism was the Inquisition, established in the Netherlands by his father, Charles V, to hunt down all those guilty or even suspected of heresy. The cities of southern Flanders had been demanding its suppression, which they declared was 'iniquitous, contrary to all laws, human and divine, surpassing the greatest barbarism which was ever practised by tyrants'. It was an impediment to trade, making it dangerous for their Protestant customers to come to market. Philip's response was to intensify the persecution, informing the Pope: 'I would lose all my states and a hundred lives, if I had them; for I do not propose nor desire to be the ruler of heretics.' In 1566, his insistence on ruthless dogmatism at a time of harvest failure and urban recession helped provoke a spectacular and widespread iconoclastic outpouring of rage against symbols of Catholicism in Flanders, wrecking churches and cathedrals.

As a consequence, Philip turned his weaponized wealth against the burghers of the Netherlands. In June 1567, muskets were carried into Europe by a 'small and stylish troop of brave and valiant soldiers', 10,000 Italian veterans of the siege of Malta commanded by the Duke of Alba. The young Abbot of Brantôme, in south-west France, used his income of 3,000 livres a year to follow excitement wherever he could, and this was a sight not to be missed. He hurried to catch them as they marched north through Lorraine. He was not disappointed by the spectacle, which identified weaponry with wealth:

'Their dress and arms were mostly gilded and the rest engraved so that they looked more like Captains than soldiers. These were the first men to be carrying great muskets, seen here for the first time going to war as an integral part of a military force on active service. They had been used in the defence of Malta, but it had been very difficult for our soldiers to get used to them.'[24]

Musketeers 'were very well dressed and highly respected, to the extent of having large strong servants who carried for them on the march, and who were paid four ducats.[25] You would have taken them for Princes, striding confidently and with great grace.' They were accompanied by 400 prostitutes on horseback who were, apparently, as fine and beautiful as princesses, as well as 800 on foot who were also finely dressed.

Musketeers did not have to look like soldiers, because their weapons had enough range to keep them safely away from the cut and thrust. The broad-brimmed feathered hat was to become a symbol of a new kind of soldier. Their courtly demeanour belied the Duke of Alba's brutal purpose, which was to enforce royal power in Flanders on the model that had been learned extracting wealth from America. In effect, the inhabitants would become a human gold mine. Alba promised Philip that he would deliver an annual income of 500,000 ducats from the confiscations he would make.

However, his attempt to crush the Low Countries backfired in the most spectacular way. Alba's army was effective and his policy was utterly ruthless, but his attempt to turn Flanders into a heavily taxed goldmine turned resistance into the unstoppable conflict that is now known as the Eighty Years' War, and ultimately led to the creation of the Dutch Protestant republic, a new economic powerhouse.

Philip's education included a simple level of arithmetic, but he had not been much interested.[26] In later life, he could not understand anything about accounts and despaired at his own bewilderment.[27] Ever since he was presented with the Spanish Empire, he had been entirely at the mercy of moneylenders; to be more specific, Genoese moneylenders, who understood numbers very well. From 1560, the wealth flowing from Potosí fell as the initial seam ran out, so the Crown was receiving less than half a million pesos a year from it.[28] Philip was defending his power and his religion against the Dutch, the English and the Ottoman Empire, and at the same time defending his territory against France. The purchasing power of the precious metal that he was spending needed to rise, but it was falling. In 1557, immediately after his accession, he was forced to renegotiate his loans from Genoese traders who could directly interfere with the flow of gold to his armies and fleets. This was not exactly bankruptcy, but the word serves. The effect was catastrophic for the whole economy of Christendom, as rulers everywhere had been sucked into the military spending contest: Spain's bankruptcy immediately triggered the bankruptcy of France,[29] and Portugal followed in 1560. Philip's total income by then was about 3 million pesos a year less than his expenditure.

The Golden Sink-hole

Instead of Flanders producing gold, it was swallowing it. The more money Philip poured in, the bigger his debts and the more profound his failure. After 1572, Spain had 70,000 troops in the Netherlands, and they were no longer anything like the courtly gentlemen Brantôme had met. They mutinied forty-six times in thirty-five years when conditions became unbearable and their pay had vanished.

By 1574, his debts and liabilities were about fourteen times his income. After Spanish troops made a 200-mile forced march with no food and won a major victory, they mutinied because they had not been paid for more than three years.[30] Supposedly awash with the whole world's wealth, Philip could only manage payments on a monthly basis to the most restive and dangerous front-line troops. To avoid the army disappearing, the government in Madrid had to agree to send bullion worth more than a million florins. The next year, Philip was obliged to stop paying his debts to his Genoese bankers, who responded by cutting off money to Flanders. Philip had other lenders, but the mutineers that year physically destroyed Antwerp.[31] It had been Northern Europe's greatest trade centre. Now the city was laid waste. The rich surface seam of silver at Potosí was exhausted around 1560, but was reinvigorated in the mid-1570s by new techniques that worked with lower-grade ores, after which he had masses of bullion, but it could never be sufficient to convert his towering piles of paper loans into coins for all the men who were owed them; or, indeed, to keep paying his gun-makers. These financial crises were fundamental manifestations of the transfer of real power in Europe from royal dynasties to networks of bankers. But of course the essence of a bankruptcy is that much, or all, of the debt is written off. Philip may have been an agent of divine will, but he has been called 'the borrower from Hell'.[32]

Although the details of Spain's fiscal records are highly untrustworthy, they do give an idea of the scale of its problem. In the century after Columbus's discovery, Spain recorded the import of around 170 tons of gold and 8,200 tons of silver, which converts to something under 200 million ducats.[33] The Crown took 20 per cent of this in tax, so in theory its revenue over the whole sixteenth century was boosted by 40 million ducats. But from 1567–1600 alone, Spain recorded spending over 80 million ducats just battling in the Netherlands. Whatever amount was actually being spent, it was an unmanageable burden. It was also a huge economic stimulus to Northern Europe, being spent very largely in the war zone.

The Armada

The rebel provinces survived because their geography and their culture of seafaring meant that Philip would have to make good his boast of being ruler of the Ocean Sea, which was impossible. In its early days, the Dutch Republic consisted entirely of a fleet of privateers, at first dependent on anchorage in England and then in the western Netherlands port of Brill. Philip's attempt to invade England with the notorious Armada of 1588 was less about imposing his rule and religion than a desperate attempt to defend his treasure shipments. Eight years earlier, Francis Drake had sailed the Golden Hind back to Devon with an unprecedented haul of plunder from Spanish ships he had met on a circumnavigation of the globe. The quantity remained a secret between him and his queen, but there was enough for her to pay off the whole of England's foreign debt, balance the national budget and invest the remaining £40,000 in a new company to trade with the East. In 1600, the latter became the East India Company, and John Maynard Keynes calculated that the huge profit generated from Elizabeth's £40,000 became the foundation of England's subsequent foreign investment.[34]

The Armada was intended to destroy this Protestant queen who was sustaining the rebels in the Netherlands, and so staunch the vast expenditure required by that war and stop the huge losses of treasure to English privateers. The Pope offered Philip a million in gold if news arrived that a landing had been effected. That, however, was a small fraction of the cost of the effort, said to be over 13 million.[35]

The Armada failed because, as one of its captains said before it left port, it set out 'in the confident hope of a miracle'. Philip's plan to embark an army onto barges in Flanders and use a largely Mediterranean fleet to shepherd them to a safe landing in England, opposed by a well-equipped and supremely confident ocean-going navy, was very dicey. It was made impossible by the absence of communication between the ships and the army, and the lack of a harbour where they could connect. Only fifty-nine of Spain's 130 ships managed to return home.

The effect was to knock down the great prop that sustained Philip II, the conviction that his gold was the material evidence of divine support. For thousands of years, people had understood kingship and divinity to be linked through gold. A crown of gold had once given the ruler a unique divine authority. As we have seen, Christian Europe shifted the power of coronation to anointment by the Church. In fact, neither Charles V nor Philip II was ever crowned King of Castile. But the gold from America, coming in such quantities to rulers who believed they were God's agents on Earth, had taken on the mystical significance of coronation. Once Charles V was able to use gold to buy election as Holy Roman Emperor, the Pope placed the gold Imperial crown on his head. Charles was the last man to wear it. American gold was their true crown, confirming Charles's and Philip's opinion that they were the ordained rulers of the globe.[36] From that flowed the duty of suppressing heresy. But in 1988, while I was making a television series on the Armada with Professor Geoffrey Parker, he discovered a previously unknown document in a private archive in Madrid. A Duke of Altamira had recognized Philip II's writing on paper he was offered for use in a bookshop toilet. When he learned that it came from sacks that had been thrown out by the royal archives and many pages had already been used, he salvaged the remaining papers. One, startlingly, was a despairing note written by Philip to his confessor on 10 November 1588, when he knew the fate of the Armada:

'I promise you, unless some remedy is found … very soon we shall find ourselves in such a state that we shall wish that we had never been born … If God does not send us a miracle, I want to die … That is what I pray for … This is for your eyes alone … If God does not come back to his cause we will see what we fear so much, sooner than anyone thinks … It can only have been permitted to punish us for our sins.'[37]

The Most Catholic King seems to have lost his belief that he could rely on God's support and empowerment. With that, the whole edifice that had bound together divine authority, earthly power and gold passed away from Europe in one long dying breath. For him, the significance of gold went far beyond its buying power; it was a magical connection to the sacred. That was why he brought alchemists from Flanders to work in the Escorial, trying to bring him the essence of alchemical gold.[38] He did not seek it for money, but as his entitlement as God's agent on Earth. Now he had lost that sense of his connection to the divine. Gold was no longer given its inherent value by sacred power. He had the material gold, but not the spiritual entitlement, and never would have. It was gone.

The mystical significance of gold was vividly demonstrated in Spanish churches. Facing the altar of Seville Cathedral, dazzled by a 20-metre-high wall of gilded carvings, it would be easy to suppose that you are being placed to adore and worship the gold itself. In fact, the sense you are supposed to feel is that the gold opens a sacred path to the sublime. It was not like that in Protestant churches, because the idea had no traction any more in the new commercial Europe.

The Flow to Amsterdam

In Protestant lands, gold had no value beyond its earthly power; when new gold appeared, it was as cargoes to be taken from Spain and used against it. After being seized by Spain in 1580, Portugal belonged in that equation; its cargoes were also worth taking from Philip. As soon as Portuguese gold-hunting ships had arrived in the Indian Ocean in the sixteenth century, they had begun transforming the region by engaging Asia in a far more extensive web of trade. They quickly began working with Malays, Chinese and Javanese, linking them to the Middle East and to more local markets. In 1592, the English captured a Portuguese galleon carrying Indian and Chinese merchandise worth nearly half the entire English treasury.

The Dutch were very interested. The revolt of the Netherlands had come close to being snuffed out in its early years as Spanish forces occupied most of the rebel territory, which had been reduced to a ship-borne republic, heavily dependent on English support and proudly adopting the Spanish sneer, 'sea beggars'. But as they pushed back the Spanish and established the new Dutch Republic, they grew into a nation of mercantile shipbuilders with control of a union of northern Low Countries provinces including Amsterdam. The sea beggars became sea wolves.

Three years after that vastly profitable English seizure, a Dutch merchant who had travelled to India with the Portuguese published detailed sailing directions in Dutch for the East Indies and Japan. That year, four Dutch ships arrived in the Far East on a carefully planned surreptitious undertaking. About a third of the crew made it back alive in 1597 with a small cargo of spices; the price obtained for them was so astronomical that it was a roaring commercial success. The money that flowed to the Netherlands through Philip's own expenditure was mobilized to finance Dutch shipping and trade, and in 1602 the merchants of the United Provinces formed the Dutch East India Company (the *Verenigde Oostindische Compagnie*, 'VOC') to put their piracy on a regular footing. By then, thirty-nine Dutch trading ships had sailed round the Cape of Good Hope and returned from the Indies, thirty-six of which were fully loaded with expensive spices.[39] One ship that they sailed home that year was the Spanish galleon *St Jago*, which they had seized in the South Atlantic off St Helena. Immediately, they minted a splendid comedy silver medal showing the seizure on one side, and on the other a leaping horse being chased off the planet by the lion of Dutch Zeeland with the inscription 'NON SUFFICIT ORBIS QVO SALTAS INSEQVAR' ('The world is not enough when you are being chased').

The Dutch were able to mobilize credit for commerce, as Protestant bankers were untroubled by the Catholic ban on usury. Dante had described moneylenders who charged interest being dragged down to the inner ring of the seventh circle of hell by the money bags round their necks. Rome's stern attitude had been manageable when these loans were for princes. Jakob Fugger made profits of 50 per cent a year lending to Charles V without charging interest, because Charles understood that he was being bribed and granted Fugger hugely valuable mining concessions.[40] But ordinary Catholic traders who needed a constant flow of loaned coins needed to borrow at interest, and only non-Christians could operate as usurers. This trade was consequently more or less reserved for Jews, though various cunning exceptions were invented.

When Jews were expelled from Spain in 1492, the Spaniards had lost an important source of credit. A favoured Jewish escape route went over the mountains to Portugal; after Spain took over that country in 1580, many ended up in the Low Countries and Venice. My own ancestors were among them.[41]

My grandmother carefully explained the whole family story to me when I was about 5, concentrating on the adventure of two brothers from Lisbon and their sister, the beautiful Maria Nunez, disguised as a man, escaping with their uncle from Porto on a ship to the Netherlands. It was captured by the English, probably in 1596. In a tale that could have been taken from Shakespeare, Maria's disguise was uncovered and she became the love interest of an unnamed English lord. The story goes that she came to the attention of Queen Elizabeth before eventually being able to make a further flight to Amsterdam. There, the family founded a synagogue and became involved in international finance.

The part of the tale that grandma did not know was that Maria's uncle was persuaded to return, under royal protection, to Madrid to help with Spain's incomprehensible financial problems after Philip II's death.

Meanwhile, Philip's enemies had equally impossible financial problems. Elizabeth of England had been rather too reliant on her seamen plundering Spanish treasure vessels. But she had thought of a solution. An emissary was sent to an Englishman, Edward Kelley, who was in Prague. Kelley was an alchemist and had produced gold like a rabbit from a hat at the court of the new Holy Roman Emperor, Rudolf II. It was time to make gold.[42]

Elizabeth needed an alchemist.

Chapter 20

Alchemy

The Basis of Transmutation

It seems obvious to us that alchemists who claimed to transmute other substances to gold were frauds. We know that there was no possible process to make a single atom of gold, let alone great lumps of the stuff. But the firm and ancient belief that this could be done had a profound impact on the way many rulers behaved and ran their kingdoms.

The belief that gold could be made from other materials was entirely rational. The world is in constant flux, and it was a common understanding that everything is naturally or divinely driven to its ultimate goal. Gold and other metals must thus be produced by some natural process, just as there is a natural process by which grass and water can turn into cows and sheep. Matter that was not gold must have turned to gold. As long as two millennia ago, this understanding was discussed in China, India and Arabia.

Today, we have a more pessimistic vision of the world and are taught that things naturally disintegrate, dissolve and will turn into an undifferentiated entropic soup. But from antiquity until recently, people preferred to believe that nature contained an inbuilt drive not towards dissolution but towards perfection. Perfectibility was a moral ambition for humans, but also a physical goal for substance. Base metals were understood to be slowly transforming into more noble ones, and gold was the noblest of all. The Chinese scholar Liu An, the grandson of the founder of the Han Dynasty, wrote the *Huainanzi*, a Taoist encyclopaedia based on a series of debates, in 139 BCE. He explained that 'gold grows in the earth by a slow process and is evolved from the immaterial principle underlying the universe, passing from one form to another up to silver, and then from silver to gold'. This opinion lay behind Herodotus's belief that gold grows in the ground, and the same expectation of gold forming underground is found today in South Africa and Papua New Guinea. There, 'the fertility of the mines must be ensured by means of sacrifice because minerals are also thought to grow'.[1] The Renaissance intellectual Paracelsus, who had worked in the Fuggers' silver mine in Austria, pictured God as a divine alchemist working in the world, separating pure from impure.[2]

Attempts to accelerate the natural transmutation of metal into its perfect form, gold, had begun in China and India around 2,000 years ago. In 144 BCE, the Han emperor Jing forbade the counterfeiting of gold, a law which has been seen as the first clear evidence of alchemy.[3]

Transmutation for the Elixir of Life

Since gold is unchanged by the passage of time, it also seemed reasonable to suppose that its immortality could be transferred to humans. In India, the emphasis was on its ability to connect humans to some form of perfection; in China, there developed a strong persuasion that a way could be found by which it could transmit its own immortality to living people. The strangeness of the substance itself, and the processes for purifying it, added to its mystery. Pure gold was usually obtained, as every Renaissance alchemist believed, by taking a naturally occurring blend of gold, silver and copper (electrum) and mixing it with mercury. In the ancient world, alluvial sediment containing electrum was amalgamated with mercury, and then burning off the mercury left pure gold. So somehow, it seemed, mercury was making gold, and there should be some way of performing this trick with just mercury. Mercury is derived from cinnabar, a brick-red ore. When heated, it gives off a toxic vapour which can be condensed in a flask. Its connection with immortality and gold has been understood by ancient peoples around the world. I first encountered it crawling into the excavation of the Mayan pyramid at Copan, to see the newly revealed skeleton of the city's first ruler, Yash-K'uk'-Mo. He lay at the end of a cramped, steamy passage, his bones still red with the cinnabar that had been painted on his corpse 1,500 years before. Breathing the dust was dangerous. Deadly, blood-coloured cinnabar was a connection between this world and the ancestors. Just as the use of gold was so similar in the tombs of many cultures, so was the use of cinnabar. Ancient Chinese burials used it the same way.

Around 135 BCE, Li Shaojun proposed to the emperor that he perform a ritual involving a stove in which he would transmute cinnabar into gold.[4] Li Shaojun proposed making crockery from the gold and said that eating and drinking from it would extend the emperor's life and enable him to become immortal. Clearly, this gold was extra-powerful, a spiritually infused material which would engage alchemists for centuries, and is referred to as 'alchemical gold'.

The pursuit of immortality through magical gold was enthusiastically taken up by Emperor Wang Mang, who seized control of China in 9 CE. According to the *Ch'ien Han Shu*, a history finished in 111 CE, he immediately set about trying to become immortal, a process which involved huge quantities of gold, much of which was required for building ritual towers and making vast offerings.[5] By

23 CE, when he was killed by desperate rebels, he had almost trebled the royal store of gold, to more than the Roman Empire possessed.[6] The currency reforms he inaugurated to do this included making private possession of gold illegal. He withdrew the gold coinage, replacing it with metal tokens, and required the export of silk for gold, creating a huge and permanent drain on the West's gold supply. The idea that money is nothing but a symbolic token was not new in China: as we have seen, this was explained in the ancient *Guanzi* text. But his reforms went much further, nationalizing land, abolishing servitude and setting up government monopolies. So as well as creating a permanent and ultimately fatal loss of gold in Rome, he triggered his own destruction by a peasant uprising that restored the Han Dynasty,

The early Chinese and Indian alchemists were interested in alchemical gold as a route to immortality rather than wealth, and this attitude would remain strong in the subsequent development of the study. Alchemy was a pursuit of perfection, seeking a spiritual transmutation. This evolved into the search for the Elixir or Philosopher's Stone, which could both work the magic of transmutation and bestow immortality. But for rulers trying to keep themselves afloat without enough money, alchemy had an obvious and less elevated appeal. If it worked, it would transform the balance of power in favour of whoever possessed this occult secret.

Elizabethan Alchemy

Alchemical texts always laid emphasis on the transcendental qualities of substances; the performance of change was understood to be dependent on a process that took place beyond, as well as within, the gross material world. This was particularly significant for gold, which had a well-known quasi-divine aspect. The division between the two values of gold – spiritual and commercial – had always been a source of tension. In the sixteenth century, European rulers who had no access to Spanish or oriental gold sought very seriously for people who could deal directly with the transcendental world, where gold existed outside time and space, and bring it back as spending money. Alchemy had a very long and mysterious history. Now it moved centre stage.

Elizabeth I's investment in alchemists was in a long tradition of royal optimism. In the thirteenth century, Michael Scot's *Art of Alchemy* was produced under the patronage of Holy Roman Emperor Frederick II von Hohenstaufen, and in the fifteenth century, Henry IV of England granted licences for men to make gold, on the basis, presumably, that he owned all mines and alchemy was a form of mining. Edward IV and Henry VI did the same. These efforts seem to have been wasted, but in a triumph of hope over experience, and in an act of desperation,

Elizabeth employed alchemists at considerable expense. Having studied the subject in depth, she clearly believed they had a worthwhile chance of success.[7] In 1565, she contracted an Italian adventurer, Cornelius Alvetanus, to manufacture 50,000 marks of pure gold a year in a laboratory in Somerset House. Two years later, his last-known letter promised to get the chemical process working if he could please be released from the Tower. Her approach to Edward Kelley in Prague, in 1588, led nowhere, but Elizabeth was still convinced enough of the possibility of success in 1594 to agree to spend £500 (about half a million in modern currency) on a 'secret menstruum' that might do the trick.[8] The Kogis' description of gold as the Earth's menstrual blood is echoed in the alchemist's use of the term 'menstruum' for gold-making solvents, with its association with fertility, and there are Sanskrit alchemical texts that speak of blending mercury and sulphur as mixing menstrual blood and semen.[9] The Kogi view of gold as the product of cosmic (and sexual) alchemy seems to have been widely shared in the recently forgotten past.

Frobisher's Gold

Five-hundred pounds was roughly the sum invested, eighteen years earlier in 1576, in two small ships and a little pinnace led by Martin Frobisher to seek out a north-west passage to the riches of the Orient.[10] His journey would bring together exploration and alchemy in an extraordinary large-scale muddle.

There were few Englishmen with any understanding of navigation out of sight of land, so the business partner of the expedition, Michael Lok, invited Queen Elizabeth's adviser in mathematics, astronomy and navigation, John Dee, to train him. Dee was keen to promote the founding of an English Empire in North America and was an immensely learned man. He was also Elizabeth's astrologer and was deeply interested in alchemy. In 1572, he had said that a brilliant light that appeared in the sky (a supernova) might signify 'the discovery of some great Treasure or the philosopher's stone', and he was happy to see his prediction proved true.[11] Soon after Frobisher's return, a Venetian assayer in England, Giovanni Battista Agnello, examined a stone brought back on his ship as a souvenir, and he found it contained gold. Agnello was an alchemist.

This is the start of a very peculiar story. Agnello had the stone from Lok, who had already sent a piece to be examined by William Humphrey, the official assayer at the Tower of London. Humphrey was the man at the heart of making English currency: he had been in charge of the complete recoinage of England's silver currency ordered in 1560 to stabilize its value. It was his job to measure the purity of precious metal for coining. Many low-quality coins had been able to enter circulation because England had too few capable and trustworthy assayers, so he decided to bring experts from Germany. Humphrey said this stone was worthless. Lok was unconvinced, but two other assayers apparently confirmed Humphrey's assessment before he found Agnello, who gave him the result he wanted. He swore Agnello to secrecy and Lok began to plot with him how they could get more from some secret expedition. Elizabeth's spymaster, Walsingham, inevitably got wind of this, and Lok revealed everything. Walsingham's own assayers found no gold, and the spymaster concluded that Agnello 'did but play the alchemist'. The real secret of playing the alchemist, as with any sleight of hand, is to help people see what they want to see rather than the whole picture, and Agnello was a master at this. Within a few months, he had convinced Frobisher and William Winter, a courtier and senior naval commander, that the supposed gold ore was valued at £240 a ton, and it could be brought back for just £10 a ton. Elizabeth invested £1,000 in a return journey, and Walsingham himself put in £200, alongside Winter. In all, nearly £4,000 was raised. John Dee was given a £100 share[12] in this enterprise of magical imperialism that should create an Empire of Albion in the New World, in which alchemists and assayers would help to sustain Gloriana, their Virgin Queen, and enable her to triumph radiantly over the dark threats and cruel empire of Philip II.

Frobisher had claimed that he had found the opening to the North-West Passage from the Atlantic to Asia, but he was instructed not to waste time on that and to bring back the ore. His crew now included thirty miners and assayers. Chief among the assayers was Christopher Schütz, a furnace engineer who had been brought to England from Saxony with twenty German-speaking assistants by Humphrey. Schütz had built England's first blast furnace.

They returned from this voyage with three captive Inuits and 200 tons of rock, taken to be gold ore. A trial smelter was built near the Tower, and the ore was tested by Schütz. He reported that two trial smeltings produced gold to the value of £40 per ton of ore. Walsingham brought in an assayer of his own, another Anglicized German named Burchard Kranich, who confirmed the presence of commercial quantities of gold.

Then Agnello was asked to perform a test assay – and found no gold at all! Two more assayers were given samples and agreed with Agnello. But Kranich had found that there actually was gold, in quantity, in the ore, and Walsingham (who was normally nobody's fool) trusted him. A third expedition was thus mounted, on a truly epic scale: there were fifteen ships, in the largest fleet to go into the Arctic before the twentieth century. This was a significant investment: £8,363. Off went the ships, and they loaded and brought home 1,000 tons of Canada, losing three ships and a mere forty men in the process. In 1578, the whole refining capacity of England was commandeered, and many months were spent trying to extract gold from rocks that, it was soon realized, had none.

Identifying Gold

This bizarre story goes to the heart of the alchemical problem, because it shows, rather surprisingly, that it was extraordinarily difficult to identify gold at all. In 1576, Jean Bodin, the French political philosopher who explained how gold from America created the 'great price rise', tried to set out a system for identifying 'false money', gold coins adulterated with copper. He published the specific gravities of the metals so that checking size against weight would reveal any fraud – but he got the numbers mixed up between different metals and it seems no one noticed. His erroneous figures were still being published in English in 1608.[13] Gold was the basis of currency and trade, the measure of national wealth, and the English government needed it desperately to pay for the necessities of survival, but they found it almost impossible to confidently recognize. Agnello, who had started the whole wild goose chase with what Walsingham believed at first to be sleight of hand, not only convinced the spymaster to invest in a second voyage but then reported that he could not find gold in what came back. It seems probable that he just could not tell. Men who assayed for the mint found gold where there was none, and then found none after the third voyage. Confidence in assaying was so frail that after the second voyage, when three assayers found no gold in the rocks brought back, a great third expedition was mounted. The Germans, Schütz and Kranich, who said there was gold, seemed for some reason to be more convincing than the English who said there was none. Perhaps German expertise was more highly regarded.

Recent archaeological studies of the second expedition's smelting site in Canada show no trace of gold there. That suggests strongly that Schütz came back from the second voyage with rocks he already knew were worthless, and someone must have added a bit of gold in some of the smelting in England.[14] It also suggests that Kranich participated in the fraud. But it is very hard to understand why they should do that. It is of course possible that the smelting site has been milked by others before the archaeologists got there. Whatever the case, the reality of gold was apparently a matter of faith.

Assaying was not a precise science. It involved heating powdered ore with lead and then boiling off the lead. It depended on accurate weighing of the ore and of the final product. The lead might itself be contaminated with gold, so it was best practice to allow for the contamination by guesswork. Contemporary texts on the processes are more like cookbooks than precise and useful guides.[15] Matters were not helped by the national definition of pounds and ounces being changed by the queen while this was going on. The assayer's workshop was a contaminated space, and both weighing and measuring were imprecise. English goldsmiths' scales had a sensitivity of 65 milligrams, 0.065 grams. That does not compare with Islamic ones; Islamic coin weights from 780 CE were accurate to within a third of a milligram, 0.0003 grams, and being made of glass could not be invisibly altered. European weights were imprecise: the standard weight of Cologne that defined the mark, made in 1703, is 0.1 per cent too heavy, and three standard 1lb Cologne weights of that date differ by the same degree.[16] With no control over the purity of the additives and apparently inadequate measuring devices, the quality of an assay depended heavily on the skill, experience and intuition of the assayer. It was not very surprising for different assayers to produce different results. There could have been fraud, but without a clear motive it was as likely to be sheer incompetence.

Gold's Ingredients

Of course, fraud was made easier by the belief that any substance could change into any other. In the fifth century BCE, a Greek poet and mystic, Empedocles, had explained that everything is made out of four immutable elements (fire, air, water and earth), and changing the proportion of elements in one substance turns it into another. By the sixteenth century, this had evolved into a belief that the four elements were an unconvincing quartet, but that the seven metals (gold, silver, copper, tin, lead, iron and mercury) 'originate from three materials, namely from mercury, sulphur and salt'.[17] Those were the words of Paracelsus, who was born in Zurich in 1493 and was taught medicine and alchemy by his father and metallurgy in the mines of Sebastian Fugger in the Tyrol, so obviously knew what he was talking about. The Fuggers' copper and silver mines were the basis of their extensive banking operations, and were where the German assaying skills so valued at the mint in the Tower of London were learned.

Since lead and gold were both believed to be composed of mercury, sulphur and salt in different proportions, changing those proportions – perhaps by heating and adding something else – might well make some gold out of lead; or lead out of gold. For example, adding gold dust to a flask of hot mercury and powdered silver will produce a golden liquid. When this is boiled away (creating highly noxious fumes), it leaves what looks like a lump of gold. This is called butter of gold. It is used for gilding, but it is not solid gold.

There were major problems in understanding the nature of gold, it was well known that there was every opportunity for fraud, and after Frobisher's third voyage the general view was that this had all been a hugely expensive swindle. Almost everyone involved with Frobisher had their reputations destroyed.

Alchemy and Government

The disaster profoundly embarrassed John Dee, who left England with the alchemist Edward Kelley in the expectation of finding gold by the other route, a journey into the mysteries of matter. Kelley was a striking charismatic cripple with cropped ears, punishment for some unspecified crime. They were carrying his Elixir of Transmutation, a tincture which he said could transform mercury into gold. He would sometimes invite audiences to watch the process,[18] which was why Lord Burghley, Elizabeth's secretary of state, wrote to him begging for some of the tincture to create gold to finance England's defence against the Armada.

The Holy Roman Emperor, Rudolf II, had set up research laboratories in his gloomy castle in Prague and was collecting alchemists, magi, astronomers and experts in the occult. He was more interested in plumbing the hidden secrets of nature than in finding an alchemical America which would give him extra wealth. Dee trusted in Kelley's mystical powers and was persuaded by his companion that spirits ordered them to hold their wives in common. Dee and his wife reluctantly acquiesced and she had a baby. Kelley was giving public demonstrations of transmutation and giving away the gold he 'made'. He refused to accompany Dee back to England and was promoted to nobility and riches by Rudolf in the expectation that he would deliver gold. His failure to do so was taken as either wilfulness or evidence of fraud, and he died in prison.

But the hope in alchemy survived. Learned men wrote at length that transmutation was certainly possible, just a mystery to be solved. The investigation of mysteries is the route to scientific discovery, and the study of alchemy remained a respectable hope for a long time. In 1644 and 1646, Christian IV of Denmark, James I's brother-in-law, minted ducats from gold which he believed had been made by his alchemist, and had more minted in 1647 to silence doubters. At the same time, Emperor Ferdinand III believed that he was having alchemical gold produced, and in 1650 performed the transmutation himself. In 1673, a German chemist, Johann Becher, proposed to make a million gold thalers a year for the States General of Holland and conducted an apparently successful trial.[19] As late as 1710, the Master of the Lyon mint was fooled into minting gold 'made' by an illiterate peasant.[20]

Queen Elizabeth had been very serious about using science to fill her treasury. In the most obvious, banal way, she was completely mistaken. We also understand, as her councillors seem not to have done, that had it been possible, the value of the metal would have plummeted. But in another, less obvious, way she was pursuing a potentially rewarding goal. Her interest in alchemy might not produce gold, but it would yield wealth in other ways. This was well understood in her own lifetime. Francis Bacon, who was born in 1561, wrote that 'alchemy may be compared to the man who told his sons, he had left them gold buried somewhere in his vineyard; where they, by digging, found no gold, but by turning up the mould about the roots of the vines, procured a plentiful vintage. So the search and endeavours to make gold have brought many useful inventions and instructive experiments to light.'[21]

The search for something like the Elixir was serious, and the serious men who took it up would eventually be known as the fathers of science. Gold was at the centre of their endeavours, and they were conscious of its mystic significance, distinguishing between 'philosophical gold', a spiritual substance at the heart of life, and 'material gold'. Few people doubted that there was a hidden key to making gold, and many rulers wanted to find it. They were just nervous that the alchemists who offered to do it were charlatans.[22] They employed them on detailed contracts, punishing breach of contract severely.

The Emergence of Science

Much of the alchemists' work was trying to achieve perfection, which meant purity. They reasoned that the first step must be to produce pure substances. They did this by distillation – heating the substance until it produced a vapour, then collecting the condensation. The processes could be unbelievably complicated. The eighth-century Islamic alchemist, Jabir ibn Hayyan, recommended one procedure that involved 700 distillations. It was alchemists who, in the painstaking search for the perfection of gold, discovered and perfected the distillation of alcohol. Alchemy might not make you rich, but you might not notice![23]

Early modern alchemists, hunting for ways to transmute metals and find the elixir of life, developed the technology of furnaces and distillation in a way that brought about an early industrial revolution with quite separate benefits. The Master of Rudolf II's Prague mint, who needed to distinguish real gold from the fake stuff, wrote a *Treatise on Ores and Assaying* in 1574 that showed an understanding of the use and nature of 'vitriol' (sulphates) that would quickly lead to the manufacture of the mineral acids fundamental to what we call chemical engineering, and so to industrial development.[24] In this way, the work of alchemists would truly remake civilization.

'Oil of vitriol' (sulphuric acid) was made by distilling 'green vitriol' (iron sulphate) in an iron retort. Nitric acid, which would become the basis of dyes, fertilizers and explosives, was an alchemical triumph, made by distilling together saltpetre and alum. This was a liquid that would completely dissolve silver and was important to sixteenth-century alchemists for purifying adulterated gold. It took longer to learn how to distil alum alone, because the condensation destroyed metal vessels. Eventually, alchemists began using glass, as the acid did not eat it away. The liquid produced, sulphuric acid, would dissolve iron and copper.

Alchemical investigations would indeed produce an ever-growing stream of wealth as they led to the development of the techniques, processes and substances that revolutionized society. Eventually, that scientific revolution would lead to the transmutation of other substances into gold, but it took a while and was not very profitable. In 2017, it was reported that the On-line Isotope Mass Separator (ISOLDE) at the European Council for Nuclear Research (CERN) has used protons accelerated to almost the speed of light in the Large Hadron Collider and smashed them into the nuclei of heavy atoms such as uranium with enough of a mighty punch to produce gold.[25] The process can create 2 million gold atoms a second. The amount of energy used is pretty huge, and 2 million gold atoms is less than you might think; it would take 50 million years of production at this rate to make 1 gram of gold.[26] After all those centuries of effort, that must seem disappointing.

In the seventeenth century, the new science sustained the image of the king as a transcendent being, identified with his own golden wealth, and Rubens painted an alchemical image of King James Stuart on the ceiling of the Whitehall Banqueting House in which the late monarch bodily ascended into heaven and was transmuted into an immortal divine form. But alchemy didn't deliver gold. No one could get enough of it even through plunder, never mind magic. The bankruptcies of Spain, France and the Netherlands in the sixteenth century demonstrated the impossibility of running a kingdom on the ruler's own resources, no matter how extensive. And the flood of gold from America was drying up. In the ten years from 1621, only one-fifth as much gold arrived in Seville as had been landed at the start of the century.[27] Something would have to give.

Chapter 21

From Lords to States

Who was Enriched?

The accumulation of gold was, in the minds of all Europeans, an increase in riches. And yet, that increase had never actually happened. The small number of rich lived well, but most Europeans were poorer at the end of the seventeenth century than the first farmers on the shores of the Black Sea in the eighth millennium BCE. They did not live longer: life expectancy at birth was generally still 30–35. They did not grow taller – in fact they were rather shorter, as they had a worse diet and more diseases. They worked harder, but their homes were more impoverished. Average wages, in real terms, were lower in England in 1650 than they had been in 1350. They were level pegging in the Netherlands and in northern Italy.[1]

Gold had changed the world in fundamental ways, and clearly Europeans believed that it was much more than a mere commodity, though its value was no longer rooted in any connection to transcendental mysteries. Further east, in Anatolia and the Middle East, Islam too had broken the ancient link between power and gold's mystical authority.

But of course, as we know very well, seventeenth-century Europeans were not set free from gold's power. On the contrary, it dominated their lives to an astonishing degree. Their mental world was affected to such an extent that they began to organize their governments around collecting, minting and exchanging gold on a completely new scale, and this impetus drove Northern Europe to transform its way of living. There was a huge movement of population into cities, where banking took on a new dimension and entirely new kinds of work appeared. Something unprecedented was happening, the invention of new machinery which would change the lives not just of people, but eventually of every living thing on Earth.

The Money Machine

This Industrial Revolution is said in Britain to have started in the middle of the eighteenth century, but that is simply not true. That story has been written by historians who identified industrialization with coal, iron and steam engines. In fact, the fundamental change happened in the sixteenth century, when the first factory was built with machines doing work that had previously been done by people. Water and wind power had been harnessed for centuries, driving mills and pumps, but here was a series of machines automating sequential tasks. It was designed for mass production, but not to make consumer goods such as textiles. The object was, quite literally, to make money, and automated minting was already up and running by the time of the Armada.

Since adopting farming, our ancestors had lived in subsistence artisanal economies. There were a small number of luxury goods such as silk, glass, precious stones, lapis lazuli and porcelain that were exchanged over long distances, and in classical times products such as blades, weapons, cloth and pottery were

Minting coins: 1516, in der Weißkönig by Maximilian I.

made for mass markets, but all were produced by the hand labour of individual artisans. It was the same with coins, which were made by artisans hammering images onto hand-made metal discs. Coins were not precision objects. Every coin was similar to the rest, but unique. Its weight needed careful checking; its design was unlikely to be exactly central. That meant that it was common for people to clip shavings off and hope no one noticed. Hand craft also limited the number of coins that could be made; in the sixteenth century, a minter would make 500 coins a day. Productivity had become a serious problem.

As the amount of money in circulation multiplied, mints struggled to keep up. Consequently, from about 1550, experimental machines were built in France, England and Germany to produce coins more quickly. The problem was most acute in Spain, where an apparently infinite quantity of treasure needed to be coined, but it was already most decisively being addressed at the other end of the Holy Roman Empire. A new silver currency had been introduced in the Tyrol, where Archduke Sigismund of Austria had taken advantage of a huge silver mine at Schwaz, north of Innsbruck.[2] The severe shortage of gold currency had been a driving force for Columbus's voyage, and six years earlier Sigismund had introduced a large new silver coin, the gulden groschen ('great guilder'), that could substitute for the gold guilder. It was a substantial and impressive disc with the same value as its gold namesake, but much bigger and weighing ten times as much. It was exceptional in its purity and quality and was in high demand – it became known as the thaler, which would mutate into 'dollar'. During the following century, the huge Schwaz mine employing around 10,000 people came to produce some 85 per cent of Europe's silver. The whole operation fell into the hands of the Fugger family, who financed the mine's expansion.

And here the problem of automated minting was solved. The Fuggers' engineers had developed very advanced hydraulic mechanical engines to try to prevent their mine from flooding, installing huge water-driven pumps in great caverns. The mines are still open to tourists; the huge, reconstructed wheels deep underground are breathtaking. Masters of the water-wheel, they invented the first successful mechanized hydraulically powered stamping mill. It was installed in 1567 in the castle mint in Hall, near Innsbruck. The entire coining process, from refining to cutting out the discs, was mechanized, and the rim was marked to make clipping impossible. This was a remarkable achievement, and Philip II wanted it in Spain. He needed it.

Quite apart from his problems of overspending, he simply could not produce enough coins to pay his troops. In 1556, the Seville mint had been the most productive in the world, but the piecework artisans in its fifteen small workshops could only deal with about 100,000 kilos of silver and gold a year.[3] This was nowhere near enough and was an expensive problem. Mints sold coins for more than their bullion value, to cover their costs and make a profit, and lacking minting capacity, Philip was sending his American bullion on the long and dangerous journey to the Hall mint. There, the Fuggers coined it and sold it back to him at a 10 per cent profit.[4] Their own mine was in decline, overpowered by unstoppable flooding, as well as the flight of miners who rejected the Catholic religion and oppression of their employers, and by the falling price of silver thanks to Philip's imports from Potosí.

Philip struck a deal with the new Archduke, his nephew Ferdinand II, for the entire manufacturing plant to be transferred to Spain.[5] This was a truly epic undertaking. In 1580, the hunt began for a Spanish site with space, security and reliable hydraulic power. The hope had been to build at Seville, but eventually the location chosen was a paper mill in Segovia, north of Madrid. In 1583, the architect of Philip's fabulous palace, the Escorial, advised by German engineers from Hall, began to erect the world's first purpose-built mechanical manufacturing factory. The ground plan was as carefully thought out as his monastic palace. It was designed to receive the machinery for each step of a departmentalized production line. Water wheels would be installed to operate giant bellows for furnaces, and to drive the rolling mills that would flatten the metal strips from which coins would be cut. More wheels would arrive for the mills that would drive the stamps to imprint the coin design onto those strips. Other wheels would be needed for the machine tools that would keep the mint running: lathes to form the steel rollers and dies, and for cutting machines to punch out the coins from the strips.[6] None of the machinery was built in Spain. It was constructed in Hall, an industrial secret protected by twenty German mint-masters and engineers.[7]

A year later, the machinery was dismantled. Hall, perhaps the most beautiful town in the Tyrol, sits in the broad Inn River valley surrounded by sharp-edged mountains. Its wealth came from salt mining ('Hall' means salt) before it became Europe's Potosí and housed a great Habsburg palace. It was a warren of narrow streets and steep-roofed houses, home to wealthy merchants, traders and officials. Navigation further upstream was deliberately blocked to collect timber floated down from Switzerland for salt-drying, and the mint was in the salt-making castle. The usual route out was downriver to Vienna. Now, though, it played host to the largest wagon train ever seen in Europe, which would go in a more challenging direction. All the castle factory's machines were loaded onto it. The inventory of the wagon train gives some idea of the scale of this enterprise:

INVENTORY OF THE MACHINERY SENT TO SEGOVIA FROM THE CECA OF HALL IN TIROL OCTOBER 1584.

LAMINATION MILLS: 3 Iron Mills: 2 for laminating and 1 for coining; with 1 wooden lantern wheel and 2 wooden collaterals each.

ROLLER DIES: 3 pairs of steel roller dies engraved for 8 reale coins; 2 pairs of steel dies engraved for 4 reale coins.

CASTING: 1 oven to melt gold and silver.

MOULDS: 4 moulds for 8 reale coins. 1 mould for 4 reale coins. 1 mould for small coin.

OTHER TYPES OF COINING PRESSES
1 hydraulic wheel-driven press for coining double gold coins.
1 pair of steel engraving dies for double gold coins.
1 hydraulic wheel-driven press for coining simple gold coins.
1 pair of engraved steel dies for single gold coins.
1 hand-operated press for coining small coins of all kinds.

CUTTER: 10 large cutters to cut large coins; 10 cutters to cut small coins.

SMITHY: 1 lathe for turning rollers.[8]

In November 1583, the oxen slowly and oh-so-carefully began to haul their massive load across the bridge over the broad River Inn and up to about 1,350 metres to cross the Brenner Pass on the Imperial road into Italy. It was evidently not closed by snow, and the procession made its way down the steep mountains to Milan and then Genoa. There, the whole enterprise took ship to Barcelona, where more oxen and wagons were required for the 750km journey to Segovia by way of Madrid. The vast, unprecedented caravan finally set down its load in June 1585, in a completely different world – the warm Sierra of central Spain.[9] The waiting factory shell had been designed and built with remarkable precision, and just four weeks after arriving, the machines began to produce coins. A modern reconstruction of the Segovia factory was completed in 2011, but the rebuilt shell turned out to be too fragile for the planned installation of modern replica machinery and stands empty at the time of writing.

The Dutch East India Company

In the years after Philip II's death, England and the Dutch Republic needed to find permanent sources of gold, rather than relying on piracy. One of the main sources was the 'gold coast' of East Africa, where the Portuguese were forcibly replaced by the Dutch, and where the British too traded. This was where Daniel Defoe's Robinson Crusoe learned his trade, selling slaves for gold to native traders. The Pacific was a far richer, more expansive and more highly organized arena, but the great problem for Europeans trading with the East had always been that there was a gold-drain. Asia did not have much enthusiasm for selling bullion; its inhabitants preferred to receive it. The delights of Eastern luxuries had to be paid for with precious metal, specifically silver. The Dutch East India Company (VOC) became a global trading force precisely because it had no source of gold or silver. It set up a global trading system, aggressively seizing Portuguese trading posts and vigorously dominating trade between the rich nations of the Pacific and Indian oceans. Its centre of operations became Jakarta (then called Batavia), and from there trade routes were plied to Indonesia, India, China and Japan, as well as Yemen and Persia. The profits earned by the fine tradition of buying (or plundering) in the cheapest markets and selling in the dearest enabled the VOC to take spices and peppers back to Europe without needing to buy them with bullion. But the bullion flow naturally increased as trade increased, creating the basis of the Dutch Golden Age and the domestic luxury of Flanders' merchants.

Their powerful, well-armed and capacious trade vessels had a disruptive impact right around the world, even if they were only a small part of the commercial and cultural territory of the vast and well-developed Indian Ocean network. Around 1700, for example, the richest port of the Mughal Empire, Surat, had a fleet of more than 100 vessels of 200–300 tons, but Europeans accounted for no more than 10 per cent of the city's estimated annual trade worth 16 million rupees.[10] Its mercantile elites included some of the richest people in the world, who now participated in the growth of global trade which the Europeans stimulated. The quantity of cash in the world increased hugely. It seems likely that an extra 8,500 kilos of gold passed through the hands of merchants every year from 1540–1640, rising to 10,000 kilos a year between 1660 and 1680. But the real game-changer was the increase in minting silver, thanks mainly to Potosí. The amount minted rose to 400,000 kilos a year in the century after 1540, transforming the scale of trade.[11] The amount of silver in Europe tripled, and the value of silver coin fell in terms of gold.

Pieces of Eight

To try to slow the inflationary influx and encourage the money to be spent abroad, Spain banned textile exports in 1552. Since Spain's domestic wealth was based on wool, this devastated its own industry, but it helped prop up the value of Spanish silver.[12] Pieces of eight (Spanish silver coins of 8 reales, also called pesos and Spanish dollars) were the coinage of world trade from the late fifteenth century for 300 years.[13] Their value was measured in gold escudos. The real was just over 3 grams of silver, the escudo a similar weight of gold and worth fifteen or sixteen times as much – more once the silver content of coins began to fall. But in China, where silver was in tremendous demand, the silver real was worth twice its weight in gold. It was the gold that kept the pieces of eight circulating.

For Europe, gold was the measure of silver and everything else. It underwrote trade and financed the progress to ever-more-costly and destructive warfare, transforming society. Gold, war and wealth were intimately bound together. Right from the beginning, in the fifth millennium BCE, gold and war had been completely intertwined. Now that there was so much more gold, there was so much more war.

The Slaughter in Europe

Wikipedia has helpfully produced an estimate of Western Europe's war dead in the century from the start of the French Wars of Religion in 1562 to the end of the Franco-Spanish War in 1659. It reckons over 11 million perished.[14]

Of course, there was a far greater death toll on the continent that was being plundered, one that crushed the brilliant civilizations of South and Central America. Europeans, on the other hand, had the opportunity to adapt and profit from the destruction of their societies. The money that paid for ever-growing armies had, after all, to go somewhere. Battlefields destroyed the wealth of communities that had lived on them, but their blood fertilized new kinds of profit.

In August 1619, an entirely new kind of book appeared in Northern Europe. It sold in thousands. It was the pocket version of a weapons training manual that had first appeared in 1607. The original had been a large, heavy volume designed for the officer class to use on the muster ground. This small, multi-lingual version, printed on successive pages in French, Dutch, German and English, was specifically aimed at young men who wanted to enlist. It taught them, in a sequence of step-by-step drawings, how to handle the weapons of modern war and make their fortunes.

Technology had transformed the battlefield. The fabulously wealthy castle-bred knights trained in horse combat, dressed to survive, had given way to gentleman-soldiers on the make who dressed to kill in every sense. Knights earned their profits from each other, in the form of ransoms. Gentleman-soldiers relied on quartermasters and contracts, so whoever was paying them had to extract the gold from the community. There was nothing new about mercenaries, but here was a new class of men being paid to fight, leaving university to become soldiers for hire. According to the booklet's preface, they had two possible ways to be promoted from a mean and low estate to 'high degrees': the study of books (which meant the law) or enlistment. Studying, Jacob de Gheyn advised, was long, hard and expensive, whereas learning how to be useful on a battlefield was quicker, 'decent and convenient'.[15]

The original text had been published to help build an army for Maurice of Nassau, the Dutch Protestant leader who had organized the rebellion against Spain that began the fatal fracturing of Europe. In 1619, when the pocket version was brought out, Europe's most powerful Protestant, Frederick V of the Palatinate, had been installed as King of Bohemia in an anti-Catholic coup. Habsburg forces were being assembled for his destruction. Frederick and his queen, James I's daughter, Elizabeth, brought 2 tons of gold to their palace in Prague to pay for their defence.

No amount of gold could ever be enough. His challenger, the Habsburg Emperor Ferdinand II, was advised that the cost of invading the Palatinate with 35,000 men would be 1,000 ducats per man – 3½ million ducats – with another 1½ million needed for the attack on Bohemia.[16] The English Privy Council made a similar calculation of the cost of sending an army to defend the Palatinate in 1620: 2,583,570 ducats for raising and transporting 25,000 men, with weapons, artillery and ammunition. The English calculation was

The Players, 1619.

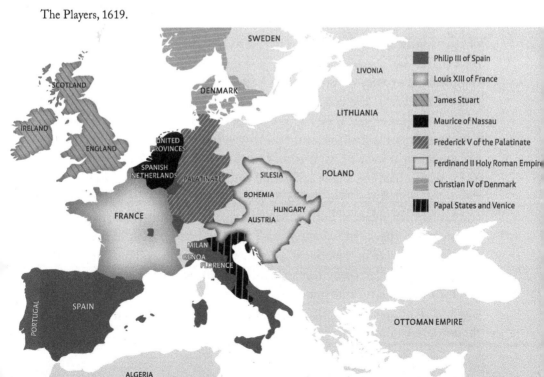

done in pounds and was very precise: monthly pay and horse hire would be a further £76,064 17*s* 8*d*. That included two chaplains, two physicians and two surgeons at 6 shillings and eightpence a day apiece, plus a couple of apothecaries at half the price.

This was an army on starvation pay; ordinary soldiers were to be given 8 pence a day, the modern equivalent of less than £5. The Lord General was to be paid 300 times that rate. But this was far beyond the resources of the country, and James I would not countenance it, even to save his own daughter (Frederick's wife).

It was also beyond anyone else's resources. But for the Catholic Habsburgs and Protestant Frederick, this was an existential threat, and they would commit to spending whatever it took. After all, the basic principle of affordability, as they understood it, was to acquire more bullion than you spent. The theory was that the success of any policy, including war, was measured by how much your gold and silver increased, and how much your opponent lost. The bigger the effort, the greater should be the reward. It was the start of a war of titans. They each sent almost 30,000 men to do battle at the White Mountain outside Prague on 8 November 1620. After two hours it was all over; Frederick's army fled. The Habsburgs had increased their wealth and power, the Protestants had lost theirs. The rebellious nobility who survived were sentenced to death, and vast wealth was transferred from losers to winners. But the Battle of the White Mountain was not the same kind of shattering Catholic triumph as Lepanto; it did not end a great clash, but rather started one. By the standards of epic conflict, the bloodshed was relatively slight; some 4,000 Protestant mercenaries lay dead, about six times as many as the Catholic corpses. But the financial arteries of Europe had been sliced open and the gush of gold drained the life of the continent. Protestant Sweden and Denmark, fearful of Catholic power, felt they had no choice but to pile in. Frederick's queen, Elizabeth Stuart, did all she could to draw in Britain, while Spain and France had too much at stake to stand aside. Thus began what is now called the Thirty Years' War. It bled the whole of Central Europe dry, killing perhaps a third of the population. Rulers received their income from borrowing, trade, plunder and taxing their subjects. Borrowing was barely credible anymore; bankers did not see much chance of being repaid. Trade does not prosper in the chaos of war, and the wealth of America to plunder was running dry. That left taxation, which had to be agreed by the population voting in their Estates, and there was little appetite for self-impoverishment to support endless war. So a new way had to be found of gathering in the gold to pay tens, even hundreds of thousands of soldiers.

Financing Limitless War

One tempting way was to lie about the amount of metal in the coinage. City-states in the Holy Roman Empire created more and more mints and issued more and more debased currency to meet the cost. It took just four months from that opening battle for Europe's first full-blown financial crisis to explode. States were not simply debasing their coins to make them seem to be worth more, they were industriously minting cheap fakes of each other's coinage, palming them off on mercenaries as far away as possible. The price of bread in Franconia rose 700 per cent between 1619 and 1622, and a theology student called Martin Bötzinger found that his annual grant of 30 florins was worth just three pairs of boots.[17]

Debasing and fakery did not work, so an attempt was made to outsource the war to contractors who would somehow drive down the cost and drive up the income. The magic of privatization has never lost its appeal, though the lesson is always the same: there is no such thing as magic.

Albrecht von Wallenstein became the supreme magician-commander of the Habsburg army for the Holy Roman Emperor, contracted to deliver what he claimed would be victory at no cost. Well, no cost to the emperor, but plenty of cost to his subjects. Wallenstein was authorized to muster regiments, inviting officers to raise forces and guaranteeing repayment of their expenses, quartering the troops in the emperor's towns. His colonels demanded food and wages from the muster towns for the forces they intended to raise as though they were already in arms – and they had the guns and manpower to enforce the demands. The emperor did not pay for feeding, equipping or clothing his army; the towns had to do it. Instead of the ruler having to pay the army once it went to war, and the soldiers supplementing their pay by plundering the conquered, Wallenstein forced the emperor's own subjects to deliver the money direct to him. His contract army was a vast horde living as a mobile camp, destroying the communities it was notionally protecting. The soldiers were accompanied by camp followers – around half were women, often with children, and many were boys making some money as weapon-carriers and ostlers.[18]

As towns and villages were driven to desperation by the demands of the alien soldiers and their dependants, Wallenstein inevitably failed to live up to his undertaking to run the army without costing the emperor cash. On the contrary, while the empire still paid 1.2 million florins a year to maintain what was now its military frontier, it paid Wallenstein 4 million florins from 1625–1630, while he also collected 3 million from Spain. He also received bribes and protection money, so Wallenstein was able to raise credit from bankers that sovereigns could not. His credit lines ran through twenty-five cities, from London to Istanbul.

The army swelled to over 100,000 by 1628, and Wallenstein's magical conjuring of gold for them out of a collapsed peasant economy was totally unsustainable. He had set up his own sovereign state, Friedland, which existed simply to make war. Friedland took over a large part of Bohemia.

Obviously, the emperor became profoundly disillusioned with his subcontractor and alarmed by his apparent intention to take control of the whole empire. Wallenstein had asked Johannes Kepler for a horoscope in 1608. The great astronomer produced one that warned of 'terrible confusion' in March 1634 and would make no predictions beyond that date. Wallenstein famously wore his horoscope as a jewelled and golden amulet. The emperor had him assassinated on 25 February 1634.

Meanwhile, on the other side, there was Ernst von Mansfeld, who used Alsace and East Frisia as his war-state territory. When his financial system collapsed, he needed to widen the war by drawing in Britain. King James had no intention of wasting his money, but Mansfeld visited England and ran a hugely successful propaganda operation which combined the appeal of chivalric defence of Princess Elizabeth, Protestant visceral anti-Catholicism and the delightful prospect of plunder. There were plenty of courtly gentlemen, headed by the Duke of Buckingham, who were entranced by Mansfeld for high-minded and most elegant reasons, but the broadsheets made it clear what most motivated the mass of people:

> 'Our Souldiers they are men of might,
> And will for gold and silver fight ...
> Come let us to the warres again
> France and Flanders make no moane,
> they get riches, we get none, ...
> Come let us to the warres again
> Some get riches, Pearls and Gold,
> We sitting still grow faint and cold
> Come let us to the warres again.'[19]

Mansfeld was fêted by London's crowd, being royally entertained, and was empowered to raise a force of 12,000 men and 200 horse. Many young men who joined up were familiar with Gheyn's handbook and abandoned their legal education to learn to drill as this new kind of soldier. But the muster that they gathered in Dover was frightening. Most of these men were not trained at all: they were pressed into service from the poor-houses. It seemed like a great way to offload them from parish poor relief until you saw thousands of raw conscripts marching towards Dover with weapons in their hands, under the guidance of local officials who simply wanted to hand them over to the army officers and be rid of them. The scale of robbery, rape and looting was sufficiently bad to scar the memories of the kingdom. In Europe, of course, things were far worse.

Economic collapse and marauding armies are not good for health. Over the course of the war, the population of Germany probably fell by 40 per cent.[20] Although the economic effects on Germany are unquantifiable, they were not at all beneficial. There had been growing prosperity; now there was disaster. One town, Werl in Westphalia, did not clear its debt from this war until 1897.

Since rulers could not gather in enough of the money that fuelled the war from their incomes or from subcontractors, each had to try to pressure their population to voluntarily hand over a share of their wealth. This was dangerous for the ruler because it meant overriding the differences between communities. Every region had its own identity, its own rules, its own way of doing things. Most people would describe themselves as belonging to a particular city or community, with their personal status defined by their trade or their title. Their rights were a form of community property, different from those of people in other communities, formulated in treasured charters, treaties and declarations. The power of kings and princes was everywhere shared with local assemblies, called Estates, Cortes, Parliaments or Diets – assemblies of nobles, clergy and burgesses which maintained the privileges of their members and had to be consulted on the grant of taxation to the ruler. In the sixteenth century, the Netherlands alone had a distinct legal code for each of over 700 communities – on average, one set of laws for every 300 adult men. But the ever-growing demands of royal money were the basis for a new form of political society – absolutism.

The Assault on Monarchy

The Netherlands had been the test bed of this approach when the Duke of Alba arrived in 1567 to demolish the privileges of Flanders and turn the population into a human gold mine. Alba completely failed, leading to Philip's bankruptcy, the mutiny of his unpaid army and the sack of Antwerp, but the theory was nevertheless very popular among Europe's crowned heads. It had been stated very firmly in France in 1576 by Jean Bodin: 'We see the principal point of sovereign majesty and absolute power to consist in giving laws to subjects in general, without their consent.'

Bodin's philosophy was not so popular among those 'subjects in general'. During the Thirty Years' War, the rebellion of Estates that had started in the Low Countries became an unstoppable epidemic of protest, uprising and revolution, different in each place as people insisted their rulers could not ignore their right to withhold consent, and confronted those rulers with righteous defences of local rights, local privileges and local traditions.

Those rulers were baffled, angry and determined, desperate for the funds to save themselves from their enemies' armies and from their own armies. Their problems were quite intractable because even if they had been able to gather in all the bullion that there was, it would not come anywhere near matching what they were spending. The coinage circulating in England, for example, rose from about £3.5 million in 1600 to some £10 million in 1640[21] – which represents an increase from about £4.15 to around £10 per household. But expenditure, on every level, increased far more. The flow of gold and silver from overseas conquests had stimulated spending that vastly exceeded what was coming in, and each kingdom in turn went bankrupt.

The clearest example was in Britain, where in 1638 Charles I was driven to find some way of funding an army to suppress a militant Calvinist rebellion in Scotland. His income was around a half a million pounds a year, which just about covered the ordinary cost of his government, but there was simply no money for an army. The original plan, for 40,000 men, would have cost almost a million pounds – a quarter of all the bullion in the country.[22] Charles asked his officials to come up with just one-fifth of that, but it was impossible. When his army assembled at York, the Treasurer at War failed to turn up with his wagonloads of gold. The citizens would not pay up, and Charles had to abandon the field. He then purged his council and relaunched his war. He brought across 'Black Tom' Strafford from Ireland; Strafford had succeeded in imposing a tough-minded colonial policy there that overrode the supposed privileges (and indeed all rights) of the landowners. Strafford knew that the King of Spain, Charles's cousin, was using England as a conduit for his gold to pay his army in the Netherlands. It was too risky to send vast quantities of bullion overland from Spain, so it was shipped to London and stored in the Tower. Strafford proposed that Charles should 'borrow' it, and ordered the mint to turn Spanish bullion into English coin.

The officers of the mint, and London's merchants, were horror-struck at the idea. There would surely be retaliation, with devastating effects on trade. Strafford relented, in exchange for a forced loan of £40,000 from the Merchant Adventurers, the largest trading company. He then turned to the idea of replacing gold coins with brass. One of England's leading diplomats, Sir Thomas Roe, insisted forcefully that a kingdom's strength was entirely dependent on the strength of its currency, so that was a non-starter. Instead, the government seized and sold a newly arrived cargo of pepper to scrape by.

Soon Strafford was so bitterly opposed by Parliament that in 1641 Charles was compelled, despite his promise of protection, to allow his chief minister to be beheaded. Eight years later, Charles himself was executed.

The dust of the Thirty Years' War settled in 1648 with the Peace of Westphalia, negotiated over four years with the new emperor, Ferdinand III, 300 or so territorial rulers of Imperial lands and the kings of France and Sweden. The deal was dominated by the bankers and merchants who had been so magnified by the power of gold. The map of Europe they constructed was a continent of states with frontiers in place of the old feudal territories with vague borders and independent cities. Power was now centralized in financial centres: Madrid, Paris, Vienna, Venice, Lisbon, Amsterdam and London. The old Christendom, whose ultimate overlords were Pope and emperor, was shattered. The treaty's significance can be seen in the Pope's blustering declaration that it was 'null, void, invalid, unjust, damnable, reprobate, inane, empty of meaning and effect for all time'.[23] It remained the basis of the map of Europe until 1914.

The New States of Europe

By 1649, when the English Parliament beheaded Charles I, royalty had almost disappeared. The French child-king, Louis, had fled to the provinces to escape rebels in Paris. The age of kings seemed over, replaced by a new sense of nationhood within many of these newly defined states. At the time of the Armada, the States-General of the Netherlands had been unique in engaging burghers in the business of national, as well as regional, government. As Queen, Elizabeth I had been compelled to seek the approval of the Commons of England for her laws, but she did so as seldom as possible and refused to allow her country to be called a 'state', as that summoned up thoughts of the States-General and popular authority. She had little interest in the welfare of her subjects and economized on the cost of her victorious fleet by imprisoning the sailors on board after defeating the Armada, so that, in the words of her adviser Robert Cecil, 'by death, by discharging of sick men, and suchlike ... there may be spared something in the general pay'.[24] Her admirals were disgusted. There had been a sense of national pride, but no political thought that England belonged to its people. The financial imperative that drove Elizabeth to value gold above the lives of her sailors would ultimately lead to Charles Stuart inventing ways to deny the right of people to resist taxation and led to the King of England being tried and condemned by his own subjects. England became a republic, and its Great Seal, which had shown Charles enthroned on one side and riding in arms on the other, was redesigned. It now showed the House of Commons in session on one side, with the Speaker's chair in place of a throne, and a map of England, Wales, Jersey, Guernsey and Ireland on the other. The map was cut off at the Scottish border. The republic of England had become a fully paid-up member of the new Europe, whose map was a net of frontiers.

By then, Philip IV of Spain had been faced with the revolt of Catalonia and the complete loss of Portugal, where a new-made king now ruled by the grace of his nobles and was never permitted to be crowned. Western Europe's only other surviving king, Frederick III of Denmark, was not placed on the throne by the nobility until he swore never to involve the kingdom in a war. There was a queen, Christina of Sweden, who made a public show of ruling by divine right while being quietly cynical about the idea. In 1654, she abdicated, changed her name and went to live in Rome. Eastern Europe was dominated by Poland, whose king would also abdicate: John Casimir was elected to succeed his popular and successful half-brother in 1648, but was such a disaster that he abdicated and joined a monastery.

Royalty would return – Charles II in Britain, Louis XIV in France, Leopold in Hungary and Bohemia, Charles XI in Sweden and Afonso in Portugal. And this royalty would all be decorated with gold. But the association with Divine Right that gold had bestowed, and which had seemed to be at the core of its value, was missing.

Each kingdom was now its own sovereign universe, and gold connected humans to government power, not God's. By 1660, the financial basis of Europe's governments was transformed. The lesson of the rebellions was a powerful one. Governments managed their servants and soldiers with the gleam and security of gold, but they had to be wary of asking for it. The only safe way to lay hands on gold was from having a share in trade. Customs duties and the part-ownership of profitable enterprises would now be government business.

Chapter 22

The Force of Oriental Gravity

China's Need for Silver

In the mid-seventeenth century, a revolutionary disruption in China changed the lives of perhaps a quarter of the world's population. The effect on Europe would be unrecognized at the time, but it was dramatic. Because China was the biggest market for silver in the world, it had a massive, if largely unacknowledged, effect on the wealth and behaviour of European rulers and governments. Since China's was the largest economy on Earth – ten times as large as Britain's – the resulting change in the Chinese demand for silver was mirrored by a change in the value of gold and upset every applecart on which Europe was now based.[1]

Marco Polo had been amazed by Kublai Khan's use of paper money, seeing it as a trick. In fact, it was a perfectly sensible financial instrument so long as it was printed in the right quantity, as the ancient text on economics, the *Guanzi*, made clear. But his suspicions were justified. Inevitably, the Mongol dynasty eventually printed much more paper money than it could justify, and the economy collapsed. When people lost faith in the paper, and not even Imperial death threats persuaded them otherwise, they turned to imported silver, which had an international market value independent of the emperor and his mandarins. The Ming Dynasty tried to reassert paper, but lacked the ruthless power needed to force people to abandon silver. By 1445, they had given up. The Chinese were now using silver, and a long period of flourishing commercial activity developed. The word 'Ming' is associated with marvellous works of art in painting, silk and porcelain. There was a great demand for silver bullion to sustain the burgeoning market economy.[2]

So when, at the end of the fifteenth century, the Portuguese finally made it around Africa to Asia, they found that China paid the highest price in the world for silver. Portuguese traders needed gold to buy the silver for China. They found it in West Africa. Without the gold there was no silver, without the silver there were no spices, and without the spices there were no profits – to be reinvested, of course, in gold.

The Portuguese realized that they could ship silver across the Pacific and make fortunes before having to sail all the way home.[3] Until the second half of the sixteenth century, Chinese ships were forbidden to trade with Japan, which allowed the Portuguese to launder Japanese silver:

'When the Portugals go from Macao in China[4] to Japan, they carry much white silk, gold, muske and porcelanes; and they bring from thence nothing but silver. They have a great caracke which goeth thither every yere, and she bringeth from thence every yere above sixe hundred thousand crusadoes; and all this silver of Japan, and two hundred thousand crusadoes more in silver which they bring yearly out of India, they imploy to their great advantage in China; and they bring from thence gold, muske, silk, copper, porcelanes, and many other things very costly and gilded.'[5]

That was written in 1591. The hunger for silver in China became extreme. In seven years from 1590, the flow to Asia from Peru and Mexico, via Manila, rose from 2–3 million pesos to 12 million. By the early seventeenth century, China was receiving 116 tons of silver a year, while the government tried to cling to the old bronze tokens. In 1631, Philip IV forbade the trade, trying to increase the flow of silver to Spain, but the ban was ineffectual – all he achieved was an increase in bribes.[6] An English merchant reported in 1635 that the Chinese in Macao were pleading for it, regarding it as precious as blood – indeed, there was a saying in Manila that 'silver is blood'.[7]

The Portuguese were suddenly cut out of this exchange in 1639 because of their missionizing. The rulers of Japan had no enthusiasm for their population developing allegiance to an alien religion, so all Japanese Christians were forced to renounce Christianity on pain of death, and all Portuguese were forbidden to enter the country. The Dutch, who had no wish to convert people, were allowed to stay, so this hugely profitable gold–silver arbitrage fell entirely into the hands of the Dutch East India Company, which was busily encouraging piracy on a huge scale where it helped keep the profits flowing. Once the Chinese embargo on Japan was lifted, up to 30,000kg of silver went to China every year.[8] Overall, for 300 years from 1500, 90 per cent of China's imports from Europe and its colonies were silver.[9] Spanish silver coins were a version of money understood by all the foreigners the Chinese were engaged with, and it was what they were being offered as payment. As Spanish silver began to flow via Manila, and Japanese silver mines stepped up production, China became fully engaged with what was, in effect, a new and entirely unregulated silver-based global economic system.

China had become enmeshed in a global system in which Europe's great ocean-spanning ships became vehicles of an entirely new economic structure, with the currency being silver and gold the key commodity. Europeans were buying in the cheapest market and selling in the dearest thousands of miles apart, arbitraging around the world. They took enormous risks. Captains often had to load cargoes in distant ports based on outdated information. The voyages were dangerous: only 70 per cent of carracks from Portugal reached Asia[10] (though they were perhaps at less risk than land travellers had been). By the time the cargo reached its destination, the price might have altered, and unloading could itself disrupt the market. But all the risks were massively outweighed by the potential profit. As the demand for silver was kept high in China, European moneymen were able to buy more gold with it. And the more gold they could get, the more spending they could do.

China was powering the world, and in the process it was becoming a tourniquet on the flow of money to Spain and Europe. It is impossible to know how large the trade was, because records were falsified and hidden in a world of smuggling and evasion. Philip IV's attempts to draw back his own silver currency were so unsuccessful that by 1642 it was priced at double its notional value.[11] Silver coins disappeared from circulation in Europe. Historians dispute whether this shortage of silver money was primarily caused by the growth in demand from trade or by the fall in supply from diminishing Spanish mines. European monarchs lacked the silver to pay their debts and revolts erupted as they tried to squeeze their populations, who were suffering as the climate changed and crops diminished. All the crises that erupted – the revolt of Portugal, the Catalan uprising, the rebellions of England, Ireland and Scotland, the French Frondes (civil wars) – were connected in this intercontinental network to the Chinese silver hunger, whose effects rippled out like distant waves on fragile shores following a tsunami.

The Manchu

Each overthrow, in country after country, was preceded by a catastrophic period of distress blamed on corruption, a ruthless nobility and unbearable taxation,[12] plus the effects of ever-growing warfare and crop failures linked to climate change. It was also linked to huge currency issues. Then the Ming Dynasty collapsed in 1644. The story played out very differently in China, of course, from Europe. Chinese cities, far larger than Europe's, were dominated by officials, not by merchants. There was no European-style struggle over religion, liberties and privileges. But everyone agrees that things went horribly wrong in China in the second quarter of the seventeenth century. Nearly 12 million people, over 11 per cent of the population, perished in the twenty years to 1646,[13] a human disaster similar to the Thirty Years' War but over a far larger area. It was sealed by the successful rebellion of a Manchu clan from north-east China. The

Manchu called their new state the 'Great Qing' (pronounced 'ching'), and it was ruthless. Men who maintained the old Ming tradition of wearing their hair long in a top-knot and refused to show their submission by shaving the front of their scalps and wearing a pigtail were executed. In one city, Jiading, almost the entire population was slaughtered. China became an even more centralized absolutist state, and all commercial and administrative power was held in the hands of the emperor. But when the Qing tried to restore the old system of a token currency, no amount of ruthless power could achieve that. Silver was what people wanted, to enable trade to function – especially their export trade to the great markets of Europe that so wanted their silks and porcelain.

So, the Chinese demand for silver increased sharply. With massive social upheaval came serious deflation – they were accepting less silver for the same goods. Those goods could then be sold for much higher prices on the other side of the world. When the value of silver rose in China, the value of gold came down everywhere. That, of course, would have consequences – especially when, in 1649, the Qing decided the best way to protect their coinage was to ban outside trade completely, evacuating coastal cities to prevent smuggling, and at the same time Japan stopped exporting silver.[14] But the Chinese smuggling continued and the Dutch were still getting silver into China, commanding ever-higher prices and using the profit to buy more gold. The trade ban was eventually ended in 1684. China was back in the world. Now it would be even more worthwhile to lay hands on Asia's store of gold.

The East India Company

The effort was in full swing, and it was driven by merchants. This was proclaimed in a magnificent piece of theatre in the coronation of Charles II in 1661, and it required the blessing of gold. The royal procession through London took over the city completely in a densely plotted pageant of wealth, glory, music and masquerade. It was presented as a vision to convey the meaning of Charles's kingdom.

When the procession reached the East India Company's office in Leadenhall Street, the king was met by a boy dressed as an Indian on a camel, 'led out by two Black-Moors, and other attendants' who scattered jewels, silks and spices among the spectators and recited a loyal offering of the Company, which expressed itself overjoyed at the new charter he had given it nineteen days earlier. This document gave the East India Company authority to make war on non-Christians in defence of its trade, to set up forts, garrisons and colonies where it would have its own courts, and to imprison any British subject trading without the Company's permission.[15] The heart of the coronation procession thus became the Company's loud declaration that 'all the Merchants of Your Realm' were being given the riches of a global empire on which the sun would never set. To hammer that home, the procession moved to the arch of naval power. On one side stood Father Thames, on the other the deck of a ship with sailors. It was a visual, speaking and singing encyclopaedia a hundred feet high that combined the projection of global power, commerce and the arts and sciences in a single bewildering performance. That included the blood-curdling song of the 'sailors' on one side of the arch, who lustily celebrated unspecified triumphs over Turks and Belgians 'Till their scuppers ran with Gore'. The fundamental message was of enthusiasm for 'trade' enjoyed as a delight in plunder on the king's behalf. Towards the end of the procession, the population saw a thousand pounds of gold – almost half a ton – physically presented to the king. It would have taken twenty people to carry it. They would have also been carrying a weight of meaning and of worth that transcends time. That little gift, which would make a block of less than one cubic foot[16] (a cube of 30cm), would cost £20 million today. After that stupendous benediction, the royal procession moved happily on to the final arch, the 'Garden of Plenty'. At no point in the performances was there any reference at all to Christianity.

England was now fully open for business, and the East India Company was its new marvellous doorway to gather gold. John Ogilby, the impresario who had choreographed Charles II's coronation, spent the early years of the restored monarchy producing guides for merchants, 'atlases' that were handbooks to India, China, Japan and America for the benefit of London's new moneymen. His readers sat at the centre of their global web, feeling the tug of every commercial thread that linked them to their ships. Ogilby began his description of Asia in 1673 by advertising that it 'may well stand in competition with the new-found World America, with all its Mines of Gold'.

Gold to Asia

The great difference was that fortunes in gold came out of America, along with fantastic quantities of silver, while barely any came from Asia. On the contrary, Asia was where these metals went, including the gold and silver of America. Gold was immortal, but gold money was not. It had its own lifecycle, which began when the metal was forcibly taken as flakes from under the gravel of South American riverbeds and ore from the darkness within mountains and was cast into shining ingots. Its rough midwives then carried these on mules and sent them by ship up the Pacific coast, before they were transported on the Camino Real, the Royal Road that crossed the rain-forested mountain spine of Panama, to reach the Caribbean coast. It was a dangerous path for soldiers and muleteers. They depended on dry weather; trying to follow it with a film crew, wading down a waist-deep Panamanian river, I was lucky enough to be lifted away by helicopter in time to see the flash flood from an unseasonable mountain storm swamp the clear water with a raging brown, unsurviveable torrent.

Once safely on the coast, the ingots were shipped to Cuba, where they were joined by coins minted in Mexico and Hispaniola[17] and sent on their great voyage to Spain.[18] But they did not rest there. Travelling always onwards, the gold had a variety of paths to follow – to Germany or the Netherlands, to the Baltic or Italy, to Alexandria or Damascus, always to be exchanged for luxuries that were coming west while it moved further and further east. It acquired some taste of Europe and the Levant until, as its short life grew steadily calmer, it settled in the vault of a noble Indian household or temple or was very likely transformed into jewellery as a wedding gift. It thus arrived at the final stop along the dark road. Once money got to India, it was effectively dead. It was not the gold and silver itself that changed the nature of European civilization; it was the process of its passage.

This has been the driving force behind gold's extraordinary effect on Europe, and so ultimately the world. It is the mechanism that gives gold universal value. It is a profound mystery; the history of the world has been shaped by the passion of Europeans and their descendants to drive gold out on this journey, to gather and then spend it on what the East can offer, and the passion of India and South Asia to sell whatever they want so that the gold can be collected and hoarded. This was the driver behind Europe's wars and revolutions, its glories and its tragedies. Economic historians struggle to understand why. Is it caused by a profound cultural difference between Western spenders and Eastern hoarders, or is there some mechanistic explanation that would be undone by pulling an invisible lever? The flow of coin one way and of otherwise unobtainable luxuries the other can be seen in the medieval business of Venice and Genoa and in the letters of the Jewish merchants of Cairo.[19] A fourteenth-century historian of Iran remarked on the mystery, saying that the gold and silver India acquired for spices, perfumes and indigo never left again.[20] A little was used to buy horses and Middle Eastern textiles, but basically what went to India, stayed in India. This was still true in the seventeenth century. French finance minister Colbert was told in 1670 that 'gold and silver, after circulating in every other quarter of the globe, come at length to be swallowed up, lost in some measure, in Hindoustan'.[21] Three years later, Ogilby made the same point for his commercial audience: 'For all the Gold and Silver which is transported thither from England, Holland, and Portugal, nothing comes in return thereof from thence but Commodities, the Money being all kept in the Countrey.'[22] Arguably, it still is. At the time of writing, in 2019, 'the Countrey' is reckoned to hold 25,000 tons of it,[23] three times the amount of gold in the USA. About 4,000 tons is thought to be sitting in temple vaults, 608 tons in the central bank, and the rest is privately owned, mostly as jewellery. That's an average of about 80 grams, worth around $4,000 for each of India's quarter of a billion households.

Indian Gold Storing

India had always been a great sink for the golden money of the West; it did not flow back again, towards Iran, Turkey or Europe until the last fifty years.[24] So what might be the root of this fundamentally important difference between European spending and Indian hoarding? The answer has been rather obscured by some historians' belief that Indians regarded gold as so sacred that they could not let people spend it. One, Peter Bernstein, assured his readers: 'Asian rulers … considered gold too important to be used as money that would be passed around from one dirty and ignoble hand to another.'[25] Yet they put Roman coins into circulation after defacing them to deny their Roman Imperial authority. Gold staters had been introduced following the arrival of Alexander and the Kushan Empire, which ruled part of what is now Afghanistan. Pakistan in the second and third century minted its own gold, recasting the Roman coins.[26] Later, until the mid-sixth century, the north Indian Gupta Empire produced fine gold coins, genuine works of art, and from 900 CE the Rajput kingdoms also produced gold coins which, like the Gupta ones, showed Lakshmi, the goddess of wealth (though now with a couple of extra arms!). They were called dinars, like Arab coins, the word derived from the Roman denarius.

So in what way was India different? The answer is not readily apparent from the original significance of gold in Hindu tradition, which is quite similar to its meaning in Europe's ancestral cultures. Since they have shared origins ('Indo-European'), that is not surprising. The *Rig Veda* speaks of the metaphysical Indus River as golden and, like so many others, Hindu creation myths link gold, water and life.[27] The *Shatapatha Brahmante*, a Vedic text from before 300 BCE (some of it very much earlier), says that the maker of an offering in a golden cup to the Brahman, the creative principle of the world, imbues himself with immortal life because gold is immortal.[28] There are clear echoes of that in Sumerian myth and at Lake Guatavita in Colombia.

The text teaches that the Creation began with a golden seed floating in the spirit-ocean; that became an egg, split open and from it was born Brahma the Creator. He is referred to as *Hiranya-garbha* – 'gold-born'. Of the two halves of that eggshell, one was of silver and the other gold. The silver half, subject to change, is the Earth. The gold, unchanging, is heaven.[29] Gold is the proper offering of respect to individuals and gods. This valuation of gold transferred from the fifth century BCE to the new philosophy of Buddhism; the oldest surviving Theravada Buddhist text, probably from the sixth century, is etched on plates of gold.[30] In that tradition, gold is the connection on Earth to the stuff of heaven, and its holy buildings are tall golden stupas. The Buddha is said to ride the spirit-ocean on a gold swan, and the modern King of Thailand rides on the royal golden swan-barge. But here we see something different from the Church's use of gold. Church architecture and any rich decoration is commissioned by the ecclesiastical authorities, who control their income and expenditure. Buddhist temples and statues have layer upon layer of gold foil laid on them by their devotees, who regard it as a necessary obligation despite often being desperately poor. It is an obligation that also lies heavy on the great. In Bangkok, there is a statue of the Buddha made, probably in the fourteenth century, from 5½ tons of gold.[31] From 1455–62 in Yangon, in Myanmar (Burma), a temple said to contain some of the Buddha's hairs was covered with the queen's weight in gold. Her successor added four times the combined weight of himself and his queen.[32]

In Indonesia, gold work was restricted to a priestly caste, and bound about with rituals, taboos, spells and sacrifices.[33] Gold jewellery there had, and still has, a special role as the carrier of family identity, able to transmit its noble character to the body and soul of the wearer. This was not simply bling: it was sacred art. And that was a perspective that extended far beyond Indonesia.

One feature of the Indian tradition (using Indian in a sub-continental sense) that differs from European is the overlap of using gold for spending, for majesty, for divinity and for women's jewellery. The connection between gold and women, understood as the female principle, was certainly present in Sumerian myth: the Lord of Aratta wore a golden crown 'for Inanna'. But the goddess was drummed out of the Judaeo-Christian tradition,[34] so there is no Western equivalent of Lakshmi, the goddess of wealth, who appeared on so many gold coins. In Hindi scriptures, she is the embodiment of all women, and every Hindu wedding is a replication of the original marriage of Vishnu and Lakshmi. Gold is laden on the bride as her gift, her right and her security. For at least the last thousand years, married Tamil women have worn a *tali*, a gold pendant necklace, probably as a link to fertility.[35] In a modern Hindu wedding, the groom ties a *mangalsultra*, a necklace with two gold pendants, around the bride's neck and, ideally, she wears so much gold that her face may be hidden by it.

This tradition of, in effect, deifying women with massive quantities of gold did not mean they were anything more than property; the practice of a widow being killed on her husband's funeral pyre is described in Greek sources from around 300 BCE, and around 1368 the inveterate traveller Ibn Battuta wrote of witnessing Indian widows ritually burned with their husbands' bodies as a sign of fidelity. He was also told that in the afterlife these women would be sanctified and given new, male bodies.[36] But the gold was the widow's property; she would dress in it for the funeral pyre and distribute gifts.[37]

The connection between gold coinage, women and jewellery can perhaps be seen in Vedic texts, where the word *nikas* may signify gold currency worn as a necklace.[38] The place of gold jewellery in Indian society goes beyond its financial meaning. It is understood as a permanent store of value, which will be recognized always and everywhere, which is in itself a blessing. It offers a divine connection not only to the great and powerful but to ordinary people. That may be a significant reason why India wanted to keep gold rather than use it to buy stuff. There was really nothing people needed more, yet from 1500 to the late nineteenth century, virtually none was being mined there.[39] Deliveries of treasure were not smooth or evenly spaced, and from time to time in the seventeenth century substantial quantities of gold would suddenly arrive in India's commercial centres, depressing its price relative to silver. But as soon as it flowed into the hands of money changers and goldsmiths, it was bought by the nobility and the price bounced right back. Its value was driven by prestige, so there was no such thing as 'too much gold'.[40]

Chapter 23

Trade as Global War

The New Law of Plunder

The need to take over ever more territory to sustain the gold demand of trading empires echoed on a global stage the old Roman need to seize territory where they could take gold. The territory the Dutch and English were particularly keen on was in the Indian Ocean, where their East India Companies physically expelled the Portuguese and set up in Java and the Spice Islands. (The English East India Company was founded in 1600, two years before the Dutch.)

That was not allowed under Papal law. Rome had declared the entire non-Christian world to be the property of Spain and Portugal, and specifically granted the Spice Islands to Portugal in the 1529 Treaty of Zaragoza. Of course, the whole existence of the Dutch Republic, and of Protestant England, was based on denying the legitimacy of the Church of Rome. It was now up to the Protestants to ground the law of nations on a new basis. They constructed an entirely new legal theory under which the world has been governed ever since. In 1609, a young Dutch lawyer working for the Dutch East India Company, Huig de Groot (or Grotius), produced a text called *The Freedom of the Seas or the Right Which belongs to the Dutch to Take Part in the East Indian Trade*, which gives a hint as to its thrust – a thrust which turned out to be far more piercing than any steel. It is the basis of the entire structure of international law, especially maritime law, which has come to rule the planet.

Grotius provided a legal excuse for the seizure and plunder of Spanish and Portuguese vessels by undermining Catholic claims to exclusive rights over the oceans. He used classical and Renaissance sources to prove, to the satisfaction of the British and Dutch, that there was an inherent right to trade and to make use of 'the freedom of the seas'. Any country that blocked that, as Spain did by blockading the Netherlands, was committing an act of war and its vessels were fair game. Might being right, and the Dutch having destroyed the Spanish fleet at the Battle of Gibraltar in 1607, Spain was in no position to argue (and conceded a twelve-year peace treaty to the Dutch). As a result, the British system of law and commerce was built in the interest of English and Dutch merchants and mercantilism. It was not decreed by the voice of God but that of gold.

Like the Portuguese, the Dutch had to find gold to buy goods in the Indian Ocean, and they too began by taking it from West Africa. They eliminated the Portuguese there and took over. The Gold Coast became the home of the Dutch West India Company. It did not actually know where the gold was found: it was brought to them from hundreds of miles inland. Between 1623 and 1674, the Company shipped out more than 9 tons of African gold. The gold bought Spanish silver – pieces of eight – which travelled on around Africa to be exchanged for East Indian delights worth vastly more in Europe. The Netherlands became, for a while, the economic powerhouse of the West. In the process, the Dutch took control of as much as they could of South-East Asia, negotiating for territory with local rulers and massacring and destroying populations of 'rebels'.

The Governor General of the Dutch East India Company explained: 'Trade without war, and war without trade cannot be maintained.'[1] In 1621, when the Banda islands of Indonesia broke an 'agreement' to trade only with them and not the English, he commanded an attack which killed almost all the 15,000 inhabitants, deporting and enslaving most of the rest and bringing slaves from Indonesia to work for Dutch planters there. The Dutch colonization of South-East Asia was underway. By 1650, they had accumulated a larger store of capital than the whole of the rest of Europe added together. Their finance was given order and stability by a new institution, the Bank of Amsterdam, which guaranteed never to lend money or bullion deposited with it. It was a treasury and an exchange, not a lending bank; there was simply a huge pile of gold in its basement.

Lending was in the hands of private banks, which funded speculation; the Dutch became famously enthusiastic about tulips, initially because they were novel and beautiful but soon just because the market for them seemed to be in endless ascent. People could buy tulips with a 20 per cent deposit, expecting to cover the cost by selling again at a higher price. It was said that a brewer in Utrecht exchanged his brewery for three bulbs.[2] When the bubble burst, as it was bound to, the story goes that the Dutch suffered a large number of bankruptcies and a recession. But there is very little evidence of that, and the solidity of the gold vaults of the Bank of Amsterdam was not shaken.[3]

The Global Gold–Silver Exchange

The English, unable to compete militarily in Indonesia, concentrated on India, where they built an extensive colonial network. Like the Dutch, they depended on West African gold to drive their trade. A few months after Charles II and his brother, James, passed through the coronation arch of naval power and plunder, the Stuarts set up the 'Company of Royal Adventurers Trading to Africa' to compete with the Dutch for access to the gold in Guinea.[4]

The entire world market for gold was powered by India, and the real opportunity for European enrichment came from the extraordinary difference between the price of gold in Europe and Asia. Asians did not want to buy Europe's stolid, unappetizing products (woollen cloth; clumsy pottery; wheat and beer – India even made more beautiful weapons). The one thing Indian traders would sell gold for was silver, because it was in such demand in China and was in short supply. Between half and three-quarters of the value of European cargo shipped to Asia in the seventeenth century was silver, mostly pieces of eight coins weighing approximately an ounce produced by Spanish mints and purchased in Cadiz, Amsterdam or London. There was a great deal of gold in India, so a pound of gold could be bought there for 160 pieces of eight. Once taken back to Europe, where there was no shortage of silver, the same pound of gold would be sold for 240 pieces of eight.[5] And off went the silver to buy half as much gold again as last time around. The voyage was expensive and dangerous, but even so, it was not that hard to make a lot of money.

The Guinea

In Britain, Charles II introduced a new gold 20-shilling piece to show that the Civil War was ended and that he was the ruler of the nation. Charles's vision was imperial; his 20-shilling coin was not a sovereign but a 'guinea', made from 22 carat gold, initially from the West African coast, with a picture of an elephant.

British currency was extraordinarily conservative: it is still called 'sterling', which was the name of the Norman silver penny a thousand years ago.[6] In 1967, I was writing radio scripts for the BBC and paid a guinea – 21 shillings – for each broadcast minute. Sterling was still calculated at 12 pennies to the shilling and 20 shillings to the pound, as it had been in the eighth century. But the guinea would change the meaning of 'sterling' from a currency based on silver to one based on gold. Then in 1666, Charles II fundamentally altered the nature of money.

That was when he took the remarkable step of selling his coinage at the exact price of its bullion content. This put coins – money – on a completely different footing from any other artefact. Mints had always charged for their work; if you took £10 worth of gold to a mint, you would get back coins whose face value was £10 but which only contained about 98 per cent of the bullion. Now, for the first time, the face value of a gold coin and its bullion value were identical. The cost of minting was now paid by the state. Gold and money had finally become one and the same thing, and money was no longer a product made by the state and sold to its people for profit. It was the state.

The international competition for wealth was on a new footing: not so much expropriation and plunder by great armies, as beggar-thy-neighbour by armed commerce. The sum of wealth was thought of as a fixed pot, from which each state's ladle of bullion could be filled by trade, reducing what was left for the others. This philosophy, 'mercantilism', equated gold, trade and power.

In June 1667, the Dutch Navy attacked the British fleet, sailing into the River Medway, burning ships at anchor and threatening London. Samuel Pepys was a leading member of the Navy Board and understood very well what might happen. His personal wealth had begun to increase sharply two years earlier, when he became treasurer of the English colony at Tangier and surveyor-general for victualling the fleet. He knew the value of money very well, and now imagined that every penny he possessed could be plundered. He hurriedly gathered as much gold as he could, which was not easy. There was a run on the banks – that is to say, the goldsmiths who looked after people's wealth were swamped and of course did not have enough coins to repay everyone. They had lent them out and could not get them back. To slow down the rush, they handed people large bags of coins which they insisted be counted on the spot, under supervision. That obviously took time – Adam Smith later reckoned that a merchant might take a week to count out £20,000[7] – and the goldsmiths deliberately got the quantities wrong, so the counting had to start all over again.

Pepys, panicked and unable to leave his office, sent his wife and father to his father's house in Cambridgeshire with £1,300 in gold stuffed into their night bag. They were instructed to bury it in the garden in total secrecy.

Four months later, on the night of 10 October 1667, Pepys's father's neighbours would have heard him quietly cursing as the three of them struggled in the dark to secretly rediscover where it had been buried. It was 'within sight of a neighbour's window, and their hearing also, being close by', and Pepys had no doubt his neighbours would become robbers. The bags had rotted, and in the dim light of a shuttered candle lantern, their spades scattered the coins in the grass. The next night they dug up the whole garden, taking the earth in pails and washing it like prospectors. Getting the coins back to London terrified him; they had to stay overnight in an inn, where Pepys was convinced that he was surrounded by brigands. His panic-stricken state is clear from his fear that the weight of the coins might break the coach floor – the coins would have weighed 12kg, about the same as a pet corgi.

Gold was not the essence of divinity on Earth, so far as Pepys was concerned. It was far more important than that. It clearly represented the very essence of wealth and nation, and without it he and his family would be rendered quite literally worthless. His terror in the garden was simple and existential.

The gold coins that Pepys buried were mass-produced on horse-powered machinery run by German experts, much improved from Philip II's money factory. Pepys had visited the Royal Mint in 1663[8] and was dazzled by the speed and precision with which 200 coin discs were flattened in a single pass in 'an engine', after which they were lettered by a secret process and then their edges were milled, to make any clipping obvious, 'on both sides at once with great exactness and speed, and then the money is perfect'.

Perfect money: its value did not require otherworldly backing. It just needed everyone in the world to be content to accept it at its face value. Machine-made money was perfect and about to become the engine of the world. As the pace of minting accelerated, it became easy to spot those who worked at the machines – they were all missing fingers.[9]

There was just one flaw in the supposed perfection of the guinea. The new coins ran into the same problem as the very first electrum ones in Lydia over 2,000 years before – a shift in the relative market values of gold and silver messed up their value to anyone who owned them. The British government had no control over the relative values of gold and silver, and it had undervalued gold.

The traditional view of English money was that the value of gold was twelve times its weight in silver, so a silver shilling was 12 pennies and a gold pound, should it be minted, should be worth 20 shillings or 240 pennies.[10] But the vast flow of American silver had led to a serious fall in its value, and the relationship to gold had become unstable. By 1660, silver in Europe was only worth one-fifteenth of its weight in gold, and merchants also had to pay a premium of up to 10 per cent to change silver for gold.[11] The guinea, decreed to be worth one pound or 240 silver pennies, contained gold worth at least 300 pennies.

In an age when Spanish silver was the currency of international commerce, and traders took as much advantage as they could of fluctuating demand for it in different parts of the world, the official measure of value throughout Europe was silver. People who had bought guineas for twenty silver shillings soon found the gold was worth more than the silver they had spent and offered the guineas at their gold value to pay their taxes. The government refused to accept them at any value over 22 shillings, though their bullion value was over 25 shillings.[12] Even at 22 shillings a pop, it was a profitable business to exchange guineas for silver and ship it east. Sir Isaac Newton was made Warden of the Mint in 1696 to restore the value of Britain's debased silver coinage and supervise the 'great recoinage'. In 1699, he became Master of the Mint, when the House of Commons was trying to protect the value of the pound by reducing the value of gold. Denying the obvious truth that gold was the real measure of money, the Commons declared:

> 'For it being impossible that more than one metal should be the true measure of Commerce; the World, by common Consent and Convenience, having settled that Measure in Silver; Gold, as well as other Metals, is to be looked upon as a Commodity, which varying its Price, as other Commodities do, its Value will always be changeable.'[13]

When gold and silver fluctuate in relative value, it must be due to a fluctuation in demand. If gold is in shorter supply than silver, you may choose to say the gold price goes up or the silver price goes down. If you want to value everything against silver, the coinage of international trade, then you have to accept that the value of gold will change. But the base of value in people's minds, whatever the government said, was gold, and what Parliament wanted to do was reduce gold's value to protect sterling, the value of a pound of silver. This firm effort to keep Britain on the silver standard was an attempt to buck the market, which never goes well. At the heart of the problem was that silver money had a long record of adulteration by rulers trying to make it go further, while the guinea delivered exactly what it said on the tin – 8.3 grams of 22 carat gold.

In 1717, Newton had another go, this time obtaining a royal proclamation that the guinea was irrevocably worth 21 shillings. That was the biggest mistake of his life. The principal victim of his other errors (staring steadily at the sun, losing £20,000 in the South Sea Bubble, wasting years on alchemy and the *Book of Revelations*) had been himself, but this one affected the global trading system. As an effort to defend the silver standard, it was a guaranteed failure. It had exactly the opposite effect, pushing Britain onto gold so thoroughly that the Master of the Mint created a situation where it stopped minting silver at all. Newton had overseen the enactment in law of a fixed value for the golden guinea, which contained gold worth more than the 21 shillings of silver it would, in law, buy. For the next hundred years, hardly anyone sold silver to the mint, and British silver money sailed away to more profitable parts of the world.[14] The gold standard, which would cause enormous disruption to the world right through into the twentieth century, had been imposed by mistake.

Newton had been the first to analyse the value of money as a science,[15] but he got it wrong and economic analysis has never recovered, just become more complicated. In 1980, some of his intellectual successors, including a member of the Bank of England's monetary policy committee, were asked at the London School of Economics by his employer's successor, Elizabeth II, why none of them had noticed the approaching collapse of the banking system. It took them eight months to compose an answer. They confessed that the problem was science itself, 'a failure of the collective imagination'.[16] In effect, they repeated Newton's reputed admission in 1720: 'I can calculate the movement of the stars, but not the madness of men.'[17] He had concluded that the value relationship between gold and silver was a mechanical balance. The great scientist thought in terms of physical forces and expected any imbalance in their prices to come into natural equilibrium over time. But there was no equilibrium. The demand for guineas outweighed the demand for silver. The ratio was enacted in law, and the balance could not right itself. As late as 1730, Newton's successor at the Royal Mint was still maintaining that silver 'always has been and ought to be' the international standard of value, but this was now evidently a moral principle of British political life (perhaps the only one) and was simply irrelevant to what went on in the world. Silver had lost its status as a measure of wealth and the gold standard was the universal standard of value, in Britain and over much of Europe and its empires.

Fashion as a Gold Mine

As we have seen, a new civilization of sovereign nation states was emerging in Europe, forged in mints of their new money and shaped by mercantile governments which understood how to use science, secular law and high fashion to create competing cosmovisions within their frontiers. The clearest exemplar of this was France, where Louis XIV used his royal authority to design a specifically French national identity through the control of literature, design, scientific endeavour, language and industry, with military strength as an adjunct to the bigger story. All Europe's states needed gold to power trade, and if the gold was not there to represent each transaction, they believed trade and their national project would crumble away. By far the greatest volume of trade in Europe was in textiles, so this was where competition was fiercest, and France determined to fill its coffers by winning the fashion wars over all Europe. Louis XIV once angrily ordered his son to burn his coat because it was made with foreign textiles.[18] His government took control of the manufacture of luxury goods in order to make them more desirable abroad than any others. His new great palace at Versailles was a showroom that persuaded the civilized world to dress in French styles and fabrics. Colbert, the minister who organized and controlled manufacturing, was perfectly clear about the purpose: 'Fashions are to France what the mines of Peru are to Spain.'[19] It was the government's job to regulate, control and ensure victory in the international trade war. The palace advertised itself as the golden home of the Sun King. The entrance to the sacred space of the Royal Courtyard from the Court of Honour was through huge golden gates. Destroyed in the revolution of 1789, they were restored in 2005 at a cost of 5 million euros. Both the originals and the restored versions were meant to be an investment that, by captivating the imagination of the world, would open its pockets.

These states were now engaged in a fierce competition for wealth, which they saw as a zero-sum game of winners and losers. The winners would accumulate treasure, at the expense of the losers. That was the logic behind the development of state-sponsored science and technology in Britain and France in the seventeenth century; nations needed better armaments and better manufacturing technology to divert their neighbours' wealth. While Louis XIV and his minister, Colbert, were winning gold through better textile machines, King Charles II ordered his Royal Society to find new ways to power and wealth by 'promoting by the authority of experiments the sciences of natural things and of useful arts'[20] – what we call R&D (Research and Development). Pepys, who ran the Royal Navy, became the Royal Society's president, which is why Isaac Newton dedicated his great work, *Principia Mathematica*, to him. Newton, very sensibly, went on to become Master of the Royal Mint. Money, utility, military development, science, mathematics and the Crown were part of a single package. Versailles, the British coronation and all the other Baroque court extravagances were homages to the true power behind the state. European governments were now not really ruled by kings or assemblies. Nor did they act in the service of the churches to which they paid lip-service. They served the imperative of trade and the accumulation of bullion. Gold was king.[21]

The competitive approach was partly shaped by the fact that Europe's stock of gold and silver was no longer fast increasing. The flow to Spain from America had peaked by 1620. By the 1660s, America's gold output had halved, the output of silver had fallen by about 30 per cent[22] and its flow from Potosí and Japan was towards China rather than Europe.[23] Spain continued to import significant quantities of bullion, but Europe's rulers felt they were struggling for shares in a static pot. The fierce resistance of their people to royal demands for higher direct taxes drove them to look for income from taxes on trade instead, which of course changed their relationship to their subjects and to each other. It also drove colonialism.

Mercantilism

Colbert was a dedicated enthusiast of the winner-and-losers understanding of power and wealth, which an eighteenth-century French economist would contemptuously term 'the mercantile system'.[24] Colbert wanted France to make fabrics not for their own sake but to seduce gold out of the hands of foreigners.

Trade was as much the business of government as was war. Each city had a role to play on this battlefield and he organized their work like a general. He issued some 200 regulations, and nearly two-thirds of them were instructions to the textile industry. In 1680, he noted happily, French-made serge and stockings cost the Dutch four million livres a year in lost trade.[25] If things went well, this was war without bloodshed, but obviously military conquest could help. So when Louis XIV set out to win glory by attacking the Dutch in 1672, it was also an opportunity to take their wealth by smashing the Dutch slave trade in the West Indies.[26] When the free city of Strasbourg was annexed in 1685, its inhabitants were given four months to stop wearing German clothes and dress in the French style, which of course meant sending a great deal of their money to France.[27] Colbert tried to organize international trade using the power of the royal court, as well as by setting up royal manufactories such as a glassworks to outdo Venice and tapestry works to compete with the Low Countries.

The British East India Company would eventually turn almost all of India into a state of its own invention, minting its own gold,[28] ruling and taxing and holding court over territories based on Madras, Bombay and Bengal. It became the largest company in the history of the world, accounting for almost half of Britain's trade.

John Ogilby's readers, who were prepared to pay very large sums for his huge, well-made guidebooks, were the men who shaped Restoration London, a city powered by the profit of trade over much of the globe, and especially from the Indies. Their meeting places were the London coffee houses where they discussed prices and shipments around the world while enjoying the taste of a brew from Java, Yemen or Mocha. These sober, club-like establishments were the newly invented emporia of global trade, filled with the scent of exotic beans, tobacco, expensive pomades and wig powder, and with the latest gossip about ships and markets, inventions and pirates, opportunities and warnings.

When the city had burned to ashes in a great conflagration in 1666, its merchants did not wait for the government to instigate rebuilding; they could not afford to hang about. Just four years later, Ogilby celebrated the city's resurrection 'from a Confused Heap of Ruines (sooner than some believed they could remove the Rubbish)' and took an office in the brand-new Royal Exchange. These merchants used and depended on goldsmiths/bankers, but most of the gold they dealt in never came to London at all, as they traded between the gold and silver markets of India, China and Japan, making huge profits on fluctuations in prices.

That was how the English Committee of Trade had been able to defend the East India Company in 1660 against the charge that it was sending precious metal abroad and diminishing the amount of money in Britain. The committee observed that the actual quantity exported was far smaller than the value of the goods acquired and re-exported, so the country's precious currency reserves were really growing, not shrinking at all.[29] Developing international trade as an instrument for magnifying the national stock of bullion became the purpose of foreign and military policy, and was at the heart of the new politics that developed in France, the Netherlands and Britain after the Thirty Years' War. With this came a fundamental change in the notion of the ideal man. In place of a courtly figure inspired by the old values of chivalry, despising the hunger for gold, a new figure appeared whose qualities were those of the proud and honest merchant, where virtue was measured by the size of his purse.

Greed is Good

There had always been gold-hungry individuals who sought to grow their personal treasure, but they were generally seen as unsavoury, not welcomed in societies that retained a vision of chivalric values. Greed had been a sin. Hieronymus Bosch's late sixteenth-century painting of a pawnbroker's final moments, surrounded by the securities for his loans, is so full of moral distaste that it is generally known as *Death and the Miser*. A man who owned a hoard in those days was a stock character unacceptable in decent society.

But in the seventeenth century, moneylenders were seen very differently. Edward Backwell, the leading British goldsmith-banker of the Restoration, was at the heart of the new world of lending on security. Like Bosch's financier, Backwell's portrait includes the elements that made him wealthy: in his case, rich fabrics and a cargo ship, an East Indiaman. But instead of being a caricature of evil, he was shown as a role model of propriety. Men like this were now at the heart of society and the state. The connection to India was fundamental to this remaking of social values and was clearly expressed in the theatrical presence of the East India Company and its gold in Charles II's coronation procession. At that moment, the Company had not seemed a likely candidate for commercial supremacy, as it had been ejected from the East Indies. The Dutch had been able to take effective control of the spice trade from Britain and Portugal; by 1663, they had trade settlements in Japan (Deshima), China (Macao), Malaysia (Malacca), Indonesia (Jacarta), Sri Lanka (Colombo) and southern India (Cochin). But the East India Company had realized that its future prosperity would not come from spices. Modern economists reckon that India produced goods and services worth ten times those of Britain,[30] and though no one at the time made that calculation, it was quite obvious that trade with India offered a source of phenomenal enrichment. By a happy chance, when in 1661 Charles II married the Portuguese Princess Catherine of Braganza, her dowry included Bombay. Portugal had no use for it, but it was the best natural harbour in South Asia and the Company had been after it for some time. In 1668, its directors instructed its factory there to concentrate on building up a cotton-weaving industry for export to Europe, and then expanded its control to Calcutta.[31] Britain accounted for less than 2 per cent of the world's annual wealth, while India produced vastly more. The greatest part of this wealth was in Bengal, dominated by Calcutta. Britain had no gold mines (the gold from Guinea was brought from indigenous mines some 300 miles inland and bartered for goods with European traders[32]), but by 1670, 40 per cent of the East India Company's exports to India were gold bullion and it was minting gold in Madras.

This was possible because gold and silver coins were no longer the currencies of local trade, but of international trade in a very diverse world. The new phenomenon of global trade was carried out at harbours dotted around the Pacific and Atlantic, which added up to a vast multi-pocketed garment worn by the East India Company, with different exchange rates between gold and silver in different pockets. Silver, bought cheaply in Europe or Mexico, was sent in galleons via the Philippines to Macao, where it commanded a far higher price and where the gold price was low. In 1711, an English publication showed that simply exchanging European silver in London for gold in China and bringing it back would yield a theoretical gross profit of 48 per cent, but the Company could do better.[33] It took the gold on the shorter, safer, less expensive journey to Bengal, where it was sold at a profit and used to pay for cotton goods at

The 'East Indies'.

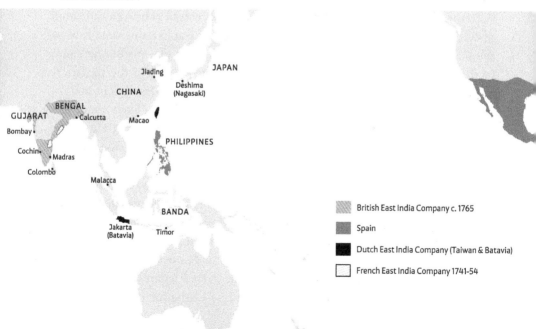

British East India Company c. 1765

Spain

Dutch East India Company (Taiwan & Batavia)

French East India Company 1741-54

low prices; these made the long voyage back to London, where the Company worked hard to establish cotton, not wool, as the fabric of fashionable clothing and décor. As the middle classes prospered, they followed fashions set by court and aristocracy. Cotton cloth, muslin, calico, chintz, dungaree and gingham built the vast profits of the Company, making it the wealthiest company in the world.[34] The shortage of currency was over, and there was coin enough to keep moneylenders confident and traders prosperous.

Creating Consumers

In order to make this work, trade needed the development of industry and of a new class of domestic purchasers, whose spending kept the money moving and shifted profit to merchants and their governments. The flow of gold around the world, and the merchants' legerdemain of silver exchange values, was transforming Britain.

France also had its East India Company, but unlike those of Britain and Holland it was a royal enterprise, run by men appointed by the Sun King whose commercial instincts were less powerful than their social ones. That was not how the new commercial world would operate. The British and Dutch East India Companies were as highly centralized as France's and also thought of trade as warfare – indeed, they were extraordinarily violent when they saw the advantage of that. But they were a new kind of commercial enterprise. These were joint-stock companies owned by their investors, able to spin credit out of thin air on the distant promise of profit, much as modern start-up companies can do in America. For them, a factory was not a place of machines and production but a trading post where their 'factor', or agent, bought and sold for them. These factories did not make anything except profits, and the fabrics, porcelain and other delights upon which their trade revolved changed the nature and quality of European domestic life for people who could live off unearned income.

By 1700, Europe's trade war for gold had been won and Britain was the dominant power in the world, controlling over a third of all trade – no other country had half as much. The value of money was officially measured in silver, but the golden guinea now commanded 25 silver shillings. In Europe, the metal was no longer thought of as magical, mystical and linked to eternity or to alchemical power, but all those faint memories still existed and reinforced its extraordinary place as the true store of value. That is, of course, completely irrational, yet even today, when our relationship to gold is supposedly completely different, the vaults of The Old Lady of Threadneedle Street hold over 5,000 tons, about one-sixth of all the gold in the world.[35]

This was a bareknuckle fight, and Europe engaged in a series of increasingly expensive military conflicts over control of the world's wealth. But since Britain was protected by its place as an island, and had the money to spend on warships, it seemed impregnable.

The political objective was empowerment through the accumulation of gold, but in truth that was not actual enrichment of a country at all. Trade and manufacturing, which was seen as the instrument to prise gold out of the world's hands, was actually far more important in improving people's lives than the gold itself. Spain and Portugal had huge inflows of treasure, but as it did not come through trade, they did not do anything to develop industry or a wider society of consumers. In terms of food, housing and the conditions of life generally, therefore, their inhabitants became relatively impoverished compared to countries that were promoting commerce.

Chapter 24

The Treaty That Changed the World

Portugal's Great Gold Strike

In the heart of the city of Porto, on a steep outcrop just below the old stock exchange, is the apparently undistinguished medieval Church of São Francisco. Step inside and you find yourself in what one guidebook describes as 'an explosion in a gold factory'.

Some 300kg of gold dust from Brazil was used to celebrate the wealth that was pouring into Lisbon and Porto during the eighteenth century. Very few people realize that by the early eighteenth century, Portugal was importing many times more gold from Brazil than Spain had ever received from the Spanish American colonies. Even fewer know what happened to it. Portugal is one of the poorest countries in Europe. The church stands in the middle of what was, at the end of the twentieth century, an impoverished, profoundly degraded and under-populated urban landscape. The country went into relative decline in the mid-eighteenth century, around the time this church was built: it entered the twentieth century with its people producing only 40 per cent as much wealth as the Western European average, and with three-quarters of them illiterate. I became connected to Porto in the 2010s, when it was in a desperate, long-neglected state. The church itself became such an embarrassment that it had been kept closed to the public for several decades, reopening in 1992.

Yet in the eighteenth century, the country was profiting from the longest gold rush of all time. Portugal's colony of Brazil had no great indigenous gold-working civilization; the forest-dwelling communities there had no cities, no hierarchies and had no apparent interest in gold's magical power to transcend the mortal world. Its potential for wealth lay in sugar, and slavers took large raiding parties into the jungle to capture and sell the inhabitants as plantation slaves. In the 1690s, slavers investigating the forested mountains north of Rio de Janeiro found rivers full of alluvial gold – both dust and nuggets. Their efforts at discretion were hopeless, and the colony's cities immediately began to empty as the largely illiterate inhabitants rushed into the jungle to fill their pockets. The small population of Portugal, well used to the idea that their only chance of improvement could come on another continent, hurried to embark in such numbers that restrictions were imposed to stop a dangerous depopulation.

The forest was felled on a huge scale, and the indigenous population was swept away.[1] Once it became clear that there were nowhere near enough indigenous slaves for the diggings, millions were imported from Africa to be worked to death extracting gold in grotesquely awful conditions. Brazil's sugar trade went into decline as the plantations, having lost their slaves to the mines, were abandoned. The newly created town of Ouro Preto – Black Gold – became the richest town in all the Americas, a wealth attested by churches like that of Nossa Senhora do Carmo, which probably contains even more gold than the Church of São Francisco in Porto. It is just one of the thirteen gold-laden churches in this small town.

The destruction of Moctezuma and Atahualpa, and the ruthless unbounded savagery of Cortés and Pizarro, resonate in Anglocentric and indigenous tales of the cruel greed of Spaniards in the name of their God. The story of the much greater plunder of Brazil has no such resonance; it does not play so well in the theatrical narrative of popular history. While Spain's loot was stripped from the glories of Tenochtitlan and Cuzco by world-conquering monsters, Portugal's far greater fortunes were scooped up in the unromantic, tediously named Minas Gerais, the General Mines.

Perhaps the Portuguese story was not told with similar righteous vigour in other countries because their investors did not come to it with clean hands, and so preferred not to dwell on it. Immeasurable suffering was inflicted on the original occupants of Brazil, but whereas the Spanish could be depicted in a 'Black Legend' of wanton cruelty and mass slaughter, the destruction of Brazilian tribes, though just as catastrophic, was bound up with African enslavement, and the British, French and Dutch were at the heart of the Atlantic slave trade. The current 'best estimate' is that during the eighteenth century, over 6 million wretched souls – more than half of all slaves carried across the Atlantic – were forcibly shipped from West Africa to Brazil, and that by far the greatest number, over 2½ million, were taken in British ships – not a process to be discussed.[2] A ship's surgeon, John Atkins, wrote a condemnation of what he had seen, but that was very unusual. 'We who buy slaves say we confer a Good,' he wrote, because the owners claimed to be improving the lives of brute and godless savages. But he insisted that carrying people off 'must be highly offending against the Laws of natural Justice and Humanity, and especially when this change is to hard Labour, corporal Punishment and for Masters they wish at the D(evi)l'.[3] He observed that the captives believed they were being shipped to be eaten.[4] The British played a full part in this story and it is reckoned that up to a quarter of the victims died in their hands. Upon arrival, survivors were sold and then taken on a terrible endurance trek to the place where their lives would end.

Another reason why popular history is rather muted about Brazil is that while the conquerors of Mexico and Peru created their story with texts, here the plunder was won by illiterate slavers; hard, tough men, life-long bachelors, who made the desperate journey to Minas Gerais in search of their fortunes and did not tell their stories, however epic. In 1726, Governor Rodrigo César de Meneses set out to visit the mines from São Paulo. His destination lay some 600km to the north, but the direct route was obstructed by the challenging forested Mantiqueira Mountains, which rise to over 2,700 metres. The journey was by river, and the rivers flow west, so he had to make a huge and extremely difficult diversion. This involved many portages of canoes and baggage past rapids and waterfalls, to eventually climb up to the watershed in the middle of the country and then make a long descent before being able to change rivers for an equally strenuous journey back eastwards. This was a five-month trip of some 3,500km. On the way, the route crossed the Pantanal, the world's largest alligator swamp, where there is certainly no shortage of competition to eat or be eaten (and where I learned to fish for piranha suppers from a canoe with a simple lump of bloody meat). It remained sufficiently remote that when I was there in 2012, some inhabitants told me that they did not learn that they were citizens of Brazil until the coming of electricity in the 1980s.

This was the journey made annually by fleets of adventurers, some with 3,000 people – mostly slaves – in 300 canoes, arriving eventually in the mineral-rich Espinhaço Mountains to extract and carry off their loot. The local Payaguá inhabitants, like uncolonized indigenous people throughout America, had no concept of monetary value; one Spaniard was able to trade a tin plate for 6lb of gold.[5] But they became incensed by the invasion and despoliation of their land, and tried to stop it. In 1730, they destroyed a flotilla carrying 400 people and 900kg of gold, most of which they donated to the water. Unsurprisingly, over the next fifty years the Payaguá were obliterated. If they had not been killed by reprisals, they would have died anyway, as the land was stripped and the water casually poisoned. The prospectors used mercury to bind the smallest fragments of gold from the gravel of the riverbeds into an amalgam, which they then evaporated, producing a small lump of gold while slowly poisoning themselves. They poured the slurry into the rivers. It is reckoned that by 1880, almost 200,000 tons of this long-lasting poison had been dumped in the rivers, much of which found its way into the food chain.[6]

The nearest we know to a legendary adventurer here was Manuel de Borba Gato, who was more like Colonel Walter E. Kurtz, as played by Marlon Brando in *Apocalypse Now*, than any conquistador. Kurtz was a military man who had taken refuge in the jungle and made himself lord over the natives; the character was based on an ivory trader in Conrad's *Heart of Darkness*, which itself was inspired by real historical figures. Gato was just such a figure, a slave trader and gem hunter who fled from his jungle estate in 1682 after murdering the Administrator General of the Mines. He spent sixteen years living deep in the forests of Minas Gerais (a province larger than France) among tribal people who came to accept him as their chief, 'like a sovereign prince'.[7] In 1698, he finally emerged, at the head of a great tribal retinue, bearing enough gold to astonish the authorities and buy his pardon. As part of the deal, he had to reveal the source of the gold, but was able to have himself installed as a lieutenant general, responsible for the organization of justice, allocation of gold mining permits and collecting of taxes for the Portuguese Crown. In 1963, he was celebrated in São Paulo with a 10-metre-high coloured statue looking like a crude children's toy. There was an ineffectual campaign to demolish it in 2008.

There is no great romantic story to tell of Minas Gerais, just a long sad tale of destruction, forest-stripping, massive pollution and the condemnation of millions of native Americans and West Africans to early and miserable deaths. But the story is actually far bigger, if that is possible, in scale and consequence than the impact of Spain's conquistadors. A graph does not stir the soul like the story of Cortés, but it can open your eyes.[8] Spanish bullion was of unique significance until the end of the seventeenth century, but then everything changed.

The quantities displayed with such apparent precision in modern studies are guesses, and likely to be on the low side. The true size of Portugal's immense windfall is, of course, unknown. The figures made public were the minimum anyone could get away with. The only people with an interest in revealing the truth were out of the loop, in Lisbon, on the far side of the world. The miners and the officials on the spot (often the same people) had every reason to conceal as much as they could. The Crown demanded a 20 per cent tax on all

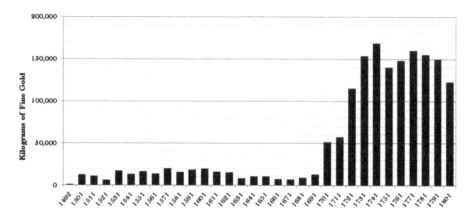

Gold imported to Europe.[9]

The Gold of Brazil.

gold taken to smelting houses. In 1701, out of the 30,000 or so people engaged in mining, only thirty-six paid the tax. The following year, that number fell to just one. With men like Manuel de Borba Gato as tax collectors, it seems surprising that the Crown received anything at all. In 1705, the king was told that he was being defrauded of millions, and that hundredweights of gold were being carried away down remote jungle tracks and smuggled through the city of Bahia.[10] Nuggets and great quantities of gold dust were simply there for the taking, and by 1703 it was being reported that 'almost every negress in Rio has gold ear-rings', some weighing 2lb. A world of excess sprang into being, in which prostitution, concubinage and extravagant display were regarded as the entitlement bestowed on strong men by the apparently limitless flow of yellow metal.[11] It is estimated that between 1720 and 1807, almost twice the weight of gold was carried to Portugal as the whole of Spain's world-shaking bonanza in the previous 200 years.[12] The scale of Portugal's colossal acquisition has only recently become clear, thanks to pioneering research in the shipping records.[13] The numbers are startling, especially in relation to Portugal's tiny population. If it had been evenly distributed, each household in the country would have received almost a kilogram of gold.[14]

Britain's Great Gold Strike

Of course, that did not happen. Portugal spent the nineteenth century dominated by the *ancién regime* of Church, aristocracy and the royal family, who used most of their riches for extravagant display. But only a small part of the gold stayed in Portugal at all. Rather astonishingly, most of this gold ended up in England. And while Portugal stagnated and declined in the depressing brilliance of its gold-smothered churches and palaces, Britain was quite transformed.

Britain had invested virtually nothing in the great ventures of global exploration by Spain, Portugal and the Netherlands, and with a relatively small army it was in no position to take much by force, but it managed to lay hands on the greatest quantity of loot on the planet.

In 1700, Portugal and Britain were both developing American colonies and trading to the Pacific, but on different trajectories. Portugal was a sliver of coast, an absolute monarchy populated by some 2 million people with very little industry. Lisbon had about 10 per cent of the Portuguese population and London about 10 per cent of the English, but Lisbon was dominated by clerics and well-connected bureaucrats. Trade was a secondary interest considered most appropriate for younger sons, and the emerging 'new rich', whose money came from commerce and investment, bought land, intermarried with the old elite, distained their past and eagerly joined the existing social system. When gold started to arrive from Brazil, the Crown used it to finance itself, celebrating its freedom from debts, obligations and the need for a parliament. King João V was proud of never summoning the Cortes.

It was not like that in Britain. London was a city of tradesmen, shopkeepers and merchants, and the East India Company was trading very profitably in the Pacific. The country was dominated by great aristocrats, but they were heavily engaged with the 1,700 or so London merchants, who maintained a well-organized commercial network with North America and the Caribbean that involved over half the city's shipping capacity.[15] The Crown's income was severely constrained. King James II had wanted to restore a more powerful throne, but in 1688 had found himself being propelled off it. The great merchants and landowners who had become Britain's kingmakers saw to it that the new rulers they invited in, William and Mary, would be completely tied to the apron strings of Parliament, which had complete authority over all taxes.[16] The sovereign had just a small personal income from hereditary revenues that were used, for example, to pay the salaries of judges and ambassadors, but eventually even that and the royal household's expenses became a form of pocket money granted by Parliament, called the Civil List. William and Mary were not given the resources to run the government, and this was hammered home when a quarter of the Anglo-Dutch fleet was destroyed by France in 1690.[17] The navy had to be rebuilt as soon as possible, but Parliament would not grant the taxes needed. The only solution was for the government to borrow the money (£1,200,000). To do that it had to hand over its present and future cash (its income from land tax and excise duties) as security. Subscribers to the loan were given bonds paying 8 per cent and formed into a new limited company called the Bank of England. There were many private banks, which were used by merchants to finance their activities, but the Bank of England was rather different. It had exclusive possession of the government's cash balances. The navy got its money in twelve days.

More unexpectedly, the Bank of England's gold deposits grew remarkably fast in the following decades. Britain found it could afford to grow into the world's dominant sea power, and the Bank could issue bank notes as personal receipts for private deposits of gold. These were not exactly currency, because, at a time when an average annual income was less than £20, the smallest note was £50. By 1760, the smallest note was still only £10, so paper money was still not for daily use, but the Bank of England was such a successful project that the navy had three times the tonnage it had lost seventy years before. The notes were easily handled cashable money-tickets, but they had to represent real bullion. The Bank said it could convert all of them to gold if asked.

This system of finance, which created a national debt managed by the Bank of England, depended on people believing that banknotes really were as good as gold because the Bank had enough gold to redeem the notes on demand. It quickly became rather precarious without a good supply of physical gold – in fact, there was a run on the Bank within two years – but London's merchants and bankers were among the first people in Europe to hear of the discovery of gold in Brazil. About a third of the directors of the Bank were importing wine from Portugal,[18] and others were selling cloth there, so they were well informed. When, in 1700, France moved to take control of Spain, Portugal desperately needed a military alliance, and London immediately offered one, tied to the most significant trade agreement in history. Oddly, it is best known for stipulating that Britain would receive port wine at a privileged rate of duty. This was highly desired at a time when England and France were at war and French wine was interdicted. But it was part of a much bigger deal. It was negotiated by John Methuen, the greatest cloth merchant in England, and Methuen also wanted the unlimited right to sell wool and cloth to Portugal and its colonies. That is what he got. In effect, all Portugal's textiles would now come from Britain, free of duties, and Britain would be paid for them in gold from Brazil.

Historians have generally regarded Methuen's trade treaty as insignificant,[19] because the Portuguese figures have not been much examined. Until the last few years, this important shift in Britain's fortunes has been overlooked. Between 1730 and 1760, British exports to Portugal and Brazil were worth possibly three times its imports from them. The difference was made up in gold. The scale of what was happening was hidden. Gold that arrived in Spain and Portugal had left a trail: it was checked and recorded (at least in theory) by royal servants. But the gold coming to England left no trail. It was being used to pay commercial debts and had nothing to do with the Crown. It was illegal to export gold from Portugal, so it was smuggled out in Royal Navy ships and the weekly packet boat to Falmouth, none of which could be examined by Portuguese officials, and it was not taxable on arrival. The gold flowed under the radar, recorded only in private ledgers.[20] A significant quantity was deposited in the Bank, allowing the national debt to grow to £52 million by July 1713. Portuguese gold was financing the power of Britain, and by the early nineteenth century it would be said, symbolically, that the streets of London were paved with gold.

Meanwhile, the Portuguese towns that had been producing textiles for Brazil simply lost their business, given away by a gold-rich king who did nothing effective to encourage trade or commerce.[21] Instead, he concentrated on impressing the Pope and other sovereigns (he spent £9,000 on his envoy's arrival procession in Rome), built up a wonderful art collection and constructed a fabulous palace. Today, the endless gloomy halls of the Palace of Mafra, with its 1,200 rooms, inspire tedium rather than awe, the presumably remarkable contents having been stripped away when the entire court was shipped to Brazil by the Royal Navy ahead of Napoleon's occupation, and by Napoleon himself. The gold did not do much for Brazil, but it left a massive legacy in Britain.

Britain takes India

In Britain, the woollen cloth that had once dressed the population was increasingly replaced by cotton fabrics imported by the East India Company from India. In the middle years of the eighteenth century, Calcutta fell to a reconquest by the Nawab of Bengal, but then a Company force, led by Robert Clive, retook it. The Nawab had profoundly alienated the dynasty of bankers who controlled the spectacular wealth of the Mughals, the Jagat Seths. He threatened their position, and they offered the Company 25 billion rupees to get rid of him – sending the offer through the Nawab's own military paymaster. When that did not seal the deal, the Jagat Seths lifted their offer to more than the entire annual revenue of Bengal.[22] That worked. In June 1757, the Company, and more specifically Clive, attacked. The Nawab assembled a vast force to confront him at Plassey, but the power of the bankers' gold was utterly decisive and the Nawab's army evaporated as Mark Antony's fleet had done at Actium. Robert Clive was presented with a decisive victory and the joint stock Company he served became the ruler of almost all India. A new form of wealth had been established, and a new form of sovereignty. That particular company is gone, but the power of companies to rule without any individual being identified as the ruler was born in Bengal.

Up to then, three-quarters of all the Company's imports to Bengal had been bullion. But now the Company collected taxes and used that money instead to pay for the goods it shipped away. India was now simply plundered (though some care was taken not to kill the goose laying its golden eggs), and having no need to make payments for what it took, the Company stopped importing gold and silver.[23] Bengal was now owned by the East India Company, its products cost the Company nothing and England kept its treasure.

It seems that the gold coinage of England trebled in eighty years;[24] a 2018 study indicates that the British coin supply grew from £10.75 million in 1700 to £44 million by 1790.[25] Between 1720 and 1807, Portugal sent around 370 tons of gold to England to buy woollens and other manufactured goods, as well as dried cod from Newfoundland – which remains a staple of Portuguese diet – and butter and beef from Ireland.[26] That means that in less than ninety years, England took in twice the quantity of gold that Spain acquired in 150 years, from 1500–1650. Most of it came as minted coins. Some were taken to the mint to be turned, free of charge, into British currency, but many circulated unaltered. Almost all the gold coins used to pay British taxes were Portuguese, and in the middle of the century most of the gold coins in circulation in Britain had been minted in Portugal. This was particularly true in the west of England, the territory of the great wool merchants.[27] Although John Methuen died a man of comfortable but modest fortune soon after the treaty was signed, his son made a colossal fortune out of it and left a quarter of a million. Something quite new then happened to wealth.

Living in Debt

In Britain, as with Spain in the sixteenth century, however much gold arrived it was very far from enough. Since the flow appeared to be unlimited, everyone acted, quite reasonably, as though there was vastly more on the way. Both the Bank of England and private citizens survived by confidently promising to clear their obligations with sovereigns that did not yet exist. The import of gold was on an astonishing scale, but the promises of future payment far exceeded what could be delivered. There was no way of getting enough coin into circulation. That did not matter so long as there was confidence that people would generally be able to repay whatever they borrowed. Credit was the act of faith by which people lived, on a quite novel scale.

There was nothing new about credit. It had always been a vital part of trade. If payment for purchases could not be postponed until buyers had sold the goods they bought, or until rents were paid, then all trade since the age of Babylon would have been crippled. Without collateral – something or someone that was held by the lender as security until the debt was paid – credit was dependent on the confidence the lender had in the borrower. That is why loans were usually only made between people with long-established networks, family connections or religious links. A lender had to know and trust the borrower, and also know where to find them or their agent whenever necessary.

The only way to make credit go farther was to extend confidence in borrowers to more distant acquaintances, or to make the penalties for default crushing. Britain was now doing both. The combination of the national debt and debtors' prisons did the trick, and there was a huge surge in lending. Respectable families with very ordinary incomes could get their shopping with a simple promise to pay. Speculators found they could raise capital from the better-off for new ventures. Stocks were being sold by brokers to raise capital as credit became available on a scale that could never have been conceived before.

Britain was getting rich on the basis of promises to pay. There was nothing like enough coin to finance the business being done. In the first eighty years of the eighteenth century, the supply of gold sovereigns may have quadrupled, to about 44 million, but Britain's gross domestic product, the measure of economic activity, is estimated to have risen to over four times that. There was nowhere near enough coin to cover the difference. Everyone was, and needed to be, in debt. Just as with Philip II's military expenditure in the sixteenth century, gold that did not yet exist was now driving everything.

No matter how much gold was sucked in, there was a desperate shortage of it, which had to be overcome to allow all this buying and selling to happen. The problem was not just at the level of great traders and investors, but a serious issue in ordinary daily life. Bread and shoes had to be bought on credit. Wages were generally unpaid for years. The wealthier the family, the greater their use of credit. The weaker the position of their creditor, the longer it would be before the debt was paid. In 1754, a 9-year-old Edinburgh beggar called John MacDonald was taken on by the coachman of a great landowner called John Hamilton. Hamilton was extremely rich; his estate was worth £4,000 a year and his marriage brought him another £10,000. Young MacDonald was dressed, as were all Hamilton's servants, in an expensive and showy costume, a scarlet jacket trimmed with gold. As an experienced postilion, he was helping to manage an expensive custom-built coach. His pay was £2 a year, but he did not receive a penny until he left five years later. All he was given in those five years was a third of any tips.[28] Hamilton's household ran entirely on credit, and that was perfectly normal. The only payments a gentleman was expected to make promptly were gambling debts. John MacDonald had no access to his wages for five years, and his enforced savings could not be regarded as his own until he was actually paid. Gold on the books was not real gold.

The desperate lack of coins meant that no matter how much came from Portugal, the entire economy was operating on a skeleton supply. Tradesmen had no choice but to extend credit to their customers and relied on credit from their suppliers. All this debt was represented by various forms of credit notes, but none of these were understood to be alternatives to real money. They were simply ways of confirming that payment was deferred. Without collateral, the only enforcement of debt came from the threat of a damaged reputation and, in extremis, the debtors' prison. That, of course, was a severe and intimidating penalty which might focus the mind of the debtor, but once invoked it did nothing to help get the debt repaid.

In the modern economy, unsecured debt, especially credit card debt, is part of the money supply. In 2023, Americans owed almost a trillion dollars on their cards. Most of it is not expected to be repaid, just rolled over while interest is paid. But in the eighteenth century, unsecured debt was regarded as a temporary loan, and it would have to be to be repaid in coin. Nevertheless, its ready availability encouraged people to borrow to start businesses on the flimsiest basis, and Britain was awash with scams and get-rich-quick schemes, all of which floated on a sea of unsecured optimism.

We see this kind of sleight-of-hand credit popping up as soon as William and Mary began borrowing from bankers in the early 1690s, a process which quickly led to the Bank of England being set up. In 1692, a young man called Daniel Ffoe, having seized the opportunity, borrowed and swiftly lost £17,000 (roughly £3 million today) in his business ventures. Undeterred, he tried to recoup his fortune by investing in seventy civet cats.[29] The musk scraped from a gland near their anuses was valued for perfume and balm, and a single ounce was worth a year of a postilion's pay. It was a desperate idea and a pretty horrible process. The creature was caged, and to get the musk it was hooded so that its rear end could be pulled out to expose the gland at the base of its tail and squeezed. It would take several minutes to collect the musk. The creatures were frequently injured and do not breed in captivity. It was not likely to be a profitable enterprise, but Ffoe was able to contract to buy the caged civets for over £850, without security or of course having the cash. Inevitably, he then borrowed more until his creditor lost patience and called in the sheriff. Ffoe was bailed out by his mother-in-law, and then to her shock a creditor appeared who insisted that he had been the owner of these poor creatures the whole time and that Ffoe's purchase had been a deceit.

Ffoe is now better known as Daniel Defoe, who a few years later literally wrote the book on what debt offered. He produced a series of articles and pamphlets, starting in 1710, which created a powerful literary image of 'Lady Credit', the daughter of Prudence. Credit 'turn'd nothing into something' and determined England's domestic and foreign strength. At home, said Defoe, credit made everyone – small shop-owners and large estate-holders – prosper; abroad, it made England a force to be taken seriously. Credit was essential to trade, war and government, but, Defoe insisted, was not to be mistaken for actual money: ''Tis the Sun-shine, not the Sun.'[30]

Of course, it followed logically that total indebtedness in Britain far exceeded assets, and that applied to most households as well as the country as whole. And since debt always had to be repaid with actual money, there was no escaping the constant risk of crashes – individual and of whole markets, such as in the South Sea Bubble.

Buying Scotland

There has been a long-lasting debate about why the Industrial Revolution took off in England rather than any other country, and why the island of Britain, half the size of Minas Gerais, thereby became the world's dominant economic and military power through the nineteenth century. Many factors have been proposed to explain the startling acceleration of Britain's economy in the eighteenth century, one recent study pointing to the arrival of potatoes.[31] But attention has only now turned to this huge influx of gold. Historians simply assumed that changes in the supply of coinage were minor details without significant consequences. Important publications by Nuno Palma, starting in 2012 and still ongoing, have demonstrated that this has been a serious oversight. In his words, 'the "big picture" message is that changes in money supply can have causal, persistent, quantitatively large effects on the performance of the economies affected'.[32] This huge change in the number of gold coins had massive, long-lasting effects. Apparently unnoticed, these coins remade Britain in the eighteenth century and brought the world the blessings and curses of modernity.

The immediate result of Portuguese gold saving the Bank of England was that England acquired the resources and confidence to, in effect, buy Scotland. The crowns of the two kingdoms of Britain had been united for a century, since James VI of Scotland became James I of England, though there had been deep resistance to his desire for a unified kingdom. But the risk of a French invasion, nominally in support of the overthrown Stuart dynasty, was a permanent drain on English resources and attention. In 1700, Scotland suffered a financial catastrophe when a commercial company representing the kingdom, the Company of Scotland, failed in its attempt to set up a colony spanning the Panama isthmus. The East India Company did what it could to sabotage it, and the Spanish military destroyed it. At least 20 per cent of all the money in Scotland – perhaps even half of it – had been invested in the so-called Darien project, and the country was ruined. England, with its new wealth, rescued Scotland with an offer it could not refuse. It bought out the company, paying compensation, provided the Scots with additional compensation for handing them a share in the national debt and made sure that the great Scottish political figures would vote their country out of existence as a sovereign state by giving them English peerages, offices, pensions and hard cash where required.

The men who ran England now believed Britain was secure against foreign-inspired division – and also had the use of Scots in their nation's armed forces, a necessary blessing. Money changes everything.

The Hidden Flow of Gold to Britain

It certainly changed itself. Silver, which had been the basis of English money for about a thousand years, was now simply understood as small change. In 1730, the Master of the Mint said that more than 90 per cent of all payments in England were made in gold.[33] That cannot have been the experience of daily life, as the smallest gold coin, a half-guinea, was about five days' pay for a London labourer, but it does explain why the value of money stopped being spoken of as silver and Britain was squarely based on the 'gold standard'.

The association between the sixteenth-century influx of Spanish bullion and inflation is well known and seems unsurprising. The more bullion that arrived, the less it was worth. But the much larger quantity that poured into Britain as gold in the eighteenth century held its value. This is a puzzle. In 1752, the social scientist David Hume wrote an essay on money discussing the time lag between extra money appearing and its value changing.[34] He was trying to make sense of the inflation that had been caused by Spanish bullion. Everyone knew about Spanish gold and silver because of the stories of looted empires, raided galleons and a magical mountain of silver. There were no statistics published to show how the money supply had actually grown. He was not interested in inflation during his own lifetime, because it was negligible. Prices fluctuated considerably from year to year, down as well as up, and the real value of a pound in 1780 was roughly the same, give or take a couple of shillings, as it had been in 1700. But the logic of Hume's own essay was that this was impossible. He did not realize this because he did not know the scale of gold imports to Britain, and his friend, the economist Adam Smith, although remarking that, 'Almost all our gold, it is said, comes from Portugal', also had no clear idea of how much that was and thought the amount reported to arrive in the Lisbon packet boat was not credible.[35] So the absence of inflation seemed unremarkable. In fact, it was extraordinary. The explanation lies in the remarkable truth that the supply of things to buy grew as fast as the money supply. Instead of pushing up prices, this steady flood of cash increased the amount of buying and selling, changing what people bought, what work they did, what their homes were like, what journeys they made, the clothes they wore and the vehicles they used. Rural communities which had been engaged in barter and sharing became monetized; peasants disappeared as landowners invested in enclosing common land, offering small landholders wage labour instead.[36]

Rural Transformation

One example of this process was Stanwell in Middlesex. In the seventeenth century it had been a village on the medieval pattern, its cottages occupied by freehold farmers with strips of land in the common fields and grazing rights on the common land, Hounslow Heath. They ploughed its heavy soil with oxen and grew food mostly for subsistence. Stanwell had some artisans, but little money flowed. It was managed by the reeve through the Court Leet, which measured out the boundaries of the villagers' strips and supervised their use of the common land on the heath. Like thousands of villages, Stanwell was run by its farming families and traditional law.

But in the eighteenth century, that changed. The first effect Stanwell felt from the increase in money was a dramatic growth of traffic along the muddy track at the bottom of the common land, which was the main road to London from the west. As more people were drawn to the capital, they needed food and clothing, and all roads from the countryside carried growing quantities of malt for beer, timber for building and animal fodder to be used in the busy city. But this particular road also carried the vastly increased volume of textiles now produced in the West Country for Portugal and Brazil.[37]

The Methuen treaty of 1703 increased Britain's cloth exports dramatically;[38] by the late 1710s, Portugal had become England's largest export market.[39] The cloth was mostly shipped over Hounslow Heath to London's docks. The wagons got bogged down, so a Turnpike Trust took over the work of maintaining the road from Stanwell to Kensington. The village was now well connected to London markets, which hugely increased the potential value of the land and opened the door to a social revolution.

From being quite literally stuck in the mud, Stanwell turned into a suitable target for new wealth owned by distant investors. In 1720, the manor, now part of the new Kingdom of Great Britain, was bought by a Scottish earl. The Earl of Dunmore's father had voted for the Act of Union and been paid for doing so,[40] a transaction made possible by the same Portuguese gold that had upgraded the road. The new earl, John Murray, invested his money, and borrowed more, to move close to London and the king.[41] His eyes were fixed on the future in a prosperous Georgian England, where the value of land came from the sale of its produce rather than the loyalty of its tenants.

Farmers living off 1-acre strips and scraggy sheep that looked like greyhounds did not have a place in that future. I once asked the court reeve of Laxton in Nottinghamshire, the last open-field village in England, how long ago the strip boundaries had been fixed, and was told: 'Those stones were there when Adam was a boy.' Murray's aim was to lift the stones and step out of antiquity into the new cash economy.

The effect of the growing money supply was not to increase incomes generally – agricultural labourers had the same income, with annual fluctuations, in 1755 as in 1710 (though many made more by taking fewer days off).[42] So did miners, skilled workers and teachers, although clergymen got poorer. But by that date, government employees were about a third better off, clerks saw about a 50 per cent rise and lawyers doubled their incomes. So did those who looked after them – police, guards and watchmen.[43] This growing inequality spurred a very significant increase in domestic indulgence, and London shopkeepers made serious profits. While the rich pursued elegance in clothing, furniture and décor, lesser folk became much more conscious of style and manners. The influx of gold was absorbed to a significant extent by colonial production, offering new things to be bought and a new way for the English to live. The 'middling class' were eating richer food, putting more fabrics in their homes, storing linen in their chests of drawers, drinking from glasses, showing off clocks and mirrors and wearing finer jackets, dresses and hats. They were also indulging in more exotic groceries – tobacco, sugar, tea, coffee and chocolate[44] – and buying more fruit and vegetables. Stanwell was well placed to profit from a city that was unlike any other in the world, dominated by a class that was uniquely English. By sheer numbers, there was more money to be made from them than from the truly rich.

This was part of a commercial and agricultural revolution. Murray persuaded many freeholders to sell up, especially those with land and common rights in the Town Field. Up came the boundary stones and in came the new enlightened farming regime that was being encouraged in intellectual and aristocratic circles, with large fields, cross-ploughing, ditching, winter fodder and, of course, profits. By 1748, some two-thirds of the village fields had been transferred to Murray's ownership and were enclosed. But in 1745, his brother took part in the doomed Scottish Jacobite rebellion to put a Stuart back on the throne, and Murray was forced to sell Stanwell. In another sign of the new economy, it was bought by a plantation owner from Barbados who wanted to make his son, John Gibbons, into an English gentleman.

Sugar and Slavery

Gibbons's fortune was not based on the mercantilist notion of winning a bigger share of someone else's market. It came instead from the new consumer market that had arisen as people had more gold in their purses. The plantation owners of Barbados had grown rich providing new luxury to the life of middling folk in England. Their island was devoted entirely to sugar; its dense rainforest had been completely stripped away to supply an English market where sugar was becoming quite literally the mark of the sweet life as people learned the pleasures of home-made jams and candies and discovered a need to sweeten tea and coffee from their new silver pots. English sugar consumption rose by more than 600 per cent in the eighteenth century, and by the 1740s it was Britain's most valuable import.

Britons had become relatively wealthy, and the sugar was being purchased with Portuguese gold. John Gibbons's father, who was the Speaker of the Barbados House of Representatives, became an immensely rich man. This did not require much care on his part. The plantation, like all sugar plantations, was worked by African slaves under inadequate overseers, 'a dreadful example of absentee ownership, of a property constantly abused by lazy owners, underpaid overseers, irresponsible short-term partners, and dishonest Jamaican factors'.[45]

In 1754, John Gibbons brought two adult slaves to Stanwell church to be baptized, which startled the rector and alarmed the congregation. The story of slavery which lay behind the gold and sugar had suddenly come to look them in the face. Were they now also to be considered as slaves? The churchgoers were now literate, and some were well-read; one had set up his son as a fruit seller in London. Their suspicions were justified. John Gibbons owned 'an immense fortune in land and money', and in 1761 paid a huge bribe to be made a Knight of the Bath. John Wilkes, the radical campaigner for English liberty, stood for election in Middlesex and described him as a monster.[46]

He was the kind of monster who wanted to increase his assets and understood Stanwell's potential, socially and economically. The more freeholders Gibbons could evict, the more valuable his estate and the more he could show off his wealth through his house. He was creating a park fit for a gentleman on the old fields around it, which he was reshaping.

What was happening in Stanwell was going on all over the country. The village blacksmith, Richard Ride, came from a family of farmers who in the seventeenth century had lived on the produce of their land and given their daughter a dowry including orchards, pastures and farmland. By 1765, the villagers were almost entirely dependent on cash for survival; the vast growth of gold had made them poorer while creating a cash-based consumer society.

Gibbons tried to fence off the common for his park but was defeated by the combined efforts of the village freeholders around the heath, who marched on Parliament. He eventually found a way to complete the consolidation of the land. Investment trumped over ancient rights, and the open fields vanished. The medieval subsistence parish was now a rich man's estate with a fine house, an elegant park and fields that supplied fruit and vegetables to Covent Garden. The freeholders of Stanwell were swept up in a wave of change which removed some 6,000 village commonwealths and remade England as a cash-in-hand country whose working rural families had no resources and were available for hire by whoever had access to gold and the will to profit from a new market.[47] Soon afterwards, a Mrs Ride is listed as receiving poor relief from Stanwell parish.

At the time of writing, the population around Hounslow Heath are protesting once more against a land-grab that will profit distant investors and serve a much wider society by changing their lives. This is now the battleground for the further expansion of Heathrow Airport.

Without the great flood of gold, none of this could have happened. And without this 'agricultural revolution', the British Industrial Revolution would have been very different, if it happened at all. The increase in domestic and colonial production provided the capital for a complete transformation, first of England, then of Europe – leading, as we will see, to the finance that freed North America from Britain and created the United States, and to the collapse of France and the invention of modern political revolution. That, and the struggle to break free of gold, is the subject of the next chapter.

Part V

Virtual Gold

Chapter 25

Paper Gold

John Law and the Abolition of Gold

In 1685, Louis XIV, the Sun King, had intended to visibly proclaim his power as 'the greatest monarch of the universe' by commissioning a throne of pure gold. He had already overseen the creation of an astonishing suite of furniture of solid silver for the State Apartments at Versailles, created over fifteen years. But unlike Britain, France had no access to a vast pot of precious metal. It had to come from trade or conquest, and both failed. In 1689, all the silver furniture – 20 tons of it – had to be melted down for coins to pay his army. The gold throne never materialized. When Louis died in 1715, it was very painfully obvious that the country had completely run out of gold, and its annual deficit was twice its income. The infant Louis XV's regent, the Duc d'Orléans, thus felt obliged to rethink the whole idea of coined money. Could they manage without it? Paper receipts for gold had been around since the mid-seventeenth century, and once people began exchanging them to pay debts, the notion of paper money was clearly in circulation. An English speculator, Nicholas Barbon, wrote a *Discourse of Trade* in 1690 explaining that money is simply an imaginary value given legal force, to make exchange easier.

The idea that money requires faith in authority evidently came naturally to Barbon, a Puritan from a community which named its children with faith-commanding mottos. He was the son of a leather worker and firebrand Puritan called Praise-God Barebone (who gave his name to the 1653 parliament that preceded Cromwell's Protectorate). Nicholas's middle name was 'If-Jesus-Christ-had-not-died-for-thee-thou-hadst-been-damned'. In place of gold as the link to divine power, in Barbon's world it was faith, and he understood money in a similar way, as a representation of credit, belief. He responded to the Great Fire of London by inventing fire insurance and speculated in the rebuilding boom. Credit could be represented by gold, but it could also be represented by anything else that had legal authority. This had something in common with the Chinese understanding of value that had so baffled Marco Polo. Was gold really the reservoir of wealth? What is wealth? Why should anyone think gold was more valuable than a piece of paper? Puritan conviction took on a new form in this age of reason; perhaps it was reasonable to go further in separating the idea of value from tangible gold.

Could paper ever replace gold? Not yet in England, where gold was now apparently the throne on which were based both finance and the constitution. In 1711, Joseph Addison published a nightmare in which the Great Hall of the Bank of England was occupied by a virgin called Public Credit, seated on a golden throne, surrounded by Magna Carta and other statutes that defined the Constitution, and by great heaps of bags of gold. The Great Hall was then invaded by ferocious spectral political figures. The virgin had a fit of the vapours and the gold turned to worthless paper.[1]

Four years later, the Duc d'Orléans assumed the regency of France, where there were no sacks of gold, the government had debts of over 2 billion livres and interest payments of 90 million, and there was not enough bullion in the country to keep trade going.

The Regent tried imprisoning and executing financiers and thought about a total state bankruptcy, but the catastrophic consequences of that were very clearly explained by his good friend John Law. An impulsive, adventurous Scot, Law lived very successfully on his wits. He had escaped to France from Newgate gaol so as not to be hanged on a murder charge for a lovers' duel. He was an attractive, entertaining social ornament, a delightfully brilliant economic theorist, mathematician, and successful gambler and speculator. He was deeply and seriously interested in theories of money, and in 1715, when the subject of alchemy arose, Law said that he knew the secret: 'I shall make gold out of paper.' This was not a joke or a fraud, but expressed his delight in paradox. He had written a book in 1705 in an attempt to establish a bank in Britain, in which he set out (unknowingly) the ancient Chinese understanding, explained in the *Guanzi*, that money had to balance the purchasing power of the population with the availability of goods.[2] Gold and silver had failed France, because there was not enough to allow trade to function. Replacing bullion with paper in the right quantities would allow trade to find its natural level. Orléans decided to support him in setting up an extraordinary bank which was designed to issue receipts that would function as currency. It all depended on credit in the sense of belief, and because Orléans had belief in John Law, investors believed in his bank. Law's idea was to print bank notes to increase the money supply sufficiently for trade to revive, and the government would be financed without relying on gold at all. In 1718, a new law demanded that transactions over 600 livres must be banknotes or gold, and as gold was in short supply, paper money was fully established. Within five months, eight printers were working day and night printing notes of 100, fifty and ten livres.[3] In 1717, Law was also allowed to set up what was known as the Mississippi Company, with shares costing 500 livres, to make everyone's fortunes from the imagined resources of the central third of North America that was legally French, from the Caribbean to Canada.

He was out to reinvent money, credit and commerce by simultaneously creating a country without coinage, and a consumer society based on shareholding. This was a spectacular intellectual experiment, revolutionary in the sense that it would cut the cord that tied France to the whole of economic history, and abolish bullion completely. The result was what people now call 'a learning experience'. In 1738, Voltaire wrote:

> 'Commerce has been better understood in France in the last twenty years than ever before … It used to be a hidden art, a kind of alchemy in the hands of three or four men who, in effect, made gold and who did not reveal their secret. Most of the nation was in such deep ignorance about this important secret that there was hardly a minister or judge who understood the terms *options, bonuses, exchange, dividend*. It took a Scotsman called John Law, who had come to France, to upset the entire economy of our government to instruct us.'[4]

The upset was total. Law's bank became the state bank and he became the controller general of finance, but disastrously, the state took over the bank and he lost control of the printing presses. Enthusiastic purchasers of his company shares, which were purchased in affordable fractions, pushed their value up fifty-fold. Fortunes were made by servants and ordinary workers who struck lucky. A diarist recorded that a servant sent to sell 250 shares at 8,000 livres found they had risen to 10,000, kept the half-million difference and then reinvested it for himself, making 2 million a few days later.[5] In 1720, the word 'millionaire' was invented to describe the richest of the newly enriched 'Mississippians'. Coins were outlawed. France now had only a paper currency, which people were told was backed by the bank's bullion reserves, and Mississippi shares were made exchangeable for bank notes It became illegal to own any gold or silver, and homes and palaces were officially searched. France decreed the triumph of reason over history, tradition and people's visceral understanding of value. It would recreate society on a new and more intelligent basis.

A few months later, the bubble burst. People became afraid, reasonably enough, that the 2.7 billion livres that had been printed were not really backed by bullion in the bank. Law tried to calm them by reducing the quantity of paper money. Between 28 June and 29 August 1720, over 700 million was publicly burned in front of the Hôtel de Ville in Paris.[6] Law had clearly failed to understand the difference between creating confidence and destroying it. The bank collapsed, and so did the company. The government backed away from their financial genius and withdrew all paper money, leaving people without any money at all until coins reappeared. There was overwhelming rage in the streets. Large businesses had been forced to use bank accounts; now their value was reduced by 75 per cent. Mississippi shares that had been worth 9,000 were now worth 2,000. John Law escaped with his life, while gold resumed its proper place.

Voltaire believed that an opportunity had been wasted, a great turning point missed, and Law should be admired:

'In the middle of the most horrible confusion of our finances, in a time of extreme general scarcity, he dared to establish a bank and a company of the Indies. It was an emetic for the sick; we took too much, and we went into convulsions … What would the result have been if we had only taken the right amount of his drug? The body of the state would be, I believe, the most robust and the most powerful in the universe.'

Voltaire was a man of reason, and Law's financial system was rational; but society is not. Voltaire rejected religion, but John Law had apparently proved that money and shares get their value entirely from belief. In this case, belief in John Law and the ruler of France. Neither faith lasted more than five years.

Russia Abolishes Gold

Law's legacy in France was a horror of paper money, which was not overcome until the pressure of necessity during the Revolution.[7] But in Russia, the possibility of basing currency on 'fiat money', with a value proclaimed by the state instead of the international price of bullion, was seen as a real way forward. The year after Law's system crashed, Peter the Great tried to tempt him to Russia with the offer of a princely title, 2,000 peasant households and the right to build his own new town populated with foreigners.[8] Law was not interested, having been scared half to death, but Voltaire's judgement carried weight for enlightened despots. Catherine the Great, who greatly admired Voltaire's writings and began a correspondence with him in 1763, was more impressed with his enthusiasm for the economic literacy of Law's system and Voltaire's conclusion that, had it not been destroyed by the state taking foolish advantage, France could have had a successful economy without needing bullion. At the time, military expenditure consumed three-quarters of Catherine's budget. Voltaire approved wholeheartedly of her war against the Turks, but she could not afford it, so in 1769, in Moscow and St Petersburg, Russia began issuing paper roubles.[9] John Law's currency theories were coming back to life.

At the same time as Law's system had literally crashed and burned in France, Britain experienced its own disastrous speculative eruption now known as the South Sea Bubble. In 1720, the South Sea company managed, on a false prospectus, to take control of the national debt; its shares were wildly inflated by overenthusiasm, manipulated by insider trading, bribery and the use of company money to buy its own shares. Reports of the resulting crash were magnified by the noisy distress of particularly wealthy investors. The directors were arrested, the Postmaster General committed suicide and the Chancellor of the Exchequer was expelled from Parliament, but the nature of money was never challenged as it was in France.[10]

Britain Wins the Trade War

As France went back to the struggle to use trade to accumulate physical gold at the expense of other countries, it needed to project military power to secure and control trading rights around the world. But the French simply could not compete with the power of the British Royal Navy, which was fed and fattened on the gold it carried from Portugal. While French and Spanish policy was made by royal courts, the British and Dutch were driven by merchants, who placed ocean routes at the heart of their interest. The British government was able to borrow with confidence, increasing the national debt at will. In 1700, the British and French navies were about equal in size, with the Dutch about 60 per cent of that size, but by 1720 the Royal Navy had more than three times the tonnage of the French and more than seven times that of Spain.[11] That was just the start. By 1792, the Royal Navy had almost as many vessels as France, Spain and Holland combined.[12] This enabled Britain to dominate the ocean trade routes and create a global colonial economy. The money spent on the navy had a huge effect on the structure of the country; ships needed a great deal of iron for nails and fittings, as well as cannon, and iron-working became big business. Ambrose Crowley's water-powered ironworks in north-east England, whose main customer was the Royal Navy, rapidly became the biggest civilian enterprise in the country.

Britain's Portuguese gold had not just bought Scotland; it had turned the country into the first global superpower. By far the largest demand for the cotton of the East India Company came from Europe's colonies, especially in North and South America and the Caribbean. Indian cotton was too delicate for pure cotton cloth to be woven in Britain. There was an obvious opportunity for anyone who could solve that problem. The answer came with new spinning and weaving machines, which became the core of the Industrial Revolution that developed in the Midlands and Lancashire in the later decades of the century.

Consumer Capitalism

Of course, new manufacturing depended on having capital, and the routes by which capital flowed from gold-rich London to entrepreneurs around the country were subtle and ubiquitous. The increase of trade that accompanied the growth in the money supply supported John Law's argument that the more money there is to use, the more trade will grow. It was just that the money did, it seems, have to be gold. As it coursed through the hands of Britain's country merchants and manufacturers, they began to replace London goldsmiths as sources of finance, and they were people with a helpful understanding of the world away from London's coffee houses. Quakers such as the Lloyds, who were Birmingham ironmasters, linen makers like the Backhouses in Darlington and wool merchants such as the Gurney family in Norfolk were examples of a new kind of banker who could push money towards innovation.[13] Richard Arkwright's cotton mill, the archetypal industrial cotton factory, was made possible by the investment of Jedediah Strutt, who made his fortune from his own invented device for knitting ribbed cotton stockings. Strutt had been able to start his business because his wife, who had been a domestic servant, went to her old employer, a Puritan minister in East London, for help. He was not at first sight an obvious source of investment, but his ministry in Crutched Friars was next door to the Navy Office and to a bank owned by a merchant trading with Madeira, the Azores and Brazil. Mrs Strutt got the gold, one thing led to another, and with a thousand such transactions, Britain became the workshop of the world.

Instead of this flood of gold simply driving up prices, the British were producing more goods to soak up the money. Instead of the country being largely unchanged and money changing its value, as had happened in Spain, money was keeping its value while the country changed. There was a significant shift of population out of the countryside into urban work, and a new consumer economy.[14] So despite the vast increase in Britain's bullion, the purchasing power of the pound fell only slightly from 1750 until 1789.

The Destruction of the Ancien Régime

But in a world where trade depended on currency, because every transaction had ultimately to be paid for in bullion, and most of that currency was being paid to Britain, the rest of Europe was starved of gold and its trade was damaged. Almost every country on the continent was having to borrow from Britain. The continent was going broke.

When France tried to break British power in the middle of the century, it was a disaster. The treaty that ended the Seven Years' War (1756–63) saw Britain and Spain strip France of its colonies in Africa, India and all of North America (the colony of Nouvelle-France there was extinguished). The French then made a last desperate effort to break what now looked like a British stranglehold on global trade. The French finance minister, Necker, understood the struggle entirely in terms of money: he saw what he called 'The English System' as 'a dictatorship of finance cleverly disguised as a "crowned republic".'[15] In 1776, when British colonists in America demanded their independence, he poured everything France had into supporting them against the British Goliath. Spain did the same. Their project of throwing enough money across the Atlantic to create a new nation there and leave Britain bereft of America was one of the most successful enterprises in history. Without France's massive and determined investment, the United States would have been crushed at birth and the history of the world would be unimaginably different.

As a financial investment, it was one of the most unsuccessful ever made, and ended up destroying not Britain but France. The French government had financed the war by borrowing on an impossible scale, almost 2 billion livres. Most of this had been gathered in by selling unaffordable debt to its own citizens. In 1788, the government was told that more than 60 per cent of its income would now be swallowed by interest payments.[16] Every proposed remedy was rejected by the assemblies of clergy and nobility, who represented socially important people, about 4 per cent of the population. In desperation, the king was obliged to call an assembly representing the other 96 per cent, the 'Third Estate' of peasants, urban workers, traders, lawyers and the bourgeoisie, to try to find a way out. Prices had risen sharply and there was real starvation; the financial system was collapsing. Hippolyte Taine, in his stirring and magisterial *La Révolution* a hundred years later, powerfully set out the horror, with huge mobs pillaging markets – 'the famished people are on the point of risking life for life' – in a country overwhelmed by fear of its masters, '*la grande peur*'.

The Assembly of the Third Estate took control of government business, and when the king attempted unsuccessfully to block them by force, they set about reinventing the state at every level.

Assignats

The revolution that followed was born out of financial desperation: it offered a way out of the impasse by renouncing gold as the essence of value. Joseph Addison's nightmare, which had seen constitutional authority as the furniture of the house of gold, became visible reality. When gold fell, so did the pillars of the kingdom. Feudal privileges were abolished and the state took over the Church. The lands seized were supposedly worth over twenty times the deficit, but selling them in a scared, starving and ungoverned country would not yield anything like that. The proposed solution was to do what John Law had always wanted to do: use the land as the backing for paper money. Like gold, land is indestructible. Unlike gold, it is genuinely useful. Of course, it is not very portable, but the documents of ownership are. In September 1790, France issued a land-backed paper currency called *assignats*, whose value was supposedly limited to around a third of the state's landholdings.[17] Markets reopened and life returned to some kind of normal. But people gradually became aware of a problem: there was no way to redeem the *assignats* for land or bullion.

The result was just the same as the Mississippi share bubble in 1720; trust in these banknotes disappeared. Prices rose again, and popular anger grew again. Coin went into hiding as people tried to spend their depreciating paper notes. In January 1793, the king was executed, war was declared with Britain, and the *assignat* began a precipitous collapse as ever more were printed. By February, their notional value equalled almost all the land the French state possessed.[18] By August, their value had dropped by 80 per cent. More were printed, inflation was manufactured and famine was created – and with it the fury of the Committee of Public Safety, which declared 'Terror the order of the day' to stabilize the state with a form of economic dictatorship that would enforce price controls and demolish the rich.[19] By 1795, inflation was 600 per cent. Whereas John Law had burned paper money to try to restore confidence in it, now people were burning *assignats* to keep warm. France had to go back to the drawing board once more. It seemed that without gold, the Revolution would perish.

They would not be able to earn it by returning to trade. There was now a degree of contempt in France for the very idea of trade, rather than honest self-sufficiency. In 1794, Robespierre blustered about the superiority of France over England, saying 'we shall see if a people of merchants is a match for a people of farmers'.[20] Foreign trade was not really an option, as it could only be conducted in gold and silver, and from 1792 until 1797, France minted very little silver and no gold at all.[21] But then Napoleon appeared and offered a way of restoring economic life not through trade or farming, but conquest. His first victory, in 1797, looted the treasures of Venice as comprehensively as Venice had once looted Constantinople, and sent vast hoards of treasure to France, including 2 million francs in gold bullion. He also sent about a million francs to the Army of the Rhine.[22]

Paper Pounds

Now it was Britain that would be driven to use paper and abandon gold. The country was faced with a huge war debt to finance its struggle for survival, just as France had been in 1789. In 1797, following financial panics and being desperately short of gold now that Napoleon was raking in so much, Prime Minister William Pitt the Younger introduced £1 notes to replace sovereigns. Britain would shift from coins to paper, and this paper money would not be exchanged for gold. This was an act of astonishing courage born of desperation. France's attempt to inject value into worthless paper and declare that it was real money had collapsed, and the *assignat* was a very immediate example. The British knew that Russia was having rather more success with its own *assignats*, introduced by Catherine II to finance her war debts. There, the coinage circulated alongside the paper, but even so, the paper rouble had lost 20 per cent of its value against the coin.[23]

Britain would abandon gold coin completely. In response, 'bullionists' loudly declared that only bullion could possess the mystic authority of inherent worth. Addison's nightmare was republished in blank verse, eighty-five years after its warning first appeared.[24] The vision of gold turning into scraps of paper might have been wonderfully rational, but Europeans' visceral attachment to the heaviest metal had a pounding resonance that could not be quietened. There was an immediate financial panic in America, with prominent merchant firms and financiers going bankrupt. But in Britain, the money men were forming a united front to insist that everything was for the best in the best of all possible worlds.

Many years later, the Confederate States in America tried to finance their war of secession from the Union by a similar trick, and failed utterly. The Confederate paper dollar collapsed long before the Confederacy was defeated. In 1862, the *New York Times* published a careful analysis of how Britain had succeeded in 1796, for the first time in known history, in making unconvertible paper money as good as gold.[25] It concluded that the meaning of value had been changed by a deliberate conspiracy at the heart of the City of London: 'Immediately on the appearance of the Order in Council, a meeting of the principal London bankers, merchants, and traders passed a unanimous resolution pledging themselves to use every means to cause the Bank of England notes to be accepted as cash in all transactions.' That resolution, on 27 February 1797, was published nationally and backed up by another 4,000 signatures. They would simply say, and behave as though, the banknotes were quite certainly and obviously as valuable as gold. In the peculiar circumstances of a country unified by the spectre of Napoleon, England's financial masters had the cultural power once exercised by the Church. Within the framework set by the Bank of England's reputation for prudence, they had enough sway over people's beliefs to change their convictions, at least for a while.[26] The country was actually producing more, with industrial and agricultural production increasing, so just as the gold supply had grown without creating inflation, the paper money supply could do the same. The bullionists were scornfully marginalized. This kept paper money afloat, with a few wobbles, until people had a reasonable expectation that it would be made convertible again. Which it was, and to an audible sigh of relief, gold was back in the saddle.[27]

Gold Napoleon

By a wonderful irony, just at the point where Britain, the richest country in Europe, went off the gold standard, France – which had been a country of paper money – took it up again. After the *assignats*, France did not have anyone's confidence that it could be trusted with debt. Not even Napoleon believed that. He modelled himself on a Roman emperor, with a financial system based on issuing gold coins with riches taken from the French Empire's conquests. The Napoleonic Wars were resurrections of Rome's conquests, and for the same reason. The rhetoric of extending the empire's values – glory, the creation of a new rational order, the establishment of a universal empire of citizens – justified the extraction of as much gold as possible from lands seized, to sustain the new aureus, the Gold Napoleon, a 20-franc gold piece with his face on it. His need for gold was so desperate that in 1803 he sold the Louisiana Territory (retaken from Spain), about 830,000 square miles between the Mississippi and the Rocky Mountains, to the United States for just 60 million francs. That deal would literally and fundamentally reshape the USA. The land was not France's to profit from, but that applied to Napoleon's European territories too. Austria and Prussia were 'taxed' of well over half a billion francs by the time Napoleon's star fell in 1812.[28]

Fourteen hundred years before, when the gold had run out, Rome had withered and died. For Napoleon, the gold ran out when the phenomenal gamble of invading Russia simply swallowed all the money there was.[29] He had adopted very Roman poses, not quite to the extent of being deified, but certainly sanctified.[30] He made himself St Napoleon and had Christians recognize him as God's anointed representative.[31] His empire placed itself in the mould of the Roman Empire, which had died when its gold was drained away and its army evaporated, which is what happened to Napoleon's realm too. Wellington, sent to war by a country that had abandoned the gold standard and convinced the world to trust its paper money, trumped Napoleon, who relied on faith in gold and had none of it left.[32] News of the French defeat at Waterloo was rushed to the City of London, and anti-Semitic propaganda said that the banker Nathan Rothschild used his inside information to make a new fortune. He did make a fortune, but it came from lending Britain the money that was used to pay Wellington's army.[33] This was a war of money, and Napoleon, having sacrificed a huge proportion of his country's young men and horses, did not have enough to fund it. The Hundred Days, running from Napoleon's return from Elba to his downfall at the Battle of Waterloo, were the most expensive so far in the history of France, and France fell, as Babylon and Rome had done, for want of gold.

Chapter 26

Famine and Feast

The Rebirth of Golden Coins

The grip of gold in the modern world is a deeper puzzle than its value in antiquity. There, after all, it was understood as the connection between the mortal world and the gods, associated with the welfare of the land and of society, with status and power. But what was gold for in the age of industry and global commerce? By 1815, when the great European war was settled, not a single nation based its currency solely on gold. In Britain, for the first time anywhere, the replacement of coins by banknotes had not produced inflation; there was no catastrophic breakdown in the meaning of money in Britain during the Napoleonic Wars. Britain had been able to live self-sufficiently, its currency cut off from the world and without any need for gold. Yet by the end of the century, every significant trading country in the world apart from China had turned to gold coinage. International trade and economic growth was rooted in irrationality.

In the middle of the Napoleonic Wars, when the British economy was booming, a Parliamentary Committee investigated the price of gold, and its report has been said to be the most famous public document in the history of economics, reprinted six times in the next 150 years.[1] This is the foundation text for the notion that gold contains the mystery of value, independently of any human agency, and has something approaching a religious authority. It asserted that gold is the foundation of the currency and that 'in this Country, Gold is itself the measure of all exchangeable value, the scale to which all monetary prices are referred'.[2] Yet once Britain had stopped converting bank notes for coin, the shortage of gold had been replaced by a surge in banknotes. By 1815, there would be ten times as much paper money in circulation as gold in the bank. The price of gold, of course, had risen sharply – Napoleon collected as much as he possibly could – but in Britain, gold was no longer money.

That terrible realization had dawned on the wretched committee, which having stated firmly that 'gold is still our measure of value and standard of prices', saw that something was horribly wrong. 'It may indeed be doubted, whether ... Gold has in truth continued to be our measure of value; and whether we have any other standard of prices' than bank notes. The issue was not whether this worked, but whether humans dared to change the value of gold.

> '... but Gold rendered more variable than it was before in consequence of being interchangeable for a paper currency which is not at will convertible into Gold, it is ... most desirable for the public that our circulating medium should again be conformed, as speedily as circumstances will permit, to its real and legal standard, Gold Bullion.'

The argument was not expressed by reason, but by the significance of capital letters. One witness, a 'very eminent Continental Merchant' whose business was disrupted by variable exchange rates, complained that the Bank of England was not letting gold 'perform those functions for which it seems to have been intended by nature'. The British had got shot of gold and taken charge of their own system of exchange, but men outside the financial loop were frightened. The fact that their country was prospering was neither here nor there. They could see that the Bank directors insisted that everything was absolutely fine, sustaining the 'conspiracy' that kept Britain afloat by insisting that paper money was trustworthy, valued and acceptable by everyone. But 'bullionist' economic theorists and foreign exchange merchants were shouting as loudly as they could that the emperor had no clothes, while the Bank's directors very properly stuck their fingers in their ears and sang 'La-la-la' to the tune of *God Save the King*. Had they faltered, the entire system would have disintegrated.

In their support was the obvious fact that changing the value of the pound to match the price of gold would have been ruinous. But once the war was over and Napoleon was safely locked up on a distant island, the price of gold collapsed and the roar of the bullionists could not be gainsaid. The government decided that it dared not push its luck. It made notes exchangeable for gold again, and bullion once more was allowed to 'perform those functions for which it seems to have been intended by nature'. They were not necessarily benevolent.

The expectation was that since these notes were now convertible, the world would flock to buy them and gold would flood in to enjoy the security of this proud new, nationalistic gold standard. Bank notes remained legal tender, but 'the sole standard measure of value and legal tender for payment, without any limitation of amount' was now to be gold coins from the Royal Mint. Even silver, which had actually been the main coinage in circulation, would only be legal tender for payments up to £2. The first country to follow the British lead was Portugal; the others all used silver, either alone or jointly with gold. But they would fall into line, because Britain engaged far more in long-distance trade than any other country and the simplicity of using the highly compressed store of value that was represented by gold coins made its trade significantly more profitable. As late as 1831, well over half the international trade in the world was with Britain,[3] and when every payment had to be settled, sooner or later, with bullion, it was obviously much cheaper to send one shipload of gold than fifteen of silver. The British crown and the British sovereign were equally majestic. London was now the largest gold market in the world, and since Napoleon had been crushed, Britain and its gold dominated the globe. The gold standard carried an ideological charge that meant it would be extremely painful to give up.

The Gold Shortage

The problem was that the price of gold quickly rose again because it was in short supply. There was simply not enough gold to back all that paper, and even raising interest rates to painful levels could not attract gold that did not exist. As the quantity of paper money was brought down to something approaching the available supply of gold, trade was strangled. The world's stock of the metal was pretty well static,[4] while new industrial production, the post-war opportunities for global trade and more efficient agriculture all increased the need for money. Brazil's gold production had already fallen by about 70 per cent by the start of the Napoleonic Wars, and many of its mines were no longer profitable.[5] In 1807, the entire Portuguese court had in any case fled to Brazil in Royal Navy ships, as a consequence of the Napoleonic invasion during the Peninsular War, so Portugal was not the milch-cow it had been.

To make the situation worse, the British Army saw its budget cut from £43 million at the time of Waterloo to just £10 million five years later, so the vast majority of its 250,000 soldiers were dismissed, along with huge numbers of contractors and administrators. All these people needed work. Thanks to the new rational agriculture, there was less work available on the land: one-in-five farm jobs that existed in 1755 had vanished.[6] This might have been compensated for by the rapid growth of industrial production, especially cotton manufacturing, which increased in value by 4,000 per cent in the sixty years from 1770.[7] But cotton mills relied on the cheapest and most docile labour available: women and poorhouse children. And the mills were over-producing; in the new shrinking market, the selling price of 1lb of spun cotton, which had been about eleven shillings before the French Revolution, fell to two shillings and sixpence by 1812. After Britain went back on the gold standard, it plunged to less than a shilling.[8]

Gold Strikes

The new consumer economy of Europe, which now reached across the globe, was producing more goods than there was money to buy them. In 1839, the world's annual gold production averaged £5 million, which has been estimated only to represent about half of the world's GNP.[9] A gold strike in the American state of Georgia saw thousands of miners wresting about 8.5kg a day from Cherokee land in 1830. Desperation for the metal was enough for the US to pass the Indian Removal Act and throw the inhabitants out, selling their land in a lottery. This was the start of the 'Trail of Tears' that propelled some 60,000 people on a forced migration across the Mississippi, killing about 4,000. European settlers had long believed in their right to take indigenous lands, but now the gold of Georgia financed the genocidal racialism that became structural in American polity. Many, including Davy Crockett, denounced this policy, but the deadly momentum of occupation was irresistible. It would continue once gold was found in California.

Britain actually had access to a new source of the precious metal from its penal colony in New South Wales, but it is said that when a surveyor reported gold around Fish River in 1823, he was told to stay quiet. Under British law, all gold finds belonged to the Crown. The governor, a brutal disciplinarian, was well aware of what would happen if his tens of thousands of ex-convicts heard about it. He had just one detachment of a foot regiment, with another on the island of Tasmania and a third arriving from England, to control some 40,000 Europeans, about half of whom were still convicts.[10] He could not be even sure of the loyalty of his small military force, themselves effectively condemned to a long exile. This policy of suppressing knowledge of the gold apparently remained in force for the next twenty-eight years, despite successive finds. In 1844, the geologist, headmaster and clergyman William Clarke told the governor that he had discovered the country was 'abundantly rich in gold'. He was instructed: 'Put it away, Mr. Clarke, or we shall all have our throats cut.' Four years later, a shepherd, Thomas Chapman, went into a Melbourne jewellery store with a stone he had found containing 38oz of 90 per cent pure gold, worth £135, perhaps four years' income. It sparked a mini-gold-rush. Mounted police were sent to take over the land and prevent any further digging. The press reported the gold to be a hoax, and that the shepherd 'came to an untimely end'.[11]

So Australia offered no succour. By the time that Chapman's discovery was discredited, the only gold rush happening was in Siberia, where 30 tons a year were being panned through the summer by paid labourers, working for the contractors of great landlords and their tsar, who had colonized this sparsely populated and hostile cold forest wilderness.[12] The gold-bearing rivers needed mechanical pumping, and since Russia had no industrial capacity, the tsar brought English expertise.[13] In 2018, a steam engine from Suffolk was found rusting in the forest over 2,500 miles east of Moscow. The arrival of machinery was a significant culture shock, and output trebled.

There was a desperate need for money in Russia. It had been supplementing coins with paper roubles since 1769. These documents were called *assignatsia* banknotes. The quantity was supposed to be limited, but Russia simply increased the production of *assignatsia* as needed, and the only coins left in circulation were copper. By 1815, there were over 825 million paper roubles in circulation, and their value dropped to 20 per cent of a silver rouble. In the 1840s, when Siberian gold production was at its peak, the *assignatsia* collapsed into worthlessness. Great estates, with their huge workforces of serfs, sank into debt and lost their independence. By 1850, over half of all privately held serfs had been mortgaged to the state by their owners. For ambitious civil servants, a steadily increasing supply of foreign commodities made it more and more difficult for salaried people to afford the lifestyle necessary to seek promotion.[14] Little if any of this gold increased prosperity, except for dealers in champagne and cigars. Much was stolen away in the remote wilderness by the indigenous forest dwellers, Siberian Tatars, for their own spending in the Far East, and the rest was used by the tsar and his nobility to gild their lavish existence. This is when St Isaac's Cathedral in St Petersburg was given the largest gold-covered dome in the world. The cathedral cost a million roubles. That was a bagatelle compared with the cost of rebuilding the Winter Palace, which was burned down in 1837, then fully restored and made more lavish in just 15 months at a cost of 15 million roubles.[15]

Russia's gold did not significantly ease the world shortage or stimulate its own economy. It just served to magnify the tensions which would eventually destroy the Romanovs. But in the 1840s, tensions were even higher in Britain.

Protecting the Pound

As gold was in short supply, its value rose, which is the same as saying that prices and wages fell. Even worse, Britain's restored freely exchangeable currency could be used to buy cheap goods from anywhere and kill off domestic production. If gold was allowed free rein, all those aristocratic British landowners who had been making fortunes selling their grain at high prices thanks to Napoleon's blockade – prices which had been affordable because of the temporary flood of paper money – were now terrified that they would be swamped by a tidal wave of dirt-cheap corn bought with gold from Europe, particularly Poland.[16]

The solution was to protect landowners by barring the import of corn unless the domestic price rose to stratospheric levels. The Corn Laws isolated corn from the general fall in prices, so at a time when 80 per cent of lower-class incomes went on grain, and in Ireland potatoes, people had to spend more of their income on basic food and had less to spend on anything else.

On 28 September 1822, the political journalist William Cobbett addressed a dinner party of farmers in the ancient capital of England, Winchester. They were desperately worried about wages, prices, incomes and the value of their land, and he said that their bankers had fully expected the government to abandon its disastrous return to the gold standard. But at the last minute, the government lacked the courage to break the stranglehold of gold. 'The reason for their giving way,' Cobbett explained, 'had its principal foundation in their perceiving, as the public would clearly see, that such a measure would make the paper-money merely *assignats*.' That dread word summoned the image of French fireplaces filled with a worthless currency protected by tumbrils and the guillotine. So banknotes in Britain would remain convertible for gold. In his view, the Corn Laws would collapse under the weight of gold pressing on them, like a frail sea wall being swept away by an ever-rising tide:

'That two countries so near together [as England and France], both having gold as a currency or standard, should differ very widely from each other, in the prices of farm-produce, is next to impossible; and therefore, when our legal tender shall be completely done away, to the prices of France you must come ... You know, as well as I do, that it is impossible, with the present taxes and rates and tithes, to pay any rent at all with prices upon that scale.'

Something would have to give, and 'it would be cruelly unjust to wring from the labourer the means of paying rent ... The labourers' wages have already been reduced as low as possible.'[17]

England had fought and won the war by escaping the grip of gold, but it did not have the confidence to stay away from it. By basing its currency on gold once more, it ushered in forty years of misery and revolutionary anger which eventually smashed the political system. In 1825, the difficulties of managing this financial system, with its opportunities for huge speculative gains and losses, resulted in a major crash in which seventy banks folded and the Bank of England had to be saved by a huge loan from France. In 1832, it became clear that a parliament dominated by agricultural landlords would no longer be tolerated, and new manufacturing centres were given parliamentary representation, but still the Corn Laws remained. Political pressure to remove them grew massively, and the appearance of potato blight in 1845, leaving many of the poorest people in Ireland without anything to eat, made the situation unsustainable.

The terrible spectre of mass starvation being enforced to protect the incomes of great English landlords was intolerable. Prime Minister Sir Robert Peel, who had staunchly defended the Corn Laws, dramatically reversed his position and declared their abolition in 1846, destroying his own Conservative Party. But it was too late for the Irish.

The next year the *Illustrated London News* published a reporter's account of what was happening:

> 'I saw the dying, the living, and the dead, lying indiscriminately upon the same floor, without anything between them and the cold earth, save a few miserable rags upon them. To point to any particular house as a proof of this would be a waste of time, as all were in the same state; and not a single house out of 500 could boast of being free from death and fever, though several could be pointed out with the dead lying close to the living for the space of three or four, even six days, without any effort being made to remove the bodies to a last resting place.'[18]

The problem was out of control, made more severe by a gruesome lack of poor relief and the decision of some landlords (often absentee) to evict tenants who could not pay rent. The government allowed some corn to be sold at subsidised

THE VILLAGE OF MIENIES.

Potato famine, *Illustrated London News*, 20 February 1847.

prices, but it was tightly restricted. 'This food, it appeared, was being doled out in miserable quantities, at "famine prices", to the neighbouring poor, from a stock lately arrived in a sloop, with a Government steamship to protect its cargo of 50 tons; whilst the population amounts to 27,000; so that you may calculate what were the feelings of the disappointed mass.'

Of course, the potato blight was not restricted to Ireland, but its effect in countries without the Corn Laws, while very grave, were on a much smaller scale. Some 40,000–50,000 died in Belgium, and a similar number in Prussia. Perhaps 10,000 perished in France. But the attempt to keep a gold standard for everything except corn in Ireland brought about perhaps a million deaths from starvation and accompanying diseases, in scenes of grotesque horror; another 1.3 million emigrated, leaving Ireland with a legacy that would continue to damage Britain for over 150 years.[19] The population of Ireland was around 3 million fewer in 2017 than at the start of the famine. The repeal of the Corn Laws did allow a massive surge in grain imports,[20] caused both by the need for more food and the fact that the price was now at last determined by the free market, which was a way of saying gold. It was finally being allowed, as that financier had put it in 1810, to 'perform those functions for which it seems to have been intended by nature'. In this particular case, that resulted in corn shortages across Northern Europe. England experienced a shortage of gold as it paid for the imports, and that fall in the supply of money caused a slowdown in industrial investment across the continent. French and German grain shortages meant cutbacks on railway building, interest rates went up, it became harder to borrow and there were financial shockwaves in Austria and Hungary.

The mounting price of food across these countries, resulting from Britain's surrender before the power of gold to determine its food prices, created a similar effect in 1848 to the British demand for parliamentary reform in 1832, but with more violent energy. The growing liberal demands in Germany, France, Austria, and Hungary for political power to be stripped from their great landowning dynasties and transferred to the new educated urban middle class, who would manage affairs for the benefit of ordinary people, erupted in revolutions which can be, and have been, mapped onto the price of corn.[21]

California

In March 1848, Karl Marx and Frederick Engels published their *Demands of the Communist Party in Germany*, under the slogan 'Workers of all countries, unite'. It demanded the setting up of a single state bank issuing paper money in place of gold and silver: 'This measure will make it possible to regulate the credit system in the interest of the people as a whole and will thus undermine the dominion of the big financial magnates.'

Revolution was, they said, inevitable – a compelling message while the streets of Berlin, Paris, Vienna and Budapest were barricaded, and the Chartists were arming and drilling in England. Gold coins, now in such short supply, were no longer fit for purpose and their days as money were beginning to look numbered. But perhaps nature really had intended gold to play a central role in human affairs, as a new source of shining metal appeared. Is there any such thing as coincidence?

Australia did not have a monopoly on secret untapped gold. California also had a good share, and that was made manifest in 1848. Between 1849 and 1852, gold worth more than $200 million was taken out of California, just when it was most needed. By a further apparent coincidence, it was discovered just as Mexico surrendered that land to the United States. I am prepared to think that the discovery of a vast quantity of gold broadly around the time that currency was collapsing was coincidence. I have no alternative explanation.[22] But the fortuitous date of the California gold strike deserves closer examination. On 24 January 1848, James Marshall, a carpenter from New Jersey, saw gold in California at the sawmill of his employer, a US colonial settler called Sutter. This was still in Mexican territory – just. The USA's Mexican War was over, but the treaty would not be signed for another nine days. Although US settlers in California had rebelled and submitted to the US, Mexico did not recognize that. Four days later, Marshall arrived with a sample at Sutter's fort 45 miles away, where tests learned from an encyclopaedia confirmed that it was at least 96 per cent pure. He was told to keep it quiet.

There is very strong circumstantial evidence that gold had already been found close to Sutter's fort, that Washington was well aware of it, and that those in the know were no keener to have it made public than was the Governor of New South Wales. Here, though, the fear was not that it would overthrow the social order but that it would preserve the political one. The gold was on Mexican land; Mexico needed to surrender it without knowing what it was giving up. The USA was desperate for it.

The British gold shortage had echoed around the world, causing American banks to restrict their lending, reducing the British finance that had been supporting westward expansion. To compensate, American state banks issued paper money which was not necessarily backed by any gold or silver reserves. This was used to create a real-estate boom in the new territories that the USA had bought from Napoleon. The unregulated flood of paper currency encouraged American citizens to drive native inhabitants off their lands and speculators to move in. To stop this, Andrew Jackson had passed a decree in 1836 which insisted that western lands could be purchased only with coin. But there were simply not enough coins in circulation. The inevitable result was a price crash and the emptying of bank vaults. Half the banks in the country failed and depression spread. Recovery was slow, and it would clearly need a significant injection of gold from somewhere to get America growing again.

It was not at all clear where that might come from, but in 1841 a party on its way back from a four-year US naval Pacific research expedition investigated the coast from what is now Portland to San Francisco, which was then a village of some forty people called Yerba Buena, 'good herb'. They studied the Sacramento valley and went on to stay at the remote ranch of Nueva Helvetia, founded two years earlier as a Swiss colony on the Rio de los Americanos.[23] It had been built by a Swiss naturalized American, Johann August Sutter, who had briefly been an under-lieutenant in the Berne army reserve; he now claimed to have been a fighter in the Swiss Guard, had become a Mexican citizen and was known as Captain John Sutter.[24] The visiting party included James Dana, a geologist from Yale, who examined the territory. Sutter's fort was in the water meadows of the valley, but Dana knew that Jesuits had long ago mined some gold in the region and he saw that the mountains further upriver were typical gold-bearing formations.[25] Dana did not publish this for eight years, when the world already knew what was there, and he insisted that his observations had been purely speculative. Obviously, therefore, no gold was reported to anyone.

If Sutter knew about the gold, then like the Governor of New South Wales he would not want it to be made public unless he was confident of his armed strength. In 1841, he began expanding Nueva Helvetia into something like an independent kingdom. The Russians had chartered trading stations in California, but as the charters expired, they were moving out, and Sutter took over whatever they were leaving, paying next to nothing in cash plus an IOU. He had chosen the site for his settlement because of its navigable water; now he acquired a 20-ton schooner from the Russians, plus forty cannon and a lot of old muskets, together with about 2,000 cattle and 500 horses.[26] He employed Native Americans as his labourers and guards, on terms close to serfdom,[27] converting his isolated ranch into a fortress and spending three years building a military base defended by cannon that could hold a garrison of 1,000 men. His stronghold was reported in 1844 by Major Frémont of the US Army, who visited on a geographical expedition.[28] Frémont was part of an undercover presidential plan to prepare for the conquest of Mexico. Pro-US settlers were being armed and funded to overthrow Mexican rule in a playbook similar to the twenty-first-century Russian takeover of eastern Ukraine. In 1847, Mexico offered Sutter the incredible sum of $100,000 for the property. A straight inflation adjustment suggests that would today be over $3 million, and in terms of income replacement, at least ten times that.[29] But he turned it down. He could see a grander future, and was even paying his employees with his own token currency. It was evident to Frémont that Sutter was waiting for Mexican rule to collapse and hoped to rule all or part of a Republic of California based on – gold? But what gold?

Like the geologist three years earlier, Frémont supposedly knew of no reason to believe there was gold.[30] But for some reason he could not resist renaming the strait into San Francisco Bay as 'The Golden Gate'.[31] In 1846, his agent had bought a large nearby estate for him from the Mexican governor. It was remote and unusable, and Frémont insisted he was mystified by the choice.[32] Apparently no one knew until after the war ended that it sat on the motherlode.[33] In the meantime, Frémont was the conqueror, there was no Republic of California and Sutter was appointed as a US lieutenant in his own fort on $50 a month. He was nearly ready to reveal the gold. He contracted a carpenter called James Marshall, who happened to have been thrown out of Frémont's battalion, to build a sawmill two days' ride upstream from the fort. Marshall found gold there. Sutter tried to persuade Marshall to remain silent, but failed. The gold was no longer Mexico's.

A newly arrived Mormon, Sam Brannan, had founded a newspaper for the 450 inhabitants of San Francisco the year before, and he rode up to the mill to check it out. He gathered a little gold, and rather than rush into print, bought up all the picks, shovels and pans that he could find and set up a store in the fort. They cost a few cents each. He then brought some gold in a quinine bottle back to San Francisco, now legally owned by the United States, waved it in the air and famously proclaimed: 'Gold, gold on the American River!' This was supposed to be the headline in his paper, but that collapsed as his staff flocked to Sutter's Fort. San Francisco and the other small settlements of northern California were abandoned as men went up to buy Brannan's $10 shovels and $15 panning dishes and bring back hundreds of dollars in gold. San Jose's jail was abandoned, and only two men were left in the town. The news reached the New York and Washington press in September and London in October, and about 300,000 gold-hunters went there as fast as they could. Inevitably, most made nothing, but in eight years San Francisco's population multiplied by 72,000 per cent.

The US did not attack Mexico for its possible resources; profound racist and religious contempt for Spaniards was quite enough to animate it.[34] United States newspapers had argued that it was their country's 'manifest destiny' to annex the remaining land all the way to the Pacific – most specifically in a newspaper article titled 'Annexation' in 1845.[35] Why it should be their destiny rather than that of the Spaniards or the Native Americans barely merited a thought. But it seems very likely that access to gold was an additional covert war aim, to be kept secret until the peace was signed. Brannan became California's first millionaire[36] and Frémont made an immense fortune, but Sutter and Marshall found themselves unprotected and were ruined by their political masters. Sutter had supposedly been warned by the chief of the local Coloma Nisenan people that the gold belonged to a demon who devoured all who searched for it, but the call of the prize was of course not to be gainsaid – and in any case, whatever happened to Sutter was insignificant compared to the mass murder and determined rape of the indigenous inhabitants.[37]

Of course the real searchers for gold were the settler population and the ultimate effect of the demon's curse could be said to be working its way through the later generations.[38] The discovery transformed the United States, as people flooded through the prophetically named Golden Gate. Gold flowing into the pockets and bank accounts of Americans, it seems, had propelled the manifest destiny of the United States and rescued the global economy. California had produced gold, and gold had given birth to the Golden State of California. The vast lands of the 'Mexican Cession' to the USA included what would become Nevada, Utah, most of Arizona, about half of New Mexico, about a quarter of Colorado and part of Wyoming, but by 1850 only California was established as a state. As gold was sent east, trade picked up, deflation ended, employment increased, and the chartists and revolutionaries lost their hold on popular imagination. They were replaced by gold fever, which would last through the rest of the century. The emergence of new financial institutions, new urban centres and new businesses in America laid invisible fuses which were now all connected to California, and once they were lit with the golden spark, thousands of new businesses, banks and financial institutions immediately sprang into being. The pace of agricultural expansion accelerated, the volume of trade and commerce quickened and there were pressing demands for new forms of transportation.[39] When misery had overwhelmed Northern Europe in 1848 and produced a flowering of optimistic revolutions, they had been crushed by armies enforcing established power. Now America, with its vast empty lands, had money coming out of the ground. The word 'America' was given new meaning, summoning a new kind of possibility for working people, the possibility of striking it rich. Californian gold inspired a dream that America, unlike anywhere else, could offer the chance of 'instant wealth, won in a twinkling by audacity and good luck'.[40]

The Gold Rushes

This was how America became seen, in the eyes of millions of Europeans, as the land of opportunity. It had long attracted the adventurous and desperate, but now the largest peacetime movement of population ever known began, as fleets of packet boats sold cheap steerage tickets for their dark, infested hold space, where the emigrants were given oatmeal, flour and rice to cook. A million Germans and 500,000 Britons sailed to the East Coast of the US in the 1850s. It was, of course, a major challenge to reach the West Coast. The horrible journey round Cape Horn took five to eight months. The overland route across the western half of the continent was dangerous and difficult, and took around the same time. But 50,000 Britons, many of them experienced miners, and about 30,000 Germans reached the Golden State in the 1850s, and by 1860 about one Californian in every seven was German. New gold flowing into the world's markets increased the opportunities for British manufacturing, powering industry and raising workers' wages.

Meanwhile, Edward Hargraves, a failed would-be California gold-digger, had gone back to Australia and started rediscovering the gold that had been found there so many times before. Australia was by then a very different place from 1823; its population was over 600,000 and California had magnified the desire for gold. The British were nervous of their colony being depopulated if the only gold rush was across the Pacific. Hargraves was allowed to publish immediately, and then the British had their own gold rush. The world's annual gold production shot up to over £30 million by 1853.[41] Britain obviously benefitted hugely. The greatest Australian discovery was the Mount Alexander goldfield. It yielded around 110 tons of gold, most of it in the first two years of the rush and within 5 metres of the surface. At first the reports were not believed in London, but when 8 tons arrived in April 1852, *The Times* declared: '...this is California all over again, but, it would appear, California on a larger scale.' Just as gold created California, it also created Australia. Immigration soared; 290,000 Britons sailed right around the world to Victoria by 1860. Industry and agriculture prospered, infrastructure was constructed and the old convict colony disappeared into memory. By 1860, Australia had more than a million inhabitants. One Mount Alexander gold field, Bendigo, produced the most gold in the world over the next fifty years. Today, the amount found there would be worth around $9 billion.

There had been a step-change in the amount of gold in circulation. The literature speaks of a 'gold shock'. During the mid-eighteeth century, Brazil's most productive period, which had so transformed Britain, the world output was about 20 tons a year. That was unprecedented, but in the 1850s it shot up to ten times that, some 200 tons a year.[42]

Gold was suddenly abundant as never before. US currency had been the silver dollar, a direct descendant of the Spanish pieces of eight, though it was legally valued in gold, a practice known as bimetallism that applied to many

The Gold Shock.

other countries, including France and Italy. But now the US began minting gold dollars, tiny coins worth a quarter of a sovereign, and high-value silver coins began to disappear. Gold was so readily available that it was cheaper than the official 16:1 price ratio. There was no formal plan to put America on the gold standard. It was just that people really liked having gold coins.[43] It was, however, necessary to somehow bring California closer to Washington and New York. The Pony Express sprang into being, but the obvious answer was to build a railway as soon as possible.

The Civil War

In 1854, Congress passed the Kansas-Nebraska Act, devised by Senator Steven A. Douglas, with the express purpose of opening up land for a transcontinental railway. Douglas owned a significant chunk of Chicago, and a railway connecting his property there with San Francisco would obviously be good for him and for America. The introduction of his Act to Organize the Territories of Nebraska and Kansas ran headlong into the most existential dispute in United States history: the legitimacy of slavery. The Southern states were built on it, but for the Northern states it was unconscionable. Great political blocs were built on that division, and their balance would be overthrown by the admission of new states on one side or the other. The 'Missouri Compromise' had been agreed, drawing a line at latitude 36°30' north. New territory could only allow slavery if it was south of the line. Douglas's proposed new territories of Kansas and Nebraska were both north of the line, so the Southern bloc was faced with losing power and opposed the Act. Douglas, who owned 140 slaves but claimed to be disinterested in the issue, set out to dump the Missouri Compromise. He got the South to support his bill by steering legislation through Congress which applied a new concept of 'popular sovereignty', whereby the people of each territory would decide whether or not slavery would be permitted there. In effect, he had engineered an expansion of American slave ownership to get the land for his link to the gold fields. For him, the pull of the gold was felt far more strongly than the need for caution, and he was desensitized to the rage he engendered in the north-east. The cost of this railway would be millions of lives, as well as dollars. On 4 July 1854, the publisher of the Boston newspaper *The Liberator* burned a copy of the Constitution before a large crowd roaring 'So perish all compromises with tyranny!' Kansas became a battleground as large armed invading mobs fought for control of popular sovereignty. America moved from radical division to legitimized ferocity. Lincoln defeated Douglas for the presidency, saying: 'A house divided against itself cannot stand.' Before the railway could be built, the United States blew up in a devastating civil war.

Instead of travelling by rail, Californian gold for the Union's war effort had to be transported east by ship via Panama. There, the Panama Railway had been built over the isthmus in 1855, at the cost of the lives of at least 6,000 desperate immigrant workers,[44] with the express purpose of carrying migrants and goods bound to, and gold from, California. There were oceangoing steamers at its terminus. These ships could carry between $750,000 and $1 million of gold. At their peak in 1864, the shipments were $45 million, nowhere near enough for the war. The Federal Government's direct expenditure was $1.8 billion.[45]

To protect what gold it had, and cover these prodigious costs, in July 1861 the Union copied the British wartime expedient of switching to paper money. Gold may have turned up at Sutter's Mill in the nick of time to escape being junked as a basis for money, but now it was back on the rack. In its place were 'greenbacks', bills of one, five, ten and twenty dollars. They were called 'on demand' notes, because they were supposed to be redeemable for gold on demand, but that promise only lasted a short while. They were soon replaced by very similar legal tender notes that bore the familiar 'promise to pay', but in reality were not redeemable for gold and were backed simply by the confidence people had in the United States government's good sense and firepower. That was when the *New York Times* analysed so carefully how Britain had made its paper money work in the Napoleonic Wars, explaining the conspiracy of London's moneymen to make everyone believe that there was no problem at all. The lesson was well learned in the North. Confidence in the greenback fluctuated with the fortunes of war, but it carried on being treated as real money, and there was no dreadful collapse.

The story in the South was very different. The Confederacy started with only half a million dollars in its treasury and no access to more. In 1861, the Confederate Army needed $162 million for pay and supplies, and the new Confederate Navy needed ships and weapons. One solution considered was simply to loot the Union's supply. The Confederacy tried and failed to make an overland assault on California, and then turned to intercepting the sea route, with an equal lack of success.[46]

The Confederacy managed, by various devices, to keep its cash spending down to 'a trivial half billion dollars'.[47] But it had nothing at all, so it too was issuing paper money. Its bills were called 'greybacks'. Their value plunged when people lost confidence in a Confederate victory. By the end of the war in April 1865, the cost of living in the South was ninety-two times what it had been before the war started.[48] The Confederate dollar became worthless.[49] With victory, the greenback recovered full strength, so that by 1873 a dollar bill, even though it was not redeemable for gold, would buy a golden dollar. That year, the United States Coinage Act stopped the minting of silver dollars, meaning that the USA was moved off a gold-and-silver currency and onto the gold standard. And then everyone else did the same. Gold had triumphed completely and now ruled the world. Given the grim vision offered by the South's experience, it is not surprising that in 1879 the United States completed the golden victory by restoring convertibility from paper money to gold coin, a painless act.

The Elimination of Distance

The Civil War had also driven a technological revolution that tied the world together more tightly than even railways could, and further increased the demand for gold. It was a process that had started in the days when Douglas was trying to bring California closer to Chicago by rail. In 1851, an electric cable which could carry Morse code messages was laid under the English Channel.

The importance of getting price-sensitive information from France to London had been made a subject of conversation in 1846 when a widely read French pamphlet by 'Satan' repeated the old fiction that Nathan Rothschild had made a fortune in 1815 by bringing the result of the Battle of Waterloo to London ahead of anyone else. Rothschild was said to have watched the battle in person, having already prepared the speediest possible transport. Satan asked: 'Does greed admit anything is impossible?' In this anti-Semitic tale, Rothschild used his duplicitous cunning to make a killing on the Stock Exchange: 'In a single coup he gained 20 million.'[50]

In truth, there had been plenty of people trying to get the news to London, but Rothschild was not one of them. It took three days, because there was a dead calm in the Channel. But Satan's fiction became an unintended sales pitch for the undersea telegraph. By 1851, the fastest way for an agent to get price-sensitive news from the London Stock Exchange to the Paris Bourse was to go by carriage across the Thames to London Bridge station. Then he would catch a train to Brighton, taking two-and-a-half hours, followed by a short journey on a branch line to Shoreham. There he had to board a steamer to Dieppe, where a *'diligence'* (a large stagecoach) would take passengers to Rouen. They could continue by train to Paris. In good conditions, a determined agent could do it in a day and a night.[51] Suddenly, in 1851, thanks to the electric telegraph, real-time opening and closing prices at one *bourse* could be known at the other in minutes. All those thrilling adventurers were now stuck in offices, where everyone could make telegraphic bids and the profit could be enormous.

A new kind of commerce was appearing, which would change the very nature of credit and money. Merchants would be able to do business with people hundreds, even thousands of miles away in a matter of hours. All it needed was the creation of a global communications infrastructure. Engineers and technicians could make it work, but in reality it would need a cotton merchant to ensure it happened.

John Pender had the vision, energy and determination required. He had been born in an impoverished cotton-printing Scottish township, worked his way up through a factory apprenticeship in Glasgow and became the factory manager by the time he was 21. A few years later he set up as a dealer in Manchester. He knew how to take advantage of commercial opportunities. Travelling widely to learn his business and make contacts, in ten years he built his business up very successfully, importing cotton from America and trading printed cloth with India and China. Looking for ways to diversify his interests, he was given the opportunity in 1852 to invest in the new and highly risky business of undersea telegraphy. There were places to connect, apart from London and Paris.[52]

By the end of 1856, Pender was one of the founder investors in the Atlantic Telegraph Company. He then became the Chairman of the British and Irish Magnetic Telegraph Company Ltd. The Atlantic was expected to become narrower than the Thames. The laying of the cable, weighing over a ton per mile, across 1,696 nautical miles of ocean was a phenomenal feat, which took several attempts.[53] It was unspooled from two ships, one from each side of the ocean, and perilously connected in the middle of the North Atlantic. On 16 August 1858, Queen Victoria exchanged messages with President Buchanan. But three weeks later the cable stopped working. It was irreparable, and the Atlantic was as wide as ever.

The inevitable recriminations were followed by allegations of fraud and chicanery, and the project was dead in the water. Pender resigned and returned to being a cotton merchant. But everything changed when the American Civil War broke out, because cotton was then weaponised. The Confederacy tried to force Britain to support it by holding the crop hostage. From 1860 to 1863–64, its price rose by 1,900 per cent. At the same time, the value of Confederate money spiralled down. The longer a trade took, the more it cost, and improving the speed of communication became an absolute priority. The cable had to be laid, regardless of the physical challenge. Pender returned to the board of the Atlantic Telegraph Company and they bought the largest ship in the world, Brunel's *Great Eastern,* at a knockdown price. England and America were finally connected in 1866. Instead of taking nine days to cross the Atlantic at a cost of £15, a ten-word message could be sent in less than two minutes for £2 10 shillings.

Suddenly, the basis of trade was revolutionized. Pender now knew that he could connect the entire planet. He founded thirty-two telegraph companies that joined London to East and South Africa, the Azores and South America, Australasia and China, and of course Europe and India. All of it British-owned and all of it running safely under the sea. This was the nervous system of the British Empire, hidden and little known, and the key to controlling global resources. London was firmly established as the hub through which the world's money flowed.

Cable connection replaced, to a significant extent, personal connection. Deals that had relied on documents that took weeks to arrive and required high levels of personal trust and patience were now concluded in minutes between strangers, with more confidence and certainty about where the parties could be found and whether the deal had actually gone through. This brought about by far the most fundamental change in the nature of money, and eventually became the network on which we all depend. Around 30 per cent of all business was done on the internet in 2023, which exists almost entirely through the undersea cable system. Satellites are only of marginal importance. The cable carries some 99 per cent of the internet's intercontinental traffic, and the day before I wrote these words, that included the trade of $131,000,000,000 of gold.

But none of it was bullion. So what has happened?

Chapter 27

The Violent Journey to Leaving Gold

Seizing the Plains

Following the massive increase in gold and trade, once the American Civil War (1861–65) was over the world was dramatically refashioned. The transcontinental Pacific railway was built, and the United States came into being as a coherent entity. Britain and France, meanwhile, imposed their power in an entirely novel ways across Africa and Asia. All this was driven by new industries – iron, steel and steam – and all of it was connected to the flow of gold.

Gold's wonderful effect on prosperity was of course less wonderful for those who got in the way. The great North American plains, land which Napoleon had exchanged for the gold he so desperately needed, were the territory of a large population of indigenous people. Around 75,000 had ancestors who had lived there (in far larger numbers) before 1800, and another 84,000 had been transplanted there from their homes further east to clear them out of the way of settlers. A further 200,000 or so lived on lands conquered, purchased or annexed in the 1840s.[1] By 1850, there were 20 million Anglophones in the USA, and for them to make use of this land the indigenous people would be cleared off it. Plains Indians, especially on the lands taken from Mexico, resisted strongly, and were seen as a serious impediment to the wagon trains heading to the gold wealth of California. In 1849, for the first time, the US Congress authorized minting gold dollars, which of course came from California. They bore the head of 'Liberty'. A war of extermination was set in motion in the Golden State, carried out with hunting parties. On 6 January 1851, the Governor of California, Peter Hardeman Burnett, explained that a campaign of genocide was in progress which would make 'the Indian race' extinct.[2] He supported it. The native population was reduced in ten years from over 100,000 to just 35,000 starving refugees hiding in the mountains.[3] Without any apparent sense of irony, in 1854 the head of Liberty on the dollar was transformed into an imagined Indian princess in a feathered coronet.

The destruction of the Native Americans of the plains was the first triumph of industrial America, and the first weapon was the plough. Wooden ploughs with cast iron ploughshares made by blacksmiths could not bite into the dense sticky soil of the prairies, bouncing off the sturdy roots of the tough grass, but the factory-produced steel plough mouldboard was invented by John Deere in 1838, allowing farmers to slice through the tough, interconnected root system of the tallgrass prairie. The flowering grassland ranges where vast herds of bison roamed were turned into fields of grain. The next weapon was more direct. Single-shot weapons were less effective, and slower to load than bows and arrows, but in 1841 Samuel Colt's invention, the revolver, arrived in Texas, carried by Texas Ranger John Hays. Hays became separated from his men and was trapped by a group of Comanches on a dome of rock (now called Enchanted Rock). He sheltered in a depression, while his assailants waited for him to fire his single shot before rushing him. He took them completely by surprise by emptying the five-shot chamber and swiftly swapping it for another. Sam Colt understood marketing and spread the tale widely.[4]

The prairies led to Californian gold, and in 1851 the US government made a patchy agreement with the tribes of the area, the Fort Laramie Treaty, defining a large area of the northern plains as tribal territory, with safe passage for migrants to California. Invasion and colonization paid little regard to the treaty, which was to have a coach and iron horse driven through it. Most of the enthusiasm to colonize these lands was driven by the business model of railway construction, which had the primary purpose of connecting to the gold fields and their cities. Railway building across the plains was financed by sales or pledges to bondholders of millions of acres of Native American land beside the track. It was gifted to the companies from 1855 by the government, and from Ohio to Iowa, over 80 per cent of farms were set up within 5 miles of a railway.

After the Civil War, ex-Union soldiers, often European immigrants with limited English, were employed by the US Army in a series of Indian Wars on what was called 'the frontier'. Some were armed with newly invented repeating rifled muskets, as well as Sam Colt's revolvers, which were made in the first machine-engineered mass production line factory. From Colt's factory came the engineers who would eventually build bicycles, automobiles and aeroplanes. The cowboys who moved the herds from *post-bellum* Texas to the railheads in Kansas, where they were shipped for slaughter in Chicago, were similarly armed. There was no real contest between cowboys and Indians. The whole colonizing operation was driven by finance, the gold dollar and factory-made weapons.

A new Fort Laramie Treaty was attempted with Sioux and Cheyenne groups in 1868, establishing the Great Sioux Reservation, which included the Black Hills, where there are places the Lakota Indians believe to be the original home of their ancestors and where solemn community offerings must be made. The protection of this treaty would last only six years. In 1869, the Union Pacific Railroad opened, creating a swift route to California. The destruction of the

Plains Indians then began in earnest. The next year, bounty-hunting buffalo killers began a gruesome fourteen-year campaign, spending long tedious days in continuous slaughter on the shortgrass prairie, shooting the hundreds of millions of bison that had sustained the Native Americans. I once spent some time being taught about their lonely lives, discovering to my surprise that I could see the 2.5in (65mm) slow-moving cartridges all the way as they travelled 200 metres from me to their target, and their recoils left me pretty bruised. One hunter was reported to kill 250 bison a day.[5]

Over 3 million bison were killed in 1872–73 alone.[6] Altogether, some 25 million died, mostly left to rot. The land was turned over to European cattle or to grain. By 1872, the Department of Indian Affairs reported that half of the surviving Native Americans were safely secured in reservations under the control of government agents. But there were still 78,000 who were deemed 'wholly barbarous'. The Department did not explain how they were counted, or why all the numbers were beautifully rounded.

In 1874, an expedition was sent under General Custer from the new settlement of Bismarck, founded two years earlier by the Union Pacific Railroad, south into the Black Hills, ostensibly to find a site for a new fort. The Sioux reservation was already ringed by at least six forts.[7] Custer's force was almost 1,000 strong and clearly provocative. It was heavily armed to deal with the resistance anticipated (twelve companies, three Gatling guns and a cannon). The native culture has deep and proud warrior traditions. I was surprised when I attended the North Dakota pow-wow to see the transposition of that pride into a celebration of their modern military service: Native Americans serve in the United States armed forces at five times the national average. There was no resistance to Custer's incursion. However, the expedition was intended to make a public splash even if it met no resistance, which was why it included reporters, a photographer, the president's son and his two younger brothers, as well as a sixteen-piece band.[8] Its true purpose was clear from its composition, which also included scientists and miners. Gold was known to be in the reservation, and the country was in the middle of a recession. The object was to noisily proclaim the discovery of gold, trigger a stampede of prospectors into the Sioux's final redout and revive the economy. That duly happened.

The Black Hills gold strike turned out to be truly massive. By the time it closed in 2002, the principal mine, Homestake, had produced 1,240 tons.[9] Native Americans were removed and the federal government swiftly invented a pretence to delegitimize their treaties. They now had to accept Americanization in reservations or extermination. They tried to block their elimination, of course, under the leadership of Sitting Bull and Crazy Horse. That led to Custer's attempt to slaughter them in 1876 at Little Bighorn. He was killed, and five of his twelve companies were annihilated at what became celebrated as a heroic tragedy, 'Custer's Last Stand'. It was much closer to being the Native Americans' last stand, and was a decisive step towards the final elimination of their independence. The battle shocked and enthralled the factory-dominated cities which made the guns and ploughs, whose inhabitants were being entertained with Wild West fantasies. The Buffalo Bill show, which showed a pantomime of the battle, included Sitting Bull himself, and there was an entire genre of popular literature which demonized Native Americans. It would be extended into movies and taught generations of children in eastern cities how they should understand 'the red man'. Part of the fantasy was the projection of a new kind of white man, the Westerner, a rugged individualist without dependants, antecedents or property, whose identity was connected to the firearm he carried. He was an entirely fictional, well-spoken and authoritative working-class isolate, a new hero without master or followers, whose manners and opinions were far removed from the world of wigs and pens that had given birth to the American constitution.

By 1880, the tallgrass prairies of the Midwest, which had been the ecosystem of central North America, were disappearing, and the bison that lived on them were virtually exterminated. Thousands eventually reappeared in 1901, not in the flesh but as an image on the $10 bill. The artist had to work from a survivor in New York Zoo. The word 'bison' no longer conjured the idea of the animal that had sustained the native people of the plains. It now conjured the value of 16.7g of gold, expressed on a piece of paper. It was gold that had taken the bison's territory. Today, 99 per cent of the tallgrass prairie has been ploughed up. In 1986, I was taken to see a relic of prairie being carefully preserved in the one place where it would be safe, on the 150 hectares contained within the 2-mile circumference of the particle accelerator complex ring at Fermilab, Chicago.[10]

The Golden Reich

The transformation of Europe by growing wealth was undoubtedly less brutal, for the time being, but it was still drastic. In 1871, a new country which had no gold, but which decided to make gold the basis of its currency, was born in Europe. The new German Reich was forged by Prussia out of twenty-four states which had used silver. Now, suddenly, they were all instructed to abandon silver and turn only to gold.

That decision produced a great economic depression and set Europe on the path to war and revolution on an unprecedented scale. We have still not emerged from its shadow. Although this was the supreme example of humans taking charge of their destiny and deliberately placing themselves in golden fetters, no one really understands why it happened.

The process that gave rise to the golden Reich had begun shortly before the American Civil War, when gold fell and silver rose. As California and Australia made gold abundant, and therefore cheaper, silver bought more than it had done. In 1834, a pound of silver had been worth just an ounce of gold, but by 1864 it would buy about 2.3 ounces in the United States. Britain could have bought its cotton from America very cheaply with gold if the American Civil War had not cut off trans-Atlantic trade. Britain had to buy all the cotton for its ever-more-demanding mills from India, much to the profit of Indian growers,[11] paying with silver rupees. Silver's increased value was also good news for the states of Germany, whose currency was still tied to a medieval silver standard. Industrial areas engaged in high-value transactions would have found gold more convenient, but it was likely to keep losing value, so the value of gold coins in Germany was allowed to fall in line with their silver value.[12] While silver was doing well, Prussia prospered. It had coal in the Ruhr, and so developed steam power. By 1870, it had hundreds of steel mills and more than 11,000 miles of railways; Berlin was transformed. Millions of silver thalers were spent on military investment, as Prussia set about taking over the other North German states, who together had only a fifth of its population. The North German Confederation had been proclaimed in 1867 after two very short wars, and was essentially an expanded Prussia, absorbing twenty states. But Prussia's economy had lost impetus seriously in the late 1860s, when the Civil War ended and the value of silver began to fall.

That happened because Britain and the US did their deals in gold, and once trans-Atlantic trade resumed, the need for silver fell. During the war, a huge silver deposit in what is now Nevada had massively increased the supply. It had been discovered in 1859 and sparked a silver rush that accelerated the growth of San Francisco and created Nevada City. At least $400 million from this lode had been used to finance the Union war effort. As soon as the war was over, Nevada became a state and silver began to lose value.

At this point, as often happens when a country is in financial trouble, Prussia decided it needed a serious war to ensure popular support. Germany had emerged from the Napoleonic Wars as a conglomeration of thirty-nine states, including Prussia and Austria. Prussia's ambition was to bring all German states west of Austria under its rule, and its swift war with Austria in 1866 gave it control of the twenty-two northern states, but it was blocked by the patriotism of the still proudly independent states of southern Germany. The solution was to inspire a German nationalism that would overwhelm regional loyalty, and that was achieved by rallying all Germany around a deliberately engineered war with France. Anti-German fervour was whipped up in France by creating what we now call 'fake news'. Prussian chancellor Bismarck falsified diplomatic correspondence and made sure that a phoney and insulting French document filled newspaper front pages.[13] France was pushed into becoming the aggressor, and all Germany stood by what was presented as poor, victimized Prussia. The result was a catastrophic defeat for France in 1870 and the slaughter of the Paris Commune, whose citizens refused to accept the government's surrender. Their fate was immortalized by the construction of the shining white church of Sacré Coeur, celebrating the crushing of the godless revolutionary Communards. All Germany except Austria had now fallen into the embrace of Prussia, and the new German Reich was established in the heart of Europe on the basis of a lie and a war.

The Impact of the Gold Mark

There was too much silver and not enough gold. There was no need for silver in America, which had abandoned its silver dollar in February 1873. But from 1871–73, the new Germany switched its currency from the silver thaler to the gold mark, and the international financial system toppled over. In May 1873, the Vienna stock market collapsed. Banks failed, in Berlin a great railway empire crashed, and when the French indemnity payments came to an end in September, there was a German financial panic. That month an attempt to raise several million dollars on the New York exchange for the Northern Pacific Railway failed disastrously.[14] The panic forced the New York exchange to close for ten days, and over the next year 115 American railroads went bankrupt. Between 1875 and 1878, American unemployment more than doubled.[15] Britain got off relatively lightly; as the economic historian Eric Hobsbawm put it, the country did not crash into ruins quite as dramatically as the USA and Central Europe, but the boom evaporated and the economy drifted downwards.[16]

There were other causes besides Germany's creation of the gold mark, but if that decision had not been taken the crash may well not have happened. Creating a new gold currency for what was suddenly the most populous country in Europe was bound to upset the golden applecart.[17] What had induced Germany to do it? Economic historians struggle to understand what was, from a purely economic perspective, quite irrational behaviour.[18]

But shortly before the creation of the Reich, Germany was gifted a new mythological identity by Richard Wagner, and gold was at its very heart. Wagner, from Saxony, described himself as the embodiment of the German spirit, and saw it as his role and duty to promote a mystical national identity expressing the character and aspirations of the people as they emerged onto the world stage. To this end, he invented a new form of spectacular music drama, through which he believed society would be served and bettered. It was hugely popular and had a profound influence on the intellectual life of German imperial identity. His crowning glory was *Der Ring des Nibelungen*, constructed out of a mélange of Nordic, Icelandic and Germanic legends.[19] The ring at its heart is forged by a dwarf from gold stolen from the Rhine maidens in their river. It is a talisman with power over fertility through the denial of love. The god Wotan steals the ring from the dwarf, but is forced to hand it over to giants in payment for building Valhalla. If he fails, they will take Freia, who provides the gods with the golden apples that keep them young.

The first part, *Das Rheingold*, was first performed in 1869, at the firm request of the King of Bavaria. So the idea of gold as the essence of German identity – the true property of the Rhine, the guarantor of love, fertility and the immortality of Germany's ancestral deities – was firmly welded into the new nation's consciousness well before the first performance of the entire four-day epic, after five years of preparation, in 1876. It was considered by many the musical event of the century, and the Kaiser attended the dress rehearsal. In 1873, it was right, proper and obvious that the fresh-born Reich should express itself in a golden currency, with coins of 10 and 20 marks (20 marks being a British sovereign).

The Gold Standard

Germany did not choose to adopt the gold standard because it made economic sense. It was a disaster. But living through the Brexit referendum in Britain in 2016, I saw for myself how a country can choose economic disaster and impoverish itself in the name of national pride and self-assertion.[20] In 1873, the attraction of gold was powerful enough to overwhelm reasoned argument and understanding. How could Britain be on the gold standard and not the Reich? Besides, France might switch to a gold standard first, causing the value of silver to fall and a silver mark to lose its value.[21] The Reichsbank and ministers advising Bismarck were 'dazzled' enthusiasts. Gerson von Bleichröder, a powerful banker who was Bismarck's close friend, warned him that there were few people with any practical understanding in the Reichstag, and that it would cause severe harm to industry.[22] But national pride was given a golden vehicle to ride, and it was more important to climb aboard than to care about the consequences. It was one more grim step along our 7,000-year journey in which people did not really use gold but let it use us.

The fastest vehicle towards a precipice is a bandwagon. Virtually the whole world boarded the gold standard. Silver had been abandoned, which meant that the total supply of specie for gold had been dramatically reduced and money was made scarce. Sixty per cent of the iron-making furnaces in England had closed by 1879. Then came big iron orders from the US and work resumed, but prices stayed low. The money supply was not keeping up with the growth in demand for it, so there was deflation.

The value of money – the price of gold – rose, and broadly speaking, prices fell by about a third over the next twenty years.[23] Investors from Britain, France and Germany looked for new ways of making their money grow and protecting markets and supplies from competition. They set out to use military power to take control of the resources of swathes of Africa. Their machine-made guns gave them brutal authority.

The collapse in agricultural prices was dramatic enough to reshape society. Agricultural land, the bastion of the power of aristocrats in Europe and Russia and of the great land-grabbers of America, was plunged into depression. The argument was heard in many countries that the gold standard was not, after all, what they needed. Deflation that pushed down prices for manufactured and agricultural produce also pushed down pay in factories and on the land. In the 1870s, the money supply was growing at half the rate of the supply of goods. Golden money was increasingly seen as a straitjacket imposed by antiquated superstition and the interests of bankers. The argument was that a more plentiful metal would increase the amount of money and of trade, and the demand to abandon gold for silver briefly became a political hurricane in the United States. 'Populism' became a political movement which claimed to be the voice of the urban and rural poor, demanding that the metropolitan elite world of bankers and tycoons – supposed masters of gold – be obliged to accept the minting of silver dollars and hand power to the people. The abolition of the silver dollar by the Coinage Act of 1873, which had attracted no notice when it was passed, was now discovered to be 'The Crime of 1873', described in 1890 as 'the greatest legislative crime and the most stupendous conspiracy against the welfare of the people of the United States and of Europe which this or any other age has witnessed'.[24] The 1896 Presidential election was played out as a war between 'gold men' and 'silverites', with a barnstorming Democratic Convention speech against the financial elite by William Jennings Bryan, a former congressman from Nebraska: 'You shall not press down upon the brow of labor this crown of thorns; you shall not crucify mankind upon a cross of gold.'[25]

The New Gold Rushes

Gold was not so easily pushed aside. The whole debate was made irrelevant by the discovery of huge new gold deposits in Alaska, Australia and South Africa, so the shortage of currency disappeared. The populist wave faded away, but it had injected a tone into United States political discourse which would remain, the voice of the left-behind, encouraged to trample on democratic debate and call out opposition as criminal.

Although South African gold was first recorded on a farm in 1852, it had been hushed up. The British, who had supplanted the Dutch settlement at the Cape of Good Hope after the defeat of Napoleon, had just recognized the independence of the Dutch who had trekked to Transvaal, north of the Vaal River. The last thing those Dutch farmers wanted was to give Britain a reason to change its mind, so the miner was thrown out of the country and his find kept quiet. But then diamonds were discovered, and in 1877 the British announced the annexation of the Transvaal without knowing about the gold. To their great surprise, their volley-firing regiments were decisively beaten back by the Boer farmers' precision marksmanship, so the British were forced to agree to complete Boer self-government under nominal British suzerainty. Now the Boers needed finance, and to get it they revealed the gold. Within a few years, the world's largest gold rush began. By October 1886, a new mining village had formed, named Johannesburg. The gold was encased in a reef of quartz, far larger and deeper than expected. Extraction needed large-scale investment, which was undertaken by German, French and especially British companies. African labourers were attracted by the earning opportunities. However, they soon regretted coming as they were treated ruthlessly, and to ensure they stayed the largest corporation, De Beers, put them in enclosed compounds, open-air prisons where workers were forced to adhere to their contracts in exchange for food, accommodation and cheap beer. There were many deductions from their low wages, and the compounds became notorious for disease, malnutrition and death.

The Kimberley mines needed a new technology to separate the precious gold molecules in the crushed ore being extracted – an ounce of gold from every 3 tons. This was achieved with a solution of cyanide. It was less immediately toxic to the workers than the existing use of mercury amalgam (which was ineffective with this ore), but of course cyanide, like mercury, is not good stuff to have in the water. The biggest killers encountered in the narrow shafts a mile underground, though, were thick dust and pathogens, resulting in silicosis and epidemic tuberculosis. The rewards to the mining companies for their ingenuity, investment and the sacrifice of their (largely black) workers were immense. In 1892, when work was just getting into its stride, the mines produced over 30 tons. Six years later, production was over 108 tons, worth £16 million ($80 million).[26] Nothing like this had ever been known. By 1914, output was around 250,000kg a year, peaking in 1970 at an incredible million – a thousand tons of gold in a single year. The Witwatersrand reef has now slowed right down, but it is said to have produced, at the time of writing, about 40 per cent of all the gold ever mined on Earth.[27] So all humanity's gold before 1890, from every continent, dating back to Varna, barely amounted to what came out of the unique geological structure of Witwatersrand.

As ever, the more gold there was, the more war there was: 1899 saw the start of Britain's longest and most expensive struggle since Napoleon, as the richest country in the world fought the Boers for their gold field. This time, London had no intention of losing. In three years, it spent about £200 million, as much gold as the strike would deliver in its first twenty years. More than 500,000 troops took on fewer than 65,000 Boer fighters, and nearly lost. They made war on the whole population, burning their farms and herding families into concentration camps, until eventually the gold and the remains of the land were surrendered. The story was reported patriotically by the soldier/journalist Winston Churchill. Public enthusiasm in Britain, though, was not so great, and the government spectacularly lost the 1906 election.

South Africa was not the only gold rush of the period. A series of discoveries, starting in another Kimberley, in Western Australia, in 1885 – and going on through the 1890s – meant that by the end of the century more than a third of Australia's population was in the goldfields there. Many dreamed of a find like the 13kg nugget found lying in the sand by a lucky prospector at Wiluna, on the edge of the Western desert. By 1900, the original Australian gold fields were failing and were replaced by new finds in Western Australia, which produced 50 tons in 1903. But neither Australia nor South Africa created a gold rush to fill the dreams of desperate Europeans and Americans like that of the Klondike. In 1896, gold was discovered deep in the Canadian Arctic. It was not the biggest, but it lived on in a way no other gold rush has ever done.

The Klondike

The Klondike changed the meaning of gold. My grandmother, who grew up in the grim poverty of London's Whitechapel in the 1890s, told me that she and her siblings were put in an orphanage when her father, 34 years old, went off to seek his fortune in the Klondike. She remembered being taken to meet him on his return, expecting to greet a rich man and encountering instead a beggar.

There was a sea route from the American west coast to the Klondike, which was how those who had substantial funds could get there quickly and pick up a fortune. The first successful gold-hunters arrived back in Seattle in July 1897.

But most people had to go overland. For them, it became a trip to hell. Of the estimated 100,000 desperate men and women who set out to cross the Arctic, 70,000 did not make it, either dying on the way or turning back, most of them humiliated. Today, we have become familiar with the death-risking journeys, in

GOLD! GOLD! GOLD!

Sixty-Eight Rich Men on the Steamer Portland.

STACKS OF YELLOW METAL!

Some Have $5,000, Many Have More, and a Few Bring Out $100,000 Each.

Headline in the *Seattle Post Intelligencer,* 17 July 1897

open boats and refrigerated trucks, for which desperate families have borrowed huge sums of money so that a young man or woman can take the chance that might give them a life worth living. The journey to the Klondike was something akin to that, with the dealers and promoters who sold them their kit selling false hope at high prices. Gold seekers were obliged to set out on the trek with a year of gear and supplies, weighing a ton, and then struggle to move them through mountains and across icy wildernesses, and paddle them down lakes and rivers. The route from Edmonton was advertised by the local Board of Trade as the easy track, taking just ninety days.[28] In fact, it was 2,000 miles, with no real trails. Pack horses were often poorly loaded by the adventurers, who usually knew only urban work, and with fodder hard to find, the animals died in their hundreds along the way. If the journey lasted into the winter, as often happened, temperatures dropped to minus 50, at which it makes no difference whether you use Centigrade or Fahrenheit. By 1898, the destination, Dawson 'City', housed 30,000 people, without running water or sewage. Of the more than 2,000 who left Edmonton, perhaps 160 eventually reached Dawson alive. In all, only about 30 per cent of the migrants completed their journey. Behind the fantasy told to my grandmother was a short-lived horror story. The early arrivals on their expensive steamships had easy pickings, but the production of gold peaked in 1900. Some 2½ million ounces had been taken since 1897, worth over $22 million.[29] Then heavy industry took over excavation and the gold seekers went away. The destruction of the delicate Arctic environment along the trails and at Dawson City was nightmarish. Out of the 100,000 who tried to make the journey, probably only 400 returned rich.

The journey to the Klondike became mythic, conjuring stories of heroism and endurance in the terrible struggles of urban workers to break free from hopelessness into the magical dream of riches, but in this strange landscape the protagonists were not acting freely. They were enslaved by hope transformed into an incomprehensible drive towards their own destruction. In 1920, Franz Kafka would write: 'No people sing with such sweet voices as those who live in deepest hell; what we take for the song of angels is their song.'[30] By then, after the apocalyptic colonization of Northern Europe by the hell of machine-powered war, that song had been heard by millions. But a quarter-century earlier, it drifted on the winds of newspaper gossip as strange, exotic, intriguing – the song of the salesmen of the Klondike, who advertised around the world, offering gold for the taking.

Failing to Leave the Gold Standard

The magnetic horror became an entire genre, lighting the way to dread. Jack London's children's story of 1902, *To Build a Fire*, was followed by a continuous stream of narratives, including Charlie Chaplin's *Gold Rush* (the highest-grossing silent movie). It still goes on, up to and beyond the Discovery Channel's 2014 miniseries *Klondike*. Gold is not what it was.

For a start, it was no longer in short supply. By the start of the twentieth century, there was vastly more gold than there had ever been before, and every country except India and China was on the gold standard, using similar coins decorated with different national images. The sovereign was virtually interchangeable with a 20-mark coin and close to the value of a $5 piece. The gold shortage that had pushed prices down before 1890 and had made the gold standard seem a really bad idea was over. Lubricated by a good flow of coin, prices recovered and economies grew at remarkable speed. That speed varied according to their potential and the effect of competition, so the US and Germany outpaced Britain and France.

But the core story is that the more money there was, the faster trade grew; people were able to afford more children, they were better looked after and lived longer, and industrial development soared. Money is really weighed on scales of confidence, and the need for heavy golden weights began to fade as confidence grew. Life did seem to be getting better. The pressure to make these wonderful things happen was so great that money was being decoupled from gold.

Up until the invention of *assignats*, money outside China had been nothing but precious metal or promises of it. That was the meaning of value, and any change in the supply of precious metal was a change in the supply of money. But although there was far more gold available for spending after 1900, most people, most of the time instead used bits of paper which claimed to represent gold. The growth of paper equivalents to money, in the form not just of banknotes but also stocks, shares, letters of credit and other banking instruments, meant that the place of gold was increasingly in the deposits of institutions rather than the purses of individuals.[31]

The developed, industrial countries were more interconnected than ever before, and the money supply they exchanged and traded with was now growing independently of monetary gold. In 1913, there was eight times as much money as gold in the USA and Britain, most of it being credit and bank deposits. And then it all came crashing down.

One reason was the traditional one of more gold, more war. Growing economies created growing fears; Germany had been made by Prussia conquering its neighbours, and that invited suspicion. Tensions were growing continually. Germany was clearly preparing to defend itself, perhaps to make a pre-emptive strike. German military spending doubled from 1911–13, and its expenditure per soldier rose by 60 per cent, far more than any other Great Power.[32]

When the First World War began, each nation needed to bolster confidence in its money. Most of the vast quantity of gold that they had acquired was in the bank accounts of their citizens. There were $2 billion of gold in the United States, but only 13 per cent of that was held by the government. Germany and Austria-Hungary had about the same inadequate amount in their national reserves, and Britain had even less, only about $170 million.[33] Merchants and bankers were enormously rich and the middle classes were more comfortably off than ever before, their bank accounts doing fine, but national banks did not have the cash to pay for a major war.

The British government immediately announced that there was nothing it needed as much as gold, and it should all be lent to the nation. Prime Minister David Lloyd George declared: 'Anyone who ... goes out of his way to attempt to withdraw sums of gold and appropriate them to his own use is assisting the enemies of his native land ... more effectively probably than if he were to take up arms.'[34]

The gold was needed to pay allies and could not be spared for the luxury of private shopping. A hundred million gold sovereigns vanished from circulation, to be replaced by banknotes which were no longer convertible to gold. Britain, and most other countries, went off the gold standard. The fact that they still insisted on gold for inter-governmental dealing reassured people that their banknotes represented 'real' worth. Nevertheless, the value of these notes halved in Britain by 1918.

By then, the Great War that had raged out of control since 1914 had been so devastating that it was thought humans would never conduct large-scale war again; at least, not between industrial powers with massive firepower and devastating explosive weapons. Battlefield deaths were over 8 million, including a third of Germany's young men between the ages of 18 and 22. Fifteen million were disabled. Britain's national debt had multiplied by fourteen times, and it had a huge number of discharged troops without work. In France, paper money had created 300 per cent inflation, and the nation's foreign debt was higher than its GDP.

The war had not only ruined Europe, but had vastly increased the width of the Atlantic. In 1913, Europe's banks held about $1.5 billion in gold, nearly six times as much as the US Treasury and Federal Reserve banks. But the power of gold, which had played such a huge part in pushing industrial societies towards this apocalypse, remained undimmed. America had suffered no damage at all, and its war dead were less than 2 per cent of Europe's. It had not spent gold on anything like the same scale: on the contrary, it had been gathering it in, especially by selling arms, grain and oil to Britain and France. By 1918, US gold reserves stood at $2¼ billion dollars; more than a third of a billion more than the whole of Europe added together.[35] In 1919, the USA went back onto the gold standard.

It had plenty of gold and looked forward to more. Europe owed America some $10 billion, about 8,000 tons of gold. About 5½ tons of it was owed by Britain, which hoped to recover 1,600 tons from France and the rest from Italy and Russia. France owed America 2,400 tons and was relying on getting it from Germany. Germany was presented with a bill of 132 billion gold marks (about 25,000 tons of gold) in reparations.

The yawning gulf of gold between America and Europe would now create a yawning gulf between their experiences.

Since the largest quantity of gold was now in America, that was where Europe generally, and Germany in particular, would need to earn it to pay their debts. Every country in Europe needed to sell to the US rather than buy from it. When they started to succeed, the United States was hit by a sharp fall in industrial production and farm incomes. It responded by raising tariffs by 60 per cent and sucking back gold by offering raised interest rates. That put its economy back on track but cut Germany off from earning the gold demanded for war reparations.[36]

Germany then tried to buy the gold it was supposed to deliver by printing vast quantities of banknotes. It defaulted, nonetheless. France, whose land had been devastated and was being pressed for repayment of its own debts, played the role of repo man and occupied the Ruhr, the German industrial heartland, in 1923. Germany responded by, in effect, backing a general strike, and printed 400 quintillion paper marks to support its people (that's 400 followed by eighteen zeroes!) – making the currency worthless. A 1lb loaf of bread that cost 0.13 marks in 1914 cost 80 billion marks on 15 November 1923. You might get change from a new 100 billion paper mark note, but as the bread had just gone up by 77 billion in a fortnight you had better spend it fast.[37] By the end of the month, the entire currency had been replaced: 4.2 trillion paper marks became one gold rentenmark, worth a dollar, which was a return to the pre-war rate of 4.2 marks to the dollar. By the magic of fictional accounting, Germany was lifted out of the hole.

Meanwhile, Wall Street wallowed in gold and filled with confidence. Urban America was transformed by automobiles, electricity and broadcasting, by new domestic appliances, new suburban communities and by Hollywood movie studios. It was a story epitomized by *The Great Gatsby*, with images of extravagance and enthusiasm, of Charlestons and Rockefellers, of Wall Street, gangsters, cheap money and jazz. The meaning of a 'gold digger' was transformed. Alaskan prospectors became comic figures in Chaplin's 1925 movie, but *The Gold Diggers* at the Lyric Theatre on Broadway in 1925 were a far more successful breed, chorus girls staking out their claims to the bank accounts of rich New Yorkers.

Britain's Return to Gold

Britain moved back to the gold standard in 1925, locking itself into a period of grim austerity quite unlike the American experience. Britain's golden age before 1913 was remembered as a time of solid reliability. Everyone in authority understood that tying money to gold was the mark of discipline. An official committee was set up in 1918 under the Governor of the Bank of England to advise on returning to normality, and its message was a repeat of the one given at the end of the Napoleonic Wars: 'The conditions necessary for the maintenance of an effective gold standard should be restored without delay.'[38] That meant restricting – in fact reducing – the supply of money to keep it in line with the store of real gold the country possessed. The alternative was a lack of discipline, an unfettered expenditure of money which might or might not have any basis in 'reality', leading ultimately to the nightmare that had engulfed Germany. This discipline would be painful, especially for the poorest, but they needed to understand that it was a price worth paying. Parliament decreed it in 1920 and the Chancellor of the Exchequer, Winston Churchill, was determined to bring the pound back to 'real' value in 1925. This did not mean issuing new sovereigns, but it did mean making banknotes convertible on request. The trouble was that the gold had been used up, so Churchill had to borrow it. To do that, it was necessary for the state to get back to a balanced budget, no matter how brutal the cuts required to do it. The last time Britain had gone back to gold, in 1821, the pound had been worth much the same as when it had gone off gold to go to war. Now, however, the US was still on the gold standard, and the dollar defined the value of gold. That was a problem, as the pound had halved in value but the dollar – and therefore the price of gold – had fallen less sharply. Gold was more expensive than in 1914, which meant everything else was worth less. If prices in Britain were now to be set in gold and based on the old exchange rate with the dollar, they would have to go down; sharply.

That did not necessarily need to happen. Britain could have simply redefined the pound. It had been worth $4.86 in 1913; perhaps now it should be $4, which was its market value in 1920.[39] But Germany had shown how fragile was the confidence that sustains the value of money. The bank wizards demanded, in resonant voices at important committees, that the pound should be what it had always been; once you lowered its value to a different level, you might open a Pandora's box of mistrust. That was not a risk worth taking.

The year after Britain went back to gold, the problem of an overvalued pound brought the country to a standstill. Prices were driven down, so wages were driven down, and that provoked a national strike in 1926. The strikers were defeated in what they saw as a class war. The Roaring Twenties were fine for Bertie Wooster, for flappers and men with top hats, but they were not so great for miners, housewives and men with flat caps.

The End of the Gold Standard

Then the dollar, to which Britain had bound itself so firmly, broke. In 1929, the overheated American stock market collapsed. By then, US output had vastly exceeded the capacity of the market, and businesses had three times as much unsold stock just before the crash as a year earlier. Manufacturing output slumped by a third and a quarter of 'workers' had no work. At the same time, the great American plains, seized from the original inhabitants for farming a few decades earlier, returned from a long period of unusual rainfall to their customary arid status (the 'great American desert'), and the ploughed-up soil blew away as dust.

Now, with America in severe depression and Germany still in social crisis, with Russia in the grip of Stalin and France impoverished, the British social fabric appeared to rip. In May 1931, Austria's largest bank collapsed and Germany's banks tottered, and in July sterling was being exchanged for gold on a large scale. To borrow more and keep Britain afloat, the budget had to be balanced, which meant cutting it by more than the cost of the police and all the armed services combined, more than the total spend on education. That was now the price of the gold standard. The king persuaded the leader of the Labour Party to take charge of a Conservative government and make the cuts to save the country. George V's cousin had been the last tsar, and the king was haunted by the fear of revolution. He would do whatever it took to avoid the fate of the Romanovs. A loan was agreed from France and the US. But when it was announced that to secure it, the wages of soldiers, sailors and the police would be cut, the lower decks of the Atlantic Fleet mutinied. This was the most powerful military force in the world, and, coming not long after the communist naval mutinies of Kiel and Kronstadt, it was seen as a revolutionary moment. There was a massive haemorrhaging of gold from the Bank of England. Paris and New York, envisaging London falling to Bolsheviks, refused to lend any more. The jig was up. That night, Prime Minister Ramsay MacDonald was told by the Bank of England to abandon the gold standard.[40]

Britain's rulers believed that whatever direction they took, they were going over a precipice. To the right, they saw themselves threatened by the power of international finance, which was making the gold standard indefensible and would propel them to a paper currency collapse like the paper mark and *assignat*. To the left, they were told that the sailors were about to march on London, gathering disaffected police and soldiers on the way to establish their own soviet. The Admiralty had drawn up plans to bombard and sink their own navy.[41]

In fact, both these threats were imaginary night terrors, signs that the British government had lost contact with reality. There was no revolution, because there was no revolutionary movement in the Royal Navy. Researching the story in 1980, I interviewed more than seventy of the men involved, hoping to find the communist plot, but in fact they were all loyal to king, country and the navy, and this was, in their minds, not a mutiny but a strike. But the Admiralty and the Cabinet were trapped in their own class-war propaganda. They were convinced that revolution was at hand, and so were the men in London, Paris and New York who shaped 'market sentiment'.

The other terror, that abandoning gold would mean the pound sliding to worthlessness, also had no basis in reality. The reason *assignats* and paper marks had failed was that so many were printed they had no connection to the supply of things to buy. As the *Guanzi* had explained 2,000 years before, it did not matter what tokens were used as money, so long as the state supplied the right amount to balance the purchasing power of the population with the availability of goods. It really makes no difference whether the currency is printed on mulberry paper, stamped on blocks of tea or cut from gold strips. Abandoning the gold standard did not cause any inflation at all, and the value of a £1 note was unchanged eight years later.

But the spell of gold had been broken. It had begun with Croesus and his golden beans, where the lion and the bull went head-to-head. It had led swiftly to the plethora of coins for armies that Athenians had denounced as the currency of tyrants. Over millennia, the story of first the people of Europe, North Africa and the Levant, and then all humanity, was powered by the ebb and flow of the golden tide through the hands of the mighty, creating fantasies of wealth and realities of ruin. Now, those little gold discs were finally being dumped

– not because of the urgency of war or revolution, but because the people at the bottom of the social order were making their power felt as never before. Twenty-four countries immediately joined Britain in stopping the conversion of their banknotes into gold. Another eighteen followed within the year. The United States was not long behind, and by 1937 there was not a country in the world that had a gold currency. Without meaning to, the ordinary seamen of the Atlantic Fleet killed off the gold sovereign and began putting an end to the long, long history of mankind's use of golden money. They were very much more revolutionary than they thought.

Chapter 28

The Grip of Gold

The Crash

In July 1926, at the height of the Jazz Age boom, a musical revue called *Americana* opened on Broadway. The *New York Times* called it a sophisticated evening of fun-making. It reappeared in October 1932, with a very different mood. The new librettist, Yip Harburg, had been running a company selling domestic electrical appliances which collapsed in the 1929 crash. He was left with debts worth, in modern terms, around a million dollars. He was determined to pay them off, but also had to support his wife and children. His childhood friend, Ira Gershwin, convinced him to try writing song lyrics:

'Once I built a railroad, I made it run
Made it race against time
Once I built a railroad, now it's done
Brother, can you spare a dime?'

The *New York Times* now spoke of *Americana*'s heart-breaking anguish. That song became the anthem of the Great Depression.

The Great Depression had a global impact and shaped the terrible events that followed. For fifty years, it was understood as a direct consequence of the human follies and stupidities of bankers. The fact that every country was on the gold standard was only relevant because it spread the problem. As with every rise and fall throughout history, people thought they were in charge of their own destiny, and those who inherit the mess seem entitled to hand out praise and blame. But, as I have been trying to show, the flow of gold has shaped history without being particularly susceptible to deliberate policies. A great body of research since the 1980s has now made it evident that gold, operating through the gold standard, actually brought about the catastrophe. The only role for bankers and politicians was to try to comprehend and limit it.[1]

The problem was not even a result of the Wall Street crash: the world's economies were already tottering by then. Between June 1919 and February 1929, North America, Chile, Japan and every country in Europe and the British Empire had returned to the gold standard and began to suffer the downward pressure on prices and wages that its discipline demanded.[2] The last one to clamber aboard, in February 1929, was Romania. Bad luck! The crash came in October.

By the time *Brother Can You Spare a Dime* made its debut, the British Empire, Scandinavia, Japan, Austria, Germany and Eastern Europe had all abandoned the gold standard once more and were starting on recovery. The USA had not. The great infrastructure projects that had given Americans money to spend had collapsed. World trade was down by 65 per cent. There was falling confidence in banks and the dollar; thousands of banks collapsed in panic as they continued attempting to pay out gold for dollars. President Herbert Hoover felt no responsibility for the disaster; he was sure that it was caused by European bankers taking control of the Federal Reserve for their own advantage.[3] When the election came, he was defeated in a landslide. The show's lullaby of disillusion, recorded by Bing Crosby, became the background music to the election of Franklin Delano Roosevelt, who made it plain that he would try to shape events rather than watch them.

Britain had run out of gold two years earlier; now it was America's turn. The US government's gold stock went down by $320 million between 1 February and 3 March 1933, and commercial banks had to redeem $280 million for gold in the same period. By 4 March, the day of FDR's inauguration, all America's banks had been ordered to close.

Sparing a dime, making money available again and spending the country out of recession was what was needed, and that was what FDR intended to do. The ghostly voice of 1896 arose again: 'You shall not press down upon the brow of labor this crown of thorns; you shall not crucify mankind upon a cross of gold.'

The new president was decisive. In 1933, it was simply made illegal for any American to own bullion. Only foreign buyers could exchange paper dollars for gold. About $400 million was surrendered by Americans for bank notes. At the start of the next year, all the gold held by the Federal Reserve (the US central bank) was seized by the Treasury. Gold was officially revalued at $35 an ounce, an increase of about 70 per cent. Roosevelt was sure that what was required was the creation of confidence: 'We have nothing to fear but fear itself.' The Director of the budget was horrified and said it was the end of Western civilization.[4] Western civilization was indeed entering an apocalyptic collapse, but not because of FDR. The descent into barbarism was on the other side of the Atlantic, in Germany. What happened there was rabid and rapid, and was powerfully affected by what had happened to gold in America.

Second World War

The year before the Wall Street crash, German National Socialists were insignificant, winning less than 3 per cent of the vote in the elections. Germany could see a path to emerging from its debt mountain, earning gold from exporting to the USA. But when the crash came, America pretty well stopped importing anything. The consequences for Germany were immediate: its industrial production fell by a catastrophic 55 per cent over the next thirty months. This reduced a significant part of the population to desperation and beggary, creating the sense of being plunged back into hopelessness, with bitter resentments. The extreme right was already in power in Italy; now it took wing in Spain, Portugal, Czechoslovakia, Belgium and, more than anywhere, Germany. In July 1932, the Nazis, offering a home to the hopeless, angry and resentful, soared and became the largest party. Now that no one would willingly spare a dime, the Nazis made it clear that their state should take what it needed by conquest. They cut Germany off from the world's banking arrangements by establishing exchange controls, privatizing state industries, building a tariff wall and demanding national self-sufficiency. They shed virtually all the country's gold. So did Fascist Italy. German industrial production began to grow more steadily and rapidly than any other country, and in six years average wages rose by 19 per cent. If you did not know what else was happening, and what would follow, you might think that extreme, totalitarian nationalism was a way to solve the economic problem. Germany achieved this growth largely by increasing its military spending faster than any other state in peacetime, using loans that were meant to be paid off by plunder. In 1938, Hitler would seize the gold reserves of Austria, then do the same with Czechoslovakia the following year. Then the face of barbarism would be revealed.

The situation was made more dangerous by America only leaving the gold standard in a half-hearted way. It had stopped the use of gold as currency but had not stopped using it to sustain the dollar internationally. Roosevelt certainly intended to make more money available to Americans – not just to lend dimes, but to offer dollars to people on government work programmes. But to increase the supply of money, he still had to get more gold. That was why he had raised what America paid for gold, reducing the value of the dollar by almost 70 per cent. Gold mines around the world increased production to buy cheap dollars; the new mining technology, ruthlessly tearing up South Africa in particular, meant that every year a new record was broken. You may recall that, in the century after Columbus's discovery, Spain recorded the import of around 170 tons of gold. In just one year, 1932, 500 tons was mined. In 1938, it was more than twice that amount. In addition, Europeans, not trusting their own governments, sold gold to America at the new high price. So did their governments. From 1934–39, Britain sent over $4 billion in gold across the Atlantic. France and the Netherlands shipped over $2,630 million worth to safety, Japan (at war with China) sent $500 million and other countries $2 billion. India broke with millennia of tradition and instead of hoarding gold, sold it to the US. China and India sold $1.5 billion worth of gold.[5] This golden avalanche allowed the US government to print more money – 37 per cent more in three years. America began to recover, and the rest of the world had reason for hope. But the inflow was too fast, the money supply was rising faster than the supply of goods, and inflation loomed. To inoculate itself, the Federal Reserve 'sterilized' the gold reserves. Whatever gold came in would no longer count towards backing the currency. No more could be printed.

This was confusion on an epic scale. Gold had been scrapped as currency because it was hurting the dollar: now the government was frightened of gold and frightened of the dollar. The recovery stopped dead; there was a new stock market collapse and a new recession in 1937.[6] Germany, isolated, was untouched.

Fort Knox

With the entire world no longer using gold coins, was the age of gold finally at an end? Had its magic evaporated and become unnecessary?

Not really. American's foreign debt was still underwritten by gold. By the time America went to war in 1941, the heart of the country was its gold deposit, the most complex fortification it could devise. Fort Knox contained half the monetary gold in the world. The US government's bullion stock had been taken out of circulation and was safely imprisoned in this specially built correctional facility where it could do no harm. It was not allowed visitors. All that elaborate security was a theatrical device to ensure that gold was still seen to be valued and the world would understand it backed the dollar. No American could actually have any of it, and no one could go to see it. The dynamo of American power in the Second World War was, in effect, a religious totem. This was like the gold of the alchemists – philosophical gold, not to be spent. You didn't need to know there was gold in there; just to believe it.

The war ended with the old world in ruins. Only one European country, Britain, had its pre-war government still functioning – but with its warlord Churchill removed and a Labour government representing working-class interests and declaring: 'We are the masters now.' The lands from China and Siberia to the middle of Europe were closed to trade, and indeed to contact; their Communist regimes regarded every foreigner as suspicious. Japan had been subject to two atom bombs, all continental Europe and much of Asia had been a battleground, and in England more than one building in ten had bomb damage. More than a million Africans had been taken to fight for their colonial masters. It is thought that the war dead totalled 85 million.

Sixteen million Americans had served in the armed forces, but the cities and infrastructure of the United States were undamaged. Everyone else was ruined, while America was rich, with production 30 per cent higher in 1947 than 1941 and with three-quarters of the world's monetary gold locked up in Fort Knox. The Soviet Union and China were determined to manage their own destinies, but for everyone else, Uncle Sam would have to be their saviour. In 1944, for the first time ever, a global currency system was crafted to keep gold under control and allow nations to grow prosperous together. Shattered and overwhelmed, delegates from forty-four countries assembled at Bretton Woods, a comfortable resort in New Hampshire, to create a path to prosperity in which policymakers intended to work together to manage money. The money in question was America's, and it was in control.

The value of each national currency was now always to be expressed in dollars, underwritten by America's gold. Vast loans were made available on that basis. No one would intentionally go to the shops in Berlin, London or Tokyo with a gold dollar – but in reality, they all did. Their banknotes were multiples of dollars with different names, and represented gold in the Federal Reserve. There was some flexibility in the way countries set the dollar value of their currencies, to avoid the old gold straitjacket, and an International Monetary Fund to finance short-term loans when there were problems. But fundamentally the dollar was to play the role of gold in what was called the 'gold exchange standard'. It was convertible to gold by other states, confident of the vast magical gold-heap in Fort Knox.

But it turned out that Fort Knox was not much of a prison. As other countries grew prosperous, America invested overseas and foreigners acquired huge quantities of dollars – $20 billion by 1960, to set against US gold reserves of $22 billion. Then the United States took on the role of the world's defender against the political heresy of Communism, just as Philip II of Spain had tried to put down the heresy of Protestantism. In March 1961, John Fitzgerald Kennedy was inaugurated as US President, having pledged 'we shall pay any price, bear any burden, meet any hardship' to defeat what America believed was the existential threat of communist insurrection. His predecessor, Eisenhower, had reduced US military expenditure by almost $100 billion a year, saying: 'Every gun that is made, every warship launched, every rocket fired signifies, in the final sense, a theft from those who hunger and are not fed, those who are cold and are not clothed.'[7] But the accumulation of gold has always magnified war, and subsequent presidents began to believe that there was no need for such a rich nation to make a choice between, as Goebbels had put it, guns and butter. It could, and would, have both.

In May 1961, Kennedy sent helicopters and 400 Green Berets to Vietnam, authorizing secret operations against the Viet Cong, America's rebranding of the newly formed anti-government National Liberation Front in South Vietnam. The US expenditure in Vietnam started small, but his pledge echoed Philip II's declaration before sending musketeers to the Low Countries, that 'I would lose all my states and a hundred lives, if I had them' to eliminate what he had seen as the existential threat of Protestantism, and Kennedy's overall military expenditure immediately rose by $20 billion.[8] (That increase was over four times the total British defence spending.) Like Philip, Kennedy dedicated vast wealth to the struggle, and proclaimed that the world was not enough. In May 1961, JFK told a special session of Congress that America was sending a manned mission to the Moon. He believed the Viet Cong were a creation of the USSR, and the space race was part of the struggle.

Vietnam became America's United Provinces, the interminable unwinnable war which sucked all the gold from the richest state on Earth. When the war started, the US had some $15 billion in gold reserves. Kennedy's successors, Lyndon Johnson and Richard Nixon, vastly increased American expenditure in Vietnam, and the war's cost from 1965 until the end of 1971 was $126 billion.[9] By then, the US gold stock had fallen to less than one-sixth of its liabilities. It had after all to be either guns or butter. And then its foreign trade collapsed. Seeing the likelihood that the US would print more dollars and thereby devalue dollar holdings around the world, other nations began to return their dollars for gold. Switzerland redeemed $50 million in July. France cashed $191 million for gold. Its price had risen to over $40 an ounce.

Nixon's Gold Shock

It all came to an end on Sunday, 15 August 1971. That was when viewers tuning in to America's most popular TV programme, *Bonanza*, saw instead President Nixon speaking from the Oval Office, formally declaring that dollars no longer represented a fixed value of gold.[10] The president announced that this exchange would no longer be possible. The dollar was not worth gold; it was worth itself. The American public was generally pleased to have escaped the supposed grip of foreign 'price-gougers'. Of course, the dollar's value against other currencies fell heavily and those currencies, unmoored from their common anchor, were free to fluctuate against each other without any common yardstick of value. The Swiss kept their franc pegged to gold for international transactions, and its price in dollars trebled in five years.

The USA did not grasp that the fall of Saigon in 1975 marked the start of its own decline. It was cheered by a false dawn when the USSR collapsed in 1991; political scientist Francis Fukuyama proclaimed the triumph of liberal democracy and 'The End of History'. But within a few decades, it was clear that history had some way to go.

The year that America abandoned gold, 1971, was the year my wife and I bought our little terraced house in London. It had been built in 1925, when housebuilding was booming, but forty-six years later this was not the case. Demand outstripped supply and people were 'gazumping', breaking agreements with better offers. We paid 50 per cent more, in real terms, than the house's original price. Since then, inflation should have raised prices and incomes together, but something has gone very badly wrong. Our home, like all London houses, has risen in value to ten times what we paid, adjusted for inflation. Few people made the connection, but the end of the gold standard would turn certain assets into stores of value that far outstripped most other possessions. Housing in London was an example, leading people to save for their old age with houses rather than money.

After the 'Nixon shock', no one really knew what to make of the value of money anymore. The most significant immediate impact was felt in the price of oil. US oil production had collapsed, and OPEC controlled over 70 per cent of the world's oil reserves, on which the industrial world depended. Now the dollar fell, and OPEC found that the value of its oil, priced in falling dollars, was shrinking. In the words of the Kuwaiti Oil Minister in 1973, 'What is the point of producing more oil and selling it for an unguaranteed paper currency?'[11] Gold would have been the guarantee.

OPEC found a pretext to raise its price by embargoing oil to countries which had supported Israel in that year's Yom Kippur War. Many people were convinced that the paper dollar was doomed. What could replace it?

There was a man who thought he knew. In early 1974, the new owner of the Circle K ranch in Texas, Randy Kreiling, rounded up his cowboys for a shooting competition. Randy was a 26-year-old lawyer turned speculator and cattle-breeder who was brother-in-law to Nelson Bunker Hunt. Bunker and his brothers needed the twelve best marksmen they could find to ride shotgun on a large delivery of precious metal. Now that gold had fallen, it must be time for silver to return. They were moving 40 million ounces of it from the US to Switzerland, in three Boeing 707s and convoys of armoured trucks.[12] They feared its confiscation. The brothers were billionaires, but not billionaires in the twenty-first-century sense. A mere $190 million in 1970 converts to a billion today. Nelson alone was reckoned to be worth $16 billion at that time, which is getting on for $90 billion in our terms and probably made him the richest man in the world.

Nelson Bunker Hunt was born in El Dorado, Arkansas, a small town named for the conquistadors' dream of gold. By chance, El Dorado turned out to be on the edge of America's largest oil field, and his father became spectacularly wealthy. His children learned to think as conquistadors, aggressively seeking the most fabulous fortunes without limit by risking everything. They had no particular need for vast wealth, or ideas of what to do with it. It was just how they scored their winnings. Their plan now was to bring the game to a conclusion by taking over the world's supply of the money of the future. By 1980, the brothers probably owned half the portable silver on Earth.

The object was to make money in the most literal sense. Nelson Bunker Hunt was a Christian fundamentalist with a survivalist perspective. As the brothers bought all the silver they could, borrowing far beyond their own resources to do so, its price rose from $2 an ounce to $50.[13]

From their perspective, the rising price of silver was simply a collapse in the value of the dollar. By March 1974, the price of oil to the US, the UK and Japan had quadrupled. Saudi Arabia, the dominant exporter, had reserves of 173 billion barrels worth over $2 trillion.[14] (That was getting on for fifty times the world's gold reserves.[15]) But the dollar's defences were stronger than they realized. If America could take control of OPEC, it could exercise this 'oil weapon' in its own favour and use black gold as an effective replacement for yellow metal. Dollars could be printed in huge quantities, as oil provided so much more backing than mere gold.

Oil and Gold

Saudi Arabia is not really a state; it is the personal fief of the head of the House of Saud. In July 1974, Nixon and his *éminence grise*, Henry Kissinger, dispatched an aggressive bond trader named William Simon, given the novel title 'US Treasury Secretary', to make Saudi's King Faisal an offer he could not refuse. Nixon guaranteed to permanently commit the entire military might of the US to the protection of Faisal, his family and their oil fields against all enemies, especially against Israel and Shia Arabs. In return, the Saudis agreed to price their oil exclusively in United States dollars. They would invest surplus oil proceeds (which were vast) in US government debt securities, and the US would keep those investments secret, which it did until 2016.[16] By 1975, all of OPEC had agreed to price their oil in dollars.[17] With all international transactions for oil being in dollars, the US was able to borrow from almost the entire world without preparing to make repayment.

The paper dollar, bolstered, survived, and the New York metal exchange pulled out the rug under the Hunt brothers in a simple but decisive way. It restricted the purchase of commodities on credit, and on 27 March 1980, the brothers suddenly had to repay their huge borrowings. The way to do that would have been by selling the silver, but of course the price immediately crashed. The day became known as Silver Thursday. There was a market panic, and that, effectively, was the end of their story. The US did not return to the silver dollar, or to gold, and the Hunts did not make money in any sense at all.

But that did not mean a dollar collapse was impossible. The democracies of Europe, having lost confidence in reliance on the USA and recovered from the devastation of war, had established a free trade area, and in 1999 launched a common currency, the Euro. In 2000, Saddam Hussein stopped selling Iraq's oil for dollars and shifted to the new currency. The Euro had no fixed value in reserves; it relied on confidence in the many different European democracies that shared it (Britain remained outside). The US was still the world's largest oil importer, and though it was importing more from Venezuela, Canada and Mexico, it remained very dependent on Saudi oil.[18] If other countries followed Iraq's lead, the stability of the dollar would be endangered. An unnamed senior London banker is quoted as saying that Saddam Hussein had made a declaration of war against the dollar, which is probably why the US orchestrated the destruction of Iraq on the pretext that Saddam was developing weapons of mass destruction.[19]

The great difference between using gold as the essence of value and using oil is that oil is consumed, and its value is dependent on need. Gold's value was never dependent on the need to physically consume it. In 1940, it had been observed that the industrial use of gold was falling while the American gold hoard was rising. It was said that soon the only use left for gold would be monetary.[20] So it was assumed by people of a logical disposition that once gold stopped being the value behind money, it should become far less valuable. Under the impact of the 'Nixon shock', the gold price rose to over $800 by 1980, but then dropped to about $225 in 2001, while the petrodollar held steady. In May 1999, the *New York Times* wrote that 'Dollarization (*i.e.: the petrodollar*) ... amounts to a sort of a gold standard without gold', and Gordon Brown, the British Chancellor, began selling more than half his country's gold reserve at an average price of $275 an ounce. That, though, turned out to be exactly when confidence in the petrodollar began to waver. Like Newton, the Chancellor failed to calculate the madness of men. As confidence crashed in banks and currencies, gold's value soared to nearly $1,700 an ounce in 2011.[21] In the first twenty years of the twenty-first century, its value rose over five times faster than inflation – not as fast as London housing, but enough to show that money had lost its foundations.

The logic of the US–Saudi relationship began to unravel after 2007 because the consumption of oil began to fall and the US discovered its own oil Klondike, in the form of shale production. The dollar's value no longer needed to be underwritten by the Saudis. So long as it is the world's reserve currency, America can enforce its foreign policy through sanctions. Meanwhile, gold has taken a completely different grip on our society. On 15 November 1971, eighty-two days after Nixon decoupled gold from the dollar, an advertisement appeared in *Electronic News* 'Announcing a New Era'. It was the truth. Intel was selling the first microprocessor, and this was the new home of gold. These devices changed and multiplied, and now there are uncountable billions of microprocessors embedded in every aspect of human life. Every one of them is powered through gold: the gold keeps it alive. But this is gold in a new form, hidden in a new way.

It's in the circuitry.[22] Every piece of electronics functions with gold. It is so ductile that it can be used with absolute precision in infinitesimal spots, it creates contacts that offer virtually no resistance to the flow of electricity, it conducts excess heat away rapidly and it will continue serving its purpose forever without degenerating or tarnishing. This was realized by the very first researchers in electronics, and the first transistor was made with gold leaf. Well over 300 tons of gold a year now serve in the tiniest quantities to sustain the flow of energy in the technology and electronic devices that we make.[23]

Gold, which was always useless in any practical sense, now keeps us alive, in computers, mobile phones, electronic memories and the keyboards that access them. Electrons travel through unresisting and incorruptible gold. Other conduction metals, like silver and copper, soon lose their power. Gold does not tarnish or corrode; the flow goes on forever.

The Giant Digital Puffball

There is a little-known facility in Las Vegas that has more in common with Fort Knox than a casino. Its 6-metre-high perimeter wall is continuously patrolled by armed military guards in Humvees and seals off an area of 3.5 million square feet (more than sixty football pitches). Inside, a group of enormous futuristic structures are guarded by combat-trained armoured guards in full battle dress. This is one of nine structures in Las Vegas which together make up 'The Core' of Supernap, the largest data processing operation outside China. It is linked to four other secretive hubs around the United States, called 'The Citadel', 'The Pyramid', 'The Keep' and 'The Rock'. What is being guarded is wealth on an unimaginable scale, but this is not gold. It is data, and these are data centres. It is a key part of 'the cloud', which is now the bank vault and information exchange of the US-based financial system. The company that owns Supernap, Switch, is controlled by a very secretive man named Rob Roy.

Gold appears to have been entirely displaced as currency. Banks used to rely on physical vaults of gold bars, coin and banknotes, represented in bound ledgers. Banks still need vaults, but their assets are mostly held in digital ledgers stored on computers scattered around the world and managed by trans-global entities with names like Google and Amazon Web Services, which connect to Supernap. The customers' assets no longer exist as a physical presence, and there is nowhere they can be visited. The closest most people will now ever get to their bank deposit is seeing a number on an app or extracting a few notes from the shrinking number of bank cash dispensers.

Mr Roy's position as the spider at the heart of the web was the opportunistic result of a stroke of luck. In 2002, one of the USA's mightiest companies, Enron, collapsed in ruins, its massive growth having been based on accounting fraud. Enron had discovered the profits to be made in selling 'derivatives', contracts whose values are linked to assets but which can be traded without owning those assets. It had started out as an energy company, turned to trading energy derivatives and its next target, a closely guarded secret, was to be broadband derivatives. To that end, Enron invested many millions in a data centre built on top of a major broadband hub in Nevada. Rob Roy was an enthusiastic 29-year-old telecoms inventor and entrepreneur with an office across the road, and he was one of the few outsiders who heard about the project. In 2002, when Enron collapsed, the facility was auctioned and he was the only bidder.

He used his own technical knowledge to create a functioning and rapidly growing data management system. Almost all US data now connects to his 'ecosystem'. He acquired enough control of the internet to ensure that he is virtually invisible apart from the very limited information he chooses to place on the company website. Rob Roy is Croesus, maker of our money, and the post-gold Midas. Everything he touches turns to data; which is, by its nature, ephemeral.

The world's financial institutions believe that money now lives in circuitry, but that does not mean that it is free from gold. The circuitry itself is completely dependent on it, and around 1 per cent of all the gold mined is used in electronic circuitry. If it was not absolutely essential, it would not be there. Gold is no longer money, but it exercises more market power through circuitry than coinage ever could. It has made possible a connected global marketplace where the cunning and determined can present themselves to untold millions, even billions of customers in a space beyond dimensions. In this new space, it has become possible for the supposed value of things to float to an incomprehensible level. As money itself has become digital, it has bloomed like a giant puffball. In 1971, there was about $163 billion in physical money in the world. Over the next thirty-eight years, that grew by a little over 9 per cent a year.[24] Then it took off, growing by 24 per cent a year so that in 2022 there was reckoned to be $40 trillion.[25] Inflation would have turned 1971's physical money into $1.2 trillion, but it has multiplied over thirty-three times.[26] That is far beyond any growth in the physical wealth in the world. And that was just the tip of the 2018 moneyberg, because credit has grown much faster. One attempt to add it all up came up in 2022 with an extra $1.3 quadrillion (that's fifteen zeroes!) of investments, derivatives and cryptocurrencies. That would be $10,000 for every star in the Milky Way. No one knows.

The situation is made more unknowable by cryptocurrencies, whose value fluctuates wildly. Crypto 'coins' are tokens registered on a currency's blockchain, a coded digital structure. A new species of web-based company sells itself rather than its product, and so helps to make the world's notional wealth unknowable. Between 2010 and 2019, more than 100 companies backed by venture capitalists launched with valuations of over $1 billion. Sixty-four per cent of them lost money, but they were sustained by the belief of their backers in fortunes yet to appear, the same principle relied on by the men who financed Charles V and Philip II. Money-losing start-ups actually fared better on the stock exchange in 2018 than money-earning businesses.[27] Apparently outside the 'real' economy, these operations seem not to create money-busting inflation – until they do.

The incomprehensible mystery, until 2022, was that this huge expansion of the money supply had not produced inflation: on the contrary, there was no inflation, no growth and banks had run out of customers wanting to borrow billions, even at historically low interest rates. Some assets had gone up – gold and housing, along with the cost of medicine and education – but the cost of shopping had barely changed since 2008. That was partly because the people who would drive up prices were not the ones with money to spend. Much of whatever wealth had been in the hands of poorer people had steadily been shifted to the rich. In the US from 1980–2014, the share taken by the richest 1 per cent roughly doubled from 20 to almost 40 per cent,[28] while in the UK in 2018 the richest 1,000 people (out of 66.5 million) owned more than the poorest 26 million and had seen their wealth rise by nearly 40 per cent in five years. The greed of those with power was evidently insatiable. Attention is paid by the media to the 'richest in the world' – Musk, Bezos, Gates – but they have smaller fortunes, adjusting for inflation, than Carnegie and Rockefeller a century earlier. A better indicator is that in 2022, 100 CEOs each received median 'compensation' of $30.5 million, a 32 per cent increase in one year.[29] While the rich have little to buy, the rest have less to spend, and individual impoverishment has increased.

Then in 2022, the Ukraine war created a massive shortage of Russian oil and gas. It also took out a significant percentage of the world's grain, and climate change meanwhile affected crops badly in many regions.[30] The inflation pigeons finally came home to roost on every chimney. The world still had a memory of the so-called inflation of 1923 in Germany, when the mark simply stopped being regarded as money. The only way of paying for food and housing became consumables: coal, potatoes, butter. Without those, you starved. Only a tiny percentage of people now have anything to offer for exchange if money vanishes. In 1923, the rest of the world still had useful money, so it was possible for Germany to be hauled out of the pit. Next year could be the occasion for a bigger problem.

Bigger than inflation.

Chapter 29

Nature and Death

Pandemic, Climate Change and Hoarding Gold

'People become ill, many new illnesses will appear, there will be no cure for them. And the reason is that Younger Brother is violating fundamental principles, continually and totally. Drilling, mining, extracting petrol, minerals. Stripping away the world. We know that this is destroying all order and damaging the world.'[1]

That was what Kogi Mamas said in 1990. The warning went unheeded, of course. In 2022, to refine around 3,100 metric tons of gold, more than 6 billion tons of rock and soil were extracted and pulverized. Visiting Mongolia in 2010, I was told of the new Oyu Tolgoi copper and gold mine in the Gobi Desert, said to be the world's largest, an open pit and deep tunnels covering a space the size of Luxembourg.[2] Its production was being accelerated to produce the gold medals for the London Olympics of 2012. Gold is the necessary prize of excellence, and it seems clear to many (though not to Rio Tinto Zinc) that there is sense in the observation that such plunder is destroying all order and damaging the world.

Rainfall in this area is between zero and 50mm per year. Mongolians are the last great nomad culture; 40 per cent of them were nomads when I was there. These people are herders, with good reason to worry. Oyu Tolgoi is draining the region's water supply, using more than a billion gallons a month.[3] I was taken by a bus driver on a spontaneous visit to the country's most prominent shaman, Byampadorj Dondog.[4] He was holding a clinic in his ger, a large circular felt tent supported by poles resting on the ground. It was a dramatic visit in a torrential storm, the ger reached by wading through deep channels with lightning flashing. He told me of his profound respect for Genghis Khan, who is celebrated over the whole of Mongolia. He explained that the very basis of Mongolian culture is respect for the Earth, which is why the poles of the ger stand on the surface and are not sunk into it. It is an insult to the Mother to make a hole. The mine is exploiting copper and gold deposits thought to take up an area larger than the state of Florida.[5] It is the biggest man-made hole on Earth. He was not optimistic.

A thousand years ago, it was universally believed that there is a link between gold, status and the transcendent energy of life, and this was as strongly felt in Mongolia as anywhere else. In 1986, archaeologists found an untouched imperial Liao Dynasty tomb in Inner Mongolia. The epitaph within revealed that it dated to 1018 and belonged to the 17-year-old Princess of Chen and her husband, Xiao Shaoju.

Her delicate gold burial mask belongs to a tradition shared across Asia, Europe, Africa and America; a tradition that linked the pinnacles of society to worth, value, transcendence and gold.

The question at the heart of this book is not 'what have we done with gold?' but 'what has gold done with us?'. And what is it doing now? Gold has been regarded as the repository of eternal value, and the story told here shows those who collect it find that it destroys value. Instead of making the life of humanity easier and more harmonious, it has produced disastrous uncontrolled economic and social consequences. We can now add to the unforeseen damage the twenty-first-century impact of climate change and eruptions of diseases from obscure reservoirs of animal pathogens. The Kogi are emphatic that gold itself is involved in these processes. They think of the planet as a quasi-biological entity, with gold connecting precise locations with life and cosmic consciousness, and see the coronavirus, for example, as an inevitable mechanistic consequence of our plunder. Their view of this is rooted in a rational cosmography, but their cosmographic knowledge is not the same as that taught in universities. The academic response from those institutions, which read different connections and sets of forces, is that we have no evidence that they are right. The Kogi assertion that gold plays a fundamental positive role in the biosphere, which is wrecked by extracting it, is not one that has any traction in modern scientific understanding. We can certainly see a correlation between the massive increase in gold mining of the last thirty years and the startling acceleration of climate change, extreme weather events and pandemic disease eruption, but we see no causal mechanism. Of course, that does not mean there is none: it may be that we just do not know where to look. In a modern form of Pascal's wager, without firm evidence either way, it might make more sense to bet on the Kogi being right than to hope they are wrong.[6] What harm would it do to pause the plunder?

The reductionist balance may be tilting towards the Kogi. Academic science is learning that gold is not irrelevant to life processes. Evidence is growing that it plays a significant and poorly understood role in micro-organisms that are fundamental to the biosphere. Gold is evidently taken up and altered by algae as well as other organisms that sustain the oceanic food chain, including sea urchins, sea stars and crabs. It is also accumulated and transformed by plants; up to 1.5 grams of gold may be accumulated in every 1,000kg of tree bark.

Amino acids, the basis of all life, dissolve gold; so do the nucleic acids from which they are made, especially ribonucleic acid, which is, as it happens, what coronavirus is made of.[7] There are processes here whose significance is not yet understood. If we were given the power to remove every atom of gold from the world, even before we needed it for electronics, for all we know we might have inadvertently removed life itself.

But the ancient belief that gold is a store of value still outweighs all that. Logically, it is clear that it has no more innate value than mulberry bark or bitcoin, except for one significant detail: it continues to exist all by itself, forever. Paper money and cryptocurrency are ephemera, whose existence is sustained for a while by the market where they can be traded but which are at perpetual risk of disappearing. The thousands of miners currently scouring the bed of the Madeira River, a Brazilian Amazon tributary, to pick up a daily gram of gold would be unlikely to surrender their golden flakes for cryptocurrency tokens, even if they could access them.

The Kogi told me of their understanding of the connection between life and gold with reference to the looting of Tairona burials, but we can also see that modern gold mining is catastrophic on a much cruder measure. In Brazil, as in many parts of the world, mercury is used in huge quantities to amalgamate the crushed ore. Ten years ago, that was banned in Mongolia, but the alternative is no improvement. In the late nineteenth century, a new process for its extraction was discovered involving large quantities of cyanide solution. It means that gold can be recovered from what were impossible locations. Most extraction is in China, followed by Russia and Australia. In 2020, more than 125 million ounces was mined.[8] Each ounce involves creating about 20 tons of toxic waste, so in a single year, mining produces 2.5 billion tons of grey sludge dense with cyanide or mercury. It can be visualized as 750 toxic heaps, each the size of the Great Pyramid, being dumped every year; well, it probably can't. According to Plutarch, King Midas's cursed touch led to his suicide, effected by drinking a poison called Bull's Blood.[9] Now, it seems, the touch of Midas has been democratized and the poison made vastly more extensive.

Perhaps a clearer visualization comes from individual locations. Papua New Guinea is a barely explored tropical paradise with spectacular cultural and biological diversity. It is also, thanks to mining, one of the fastest-growing economies in the world. The Lihir gold mine dumps over 5 million tons of toxic waste into the Pacific Ocean each year, with devastating effects on marine life. The beaches are gone, as are all the sources of fresh water.[10] Or we can look at the Grasberg Mine in Indonesia, which dumps about 80 million tons of poisonous slurry into the Ajkwa River system every year.[11] In the Madre de Dios region of Peru, where around a third of all the gold is illegally mined in grotesque, nightmarish conditions, more than 50,000 hectares of Amazon forest have been destroyed, and mercury and cyanide contaminate rivers, fish and people.[12] In South Africa the story is similar.[13]

In Colombia, illegal mining proliferates; by 2018, its profits exceeded cocaine production. Officially, the country produces over 2 million ounces, but 70 per cent of Colombia's output is illegal. Almost 90,000 hectares – about 350 square miles – is being ripped up by mining machines and poisoned by criminal groups, *barranqueros* ('burrowing parrots'), who execute many of those who complain.[14]

The use of vast quantities of toxic mercury and cyanide in gold extraction could be replaced by cheaper and much faster processes which leave no toxic waste at all.[15] One uses corn starch![16] Sir Fraser Stoddart, who was awarded a Nobel Prize in 2016, has now set up a company to develop its commercial application and it is being tested in numerous gold fields.[17]

But that will not slow down the mining or ameliorate the other forms of damage it creates. The vast scale of what is happening is probably best measured in the sewers of Switzerland. Seventy per cent of all newly excavated gold is sent to that little country for refining and shaping into the stamped bars that are guaranteed for purity and weight. About half comes, rather suspiciously, from places without gold mines – Britain, the United Arab Republic and Hong Kong. The gold they send reappears refined, stamped and untraceable. A large but unknown quantity comes from conflict zones or from profoundly sordid and destructive illegal workings. In this gold-laundering process, microscopic flakes are inadvertently washed into the refineries' drains. In 2017, researchers found that 43kg a year of this untrappable waste is going into Switzerland's sewers. That would make a cube with 13cm sides worth some \$2 million,[18] roughly enough gold to make 8,000 wedding rings a year. Its production involved the creation of about 170,000 tons of toxic waste, yet it is such a tiny percentage of the total being refined that its loss is unnoticed.

The hunger for gold has become world-consuming. We no longer need to think that gold is the basis of value, or that it connects us to divinity. But we rely on the flow of energy through it. We depend on that for our electronic circuitry, so this is the first time in human history when we can be quite certain that if gold vanished from the universe we would rapidly die. We would lose communications, water, power, all our machines and of course all our money. But that is not why so much is extracted. We hoard it because we do not trust anything else as a store of value.

No one can digest gold, and it can no longer be thought of as sustaining the health of the land and humanity. We have wrenched it from the Earth, poisoning land and sea to store up imagined value, and our confidence that it served no purpose in the ground might be terribly mistaken.

The Kogi alarm at gold extraction is part of their vision of the desolation resulting from our plunder. We determinedly disrupt all order and balance for imaginary wealth. I was startled by a Mama saying 'We know what you have done. You have sold the clouds.' They see a web of natural connections binding life together. We inhabit a new web of global supply chains, exploitation, transportation, and tourism which makes ours the least sustainable culture that ever existed. Not long ago, most people lived in more-or-less autonomous communities. Now we have turned ourselves into marionettes all operating each other's strings, dependent for survival on piped water, electricity, Wi-Fi, telecommunications, satellites, aircraft, just-in-time food transport and an electronic banking system. When Covid-19 briefly cut those threads we learned how fragile we have become. And how helpless.

The only prediction that can be made with certainly is that all our forecasts will be wrong. Our pontificators, building their imaginary bridges to a later date, calculate how long it will take for normal life to begin again, with a few adjustments that may be profitably anticipated. But the impact of the disease is still being felt, and they have no ground to start from. Disruption on this scale could involve the collapse of major industries and commercial operations. It may precipitate the disintegration of healthcare, social welfare, and indeed entire countries, the multiplication of unaffordable debt and the collapse in many regions of all political authority. This pandemic began by forcefully shutting half the world away from the sky and the sea and goes far beyond our comprehension of economics. It changed all human relations. The shape of the recovery curve is not and will not be as expected. Perhaps it will not even be recognizable. We have an impressive track record of being completely and confidently wrong.

We may be on the brink of a new skeleton horizon, caused by relentless over-exploitation, the death of the natural world and the brutal magnification of authority. The obsessive plunder of gold is driven by fear that our economic system is fragile. But its possible collapse should not take us back to coinage, or anything that represents coinage. Perhaps our best hope is for modern societies to understand and learn from the civilizations that flourished in the Americas before Columbus, where large cities flourished, law functioned and goods were exchanged over huge distances without any need for market prices or currency. The great oceans that cut off America from Afro-Eurasia created the space for two fundamentally different pasts. We have imposed one, and almost completely eliminated the memory of the other. But there is still time to open our eyes and look at the alternative.

Chapter 30

The New Place of Gold

I write this fifteen months after the Russian invasion of Ukraine. The shockwaves of the attack, and the response by Ukraine and the rest of the world, have been huge, and it appears that, along with much else, the place of gold has been fundamentally altered. A determined attempt was made to render Russia's gold reserves effectively worthless by a dramatic and uniquely forceful international sanctions regime.

In a united action, US, UK and European Union institutions were suddenly blocked from doing business with Russia's central bank. The US Senate then scared off potential private purchasers of Russia's gold with threats of penalties and reputational damage. This gold was supposedly rendered internationally worthless. The US knew that banks and dealers in India and China may be willing to buy it at a big discount, but hoped they would not risk sacrificing their holdings of dollars or euros for that tainted metal. Russia produces a good deal of gold itself – the second-biggest mine in the world is in Kyrgyzstan – but to be sold to banks it needs to be stamped by an accredited refinery, and that was supposed to be impossible.

The effort to remove value from Russian gold was not made because humankind has become more rational, but as an act of war, to cripple Putin's war machine. It failed, and instead of removing the final traces of monetary gold from the world, it brought the ancient story of value roaring back. A new monetary coalition appeared, hostile to the dollar and to liberal democracies, in which gold is the basis of business.

The latest figures show central banks accumulating gold at the fastest rate on record, with the biggest buyers being Singapore, Turkey, China, Russia and India. The effect of American sanctions has been to promote the emergence of a China-centric community of countries wealthy enough to challenge American supremacy.

Gold is now the support for their currencies. More and more global trade is now being conducted in the Chinese yuan, and there are reports that these countries, and South Africa, are a considering developing a new currency backed by gold 'and other rare-earth elements'.

As the pace of gold mining accelerates, we are all conscious of a sense of approaching crisis – climate crisis, economic crisis, social crisis and global military crisis. Gold is here to stay, apparently, and its damaging power seems set to outlast us.

But there is a paradox. Up to the last few years we thought of money in very concrete terms, as actual physical stuff that we carried around and exchanged in shops and markets. In the twentieth century the coins ceased to be made of bullion, and were mostly represented by bank notes, but money was still physical stuff.

That is clearly ending. In 2021, only one in five payments in the US were made with cash. The rest were cards and electronic payments. Fifteen countries, seven in Europe, plan to abandon physical money by 2030. That project, and the very future of digital money, was thrown into doubt on the night of 18 July 2024. That is when a global cyber security company in Texas called CrowdStrike remotely installed a defective update on over 8 million Windows computers around the world. Within hours they all stopped working. The problem was quickly identified, and the process of repair initiated, but the lesson was startling and unexpected. Among the many government and private organizations that were paralyzed were banks, financial institutions and payment systems. Countries expecting to become entirely cashless were made dramatically aware that digital money hangs by a very delicate thread to which they have no access and which can totally and instantly vanish.

Meanwhile, the fall-back stockpiles of physical gold rise, and it is being suggested that the remainder is being extracted so fast that in a few decades no useable deposits will be left.

There could be serious trouble ahead. Gold seems to be in charge. How close is the skeleton horizon?

Notes

Introduction

1. Benati, G., & Jansen, M., 'On the Beginnings of Gold Use in Southern Mesopotamia: the Rediscovery of an Artifact from the al-'Ubaid Stratum at Ur in the Collections of the Penn Museum', in *Metallurgica Anatolica. Festschrift für Ünsal Yalçın anlässlich seines 65. Geburtstags*, publisher Ege Yayınları, pp.319–22.
2. ARMT (The Royal Archives of Mari) XXV 815: Villard, P., *Parade militaire dans les jardins de Babylone*, Florilegium Marianum (= Mél. M. Fleury), 1992.
3. https://www.ipcc.ch/report/sixth-assessment-report-cycle/.
4. World Gold Council, https://www.gold.org/about-gold/gold-supply/gold-mining/how-much-gold.
5. Dubey, A.K., *Great Treasures* (Pustak Mahal, 1993), p.42.
6. TV programme *From The Heart of the World: The Elder Brothers' Warning* (BBC1, 4 December 1990; BBC2, 3 March 1991).
7. Garside, M., *Statista*, 16 June 2020, https://www.statista.com/statistics/299603/gold-demand-by-sector/.
8. The US government ordered gold mining to stop during the Second World War to redirect labour and mining effort into production for the war effort. Gold was not a war material.
9. Keynes, J.M., *A Tract on Monetary Reform* (Macmillan, 1923).
10. https://www.nytimes.com/2017/10/16/science/ligo-neutron-stars-collision.html.
11. https://www.caltech.edu/news/caltech-led-teams-strike-cosmic-gold-80074.
12. Pitcairn, I., *Gold distribution in the Earth's crust*, Stockholm University Geological Sciences Project Archive, URL http://www.geo.su.se/index.php/en/project-archive/489-gold-distribution-in-the-earth-s-crust consulted 4/3/2018.
13. 'Gold in Melbourne Streets', *Geelong Advertiser*, 14 August 1851.
14. Parisi, A.F., *et al.*, 'Can the Late Heavy Bombardment hypothesis be resuscitated?', *American Geophysical Union*, Fall Meeting 2020, abstract #DI019-0012 December 2020, URL https://ui.adsabs.harvard.edu/abs/2020AGUFMDI190012P/abstract; consulted 19 November 2021.
15. Willbold, M., Elliott, T., and Moorbath, S., 'The tungsten isotopic composition of the Earth's mantle before the terminal bombardment', *Nature* 477 (2011), pp.195–98.
16. http://www.livescience.com/15938-earth-precious-metals-space-origin.html; Willbold, M., Elliott, T., and Moorbath, S., 'The tungsten isotopic composition of the Earth's mantle before the terminal bombardment', *Nature* 477 (2011), pp.195–98.
17. Smithsonian Environmental Research Center, Forces of Change, Atmosphere, https://forces.si.edu/atmosphere/02_02_01.html; consulted 17 April 2021.
18. The earliest evidence of microbial life on earth is from 3.7 billion years ago. Nutman, A., Bennett, V., Friend, C. *et al.*, 'Rapid emergence of life shown by discovery of 3,700-million-year-old microbial structure', *Nature* 537 (2016), pp.535–38.
19. S. Cockell, 'The Origin and Emergence of Life under Impact Bombardment', *Philosophical Transactions: Biological Sciences*, Vol. 361, No. 1474, Conditions for the Emergence of Life on the Early Earth (29 October 2006), pp.1845–56; Abramov, O., and Mojzsis, S.J., 'Microbial habitability of the Hadean Earth during the late heavy bombardment', *Nature* 459 (2009), pp.419–22.

20. Pitfield, P., and Brown, T., *Tungsten* (British Geological Survey, 2011), www.mineralsuk.com.
21. Gwynne, P., 'Microbiology: There's gold in them there bugs', *Nature* 495 (20130, S12–S13.
22. http://adamwbrown.net/projects-2/the-great-work-of-the-metal-lover/#:~:text=The%20 Great%20Work%20of%20the%20Metal%20Lover%20is,gas%20tank%20filled%20with%20 carbon%20dioxide%20and%20hydrogen; consulted 17 April 2021.
23. Crocket, J.H., 'Distribution of gold in the Earth's crust', in *Gold metallogeny and exploration* (Springer, Boston, MA, 1991).
24. Kerrich, R., 'Nature's Gold Factory', *Science*, New Series v.284 no.2453 (25 June 1999), pp.2101–02; Bütof, L., *et al.*, 'Synergistic gold–copper detoxification at the core of gold biomineralisation in Cupriavidus metallidurans', *Metallomics* 10 (2018), pp.278–86.
25. Herodotus, *Histories*, 3, 116.
26. *Ibid.*, 3, 102–105.
27. Gilgamesh, Tablet 6, ll.24–5.
28. Hawthorne, N., *A Wonder-Book for Boys and Girls* (Boston, USA, 1852).
29. Roller, L.E., 'The Legend of Midas', *Classical Antiquity*, Vol. 2, No. 2 (9 October 1983), pp.299–313.
30. *The Electronic Text Corpus of Sumerian Literature*, https://etcsl.orinst.ox.ac.uk/section1/tr1823. htm.

Chapter 1

1. Jaru, O., 'Egyptian mummies covered in gold are rare, and we may have just found the oldest', Livescience (31 January 2013), URL https://www.livescience.com/oldest-gold-covered-egyptian-mummy.
2. For a discussion of the construction of the body as a political, social and cultural object in relation to Varna, see D.W. Bailey, 'Neolithic bodies beyond the grave; corporealities of being', in V. Slavchev (ed.), *The Varna Eneolithic Necropolis and Problems of Prehistory in Southeast Europe* (Acta Musei Varnaensis 6, 2008), pp.57–74.
3. Zbenovich, V.G., 'The Oldest Gold in the World (on the occasion of the exhibition in the Israel Museum)', *Mitekufat Haeven: Journal of the Israel Prehistoric Society* (1994–95), pp.159–73.
4. Krauß, R., Schmid, C., Kirschenheuter, D., Abele, J., Slavchev, V., and Weninger, B., 'Chronology and development of the Chalcolithic necropolis of Varna I', *Documenta Praehistorica* XLIV (2017).
5. Ifantidis, F. and Nikolaidou, M., 'Spondylus in Prehistory: New Data and Approaches – Contributions to the Archaeology of Shell Technologies', *British Archaeological Reports*, Int. Ser. 2216 (2011).
6. www.archaeo.museumvarna.com/en/category/list?category_id=3&id=6 consulted 31/03/2020.
7. Higham, T., Slavchev, V., Gaydarska, B., and Chapman, J., 'AMS dating of the Late Copper Age Varna cemetery, Bulgaria', *Radiocarbon*, 60 (02) (2018), pp.493–516.
8. Stratton, S., '"Seek and you Shall Find." How the Analysis of Gendered Patterns in Archaeology can Create False Binaries: a Case Study from Durankulak'. *Journal of Archaeological Method and Theory*, 23, pp.854–69 (2016).
9. Boyadziev, V., 'Changes of the Burial Rites Within the Transition from Hamangia to Varna Culture', in V. Slavchev (ed.), *The Varna Eneolithic Necropolis and Problems of Prehistory in Southeast Europe* (Acta Musei Varnaensis 6, 2008), pp.85–94.
10. Slavchev, V., 'The Varna Eneolithic Cemetery in the Context of the Late Copper Age in the East Balkans', in D.W. Anthony (ed.), *The Lost World of Old Europe; The Danube Valley, 5000–3500 bc* (Princeton University Press, 2010), pp.192–211 (p.200).
11. Watson, E., and Gaydarska, B., 'Little Cucuteni pots of hope: a challenge to the divine nature of figurines', *Studii de Preistorie*, 11 (2014), pp.115–24.

12. 'But thereafter he [Odysseus] shall suffer whatever Fate and the dread Spinners spun with their thread for him at his birth, when his mother bore him.' (Odyssey 7.198, http://data. perseus.org/citations/urn:cts:greekLit:tlg0012.tlg002.perseus-eng1:7.152-7.197).

13. See 'Varna Gold Treasure and Varna Chalcolithic Necropolis – Black Sea Coast, Varna, Bulgaria', URL http://archaeologyinbulgaria.com/varna-gold-treasure-varna-chalcolithic-necropolis-varnabulgaria/; consulted 15 May 2021.

14. Peev, P., Farr, R.H., Slavchev, V., Grant, M.J., Adams, J., and Bailey G, 'Bulgaria: Sea-Level Change and Submerged Settlements on the Black Sea', in G. Bailey, N. Galanidou, H. Peeters, H. Jöns, and M. Mennenga (eds), *The Archaeology of Europe's Drowned Landscapes* (Coastal Research Library, vol. 35).

15. Alva, W., 'The Royal Tombs of Sipán: Art and Power in Moche Society', *Studies in the History of Art*, Vol. 63, Symposium Papers XL: Moche Art and Archaeology in Ancient Peru (2001), pp.222–45; S. Bourget and K.L. Jones (eds), *The art and archaeology of the Moche: an ancient Andean society of the Peruvian north coast* (University of Texas Press, 2009).

16. Alva, W., (*op. cit.*); for problems in understanding the nature of Moche polities, see Quilter, J., 'Moche Politics, Religion and Warfare', *Journal of World Prehistory*, Vol. 16, No. 2 (June 2002), pp.145–95.

17. There have been speculative claims of transatlantic contact with Phoenicians, Romans and Africans, and these cannot be definitively ruled out. The Larco Museum in Lima, which houses a vast collection of highly realistic Moche portrait pots, has one which depicts a drummer with a captive's haircut who looks (to my eye) distinctively African (Cat. ML012837).

18. Van Buren, E. Douglas, 'The Sceptre, its Origin and Significance', *Revue d'Assyriologie et d'archéologie orientale*, Vol. 50, No. 2 (1956), pp.101–03.

19. https://www.justcollecting.com/miscellania/antiquities-saleroom-auction-to-offer-40-000-mochegold-sceptre; accessed 12 June 2017; Rovira, S., 'Pre-Hispanic Goldwork from the Museo de América, Madrid: A New Set of Analyses', in D.A. Scott and P. Meyers (eds), *Archaeometry of Pre-Columbian Sites and Artifacts* (Getty Publications, 1994), p.342.

20. Consuming very large quantities of gold in solution, or being injected with it regularly as a medical treatment, can have toxic effects.

21. Nutting, J., and Nuttall, J.L., 'The malleability of gold; An explanation of its unique mode of deformation', *Gold Bulletin* 10, 2–8 (1977).

22. Private communication.

23. Leusch, V., *et al.*, 'On the Invention of Gold Metallurgy: The Gold Objects from the Varna I Cemetery (Bulgaria) – Technological Consequence and Inventive Creativity', *Cambridge Archaeological Journal*, 25 (2015), fig.11, p.364.

24. The evidence of Anatolian origin is seen particularly in their pottery. See M. Nica on the unity and diversity of Neolithic cultures along the lower Danube in 'Unitate şi diversitate în culturile neolitice de la dunărea de jos', *Revista Pontica* vol. 30 (1997), pp.105–16. https://drive.google.com/file/d/0BwmOVzh5qKnCWHlRdV9YVmNjbGc/view; consulted 20 April 2021.

25. Müller, J., 'Movements of Plants, Animals, Ideas, and People in South-East Europe', in C. Fowler *et al.* (eds), *The Oxford Handbook of Neolithic Europe* Oxford University Press (2015), pp.63–80.

26. Nikolov, V., 'The prehistoric salt-production and urban center of Provadia-Solnitsata, Northeastern Bulgaria', *Méditerranée* 126 (2018), pp.71–78.

27. Boyadziev, K., 'Warfare in the Chalcolithic of Bulgaria', in K. Bacvarov and R. Gleser (eds), *Southeast Europe and Anatolia in prehistory. Essays in honor of Vassil Nikolov on his 65th anniversary* (Verlag Dr. Rudolf Habelt GmbH, Bonn, 2016), pp.261–68.

28. Nikolov, V. (2018), paras 29–33.

29. Chernakov, D., 'A New-Found Hoard of Chalcolithic Heavy Copper Tools from Northeastern Bulgaria', *Archaeologia Bulgarica* XXII, 2 (2018), pp.1–13. E.g. Todorova, K., 'The eneolithic period in Bulgaria in the fifth millennium B.C.', trans. V. Zhelyaskova, *British Archaeological Reports* (Oxford, 1978).

30. Kienlin, T.L., 'Copper And Bronze: Bronze Age Metalworking in Context', in H. Fokkens and A. Harding (eds), *The Oxford Handbook of the European Bronze Age* (Oxford University Press, 2013), pp.416–19.

31. Plutonium is heavier but was unknown until the eighteenth century.

32. Leusch, V., Armbruster, B., Pernicka, E. and Slavčev, V., 'On the Invention of Gold Metallurgy: The Gold Objects from the Varna I Cemetery (Bulgaria) – Technological Consequence and Inventive Creativity', *Cambridge Archaeological Journal*, 25 (2015), p.359.

33. Lordkipanidze, O., 'The Golden Fleece: Myth, Euhemeristic Explanation and Archaeology', *Oxford Journal of Archaeology* (2001), pp.2–38.

34. Saville, M.H., 'The goldsmith's art in ancient Mexico', *Indian Notes and Monographs* (Museum of the American Indian, 1920), p.14.

35. Sillitoe, R.H., 'Giant and Bonanza Gold Deposits in the Epithermal Environment: Assessment of Potential Genetic Factors', in B.H. Whiting, C.J. Hodgson and R. Mason (eds), *Giant Ore Deposits* (Society of Economic Geologists, 1993).

36. The first wheelbarrow appeared in Greece 3,000 years later.

37. Armbruster, B., 'Gold technology of the ancient Scythians – gold from the kurgan Arzhan 2, Tuva', *ArcheoSciences*, 33 (2009), online since 10 December 2012; connection on 1 October 2016. URL http://archeosciences.revues.org/2193; DOI: 10.4000/archeosciences.2193.

38. R. Roberts (ed.), *Gold of the Great Steppe* (The Fitzwilliam Museum, Cambridge, 2021), pp.148–49.

39. Juras, A., Krzewińska, M., Nikitin, A.G. *et al.*, 'Diverse origin of mitochondrial lineages in Iron Age Black Sea Scythians', *Scientific Reports* (2017), 7:43950. http://doi.org/10.1038/srep43950.

40. http://www.nomadexhibitions.com/blog/2016/4/1/object-focus.

41. It was one of seven funerary masks discovered there by Heinrich Schliemann in 1876. It became famous enough to be described as a possible forgery planted among the others, but no evidence or cause for Schliemann doing that has been advanced. Harrington, S.P.M., 'Behind the Mask of Agamemnon', *Archaeology*, Vol. 52, No. 4 (July/August 1999).

42. Kelder, J., 'The Egyptian interest in Mycenaean Greece', *Annual of Ex Oriente Lux (JEOL)* (2010), p.125.

43. Bonsall, C., Gurova, M., Elenski, N., Ivanov, G., Bakamska, A., Ganetsovski, G., Zlateva-Uzunova, R., and Slavchev, V., 'Tracing the source of obsidian from prehistoric sites in Bulgaria', *Bulgarian E-Journal of Archaeology* 7, 1 (26 June 2017), accessed 21 July 2017.

44. Chapman, J., 'From Varna to Brittany via Csőszhalom – Was There a "Varna Effect"?', in A. Anders *et al.*(eds), *Moments in Time* (Hungary, 2013), pp.323–36.

45. Cassen, S., 'To import, to copy, to inspire? Central-Europeans objects signs in the Armorican Neolithic Age', *L'anthropologie* 107 (2003), pp.255–70.

46. Chapman, J. (2013).

47. Kustov, R., 'Gem minerals and materials from the neolithic and chalcolithic periods in Bulgaria and their impact on the history of gemmology', *Scientific Annals, School of Geology, Aristotle University of Thessaloniki Proceedings of the XIX CBGA Congress*, Special volume 100 (Thessaloniki, Greece, 2010), pp.391–97.

48. Krauß, R. *et al.* (2017).

49. Tringham, R., 'Fire – Friend or Fiend in Human History', Annual Pitt Rivers Lecture (2019).

50. Zäuner, S.P., 'The Dark Side of the Chalcolithic. Evidence for Warfare at Tell Yunatsite? – An anthropological approach', in Y. Boyadzhiev and St. Terzijska-Ignatova (eds), *The Golden 5th Millennium: Thrace and its neighbour areas in the Chalcolithic* (Sofia, 2011), pp.49–57.

51. Balabina, V., and Mishina, T., 'Considering the Destruction of the Latest Eneolithic Village at Tell Yunatsite', in Y. Boyadzhiev and St. Terzijska-Ignatova (eds), *The Golden 5th Millennium: Thrace and its neighbour areas in the Chalcolithic* (Sofia, 2011), pp.39–48.
52. Boyadzhiev, K., 'Weapons from the Chalcolithic period in Bulgaria', *Dissertations*, Vol. 9 (Bulgarian Academy of Sciences, 2014).
53. Woodward, A., and Hunter, J., *Ritual in Early Bronze Age Grave Goods* (Oxbow Books, 2015), ch.6.
54. Thom, A. *et al.*, 'The Bush Barrow gold lozenge: Is it a solar and lunar calendar for Stonehenge?', *Antiquity*, 62 (236) (1988), pp,492–502.
55. https://www.smithsonianmag.com/smart-news/heres-what-happens-all-coins-tossed-fountains-180959314/; accessed 9 April 2018.
56. http://uk.businessinsider.com/how-much-money-is-thrown-into-romes-trevi-fountain-and-where-it-goes-2017-6; accessed 9 April 2018.

Chapter 2

1. Klemm, D., Klemm, R., and Murr, A., 'Gold of the Pharaohs – 6000 years of gold mining in Egypt and Nubia', *African Earth Sciences* 33 (2001), pp.643–59.
2. Midant-Reynes, B., 'The Naqada Period (*c.*4000–3200 BC)', in I. Shaw (ed.), *The Oxford History of Ancient Egypt* (Oxford University Press, 2000), p.55.
3. Reichel, C.D., 'Excavations at Hamoukar Syria', *Oriental Institute Fall 2011 News and Notes*, no. 211 (2011), pp.1–9, https://oi.uchicago.edu/sites/oi.uchicago.edu/files/uploads/shared/docs/nn211.pdf; consulted 29 August 2020.
4. Bogdanos, M., 'The Casualties of War: The Truth about the Iraq Museum', *American Journal of Archaeology*, Vol. 109, No. 3 (July 2005), pp.477–526.
5. Basmachi, F., *Treasures of the Iraq Museum* (al-Jumhuriya Press, Baghdad, 1975–1976).
6. The oldest historical text from Egypt is probably the Palermo stone, which is around the same date. There is an older king-list of Egyptian first dynasty rulers, found on a seal in the tomb of Den, dating from around 3000 BCE.
7. Leick, G., *Mesopotamia: The Invention of the City* (Penguin Books, 2002), p.xvii.
8. That is presumably why his is the first name, apart from the mythical Gilgamesh, on the Metropolitan Museum's List of Rulers of Mesopotamia, url http://www.metmuseum.org/toah/hd/meru/hd_meru.htm; consulted 21 August 2017.
9. http://sumerianshakespeare.com/56701.html; consulted 9 June 2021.
10. Millerman, A.J., 'The Spinning of Ur: How Sir Leonard Woolley, James R. Ogden and the British Museum interpreted and represented the past to generate funding for the excavation of Ur in the 1920s and 1930s' (PhD thesis, University of Manchester, Humanities, 2015).
11. URL http://data.worldbank.org/indicator/SP.RUR.TOTL.ZS?view=mapx; consulted 21 August 2017.
12. Philip, G., and Rehren, T., 'Fourth millennium BC silver from Tell esh-Shuna, Jordan: archaeometallurgical investigation and some thoughts on ceramic skeuomorphs', *Oxford Journal of Archaeology* 15 (2) (1996), p.143.
13. Levey, M., 'The Refining of Gold in Ancient Mesopotamia', *Chymia*, Vol. 5 (1959), p.35.
14. Gale, N.H., and Stos-Gale, Z.A., 'Ancient Egyptian Silver', *The Journal of Egyptian Archaeology*, Vol. 67 (1981), pp.103–15; Powell, M.A., 'Money in Mesopotamia', *Journal of the Economic and Social History of the Orient*, Vol. 39, No. 3, 'Money in the Orient' (1996), pp.224–42.
15. Crawford, H., 'Trade in the Sumerian World', in H. Crawford (ed.), *The Sumerian World* (Routledge, 2013).
16. Maxwell-Hyslop, K.R., 'Sources of Sumerian Gold: The Ur Goldwork from the Brotherton Library, University of Leeds. A Preliminary Report', *Iraq*, Vol. 39, No. 1 (Spring 1977), pp.83–86.
17. Powell, M.A., 'Money in Mesopotamia', *Journal of the Economic and Social History of the Orient*, Vol. 39, No. 3, 'Money in the Orient' (1996), pp.224–42.

18. Maxwell-Hyslop, K.R., 'The Ur Jewellery. A Re-Assessment in the Light of Some Recent Discoveries', *Iraq*, Vol. 22, 'Ur in Retrospect'. In Memory of Sir C. Leonard Woolley (Spring–Autumn 1960), pp.105–15.
19. Powell, M.A., 'Money in Mesopotamia', *Journal of the Economic and Social History of the Orient*, Vol. 39, No. 3 (1996), pp.224–42.
20. *Ibid.*, p.229.
21. Leverani, M., *Uruk, the First City* (Equinox, 2006).
22. Crawford, H., *Sumer and The Sumerians* (Cambridge University Press, 2004), p.139.
23. Herodotus, *The Histories*, 1.181–1.182, 1.199.
24. Crawford, H., 'Trade in the Sumerian World', in H. Crawford (ed.), *The Sumerian World* (Routledge, 2013), p.449.
25. Levey, M., 'The Refining of Gold in Ancient Mesopotamia', *Chymia*, Vol. 5 (1959).
26. Joannes, F., '108) Medailles d'argent d'Hammurabi?', *Nouvelles Assyriologiques Breves et Utilitaires*, No. 4 (December 1989), pp.80–81.
27. Keynes, J.M., *A Treatise on Money*, Vol. 2 (Macmillan, 1958), p.150.
28. Daumas, F., 'Le problème de la monnaie dans l'Egypte antique avant Alexandre', in *Mélanges de l'Ecole Française de Rome*, Vol. 89, Nos 89–92 (1977), pp.425–42.
29. https://www.ucl.ac.uk/museums-static/digitalegypt//literature/sanehat/text.html.
30. Moran, W.L., *The Armana Letters* (Johns Hopkins University Press, 1992).
31. In the *Odyssey* 4.73, the brilliance of the halls of the palace of Menelaus was ascribed to the flashing of 'elektrum'.
32. Klemm, R. and D., 'Gold and Gold Mining in Ancient Egypt and Nubia: Geoarchaeology of the Ancient Gold Mining Sites in the Egyptian and Sudanese Eastern Deserts', in Springer, *Science & Business Media* (2012), p.21.
33. Brinkman, J.A., 'Foreign Relations of Babylonia from 1600 to 625 B.C.: The Documentary Evidence', *American Journal of Archaeology*, Vol. 76, No. 3 (July 1972), pp.271–81.
34. Brinkman, J.A., 'Administration and Society in Kassite Babylonia', *Journal of the American Oriental Society*, Vol. 124, No. 2 (April–June 2004), pp.283–304.
35. Kleber, K., 'The Kassite Gold and the Post-Kassite Silver Standards Revisited', in K. Kleber and R. Pirngruber (eds), *Silver, Money and Credit* (Leiden 2016), pp.42–43.
36. Brinkman, J.A., 'Babylonia under the Kassites: Some Aspects for Consideration', in A. Bartelmus and K. Sternitzke (eds), *Kardunias̆. Babylonia Under the Kassites* (de Gruyter, 2017), v.1, pp.12–13.
37. Thompson, C.M., 'Sealed Silver in Iron Age Cisjordan and the "Invention" of Coinage', *Oxford Journal of Archaeology* 22(1) (2003), pp.67–107.
38. Bass, G.F., 'Troy and Ur: Gold Links between Two Ancient Capitals', *Expedition* 8 (4) (1966), pp.26–39.
39. Guerra, M.F., and Rehren, T., 'In-situ examination and analysis of the gold jewellery from the Phoenician tomb of Kition (Cyprus)', *ArcheoSciences*, 33 (2009), pp.151–58.
40. Roller (1983).
41. Xenophon, *Anabasis*, 3.4 (7–12).

Chapter 3

1. For China, see 'Eastern Zhou Political and Economic History', in Lander, B.G., *Environmental Change and the Rise of the Qin Empire: A Political Ecology of Ancient North China* (PhD thesis, Columbia University, 2015); for Mesopotamia, Schneider, A., and Selim, A., '"No harvest was reaped": demographic and climatic factors in the decline of the Neo-Assyrian Empire', *Climatic Change*, 127 (2014), pp.435–46.
2. Horesh, N., *Chinese Money in Global Context: Historic Junctures Between 600 BCE and 2012* (Stanford University Press, 2013), p.22.

3. Kakinuma, Y., 'The Emergence and Spread of Coins in China from the Spring and Autumn Period to the Warring States Period', in P. Bernholz and R. Vaubel (eds), *Explaining Monetary and Financial Innovation. Financial and Monetary Policy Studies, vol 39* (Springer, 2014).

4. Herodotus, *The Histories*, 1.94.

5. Radet, G., *La Lydie et le Monde Grec* (1893), p.295 ff.

6. Herodotus, *The Histories*, 1.94.

7. Craddock, P.T. and Cahill, N., 'The Gold of the Lydians' in *Metallurgy in Numismatics 6: Mines, Metals, and Money, Ancient World Studies in Science, Archaeology and History*, (K. Sheedy and G. Davis eds.), Royal Numismatic Society, London (2020). pp.165–174.

8. Ovid, *Metamorphoses* Book XI, 145.

9. Craddock and Cahill.

10. Velde, F.R., 'A Quantitative Approach to the Beginnings of Coinage', in van Alfen, P., and Wartenberg, U., *White Gold: Studies in Early Electrum Coinage* (The American Numismatic Society, 2020), p.512.

11. Seaford, R., *Money and the Early Greek Mind: Homer, Philosophy, Tragedy* (Cambridge University Press, 2004), p.31.

12. *Iliad*, Bk II.

13. Achilles offered a half-talent as third prize for a race: the first was a fabulous great silver bowl that had ransomed a warrior, the second a great fatted ox (*Iliad* 23.751). If the third prize was half the second, then a talent was the value of a good ox and ten talents was a phenomenal gift. In the seventh-century Athenian constitution, it was the property qualification to be a city treasurer.

14. *Odyssey*, Bk. VII.94.

15. Seaford, R. (2004), pp.30–34.

16. Van der Spek, R.J., van Zanden, J.L., and van Leeuwen, B., *A History of Market Performance: From Ancient Babylonia to the Modern World* (Routledge, 2014), p.545.

17. E.g. the looting of Nineveh in 612 BCE; Luckenbill, D.D., *Ancient Records of Assyria and Babylon* (University of Chicago Press, 1927), v.II, p.420.

18. That is by volume. Since gold is heavier, only 45 per cent of the weight of the coin was silver. Millman, E., 'The Importance of the Lydian Stater as the World's First Coin', *Ancient History Encyclopedia* (27 March 2015. Retrieved from https://www.ancient.eu/article/797/.

19. Cahill *et Al.* (2020), p.297.

20. Cahill, N., Hari, J., Önay, B., and Dokumacı, E., 'Depletion Gilding of Lydian Electrum Coins and the Sources of Lydian Gold', p.319, and Blet-Lemarquand, M., and Duyrat, F., 'Elemental Analysis of the Lydo-Milesian Electrum Coins of the Bibliothèque Nationale de France Using LA-ICPMS', pp.358–61, in van Alfen (2020).

21. Other forms of currency are 'commodity' currency, such as gold coins, which has the value of the market price of the stuff it is made from, and 'fiat' currency, such as modern banknotes, which must be accepted by law at the value it shows, and its redemption for gold cannot be demanded.

22. Van Alfen, P., and Wartenberg, U., *The Planchet*, Season 1, Episode 3, podcast, http://numismatics.org/planchet/01-03/, 12.00–12.19.

23. Bresson, A., 'The Choice of Electrum Monometallism: When and Why', in van Alfen (2020), p.489.

24. https://www.cointalk.com/threads/the-smallest-electrum.265593.

25. Velde, F.R., 'A Quantitative Approach to the Beginnings of Coinage', in van Alfen, P., and Wartenberg, U., *White Gold: Studies in Early Electrum Coinage* (The American Numismatic Society, 2020), p.506.

26. De Callataÿ, F., 'White Gold: An Enigmatic Start to Greek Coinage', *American Numismatic Society*, Issue 2 (2013), p.9.

27. A small number of mints did produce more electrum coins in small quantities. Wartenberg, U., 'Was there an Ionian Revolt Coinage? Monetary Patterns in the Late Archaic Perod', in van Alfen, P., and Wartenberg, U., *White Gold: Studies in Early Electrum Coinage* (The American Numismatic Society, 2020), p.512.

28. The small community of 'Israelite Samaritans' based on Mount Holon, near Nablus, self-identify as survivors of these lost tribes and maintain a form of Israelite text-based religion which does not accept the subsequent development of Judaism.

29. Sapir-Hen, L., Gadot, Y., and Finkelstein, I., 'Animal Economy in a Temple City and its Countryside: Iron Age Jerusalem as a Case Study', *Bulletin of the American Schools of Oriental Research* 375, 103 (May 2016).

30. Finkelstein, I., and Silberman, N.A., 'Temple and Dynasty: Hezekiah, the Remaking of Judah and the Rise of the Pan-Israelite Ideology', *Journal for the Study of the Old Testament*, Vol 30.3 (2006), pp.259–85.

31. Ezekiel 1.4. The Hebrew *chashmal*, yellow shining metal (?), is *elektron* in the second-century BCE Greek translation and *electri* in the fourth-century CE Latin, but *amber* in the King James Bible. Zimmerli, W., *Ezekiel: A Commentary on the Book of the Prophet Ezekiel, Volume 1* (Fortress Press, 1979).

32. Exodus, 25.18.

33. Exodus, 39.30.

34. Babylonian Talmud Zevachim 17.B.

35. https://etcsl.orinst.ox.ac.uk/section1/tr1823.htm, pp.38–64.

36. 2 Kings, 23.

37. Deuteronomy, 1.1.

38. Schuster, R., 'Rare Jewel Found on Mt. Zion Reveals Babylonian Destruction of Jerusalem', *Haaretz*, 11 August 2019, https://www.haaretz.com/archaeology/.premium-rare-jewel-found-on-mt-zion-reveals-babylonian-destruction-of-jerusalem-1.7658563?v=1594820159134; consulted 15 July 2020.

39. Pearce L.E., and Wunsch, C., *Documents of Judean Exiles and West Semites in Babylonia in the Collection of David Sofer* (CaDL Press, 2014).

40. A typical inscription on the lintel of a tomb entrance says: 'There is no silver or gold here.' Olyan, S.M., 'Some Neglected Aspects of Israelite Interment Ideology', *Journal of Biblical Literature*, Vol. 124, No. 4 (Winter 2005), pp.601–16.

41. Alstola, T., 'Judean Merchants in Babylonia and Their Participation in Long-Distance Trade', *Die Welt des Orients* 47 (2017), pp.25–51.

42. Herodotus, *The Histories*, 1.50.

43. Craddock, P.T., and Cahill, N., 'The Gold of the Lydians' in *Metallurgy in Numismatics 6: Mines, Metals, and Money, Ancient World Studies in Science, Archaeology and History*, (K. Sheedy and G. Davis eds.), Royal Numismatic Society, London. pp.165–174.

44. Ramage, A., and Craddock, P.T., *King Croesus's Gold: Excavations at Sardis and the History of Gold Refining* (Harvard University Press and the British Museum, 2000).

45. Baughan, E., *Lydian Burial Customs*, URL http://www.sardisexpedition.org/en/essays/latw-baughan-lydian-burial-customs#introduction; consulted 25 August 2017.

46. This may also explain Herodotus's assertion that all Lydian girls had to serve as prostitutes before marriage. That may have begun as a religious obligation, with temple rituals requiring sacred prostitution.

47. Pausanias, *Description of Greece*, 7.7–8.

48. Melcher, M., *et al.*, 'Investigation of ancient gold objects from Artemision at Ephesus using portable μ-XRF', *ArcheoSciences* 33 (2009), URL http://journals.openedition.org/archeosciences/2172, consulted 26 February 2018; DOI: 10.4000/archeosciences.2172.

49. Herodotus, *The Histories*, 1.155.4.

50. https://www.dailysabah.com/real-estate/2015/08/16/istanbuls-most-expensive-place-to-rent-property-the-grand-bazaar; consulted 28 August 2017.

51. Yalichev, S., *Mercenaries of the Ancient World* (Constable, 1997).

52. English, S., *Mercenaries in the Classical World: To the Death of Alexander* (Pen & Sword, 2012), ch.2.

53. Bassi, K., 'Croesus's Offerings and the Value of the Past in Herodotus' *Histories*', J. Ker and C. Pieper (eds), *Valuing the Past in the Graeco-Roman World* (Brill, 2014), pp.173–98; Parke, W., *Croesus and Delphi* (1984), URL grbs.library.duke.edu/article/download/5491/5297; consulted 25 August 2017.

Chapter 4

1. Briant, P., *From Cyrus to Alexander: A History of the Persian Empire* (Eisenbrauns, 2002), p.33.

2. Diodorus Siculus, *Library*, 9.32.

3. Xenophon, *Cyropaedia*, 6

4. Evans, J.A.S., 'What Happened to Croesus?', *The Classical Journal*, Vol. 74, No. 1 (October–November 1978), pp.34–40.

5. Xenophanes of Colophon, cf. Evans (1978).

6. As I write this, 'rich as Croesus' has been recently used by *Vogue* (14 August 2017) of Oprah Winfrey, *The Times* (8 July 2017) of Bill Gates and the *Telegraph* (15 November 2016) of, inevitably, Donald Trump.

7. Kurke, L., *Coins, Bodies, Games and Gold* (Princeton University Press, 1999), p.7.

8. Bresson, A., 'The Origin of Lydian and Greek Coinage: Cost and Quantity', *Historical Research*, 5 (2006), pp.149–65 (in Chinese translation), https://economics.yale.edu/sites/default/files/files/Workshops-Seminars/Economic-History/bresson-090921a.pdf; consulted 15 May 2020.

9. Herodotus, *The Histories*, 1.191.

10. The Cyrus Cylinder was deliberately buried in the wall of Babylon, a foundation deposit by the conqueror. The other cuneiform texts are the closely contemporary Nabonidus Chronicle, the Verse Account of Nabonidus and the post-Alexander Dynastic Prophecy.

11. Hasel, G., 'New Light on the Book of Daniel from the Dead Sea Scrolls', *Bible and Spade* (Spring 2011).

12. For a thorough analysis, see Dougherty, R.P., *Nabonidus and Belshazzar* (Yale University Press, 1929).

13. Babylonians in this period counted in sixties, hence our units of time; the prophet Ezekiel was supposedly in Babylon at the time and the 'Book of Ezekiel' mentions a mina as sixty shekels.

14. Forbes, R.J., *Metallurgy in Antiquity: A Notebook for Archaeologists and Technologists* (Brill, 1950).

15. The writing is reported in Aramaic, the script and language of business, not the cuneiform Akkadian of sacred or government texts. The words were written without vowels, so appear as 'MN. MN, SKL, VPRSYN'. 'PRSYN' means 'divided' or 'halved', and its root, 'PRS', was a noun signifying half the weight of a mina.

16. Wolters, A., 'Untying the King's Knots: Physiology and Wordplay in Daniel 5', *Journal of Biblical Literature* Vol. 110, No. 1 (Spring 1991), pp.117–22. This despite the fact that neither Belshazzar nor his scribes could read the words drawn on the plaster, suggesting that they could not read the Aramaic script used by merchants, Jews and, apparently, the hand of their disembodied God. Though Daniel's interpretation is more abstract in the biblical story, the literal translation of those words is purely monetary.

17. Linssen, M.J.H. *The Cults of Uruk and Babylon: The Temple Ritual Texts as Evidence for Hellenistic Cult Practices* (Brill, 2004), p.73.

18. A comparison can be made with the Jewish New Year and Day of Atonement on the same dates: see Milgrom, J., *Leviticus 1–16: A New Translation with Introduction and Commentary*

(Doubleday, 1991), pp.1067–69, 1077–78; Gane, R., *Cult and Character: Purification Offerings, Day of Atonement, and Theodicy* (Eisenbrauns, 2005), pp.355–78.

19. Wolters, A., 'Belshazzar's Feast and the Cult of the Moon God Sîn', *Bulletin for Biblical Research* 5 (1995), pp.199–206.
20. http://oracc.museum.upenn.edu/amgg/listofdeities/marduk/; consulted 13 June 2021.
21. Lewy, J., 'The Late Assyro-Babylonian Cult of the Moon and its Culmination at the Time of Nabonidus', *Hebrew Union College Annual*, Vol. 19 (1945–46), pp.405–489, see n.222.
22. We know that in the late fourth century BCE, the temple employed at least fourteen scribes on these records.
23. Mazdaism dates back to at least 1000 BCE; see Briant, p.94.
24. Herodotus, *The Histories*, 1.153, quoted in Burn, A.R., *Persia and the Greeks: The Defence of the West, C. 546–478 B.C.* (Stanford University Press, 1984), p.44.
25. Herodotus, *The Histories*, 1.153.1, quoted in Kurke, L., *Coins, Bodies, Games and God* (Princeton University Press, 1999), pp.73–74, as symptomatic of Greek aristocratic disapproval of trade and the trivialization of gold.
26. Boucharlat, R., 'Pasargadae', *Iran*, Vol. 40 (2002), pp.279–82.
27. http://www.livius.org/sources/content/arrian/anabasis/alexander-and-the-tomb-of-cyrus/.
28. Ezra 1:8.
29. The Farsi name of Persepolis is Parsa, the name of the province and people.
30. Cool Root, M., 'Evidence from Persepolis for the Dating of Persian and Archaic Greek Coinage', *The Numismatic Chronicle*, Vol. 148 (1988), pp.1–12.
31. Nimchuk, C.L., 'The "Archers" of Darius: Coinage or Tokens of Royal Esteem?', *Ars Orientalis*, Vol. 32, *Medes and Persians: Reflections on Elusive Empires* (2002), pp.55–79; Briant, P., *From Cyrus to Alexander: A History of the Persian Empire* (Eisenbrauns, 2002), p.409.

Chapter 5

1. Grant, D.D.G., 'Orphic Masks and Burial Rituals: Homer, Vergina and the Cremation of Philip II of Macedon', *Ancient Origins* (2020), https://www.ancient-origins.net/history/king-philip-ii-macedon-0013034; consulted 13 June 2021.
2. Castañada, J.E., 'New estimates of the stock of gold, 1493–2011' (2013), https://www.researchgate.net/publication/266390495_New_estimates_of_the_stock_of_gold_1493-2011.
3. Manning, J.G., 'Coinage as "Code" in Ptolemaic Egypt', *Princeton/Stanford Working Papers in Classics* (December 2006).
4. Its restoration may have resulted from Seleucid compromise rather than surrender. Ma, J., 'Re-Examining Hanukkah', *Marginalia* (9 July 2013), https://marginalia.lareviewofbooks.org/re-examining-hanukkah/3/; consulted 13 June 2021.

Chapter 6

1. Pliny, *Natural History*, 33.1.
2. Gallagher, R.L., 'Metaphor in Cicero's "De Re Publica"', *The Classical Quarterly*, Vol. 51, No. 2 (2001).
3. Pliny, *Natural History*, 33.4.
4. *Ibid.*, 33.13.
5. They could barely raise Brennus's ransom of 1,000 pounds' weight of gold. A Roman pound weighed about 330g, and 1,000 pounds occupied just two-hundredths of a cubic metre.
6. Pope, R., 'Re-approaching Celts: Origins, Society, and Social Change', *Journal of Archaeological Research* (9 February 2021), https://doi.org/10.1007/s10814-021-09157-1.
7. For example, the Samnites of south-central Italy, who had a tribal and transhumant culture, had very different values from the hierarchical and urban people of Rome, and fought three wars against them in the fourth and third centuries BCE, eventually being defeated, assimilated and ceasing to exist as different from Romans.

8. Livy, *History of Rome*, 49.
9. Suetonius, *Tiberius*, Bk.3.
10. Cunliffe, B., *The Ancient Celts* (Oxford University Press, 2018), 'The Celts in Asia Minor, Third Century bc to Fourth Century ad'.
11. Cassius Dio, *Roman History*, Bk.27 (90).
12. Trundle, M.F., *The Classical Greek Mercenary and his Relationship to the Greek Polis* (McMaster University dissertation), URL http://hdl.handle.net/11375/13924; accessed 8 October 2017.
13. Fröhlich, J., 'Vzácny Nález Statéra Filipa II Macedónskeho v Moravskom Laténskom Centre Němčice Nad Hanou', *Folia Numismatika* 28/1. Supplementum ad Acta Musei Moraviae, Scientiae sociales XCIX (2014), pp.11–26; see MacGonagle, B., 'AB OVO – The First Celtic Coinage', https://www.academia.edu/25857737/AB_OVO_The_First_Celtic_Coinage; consulted 10 July 2021.
14. MacGonagle, B., 'The Kingmakers – Celtic Mercenaries', https://www.academia.edu/4910243/THE_KINGMAKERS_Celtic_Mercenaries; consulted 10 July 2021.
15. Charles-Picard, G. and C., tr. A.E. Foster, *Daily Life in Carthage at the Time of Hannibal* (Allen & Unwin, 1981), p.176.
16. Frey-Kupper, S., 'Coins and their use in the Punic Mediterranean: case studies from Carthage to Italy from the fourth to the first century BCE', in J. Crawley Quinn and N.C. Vella (eds), *The Punic Mediterranean* (Cambridge University Press, 2014), p.98.
17. Watts, D., *Christians and Pagans in Roman Britain* (Routledge, 1991), p.192.
18. Garrard, T.F., 'The Early Trans-Saharan Gold Trade', *The Journal of African History*, Vol. 23, No. 4 (1982), pp.443–61.
19. Herodotus, *The Histories, Melpomene* IV, 196. This is often supposed to mean sub-Saharan Africa, but there is no evidence to support that idea. Medieval Arab writers reported the same form of dumb barter, salt for gold, in the 'Sudan', but none had observed it themselves and this may be simply travellers' tales based on Herodotus. See de Moraes Farias, P.F., 'Silent Trade: Myth and Historical Evidence', *History in Africa*, Vol. 1 (1974), pp.9–24.
20. Xella, P., Quinn, J., Melchiorri, V., and van Dommelen, P., 'Cemetery or sacrifice? Infant burials at the Carthage Tophet: Phoenician bones of contention', *Antiquity*, Vol. 87, Issue 338 (1 December 2013).
21. Diodorus Siculus, *Library of History*, 20.14. The reality of child sacrifices has been supported by archaeological evidence: Quinn, J., 'Cemetery or sacrifice? Infant burials at the Carthage Tophet', *Antiquity*, Vol. 87, Issue 338.
22. Beck, H., 'Wealth, Power, and Class Coherence. The ambitus Legislation of the 180s B.C.', in H. Beck *et al.* (eds), *Money and Power in the Roman Republic* (Brussels, 2016), p.147.
23. Markowitz, M., 'The Coinage of Carthage', *CoinWeek* (7 July 2014). Markowitz converts the penalty of 3,000 Euboean gold talents into their weight. Euboean talents, as opposed to Babylonian talents, were weights of gold; Herodotus, *The Histories*, III, 89–97, quoted in Kuhrt, A., *The Persian Empire: A Corpus of Sources from the Achaemenid Period* (Routledge, 2013), p.673.
24. Polybius, *Histories*, 66–88.
25. 'Punic' is derived from Phoenician.
26. Friedberg, A.L. and I.S., *Gold Coins of the World: From Ancient Times to the Present : an Illustrated Standard Catalogue with Valuations* (Coin & Currency Institute, 2009), p.32.
27. 'The Dioscuri on Reverses' *The Numismatic Journal* 1 (1836), p.133; http://www.jstor.org.ezproxy.uwtsd.ac.uk/stable/42679077.
28. The Attic talent was about 26kg, the Roman pound about 330 grams.
29. Kiernan, B., 'The First Genocide: Carthage, 146 BC', *Diogenes* 203 (2004), pp.27–39. It was not the first time brute force was used to destroy an entire culture; for example, the

Athenians wiped out the population of Melos, eliminating its culture as a demonstration of ruthless power.

30. Cicero, *De Officiis* 3.xx; URL https://warwick.ac.uk/newsandevents/pressreleases/research_team_sheds (6 April 2022); consulted 13 January 2024.

31. Calvet, M., and Roesch, P., 'Les Sarapieia de Tanagra', *Revue Archéologique*, Nouvelle Série, Fasc. 2 (1966), pp.297–332.

32. See for instance Krause, D., *et al.*, 'The "Keltenblock" project: discovery and excavation of a rich Hallstatt grave at the Heuneburg, Germany', *Antiquity*, Vol. 91, Issue 355, pp.108–23.

33. Fitzpatrick, A.P., 'The roles of Celtic coinage in south east England', in M. Mays (ed.), *Celtic Coinage: Britain and Beyond*, BAR British Series 222 (1992), pp.1–32.

34. Leins, I., 'Coins in Context: Coinage and Votive Deposition in Iron Age South-East Leicestershire', *British Numismatic Journal* 77 (2007), pp.22–48.

35. Williams, M., and Creighton, J., 'Shamanic practices and trance imagery in the Iron Age', in P. de Jersey (ed.), *Celtic Coinage: New Discoveries, New Discussion*, BAR International Series 1532 (2006), pp.49–60.

36. Cauuet, B, Tămaş, C.G., Boussicault, M., and Munoz, M., 'Quantités et contrôle de l'or produit à l'âge du fer en Gaule du Centre-Ouest', *Mélanges de la Casa de Velázquez*, 48-1 (2018), pp.13–42.

37. Wells, P.S., 'Settlement and Social Systems at the End of the Iron Age', in B. Arnold and D. Blair Gibson (eds), *Celtic Chiefdom, Celtic State: The Evolution of Complex Social Systems in Prehistoric Europe* (Cambridge University Press, 1995), p.94; Wellington, I., 'The role of Iron Age coinage in archaeological contexts', in de Jersey (2006), pp.81–95, concludes that gold coinage was largely reserved for ritual deposits and hoards.

38. Edwards, G., and Dennis, M., 'The Silsden hoard; discovery, investigation and new interpretations', in de Jersey (2006), pp.249–60.

39. Pliny, *Natural History* XXXIII, 17, 55.

40. Veyne, P., 'Rome devant la prétendue fuite de l'or: mercantilisme ou politique disciplinaire?', *Annales. Histoire, Sciences Sociales*, 34e Année, No. 2 (February–March 1979), p.215, accepts Pliny's figures as evidence that Rome was extraordinarily rich in gold, and his unusual precision indicates that modern very low estimates of gold extracted before Columbus are unconvincing.

Chapter 7

1. Harl, K., *Coinage in the Roman Economy 300 B.C. to A.D. 700* (Johns Hopkins University Press, 1996), p.48.

2. Appian, *The Mithridatic Wars* 4 (sec. 22).

3. Telford, L., *Sulla, A Dictator Reconsidered* (Pen Sword Books, 2014), p.120. Telford argues that he believed he was simply borrowing from the gods and repaid the money, but it was not repayment in kind or from his own pocket. His loot from the temples of Epidavros, Olympia and Delphi was repaid with half the territory of the Thebans (Pausanias, *Description of Greece*, 9.7.5).

4. Polybius, *World History*, 10.40.2–5.

5. Later Roman accounts said he executed 4,700, but modern historians have reduced the death toll.

6. Marshall, B.A., *Crassus: A Political Biography* (Amsterdam, 1976).

7. Appian, *Civil Wars*, II, 8.

8. Diodorus Siculus III, 38.

9. Lewis, P.R., and Jones, G.D.B., 'Roman Gold-Mining in North-West Spain', *The Journal of Roman Studies*, Vol. 60 (1970), pp.169–85; Redondo-Vega, J.M., Alonso-Herrero, E., Santos-González, J., González-Gutiérrez, R.B., and Gómez-Villar, A. (2015). La Balouta

exhumed karst: a Roman gold-mine-derived landscape within the Las Médulas UNESCO World Heritage Site in Spain. *International Journal of Speleology, 44* (3), p.267.

10. Suetonius, *The Lives of the Caesars: Julius Caesar*, 54.

11. Strabo, *The Geography*, Book IV, 1.13.

12. Diodorus Siculus, V, 27.

13. Cunliffe, B., and Chadwick, N., *The Celts* (Penguin, 1997).

14. Roymans, N., and Fernandez-Gotz, M., 'Fire and Sword. The archaeology of Caesar's Gallic War', *Military History Monthly*, 56 (2015), pp.52–56.

15. Creighton, J., *Coins and Power in Late Iron Age Britain* (Cambridge University Press, 2000).

16. van de Goot, F.R.W., ten Berge, R.L., and Vos, R., 'Molten gold was poured down his throat until his bowels burst', *Journal of Clinical Pathology*, 56 (2003), p.157.

17. Harl, K., *Roman Economy 300 B.C. to A.D. 700* (Johns Hopkins University Press, 1996), p.52; Watson, G.R., 'The Pay of the Roman Army. The Republic', *Historia: Zeitschrift für Alte Geschichte*, Bd. 7, H. 1 (January 1958), pp.113–20.

Chapter 8

1. Harl, K., *Coinage in the Roman Economy, 300 B.C. to A.D. 700* (Johns Hopkins University Press, 1996), p.71.

2. Cassius Dio, *Roman History*, 47, 47–49.

3. Plutarch, *Life of Antony*, 76; Cassius Dio, *Roman History*, 51.

4. Lange, C.H., *Triumphs in the Age of Civil War: the Late Republic and the Adaptability of Triumphal Tradition* (Bloomsbury Academic, 2016).

5. Harl, p.73.

6. White, R.T., 'Luxury at Rome: avaritia, aemulatio and the mos maiorum', *Ex Historia*, Vol. 6 (2014), pp.117–43.

7. Dignas, B., and Winter, E., *Rome and Persia in Late Antiquity: Neighbours and Rivals* (Cambridge University Press, 2007).

8. Davies, P.J.E., *Architecture and Politics in Republican Rome* (Cambridge University Press, 2017), p.263.

9. Seneca the Elder (*c.* 54 BCE–39 CE), *Declamations*, Vol. I.

10. Suetonius, *Twelve Caesars*, 'Tiberius', 48.

11. Southern, P., *Augustus* (Routledge, 2013), p.314.

12. Tacitus, *Annals*, 2.87.

13. *Ibid.*, 6.13–16.

14. Rodewald, C., *Money in the Age of Tiberius* (Manchester University Press, 1976). Rodewald ignores the evidence of the food riots and political protests which accompanied the attempts to have loans declared illegal. Those were caused by the land bubble bursting.

15. Talbert, R.J.A., 'Augustus and the Senate', *Greece & Rome*, Vol. 31, No. 1 (April 1984), pp.55–63.

16. https://fred.stlouisfed.org/series/GDIA; consulted 27 November 2017.

17. https://fred.stlouisfed.org/series/PSAVERT; consulted 27 November 2017.

18. Lightner, O.C., *The History of Business Depressions* (The Northeastern Press, 1922), p.24.

19. Luke, 23: 20–24.

20. Breglia, L., 'Circolazione monetale ed aspetti di vita economica in Pompeii', *Raccolta di studi per il seconda centenario degli scavi di Pompei* (1950), pp.41–50.

21. Strabo, *Geography*, IV, 5.3.

22. Fitzpatrick, M.P., 'Provincializing Rome: The Indian Ocean Trade Network and Roman Imperialism', *Journal of World History*, Vol. 22, No. 1 (March 2011), pp.27–54.

23. Appian, Preface 1.5.

24. Boon, G.C., '"Plumbum Britannicum" and Other Remarks', *Britannia*, Vol. 22 (1991), pp.317–22

25. Tacitus, *Annals*, 14.33.

26. Levick, B., *Vespasian* (Routledge, 2016).
27. Suetonius, *The Twelve Caesars*, 'Vespasian' 16. It has been suggested that Suetonius multiplied the number by ten, because it seems so incredible.
28. Suetonius, *The Twelve Caesars*, 'Vespasian', XVIII.
29. Rutledge, S.H., 'The Roman Destruction of Sacred Sites', *Historia: Zeitschrift für Alte Geschichte*, Bd. 56, H. 2 (2007), pp.179–95.
30. Puttnam, B. and Wood, J.E., *The Treasure of Rennes-le-Château. A Mystery Solved* (Stroud, 2003). The resonance of the myth is laid out in Kingsley, S., *God's Gold: The Quest for the Lost Temple Treasure of Jerusalem* (John Murray, 2006).
31. Duncan-Jones, R., *Money and Government in the Roman Empire* (Cambridge University Press, 1998), pp.10–14.
32. Duncan-Jones (1998).
33. *Historia Augusta*, 'Life of Didius Julianus', 3.2–5.
34. De Blois, L., 'The Perception of Emperor and Empire in Cassius Dio's "Roman History"', *Ancient Society*, Vol. 29 (1998–1999), pp.267–81.
35. Cassius Dio, *Roman History* LXXVII, 10.4.
36. Scheidel, W., *Roman Economy* (Cambridge University Press, 2012), p.271.
37. Elton, H., *Warfare in Roman Europe, CE 350–425 (Oxford University Press*, 1996), pp.144–45.
38. Harl, p.156.
39. Depeyrot, G., 'Economy and Society', in Lenski, N., *The Cambridge Companion to the Age of Constantine* (Cambridge University Press, 2012), p.236.
40. Littman, R.J., and Littman, M.L., 'Galen and the Antonine Plague', *The American Journal of Philology*, Vol. 94, No. 3 (Autumn 1973), pp.243–55.
41. Cyprian, *Writings, Bp. of Carthage, Cyprianus*, v.2, tr. E. Wallis (Edinburgh, 1869).

Chapter 9
1. https://www.livemint.com/Opinion/yLqLISrnY6OAt9xtH13rnM/Who-are-the-biggest-buyers-of-gold-in-India.html; accessed 18 April 2012.
2. http://www.business-standard.com/article/economy-policy/tirumala-tirupati-devasthanams-deposits-2-780-kg-gold-with-sbi-under-gms-117082900736_1.html; consulted 17 April 2018.
3. https://www.washingtonpost.com/world/asia_pacific/india-wants-its-rich-temples-to-part-with-their-gold-and-help-the-economy/2015/04/21/4b7f5eda-e29c-11e4-ae0f-f8c46aa8c3a4_story.html?noredirect=on&utm_term=.defeb3bf2c9d; consulted 19 April 2018.
4. https://www.bullionstar.com/blogs/koos-jansen/estimated-chinese-gold-reserves-surpass-20000-tonnes/; consulted 19 April 2018.
5. Halpern, J., 'The Secret of the Temple', *New Yorker* (30 April 2012).
6. Rathbone, D., 'The Muziris papyrus (SB XVIII): financing Roman trade with India', in Alexandrian Studies II in Honour of Mostafa el Abbadi, *Bulletin de la Societe d'Archeologie d'Alexandrie* 46 (2000), pp.39–50.
7. Petronius, 76.
8. http://news.xinhuanet.com/english/2015-11/17/c_134826435.htm; consulted 5 December 2017.
9. Marquis of Haihun's tomb of the Western Han Dynasty in Nanchang, Jiangxi (2017), 17(1), pp.44–59. Retrieved 5 December 2017 from doi:10.1515/char-2017-0004.
10. Scheidel, W., 'The Monetary Systems of the Han and Roman Empires', in W. Scheidel (ed.), *Rome and China: Comparative Perspectives on Ancient World Empires* (Oxford University Press, 2009), p.165.
11. Tye, R., *Wang Mang*, https://www.academia.edu/356703/Wang_Mang (2013).
12. Rodewald, C., *Money in the Age of Tiberius* (Manchester University Press,1976).

13. Taube, K., 'The Symbolism of Jade in Classic Maya Religion', *Ancient Mesoamerica*, 16(1) (2005), pp.23–50; doi:10.1017/S0956536105050017; consulted 13 April 2018.
14. J.C.S. Lin (ed.), *The Search For Immortality: Tomb Treasures of Han China* (Cambridge University Press, 2012), pp.49–50.
15. Huaizhi, Z., and Yuantao, N., 'China's ancient gold drugs', *Gold Bull* 34 (2001), p.24; https://doi.org/10.1007/BF03214805; consulted 4 December 2017.
16. Hung, Ko, Wu, Lu-Ch'iang, and Davis, Tenney L., 'An Ancient Chinese Alchemical Classic. Ko Hung on the Gold Medicine and on the Yellow and the White: The Fourth and Sixteenth Chapters of Pao-P'u-tzǔ', *Proceedings of the American Academy of Arts and Sciences*, Vol. 70, No. 6 (December 1935), p.236.
17. Bunker, E.C., 'Gold in the Ancient Chinese World: A Cultural Puzzle', *Artibus Asiae* 53, 1/2 (1993), p.35.
18. Walker, A., 'Forgeries and Inventions of Parthian Coins', *Bulletin on Counterfeits*, Vol. 19, No. 2 (1994–95).
19. Trajan's *Dacia Traiana* was evacuated by Aurelius around 275 CE. To obscure the humiliation, he renamed the province of Lower Moesia, south of the Danube, calling it *Dacia Aureliana*.
20. Bardill, J., *Constantine, Divine Emperor of the Christian Golden Age* (Cambridge University Press, 2012), p.87.
21. Rowden, G., 'The Last Days of Constantine: Oppositional Versions and Their Influence', *The Journal of Roman Studies*, Vol. 84 (1994), pp.146–70.
22. *De Rebus Bellicis*, *c.* 368 CE, quoted in Depeyrol (2012), p.238.
23. Freeman, C., *The Closing Of The Western Mind* (Random House, 2011), p.177.
24. Eusebius Caesariensis, *Vita Constantini*, LVIII.
25. The ziggurat was 91m high and 91m on each side. Constantine's palace covered 19,000sqm and rose on terraces to 33m.
26. Eusebius Caesariensis, *Vita Constantini*, LX.
27. Leone, M., and Parmentier, R.J., 'Representing Transcendence: The Semiosis of Real Presence', *Signs and Society*, Vol. 2, No. S1 (Supplement 2014), pp.S1–S23, S12.
28. Depeyrot, G., 'Economy and Society', in Lesky, N., *The Cambridge Companion to the Age of Constantine* (Cambridge University Press, 2012), p.238.
29. Guest, P., 'Roman Gold and Hun Kings: the use and hoarding of solidi in the late fourth and fifth centuries', in A. Bursche *et al.* (eds), *Roman Coins Outside The Empire* (Moneta, Wetteren, 2008), pp.299–300.
30. Ammianus Marcellinus, XXXI, 6.
31. *Suda* mu. 405, tr. D. Whitehead, https://www.cs.uky.edu/~raphael/sol/sol-html/index.html; consulted 7 July 2021.

Chapter 10

1. Harrell, J.A., and Brown, V.M., 'The World's Oldest Surviving Geological Map: The 1150 B.C. Turin Papyrus from Egypt', *The Journal of Geology* 100(1) (1992), pp.3–18. The map is in the Egyptian Museum in Turin; it was found around 1820 near Thebes.
2. Meyer, C., *Bir Umm Fawakhir 3: excavations 1991–2003* (Oriental Institute of the University of Chicago, 2014); https://oi.uchicago.edu/research/projects/bir-umm-fawakhir-project; consulted 28 December 2017.
3. Laiou, A.E., and Morrison, C., *The Byzantine Economy* (Cambridge University Press, 2007), Map 4; C. Meyer.
4. Grierson, P., and Blackburn, M., *Medieval European Coinage; The Early Middle Ages (5th–10th Centuries)* (Cambridge University Press, 2007), p.9.
5. Grierson (2007), p.150.

6. Paul Veyne has argued that there probably was a balance of trade between Asia and the Empire so that there was no significant outflow of gold, and that Romans were mistaken to be worried; Veyne, P., 'Rome devant la prétendue fuite de l'or: mercantilisme ou politique disciplinaire?', *Annales. Histoire, Sciences Sociales*, 34e Année, No. 2 (February–March 1979), pp.211–44). But his list of Rome's exports – wines, copper, tin, lead, textiles and Egyptian flax – are all relatively low value. In Diocletian's list of maximum prices, top-quality wine was cheaper than olive oil. Copper, tin and lead were obviously low value, pound for pound, compared with gold, and it would have taken phenomenal quantities of textiles and flax to balance the trade in silk and expensive spices.

7. 'The Trans-Saharan Gold Trade (7th–14th Century)', The Metropolitan Museum of Art, Department of the Arts of Africa, Oceania, and the Americas, October 2000, https://www.metmuseum.org/toah/hd/gold/hd_gold.htm; consulted 16 July 2021.

8. Pliny, *Natural History*, 5.34.

9. Cosmas Indicopleustes, *Christian topography*, Book XI, 338.

10. Gibbon, E., *The History of the Decline and Fall of the Roman Empire*, Vol. 3 (1789), p.XX.

11. Procopius, *De Aedificiis*, I, 26.54.

12. Pseudo-Dionysius, *On the Heavenly Hierarchy*, cII, s.III.

13. James, L., *Mosaics in the Medieval World: From Late Antiquity to the Fifteenth Century* (Cambridge University Press, 2017).

14. Procopius, *De Bella Gothica*, III, 33.

15. Haldon, J., *Byzantium in the Seventh Century: The Transformation of a Culture* (Cambridge University Press, 1990), pp.147 ff., 223 ff., and his 'Production, distribution and exchange in the Byzantine World c. 660–840', in I.L. Hansen and C. Wickham (eds), *The Long Eighth Century* (Brill, 2000), p.232.

16. Cherniss, M.D., 'The Progress of the Hoard in Beowulf', PQ 47 (1967), pp.473–86.

17. Translation from URL http://www.anglo-saxons.net/hwaet/?do=get&type=text&id=wdr; consulted 8 March 2018.

18. Silber, P., 'Gold and its Significance in Beowulf', *Annuale Medievale*, Vol. 18 (1977).

19. Musset, L., Bouvris, J-M., and Gazeau, V., 'Sept essais sur des Aspects de la société et de l'économie dans la Normandie médiévale (Xe–XIIIe siècles)', *Annales de Normandie* 22 (1988), pp.68–76.

20. Jones, S.R.H., 'Transaction Costs, Institutional Change, and the Emergence of a Market Economy in Later Anglo-Saxon England', *The Economic History Review*, New Series, Vol. 46, No. 4 (November 1993), pp.658–78.

21. Edberg, Rune. *Runriket Täby-Vallentuna – en handledning* (in Swedish); stockholms.lans.museum.

22. Jansson, S.B., *Runstenar* (Stockholm, 1980), p.35.

23. Spufford, P., *Money and Its Use in Medieval Europe* (Cambridge University Press, 1988), p.63.

24. *Rectitudines singularum personarum*, a tenth-century Anglo-Saxon explanation of the social structure, see http://www.earlyenglishlaws.ac.uk/laws/texts/rect/view/#edition,1_0_c_1/translation,1; consulted 12 January 2018. It is now recognized as being evidence of a feudal structure in England considerably before 1088; Harvey, P.D.A., 'Rectitudines Singularum Personarum and Gerefa', *The English Historical Review*, Vol. 108, No. 426 (January 1993), pp.1–22.

25. Douglas, D.C., *William the Conqueror: The Norman Impact Upon England* (University of California Press, 1964), p.51.

26. Musset, L., Bouvris, J-M., and Gazeau, V., *Sept essais sur des Aspects de la société et de l'économie dans la Normandie médiévale (Xe–XIIIe siècles)* (Annales de Normandie 22 (1988) ; the map on p.80 indicates the extent to which Caen replaced Rouen as a trade hub, at least in terms of surviving contracts.

27. B.B. Bachrach, 'On the Origins of William the Conqueror's Horse Transports', *Technology and Culture*, Vol. 26, No. 3 (July 1985), pp.505-531

28. On the basis of a corn price of 2d., or 3 gm. of silver per kg. The price is taken from https://regia.org/research/misc/costs.htm, and is no more than a vaguely representative figure. To continue the estimate, since a penny can be regarded as having a modern value of around £20, we are talking of a daily porridge bill of about £100,000.

29. Bachrach, 'Logistics in Pre-Crusade Europe,' in J.A. Lynn (ed.), *Feeding Mars; Logistics in Western Warfare from the Middle Ages to the Present*, Westview Press (1993), 72.

30. N. Gelb, *The Jews in Medieval Normandy: A Social and Intellectual History*, Cambridge University Press, 1998

31. Sawyer, P., *The Wealth of Anglo-Saxon England* (Oxford University Press, 2013).

32. At the Assize of Moneyers, Winchester, Christmas 1124. Stewart, I., 'Moneyers In The 1130 Pipe Roll', *British Numismatic Journal* 61 (1991), pp.1–8.

33. Quiring, H., *Die Geschichte des Goldes. Die goldenen Zeitalter in ihrer kulturellen und wirtschaftlichen Bedeutung* (Stuttgart, 1948), p.197, reckons that from 501–1260 CE, Europe acquired 38 tons, or 1.9 cubic metres. A standard bath holds 1.8 cubic metres.

34. Bagnoli, M., 'The Stuff of Heaven: Materials and Craftsmanship in Mediaeval Reliquaries', in M. Bagnoli (ed.), *Treasures of Heaven: Saints, Relics and Devotion in Medieval Europe* (British Museum, 2011), p.138.

35. Talbot Rice, D., in L. Vitali (ed.), *Il tesoro del Duomo di Monza* (Banca Popolare di Milano, 1966), pp.31–32.

36. Spufford, P., *Money and Its Use in Medieval Europe* (Cambridge University Press, 1988), p.19.

37. https://fireina55gallondrum.wordpress.com/2013/06/27/al-muallaqat-1-stop-friends-by-imru-al-qais/.

38. Peters, F.E., *Muhammad and the origins of Islam* (SUNY Press, 1994), p.109.

39. Greif, A., 'Reputations and Coalitions in Medieval Trade', *Journal of Economic History*, Vol. 49, no. 4 (December 1989), pp.857–82. This is an analysis of eleventh-century Jewish traders from Cairo, but the issues are not dissimilar.

40. Ibrahim, M., *Merchant Capital and Islam* (University of Texas Press, 2011).

41. Nahon, K., and Hemsley, J., *Going Viral* (Cambridge, 2013).

42. *Qur'an* 8.1, tr. Muhammad Sarwar, https://corpus.quran.com/translation.jsp?chapter=8&verse=1.

43. Hassan, A.A.H., *Sales and Contracts in Early Islamic Commercial Law* (The Other Press, 2007), Ch.3, 'International Monetary Co-operation Since Bretton Woods'.

44. Fouracre, P., *The Age of Charles Martel*, ch.5, s. Precaria (Longman, 2000).

45. Einhard, *The Life of Charlemagne*, s.13.

46. Coupland, S., 'Charlemagne's coinage: Ideology and Economy', in J. Story (ed.), *Charlemagne: Empire and Society* (Manchester University Press, 2005).

47. Butt, J.J., *Daily Life in the Age of Charlemagne* (Greenwood Press, 2002), p.97; Metcalf, D.M., 'How Large was the Anglo-Saxon Currency?', *The Economic History Review* Second Series, Vol. XVIII, No. 3 (1965), pp.475–82.

48. Grierson (1986), p.198.

Chapter 11

1. De Urbel, J.P., *Los monjes españoles en la Edad Media* (1933), II, 416 ff., in Castro, A., *The Spaniards: An Introduction to Their History* (University of California Press, 1985), p.423.

2. Castro, A., *The Spaniards: An Introduction to Their History* (University of California Press, 1985), p.427.

3. Murray, A., *Reason and Society in the Middle Ages* (Clarendon Press, 2002), p.55.

4. Balaguer, A.M., *Història de la moneda dels comtats Catalans* (Institut d'Estudis Catalans, 1999), p.71.

5. Watson, A.M., 'Back to Gold – and Silver', *The Economic History Review*, New Series, Vol. 20, No. 1 (April 1967), pp.1–34.

6. Nicholson, H.J., *The Knights Hospitaller* (Boydell & Brewer, 2001), pp.2–3.

7. Cazel, F.A., Jr., 'Financing the Crusades', in K.M. Setton (ed.), *A History of the Crusades*, Vol. VI, pp.116–49.

8. He records using 42 marks of gold on the front of the altar, 40oz on the rear and 'the whole outside container', around 80 marks, on the cross, requiring between five and seven goldsmiths to work for two years, and a chalice of 140oz of gold. A mark was a unit of weight: 8oz. D. Burr (tr.), *The Book of Suger Abbot of St. Denis on What Was Done During his Administration*, URL http://www.medart.pitt.edu/texts/Saint-Denis/SugerAdmin.html; consulted 3 April 2018.

9. Fulcher of Chartres, *Historia Hierosolymitana* (1095–1127), ed. H. Hagenmeyer (Heidelberg, 1913), III, 37, pp.2–8, quoted in Tal, O., Kool, R., and Baidoun, I., *Hoard Twice Buried? Fatimid Gold from Thirteenth Century Crusader Arsur (Apollonia-Arsuf)* (The Royal Numismatic Society, (2013).

10. Gasper, G.E.M., and Gullbekk, S.H., *Money and the Church in Medieval Europe, 1000–1200: Practice, Morality and Thought* (Routledge, 2016), p.30.

11. Friedman, Y., *Encounter Between Enemies: Captivity and Ransom in the Latin Kingdom of Jerusalem* (Brill, 2002), p.155.

12. Jones, T., and Ereira, A., *Medieval Lives* (BBC Books, 2005), pp.27–28; Bartlett, R., *The Making of Europe: Conquest, Colonization and Cultural Change, 950–1350* (Princeton University Press, 1993), p.125.

13. Lopez, R., 'Aux origines du capitalisme génois', *Annales d'histoire économique et sociale*, T. 9, No. 47 (30 September 1937), pp.429–54.

14. De Vivo, F., 'Historical Justifications of Venetian Power in the Adriatic', *Journal of the History of Ideas*, Vol. 64, No. 2 (April 2003), pp.159–76; Korsch, E., 'Renaissance Venice and the Sacred-Political Connotations of Waterborne Pageants', in M. Shewring (ed.), *Waterborne Pageants and Festivities in the Renaissance: Essays in Honour of J.R. Mulryne* (Routledge, 2017).

15. Jones, T., and Ereira, A., *Crusades* (Penguin Books, 1996), pp.155–57.

16. *Ibid.*, p.167.

17. Cohen, M., *The Sainte-Chapelle and the Construction of Sacral Monarchy: Royal Architecture in Thirteenth-Century Paris* (Cambridge University Press, 2015).

18. Nicol, D.M., *Byzantium and Venice* (CUP, 1988), p.185.

19. The accounts of Peter Chaceporc, a royal treasurer, show that in 1243–44 only 1.5 per cent of the gold received as gifts and fines was in the form of coins.

20. Moore, T.K., 'Credit Finance in the Middle Ages', Economic History Society Conference 2009, URL www.ehs.org.uk/dotAsset/2198856a-47ce-475b-8e49-0917b3b1f0d7.pdf; consulted 2 April 2018.

21. Carpenter, D.A., *The Reign of Henry III* (A&C Black, 1996), p.127.

22. For the estimated death toll, see Frey, R.J., *Genocide and International Justice* (Infobase Publishing, 2009), p.335; for world population estimates, see Ecology Global Network, http://www.ecology.com/population-estimates-year-2050/; consulted 4 April 2018.

23. By which I mean Eurasia and Africa, the world then known to Asians and Europeans.

24. Aigle, D., *The Mongol Empire between Myth and Reality: Studies in Anthropological History* (Brill, 2014), p.3.

25. Rickett, W. Allyn, *Guanzi: Political, Economic, and Philosophical Essays from Early China*, v.2 XXII, 76 (VIII), p.416. The origin of the text is attributed to Guan Zhong (*c.* 720–645 BCE), chief minister to Duke Huan of Qi, but the version we have is the later edit.

26. Ciocîltan, V., *The Mongols and the Black Sea Trade in the Thirteenth and Fourteenth Centuries* (Brill, 2012), pp.107–08.
27. Lindemann, A.S., and Levy, R.S., *Antisemitism: A History* (Oxford University Press, 2010).
28. Kaeuper, R., *Bankers to the Crown: The Riccardi of Lucca and Edward I* (Princeton University Press, 2015); Padgett, J.F., and Powell, W.W., *The Emergence of Organizations and Markets* (Princeton University Press, 2012).
29. Streyer, J.R., *The Reign of Philip the Fair* (Princeton, 1980); Lynch, J., *The Medieval Church: A Brief History* (Routledge, 2013), p.323.
30. Jordan, W.C., 'Administering Expulsion in 1306', *Jewish Studies Quarterly*, Vol. 15, No. 3 (2008), pp.241–50.
31. Spufford, P., *Money and its Use in Medieval Europe* (CUP, 1988), p.271.
32. Lane, F.C., and Mueller, R.C., *Money and Banking in Mediaeval and Renaissance Venice, Vol. 1* (Johns Hopkins University Press, 1985), p.283.
33. Christiansen, K., *Duccio and the Origins of Western Painting* (Metropolitan Museum of Art, 2008).
34. Hourihane, C., *The Grove Encyclopedia of Medieval Art and Architecture*, Vol. 2 (OUP, 2012), p.163.
35. Usher, P., *The Early History of Deposit Banking in Mediterranean Europe* (Harvard University Press, 1943), pp.240, 242.

Chapter 12

1. http://www.davidmus.dk/en/collections/islamic/dynasties/mamluks/coins/c141?back=1&show=comment; consulted 20 April 2018.
2. Gibb, H.A.R., *The Encyclopaedia of Islam* (Brill Archive, 1954), p.965.
3. Gomez, M.A., *African Dominion: A New History of Empire in Early and Medieval West Africa* (Princeton University Press, 2018), p.31.
4. Ancient Ghana was inland. Modern Ghana was created in 1957, and includes the area called the Gold Coast in colonial times, because that is where the gold from the lands of ancient Ghana was brought for European trade ships.
5. Gomez (2018), p.35.
6. *Ibid.*, p.85.
7. K. Shillington (ed.), *Encyclopedia of African History*, I, (Fitzroy Dearborne, 2005), p.585.
8. Devisse, J., 'Trade and trade routes in West Africa', in M. Efasi (ed), *General History of Africa, III: Africa from the Seventh to the Eleventh Century* (UNESCO, 1994), p.389.
9. Department of the Arts of Africa, Oceania, and the Americas, 'The Empires of the Western Sudan: Ghana Empire', in Heilbrunn, *Timeline of Art History* The Metropolitan Museum of Art, New York, 2000), http://www.metmuseum.org/toah/hd/ghan/hd_ghan.htm; accessed October 2000.
10. Dévisse, J., 'Une enquête à développer: le problème de la propriété des mines en Afrique de l'Ouest du VIII au XVI siècle', *Miscellanea Charles Verlinden (Bulletin de l'Institut Historique Belge de Rome)*, 44 (1974), pp.201–19.
11. Dramani-Issifou, Z., 'Islam as a social system in Africa since the seventh century', in M. Efasi (ed.), *General History of Africa, III: Africa from the Seventh to the Eleventh century* (UNESCO, 1994), p.102.
12. Abitbol, M., 'Juifs maghrébins et commerce transsaharien du VIIIe au XVe siècles' in *2000 ans d'histoire africaine. Le sol, la parole et l'écrit. Mélanges en hommage à Raymond Mauny. Tome II* (Société française d'histoire d'outre-mer, 1981), pp.561–77.
13. Horton, M., 'Egypt', in J. Middleton (ed.), *Encyclopedia of Africa South of the Sahara* (Scribners, 1997), v.2, p.31.

14. Schultz, W., 'Mansa Musa's Gold in Mamluk Cairo', in J. Pfeiffer and S.A. Quinn (eds), *History and Historiography of Post-Mongol Central Asia and the Middle East* (Harrassowitz Verlag, 2006), pp.428–47.

15. Gråberg, G., *Annali di geografia e di statistica* (Genoa, 1802), vol. II, p.290.

16. Levtzion, N., 'Sudanic Empires of Western Africa', in J. Middleton (ed.), *Encyclopedia of Africa South of the Sahara* (Scribners, 1997), v.4, p.179.

17. Nightingale, P., 'Monetary Contraction and Mercantile Credit in Later Medieval England', *The Economic History Review*, Vol. 43, No. 4 (November 1990), pp.560–75; Spufford, P., *Money and its use in Medieval Europe* (CUP, 1988).

18. Etting, V., *Queen Margrete I, 1353–1412, and the Founding of the Nordic Union* (Brill, 2004), p.27. As employees were forbidden to marry local girls, the term became synonymous with 'bachelor'.

19. Platt, p.357.

20. Green, M.H., *Taking 'Pandemic' Seriously: Making the Black Death Global* (TMG 1, 2014): *Pandemic Disease in the Medieval World: Rethinking the Black Death*, ed. Monica Green (2014). *The Medieval Globe Books*, 1. URL https://scholarworks.wmich.edu/medieval_globe/1; consulted 29 December 2019.

21. Tignor, A., *et al.*, *Worlds Together, Worlds Apart, Volume 1: Beginnings to the 15th Century* (W.W Norton & Company, 2014), p.407; *Raoult, D., Paleomicrobiology: Past Human Infections (Springer, 2008)*, p.152.

22. Haensch, S., *et al.*, 'Distinct Clones of Yersinia pestis Caused the Black Death', *PLoS Pathog*, 6 (10) (2010).

23. Miskimin, H.A., *The Economy of Early Renaissance Europe, 1300–1460* (Cambridge University Press, 1975); Platt, C., *King Death* (UCL Press, 1996). In the forty years after 1369, England's coin production fell by 85 per cent. Nightingale, P., 'Monetary Contraction and Mercantile Credit in Later Medieval England', *The Economic History Review*, Vol. 43, No. 4 (November 1990), p.561.

24. Cowen, R., 'Medieval Silver and Gold', http://mygeologypage.ucdavis.edu/cowen/~gel115/115CH7.html.

25. Miskimin, p.146.

26. Spufford, p.345.

27. These are the figures for Torre Vedras and Sintra; Rodrigues, Ana Maria S.A., 'The Black Death and Recovery 1348–500', in D. Freire and P. Lains (eds), *An Agrarian History of Portugal, 1000–2000: Economic Development on the European Frontier* (Brill, 2017), pp.45–70.

28. Broadberry, S., Campbell, Bruce M.S., and van Leeuwen, Bas, 'English Medieval Population: Reconciling time series and cross-sectional evidence', University of Warwick unpublished manuscript (2010), URL https://warwick.ac.uk/fac/soc/economics/staff/sbroadberry/wp/medievalpopulation7.pdf; consulted 2 July 2018.

29. De Oliveira Marques, A.H., *Daily Life in Portugal in the Late Middle Ages* (University of Wisconsin Press, 1971).

30. Rodrigues, p.56.

31. Azurara, *Crónica de Ceuta*, ch. 9, cited in Diffie, B.W., *Foundations of the Portuguese Empire, 1415–1580* (University of Minnesota Press, 1977).

32. Phillips, W.D., Jr., *Slavery in Medieval and Early Modern Iberia* (University of Pennsylvania Press, 2013).

33. Axelson, E., 'Prince Henry the Navigator and the Discovery of the Sea Route to India', *The Geographical Journal* 127, 2 (June 1961), pp.145–55.

34. A squire, *escudeiro*, was a commoner under royal patronage entitled to his own stable and retinue. Azzam, A.R., *The Other Exile: The Remarkable Story of Fernão Lopes, the Island of Saint Helena, and a Paradise Lost* (Icon Books, 2017), ch.2.

35. Schwarz, G.R., *The History and Development of Caravels* (unpublished MA thesis, University of Texas A&M University, 2008).

Chapter 13

 1. Vilar, P., *A History of Gold and Money, 1450 to 1920* (Verso, 1991), pp.44–45.
 2. Nicolai, R., *The Enigma of the Origin of Portolan Charts: A Geodetic Analysis of the Hypothesis of a Medieval Origin* (Brill, 2016); Blackler, A., *Conference Review – First International Workshop on the Origin and Evolution of Portolan Charts, Lisbon, June 2016*, e-Perimetron, v.12 (1) (2017), pp.37–39, includes the information that the earliest known portolan chart has been carbon-dated to a likely twelfth-century date. This appears to tie in with changes in Italian navigators' ability to ship crusaders to the Holy Land spelt out in Pryor, J.H., 'A Medieval Mediterranean Maritime Revolution: Crusading by Sea ca. 1096–1204', in Carlson, D.N. *et al.*, *Maritime Studies in the Wake of the Byzantine Shipwreck at Yassiada, Turkey* (Texas A&M University Press, 2015), pp.174–88.
 3. http://cartographic-images.net/Cartographic_Images/249_Fra_Mauros_Mappamundi.html.
 4. Feinberg, H.M., 'Africans and Europeans in West Africa: Elminans and Dutchmen on the Gold Coast During the Eighteenth Century', *The American Philosophical Society*, Vol. 79, Part 7 (1989), p.27.
 5. Chouin, G., 'The "Big Bang" Theory Reconsidered: Framing Early Ghanaian History', *Transactions of the Historical Society of Ghana*, New Series, No. 14 (2012), pp.13–-40.
 6. Birmingham, D., 'The Regimento Da Mina', *Transactions of the Historical Society of Ghana*, Vol. 11 (1970), pp.1–7.
 7. Matsukawa, K., 'European Images of India before the Rise of Orientalism in the Late Eighteenth Century' (M. Phil thesis, London School of Economics, 2000), URL http://etheses.lse.ac.uk/1600/1/U148238.pdf; consulted 15 November 2009.
 8. *The Travels of Marco Polo: The Complete Yule-Cordier Edition* (Courier Corporation, 1993), p.287. It is reckoned today as the sixth-largest island.
 9. Ibn Battuta, *The Travels of Ibn Battuta: in the Near East, Asia and Africa, 1325–1354* (Courier Corporation, 2013).
10. https://www.indephedia.com/2019/09/history-of-naming-sumatra-island.html; consulted 13 November 2021.
11. Crowley, R., *Conquerors: How Portugal Seized the Indian Ocean and Forged the First Global Empire* (Faber & Faber, 2015).
12. Khan, I. Alam, 'Coming of Gunpowder to the Islamic world and North India: Spotlight on the role of the Mongols', *Journal of Asian History*, Vol. 30, No. 1 (1996), pp.27–45.
13. A. Pertusi, (ed.), *La Caduta di Costantinopoli* (Fondazione Lorenzo Valla, Verona, 1976).
14. Camões, Luís Vaz de, *The Lusiads* Canto Four, v. 94 Camões 99, tr. Landeg White (Oxford University Press, 1997).
15. Ndoro, W., 'Great Zimbabwe', *Scientific American*, Vol. 277, No. 5 (November 1997), pp.94–99.
16. Gayre, R., *The Origin of the Zimbabwean Civilization* (Galaxie Press, Rhodesia, 1972). The history of Great Zimbabwe has been massively overlaid by racist efforts to prove that the city cannot have been built by Africans – this has resulted in the destruction of most of the archaeological site and the creation of a deliberately falsified history, to which Gayre made a very significant unfortunate contribution. But he may be right about the gold.
17. Mearns, D.L., *et al.*, 'A Portuguese East Indiaman from the 1502–1503 Fleet of Vasco da Gama off Al Hallaniyah Island, Oman: an interim report', *International Journal of Nautical Archaeology*, 45 (2016), pp.331–50.
18. Corrêa, G., *The Three Voyages of Vasco da Gama, and his Viceroyalty: from the Lendas da India of Gaspar Corrêa* (Hakluyt Society, 1869), p.87.
19. Crowley, R., *Conquerors: How Portugal Seized the Indian Ocean and Forged the First Global Empire* (Faber & Faber, 2015), p.74.

20. Crowley (2015), p.90.
21. O'Connell, J., *The Book of Spice: From Anise to Zedoary* (Profile Books, 2015), Introduction.
22. Freedman, P., *Out of the East* (Yale University Press, 2008), p.4.
23. *The Suma Oriental of Tomé Pires* (Hakluyt Society, 1944), II, p.285.
24. Corrêa, G., *The Three Voyages of Vasco da Gama, and his Viceroyalty: from the Lendas da India of Gaspar Corrêa* (Hakluyt Society, 1869), p.295.
25. Corrêa (1869), p.299.
26. Corrêa (1869), pp.331–32.
27. Smith, R., 'Shipwreck in the Forbidden Zone', *National Geographic* (October 2009); CTV news, 15 September 2017, URL https://www.ctvnews.ca/sci-tech/in-namibia-1533-portuguese-shipwreck-s-relics-hidden-away-1.3590932; consulted 17 July 2018.
28. 'Portuguese 400 year old shipwreck found off Cascais', BBC News, 24 September 2018, URL https://www.bbc.co.uk/news/world-europe-45630260; consulted 15 November 2019.
29. The word '*saudade*' can be found in poetry of the fourteenth century and is associated originally with the crusades of the conquest, but the 'age of discoveries' burned it into the character of Portuguese civilization.
30. Tripe eating is seen as a symbol of Portuguese loyal endurance; the fourteenth-century chronicler Fernão Lopez said that it had to be eaten in Lisbon during the siege of 1384, and it is also said to have been all that the people of Porto left themselves with when they supplied ships for the invasion of Ceuta in 1415. In this version it becomes their willing sacrifice for the profit of the kingdom.
31. Halikowski Smith, S., 'Portugal and the European spice trade, 1480–1580' (European University Institute, 2001), EUI PhD theses, Department of History and Civilization, p.361. Retrieved from Cadmus, European University Institute Research Repository, at http://hdl.handle.net/1814/5828, 22 April 2020.
32. Wake, C.H.H., 'The changing pattern of Europe's pepper and spice imports, ca 1400–1700', *Journal of European Economic History*, Vol. 8, Edition 2 (1979), pp.361–403, 374.
33. Godinho, V.M., *Os Descobrimentos e a Economia Mundial* (Lisbon, 1982–84), vol. 3:10, quoted in Costa, L.F., *et al.*, *An Economic History of Portugal, 1143–2010* (Cambridge University Press, 2016), p.86.
34. Palma, N., and Reis, J., 'From Convergence to Divergence: Portuguese Economic Growth, 1527–1850', *Journal of Economic History* 79 (2) (2019), pp.477–506.
35. Costa, L.F., Palma, N., and Reis, J., 'The great escape? The contribution of the empire to Portugal's economic growth, 1500–1800', *European Review of Economic History*, 19(1) (2015), pp.1–22.
36. Halikowski Smith, S., '"Profits sprout like tropical plants": a fresh look at what went wrong with the Eurasian spice trade c. 1550–1800', *Journal of Global History* 3 (2008), pp.389–418.
37. Severy, M., 'Portugal's Sea Road to the East', *National Geographic* 182, 5 (November 1992), p.78.
38. Zamora, M., *Reading Columbus* (University of California Press, 1993), p.19.
39. E.G. Bourne (ed.), *The Northmen, Columbus and Cabot, 985–1503: The Voyages of the Northmen; The Voyages of Columbus and of John Cabot* (Charles Scribner's Sons, 1906), p.412.
40. Morison, S.E., *Christopher Columbus; Admiral of the Ocean Sea* (Oxford University Press, 1942), p.34. The true distance is closer to 11,000 nautical miles.
41. Masakatsu, M., 'The Legend of "Zipangu", the Land of Gold', *Nipponia* No. 45 (15 June 2008).
42. Vilar, p.56.

Chapter 14

1. http://columbuslandfall.com/ccnav/longi.shtml; consulted 28 July 2018.
2. Olson, D.W., 'Columbus and an eclipse of the Moon', *Sky & Telescope* (October 1992), pp.437–40.
3. Thomas (2003), p.219.
4. Estevez, J., 'Origins of the word Taino', researchgate.net, 28 September 2016.

5. Van Wyck Brooks (tr.), *Christopher Columbus: the Journal of his First Voyage to America. (An abstract of the original journal made by ... Las Casas* (Jarrolds, 1925).

6. They were called Island Arawacs, but since the 1980s they have been known as Taino to avoid confusion with the Arawacs of South America. According to William Keegan, 'the name glosses as "noble" or "good" in the native language'. Keegan, W.F., 'The "Classic" Taino', in W.F. Keegan and C.L. Hofman (eds), *The Oxford Handbook of Caribbean Archaeology* (Oxford University Press, 2013), pp.70–83. Bartolomé de las Casas estimated the first contact population at 4 million: modern estimates are between 100,000 (Rosenblat, A., 'The population of Hispaniola at the time of Columbus', in W. Denevan (ed.), *The Native Population of The America in 1492* (University of Wisconsin Press, 1992) and 8 million (Cook, S.F., and Simpson, L.B., *The Population of Central Mexico in the Sixteenth Century* (AMS Press, 1948).

7. Gonzales Fernandez de Oviedo, quoted by Guerra, F., 'The Earliest American Epidemic: The Influenza of 1493', *Social Science History*, Vol. 12, No. 3 (Autumn 1988), pp.305–25.

8. Cook, N.D., 'Sickness, Starvation, and Death in Early Hispaniola', *The Journal of Interdisciplinary History*, Vol. 32, No. 3 (Winter 2002), pp.349–86.

9. Colombo, C., 'Memorial que para los Reyes Católicos dio el Almirante a don Antonio de Torres' (30 January 1494), in Ignacio Anzoátegui (ed.), *Los cuatro viajes del almirante y su testamento* (Madrid, 1971), p.158.

10. Cook, N.D., *Born to Die: Disease and New World Conquest, 1492–1650* (Cambridge University Press, 1998), p.35.

11. Earle, R., '"If You Eat Their Food ...": Diets and Bodies in Early Colonial Spanish America', *The American Historical Review*, Vol. 115, No. 3 (June 2010), pp.688–713.

12. Molina-Cruz, A., and Barillas-Mury, C.,. 'The remarkable journey of adaptation of the Plasmodium falciparum malaria parasite to New World anopheline mosquitoes', *Memórias do Instituto Oswaldo Cruz*, 109(5) (2014), pp.662–67.

13. Leathlobhair, M.N., *et al.*, 'The evolutionary history of dogs in the Americas', *Science*, Vol. 361, Issue 6397 (6 July 2018), pp.81–85.

14. Earle (2010), p.703.

15. Diamond, J., *Guns, Germs and Steel* (New York, 1997), p.210; Harper, K.N., Ocampo, P.S., Steiner, B.M., George, R.W., Silverman, M.S., Bolotin, S., *et al.*, 'On the Origin of the Treponematoses: A Phylogenetic Approach', *PLoS Negl Trop Dis* 2(1) (2008), e148, https://doi.org/10.1371/journal.pntd.0000148.

16. Chaunu, H. and P., *Séville et l'Atlantique, 1504–1650*, vol. 8 (Paris, 1959), p.104.

17. Smith, R.C., 'Colonial Towns of Spanish and Portuguese America', *Journal of the Society of Architectural Historians*, Vol. 14, No. 4, Town Planning Issue (December 1955), pp.3–12.

18. PARES, Portal de Archivos Españoles – Archivo General de Indias, *INDIFERENTE*, 418, L.1, F. 41V. See 'First Blacks in the Americas: the African Presence in the Dominican Republic', The Dominican Studies Institute, http://firstblacks.org/en/summaries/timeline/; consulted 28 July 2021.

19. PARES, Portal de Archivos Españoles, Archivo General de Indias, *INDIFERENTE*, 418, L.1, F.180V-181V-1-Imagen Núm: 1/3.

20. Guerra (1988), p.319. His argument that this was an old world epidemic is aggressively debunked in Henige, D., *Numbers from Nowhere: the American Indian Contact Population Debate* (University of Oklahoma Press, 1998), pp.168–75.

21. Varela, C., and Aguirre, I., *La caída de Cristóbal Colón: el juicio de Bobadilla* (Marcial Pons Historia, 2006).

22. Hamilton, E.J., 'Imports of American Gold and Silver Into Spain, 1503–1660', *The Quarterly Journal of Economics*, Vol. 43, No. 3 (May 1929), pp.436–72.

23. El Rey al Almirante, Sevilla 6 de Junio de 1511. MSS. Coleccion de Munoz, tomo 90, quoted in Helps, A., *The conquerors of the New world and their bondsmen: being a narrative of the principal events which led to negro slavery in the West Indies and America* (London, 1848–52), p.232.
24. Deagan, K.A., and Mari a Cruxent, J., *Archaeology at La Isabela: America's First European Town* (Yale University Press, 2002).
25. Anderson-Córdova (2017), pp.89–91.
26. The epidemic is well documented. Cook, N.D., 'Sickness, Starvation, and Death in Early Hispaniola', *The Journal of Interdisciplinary History*, Vol. 32, No. 3 (Winter 2002), pp.349–86.
27. Technically, he was an '*encomendero*' with a grant of ownership of a number of indigenous people from whom he could demand work in exchange for religious instruction.
28. Anderson-Córdova, K.F., *Surviving Spanish Conquest: Indian Fight, Flight, and Cultural Transformation in Hispaniola and Puerto Rico* (University of Alabama Press, 2017), p.60.
29. Geggus, D., *Haitian Revolutionary Studies* (Indiana University Press, 2002), p.208.
30. Ozuna, A., 'Rebellion and Anti-colonial Struggle in Hispaniola: From Indigenous Agitators to African Rebels', *Africology: The Journal of Pan African Studies*, vol. 11, no. 7 (May 2018).
31. De Charlevoix, P.F. Xavier, *Histoire de l'isle espagnole ou de Saint Domingue* (Amsterdam, 1733), 2: pp.219–33, referenced in Geggus, D. (2002), p.212.
32. Happel, E., 'Community Organizations in Haiti Say "NO" to Newmont', 18 May 2020, https://www.earthworks.org/blog/community-organizations-in-haiti-say--to-newmont/; consulted 30 July 2021.

Chapter 15

1. It was discovered in a Paris bookshop in the winter of 1831–32. Merás, L.M., 'La carta de Juan de la Cosa: interpretación e historia', *Monte Buciero (Ayuntamiento de Santoña)* 4 (2000), pp.71–86.
2. There is an overlay of modern mapping in Robles Macias, L.A., 'Juan de la Cosa's Projection: A Fresh Analysis of the Earliest Preserved Map of the Americas', *Coordinates* (24 May 2010), p.18, http://purl.oclc.org/coordinates/a9.htm; consulted 5 January 2020.
3. Siebold, J., 'Monography on the Portolan World Map, Juan de la Cosa, 1500' (1998), URL http://cartographic-images.net/Cartographic_Images/305_de_la_Cosa.html; consulted 26 July 2018.
4. Martín-Merás, L., 'La Carta de Juan de la Cosa: interpretación e historia', *Monte Buciero* 4 (2000), pp.71–85.
5. Fernanádez-Armesto, F., *Amerigo: The Man Who Gave His Name to America* (Random House, 2008).
6. Lester, T., *The Fourth Part of the World: The Race to the Ends of the Earth and the Epic Story of the Map that gave America its Name* (Profile Books, 2009), p.322.
7. Nowell, C.E., 'The Discovery of Brazil – Accidental or Intentional?', *The Hispanic American Historical Review*, Vol. 16, No. 3 (August 1936), pp.311–38.
8. R. E. de Azevedo Basto (ed.), Pereira, D.P., *Esmeraldo de situ orbis* (Lisbon, Imprensa Nacional, 1892).
9. The arguments are set out and rebutted in Greenlee, W.B., *The Voyage of Pedro Álvares Cabral to Brazil and India: from Contemporary Documents and Narratives* (Routledge, 2017), but the debate remains open.
10. Popescu, O., *Studies in the History of Latin American Economic Thought* (Routledge, 2001), p.75.
11. De Oviedo y Valdés, G. Fernández, *Oviedo on Columbus* (Brepols, 2000), p.83.
12. De Las Casas, B., *Historia de las Indias*, Vol. 5 (Madrid, 1875), p.496. A *castellano* was 4.6 grams of gold.
13. *Tumbaga* is a word adopted by the Spanish in the nineteenth century from the language of Manila. Blust, R., 'Tumbaga in Southeast Asia and South America', *Anthropos*, Bd. 87, H. 4/6 (1992), pp.443–57.

14. Martinón-Torres, M., Valcárcel Rojas, R., Sáenz Samper, J., and Filomena Guerra, M., 'Metallic encounters in Cuba: The technology, exchange and meaning of metals before and after Columbus,' *Journal of Anthropological Archaeology*, Vol. 31, Issue 4 (2012), pp.439–54, http://www.sciencedirect.com/science/article/pii/S0278416512000268.

15. Keegan, W.F., *Taino Indian Myth and Practice: The Arrival of the Stranger King* (University Press of Florida, 2007).

16. Keegan, W.F., (2007).

17. The Tairona lived in the lower region of the Sierra and were wiped out by the Spanish in a genocidal campaign early in the seventeenth century. The Kogi remember these inhabitants as Nañi. Their own ancestors lived above 600 metres, and see themselves as guardians of Nañi knowledge. See Falk Xué Para Witte, 'Living the Law of Origin: The Cosmological, Ontological, Epistemological, and Ecological Framework of Kogi Environmental Politics' (PhD thesis, Downing College, Cambridge, 2017), p.172.

18. Keegan, W.F., 'The "Classic" Taino', in Keegan *et al.* (eds), *The Oxford Handbook of Caribbean Archaeology* (Oxford University Press, 2013).

19. MacNutt, F.A., *De Orbis Novo: The Eight Decades of Peter Martyr D'Anghera* (G.P. Putnam, 1912), Vol. I, p.220.

20. Squier, E.G., 'More about the gold discoveries of the isthmus', *Harper's Weekly* (20 August 1859), p.7.

Chapter 16

1. https://www.nytimes.com/1981/04/19/world/gold-bar-found-in-mexico-thought-to-be-cortes-s.html?module=ArrowsNav&contentCollection=World&action=keypress&region=FixedLeft&pgtype=article; consulted 24 July 2018; https://www.upi.com/Archives/1981/03/27/A-32000-chunk-of-Montezumas-Treasure-is-found/9719354517200/; consulted 24 July 2018.

2. Colección de documentos inéditos relativos al descubrimiento, conquista, y organisación de las posesiones españolas de ultramar, Madrid (1880–1932), XXXIX, p.241, quoted in Thomas, H., *Rivers of Gold; The Rise of the Spanish Empire* (Weidenfeld & Nicolson, 2003), p.289.

3. Ávila, A., *et al.*, 'Cinnabar in Mesoamerica: poisoning or mortuary ritual?', *Journal of Archaeological Science*, 49 (2014), pp.48–56.

4. Panama was a fishing port, and the indigenous word meant 'plenty of fish'.

5. 200,000 according to Smith, M.E., 'City Size in Late Postclassic Mesoamerica', *Journal of Urban History* (2005), pp.403–34, 50,000 according to Townsend (2019). The city covered 5.4 square miles, and Smith suggests a population of 40,600 per square mile, which is similar to modern Seoul or Cairo. S.T. Evans, in *Ancient Mexico and Central America: Archaeology and Culture History* (Thames & Hudson, 2013), p.549, suggests in effect a density of under 17,000. Manilla has about 20,000 to the square mile, so the argument is debatable.

6. Moctezuma, E. Matos, 'Archaeology & Symbolism in Aztec Mexico: The Templo Mayor of Tenochtitlan', *Journal of the American Academy of Religion*, Vol. 53, No. 4, (December 1985), pp.797–813.

7. http://www.mexicolore.co.uk/aztecs/ask-us/how-much-gold-did-the-conquistadores-get.

8. There is, of course, a huge literature on the Spanish conquest of Mexico. I have primarily used Townsend, C., *Fifth Sun: A New History of the Aztecs* (Oxford University Press, 2019), Restall, M., *When Montezuma met Cortés* (Harper Collins, 2018), Thomas, H., *The Conquest of Mexico* (Pimlico, 1993) and *Rivers of Gold; The Rise of the Spanish Empire* (Weidenfeld and Nicolson, 2003), together with Van Tuerenhout, D.R., *The Aztecs. New Perspectives* (ABC-CLIO, 2005)'

9. Mexica (Aztec) & Tlaxcala accounts of the Spanish Conques, 1500s, URL https://nationalhumanitiescenter.org/pds/amerbegin/contact/text7/mexica_tlaxcala.pdf; consulted 15 January 2024; Townsend, C., *Fifth Sun: A New History of the Aztecs* (Oxford University Press, 2019), p.102.

10. Thomas (2004), pp.178–87.
11. http://www.mexconnect.com/articles/1238-did-you-know-lots-of-real-aztec-gold-was-only-tumbaga; consulted 7 August 2018.
12. Dürer, Albrecht, *Diary of his Journey to the Netherlands. 1520–21* (Lund Humphries, 1971).
13. Atwood, R., 'Aztec Warrior Wolf', *Archaeology* (11 December 2017), URL https://www.archaeology.org/issues/281-1801/features/6170-mexico-aztec-wolf-burial; consulted 8 August 2018.
14. H. Cortés and, M.J. Baynard (ed. and trans.), *Five Letters of Cortés to the Emperor* (Norton, 1969), p.70.
15. McCaa, R., 'Spanish and Nahuatl Views on Smallpox and Demographic Catastrophe in Mexico', *The Journal of Interdisciplinary History*, Vol. 25, No. 3 (Winter 1995), pp.397–431.
16. M. León Portilla (ed.), *The Broken Spears: The Aztec Account of the Conquest of Mexico* (Beacon Press, 2006).
17. F.A. MacNutt (ed. and tr.), *The Five Letters of Relation from Fernando Cortes to the Emperor Charles V* (G.P. Putnam's Sons, 1908), v.2, p.126.
18. MacNutt (1908), v.2, p.130. A *castellano* weighed 4.11 grams.
19. Hamilton (1929).
20. Alcalá, M., *César y Cortés* (Mexico, 1950).
21. Elliott, J.H., 'The Mental World of Hernán Cortés', *Transactions of the Royal Historical Society*, Vol. 17 (1967), pp.41–58.
22. The Latin of 'Genesis', 1:28.
23. Davis, W., *One River: Explorations and Discoveries in the Amazon Rain Forest* (Random House, 2014), p.34.
24. Ereira (1990), pp.140–41.
25. Friede, J., 'The Catálogo de Pasajeros and Spanish Emigration to America to 1550', *The Hispanic American Historical Review*, Vol. 31, No. 2 (May1951), pp.333–48.
26. Vilches, E., *New World Gold: Cultural Anxiety and Monetary Disorder in Early Modern Spain* (University of Chicago Press, 2010).

Chapter 17
1. De Andagoya, Pascual, *Narrative of the Proceedings of Pedrarias Davila*, tr. C. Robert Markham (Haklyut Society, 1865).
2. Xeres, F., 'Narrative of the Conquest of Peru', in C. Markham (ed.), *Reports on the Discovery of Peru (Cambridge Library Collection – Hakluyt First Series)* (Cambridge University Press, 2010).
3. Stirling, S., *Pizarro, Conqueror of the Inca* (Sutton Publishing, 2005), p.31.
4. Xeres (2010), p.34.
5. Xeres (2010), p.36.
6. Hernando Pizarro, quoted in Hemming, J., *The Conquest of the Incas* (Macmillan, 1970), p.39.
7. Xeres (2010), p.52.
8. This statement appears in an undated memorial sent to the king by Benardino de Minaya and found in the Archive General de Simancas, Seccion de Estado, Legajo 892, foL 197 ff., quoted in Hanke, L., *The Spanish Struggle for Justice in the Conquest of America* (University of Pennsylvania Press, 1949), p.7.
9. Stirling, S., *Pizarro, Conqueror of the Inca* (Sutton Publishing, 2005), p.42.
10. Silver, J., 'The Myth of El Dorado', *History Workshop*, 34 (1992), pp.1–15.
11. Bauer, R., *The Alchemy of Conquest: Science, Religion, and the Secrets of the New World* (University of Virginia Press, 2019).
12. Hemming, J., *The Search for El Dorado* (Phoenix Press, 1978).
13. *Aluna*, documentary, 1.10.40–1.12.59, https://vimeo.com/54434492; consulted 3 August 2021.
14. McEwan, G.F., *The Incas: New Perspectives* (ABC-CLIO, 2006).

15. Chaliand, G., *Mirrors of a Disaster: The Spanish Military Conquest of America* (Routledge, 2019).

16. On 26 June 1548, a would-be tax collector of the province, Miguel Diaz de Armendáriz, wrote to the king requesting a stamp to mark very small gold coins 'since there is no currency'. Langebaek, C.H., *Mercados, Poblamiento e Integración Étnica Entre los Muiscas, SIGLO XVI* (Banco de la Republica, Columbia, 1987), p.127.

17. De Oviedo, Gonzalo Fernández, *General and Natural History of the Indies, Islands and The Mainland Ocean* (Madrid, 1548/1852), II, p.407.

18. Ereira, A., and Attala, L., 'Zhigoneshi: A Culture of Connection', *Ecocene*, Vol. 2, Issue 1 (June 2021), https://ecocene.kapadokya.edu.tr/index.php/ecocene/article/view/63/49; accessed 5 August 2021.

19. These were not bankruptcies in the sense that a business or an individual goes bankrupt. The sovereign's debt could be repaid when more cash arrived, but it had not arrived in time. It is conventional to refer to these events as bankruptcies. Drelichman. M., and Voth, H.-J., 'Lending to the Borrower From Hell: Debt and Default In the Age of Philip II', *The Economic Journal* Vol. 121, No. 557 (December 2011), pp.1205–27.

20. Drelichman, M., and Voth, H.-J., 'The Sustainable Debts of Philip II: A Reconstruction of Castile's Fiscal Position, 1566–1596', *The Journal of Economic History*, vol. 70, no. 4 (2010), pp.813–42. JSTOR, www.jstor.org/stable/40984779; accessed 13 January 2020.

Chapter 18

1. In 1500, GDP per capita was very similar in England, Spain and Portugal. By 1800, GDP per capita had doubled in England, but had not grown at all in Spain or Portugal. Palma, N., and Santiago-Caballero, C., 'Patterns of Iberian Economic Growth in the Early Modern Period' in *An Economic History of the Iberian Peninsula, 700–2000* (Cambridge University Press, 2004).

2. Álvarez-Nogal, C., and Prados de la Escosura, L., 'The decline of Spain (1500–1850): conjectural estimates', *European Review of Economic History*, 11 (2007), p.350.

3. Hume, D., *Essays, Moral, Political, and Literary* (Edinburgh, 1742), II, III.6.

4. Palma, N., 'American Precious Metals and their Consequences for Early Modern Europe', in S. Battilossi, Y. Cassis and K. Yago (eds), *Handbook of the History of Money and Currency* (Springer, 2020).

5. Karl, T.L., 'The Perils of the Petro-State; Reflections on the Paradox of Plenty', *Journal of International Affairs*, Vol. 53, no.1 (Fall 1999), pp.31–48.

6. *Cortes de los antigua reinos de León y Castilla*, Actas vol. 8,(1586), p.52, and Actas vol. II (1588–93), p.535. quoted in Villar, P., *A History of Gold and Money, 1450 to 1920* (Verso, 1991), p.166.

7. De Azpilcueta, Martín, *Comentario Resolutorio de Cambios* (1556); Bodin, Jean, *Response to the Paradoxes of Malestroit* (Paris, 1568). The rule only holds if the supply of goods remains the same.

8. 'His deseign is to make himselfe monarche of Christendome', H. Middelmore, Letter of 17 June 1572, in Ellis, H., *Original Letters, Illustrative Of English History V3: Including Numerous Royal Letters* (1827), 2nd Ser. III, 5.

9. Albert of Brandenburg, Elector of Mainz; Richard von Greiffenklau zu Vollrads, Elector of Trier; Hermann of Wied, Elector of Cologne; Louis II of Hungary, King of Bohemia; Louis V, Elector Palatine, Elector of the Electoral Palatinate; Frederick III, Elector of Saxony, Elector of Electorate of Saxony; and Joachim I Nestor, Elector of Brandenburg.

10. Knecht, R.J., *Renaissance Warrior and Patron: The Reign of Francis I* (Cambridge University Press, 1994), p.286.

11 Vilches, E., *New World Gold: Cultural Anxiety and Monetary Disorder in Early Modern Spain* (University of Chicago Press, 2010), p.25.

12. De Santa Cruz, A., *Crónica del emperador Carlos V (1551–60)* (Whitworth Press, 2018).

13. De Cieza De Leon, Pedro, *Travels*, tr. C.R. Markham (The Hakluyt Society, 1864), p.77.

14. Anonymous account from an inhabitant of Lille, from Rowen, H.R., *The Low Countries in Early Modern Times: A Documentary History* (Harper & Row, 1972), pp.17–25.

15. Kleinschmidt, H., *Charles V: The World Emperor* (Sutton Publishing, 2004), p.146.

16. Hamilton, E.J., *American Treasure and the Price Revolution in Spain* (Cambridge, Mass., 1934), p.41.

17. Koch, A., *et al.*, 'Earth system impacts of the European arrival and Great Dying in the Americas after 1492', *Quaternary Science Reviews*, Vol. 207 (1 March 2019), pp.13–36. This article argues that the scale of mortality led to the collapse of American indigenous agriculture and had a significant impact on the climate.

18. Kleinschmidt, p.146.

19. Quoted in Deckard, S., *Paradise Discourse, Imperialism, and Globalization: Exploiting Eden* (Routledge, 2009), p.29.

20. De Orsúa y Vela, B. Arzáns, *Tales of Potosí* (Brown University Press, 1975).

21. Lane, K., *Potosi: The Silver City that Changed the World* (University of California Press, 2019).

22. Braudel, Ferdinand, *Capitalism and Material Life* (London, 1973), quoted in Zorach, Rebecca, *Blood, Milk, Ink, Gold: Abundance and Excess in the French Renaissance* (University of Chicago Press, 2005), p.197.

23. Gardner, Victoria C., 'Homines non nascuntur, sed figuntur: Benvenuto Cellini's Vita and Self-Presentation of the Renaissance Artist', *The Sixteenth Century Journal*, Vol. 28, No. 2 (Summer 1997), pp.447–65.

24. Cellini, *Vita*, Bk 2, XXXVI.

25. Cellini, *Vita*, Bk 2.

26. Allen, R.C., 'The Great Divergence in European Wages and Prices from the Middle Ages to the First World War', *Explorations in Economic History* 38 (2001), pp.411–47.

27. Baulant, M., 'Prix et salaires a paris au XVIe siècle', *Annales*, 31e Année, No. 5 (September–October 1976), pp.954–95.

28. Hoskins, W.G., 'The Rebuilding of Rural England, 1570–1640', *Past & Present*, No. 4 (November 1953), pp.44–59.

29. Allen, R.C., (2001).

30. Kershaw, S.E., 'Power and Duty in the Elizabethan aristocracy: George, Earl of Shrewsbury, the Glossopdale Dispute and the Council', in G.W. Bernard (ed.), *The Tudor Nobility* (Manchester University Press, 1992), p.269.

31. *Ibid.*, p.71.

32. Pamuk, Ş., 'The Price Revolution in the Ottoman Empire Reconsidered', *International Journal of Middle East Studies*, Vol. 33, No. 1 (February 2001), pp.69–89.

33. http://www.dailysabah.com/real-estate/2015/08/16/istanbuls-most-expensive-place-to-rent-property-the-grand-bazaar, with gold at £32,000 a kilo.

34. Pastor, L., *The History of the Popes from the Close of the Middle Ages*, vol. VIII (Herder Book Co., 1950), p.361.

35. Kiermayr, R., 'How Much Money was Actually in the Indulgence Chest?', *The Sixteenth Century Journal*, 17, No. 3 (Autumn 1986), pp.303–18.

36. Atherstone, A., and Benson, K., *Reformation: A World in Turmoil* (Lion Books, 2015), p.26.

37. J.C. Olin (ed.), *The Catholic Reformation: Savonarola to Ignatius Loyola* (New York, 1992), p.80.

38. The phrase does not appear in Tetzel's surviving writings but was widely reported and formed part of Luther's ninety-five theses.

39. Edwards, M.U., *Printing, Propaganda and Martin Luther* (University of California Press, 1994), p.16.

40. He said: 'I, the German prophet seek salvation and blessedness not for myself but for the Germans.''Address To The Nobility of the German Nation' (1520), from the Internet History Sourcebooks Project, tr. C.A. Buchheim.

41. Luther, M., *On trading and usury* (1524), from *Works of Martin Luther* (A.J. Holman Company, 1915), vol. 4.

42. Maltby, W., *The Reign of Charles V* (Palgrave, 2002), p.103.

Chapter 19

1. The Treaty of Tordesillas of 1494 left the Pacific without a dividing line, so that was drawn in the Treaty of Zaragoza in 1529. It was well known that no one could establish longitude in the ocean, and as some Portuguese walked to the negotiations, 'a little boy who stood guarding his mother's washing asked whether they were the men that were dividing up the world with the Emperor. When they answered "Yes", he pulled up his shirt and showed them his bare arse, saying: "Come and draw your line here down the middle."' Mártyr de Anglería, P., *Décadas del Nuevo Mundo* (Maxtor, 2012), p.493.

2. Israel, J., 'López Pereira of Amsterdam, Antwerp And Madrid: Jew, New Christian, and advisor to the Conde-Duque de Olivares', *Studia Rosenthaliana*, Vol. 19, No. 2 (October 1985), pp.109–26; idem., *Empires and Entrepots: Dutch, the Spanish Monarchy and the Jews, 1585–1713* (Bloomsbury, 1990), pp.250–53.

3. I later discovered that this was a Rabbinic teaching from Yoshua ben Sira in the second century BCE: 'Do not lend to one more powerful than yourself; or if you lend, count it as lost' (Ben Sidra 8:12), evidently passed down the generations as Jews rejected the text as non-Biblical. F. Braudel, in *The Mediterranean and the Mediterranean World in the Age of Philip II* (Glasgow, 1966), p.362, argued that Philip's bankruptcies cost his bankers dear. The economic historians M. Drelichman and H.-J. Voth, in the splendidly titled *Lending to the Borrower from Hell* (Princeton University Press, 2014), p.149, argue that Braudel was mistaken and his bankers carried on lending willingly, but the Fuggers have evidence of refusal. When Philip asked Marx Fugger for a new loan of a million ducats in 1575, the firm totalled up his outstanding liability to them at 6 million ducats and prevaricated. 'This is essentially sort of the beginning of the end, at least in terms of the financing relationship between the Fugger firm and the Habsburg family' (Count Alexander Fugger Babenhausen, *Titian: Behind Closed Doors*, BBC2, 4 April 2020). Conscious of my grandmother's advice, I have never deliberately lent money to princes.

4. For comparison, US military expenditure in 2015 was \$0.6 trillion, 18 per cent of total Federal revenues.

5. The term derives from *Marui*, which Strabo gave as the native name for the inhabitants of Mauretania. It came to mean the inhabitants of the Roman province of Africa and thus, eventually, the Islamic invaders of Iberia.

6. Fleet, K., 'Ottoman expansion in the Mediterranean', in S. Faroqhi and K. Fleet (eds), *The Cambridge History of Turkey*, (Cambridge University Press, 2012), pp.141–72.

7. Serim, N., 'The Causes of the Financial Crisis That Began in the 16th Century and Continued until the Tanzimat Era in the Ottoman Empire', *Yönetim Bilimleri Dergisi* (2012), Cilt 10, Sayı 20, pp.181–94, URL http://dergipark.gov.tr/download/article-file/46291; consulted 3 April 2019.

8. Durucu, N., 'Suleiman The Magnificent: an Ottoman Sultan and Jeweler' (2017), https://www.researchgate.net/publication/335420655_Suleiman_the_Magnificent_An_Ottoman_Sultan_and_Jeweler; consulted 5 August 2021.

9. Clot, A., *Suleiman the Magnificent* (Saqi Books, 2005), Ch.10.

10. İnalcık, Halil, 'Osmanlı Para ve Ekonomi Tarihine Toplu Bir Bakış, Makaleler-I' ['A Synopsis of the Ottoman Money and Economy History, Articles-1'], (Ankara, Dogu-Bati Publications, 2005), p.172.

11. Hall, B.S., *Weapons and Warfare in Renaissance Europe: Gunpowder, Technology and Tactics* (Johns Hopkins University Press, 1997), pp.176–78.

12. Guilmartin, J.F. Jr., *Gunpowder and Galleys: Changing Technology and Mediterranean Warfare at Sea in the Sixteenth Century* (Cambridge University Press, 1974), p.275.

13. Drelichman, M., and Voth, H.-J., 'The Sustainable Debts of Philip II: A Reconstruction of Castile's Fiscal Position, 1566–1596', *The Journal of Economic History*, Vol. 70, No. 4 (December 2010), pp.813–42, Fig.4, quoted in Serim (2012).

14. Elizabeth was making massive borrowings in Antwerp to sustain a budget of £14,000 a year on the navy, £45,000 in Ireland and £36,000 a year on Berwick; Hammer, P.E.J., *Elizabeth's Wars: War, Government and Society in Tudor England, 1544–1604* (Palgrave, 2003), 'The Cost of War, 1559–69'. A pound was 3 ducats.

15. Cressy, D., *Saltpeter, The Mother of Gunpowder* (Oxford University Press, 2013), p.51.

16. L'Abbé de Vertot, *The History of the Knights of Malta* (London, 1728), II, p.13.

17. Cantemir, D., trans. N. Tinda, T*he History of the Growth and Decay of the Othman Empire* (London, 1734), pp.223–24.

18. Capponi, N., *Victory of the West: The Story of the Battle of Lepanto* (Macmillan, 2006), p.201.

19. Grell, O.P., *Brethren in Christ: A Calvinist Network in Reformation Europe* (Cambridge University Press, 2011).

20. Olson, J.E., 'Calvin and socio-ethical issues', in D.K. McKim (ed.), *The Cambridge Companion to John Calvin* (Cambridge University Press, 2004), p.168.

21. Treasure, G., *The Huguenots* (Yale University Press, 2013), p.107.

22. Scoville, W.C., 'The Huguenots in the French Economy, 1650–1750', *The Quarterly Journal of Economics*, Vol. 67, No. 3 (August 1953), pp.423–444.

23. Grell.

24. De Bourdeile, P., Seigneur de Brantome, *Memoirs* (Leiden, 1665), pp.75–79.

25. The cost of a musket was less than 2 ducats; Carrion Arregui, I.M., Lette, M. and Oris, M., 'Sixteenth and Seventeenth Century Arms Production in Gipuzkoa', *Technology and Engineering: Proceedings of the XXth International Congress of History of Science (Liège, 20–26 July 1997) Vol. VII* (Brepols, 2000), pp.265–79, table 2.

26. Kamen, H., *Philip of Spain* (Yale University Press, 1998), p.5.

27. Parker, G., *Philip II* (Penguin, 1979), pp.123–24.

28. Conklin, J., 'The Theory of Sovereign Debt and Spain under Philip II', *Journal of Political Economy*, Vol. 106, No. 3 (June 1998), pp.483–513.

29. Spooner, F.C., *The International Economy and Monetary Movements in France, 1493–1725* (Harvard University Press, 1972), Ch.3.

30. Parker, G., 'Mutiny and Discontent in the Spanish Army of Flanders 1572–1607', *Past & Present*, No. 58 (February 1973), pp.38–52.

31. Harreld, D.J., *High Germans In The Low Countries: German Merchants And Commerce In Golden Age Antwerp* (Brill, 2004), p.182.

32. Drelichman, M., and Voth, H.J., *Lending to the Borrower from Hell: Debt, Taxes, and Default in the Age of Philip II* (Princeton University Press, 2014).

33. Walton, T.R., *The Spanish Treasure Fleets* (Pineapple Press Inc., 2002), p.85. A gold ducat weighed 3.5 grams and had a value equivalent to 60 grams of silver.

34. Keynes, J.M., 'Economic Possibilities for Our Grandchildren' (1930), in *Essays in Persuasion* (Palgrave Macmillan, 2010).

35. Scully, R.E., '"In the Confident Hope of a Miracle": The Spanish Armada and Religious Mentalities in the Late Sixteenth Century', *The Catholic Historical Review*, Vol. 89, No. 4 (October 2003), pp.643–70.

36. For Philip's understanding that he was divinely appointed to this messianic role, see Parker, G., 'The Place of Tudor England in the Messianic Vision of Philip II', *Transactions of the Royal Historical Society*, 12 (2002), pp.167–221.

37. Martin, C., and Parker, G., *The Spanish Armada* (Hamish Hamilton, 1988), p.258, https://www.youtube.com/watch?v=wf1hwxa0494.

38. Sarmiento, P., 'La panacea áurea: alquimia y destilación en la corte de Felipe II (1527–1598)', *Dynamis*, 17 (1997), pp.107–40.

39. Laarhoven, R., and Pino Wittermans, E., 'From Blockade to Trade: Early Dutch Relations with Manila, 1600–1750', *Philippine Studies*, Vol. 33, No. 4 (Fourth Quarter 1985), pp.485–504.

40. Koenigsberger, H.G., Mosse, George L., and Bowler, G.Q., *Europe in the Sixteenth Century* (Routledge, 2014), p.55.

41. Israel, J., *Empires and Entrepots: Dutch, the Spanish Monarchy and the Jews, 1585–1713* (A&C Black, 1990).

42. Guenther, G., *Magical Imaginations: Instrumental Aesthetics in the English Renaissance* (University of Toronto Press, 2012), pp.31–33; Parry, G., *The Arch-Conjuror of England, John Dee* (Yale University Press, 2011), pp.200–02.

Chapter 20

1. Mbogoni, L.E.Y., *Human Sacrifice and the Supernatural in African History* (Dar-es-Salaam, 2013), p.129.

2. Debus, A.G., 'Iatrochemistry and the chemical revolution', in von Martels, Z.R.W.M., *Alchemy Revisited; Proceedings of the International Conference of the History of Alchemy at the University of Groningen 17–19 April 1989* (Brill, 1990), p.54.

3. Pregadio, F., *Great Clarity: Daoism and Alchemy in Early Medieval China* (Stanford University Press, 2006), ch.1.

4. Dubs, H.H., 'The beginnings of Alchemy', *Isis*, Vol. 38, No. 1/2 (November 1947), pp.62–86.

5. J. Needham, *Science and Civilisation in China: Spagyrical discovery and invention; : historical survey, from cinnabar elixirs to synthetic insulin*, Cambridge University Press (1974) p.37

6. Dubs (1947). p.82 (n.)

7. Parry, G., 'John Dee, Alchemy and Authority in Elizabethan England', in M. Harmes and V. Bladen (eds), *Supernatural and Secular Power in Early Modern England* (Ashgate Publishing Limited, 2015), p.26.

8. Thompson, C.J.S., *Alchemy and Alchemists* (David & Charles, 2002), pp.143–44. It was sent in great secrecy in vials from Germany, and as no instructions could be found she sent it back without paying. The entertaining operation is detailed in State Papers Elizabeth Vol. CCXLV. 130; CCXLVII. 36; CCXLVII. 72; CCL. 9; CCLI. 57; CCLIV. 46. The mysterious menstruum was described in 'The Humid Path or a Discourse Upon the Vegetable Menstruum of Saturn' in A.E. Waite's *The Alchemical Writings of Edward Kelly* (London, 1893). The 'menstruum' is a menstrual liquid derived from lead, and the transmutation involves a mystical generative energy.

9. E.g. Magee, M., *Shri Matrika Bheda Tantra* (Indological Book House, 1989), p.13.

10. Based on the accounts of Martin Lok, who financed the expedition. Mariner's Museum, *Exploration Through the Ages*, 'Martin Frobisher' (2004), URL ushistoryatlas.com/era1/USHAcom_PS_U01_frobisher_R2.pdf.

11. Parry, G., *The Arch Conjuror of England: John Dee* (Yale University Press, 2012), p.98.

12. McGhee, R., *The Arctic voyages of Martin Frobisher: an Elizabethan Adventure* (Canadian Museum of Civilization, 2001).

13. Pastorino, C., 'Experimental Histories and Francis Bacon's Quantitative Program', *Early Science and Medicine*, 16 (6) (2011), pp.559–60.

14. Baudoin, G., and Auger, R., 'Implications of the mineralogy and chemical composition of lead beads from Frobisher's assay site, Kodlunarn Island, Canada: prelude to Bre-X?', *Canadian Journal of Earth Sciences*, 41, 6 (June 2004), pp.669–81.
15. Mongiatti, A., 'Analysing and smelting noble metals in sixteenth century Austria: a comparative analytic study' (PhD Thesis, Institute of Archaeology, University of London, 2010), URL discovery.ucl.ac.uk/18710/1/18710.pdf.
16. Kisch, B., *Scales and Weights: A Historical Outline* (Yale University Press, 1965), pp.8–9.
17. Holmyard, E.J., *Alchemy* (Penguin Books, 1968), p.175.
18. Wilding, M., 'A Biography of Edward Kelley, the English Alchemist...', in S.J. Linden (ed.), *Mystical Metal of Gold* (AMS Press, 2007).
19. Becher was the man who transformed chemistry by advancing the theory that flammability depended on materials having to contain a previously undetected substance called phlogiston. This is consumed when the material burns. The theory went up in smoke when it was discovered that the ash and smoke of burned paper weigh more than the unburned paper, which could only be explained if phlogiston has a negative weight. Or, of course, if the burning adds oxygen to the paper residues. Becher was a laughing stock through the twentieth century, but as I write, the mathematics of dark matter and dark energy have been shown to make perfect sense if they have negative mass. Come back phlogiston, all may be forgiven?
20. Holmyard, *Alchemy*, pp.126–34.
21. Bacon, F., *Of the Proficience of the Advancement of Learning, Human and Divine* (London, 1605), Bk.1, IV (11).
22. Nummedal, T., *Alchemy and Authority in the Holy Roman Empire* (University of Chicago Press, 2007).
23. Holmyard, *Alchemy*, p.52.
24. Karpenko, V., and Norris, J.A., 'Vitriol in the History of Chemistry', *Chem. Listy* 96 (2002), pp.997–1,005.
25. https://glintpay.com/gold/modern-day-alchemy-making-gold-atoms-cern/.
26. https://www.realclearscience.com/blog/2012/09/modern-day-alchemists-routinely-make-gold.html.
27. Vilar, p.193.

Chapter 21

1. Clark, G., *A Farewell to Arms* (Princeton University Press, 2007), p.47.
2. Breitenlechner, E., *et al.*, 'Reconstructing the History of Copper and Silver Mining in Schwaz, Tirol', in F. Uekoetter (ed.), *Mining in Central Europe: Perspectives from Environmental History* (RCC Perspectives, 2012, no. 10), pp.7–20.
3. http://www.segoviamint.org/english/technology.htm; consulted 25 May 2019.
4. Graulau, J., 'Finance, Industry and Globalisation in the Early Modern Period: the Example of the Metallic Business of the House of Fugger', *Rivista di Studi Politici Internazionali*, Nuova Serie, Vol. 75, No. 4 (300) (October–December 2008), pp.554–98.
5. Fantome, G.S.M., 'Reutilization of our industrial heritage: The unique example of Royal Segovia Mint in Spain (1583)', in J.M. de la Portilla and M. Ceccarelli (eds), *History of Machines for Heritage and Engineering Development* (Springer, 2011), pp.1–45.
6. Murray, G., 'The Segovia Mint Project: Recovering the activity in a Sixteenth-century Mint', *Proceedings of the ICOMON meetings held in Madrid, Spain, 1999* (Museo Casa de la Moneda, Madrid, 2001), pp.329–46.
7. Private communication from Werner Nuding.
8. Ministerio de Cultura, Archivo General de Simancas Estado leg. 671 fol.7.
9. Fantom, G.S.M., *El Real Ingenio de la Moneda de Segovia: maravilla tecnológica del siglo XVI* (Fundación Juanelo Turriano, 2006).

10. Parthasarathi, P., and Riello, G., 'The Indian Ocean in the Long Eighteenth Century', *Eighteenth-Century Studies*, Vol. 48, No. 1, Special Issue: 'The Maritime Eighteenth Century' (Fall 2014), pp.1–19, p.10.

11. Vilar (1991), p.197.

12. Moisés, R.P., 'The Rise of the Spanish Silver Real', *Sigma: Journal of Political and International Studies*, Vol. 23, Article 5 (2005), https://scholarsarchive.byu.edu/sigma/vol23/iss1/5; consulted 10 May 2020.

13. *Ibid.*

14. https://en.wikipedia.org/wiki/List_of_wars_by_death_toll#Modern_wars_with_greater_than_25,000_deaths_by_death_toll; consulted 3 February 2019.

15. Gheyn, Jacob de, *The exercise of armes for calivres, mvskettes, and pikes: after the ordre of his excellence Maurits Prince of Orange* (Zutphen, 1619).

16. Pursell, Brennan C., *The winter king: Frederick V of the Palatinate and the coming of the Thirty Years' War* (Routledge, 2017), 'The Tide Turns'.

17. Bötzinger, Paster Martin, 'Vitae curricula', *Beyträge zur Erläuterung der Hochfürstl*, Sachsen-Hildburghäusischen Kirchen-, Schul- und Landes-Historie, 1 (1750), p.349.

18. Wilson, P.H., *Europe's Tragedy: A New History of the Thirty Years War* (Penguin, 2009), p.401.

19. 'Gallants to Bohemia', in H.E. Rollins (ed.), *A Pepysian Garland: Black-Letter Broadside Ballads of the Years 1595–1639* (Cambridge University Press, 1922), pp.416–17.

20. Rabb, T.K., 'The Effects of the Thirty Years War on the German Economy', *The Journal of Modern History*, Vol. 34, no.1 (March 1962), p.48.

21. Muldrew, C., 'Hard Food for Midas: Cash and Its Social Value in Early Modern England', *Past & Present*, No. 170 (February 2001), pp.78–120.

22. Fissel, M.C., *The Bishops' Wars: Charles I's Campaigns Against Scotland, 1638–1640* (Cambridge University Press, 2011), p.111.

23. Holsti, Kalevi Jaakko, *Peace and War: Armed Conflicts and International Order, 1648–1989* (Cambridge University Press, 1991), p.25.

24. Martin, C., and Parker, G., *The Spanish Armada* (Hamish Hamilton, 1988), p.253.

Chapter 22

1. Bolt, J., and van Zanden, J.L., 'The First Update of the Maddison Project; Re-Estimating Growth Before 1820', Maddison Project Working Paper 4 (2013), URL http://www.ggdc.net/maddison/maddison-project/home.htm; and Maddison, A., 'Historical Statistics of the World Economy: 1–2008 AD', URL www.ggdc.net/maddison/Historical_Statistics/horizontal-file_02-2010.xls; consulted 12 July 2014.

2. The monetary history here is based on von Glahn, R., *Fountain of Fortune: Money and Monetary Policy in China, 1000–1700* (University of California Press, 1996).

3. Attman, A., *The Bullion Flow between Europe and the East, 1000–1750* (Göteborg, 1981).

4. Where they were given permission to trade.

5. Letter from Goa written by Master Ralph Fitch, 1591. Hakluyt, R., *Principal navigations, voyages, traffiques & discoveries of the English nation made by sea or over-land to the remote and farthest distant quarters of the earth at any time within the compasse of these 1600 yeerse* (Glasgow, 1903–05), v.5, p.498.

6. Kindleberger (1990), p.46.

7. Atwell, W.S., 'Another Look at Silver Imports into China, ca. 1635–1644', *Journal of World History*, Vol. 16, No. 4 (December 2005), pp.467–89, p.476.

8. R.P. Moisés, 'The Rise of the Spanish Silver Real', *Sigma: Journal of Political and International Studies*, Vol. 23, Article 5 (2005), https://scholarsarchive.byu.edu/sigma/vol23/iss1/5.

9. Pomeranz, K., *The Great Divergence: China, Europe, and the Making of the Modern World Economy* (Princeton University Press, 2001), p.273, quoted in Palma, N., 'Harbingers of

Modernity: Monetary Injections and European Economic Growth, 1492–1790' (PhD thesis, LSE, 2015/16), URL https://core.ac.uk/download/pdf/46520038.pdf; consulted 11 July 2019.

10. Van Veen, E., and Blussé, L., *Rivalry and Conflict: European Traders and Asian Trading Networks in the 16th and 17th Centuries* (Amsterdam University Press, 2005), p.15.

11. Moisés, R.P., 'The Rise of the Spanish Silver Real', *Sigma: Journal of Political and International Studies*, Vol. 23, Article 5 (2005), https://scholarsarchive.byu.edu/sigma/vol23/iss1/5; consulted 10 May 2020.

12. Atwell, W.S., 'Ming Observers of Ming Decline: Some Chinese Views on the "Seventeenth-Century Crisis" in Comparative Perspective', *The Journal of the Royal Asiatic Society of Great Britain and Ireland*, No. 2 (1988), pp.316–48.

13. Lee, H.F., and Zhang, D.D., 'A tale of two population crises in recent Chinese history', *Climatic Change*, Vol. 116, Issue 2 (2013), pp285–308.

14. Glahn (1996), p.217 ff.

15. Grant, R., *A Sketch of the History of the East-India Company: From Its First Formation to the Passing of the Regulating Act of 1773; with a Summary View of the Changes which Have Taken Place Since that Period in the Internal Administration of British India* (Black, Parry, and Company, 1813), p.64.

16. A cubic foot of 24 carat gold weighs 1,203.74lb.

17. Irigoin, A., 'Global silver: Bullion or Specie? Supply and demand in the making of the early modern global economy', *Economic History Working Papers, No: 285*, LSE (September 2018), http://eprints.lse.ac.uk/90190/1/WP285.pdf; consulted 13 May 2020.

18. Craig, A.K., and Richards, E.J. Jr., *Spanish Treasure Bars From New World Shipwrecks*, I (En Rada Publications, West Palm Beach, Florida, 2003).

19. Goitein, S.D., *Studies in Islamic history and institutions* (Leiden, 1966).

20. Haider, N., 'The Network of Monetary Exchange in the Indian Ocean Trade: 1200–1700', in H. Prabha Ray and E. Alpers (eds), *Cross Currents and Community Networks: The History of the Indian Ocean World* (Oxford University Press, 2007), p.188.

21. Bernier, F., *Travels in the Mogul Empire*, tr. Brock, ed. Constable (London, 1891), p.202.

22. Ogilby, J., *Asia* (1673), p.157.

23. 'Indian households have stocked up to 25,000 tonnes of gold: World Gold Council', *Business Today* (21 May 2019), url https://www.businesstoday.in/current/economy-politics/indian-households-have-stocked-up-to-25000-tonnes-of-gold-world-gold-council/story/348598.html; consulted 20 August 2019.

24. Haider, N., 'The Network of Monetary Exchange in the Indian Ocean Trade: 1200–1700', in H. Prabha Ray and E. Alpers (eds), *Cross Currents and Community Networks: The History of the Indian Ocean World* (Oxford University Press, 2007), pp.181–205.

25. Bernstein, P.L., *The Power of Gold* (John Wiley and Sons, 2000), p.164.

26. Kulke, H., and Rothermund, D., *A History of India* (Psychology Press, 2004), p.80.

27. The age of the *Rig Veda* is a politically charged controversy, but it seems clear that some texts were composed before 1100 BCE, making them among the oldest in any Indo-European language, perhaps similar in date to the 'Song of Miriam' in the *Book of Exodus*.

28. Satapatha-Brahmana V Kajvda 1 Adhyava, 28.

29. *Rig Veda* III, xix 1–2.

30. Stargardt, J., 'The Four Oldest Surviving Pali Texts: the Results of the Cambridge Symposium on the Golden Pali Text of Sri Ksetra (Burma), April 1995', *Journal of the Pali Text Society*, XXI, pp.199–213.

31. Venable, S.L., *Gold: A Cultural Encyclopedia* (ABC-CLIO, 2011), p.283.

32. Moore, E., *et al.*, *Shwedagon* (Thames & Hudson, 1999), p.145.

33. Richter, A., Carpenter, B.W., and Carpenter, B., *Gold Jewellery of the Indonesian Archipelago* (Editions Didier Millet, 2012).

34. Modern Biblical scholars draw attention to the discovery of goddess images in ancient Israelite sites and the expulsion of the Hebrew god's consort, Ashera, from the Jerusalem temple. See, for example, Becking, B., Dijkstra, M., Korpel, M., and Vriezen, K., *Only One God?: Monotheism in Ancient Israel and the Veneration of the Goddess Asherah* (Sheffield Academic Press, 2002).
35. Flueckiger, J.B., 'Wandering from "Hills to Valleys" with the Goddess: Protection and Freedom in the Matamma Tradition of Adhra', in T. Pintchman (ed.), *Women's Lives, Women's Rituals in the Hindu Tradition* (Oxford University Press, 2007), p.39 ff.
36. S. Lee (trans.), *The Travels of Ibn Battuta* (Darf, 1984), pp.108–10.
37. Stein, D., 'Burning Widows, Burning Brides: The Perils of Daughterhood in India', *Pacific Affairs*, Vol. 61, No. 3 (Autumn 1988), pp.465–485.
38. Bhandarkar, D.R., *Lectures on Ancient Indian Numismatics* (Asian Educational Services, 1990), p.65.
39. Grover, A.K., and Pandit, M.K., 'Ancient Gold Mining Activities in India – An Overview', *Iranian Journal of Earth Sciences* 7 (2015), pp.1–13.
40. Haider, N., 'Prices and Wages in India (1200–1800); Source Material, Historiography and New Directions', *Towards a Global History of Prices and Wages* (Utrecht, 19–21 August 2004), p.57, unpublished; URL http://www.iisg.nl/hp.

Chapter 23

1. Southworth, E., 'The Roots of the Dutch Republic's Golden Age Commercial Success' (NEH Seminar For School Teachers, 2015, University of Massachusetts Dartmouth), url http://www1.umassd.edu/euro/2015papers/southworth.pdf; accessed 16 August 2019.
2. Tvede, L., *The Psychology of Finance: Understanding the Behavioural Dynamics of Markets* (John Wiley & Sons, 22 April 2002), p.27.
3. Goldgar, A., *Tulipmania: Money, Honor, and Knowledge in the Dutch Golden Age* (University of Chicago Press, 2008).
4. Zook, G.F., 'The Company Of Royal Adventurers Trading Into Africa', *The Journal of Negro History*, Vol. IV, No. 2 (April 1919).
5. Gipouloux, F., *The Asian Mediterranean: Port cities and Trading Networks in China, Japan and Southeast Asia, 13th–21st Century* (Edward Elgar, 2011), p.138.
6. Probably because it was a *steorling* marked with four stars (*Oxford English Dictionary*).
7. Smith, A., *Lectures on Jurisprudence*, ed. R.L. Meek, D.D. Raphael and P.G. Stein (Clarendon Press, 1978).
8. Pepys, *Diary*, 19 May 1663.
9. Craig, J., *The Mint: A History of the London Mint from A.D. 287 to 1948* (Cambridge University Press, 2011), p.165.
10. Stride, H.G., 'The Gold Coinage Of Charles II', *British Numismatic Journal*, vol. 28 (1955), https://www.britnumsoc.org/publications/Digital%20BNJ/pdfs/1955_BNJ_28_28.pdf; consulted 6 May 2019.
11. Craig, J. (2011), p.157.
12. Pepys, *Diary*, 19 June 1667.
13. House of Commons Journals, XII, 511, 14 February (1699).
14. C. R. Fay, 'Newton and the Gold Standard', *The Cambridge Historical Journal*, Vol. 5, No. 1 (1935), pp. 109-117
15. I. Newton, 'Representation Third to the Right Honourable the Lords Commissioners of His Majesty's Revenue', London, 21 September 1717, reprinted in J.R, McCulloch (ed.), *A Select Collection of Rare and Valuable Tracts on Money*, Augustus M. Kelly (1966), 274-9
16. H. Stewart, 'This is how we let the credit crunch happen, Ma'am', *Guardian* 26 July 2009, https://www.theguardian.com/uk/2009/jul/26/monarchy-credit-crunch consulted 12/5/2020

17. Cherian, J., 'Influence of Isaac Newton in the Development of Economic Thought', https://medium.com/@joel.cherian/influence-of-isaac-newton-in-the-development-of-economic-thought-741683a12185; consulted 12 May 2020.
18. Marquis de Dangeau, *Journal*, II (Cleremont-Ferrand, (2002), p.225 and n., 18 November 1687.
19. Steele, V., *Paris Fashion: a cultural history* (Oxford, 1955), p.21.
20. Charter of the Royal Society, 1662.
21. It has been argued since the 1970s that the idea that imperial trade had a profound economic effect on European economies was old fashioned and 'Marxist'. New research has, however, vindicated the original view – which was also the view at the time. See Freire Costa, L., Palma, N. and Reis, J., 'The great escape? The contribution of the empire to Portugal's economic growth, 1500–1800', *European Review of Economic History*, 19 (1) (2015), pp.1–22, Fig.2.
22. TePaske, J.J., *A New World of Gold and Silver* (Brill, 2010), Table 1-2, p.20.
23. Atwell, W.S., 'Notes on Silver, Foreign Trade, and the Late Ming Economy', *Ch'ing-shih wen-t'i*, vol. 3, no. 8 (1977), pp.1–33.
24. De Riqueti, Victor, Marquis de Mirabeau (1715–89), *Philosophie Rurale, ou Économie générale et politique de l'Agriculture* (Amsterdam, 1763), p.329. Merchants were still to be sneered at by French aristocrats.
25. Mikosch, E., 'The Manufacture And Trade Of Luxury Textiles In The Age Of Mercantilism', *Textile Society of America Symposium Proceedings*, Textile Society of America (1990) 612, p.57, url digitalcommons.unl.edu/cgi/viewcontent.cgi?article=1611&context=tsaconf; consulted 10 May 2019.
26. Pritchard, J., 'The Franco-Dutch War, 1672–1678', in *In Search of Empire: The French in the Americas, 1670–1730* (Cambridge University Press, 2004), pp.267–300.
27. Von Boehn, M., *Menschen und Moden im 17 Jahrhundert* (Munich, 1920), p.151, in Mikosch (1990).
28. Thurston, E., *History of the Coinage of the Territories of the East India Company in the Indian Peninsula and Catalogue of the Coins in the Madras Museum* (Asian Educational Services, 1992).
29. Minutes of the Committee of Trade, 1660–62, BM Add, Ms. 25115, pp.44–54, cited in Chaudhuri, K.J.N., *The Trading World of Asia and the English East India Company 1660–1760* (Cambridge University Press, 1978), p.8.
30. Bolt, J., and van Zanden, J.L., 'The First Update of the Maddison Project; Re-Estimating Growth Before 1820', Maddison Project Working Paper 4 (2013), http://www.ggdc.net/maddison/maddisonproject/home.htm; and Maddison, A., 'Historical Statistics of the World Economy: 1–2008 AD', www.ggdc.net/maddison/Historical_Statistics/horizontal-file_02-2010.xls; consulted 12 July 2014.
31. Dalrymple, W., *The Anarchy: The Relentless Rise of the East India Company* (Bloomsbury, 2019).
32. Peters, W., 'Der Goldhandel und Goldbergbau im 15. bis 18. Jahrhundert an der Goldkueste (Ghana) und die Aktivitaeten der Brandenburg-Preussen', *Zeitschrift der Foerderer des Bergbaus und des Huettenwesens*, Nr. 1, 20. Jahrgang (May 1986), trans., https://e-docs.geo-leo.de/bitstream/handle/11858/00-1735-0000-0022-C2008/1TRANSLA_%C3%BCberarbeitet_von_A_Peters.pdf?sequence=1&isAllowed=y.
33. Chaudhuri, K.N., 'Treasure and Trade Balances: The East India Company's Export Trade, 1660–1720', *The Economic History Review*, New Series, Vol. 21, No. 3 (December 1968), pp.480–502, 490.
34. Douglas, A.W., 'Cotton Textiles in England: The East India Company's Attempt to Exploit Developments in Fashion 1660–1721', *Journal of British Studies*, Vol. 8, No. 2 (May 1969), pp.28–43.
35. http://www.independent.co.uk/news/business/news/gold-price-bars-hidden-in-secret-vaults-beneath-the-bank-of-england-worth-248bn-a6994276.html.

Chapter 24

1. Hemming, J., *Red Gold: the Conquest of the Brazilian Indians* (Papermac, 1995), p.389.
2. Lovejoy, P.E., 'The Volume of the Atlantic Slave Trade: A Synthesis', *The Journal of African History*, Vol. 23, No. 4 (1982), pp.473–501.
3. Atkins, J., *A Voyage to Guinea, Brasil and the West-Indies, in His Majesty's Ships, the Swallow and Weymouth* (printed in Fleet Street, London, 1735), pp.177–78. The printer was the proprietor of a York newspaper with shops there and in the coal port and spa town of Scarborough. This publication was sold specifically in Scarborough
4. Atkins (1735), p.175.
5. Hemming (1995), p.406.
6. Malm, O., 'Gold mining as a source of mercury exposure in the Brazilian Amazon', *Environmental Research*, 77 (2) (May 1998), pp.73–78.
7. Hemming (1995), p.386.
8. Palma, N., 'Harbingers of Modernity: Monetary Injections and European Economic Growth, 1492-1790' (PhD thesis, LSE, 2015/16), Fig. A6.
9. *Ibid.*, Table 2.
10. Boxer, C.R., *The Golden Age of Brazil, 1695–1750: Growing Pains of a Colonial Society* (University of California Press, 1962), pp.57–59.
11. Cardozo, M., 'The Brazilian Gold Rush', *The Americas*, Vol. 3, No. 2 (October 1946), pp.137–60.
12. Costa, L. Freire, Rocha, M. Manuela, and de Sousa, R. Martins, 'Brazilian Gold in the Eighteenth Century: A Reassessment', Working Papers GHES (Universidade de Lisboa, 2010). Hamilton, E.J., *American Treasure and the Price Revolution in Spain, 1501–1650* (Octagon, 1970), estimates that from 1503–1660, 181 tons of gold went to Spain from its empire.
13. Costa, L.F., Rocha, M.M,, and Sousa, R., *O Ouro do Brasil* (Imprensa Nacional-Casa da Moeda, 2013).
14. That entertaining but slightly specious calculation is based on 557 tons of gold being shared between 2.5 million Portuguese (the mid-eighteenth century population), with an average of four people per household. Palma, N., Reis, J., and Zhang, M., 'Reconstruction of regional and national population using intermittent census-type data: the case of Portugal, 1527–1864', *Historical Methods: A Journal of Quantitative and Interdisciplinary History* (2019), URL https://www.tandfonline.com/doi/full/10.1080/01615440.2019.1666762; consulted 18 November 2019.
15. Zahedieh, N., *The Capital and the Colonies: London and the Atlantic Economy, 1660–1700* (Cambridge University Press, 2010).
16. O'Brien, P., 'The nature and historical evolution of an exceptional fiscal state and its possible significance for the precocious commercialization and industrialization of the British economy from Cromwell to Nelson', *The Economic History Review*, 64 (2) (2011), pp.426–27.
17. Aubrey, P., *The Defeat of James Stuart's Armada, 1692* (Leicester University Press, 1979).
18. Kynaston, D., *Till Time's Last Sand: A History of the Bank of England 1694–2013* (Bloomsbury, 2017).
19. Francis, A.D., 'John Methuen and the Anglo-Portuguese Treaties of 1703', *The Historical Journal*, Vol. 3, No. 2 (1960), p.122.
20. Boxer, C.R., 'Brazilian Gold and British Traders in the First Half of the Eighteenth Century', *The Hispanic American Historical Review*, Vol. 49, No. 3 (August 1969), p.460.
21. Palma, N., 'The Cross of Gold: Brazilian Treasure and the Decline of Portugal', *Journal of Economic History* (forthcoming).
22. Dalrymple (2019).
23. *Ibid.*
24. Craig, J., *The Mint: A History of the London Mint from A.D. 287 to 1948* (Cambridge University Press, 2011/1953), p.214.

25. Palma, N., 'Reconstruction of money supply over the long run: the case of England, 1270–1870', *The Economic History Review*, 71 (2) (2018), pp.373–92.
26. Palma (2015/16), p.142.
27. *Ibid.*, p.149.
28. Ereira, *The People's England* (1981), p.41.
29. Newton, T.F.M., 'The Civet-Cats of Newington Green: New Light on Defoe', *The Review of English Studies*, Vol. 13, No. 49 (January 1937), pp.10–19.
30. Backscheider, P.R., 'Defoe's Lady Credit', *Huntington Library Quarterly*, Vol. 44, No. 2 (Spring 1981), pp.89–100.
31. Nunn, N., and Qian, N., 'The Potato's Contribution to Population and Urbanization: Evidence from a Historical Experiment', *Quarterly Journal of Economics*, 126 (2) (2011), pp.593–650.
32. Palma, N., 'The Real Effects of Monetary Expansions: Evidence from a Large-scale Historical Experiment', *Review of Economic Studies* (2022), 89, 1593–1627.
33. Challis, C.E., *A New History of the Royal Mint* (Cambridge University Press, 1992), p.431.
34. Hume, D., 'Of Money', *Political Discourses* (Edinburgh, 1752).
35. Smith, A., *Wealth of Nations* (Courier Dover Publications, 2019), Book IV, Art. III.
36. Palma, N., 'Money and modernization in early modern England', *Financial History Review*, 25 (3) (2018), pp.231–61.
37. *Ibid.*, p.38.
38. Deane, P., *British economic growth, 1688–1959: trends and structure* (Cambridge University Press, 1962), p.48.
39. Ormrod, D., *The Rise of Commercial Empires: England and the Netherlands in the Age of Mercantilism, 1650–1770* (Cambridge University Press, 2003), p.105.
40. Riley, P.W.J., 'The Union of 1707 as an Episode in English Politics', *The English Historical Review*, Vol. 84, No. 332 (July 1969), pp.498–527.
41. Whatley, C.A., *Scots and the Union: Then and Now* (Edinburgh University Press, 2014), p.35.
42. Broadberry, S., Campbell, B., Klein, A., Overton, M., and Van Leeuwen, B., *British Economic Growth, 1270–1870* (Cambridge University Press, 2015), Fig. 1.02.
43. Williamson, Jeffrey G., 'The structure of pay in Britain, 1710–1911', *Research in economic history*, Vol. 7 (1982), pp.1–54.
44. Styles, J., 'Product Innovation in Early Modern London', *Past & Present*, No. 168 (August 2000), pp.124–69.
45. Dunn, R.S., *Sugar and Slaves; the rise of the planter class in the English West Indies, 1624–1713* (Jonathan Cape, 1973), p.222.
46. https://www.historyofparliamentonline.org/volume/1754-1790/member/gibbons-john-1717-76; consulted 1 August 2019.
47. Ereira, A., *The People's England* (Routledge & Kegan Paul, 1981), pp.1–9.

Chapter 25

1. Addison, J., 'Allegory of Public Credit', *The Spectator* No. 3 (3 March 1711).
2. Law, J., *Oeuvres ... de John Law, contenant les principes sur le numéraire, le commerce, le credit et les banques*, E.F de Sénovert (ed.) (Paris, 1790) I, p.158.
3. Buvat, J., *Journal de la Régence* (Henri Plon, 1865).
4. Voltaire, 'Observations sur MM. Jean Lass, Melon et Dutot sur le commerce, le luxe, les monnaies et les impots' (1738), from *Œuvres complètes de Voltaire* (Garnier, 1879), tome 22, p.359.
5. Gleeson, J., *The Moneymaker* (Random House, 2012), Ch.5.
6. Murphy, A.E., *John Law: Economic Theorist and Policy-Maker* (Clarendon Press, 1997), p.290.
7. Spang, R.L., 'The Ghost of Law: Speculating on Money. Memory and Mississippi in the French Constituent Asembly', *Historical Relflections/Réflections Historiques*, Vol.31, No.1,

'Money in the Enlightenment' (Spring 2005), pp.3–25; Kaiser, T.E., 'Money, Despotism and Public Opinion in Early Eighteenth-Century France: John Law and the debate on Royal Credit', *The Journal of Modern History*, Vol. 63, No.1 (March 1991), pp.1–28.

8. Dixon, S., *The Modernisation of Russia, 1676–1825* (Cambridge University Press, 1999), p.63.
9. *Ibid.*, p.66.
10. Hoppit, J., 'The Myths of the South Sea Bubble', *Transactions of the Royal Historical Society*, 12, pp.141–65.
11. Glete, J., *Navies and Nations: Warships, Navies and State Building in Europe and America, 1500–1860*, 2 vols (Stockholm, 1993).
12. Britain 661, France 291, Spain 222, Holland 187, from Fulton, R., *Torpedo War, and submarine explosions* (New York, 1810).
13. Pressnell, L.S., *Country Banking in the Industrial Revolution* (Clarendon Press, 1956).
14. Crafts, N.F.R., British *Economic Growth during the Industrial Revolution* (Oxford, 1985); www.ehs.org.uk/dotAsset/15457c19-e7bd-4045-a056-30a3efac2d47.pdf.
15. McNair Wilson, R., *The Mind of Napoleon; A Study of Napoleon, Mr. Roosevelt, and the Money Power* (G. Routledge & Sons, 1934), p.33.
16. Soboul, A., *A Short History of the French Revolution, 1789–1799* (University of California Press, 1977), p.37. The accounting for this has been questioned in Harris, R.D., 'French Finances and the American War, 1777–1783', *The Journal of Modern History*, Vol. 48, No. 2 (June 1976), pp.233–58.
17. Hawtrey, R.G., 'The Collapse of the French Assignats', *The Economic Journal*, Vol. 28, No. 111 (September 1918), pp.300–14.
18. Aftalion, p.124.
19. *Ibid*, p.147.
20. Hampson, N., *The Perfidy of Albion: French Perceptions of England during the French Revolution* (Springer, 1998), p.133.
21. Aftalion, p.305.
22. Dwyer, P.G., *Napoleon: The Path to Power* (Yale University Press, 2007).
23. Dehn, W., 'The Russian Currency Reform', *The Economic Journal*, Vol. 8, No. 30 (June 1898), pp.225–33.
24. *Walker's Hibernian Magazine* (January 1796), pp.85–86.
25. 'WAR FINANCE IN ENGLAND', *NY Times* (27 January 1862), http://www.nytimes.com/1862/01/27/news/war-finance-england-bank-restriction-act-1797-suspension-specie-payments-for.html?pagewanted=all.
26. O'Brien, P.K., and Palma, N., 'Danger To The Old Lady Of Threadneedle Street? The Bank Restriction Act And The Regime Shift To Paper Money, 1797–1821', *European Review of Economic History* (November 2019), URL https://academic.oup.com/ereh/advance-article-abstract/doi/10.1093/ereh/hez008/5587705?redirectedFrom=fulltext; consulted 18 November 2019).
27. Bordo, M.D., and White, E.N., ' A Tale of Two Currencies: British and French Finance During the Napoleonic Wars', *The Journal of Economic History*, Vol. 51, No. 2 (June 1991), pp.303–16.
28. White, E.N., 'The French Revolution and the Politics of Government Finance, 1770–1815', *The Journal of Economic History*, Vol. 55, No. 2 (June 1995), pp.227–55.
29. For analysis of the money used for his armies, see Broers, M., Hicks, P., Guimerá Ravina, A., and Guimera, A., *The Napoleonic Empire and the New European Political Culture* (Palgrave Macmillan, 2012).
30. Rémond, R., *Religion and Society in Modern Europe* (Blackwell, 1999), p.81.
31. Wilson-Smith, T., *Napoleon: Man of War, Man of Peace* (Carroll & Graf, 2002), p.178.
32. Thiers, A., *History of the Consulate and the Empire of France Under Napoleon*, Vol. 3, 1812–1814, p.413.

33. Cathcart, B., *The News from Waterloo* (Faber & Faber, 2015).

Chapter 26
1. Fetter, F.W., 'The Editions of the Bullion Report', *Economica*, New Series, Vol. 22, No. 86 (May 1955), pp.152–57.
2. 'Report, together with Minutes of Evidence, and Accounts, from the Select Committee on the High Price of Gold Bullion. Ordered, by the House of Commons, to be printed, 8 June 1810', *Parliamentary Papers* (1810), Vol. III, p.5.
3. In 1831, UK exports totalled approx. £63 million, while the rest of the world exported goods worth less than £50 million; Http://ricardo.medialab.sciences-po.fr/#/world; consulted 15 October 2018.
4. Tucker, R.S., 'Gold and the General Price Level', *The Review of Economics and Statistics*, Vol. 16, No. 1 (15 January 1934), p.12.
5. Coutinho, Father Jose Joaquim da Cunha de Azeredo, *Discurso sobre o estado atual das minas do Brazil*, quoted in Machado, I.F., and de M. Figueirôa, S.F., '500 years of mining in Brazil: a brief review', *Resources Policy* 27 (2001), pp.9–24.
6. Broadberry. S., *et al.*, *British Economic Growth, 1270–1870* (Cambridge University Press, 2015), p.342.
7. Deane, P., and Cole, W.A., *British Economic Growth, 1688–1959* (Cambridge University Press, 1962), quoted in Crafts, N.F.R., 'British Economic Growth, 1700–1831: A Review of the Evidence', *The Economic History Review*, New Series, Vol. 36, No. 2 (May 1983), p.180.
8. Hosbawm, E., *Industry and Empire: An Economic History of Britain since 1750* (1968), p.58.
9. Maddison, A., *Contours of the World Economy, 1–2030 AD, Essays in Macro-Economic History* (Oxford University Press, 2007), p.379, table A.4.
10. Beckett, G.W., *A Population History of Colonial New South Wales: The Economic Growth of a New Colony* (Trafford Publishing, 2013), p.16.
11. *Port Phillip Gazette and Settler's Journal* (Wednesday, 21 February 1849), p.2; *The Argos* (16 May 1882), p.6. Blainey, G., 'Gold and Governors', *Historical Studies, Australia and New Zealand*, Vol. 9, 61 (May 1961), pp.337–50, pours scorn on this narrative, insisting that it lacks credibility and critical sense, and that these discoveries were clearly understood to be insignificant. I believe that his argument is undermined by the large discovery made by Chapman and the way it was handled
12. Blake, W.P., *Report Upon the Precious Metals* (US Government Printing Office, 1869), p.92.
13. Morrell, W.P., *The Gold Rushes* (Adam and Charles Black, 1940), pp.46–58.
14. Porter, J.E., 'Money and Mad Ambition: Economies of Russian Literature 1830–1850' (PhD thesis, UC Berkeley, 2011), https://escholarship.org/uc/item/9ng5x5qp; consulted 19 May 2020.
15. Haywood, R.M., 'The Winter Palace in St. Petersburg: Destruction by Fire and Reconstruction, December 1837 – March 1839', *Jahrbücher für Geschichte Osteuropas, Neue Folge*, Bd. 27, H. 2 (1979), pp.161–80.
16. Fay, C.R., 'Corn Prices and the Corn Laws, 1815–1846', *The Economic Journal*, Vol. 31, No. 121 (March 1921), pp.17–27.
17. Cobbett, W., *Rural Rides* (Nelson and Sons, 1935), pp.102–03.
18. Mahony, J., 'Sketches in the West of Ireland', *Illustrated London News* (13 February 1847).
19. Boyle P.P., and Grada, C.O., 'Fertility Trends, Excess Mortality, and the Great Irish Famine', *Demography*, 23 (4) (1986), p.555.
20. Boot, H.M., *The Commercial Crisis of 1847* (Hull University Press, 1984), Ch.6.
21. Berger, H., and Spoerer, M., 'Economic Crises and the European Revolutions of 1848', *The Journal of Economic History*, Vol. 61, No. 2 (June 2001), pp.293–326.

22. G. Blainey attempted valorously to undermine the general belief that new gold fields turned up by happy accident – 'A Theory of Mineral Discovery: Australia in the Nineteenth Century', *The Economic History Review*, Vol. 23, No. 2 (August 1970), pp.298–313 – but his explanation that it is connected with new settlement does not really change the oddness.

23. Named after Canadian trappers who forded the stream and were called Americanos.

24. Hurtado, A.L., *John Sutter: A Life on the North American Frontier* (University of Oklahoma Press, 2006), p.20.

25. Dana, J.D., 'Observation on some points in the physical geography of Oregon and Upper California', *American Journal of Science* (2), vol. 7 (1849), pp. 125, 262.

26. http://www.sfmuseum.net/hist2/sutdiary1.html; consulted 23 October 2019.

27. https://obrag.org/2015/03/the-great-california-genocide/.

28. Schoonover, T.J., *The life and times of Gen. John A. Sutter* (Sacramento, 1907).

29. https://www.measuringworth.com/calculators/ppowerus/; consulted 18 October 2019.

30. Gudde, E.G., *California Place Names: The Origin and Etymology of Current Geographical Names* (University of California Press, 1960).

31. http://www.321gold.com/editorials/moriarty/moriarty110614.html; Rolle, A., *John Charles Frémont: Character as Destiny* (University of Oklahoma Press, 1991).

32. http://www.yosemite.com/mariposa-county/history/.

33. There is a report that his men found gold when camped there in 1845; Radanovich, L., 'An Overview of Mariposa County History', *Mariposa Gazette* (5 November 1998).

34. Starr, K., *Americans and the California Dream, 1850–1915* (Oxford University Press, 1986), Ch.1.

35. John O'Sullivan (ed.), 'Annexation', *The United States Magazine and Democratic Review*, vol. 17 (New York, 1845), pp.5–6, 9–10.

36. http://www.legendsofamerica.com/ca-jamesmarshall.html; http://www.sierrafoothillmagazine. com/brannan.html.

37. Madley, B., *An American Genocide: The United States and the California Indian Catastrophe, 1846–1873* (Yale University Press, 2016).

38. A point made in Zorach, R., and Phillips M.W., Jr., *Gold: Nature and Culture* (Reaktion Books, 2016), p.173.

39. Nash, G.D., 'A Veritable Revolution: The Global Economic Significance of the California Gold Rush', *California History*, Vol. 77, No. 4, 'A Golden State: Mining and Economic Development in Gold Rush California' (Winter 1998/1999), pp.276–92.

40. Brands, H.W., *The Age of Gold: the California Gold Rush and the New American Dream* (Doubleday, 2003), p.442.

41. Kitchin, J., 'The Position of Gold', *The Review of Economics and Statistics*, Vol. 3, No. 8 (August 1921), p.257.

42. Morys, M., 'The emergence of the Classical Gold Standard', CHERRY Discussion Paper Series, CHERRY DP 12/01 (2012), Fig.1. URL https://www.york.ac.uk/media/economics/ documents/cherrydiscussionpapers/1201.pdf.

43. Martin, D.A., '1853: The End of Bimetallism in the United States', *The Journal of Economic History*, Vol. 33, No. 4 (December 1973).

44. http://www.panamarailroad.org/history1.html; consulted 22 October 2019.

45. Goldin, C.D., and Lewis, F.W., 'The Economic Cost of the American Civil War: Estimates and Implications', *Journal of Economic History*, 35 (2) (June 1975), pp.299–326.

46. Chatelain, N.P., 'Controlling the California Gold Steamers: The Panama Route in the United States Civil War', *UCLA Historical Journal*, 28 (1) (2017).

47. Goldin, C.D., and Lewis, F.D., 'The Economic Cost of the American Civil War: Estimates and Implications', *Journal of Economic History*, 35 (2) (June 1975), pp. 299–26, 306.

48. Rothman, J., '"A Pledge of a Nation": Charting The Economic Aspirations, Political Motivations, and Consequences of Confederate Currency Creation' (unpublished M.A.,

American History Department, Brandeis University, May 2009), URL http://bir.brandeis.edu/bitstream/handle/10192/23258/Thesis2.pdf;jsessionid=9CC930B1092FB189593899C70B5C69AA?sequence=1; consulted 4 June 2020.

49. https://inflationdata.com/articles/confederate-inflation/; consulted 22 October 2019. Some notes now have value to collectors.

50. Cathcart, B., *The News from Waterloo: The Race to Tell Britain of Wellington's Victory* (Faber & Faber, 2015).

51. 'London to Paris travel in 1843 and 1900', *The Examiner* (Saturday, 30 March 1901), p.13.

52. Ash, S., *The Cable King: the Life of John Pender* (privately published, 2018, Kindle edition).

53. Mullaly, J., *The Laying of the Cable, or The Ocean Telegraph* (New York, 1858), p.307.

Chapter 27

1. Selcer, R.F., *Civil War America, 1850 to 1875* (Infobase Publishing, 2014), p.42.

2. https://governors.library.ca.gov/addresses/s_01-Burnett2.html.

3. Selcer, p.45.

4. Luther, J., *Fort Martin Scott: Guardian of the Treaty* (Arcadia Publishing, 2013); A. Ereira documentary *Son of a Gun, or how Sam Colt Changed America* (BBCTV, 1986), https://vimeo.com/467453274; consulted 9 August 2021.

5. Fehrenbach, T.R., *Comanches: The History of a People* (Vintage Books, 2007), p.523.

6. http://www.nateamerican.co.uk/1872-3buffalo.html; consulted 9 August 2021.

7. Radabaugh, J.S., 'Custer Explores the Black Hills, 1874', *Military Affairs*, Vol. 26, No. 4 (Winter 1962–63), p.163.

8. Markley, Bill, 'Custer's Gold', *True West* (April 2018); URL https://truewestmagazine.com/article/custers-gold/; consulted 6 November 2021.

9. Wolff, D., 'Gold Mining in the Black Hills', *Black Hills Visitor Magazine* (5 August 2015).

10. Betz, R.F., Lootens, R.J,, and Becker, M.K., 'Two Decades of Prairie Restoration at Fermilab, Batavia, Illinois', URL https://web.fnal.gov/organization/ecology/Shared%20Documents/Two%20Decades%20of%20Fermilab%20Prairie%20Restoration.pdf; consulted 25 October 2019.

11. Harnetty, P., 'Cotton Exports and Indian Agriculture, 1861–1870', *The Economic History Review*, Vol. 24, No. 3 (August 1971), p.424.

12. Willis, H.P., 'The Vienna Monetary Treaty of 1857', *Journal of Political Economy*, Vol. 4, No. 2 (March 1896), pp.187–207.

13. The 'Ems telegram'. Welch, D.A., *Justice and the Genesis of War* (Cambridge University Press, 1995), p.86.

14. Harnsberger, J.L., 'Jay Cooke and the Financing of the Northern Pacific Railroad, 1869–1873', *North Dakota Quarterly* 37 (4) (1969), pp.5–13, URL https://babel.hathitrust.org/cgi/pt?id=mdp.39015014324852&view=1up&seq=577; consulted 30 October 2019.

15. Vernon, J.R., 'Unemployment Rates in Post-Bellum America: 1869–1899', *Journal of Macroeconomics* 16 (1994), pp.701–14.

16. Hobsbawm (1968), p.104.

17. 'Destabilizing the Global Monetary System: Germany's Adoption of the Gold Standard in the Early 1870s', IMF Working Paper WP/19/32, prepared by J. Wiegand (February 2019).

18. Morys, M., 'The emergence of the Classical Gold Standard', CHERRY Discussion Paper 12/01 (January 2012), URL https://www.york.ac.uk/media/economics/documents/cherrydiscussionpapers/1201.pdf; consulted 24 October 2019.

19. Haymes, E.R., '*The Ring of the Nibelung* and the *Nibelungenlied*: Wagner's Ambiguous Relationship to a Source', in Fugelso, K., *Defining Medievalism(s)* (Boydell & Brewer, 2009), pp.218–46.

20. The population of the five areas of the UK that received the most funding from the European Union, because of their relative deprivation, all voted 'Leave' and gave up that income. Dean, A., 'Which UK regions receive the most EU funding', *Prospect* (7 September 2016), https://www.prospectmagazine.co.uk/politics/43279/which-uk-regions-receive-the-most-eu-funding; accessed 4 March 2020.

21. Wiegand, J., *Destabilizing the Global Monetary System: Germany's Adoption of the Gold Standard in the Early 1870s*, IMF Working Paper WP/19/32 (February 2019).

22. Stern, F., *Gold and Iron: Bismarck, Bleichröder and the building of the German Empire* (Penguin Books, 1987), p.180.

23. Hobsbawm (1968), p.105.

24. Senator John H. Reagan, quoted in Friedman, M., 'The Crime of 1873', *Journal of Political Economy*, Vol. 98, No. 6 (December 1990), pp.1159–94.

25. https://en.wikipedia.org/wiki/Cross_of_Gold_speech.

26. Gilbert, D.W., 'The Economic Effects of the Gold Discoveries Upon South Africa: 1886–1910', *The Quarterly Journal of Economics*, Vol. 47, No. 4 (August 1933), p.558, in pp.553–97.

27. https://www.911metallurgist.com/blog/witwatersrand-gold-deposits; consulted 1 November 2019.

28. McLaughlin, L., 'The All-Canadian Route to the Klondike', URL http://hougengroup.com/yukon-history/yukon-nuggets/the-all-candian-route-to-the-klondike/; consulted 2 November 2019.

29. *Annual Report on the Mineral Production of Canada 1906*, Dept. of Mines (1908), p.24, Table 10.

30. Kafka, Franz, *Letters to Milena* (Random House, 1992), p.148.

31. Lewis W.A., *Growth and Fluctuations 1870–1913* (George Allen & Unwin, 1978), p.88.

32. Herrmann, D.G., *The Arming of Europe and the Making of the First World War* (Princeton University Press, 1997), pp.234–37.

33. 'Gold Reserves Of Principal Countries, 1913–1925', *Federal Reserve Bulletin* (April 1926), p.271.

34. David Lloyd George, House of Commons, 5 August 1914.

35. 'Gold Reserves Of Principal Countries, 1913–1925', *Federal Reserve Bulletin* (April 1926), p.271.

36. Tooze, A., *The Deluge: The Great War and the Remaking of Global Order 1916–1931* (Penguin UK, 2014), Ch.18 (4).

37. http://www.joelscoins.com/exhibger2.htm; consulted 6 November 2019.

38. *Key Documents in the History of Gold, V.2, The Heyday of the Gold Standard, 1820–1930*, p.117, URL https://www.gold.org/sites/default/files/documents/1900mar14.pdf; consulted 5 November 2019.

39. http://www.miketodd.net/encyc/dollhist.htm; consulted 5 November 2019.

40. Ereira, A., *The Invergordon Mutiny: A Narrative History of the Last Great Mutiny in the Royal Navy and How it Forced Britain Off the Gold Standard in 1931* (Routledge, 1981).

41. *Ibid.*

Chapter 28

1. Albers, T., and Uebele, M., 'A Monthly International Dataset for the Interwar Period: Taking the Debate to the Next Level' (2013), Conference paper, URL https://www.researchgate.net/publication/257413890_A_Monthly_International_Dataset_for_the_Interwar_Period_Taking_the_Debate_to_the_Next_Level/citation/download; consulted 10 November 2019.

2. Estevadeordal, A. Frantz, B., and Taylor, A.M., 'The Rise and Fall of World Trade, 1870–1939'. *The Quarterly Journal of Economics*, Vol. 118, No. 2 (May 2003), pp.359–407).

3. Hoover, H., *The Memoirs of Herbert Hoover: The Great Depression, 1929–41* (Macmillan, 1952), p.vi, URL https://hoover.archives.gov/sites/default/files/research/ebooks/b1v3_full.pdfd; consulted 8 November 2019.

4. Hoover, H., *The Memoirs of Herbert Hoover: The Great Depression, 1929–41* (Macmillan, 1952), p.397, URL https://hoover.archives.gov/sites/default/files/research/ebooks/b1v3_full.pdfd; consulted 8 November 2019.

5. Graham, F.D., and Whittlesey, C.R., *Golden Avalanche* (Princeton University Press, 1940), Ch.1

6. Irwin, D.A., 'Gold sterilization and the recession of 1937–1938', *Financial History Review*, Vol.19, 3, pp.249–67.

7. http://www.edchange.org/multicultural/speeches/ike_chance_for_peace.html; consulted 6 December 2019.

8. 'Federal Budget Outlays for Defense Functions: 1980 to 2002 Military Personnel U.S. Military Ranks', cited at www.infoplease.com/us/military-personnel/us-military-spending-1946-2009; consulted 25 November 2019.

9. Leitenberg, M., 'America in Vietnam: Statistics of a war', *Survival*, 14:6 (1972), p.272 in pp. 268–74.

10. http://www.federalreservehistory.org/Events/DetailView/33.

11. James, H., *International Monetary Co-operation Since Bretton Woods* (IMF and Oxford University Press, 1996), p.253, quoted in Hammes, D., and Wills, D., 'Black Gold; The End of Bretton Woods and the Oil-Price Shocks of the 1970s', *The Independent Review* v. IX, n. 4 (Spring 2005), p.507.

12. LaBorde, L., 'Money – Then and Now: Instalment VII: H.L. Hunt's Boys and the Circle K Cowboys', gold-eagle.com (26 January 2004), www.gold-eagle.com/article/money-then-and-now.

13. http://uk.businessinsider.com/hunt-brothers-trying-to-corner-silver-market-2016-5?r=US&IR=T; consulted 20 April 2018.

14. 143,227.40 million barrels at $11.75 a barrel, https://www.opec.org/library/Annual%20Statistical%20Bulletin/interactive/current/FileZ/XL/T31.HTM; consulted 4 December 2019.

15. Global reserves 35,274 tons, from Green, T., *Central Bank Gold Reserves: An historical perspective since 1845* (World Gold Council, 1999), p.19; price in 1974 $154 per oz, http://piketty.pse.ens.fr/files/capital21c/xls/RawDataFiles/GoldPrices17922012.pdf; consulted 4 December 2019.

16. Wong, A., 'The Untold Story Behind Saudi Arabia's 41-Year US Debt Secret', https://www.bloomberg.com/news/features/2016-05-30/the-untold-story-behind-saudi-arabia-s-41-year-u-s-debt-secret; consulted 31 May 2020.

17. Katusa, M., *The Colder War: How the Global Energy Trade Slipped from America's Grasp* (John Wiley & Sons, 2014), p.54.

18. Bahgat, G., 'Managing Dependence: American-Saudi Oil Relations', *Arab Studies Quarterly*, Vol. 23, No. 1 (Winter 2001), pp.1–14.

19. Clark, W.R., *Petrodollar Warfare* (New Society Publishers, 2005), p.32.

20. Graham, F.D., and Whittlesey, C.R., *Golden Avalanche* (Princeton University Press, 1940), p.16'

21. http://onlygold.com/m/Prices/Prices200Years.asp.

22. http://www.chipsetc.com/gold-value-in-computer-chips.html.

23. http://www.gold.org/supply-and-demand/gold-demand-trends/back-issues/gold-demand-trends-full-year-2016/technology.

24. 'All the Money in the World', *Bullion Vault* (27 October 2009), URL https://www.bullionvault.com/gold-news/all_the_money_in_the_world_102720093; consulted 12 November 2019.

25. https://www.rankred.com/how-much-money-is-there-in-the-world/; consulted 25 August 2022.

26. https://www.in2013dollars.com/us/inflation/1971?amount=163000000000; consulted 25 August 2022.

27. Clark, K., 'Unicorns aren't profitable, and Wall Street doesn't care', *Tech Crunch* (26 March 2019), https://techcrunch.com/2019/03/26/unicorns-arent-profitable-wall-street-doesnt-care/; consulted 14 May 2010.

28. https://www.washingtonpost.com/news/wonk/wp/2018/02/06/how-rising-inequality-hurts-everyone-even-the-rich/; consulted 6 December 2019.

29. Batish, A., 'Equilar – New York Times 100 Highest-Paid CEOs' (30 June 2023), https://www.equilar.com/reports/102-equilar-new-york-times-top-100-highest-paid-ceos-2023.html; consulted 28 November 2023.

30. By April 2022, price rises above the 2014- 16 average were Food price index 58.5%, cereals 69.5%, oils 137.5% https://www.reuters.com/graphics/UKRAINE-CRISIS/FOOD/zjvqkgomjvx/ consulted 18/1/2024

Chapter 29

1. 'From the Heart of the World, The Elder Brothers' Warning', BBC TV broadcast (11 December 1990), 36m.14s. –36m.36s.

2. Luxembourg is 82km x 57km.

3. Schneider, K., 'Mongolia Copper Mine at Oyu Tolgoi Tests Water Supply and Young Democracy', *Circle of Blue* (5 November 2013).

4. Mátyás, B., 'Contemporary shamanisms in Mongolia', *Asian Ethnicity* 11 (2010), pp.229–38.

5. Gordillo, E., 'Land Grabs and the Cost of Mining in Mongolia', *The Diplomat* (6 April 2023).

6. Pascal's wager was that without sufficient evidence it was better to bet on the existence of God than against it. Making this bet has only a slight downside if God does not exist, whereas if God does exist, the winnings are seriously remarkable. With this argument, he set out the basis of the sciences of probability theory, decision theory and pragmatic existentialism.

7. Korobushkina, E.D., Karavaiko, G.I., and Korobushkin, I.M., 'Biochemistry of Gold', *Ecological Bulletins*, No. 35, Environmental Biogeochemistry (1983), pp.325–33.

8. http://www.gold.org/supply-and-demand/gold-demand-trends.

9. Plutarch, *On Superstition*, 8.25. Kitchell, K.F., and Parker, L.A., 'Death by Bull's Blood, a Natural Explanation', in W.J. Cherf (ed.), *Alpha to Omega: Studies in Honor of George John Szemler on his Sixty-Fifth Birthday* (Cambridge University Press, 1993), pp.123–41.

10. http://www.brilliantearth.com/gold-mining-environment/.

11. http://www.smithsonianmag.com/science-nature/environmental-disaster-gold-industry-180949762/#7f0gzkjzMf4A5zxC.99

12. Bird, L., and Krauer, N., 'Case Study: Illicit Gold Mining in Peru', The Global Initiative Against Transnational Organised Crime (November 2017), URL https://globalinitiative.net/wp-content/uploads/2017/11/tgiatoc-case-study-peru-1878-web-lo-res.pdf; consulted 8 November 2021.

13. *The Cost of Gold: Environmental, Health and Human Rights Consequences of Gold Mining in South Africa's West and Central Rand* (Harvard Law School International Human Rights Clinic, October 2016).

14. UNODC, 'Alluvial gold exploitation; Evidences from remote sensing 2016' (May 2018).

15. https://etn-socrates.eu/leaching-and-recovery-of-gold-from-ore-in-cyanide-free-glycine-media/, referencing Altinkaya, P., *et al.*, 'Leaching and recovery of gold from ore in cyanide-free glycine media', *Minerals Engineering*, Vol. 158 (1 November 2020), 106610; consulted 8 November 2021.

16. Stoddart, J. Fraser, *et al.*, 'Cation-Dependent Gold Recovery with α-Cyclodextrin Facilitated by Second-Sphere Coordination', *Journal of the American Chemical Society*, 138, 36 (2016), pp.11,643–653.

17. https://www.fs-ventures.co.uk/investee-companies/corporate-news/relatednews/109/; consulted 7 November 2021.

18. Petroff, A., 'Scientists find gold worth $2 million in Swiss sewage', *CNN Money* (11 October 2017), https://money.cnn.com/2017/10/11/news/gold-switzerland-water-sewage-waste/index.html; consulted 29 October 2021.

Bibliography

Secondary sources

Aarts, J., 'Coins, money and exchange in the Roman world: A cultural-economic perspective', *Archaeological Dialogues* 12 (1) (2005), pp.1–28.

Abramov, O., & Mojzsis, S.J., 'Microbial habitability of the Hadean Earth during the late heavy bombardment', *Nature* 459 (2009), pp.419–22.

Addison, J., 'Allegory of Public Credit', *The Spectator*, No. 3 (3 March 1711).

Aftalion, F., *The French Revolution: An Economic Interpretation* (Cambridge University Press, 1990).

Aigle, D., *The Mongol Empire between Myth and Reality: Studies in Anthropological History* (Brill, 2014).

Albert, W., *The Turnpike Road System in England: 1663–1840* (Cambridge University Press, 2007).

Alcalá, M., *César y Cortés* (Mexico, 1950).

Aleklett, K., Morrissey, D.J., Loveland, W., McGaughey, P.L., & Seaborg, G.T., 'Energy dependence of 209Bi fragmentation in relativistic nuclear collisions', *Physical Review* C 23 (3) (1981), p.1044.

van Alfen, P., & Wartenberg, U., *White Gold: Studies in Early Electrum Coinage* (The American Numismatic Society, 2020).

Allen, R.C., 'The Great Divergence in European Wages and Prices from the Middle Ages to the First World War', *Explorations in Economic History* 38 (2001), pp.411–47.

Allyn Rickett, W., *Guanzi: Political, Economic, and Philosophical Essays from Early China*, v.2 XXII.

Alstola, T., 'Judean Merchants in Babylonia and Their Participation in Long-Distance Trade', *Die Welt des Orients* 47 (2017), pp.25–51.

Altinkaya, P., *et al.*, 'Leaching and recovery of gold from ore in cyanide-free glycine media', *Minerals Engineering*, Vol. 158 (1 November 2020), p.106610.

Alva, W., 'The Royal Tombs of Sipán: Art and Power in Moche Society', *Studies in the History of Art*, Vol. 63, Symposium Papers XL: Moche Art and Archaeology in Ancient Peru (2001), pp.222–45.

Álvarez-Nogal, C., & Prados de la Escosura, L., 'The Decline of Spain (1500–1850): conjectural estimates', *European Review of Economic History* (2007), p.11.

Anderson-Córdova, K.F., *Surviving Spanish Conquest: Indian Fight, Flight, and Cultural Transformation in Hispaniola and Puerto Rico* (University of Alabama Press, 2017).

Anthony, D.W. (ed.), *The Lost World of Old Europe: The Danube Valley, 5000–3500 BC* (Princeton University Press, 2010).

Archibald, Z., Davies, J.K., & Gabrielsen, V. (eds), *The Economies of Hellenistic Societies, Third to First Centuries BC* (Oxford University Press, 2011).

Arhin, K., 'Succession and Gold Mining at Nkwanta', *Institute of African Studies: Research Review*, Vol. 6, No. 3 (1970), pp.101–09.

Arnold, B., & Blair Gibson, D. (eds), *Celtic Chiefdom, Celtic State: The Evolution of Complex Social Systems in Prehistoric Europe* (Cambridge University Press, 1995).

Arzáns, B. de Orsúa y Vela, *Tales of Potosí* (Brown University Press, 1975).

Atherstone, A., & Benson, K., *Reformation: A World in Turmoil* (Lion Books, 2015).

Attman, A., *The Bullion Flow between Europe and the East, 1000–1750* (Göteborg, 1981).

Atwell, W.S., 'Another Look at Silver Imports into China, ca., 1635–1644', *Journal of World History*, Vol. 16, No. 4 (December 2005), pp.467–89, p.476.

Atwell, W.S., 'Ming Observers of Ming Decline: Some Chinese Views on the "Seventeenth-Century Crisis" in Comparative Perspective', *The Journal of the Royal Asiatic Society of Great Britain and Ireland*, No. 2 (1988), pp.316–48.

Atwell, W.S., 'Notes on Silver, Foreign Trade, and the Late Ming Economy', *Ch'ing-shih wen-t'i*, Vol. 3, No. 8 (1977), pp.1–33.

Atwood, R., 'Aztec Warrior Wolf', *Archaeology* (11 December 2017).

Ávila, A., *et al.*, 'Cinnabar in Mesoamerica: poisoning or mortuary ritual?', *Journal of Archaeological Science*, 49 (2014), pp.48–56.

Axelson, E., 'Prince Henry the Navigator and the Discovery of the Sea Route to India', *The Geographical Journal* 127, 2 (June 1961), pp.145–55.

Azzam, A.R., *The Other Exile: The Remarkable Story of Fernão Lopes, the Island of Saint Helena, and the meaning of human solitude* (Icon Books, 2017).

Bachrach, B.B., 'On the Origins of William the Conqueror's Horse Transports', *Technology and Culture*, Vol. 26, No. 3 (July 1985), pp.505–31.

Bahgat, G., 'Managing Dependence: American-Saudi Oil Relations', *Arab Studies Quarterly*, Vol. 23, No. 1 (Winter 2001), pp.1–14.

Balaguer, A.M., *Història de la moneda dels comtats Catalans* (Institut d'Estudis Catalans, 1999).

Bardill, J., *Constantine, Divine Emperor of the Christian Golden Age* (Cambridge University Press, 2012).

Bartelmus, A., & Sternitzke, K. (eds), *Karduniaš. Babylonia Under the Kassites* (de Gruyter, 2017), 2 vols.

Basmachi, F., *Treasures of the Iraq Museum* (al-Jumhuriya Press, Baghdad, 1975–76).

Bass, G.F., 'Troy and Ur: Gold Links between Two Ancient Capitals', *Expedition* 8 (4) (1966), pp.26–39.

Battilossi, S., Cassis, Y., & Yago, K. (eds), *Handbook of the History of Money and Currency* (Springer, 2020).

Baudoin, R., & Auger, G., 'Implications of the mineralogy and chemical composition of lead beads from Frobisher's assay site, Kodlunarn Island, Canada: prelude to Bre-X?', *Canadian Journal of Earth Sciences*, 41, 6 (June 2004), pp.669–681.

Bauer, R., *The Alchemy of Conquest: Science, Religion, and the Secrets of the New World* (University of Virginia Press, 2019).

Baulant, M., 'Prix et salaires a paris au XVIe siècle', *Annales*, 31e Année, No. 5 (September–October 1976), pp.954–95.

Beck, H., *et al.* (eds.), *Money and Power in the Roman Republic* (Brussels, 2016).

Beckett, G.W., *A Population History of Colonial New South Wales: The Economic Growth of a New Colony* (Trafford Publishing, 2013).

Becking, B., Dijkstra, M., Korpel, M., & Vriezen, K., *Only One God?: Monotheism in Ancient Israel and the Veneration of the Goddess Asherah* (Sheffield Academic Press, 2002).

Berger, H., & Spoerer, M., 'Economic Crises and the European Revolutions of 1848', *The Journal of Economic History*, Vol. 61, No. 2 (June 2001), pp.293–326.

Bernard, G.W. (ed.), *The Tudor Nobility* (Manchester University Press, 1992).

Bernier, F., tr. Brock, I., ed. Constable, A., *Travels in the Mogul Empire* (London, 1891).

Bernstein, P.L., *The Power of Gold* (John Wiley and Sons, 2000).

Bhandarkar, D.R., *Lectures on Ancient Indian Numismatics* (Asian Educational Services, 1990).

Birmingham, D., 'The Regimento Da Mina', *Transactions of the Historical Society of Ghana*, Vol. 11 (1970), pp.1–7.

Blackler, A., 'Conference Review – First International Workshop on the Origin and Evolution of Portolan Charts – Lisbon, June 2016', *e-Perimetron*, v.12 (1) (2017).

Blainey, G., 'A Theory of Mineral Discovery: Australia in the Nineteenth Century', *The Economic History Review*, Vol. 23, No. 2 (August 1970), pp.298–313.

Blainey, G., 'Gold and Governors', *Historical Studies, Australia and New Zealand*, Vol. 9, 61 (May 1961), pp.337–50.

Blake, W.P., *Report Upon the Precious Metals* (US Government Printing Office, 1869), p.92.

Blois, L. de, 'The Perception of Emperor and Empire in Cassius Dio's "Roman History"', *Ancient Society*, Vol. 29 (1998–99), pp.267–81.

Blust, R., 'Tumbaga in Southeast Asia and South America', *Anthropos*, Bd. 87, H. 4./6. (1992), pp.443–57.

Bogdanos, M., 'The Casualties of War: The Truth about the Iraq Museum', *American Journal of Archaeology*, Vol. 109, No. 3 (July 2005), pp.477–526.

Boon, G.C., '"Plumbum Britannicum" and Other Remarks', *Britannia*, Vol. 22 (1991), pp.317–22.

Boot, H.M., *The Commercial Crisis of 1847* (Hull University Press, 1984).

Bordo, M.D., & White, E.N., 'A Tale of Two Currencies: British and French Finance During the Napoleonic Wars', *The Journal of Economic History*, Vol. 51, No. 2 (June 1991), pp.303–16.

Boucharlat, R., 'Pasargadae', *Iran*, Vol. 40 (2002), pp.279–82.

Bourget, S., & Jones, K.L. (eds), *The art and archaeology of the Moche: an ancient Andean society of the Peruvian north coast* (University of Texas Press, 2009).

Bourne, E.G. (ed.), *The Northmen, Columbus and Cabot, 985–1503: The voyages of the Northmen, The voyages of Columbus and of John Cabot* (Charles Scribner's Sons, 1906).

Bower, B., 'Golden Fleece voyage may be no myth', *Science News*, Vol. 186, No. 13 (27 December 2014), p.9.

Boxer, C.R., 'Brazilian Gold and British Traders in the First Half of the Eighteenth Century', *The Hispanic American Historical Review*, Vol. 49, No. 3 (August 1969).

Boxer, C.R., *The Golden Age of Brazil, 1695–1750: Growing Pains of a Colonial Society* (University of California Press, 1962).

Boyadzhiev, K., 'Weapons from the Chalcolithic period in Bulgaria', *Dissertations*, Vol. 9 (Bulgarian Academy of Sciences, 2014).

Boyadzhiev, Y., St., Terzijska-Ignatova (eds), *The Golden 5th Millennium: Thrace and its neighbour areas in the Chalcolithic* (Sofia, 2011).

Boyle, P.P., & Grada, C.O., 'Fertility Trends, Excess Mortality, and the Great Irish Famine', *Demography*, 23 (4) (1986), pp.543–62.

Boyle, R.W., *Gold: History and Genesis of Deposits* (Van Nostrand Reinhold, 1987).

Brands, H.W., *The Age of Gold: the California Gold Rush and the New American Dream* (Knopf Doubleday Publishing Group, 2010).

Braudel, F., *Capitalism and Material Life* (London, 1973).

Breglia, L., 'Circolazione monetale ed aspetti di vita economica in Pompeii', *Raccolta di studi per il seconda centenario degli scavi di Pompei* (1950), pp.41–50.

Breitenlechner, E., *et al.*, 'Reconstructing the History of Copper and Silver Mining in Schwaz, Tirol', in *Mining in Central Europe, Perspectives from Environmental History*, ed. F. Uekoetter (RCC Perspectives, 2012), no. 10, pp.7–20.

Briant, P., *From Cyrus to Alexander: A History of the Persian Empire*, tr. P.T. Daniels (Eisenbrauns, 2002).

Brinkman, J.A., 'Foreign Relations of Babylonia from 1600 to 625 BC: The Documentary Evidence', *American Journal of Archaeology*, Vol. 76, No. 3 (July 1972), pp.271–81.

Broadberry, S., Campbell, B., Klein, A., Overton, M., & Van Leeuwen, B., *British Economic Growth, 1270–1870* (Cambridge University Press, 2015).

Broers, M., Hicks, P., Guimerá Ravina, A., & Guimera, A., *The Napoleonic Empire and the New European Political Culture* (Palgrave Macmillan, 2012).

Bunker, E.C., 'Gold in the Ancient Chinese World: A Cultural Puzzle', *Artibus Asiae* 53, No. 1/2 (1993), pp.27–50.

Burn, A.R., *Persia and the Greeks: The Defence of the West, c. 546–478 BC* (Stanford University Press, 1984).

Burns, A.R., *Money and Monetary Policy in Early Times* (Routledge, 1996).

Butt, J.J., *Daily Life in the Age of Charlemagne* (Greenwood Press, 2002).

Cahill, N.D. (ed.), *Lidyalılar ve dünyaları/The Lydians and Their World* (Istanbul: Yapı Kredi Yayınları, 2010).

Calvet, M., & Roesch, P., 'Les Sarapieia de Tanagra', *Revue Archéologique*, Nouvelle Série, Fasc. 2 (1966), pp.297–332.

Campbell, W., *Materials for a History of the Reign of Henry VII: From Original Documents Preserved in the Public Record Office* (Cambridge University Press, 2012).

Capponi, N., *Victory of the West: The Story of the Battle of Lepanto* (Macmillan, 2006).

Cardozo, M., 'The Brazilian Gold Rush', *The Americas*, Vol. 3, No. 2 (October 1946), pp.137–60.

Carlson, D.N., *et al.*, *Maritime Studies in the Wake of the Byzantine Shipwreck at Yassiada, Turkey* (Texas A&M University Press, 2015).

Carman, J., & Harding, A., *Ancient Warfare* (Sutton, 1999).

Carpenter, D.A., *The Reign of Henry III* (A&C Black, 1996).

Carrion Arregui, I.M., 'Sixteenth and Seventeenth Century Arms Production in Gipuzkoa', *Technology and Engineering: Proceedings of the XXth International Congress of History of Science* (Liège, 20–26 July 1997) Vol. VII, pp.265–79.

Carrion Arregui, I.M., Lette, M., & Oris, M., 'Sixteenth and Seventeenth Century Arms Production in Gipuzkoa', *Technology and Engineering: Proceedings of the XXth International Congress of History of Science* (Liège, 20–26 July 1997) Vol. VII (Brepols, 2000), pp.265–79.

Cassen, S., 'To import, to copy, to inspire? Central-Europeans objects signs in the Armorican Neolithic Age', *L'anthropologie* 107 (2003), pp.255–70.

Castro, A., *The Spaniards: An Introduction to Their History* (University of California Press, 1985).

Cathcart, B., *The News from Waterloo* (Faber & Faber, 2015).

Cauuet, B., Călin, G.T., Boussicault, M., & Munoz, M., 'Quantités et contrôle de l'or produit à l'âge du fer en Gaule du Centre-Ouest', *Mélanges de la Casa de Velázquez*, 48-1 (2018), pp.13–42.

Cazel, F.A., Jr., 'Financing the Crusades', in K.M. Setton (ed.), *A History of the Crusades*, Vol. VI, pp.116–49.

Chaliand, G., *Mirrors of a Disaster: The Spanish Military Conquest of America* (Routledge, 2019).

Challis, C.E., *A New History of the Royal Mint* (Cambridge University Press, 1992).

Chapman, J., 'From Varna to Brittany via Csőszhalom – Was There a "Varna Effect"?', in Anders, A., *et al.*(eds), *Moments in Time* (Hungary, 2013), pp.323–36.

Charles-Picard, G. & C., tr. Foster, A.E., *Daily Life in Carthage at the Time of Hannibal* (Allen & Unwin, 1981).

Chatelain, N.P., 'Controlling the California Gold Steamers: The Panama Route in the United States Civil War', *UCLA Historical Journal*, 28 (1) (2017).

Chaudhuri, K.N., *The Trading World of Asia and the English East India Company 1660–1760* (Cambridge University Press, 1978).

Chaudhuri, K.N., 'Treasure and Trade Balances: The East India Company's Export Trade, 1660–1720', *The Economic History Review*, New Series, Vol. 21, No. 3 (December 1968), pp.480–502.

Chaunu, H. & P., *Séville et l'Atlantique, 1504–1650*, Vol. 8 (Paris, 1959).

Chernakov, D., 'A New-Found Hoard of Chalcolithic Heavy Copper Tools from Northeastern Bulgaria', *Archaeologia Bulgarica* XXII, 2 (2018), pp.1–13.

Cherniss, M.D., 'The Progress of the Hoard in Beowulf', *PQ* 47 (1967), pp.473–86.

Chouin, G., 'The "Big Bang" Theory Reconsidered: Framing Early Ghanaian History', *Transactions of the Historical Society of Ghana New Series*, No. 14 (2012), pp.13–40.

Christiansen, K., *Duccio and the Origins of Western Painting* (Metropolitan Museum of Art, 2008).

Ciocîltan, V., *The Mongols and the Black Sea Trade in the Thirteenth and Fourteenth Centuries* (Brill, 2012).

Clark, G., *A Farewell to Arms* (Princeton University Press, 2007).

Clark, M.A., *Santería: Correcting the Myths and Uncovering the Realities of a Growing Religion* (Greenwood Publishing Group, 2007).

Clark, W.R., *Petrodollar Warfare* (New Society Publishers, 2005).

Clot, A., *Suleiman the Magnificent* (Saqi Books, 2005).

Cockell, S., 'The Origin and Emergence of Life under Impact Bombardment', *Philosophical Transactions: Biological Sciences*, Vol. 361, No. 1474, Conditions for the Emergence of Life on the Early Earth (29 October 2006), pp.1845–56.

Cohen, M., *The Sainte-Chapelle and the Construction of Sacral Monarchy: Royal Architecture in Thirteenth-Century Paris* (Cambridge University Press, 2015).

Conklin, J., 'The Theory of Sovereign Debt and Spain under Philip II', *Journal of Political Economy*, Vol. 106, No. 3 (June 1998), pp.483–513.

Cook, N.D., *Born to Die: Disease and New World Conquest, 1492–1650* (Cambridge University Press, 1998).

Cook, N.D., 'Sickness, Starvation, and Death in Early Hispaniola', *The Journal of Interdisciplinary History*, Vol. 32, No. 3 (Winter 2002), pp.349–86.

Cook, N.D., & George, W. (eds), *Secret Judgments of God: Old World Disease in Colonial Spanish America* (University of Oklahoma Press, 2001).

Cook, S.F., & Simpson, L.B., *The Population of Central Mexico in the Sixteenth Century* (AMS Press, 1978).

Costa, L.F., Lains, P., & Miranda, S.M., *An Economic History of Portugal, 1143–2010* (Cambridge University Press, 2016).

Costa, L.F., Palma, N., & Reis, J., 'The great escape? The contribution of the empire to Portugal's economic growth, 1500–1800', *European Review of Economic History*, 19 (1) (2015), pp.1–22.

Costa, L.F., Rocha, M.M., & de Sousa, R.M., 'Brazilian Gold in the Eighteenth Century: A Reassessment', *Working Papers*, GHES Universidade de Lisboa (2010).

Costa, L.F., Rocha, M.M., & de Sousa, R.M., *O Ouro do Brasil* (Imprensa Nacional-Casa da Moeda, 2013).

Craddock, P.T., 'From Egypt to Greece via India: New Insights into Bronze Casting Technology in Antiquity', in P. Eisenach *et al.* (eds), *The RITaK Conferences 2013–2014* (VML Vlg Marie Leidorf GmbH, 2017), pp.229–42.

Craddock, P.T., 'The Metal Casting Traditions of South Asia: Continuity and Innovation', *Indian Journal of History of Science*, 50.1 (2015), pp.55–82.

Craddock, P.T., & Cahill, N., 'The Gold of the Lydians' in *Metallurgy in Numismatics 6: Mines, Metals, and Money, Ancient World Studies in Science, Archaeology and History*, (K. Sheedy and G. Davis eds), Royal Numismatic Society, London, 2020.

Crafts, N.F.R., 'British Economic Growth, 1700–1831: A Review of the Evidence', *The Economic History Review*, New Series, Vol. 36, No. 2 (May 1983).

Craig, A.K., & Richards, Jr., E.J., *Spanish Treasure Bars From New World Shipwrecks* (En Rada Publications, 2003).

Craig, J., *The Mint: A History of the London Mint from AD 287 to 1948* (Cambridge University Press, 2011).

Crawford, H., *Sumer and The Sumerians* (Cambridge University Press, 2004).

Crawford, H. (ed.), *The Sumerian World* (Routledge, 2013).

Creighton, J., *Coins and Power in Late Iron Age Britain* (Cambridge University Press, 2000).

Cressy, D., *Saltpeter, The Mother of Gunpowder* (Oxford University Press, 2013).

Crowley, R., *Conquerors: How Portugal seized the Indian Ocean and forged the First Global Empire* (Faber & Faber, 2015).

Cunliffe, B., & Chadwick, N., *The Celts* (Penguin, 1997).

Dalrymple, W., *The Anarchy: The Relentless Rise of the East India Company* (Bloomsbury, 2019)

Dana, J.D., 'Observation on some points in the physical geography of Oregon and Upper California', *American Journal of Science* (2), Vol. 7 (1849), pp.125, 262.

Darling, A., *Back from the Brink: 1,000 Days at Number 11* (Atlantic Books, 2011)

Davey, J. (ed.), *Tudor and Stuart Seafarers: The Emergence of a Maritime Nation, 1485–1707* (National Maritime Museum, 2018).

Davies, P.J.E., *Architecture and Politics in Republican Rome* (Cambridge University Press, 2017).

Davis, R., *The Rise of the English Shipping Industry in the Seventeenth and Eighteenth Centuries* (Oxford University Press, 2012).

Davis, W., *One River: Explorations and Discoveries in the Amazon Rain Forest* (Random House, 2014).

Deagan, K.A., & Maria Cruxent, J., *Archaeology at La Isabela: America's First European Town* (Yale University Press, 2002).

Deane, P., & Cole, W.A., *British Economic Growth, 1688–1959: Trends and Structure* (Cambridge University Press, 1962).

De Callataÿ, F., 'White Gold: An Enigmatic Start to Greek Coinage', *American Numismatic Society* (2013), Issue 2.

Deckard, S., *Paradise Discourse, Imperialism, and Globalization: Exploiting Eden* (Routledge, 2009).

Dehn, W., 'The Russian Currency Reform', *The Economic Journal*, Vol. 8, No. 30 (June 1898), pp.225–33.

Denevan, W. (ed.), *The Native Population of The Americas in 1492* (University of Wisconsin Press, 1992).

Despini, A., Schurmann, W. & Gisler, J.-R., 'Gold Funerary Masks', *Antike Kunst*, 52. Jahrg. (2009), pp.20–65.

Diamond, J., *Guns, Germs and Steel* (New York, 1997).

Diffie, B.W., *Foundations of the Portuguese Empire, 1415–1580* (University of Minnesota Press, 1977).

Dignas, B., & Winter, E., *Rome and Persia in Late Antiquity: Neighbours and Rivals* (Cambridge University Press, 2007).

Dixon, S., *The Modernisation of Russia, 1676–1825* (Cambridge University Press, 1999).

Dolfini, A., Crellin, R.J., Horn, C., & Uckelmann, M., *Prehistoric Warfare and Violence: Quantitative and Qualitative Approaches* (Springer, 2018).

Dougherty, R.P., *Nabonidus and Belshazzar: A Study of the Closing Events of the Neo-Babylonian Empire* (Yale University Press, 1929).

Douglas, A.W., 'Cotton Textiles in England: The East India Company's Attempt to Exploit Developments in Fashion 1660–1721', *Journal of British Studies*, Vol. 8, No. 2 (May 1969), pp.28–43.

Douglas, D.C., *William the Conqueror: The Norman Impact Upon England* (University of California Press, 1964).

Drelichman, M., & Voth, H.-J., *Lending to the Borrower from Hell: Debt, Taxes, and Default in the Age of Philip II* (Princeton University Press, 2014).

Drelichman, M., & Voth, H.-J., 'The Sustainable Debts of Philip II: A Reconstruction of Castile's Fiscal Position, 1566–1596', *The Journal of Economic History*, Vol. 70, No. 4 (2010), pp.813–42.

Droysen, J.G., *History of Alexander the Great* (Berlin, 1833), tr. F. Kimmich, G.W. Bowersock & A.B. Bosworth, Transactions of the American Philosophical Society, Vol. 102, No. 3 (2012).

Drutz, E., 'Special article: Measles: Its history and its eventual eradication', *Seminars in Pediatric Infectious Diseases*, Vol. 12, Issue 4 (October 2001), pp.315–22.

Dubey, A.K., *Great Treasures* (Pustak Mahal, 1993).

Dubs, H.H., 'The beginnings of Alchemy', *Isis*, Vol. 38, No. 1/2 (November 1947), pp.62–86.

Duffy, C., *Siege Warfare: The Fortress in the Early Modern World 1494–1660* (Routledge, 2013).

Duncan-Jones, R., *Money and Government in the Roman Empire* (Cambridge University Press, 1998).

Dunn, R.S., *Sugar and Slaves; the rise of the planter class in the English West Indies, 1624–1713* (Jonathan Cape, 1973).

Duran, D., *Historia de las Indias de Nueva España e islas de la tierra firme México* (Editorial Porrúa, 1967).

Dussubieux, L., et al. (eds), *Recent Advances in Laser Ablation ICP-MS for Archaeology* (Springer-Verlag, 2016).

Dwyer, P.G., *Napoleon: The Path to Power* (Yale University Press, 2007).

Dyer, C., *Making a Living in the Middle Ages: The People of Britain, 850–1520* (Yale University Press, 2002).

Earle, R., '"If You Eat Their Food …"': Diets and Bodies in Early Colonial Spanish America', *The American Historical Review*, Vol. 115, No. 3 (June 2010), pp.688–713.

Edwards, M.U., *Printing, Propaganda and Martin Luther* (University of California Press, 1994).

Elliott, J.H., 'The Mental World of Hernán Cortés', *Transactions of the Royal Historical Society*, Vol. 17 (1967), pp.41–58.

Elton, H., *Warfare in Roman Europe, CE 350–425* (Oxford University Press, 1996).

English, S., *Mercenaries in the Classical World: To the Death of Alexander* (Pen & Sword, 2012).

Ereira, A., *The Invergordon Mutiny: A Narrative History of the Last Great Mutiny in the Royal Navy and How it Forced Britain Off the Gold Standard in 1931* (Routledge, 2015).

Ereira, A., *The People's England* (Routledge & Kegan Paul, 1981).

Espinosa, O., 'To Be Shipibo Nowadays: The Shipibo-Konibo Youth Organizations as a Strategy for Dealing with Cultural Change in the Peruvian Amazon Region', *The Journal of Latin American and Caribbean Anthropology*, 17 (November 2012), pp.451–71.

Estevadeordal, A., Frantz, B., & Taylor, A.M., 'The Rise and Fall of World Trade, 1870–1939,' *The Quarterly Journal of Economics*, Vol. 118, No. 2 (May 2003), pp.359–407.

Etting, V., *Queen Margrete I, 1353–1412, and the Founding of the Nordic Union* (Brill, 2004).

Evans, J.A.S., 'What Happened to Croesus?', *The Classical Journal*, Vol. 74, No. 1 (October–November 1978), pp.34–40.

Evans, S.T., *Ancient Mexico and Central America: Archaeology and Culture* (Thames & Hudson, 2013).

Fage, J.D., 'Ancient Ghana: a Review of the Evidence', *Transactions of the Historical Society of Ghana*, Vol. 3, No. 2 (1957), pp.3–24.

Fantom, G.S.M., *El Real Ingenio de la Moneda de Segovia: maravilla tecnológica del siglo XVI* (Fundación Juanelo Turriano, 2006).

Faroqhi, S., & Fleet, K. (eds), *The Cambridge History of Turkey* (Cambridge University Press, 2012).

Fay, C.R., 'Corn Prices and the Corn Laws, 1815–1846', *The Economic Journal*, Vol. 31, No. 121 (March 1921), pp.17–27.

Fay, C.R., 'Newton and the Gold Standard', *The Cambridge Historical Journal*, Vol. 5, No. 1 (1935), pp.109–17.

Feinberg, H.M., 'Africans and Europeans in West Africa: Elminans and Dutchmen on the Gold Coast During the Eighteenth Century', *The American Philosophical Society*, Vol. 79, Part 7 (1989).

Feinman G.M., & Price, T.D. (eds), *Archaeology at the Millennium: A Sourcebook* (Springer, 2002).

Fernanádez-Armesto, F., *Amerigo: The Man Who Gave His Name to America* (Random House, 2008).

Fernanádez-Armesto, F., *Before Columbus: Exploration and Colonisation from the Mediterranean to the Atlantic, 1229–1492* (Macmillan, 1987).

Fernanádez-Armesto, F., *Columbus* (Oxford University Press, 1991).

Ferry, S., *I am Rich Potosí, the Mountain that Eats Men* (The Monacelli Press, 1999).

Fetter, F.W., 'The Editions of the Bullion Report', *Economica*, New Series, Vol. 22, No. 86 (May 1955), pp.152–57.

Finkelstein, I., & Silberman, N.A., 'Temple and Dynasty: Hezekiah, the Remaking of Judah and the Rise of the Pan-Israelite Ideology', *Journal for the Study of the Old Testament*, Vol. 30.3 (2006), pp.259–85.

Fissel, M.C., *The Bishops' Wars: Charles I's Campaigns Against Scotland, 1638–1640* (Cambridge University Press, 2011).

Fitzpatrick, M.P., 'Provincializing Rome: The Indian Ocean Trade Network and Roman Imperialism', *Journal of World History*, Vol. 22, No. 1 (March 2011), pp.27–54.

Flandreau, M., 'The French Crime of 1873: An Essay on the Emergence of the International Gold Standard, 1870–1880', *The Journal of Economic History*, 56 (4) (1996), pp.862–97.

Fokkens, H., & Harding, A. (eds), *The Oxford Handbook of the European Bronze Age* (Oxford University Press, 2013).

Forbes, R.J., *Metallurgy in Antiquity: A Notebook for Archaeologists and Technologists* (Brill, 1950).

Foster, B. (ed.), *Gold Metallogeny and Exploration* (Springer, 1993).

Fouracre, P., *The Age of Charles Martel* (Longman, 2000).

Fowler, C., Harding, J., & Hofmann, D., *The Oxford Handbook of Neolithic Europe* (Oxford University Press, 2015).

Francis, A.D., 'John Methuen and the Anglo-Portuguese Treaties of 1703', *The Historical Journal*, Vol. 3, No. 2 (1960).

Freedman, P., *Out of the East* (Yale University Press, 2008).

Freeman, C., *The Closing Of The Western Mind* (Random House, 2011).

Freire, D., & Lains, P. (eds.), *An Agrarian History of Portugal, 1000–2000: Economic Development on the European Frontier* (Brill, 2017).

Freire, L., Costa, M., Rocha, M., & Martins de Sousa, R., 'Brazilian Gold in the Eighteenth Century: A Reassessment,' *DT/WP*, No. 42 (Universidade de Lisboa, 2010).

Frey, R.J., *Genocide and International Justice* (Infobase Publishing, 2009).

Friedberg, A.L., & Friedberg, I.S., *Gold Coins of the World: From Ancient Times to the Present: an Illustrated Standard Catalogue with Valuations* (Coin & Currency Institute, 2009).

Friede, J., 'The Catálogo de Pasajeros and Spanish Emigration to America to 1550', *The Hispanic American Historical Review*, Vol. 31, No. 2 (May 1951), pp.333–48.

Friedman, M., 'The Crime of 1873', *Journal of Political Economy*, Vol. 98, No. 6 (December 1990), pp.1159–94.

Friedman, Y., *Encounter Between Enemies: Captivity and Ransom in the Latin Kingdom of Jerusalem* (Brill, 2002), p.155.

Fugelso, K., *Defining Medievalism(s)* (Boydell & Brewer, 2009).

Gane, R., *Cult and Character: Purification Offerings, Day of Atonement, and Theodicy* (Eisenbrauns, 2005).

Garrard, T.F., 'The Early Trans-Saharan Gold Trade', *The Journal of African History*, Vol. 23, No. 4 (1982), pp.443–61.

Gasper, G.E.M., & Gullbekk, S.H., *Money and the Church in Medieval Europe, 1000–1200: Practice, Morality and Thought* (Routledge, 2016).

Gayre, R., *The Origin of the Zimbabwean Civilization* (Galaxie Press, Rhodesia, 1972).

Gelb, N., *The Jews in Medieval Normandy: A Social and Intellectual History* (Cambridge University Press, 1998).

Gibb, H.A.R., *The Encyclopaedia of Islam* (Brill Archive, 1954).

Gibbon, E., *The History of the Decline and Fall of the Roman Empire*, 6 vols. (London, 1789).

Gilbert, D.W., 'The Economic Effects of the Gold Discoveries Upon South Africa: 1886–1910', *The Quarterly Journal of Economics*, Vol. 47, No. 4 (August 1933), pp.553–97.

Gipouloux, F., *The Asian Mediterranean: Port Cities and Trading Networks in China, Japan and Southeast Asia, 13th–21st Century* (Edward Elgar, 2011).

Gleeson, J., *The Moneymaker* (Random House, 2012).

Glete, J., *Navies and Nations: Warships, Navies and State Building in Europe and America, 1500–1860*, 2 vols (Stockholm, 1993).

Goitein, S.D., *Studies in Islamic History and Institutions* (Leiden, 1966).

Goldgar, A., *Tulipmania: Money, Honor, and Knowledge in the Dutch Golden Age* (University of Chicago Press, 2008).

Goldin, C.D., & Lewis, F.D., 'The Economic Cost of the American Civil War: Estimates and Implications', *The Journal of Economic History*, Vol. 35, No. 2 (June 1975), pp.299–326.

Golson, E., 'The allied neutral? Portuguese balance of payments with the UK and Germany in the Second World War, 1939–1945', *Journal of Iberian and Latin American Economic History* 79.

Gordillo, E., 'Land Grabs and the Cost of Mining in Mongolia', *The Diplomat* (6 April 2023).

Goucher, C., LeGuin, C., & Walton, L., *In the Balance: Themes in Global History* (McGraw-Hill, 1998).

Gråberg, G., *Annali di geografia e di statistica* (Genoa, 1802).

Graham, F.D., & Whittlesey, C.R., *Golden Avalanche* (Princeton University Press, 1940).

Grant, R., *A Sketch of the History of the East-India Company: From Its First Formation to the Passing of the Regulating Act of 1773; with a Summary View of the Changes which Have Taken Place Since that Period in the Internal Administration of British India* (Black, Parry, and Company, 1813).

Graulau, J., 'Finance, Industry and Globalisation in the Early Modern Period: the Example of the Metallic Business of the House of Fugger', *Rivista di Studi Politici Internazionali*, Nuova Serie, Vol. 75, No. 4 (300) (October–December 2008), pp.554–98.

Green, M.J. (ed.), *The Celtic World* (Routledge, 1995).

Green, T., *Central Bank Gold Reserves: An historical perspective since 1845* (World Gold Council, 1999).

Greif, A., 'Reputations and Coalitions in Medieval Trade', *Journal of Economic History*, Vol. 49, No. 4 (December 1989), pp.857–82.

Grell, O.P., *Brethren in Christ: A Calvinist Network in Reformation Europe* (Cambridge University Press, 2011).

Grierson, P., *Medieval European Coinage* (Cambridge University Press, 1986).

Grierson, P., & Blackburn, M., *Medieval European Coinage; The Early Middle Ages (5th–10th Centuries)* (Cambridge University Press, 2007).

Grover, A.K., & Pandit, M.K., 'Ancient Gold Mining Activities in India – An Overview', *Iranian Journal of Earth Sciences* 7 (2015), pp.1–13.

Gudde, E.G., *California Place Names: The Origin and Etymology of Current Geographical Names* (University of California Press, 1960).

Guenther, G., *Magical Imaginations: Instrumental Aesthetics in the English Renaissance* (University of Toronto Press, 2012).

Guerra, F., 'The Earliest American Epidemic: The Influenza of 1493', *Social Science History*, Vol. 12, No. 3 (Autumn 1988), pp.305–25.

Guerra, M.F., & Rehren, T., 'In-situ examination and analysis of the gold jewellery from the Phoenician tomb of Kition (Cyprus)', *ArcheoSciences*, 33 (2009), pp.151–58.

Guilmartin Jr., J.F., *Gunpowder and Galleys: Changing Technology and Mediterranean Warfare at Sea in the Sixteenth Century* (Cambridge University Press, 1974).

Haak, W., *et al.*, 'Massive migration from the steppe was a source for Indo-European languages in Europe', *Nature*, Vol. 522 (11 June 2015), pp.207–11.

Haensch, S., Bianucci, R., Signoli, M., *et al.*, 'Distinct clones of Yersinia pestis caused the Black Death', *PLoS Pathog* 6 (10) (2010).

Haldon, J., *Byzantium in the Seventh Century: The Transformation of a Culture* (Cambridge University Press, 1990).

Halikowski Smith, S., '"Profits sprout like tropical plants": a fresh look at what went wrong with the Eurasian spice trade c., 1550–1800', *Journal of Global History* 3 (2008), pp.389–418.

Hall, B.S., *Weapons and Warfare in Renaissance Europe: Gunpowder, Technology and Tactics* (Johns Hopkins University Press, 1997).

Halpern, J., 'The Secret of the Temple', *New Yorker* (30 April 2012).

Hamilton, E.J., 'Imports of American Gold and Silver Into Spain, 1503–1660', *The Quarterly Journal of Economics*, Vol. 43, No. 3 (May 1929), pp.436–72.

Hamilton, E.J., *American Treasure and the Price Revolution in Spain, 1501–1650* (Octagon, 1970).

Hammer, P.E.J., *Elizabeth's Wars: War, Government and Society in Tudor England, 1544–1604* (Palgrave, 2003).

Hammes, D., & Wills, D., 'Black Gold; The End of Bretton Woods and the Oil-Price Shocks of the 1970s', *The Independent Review*, Vol. IX, No. 4 (Spring 2005).

Hampson, N., *The Perfidy of Albion: French Perceptions of England during the French Revolution* (Springer, 1998).

Hanke, L., *The Spanish Struggle for Justice in the Conquest of America* (University of Pennsylvania Press, 1949).

Harl, K., *Coinage in the Roman Economy 300 BC to AD 700* (Johns Hopkins University Press, 1996).

Harnetty, P., 'Cotton Exports and Indian Agriculture, 1861–1870', *The Economic History Review*, Vol. 24, No. 3 (August 1971), p.424.

Harnsberger, J.L., 'Jay Cooke and the Financing of the Northern Pacific Railroad, 1869–1873', *North Dakota Quarterly* 37 (4) (1969), pp.5–13.

Harper, K.N., Ocampo, P.S., Steiner, B.M., George, R.W., Silverman, M.S., Bolotin, S., *et al.*, 'On the Origin of the Treponematoses: A Phylogenetic Approach', *PLoS Negl Trop Dis*, 2 (1) (January 2008).

Harreld, D.J., *High Germans in The Low Countries: German Merchants And Commerce In Golden Age Antwerp* (Brill, 2004).

Harrell, J.A., and Brown, V.M., 'The World's Oldest Surviving Geological Map: The 1150 BC Turin Papyrus from Egypt', *The Journal of Geology*, 100 (1) (1992), pp.3–18.

Harrington, S.P.M., 'Behind the Mask of Agamemnon', *Archaeology*, Vol. 52, No. 4 (July/August 1999).

Harris, R.D., 'French Finances and the American War, 1777–1783', *The Journal of Modern History*, Vol. 48, No. 2 (June 1976), pp.233–58.

Harvard Law School International Human Rights Clinic, 'The Cost of Gold: Environmental Health and Human Rights Consequences of Gold Mining in South Africa's West and Central Rand' (2016).

Harvey, P.D.A., 'Rectitudines Singularum Personarum and Gerefa', *The English Historical Review*, Vol. 108, No. 426 (January 1993), pp.1–22.

Hasel, G., 'New Light on the Book of Daniel from the Dead Sea Scrolls', *Bible and Spade* (Spring 2011).

Hassan, A.A.H., *Sales and Contracts in Early Islamic Commercial Law* (The Other Press, 2007).

Hawthorne, N., *A Wonder-Book for Boys and Girls* (Boston, US, 1852).

Hawtrey, R.G., 'The Collapse of the French Assignats', *The Economic Journal*, Vol. 28, No. 111 (September 1918), pp.300–14.

Haywood, R.M., 'The Winter Palace in St Petersburg: Destruction by Fire and Reconstruction, December 1837–March 1839', *Jahrbücher für Geschichte Osteuropas*, Neue Folge, Bd. 27, H. 2 (1979), pp.161–80.

Helps, A., *The conquerors of the New World and their bondsmen : being a narrative of the principal events which led to negro slavery in the West Indies and America* (London, 1848–52).

Hemming, J., *Red Gold: the Conquest of the Brazilian Indians* (Papermac, 1995).

Hemming, J., *The Conquest of the Incas* (Macmillan, 1970).

Hemming, J., *The Search for El Dorado* (Phoenix Press, 1978).

Henige, D., *Numbers from Nowhere: the American Indian Contact Population Debate* (University of Oklahoma Press, 1998).

Herrmann, D.G., *The Arming of Europe and the Making of the First World War* (Princeton University Press, 1997), pp.234–37.

Higgins, K.J., *'Licentious liberty' in a Brazilian gold-mining region: slavery, gender, and social control in eighteenth-century Sabará, Minas Gerais* (Pennsylvania State University Press, 1999).

Hobsbawm, E.J., *Industry and Empire: The Making of Modern English Society* (Pantheon, 1968).

Holmyard, E.J., *Alchemy* (Penguin Books, 1968).

Holsti, K.J., *Peace and War: Armed Conflicts and International Order, 1648–1989* (Cambridge University Press, 1991).

Holt, F.L., *The Treasures of Alexander the Great; How One Man's Wealth Shaped the World* (Oxford University Press, 2016).

Hoppit, J., 'The Myths of the South Sea Bubble', *Transactions of the Royal Historical Society*, 12 (2002), pp.141–6.

Hoskins, W.G., 'The Rebuilding of Rural England, 1570–1640', *Past & Present*, No. 4 (November 1953), pp.44–59.

Hourihane, C., *The Grove Encyclopedia of Medieval Art and Architecture* (Oxford University Press, 2012).

Huaizhi, Z., & Yuantao, N., 'China's ancient gold drugs', *Gold Bull*, 34 (2001), p.24.

Hung, Ko Lu-Ch'iang Wu, & Davis, T.L., 'An Ancient Chinese Alchemical Classic. Ko Hung on the Gold Medicine and on the Yellow and the White: The Fourth and Sixteenth Chapters of Pao-P'u-tzŭ', *Proceedings of the American Academy of Arts and Sciences*, Vol. 70, No. 6 (December 1935).

Hurtado, A.L., *John Sutter: A Life on the North American Frontier* (University of Oklahoma Press, 2006).

Ibrahim, M., *Merchant Capital and Islam* (University of Texas Press, 2011).

Ifantidis, F., & Nikolaidou, M., 'Spondylus in Prehistory: New Data and Approaches – Contributions to the Archaeology of Shell Technologies', *British Archaeological Reports*, 4Int. Ser. 2216 (2011).

İnalcık, H., Osmanlı Para ve Ekonomi Tarihine Toplu Bir Bakış', Makaleler-I. ['A Synopsis of the Ottoman Money and Economy History', Article-1] (Ankara: Dogu-Bati Publications, 2005).

Irigoin, A., 'Global silver: Bullion or Specie? Supply and demand in the making of the early modern global economy', *Economic History Working Papers*, No. 285, LSE (September 2018).

Irwin, D.A., 'Gold sterilization and the recession of 1937–1938', *Financial History Review*, Vol. 19, 3 pp.249–67.

Israel, J., *Empires and Entrepots: Dutch, the Spanish Monarchy and the Jews, 1585–1713* (Bloomsbury, 1990).

Israel, J., 'López Pereira of Amsterdam, Antwerp and Madrid: Jew, New Christian, and advisor to the Conde-Duque de Olivares', *Studia Rosenthaliana*, Vol. 19, No. 2 (October 1985), pp.109–26.

Ivanova, M., 'Tells, Invasion Theories and Warfare in Fifth Millennium BC, North-Eastern Bulgaria', *Journal of Conflict Archaeology*, Vol. 2, 1 (2006), pp.33–48.

James, H., *International Monetary Co-operation Since Bretton Woods* (Oxford University Press, 1996).

James, L., *Mosaics in the Medieval World: From Late Antiquity to the Fifteenth Century* (Cambridge University Press, 2017).

Jansson, S.B., *Runstenar* (Stockholm, 1980).

Jersey, P. de (ed.), *Celtic Coinage: New Discoveries, New Discussion*, BAR International Series 1532 (2006).

Jiangxi Provincial Institute of Cultural Relics and Archaeology, Nanchang Museum & Xinjian District Museum, 'Marquis of Haihun's tomb of the Western Han Dynasty in Nanchang, Jiangxi', *Chinese Archaeology*, Vol. 17, Issue 117 (1) (2017), pp.44–59.

Jones, S.R.H., 'Transaction Costs, Institutional Change, and the Emergence of a Market Economy in Later Anglo-Saxon England', *The Economic History Review*, New Series, Vol. 46, No. 4 (November 1993), pp.658–78.

Jordan, W.C., 'Administering Expulsion in 1306', *Jewish Studies Quarterly*, Vol. 15, No. 3 (2008), pp.241–50.

Juras, A., Krzewińska, M, Nikitin, A.G., *et al.*, 'Diverse origin of mitochondrial lineages in Iron Age Black Sea Scythians', *Scientific Reports*, 7 (2017), 43950.

Kaeuper, R., *Bankers to the Crown: The Riccardi of Lucca and Edward I* (Princeton University Press, 2015).

Kaiser, T.E., 'Money, Despotism and Public Opinion in Early Eighteenth-Century France: John Law and the debate on Royal Credit', *The Journal of Modern History*, Vol. 63, No. 1 (March 1991), pp.1–28.

Kamen, H., *Philip of Spain* (Yale University Press, 1998).

Karl, T.L., 'The Perils of the Petro-State; Reflections on the Paradox of Plenty', *Journal of International Affairs*, Vol. 53, No.1 (Fall 1999), pp.31–48.

Karpenko, V., & Norris, J.A., 'Vitriol in the History of Chemistry', *Chem. Listy* 96 (2002), pp.997–1005.

Katusa, M., *The Colder War: How the Global Energy Trade Slipped from America's Grasp* (John Wiley & Sons, 2014).

Keegan, W.F., *Taino Indian Myth and Practice: The Arrival of the Stranger King* (University Press of Florida, 2007).

Keegan, W.F., *et al.* (eds), *The Oxford Handbook of Caribbean Archaeology* (Oxford University Press, 2013).

Kelder, J., 'The Egyptian interest in Mycenaean Greece', *Annual of Ex Oriente Lux (JEOL)* (2010), p.125.

Ker, J., & Pieper, C. (eds), *Valuing the Past in the Graeco-Roman World* (Brill, 2014).

Kerrich, R., 'Nature's Gold Factory', *Science*, New Series, Vol. 284, No. 2453 (25 June 1999), pp.2101–02.

Keynes, J.M., *A Treatise on Money V.2* (Macmillan, 1958).

Keynes, J.M., *Essays in Persuasion* (Palgrave Macmillan, 2010).

Khan, I.A., 'Coming of Gunpowder to the Islamic world and North India: Spotlight on the role of the Mongols', *Journal of Asian History*, Vol. 30, No. 1 (1996).

Kiermayr, R., How Much Money was Actually in the Indulgence Chest?', *The Sixteenth Century Journal*, 17, No. 3 (Autumn 1986), pp.303–18.

Kiernan, B., 'The First Genocide: Carthage, 146 BC', *Diogenes* 203 (2004), pp.27–39.

Kindleberger, C.P., *Historical Economics: Art or Science?* (University of California Press, 1990).

King, J.G., 'The Dioscuri on Reverses', *The Numismatic Journal* 1 (1836).

Kingsley, S., *God's Gold: The Quest for the Lost Temple Treasure of Jerusalem* (John Murray, 2006).

Kirk, G.S., *The Nature of Greek Myths* (Penguin, 1974).

Kisch, B., *Scales and Weights: A Historical Outline* (Yale University Press, 1965).

Kitchin, J., 'The Position of Gold', *The Review of Economics and Statistics*, Vol. 3, No. 8 (August 1921).

Kleber, K., & Pirngruber, R. (eds), *Silver, Money and Credit* (Leiden, 2016).

Kleinschmidt, H., *Charles V, The World Emperor* (Sutton, 2004).

Klemm, D., Klemm, R., & Murr, A., 'Gold of the Pharaohs – 6,000 years of gold mining in Egypt and Nubia', *African Earth Sciences* 33 (2001), pp.643–59.

Klemm, R., & Klemm, D., *Gold and Gold Mining in Ancient Egypt and Nubia: Geoarchaeology of the Ancient Gold Mining Sites in the Egyptian and Sudanese Eastern Deserts* (Springer Science & Business Media, 2012).

Knecht, R.J., *Renaissance Warrior and Patron: The Reign of Francis I* (Cambridge University Press, 1994).

Koch, A., *et al.*, 'Earth system impacts of the European arrival and Great Dying in the Americas after 1492', *Quaternary Science Reviews*, Vol. 207 (1 March 2019), pp.13–36.

Koenigsberger, H.G., Mosse, G.L., & Bowler, G.Q., *Europe in the Sixteenth Century* (Routledge, 2014).

Korobushkina, E.D., Karavaiko, G.I., & Korobushkin, I.M., 'Biochemistry of Gold', *Ecological Bulletins*, No. 35, Environmental Biogeochemistry (1983), pp.325–33.

Kotar, S.L., & Gessler, J.E., *Smallpox: A History* (McFarland, 2013).

Kratoska, P.H., *South East Asia, Colonial History: Imperialism before 1800* (Taylor & Francis, 2001).

Krauß, R., Schmid, C., Kirschenheuter, D., Abele, J. Slavchev, V., & Weninger, B., 'Chronology and development of the Chalcolithic necropolis of Varna I', *Documenta Praehistorica* XLIV (2017).

Krausse, D., *et al.*, 'The "Keltenblock" project: discovery and excavation of a rich Hallstatt grave at the Heuneburg, Germany', *Antiquity*, Vol. 91, Issue 355, pp.108–23.

Kulke, H., & Rothermund, D., *A History of India* (Psychology Press, 2004).

Kurke, L., *Coins, Bodies, Games, and Gold: The Politics of Meaning in Archaic Greece* (Princeton University Press, 1999).

Kustov, R., 'Gem minerals and materials from the neolithic and chalcolithic periods in Bulgaria and their impact on the history of gemmology', *Scientific Annals*, School of Geology, Aristotle University of Thessaloniki Proceedings of the XIX CBGA Congress, Special volume 100, Thessaloniki, Greece.

Kynaston, D., *Till Time's Last Sand: A History of the Bank of England 1694–2013* (Bloomsbury, 2017).

Laarhoven, R., & Pino Wittermans, E., 'From Blockade to Trade: Early Dutch Relations with Manila, 1600–1750', *Philippine Studies*, Vol. 33, No. 4 (Fourth Quarter 1985), pp.485–504.

Laiou, A.E., & Morrison, C., *The Byzantine Economy* (Cambridge University Press, 2007).

Lane, F.C., & Mueller, R.C., *Money and Banking in Mediaeval and Renaissance Venice*, Vol.1 (Johns Hopkins University Press, 1985).

Lane, K., *Potosi: The Silver City that Changed the World* (University of California Press, 2019).

Lange, C.H., *Triumphs in the Age of Civil War: the Late Republic and the Adaptability of Triumphal Tradition* (Bloomsbury Academic, 2016).

Leathlobhair, M.N., *et al.*, 'The evolutionary history of dogs in the Americas', *Science* (6 July 2018).

Lee, H.F., & Zhang, D.D., 'A tale of two population crises in recent Chinese history', *Climatic Change*, Vol. 116, Issue 2 (January 2013), pp.285–308.

Leick, G., *Mesopotamia: The Invention of the City* (Penguin Books, 2002).

Leins, I., 'Coins in Context: Coinage and Votive Deposition in Iron Age South-East Leicestershire', *British Numismatic Journal*, 77 (2007).

Leitenberg, M., 'America in Vietnam: Statistics of a war', *Survival*, 14:6 (1972).

Lemaire, A., Halpern, B., & Adams, M.J., *The Books of Kings: Sources, Composition, Historiography and Reception* (Brill, 2010).

Lenski, N. (ed.), *The Cambridge Companion to the Age of Constantine* (Cambridge: Cambridge University Press, 2012).

Leone, M., & Parmentier, R.J., 'Representing Transcendence: The Semiosis of Real Presence', *Signs and Society*, Vol. 2, No. S1 (Supplement 2014), pp.S1–S23.

Lester, T., *The Fourth Part of the World: The Race to the Ends of the Earth and the Epic Story of the Map that Gave America its Name* (Profile Books, 2009).

Leusch, V., & Pernicka, E., *Metals of Power – Early Gold and Silver*, 6th Archaeological Conference of Central Germany, 17–19 October 2013, in Halle (Saale, 2014).

Leusch, V., Armbruster, B., Pernicka, E., & Slavčev, V., 'On the Invention of Gold Metallurgy: The Gold Objects from the Varna I Cemetery (Bulgaria) – Technological Consequence and Inventive Creativity'. *Cambridge Archaeological Journal*, 25 (2015), pp.353–76.

Leverani, M., *Uruk, the First City* (Equinox, 2006).

Levey, M., 'The Refining of Gold in Ancient Mesopotamia', *Chymia*, Vol. 5 (1959), pp.31–36.

Levick, B., *Vespasian* (Routledge, 2016).

Levtzion, N., 'The Thirteenth- and Fourteenth-Century Kings of Mali', *The Journal of African History*, Vol. 4, No. 3 (1963), pp.341–53.

Lewis, P.R., & Jones, G.D.B., 'Roman Gold-Mining in North-West Spain', *The Journal of Roman Studies*, Vol. 60 (1970), pp.169–85.

Lewis, W.A., *Growth and Fluctuations 1870–1913* (George Allen & Unwin, 1978).

Lin, J.C.S. (ed.), *The Search For Immortality: Tomb Treasures of Han China* (Cambridge University Press, 2012).

Lindemann, A.S., & Levy, R.S., *Antisemitism: A History* (Oxford University Press, 2010).

Linden, S.J. (ed.), *Mystical Metal of Gold* (AMS Press, 2007).

Linssen, M.J.H., *The Cults of Uruk and Babylon: The Temple Ritual Texts as Evidence for Hellenistic Cult Practices* (Brill, 2004).

Lintern, M., Anand, R., Ryan, C., *et al.*, 'Natural gold particles in Eucalyptus leaves and their relevance to exploration for buried gold deposits', *Nature Communications* 4, 2614 (2013).

Lopez, R., 'Aux origines du capitalisme génois', *Annales d'histoire économique et sociale*, T. 9, No. 47 (30 September 1937), pp.429–54.

Lovejoy, P.E., 'The Volume of the Atlantic Slave Trade: A Synthesis', *The Journal of African History*, Vol. 23, No. 4 (1982), pp.473–501.

Luckenbill, D.D., *Ancient Records of Assyria and Babylon* (University of Chicago Press, 1927), v.II.

Lynch, J., *The Medieval Church: A Brief History* (Routledge, 2013).

Lynch, M., *Monotheism and Institutions in the Book of Chronicles: Temple, Priesthood, and Kingship in Post-Exilic Perspective* (Mohr Siebeck, 2014).

Lynn, J.A. (ed.), *Feeding Mars; Logistics in Western Warfare from the Middle Ages to the Present* (Westview Press, 1993).

Machado, I.F., & de M. Figueirôa, S.F., '500 years of mining in Brazil: a brief review', *Resources Policy*, 27 (2001), pp.9–24.

Mackenzie, D.A., *Myths of Pre-Columbian America* (Courier Corporation, 1996).

Mackie, C.J., 'The Earliest Jason. What's in a Name?', *Greece & Rome*, Vol. 48, No. 1 (April 2001).

Maddison, A., *Contours of the World Economy, 1–2030 AD, Essays in Macro-Economic History* (Oxford University Press, 2007).

Madley, B., *An American Genocide: The United States and the California Indian Catastrophe, 1846–1873* (Yale University Press, 2016).

Magee, M., *Shri Matrika Bheda Tantra* (Indological Book House, 1989).

Malm, O., 'Gold mining as a source of mercury exposure in the Brazilian Amazon', *Environmental Research*, 77 (2) (May 1998), pp.73–78.

Maltby, W., *The Reign of Charles V* (Palgrave, 2002).

Manning, J.G., 'Coinage as "Code" in Ptolemaic Egypt', Princeton/Stanford Working Papers in Classics (December 2006)

Manning, J.G., 'Volcanic suppression of Nile summer flooding triggers revolt and constrains interstate conflict in ancient Egypt', *Nature Communications*, 8, Article 900 (2017).

Manolakakis, L., Schlanger, N., & Coudart, A., *European Archaeology: Identities & Migrations* (Leiden, 2017).

Markowitz, M., 'The Coinage of Carthage', *CoinWeek* (7 July 2014).

Marques, A.H. de Oliveira, *Daily Life in Portugal in the Late Middle Ages* (University of Wisconsin Press, 1971).

Marshall, B.A., *Crassus: A Political Biography* (Amsterdam, 1976).

Martels, Z.R.W.M. von, *Alchemy Revisited; Proceedings of the International Conference on the History of Alchemy at the University of Groningen 17–19 April 1989* (Brill, 1990).

Martin, C., & Parker, G., *The Spanish Armada* (Hamish Hamilton, 1988).

Martin, D.A., '1853: The End of Bimetallism in the United States', *The Journal of Economic History*, Vol. 33, Issue 4 (December 1973).

Martín-Merás, L., 'La Carta de Juan de la Cosa: interpretación e historia', *Monte Buciero*, 4 (2000), pp.71–85.

Martinón-Torres, M., Valcárcel Rojas, R., Sáenz Samper, J., & Filomena Guerra, M., 'Metallic encounters in Cuba: The technology, exchange and meaning of metals before and after Columbus', *Journal of Anthropological Archaeology*, Vol. 31, Issue 4 (2012), pp.439–54.

Masakatsu, M., 'The Legend of "Zipangu", the Land of Gold', *Nipponia*, No. 45 (15 June 2008).

Matos Moctezuma, E., 'Archaeology & Symbolism in Aztec Mexico: The Templo Mayor of Tenochtitlan', *Journal of the American Academy of Religion*, Vol. 53, No. 4 (December 1985), pp.797–813.

Maxwell-Hyslop, K.R., 'Sources of Sumerian Gold: The Ur Goldwork from the Brotherton Library, University of Leeds. A Preliminary Report', *Iraq*, Vol. 39, No. 1 (Spring 1977), pp.83–86.

Maxwell-Hyslop, K.R., 'The Ur Jewellery. A Re-Assessment in the Light of Some Recent Discoveries', *Iraq*, Vol. 22, Ur in Retrospect. In Memory of Sir C. Leonard Woolley (Spring–Autumn 1960), pp.105–15.

Mays, M. (ed.), *Celtic Coinage: Britain and Beyond: the Eleventh Oxford Symposium on Coinage and Monetary History* (Tempus Reparatum, 1992).

Mbogoni, L.E.Y., *Human Sacrifice and the Supernatural in African History* (Dar-es-Salaam, 2013).

McCaa, R., 'Spanish and Nahuatl Views on Smallpox and Demographic Catastrophe in Mexico', *The Journal of Interdisciplinary History*, Vol. 25, No. 3 (Winter 1995), pp.397–431.

McEwan, G.F., *The Incas: New Perspectives* (ABC-CLIO, 2006).

McGhee, R., *The Arctic Voyages of Martin Frobisher: an Elizabethan Adventure* (Canadian Museum of Civilization, 2001).

McKim, D.K. (ed.), *The Cambridge Companion to John Calvin* (Cambridge University Press, 2004).

McNair Wilson, R., *The Mind of Napoleon; A study of Napoleon, Mr Roosevelt, and the Money Power* (G. Routledge & Sons, 1934).

Mearns, D.L., *et al.*, 'A Portuguese East Indiaman from the 1502–1503 Fleet of Vasco da Gama off Al Hallaniyah Island, Oman: an interim report', *The International Journal of Nautical Archaeology*, Vol. 45, 2 (2016), pp.331–50.

Melcher, M., *et al.*, 'Investigation of ancient gold objects from Artemision at Ephesus using portable μ-XRF', *ArcheoSciences*, 33 (2009).

Metcalf, D.M., 'How Large was the Anglo-Saxon Currency?', *The Economic History Review*, Second Series, Vol. XVIII, No. 3 (1965), pp.475–82.

Metcalf, W.E., *The Oxford Handbook of Greek and Roman Coinage* (Oxford University Press, 2016).

Meyer, C., *Bir Umm Fawakhir 3: excavations 1991–2003* (Oriental Institute of the University of Chicago, 2014).

Middleton, J. (ed.), *Encyclopedia of Africa South of the Sahara* (Scribner's, 1997).

Miskimin, H.A., *The Economy of Early Renaissance Europe, 1300–1460* (Cambridge University Press, 1975).

Modelski, G., *Cities of the Ancient World: An Inventory (-3500 to -1200)* (University of Washington, 1997).

Moisés, R.P., 'The Rise of the Spanish Silver Real', *Sigma: Journal of Political and International Studies*, Vol. 23, Article 5 (2005).

Molina-Cruz, A., & Barillas-Mury, C., 'The remarkable journey of adaptation of the Plasmodium falciparum malaria parasite to New World anopheline mosquitoes', *Memórias do Instituto Oswaldo Cruz*, 109 (5) (2014), pp.662–67.

Monroe, A.E., 'The French Indemnity of 1871 and its Effects', *The Review of Economics and Statistics*, Vol. 1, No. 4 (October 1919), pp.269–81.

Moore, E., *et al.*, *Shwedagon* (Thames & Hudson, 1999).

Moraes Farias, P.F. de, 'Silent Trade: Myth and Historical Evidence', *History in Africa*, Vol. 1 (1974), pp.9–24.

Moran, W.L., *The Armana Letters* (Johns Hopkins University Press, 1992).

Morganstern, A.M., 'The Pawns in Bosch's "Death and the Miser"', *Studies in the History of Art*, Vol. 12 (1982), pp.33–41.

Morison, S.E., *Christopher Columbus; Admiral of the Ocean Sea* (Oxford University Press, 1942).

Mørkholm, O., *Antiochus IV of Syria* (Gyldendal, 1966).

Morrell, W.P., *The Gold Rushes* (Adam and Charles Black, 1940), pp.46–58.

Muldrew, C., 'Hard Food for Midas: Cash and Its Social Value in Early Modern England', *Past & Present*, No. 170 (February 2001), pp.78–120.

Murphy, A.E., *John Law: Economic Theorist and Policy-Maker* (Clarendon Press, 1997).

Murray, A., *Reason and Society in the Middle Ages* (Clarendon Press, 2002).

Murray, G., 'The Segovia Mint Project: Recovering the activity in a Sixteenth-century Mint', *Proceedings of the ICOMON meetings held in Madrid, Spain, 1999* (Museo Casa de la Moneda, Madrid, 2001).

Musset, L., Bouvris, J.-M., & Gazeau, V., 'Sept essais sur des Aspects de la société et de l'économie dans la Normandie médiévale (Xe–XIIIe siècles)', *Annales de Normandie* (1988), p.22.

Nahon, K., & Hemsley, J., *Going Viral* (Cambridge, 2013).

Nash, G.D., 'A Veritable Revolution: The Global Economic Significance of the California Gold Rush', *California History*, Vol. 77, No. 4, 'A Golden State: Mining and Economic Development in Gold Rush California' (Winter 1998/99), pp.276–92.

Ndoro, W., 'Great Zimbabwe', *Scientific American*, Vol. 277, No. 5 (November 1997), pp.94–99.

Needham, J., *Science and Civilisation in China: Spagyrical discovery and invention; historical survey, from cinnabar elixirs to synthetic insulin* (Cambridge University Press, 1974).

Nelson, S.M., *Shamanism and the Origin of States: Spirit, Power, and Gender in East Asia* (Routledge, 2008).

Neto, L., Pinto, N., & Burns, M., 'Evaluating the Impacts of Urban Regeneration Companies in Portugal: The Case of Porto', *Planning Practice & Research*, 29:5 (2014), pp.525–42.

Nicholson, H.J., *The Knights Hospitaller* (Boydell & Brewer, 2001).

Nicol, D.M., *Byzantium and Venice* (CUP, 1988).

Nicolai, R., *The Enigma of the Origin of Portolan Charts: A Geodetic Analysis of the Hypothesis of a Medieval Origin* (Brill, 2016).

Nightingale, P., 'Monetary Contraction and Mercantile Credit in Later Medieval England', *The Economic History Review*, Vol. 43, No. 4 (November 1990), pp.560–75.

Nimchuk, C.L., 'The "Archers" of Darius: Coinage or Tokens of Royal Esteem?', *Ars Orientalis*, Vol. 32, 'Medes and Persians: Reflections on Elusive Empires' (2002), pp.55–79.

Nowell, C.E., 'The Discovery of Brazil – Accidental or Intentional?', *The Hispanic American Historical Review*, Vol. 16, No. 3 (August 1936), pp.311–38.

Nummedal, T., *Alchemy and Authority in the Holy Roman Empire* (University of Chicago Press, 2007).

Núñez, C.E., *Histoire Monétaire: Une Perspective Globale, 1500–1808* (Universidad de Sevilla, 1998).

Nunn, N., & Qian, N., 'The Potato's Contribution to Population and Urbanization: Evidence from a Historical Experiment', *Quarterly Journal of Economics*, 126 (2) (2011), pp.593–650.

O'Brien, P., 'The nature and historical evolution of an exceptional fiscal state and its possible significance for the precocious commercialization and industrialization of the British economy from Cromwell to Nelson', *The Economic History Review*, 64 (2) (2011), pp.408–46.

O'Connell, J., *The Book of Spice: From Anise to Zedoary* (Profile Books, 2015).

Olin, J.C. (ed.), *The Catholic Reformation: Savonarola to Ignatius Loyola* (New York, 1992).

Olson, D.W., 'Columbus and an eclipse of the Moon', *Sky & Telescope* (October 1992), pp.437–40.

Ormrod, D., *The Rise of Commercial Empires: England and the Netherlands in the Age of Mercantilism, 1650–1770* (Cambridge University Press, 2003).

Padgett, J.F., & Powell, W.W., *The Emergence of Organizations and Markets* (Princeton University Press, 2012).

Palma, N., & Reis, J., 'From Convergence to Divergence: Portuguese Economic Growth, 1527–1850', *The Journal of Economic History*, 79 (2) (2019), pp.477–506.

Palma, N., 'Money and modernization in early modern England', *Financial History Review*, 25 (3) (2018), pp.231–61.

Palma, N., 'Reconstruction of money supply over the long run: the case of England, 1270–1870', *The Economic History Review*, 71 (2) (2018), pp.373–92.

Palma, N., 'The Real Effects of Monetary Expansions: Evidence from a Large-scale Historical Experiment', *Review of Economic Studies* (2022), 89, 1593–1627.

Pamuk, Ş., 'The Price Revolution in the Ottoman Empire Reconsidered', *International Journal of Middle East Studies*, Vol. 33, No. 1 (February 2001), pp.69–89.

Parker, G., 'Mutiny and Discontent in the Spanish Army of Flanders 1572–1607', *Past & Present*, No. 58 (February 1973), pp.38–52.

Parker, G., *Philip II* (Penguin, 1979).

Parker, G., 'The Place of Tudor England in the Messianic Vision of Philip II', *Transactions of the Royal Historical Society*, 12 (2002), pp.167–221.

Parrott, D., *The Business of War: Military Enterprise and Military Revolution in Early Modern Europe* (Cambridge: Cambridge University Press, 2012).

Parry, G., *The Arch Conjuror of England: John Dee* (Yale University Press, 2012).

Parthasarathi, P., & Riello, G., 'The Indian Ocean in the Long Eighteenth Century', *Eighteenth-Century Studies*, Vol. 48, No. 1, Special Issue: 'The Maritime Eighteenth Century' (Fall 2014), pp.1–19.

Pastor, L., *The History of the Popes From the Close of the Middle Ages*, Vol. VIII (Herder Book Co., 1950).

Pastorino, C., 'Experimental Histories and Francis Bacon's Quantitative Program', *Early Science and Medicine*, 16 (6) (2011), pp.559–60.

Peissel, M., *The Ants' Gold: the Discovery of the Greek El Dorado in the Himalayas* (Harvill Press, 1984).

Pereira, D.P., & de Azevedo Basto, R.E. (ed.), *Esmeraldo de situ orbis* (Lisbon: Imprensa Nacional, 1892).

Pertusi, A. (ed.), *La Caduta di Costantinopoli* (Fondazione Lorenzo Valla: Verona, 1976).

Peters, F.E., *Muhammad and the origins of Islam* (SUNY Press, 1994).

Phillips, W.D., Jr., *Slavery in Medieval and Early Modern Iberia* (University of Pennsylvania Press, 2013).

Pintchman, T. (ed.), *Women's Lives, Women's Rituals in the Hindu Tradition* (Oxford University Press, 2007).

Piqueras-Fiszman, B., Laughlin, Z., Miodownik, M., & Spence, C., 'Tasting spoons: Assessing how the material of a spoon affects the taste of the food', *Food Quality and Preference*, Vol. 24, Issue 1 (April 2012), pp.24–29.

Pitfield, P., & Brown, T., *Tungsten* (British Geological Survey, 2011).

Platt, C., *King Death* (UCL Press, 1996).

Pomeranz, K., *The Great Divergence: China, Europe, and the Making of the Modern World Economy* (Princeton University Press, 2001).

Popescu, O., *Studies in the History of Latin American Economic Thought* (Routledge, 2001).

Portilla, J.M. de la, & Ceccarelli, M. (eds), *History of Machines for Heritage and Engineering Development* (Springer, 2011).

Portilla. M.L. (ed.), *The Broken Spears: The Aztec Account of the Conquest of Mexico* (Beacon Press, 2006).

Powell, M.A., 'Money in Mesopotamia', *Journal of the Economic and Social History of the Orient*', Vol. 39, No. 3, 'Money in the Orient' (1996), pp.224–42.

Prabha Ray, H., & Alpers, E. (eds), *Cross Currents and Community Networks: The History of the Indian Ocean World* (Oxford University Press, 2007).

Pregadio, F., *Great Clarity: Daoism and Alchemy in Early Medieval China* (Stanford University Press, 2006), ch.1.

Pressnell, L.S., *Country Banking in the Industrial Revolution* (Clarendon Press, 1956).

Pritchard, J., *In Search of Empire: The French in the Americas, 1670–1730* (Cambridge University Press, 2004).

Pursell, B.C., *The Winter King: Frederick V of the Palatinate and the Coming of the Thirty Years' War* (Routledge, 2017).

Puttnam, B., & Wood, J.E., *The Treasure of Rennes-le-Château. A Mystery Solved* (Stroud, 2003).

Quilter, J., 'Moche Politics, Religion and Warfare', *Journal of World Prehistory*, Vol. 16, No. 2 (June 2002), pp.145–95.

Quinn, J.C., & Vella, N.C. (eds), *The Punic Mediterranean* (Cambridge University Press, 2014).

Quiring, H., *Die Geschichte des Goldes. Die goldenen Zeitalter in ihrer kulturellen und wirtschaftlichen Bedeutung* (Stuttgart, 1948).

Rabb, T.K., 'The Effects of the Thirty Years War on the German Economy', *The Journal of Modern History*, Vol. 34, No. 1 (March 1962).

Radabaugh, J.S., 'Custer Explores the Black Hills 1874', *Military Affairs*, Vol. 26, No. 4 (Winter 1962–63), pp.162–70.

Radanovich, L., 'An Overview of Mariposa County History', *Mariposa Gazette* (5 November 1998).

Radet, G., *La Lydie et le Monde Grec* (1893).

Rady, M., *The Emperor Charles V* (Routledge, 2014), p.68.

Ramage, A., Craddock, P.T., & Cowell, M.R., *King Croesus' Gold: Excavations at Sardis and the History of Gold Refining* (Harvard University Press/Art Museums and the British Museum, 2000).

Raoult, D., *Paleomicrobiology: Past Human Infections* (Springer, 2008).

Rathbone, D., 'The Muziris papyrus (SB XVIII): financing Roman trade with India', in Alexandrian Studies II in Honour of Mostafa el Abbadi, *Bulletin de la Societe d'Archaeologie d'Alexandrie* 46 (2000), pp.39–50.

Reade, J., 'Assyrian King-Lists, the Royal Tombs of Ur, and Indus Origins', *Journal of Near Eastern Studies*, Vol. 60, No. 1 (January 2001), pp.1–29.

Redondo-Vega, J.M., Alonso-Herrero, E., Santos-González, J., González-Gutiérrez, R.B., and Gómez-Villar, A., 'La Balouta exhumed karst: a Roman gold-mine-derived landscape within the Las Médulas UNESCO World Heritage Site (Spain)', *International Journal of Speleology*, 44 (3) (2015), p.267.

Reis, J., 'The great escape? The contribution of the empire to Portugal's economic growth, 1500–1800', *European Review of Economic History*, 19 (1) (2015), pp.1–22.

Rémond, R., *Religion and Society in Modern Europe* (Blackwell, 1999).

Restall, M., *When Montezuma met Cortés* (Harper Collins, 2018).

Richter, A., Carpenter, B.W, & Carpenter, B., *Gold Jewellery of the Indonesian Archipelago* (Editions Didier Millet, 2012).

Riley, P.W.J., 'The Union of 1707 as an Episode in English Politics', *The English Historical Review*, Vol. 84, No. 332 (July 1969), pp.498–527.

Roberts, B., & Thornton, C. (eds), *Archaeo-metallurgy in Global Perspective – Methods and Syntheses* (Springer, 2014).

Roberts, R. (ed.), *Gold of the Great Steppe* (The Fitzwilliam Museum, Cambridge, 2021).

Robles Macias, L.A., 'Juan de la Cosa's Projection: A Fresh Analysis of the Earliest Preserved Map of the Americas', *Coordinates* (24 May 2010).

Rodewald, C., *Money in the Age of Tiberius* (Manchester University Press, 1976).

Roe, P.G., *The Cosmic Zygote: Cosmology in the Amazon Basin* (Rutgers University Press, 1982).

Rolle, A., *John Charles Frémont: Character as Destiny* (University of Oklahoma Press, 1991).

Roller, L.E., 'The Legend of Midas', *Classical Antiquity*, Vol. 2, No. 2 (9 October 1983), pp.299–313.

Rovira, S., Scott, D.A., & Meyers, P. (eds), *Archaeometry of Pre-Columbian Sites and Artifacts* (Getty Publications, 1994).

Rowden, G., 'The Last Days of Constantine: Oppositional Versions and Their Influence', *The Journal of Roman Studies*, Vol. 84 (1994), pp.146–70.

Rowen, H.R., *The Low Countries in Early Modern Times: A Documentary History* (Harper & Row, 1972).

Roymans, N., & Fernandez-Gotz, M., 'Fire and Sword. The archaeology of Caesar's Gallic War', *Military History Monthly*, 56 (2015), pp.52–56.

Rutledge, S.H., 'The Roman Destruction of Sacred Sites', *Historia: Zeitschrift für Alte Geschichte*, Bd. 56, H. 2 (2007), pp.179–95.

Sarmiento, P., 'La panacea áurea: alquimia y destilación en la corte de Felipe II (1527–1598)', *Dynamis*, 17 (1997), pp.107–40.

Schatz, E.A., 'The weight of the Ark of the Covenant', *Jewish Bible Quarterly*, 35, 2 (2007), pp.115–18.

Scheidel, W. (ed.), *Rome and China: Comparative Perspectives on Ancient World Empires* (Oxford University Press, 2009), p.165.

Scheidel, W., *Roman Economy* (Cambridge University Press, 2012).

Schmidbaur, H. (ed), *Gold: Progress in Chemistry, Biochemistry and Technology* (Wiley, 1999).

Schneider, K., 'Mongolia Copper Mine at Oyu Tolgoi Tests Water Supply and Young Democracy', *Circle of Blue* (5 November 2013).

Schoenberger, E., 'Why is gold valuable? Nature, social power and the value of things', *Cultural Geographies*, 18 (1) (2010), pp.3–24.

Schoonover, T.J., *The life and times of Gen. John A. Sutter* (Sacramento, 1907).

Scott, J.A., 'The Origin of the Myth of the Golden Fleece', *The Classical Journal*, Vol. 22, No. 7 (April 1927).

Scoville, W.C., 'The Huguenots in the French Economy, 1650–1750', *The Quarterly Journal of Economics*, Vol. 67, No. 3 (August 1953), pp.423–44.

Scully, R.E., '"In the Confident Hope of a Miracle": The Spanish Armada and Religious Mentalities in the Late Sixteenth Century', *The Catholic Historical Review*, Vol. 89, No. 4 (October 2003), pp.643–70.

Seaford, R., *Money and the Early Greek Mind: Homer, Philosophy, Tragedy* (Cambridge University Press, 2004).

Séfériadès, M.L., *Spondylus and Long-Distance Trade in Prehistoric Europe* (Centre National de la Recherche Scientifique/CNRS, 2009).

Selcer, R.F., *Civil War America, 1850 to 1875* (Infobase Publishing, 2014).

Serim, N., 'The Causes of the Financial Crisis That Began in the 16th Century and Continued until the Tanzimat Era in the Ottoman Empire', *Yönetim Bilimleri Dergisi*, Cilt 10, Sayı 20 (2012), pp.181–94.

Severy, M., 'Portugal's Sea Road to the East', *National Geographic*, 182, 5 (November 1992).

Shaps, D.M., *The Invention of Coinage and the Monetization of Ancient Greece* (University of Michigan Press, 2007).

Shaw, I. (ed.), *The Oxford History of Ancient Egypt* (Oxford University Press, 2000).

Shewring, M. (ed.), *Waterborne Pageants and Festivities in the Renaissance: Essays in Honour of J.R. Mulryne* (Routledge, 2017).

Shillington, K., (ed.), *Encyclopedia of African History* (Fitzroy Dearborne, 2005).

Sias, F.R., *Lost-wax Casting: Old, New, and Inexpensive Methods* (Woodsmere Press, 2005).

Silber, P., 'Gold and its Significance in Beowulf', *Annuale Medievale*, Vol. 18 (1977).

Silver, J., 'The Myth of El Dorado', *History Workshop*, 34, (1992), pp.1–15.

Smith, M.E., 'City Size in Late Postclassic Mesoamerica', *Journal of Urban History* (2005), pp.403–34.

Smith, R., 'Shipwreck in the Forbidden Zone', *National Geographic* (October 2009).

Smith, R.C., 'Colonial Towns of Spanish and Portuguese America', *Journal of the Society of Architectural Historians*, Vol. 14, No. 4, Town Planning Issue (December 1955), pp.3–12.

Snape, S., *Ancient Egyptian Tombs: The Culture of Life and Death* (John Wiley & Sons, 2011).

Soboul, A., *A Short History of the French Revolution, 1789–1799* (University of California Press, 1977).

Southern, P., *Augustus* (Routledge, 2013).

Spang, R.L., 'The Ghost of Law: Speculating on Money. Memory and Mississippi in the French Constituent Asembly', *Historical Relflections/Réflections Historiques*, Vol. 31, No. 1, 'Money in the Enlightenment' (Spring 2005).

Spooner, F.C., *The International Economy and Monetary Movements in France, 1493–1725* (Harvard University Press, 1972).

Spufford, P., *Money and Its Use in Medieval Europe* (Cambridge University Press, 1988).

Stargardt, J., 'The Four Oldest Surviving Pali Texts: the Results of the Cambridge Symposium on the Golden Pali Text of Sri Ksetra (Burma), April 1995', *Journal of the Pali Text Society* XXI, pp.199–213.

Starr, K., *Americans and the California Dream, 1850–1915* (Oxford University Press, 1986).

Steele, V., *Paris Fashion: A Cultural History* (Oxford, 1955).

Stein, D., 'Burning Widows, Burning Brides: The Perils of Daughterhood in India', *Pacific Affairs*, Vol. 61, No. 3 (Autumn 1988), pp.465–85.

Stern, F., *Gold and Iron: Bismarck, Bleichröder and the building of the German Empire* (Penguin Books, 1987).

Stewart, I., 'Moneyers In The 1130 Pipe Roll', *British Numismatic Journal*, 61 (1991), pp.1–8.

Stirling, S., *Pizarro, Conqueror of the Inca* (Sutton Publishing, 2005).

Stoddart, J.F., *et al.*, 'Cation-Dependent Gold Recovery with α-Cyclodextrin Facilitated by Second-Sphere Coordination', *Journal of the American Chemical Society*, 138, 36 (2016), pp.11643–653.

Story, J. (ed.), *Charlemagne: Empire and Society* (Manchester University Press, 2005).

Stratton, S., '"Seek and you Shall Find." How the Analysis of Gendered Patterns in Archaeology can Create False Binaries: a Case Study from Durankulak', *Journal of Archaeological Method and Theory*, Vol. 23, No. 3, '"Binary Binds": Deconstructing Sex and Gender Dichotomies in Archaeological Practice' (September 2016), pp.854–69.

Streyer, J.R., *The Reign of Philip the Fair* (Princeton, 1980).

Stride, H.G., 'The Gold Coinage Of Charles II', *British Numismatic Journal*, Vol. 28 (1955).

Styles, J., 'Product Innovation in Early Modern London', *Past & Present*, No. 168 (August 2000), pp.124–69.

Taber, G.M., *Chasing Gold: The Incredible Story of How the Nazis Stole Europe's Bullion* (Pegasus Books, 2014).

Tal, O., Kool, R., & Baidoun, I., 'A Hoard Twice Buried? Fatimid Gold from Thirteenth Century Crusader Arsur (Apollonia-Arsuf)', *The Numismatic Chronicle*, Vol. 173 (2013), pp.261–92.

Talbert, R.J.A., 'Augustus and the Senate', *Greece & Rome*, Vol. 31, No. 1 (April 1984), pp.55–63.

Taube, K., 'The Symbolism of Jade in Classic Maya Religion', *Ancient Mesoamerica*, 16 (1) (2005), pp.23–50.

Telford, L., *Sulla, A Dictator Reconsidered* (Pen & Sword Books, 2014).

TePaske, J.J., *A New World of Gold and Silver* (Brill, 2010).

Thomas, H., *Conquest: Cortes, Moctezuma, and the Fall of Old Mexico* (Simon & Schuster, 1995).

Thomas, H., *Rivers of Gold; The Rise of the Spanish Empire* (Weidenfeld & Nicolson, 2003).

Thomas, H., *The Conquest of Mexico* (Simon & Schuster, 2004).

Thompson, C.J.S., *Alchemy and Alchemists* (David & Charles, 2002).

Thompson, C.M., 'Sealed Silver in Iron Age Cisjordan and the "Invention" of Coinage', *Oxford Journal of Archaeology*, 22 (1) (2003), pp.67–107.

Thompson, E.A., *A Roman Reformer and Inventor, being a new text of the Treatise De Rebus Bellicis with a Translation and Introduction* (Clarendon Press, 1952).

Thurston, E., *History of the Coinage of the Territories of the East India Company in the Indian Peninsula and Catalogue of the Coins in the Madras Museum* (Asian Educational Services, 1992).

Tignor, A., *et al.*, *Worlds Together, Worlds Apart, Volume 1: Beginnings to the 15th Century* (W.W. Norton & Company, 2014).

Todorova, K., tr. V. Zhelyaskova, *The Eneolithic Period in Bulgaria in the Fifth Millennium BC* (British Archaeological Reports, Oxford, 1978).

Tooze, A., *The Deluge: The Great War and the Remaking of Global Order 1916–1931* (Penguin UK, 2014).

Townsend, C., *Fifth Sun: A New History of the Aztecs* (Oxford University Press, 2019).

Treasure, G., *The Huguenots* (Yale University Press, 2013).

Tringham, R., *Hunters, Fishers and Farmers of Eastern Europe, 6000–3000 BC* (Routledge, 1971/2015).

Tucker, R.S., 'Gold and the General Price Level', *The Review of Economics and Statistics*, Vol. 16, No. 1 (15 January 1934)'

Tvede, L., *The Psychology of Finance: Understanding the Behavioural Dynamics of Markets* (John Wiley & Sons, 2002).

Usher, P., *The Early History of Deposit Banking in Mediterranean Europe* (Harvard University Press, 1943).

Usishkin, D., 'The Ghassulian Shrine at En-gedi', *Journal of the Tel Aviv University Institute of Archaeology*, 7 (1–2) (1980), pp.1–44.

Van Buren, E.D., 'The Sceptre, its Origin and Significance', *Revue d'Assyriologie et d'archéologie orientale*, Vol. 50, No. 2 (1956), pp.101–03.

Van de Goot, F.R.W., ten Berge, R.L., & Vos, R., 'Molten gold was poured down his throat until his bowels burst', *Journal of Clinical Pathology*, 56 (2003), p.157.

Van der Spek, R.J., van Zanden, J.L., & van Leeuwen, B., *A History of Market Performance: From Ancient Babylonia to the Modern World* (Routledge, 2014).

Van Tuerenhout, D.R., *The Aztecs. New Perspectives* (ABC-CLIO, 2005).

Van Veen, E., & Blussé, L., *Rivalry and Conflict: European Traders and Asian Trading Networks in the 16th and 17th Centuries* (Amsterdam University Press, 2005).

Varela, C., & Aguirre, I., *La caída de Cristóbal Colón: el juicio de Bobadilla* (Marcial Pons Historia, 2006).

Venable, S.L., *Gold: A Cultural Encyclopedia* (ABC-CLIO, 2011).

Vernon, J.R., 'Unemployment Rates in Post-Bellum America: 1869–1899', *Journal of Macroeconomics*, 16 (1994), pp.701–14.

Veyne, P., 'Rome devant la prétendue fuite de l'or: mercantilisme ou politique disciplinaire?', *Annales. Histoire, Sciences Sociales*, 34e Année, No. 2 (February–March 1979), pp.211–44.

Vilar, P., *A History of Gold and Money, 1450 to 1920* (Verso, 1991).

Vilches, E., *New World Gold: Cultural Anxiety and Monetary Disorder in Early Modern Spain* (University of Chicago Press, 2010).

Vitali, L. (ed.), *Il tesoro del Duomo di Monza* (Banca Popolare di Milano, 1966).

Vivo, F. de, 'Historical Justifications of Venetian Power in the Adriatic', *Journal of the History of Ideas*, Vol. 64, No. 2 (April 2003), pp.159–76.

von Glahn, R., *Fountain of Fortune: Money and Monetary Policy in China, 1000–1700* (University of California Press, 1996).

Wake, C.H.H., 'The changing pattern of Europe's pepper and spice imports, ca 1400–1700', *Journal of European Economic History*, Vol. 8, Edition 2 (1979), pp.361–403.

Wali, A., *et al.*, *The Shipibo-Conibo: Culture and Collections in Context* (Field Museum of Natural History, 2016).

Walker, A., 'Forgeries and Inventions of Parthian Coins', *Bulletin on Counterfeits*, Vol. 19, No. 2 (1994/95).

Walton, T.R., *The Spanish Treasure Fleets* (Pineapple Press Inc, 2002).

Watson, A.M., 'Back to Gold and Silver', *The Economic History Review*, New Series, Vol. 20, No. 1 (April 1967), pp.1–34.

Watts, D., *Christians and Pagans in Roman Britain* (Routledge, 1991).

Welch, D.A., *Justice and the Genesis of War* (Cambridge University Press, 1995).

Whatley, C.A., *Scots and the Union: Then and Now* (Edinburgh University Press, 2014).

White, E.N., 'The French Revolution and the Politics of Government Finance, 1770–1815', *The Journal of Economic History*, Vol. 55, No. 2 (June 1995), pp 227–55.

White, R.T., 'Luxury at Rome: avaritia, aemulatio and the mos maiorum', *Ex Historia*, Vol. 6 (2014), pp.117–43.

Whiting, B.H., Hodgson, C.J., & Mason, R. (eds), *Giant Ore Deposits* (Society of Economic Geologists, 1993).

Wiegand, J., 'Destabilizing the Global Monetary System: Germany's Adoption of the Gold Standard in the Early 1870s', *IMF Working Paper WP/19/32* (February 2019).

Willbold, M., Elliott, T., & Moorbath, S., 'The tungsten isotopic composition of the Earth's mantle before the terminal bombardment', *Nature*, 477 (2011), pp.195–98.

Williamson, Jeffrey G., 'The structure of pay in Britain, 1710–1911', *Research in Economic History*, Vol. 7 (1982), pp.1–54.

Willis, H.P., 'The Vienna Monetary Treaty of 1857', *Journal of Political Economy*, Vol. 4, No. 2 (March 1896), pp.187–207.

Wilson, P.H., *Europe's Tragedy: A New History of the Thirty Years War* (Penguin, 2009).

Wilson-Smith, T., *Napoleon: Man of War, Man of Peace* (Carroll & Graf, 2002).

Witte, F.X.P., 'Living the Law of Origin: The Cosmological, Ontological, Epistemological, and Ecological Framework of Kogi Environmental Politics' (PhD thesis, Downing College, Cambridge, 2017).

Wolff, D., 'Gold Mining in the Black Hills', *Black Hills Visitor Magazine* (5 August 2015).

Wolters, A., 'Belshazzar's Feast and the Cult of the Moon God Sîn', *Bulletin for Biblical Research* 5 (1995), pp.199–206.

Xella, P., Quinn, J., Melchiorri, V., & van Dommelen, P., 'Cemetery or sacrifice? Infant burials at the Carthage Tophet: Phoenician bones of contention', *Antiquity*, Vol. 87, 338 (1 December 2013).

Yalcindag, E., *et al.*, 'Multiple independent introductions of Plasmodium falciparum in South America', *Proceedings of the National Academy of Sciences*, Vol. 109 (2) (2012), pp.511–16.

Yalichev, S., *Mercenaries of the Ancient World* (Constable, 1997).

Yanko-Hombach, V., Gilbert, A.S., Panin, N., & Dolukhanov, P.M. (eds), *The Black Sea Flood Question: Changes in Coastline, Climate, and Human Settlement* (Springer, 2007).

Yarshater, E. (ed.), *The Cambridge History of Iran. Vol. 3, The Seleucid, Parthian and Sasanian Periods* (Cambridge University Press, 1983).

Zahedieh, N., *The Capital and the Colonies: London and the Atlantic Economy, 1660–1700* (Cambridge University Press, 2010).

Zamora, M., *Reading Columbus* (University of California Press, 1993).

Zbenovich, V.G., 'The Oldest Gold in the World (on the occasion of the exhibition in the Israel Museum)', *Mitekufat Haeven: Journal of the Israel Prehistoric Society* 1994–95), pp.159–73.

Zimmerli, W., *Ezekiel: A Commentary on the Book of the Prophet Ezekiel, Volume 1* (Fortress Press, 1979).

Zinner, E., & Brown, E., *Regiomontanus: His Life and Work* (Elsevier, 2014).

Zook, G.F., 'The Company Of Royal Adventurers Trading Into Africa', *The Journal of Negro History*, Vol. IV, No. 2 (April 1919).

Zorach, R., *Blood, Milk, Ink, Gold: Abundance and Excess in the French Renaissance* (University of Chicago Press, 2005).

Zorach, R., & Phillips, M.W. Jr, *Gold: Nature and Culture* (Reaktion Books, 2016).

URLs

Albers, T., & Uebele, M., 'A Monthly International Dataset for the Interwar Period: Taking the Debate to the Next Level' (2013), Conference paper, URL https://www.researchgate.

net/publication/257413890_A_Monthly_International_Dataset_for_the_Interwar_Period_
Taking_the_Debate_to_the_Next_Level/citation/download; consulted 10/11/2019.

'All the Money in the World', Bullion Vault 10/27/2009, URL https://www.bullionvault.com/
gold-news/all_the_money_in_the_world_102720093; consulted 12/11/2019.

Armbruster, B., 'Gold technology of the ancient Scythians – gold from the kurgan Arzhan 2, Tuva',
ArcheoSciences (Online), 33 (2009), online since 10 December 2012, consulted 4 March 2024.

Baughan, E., 'Lydian Burial Customs', URL http://www.sardisexpedition.org/en/essays/latw-
baughan-lydian-burial-customs#introduction; consulted 25/8/2017.

BBC news, 24 September 2018, 'Portuguese 400 year old shipwreck found off Cascais', URL
https://www.bbc.co.uk/news/world-europe-45630260; consulted 15/11/2019.

Betz, R.F., Lootens, R.J., & Becker, M.K., 'Two Decades of Prairie Restoration at Fermilab',
https://www.osti.gov/biblio/435342. Consulted 18/05/2024.

Bird, L., & Krauer, N., 'Case Study: Illicit Gold Mining in Peru', The Global Initiative Against
Transnational Organised Crime (November 2017), URL https://globalinitiative.net/wp-
content/uploads/2017/11/tgiatoc-case-study-peru-1878-web-lo-res.pdf.

Bolt, J., &van Zanden, J.L., 'The First Update of the Maddison Project; Re-Estimating Growth
Before 1820', Maddison Project Working Paper 4 (2013), http://www.ggdc.net/maddison/
maddisonproject/home.htm.

Bonsall, C., Gurova, M., Elenski, N., Ivanov, G., Bakamska, A., Ganetsovski, G., Zlateva-Uzunova,
R. & Slavchev, V., 'Tracing the source of obsidian from prehistoric sites in Bulgaria', Bulgarian
E-Journal of Archaeology, 7, 1 (26 June 2017); accessed 21/07/2017.

Bresson, A., 'The Origin of Lydian and Greek Coinage: Cost and Quantity', based on 'The Origin
of Lydian and Greek Coinage: Cost and Quantity', Historical Research, 5 (2006), pp.149–65 (in
Chinese translation), https://economics.yale.edu/sites/default/files/files/Workshops-Seminars/
Economic-History/bresson-090921a.pdf; consulted 15/05/2020.

Broadberry, S., Campbell, Bruce M.S., and van Leeuwen, Bas, 'English Medieval Population:
Reconciling time series and cross-sectional evidence', University of Warwick unpublished
manuscript (2010), URL https://warwick.ac.uk/fac/soc/economics/staff/sbroadberry/wp/
medievalpopulation7.pdf; consulted 2/7/2018.

Burr, D., (tr.), 'The Book of Suger Abbot of St. Denis on What Was Done During his
Administration', URL http://www.medart.pitt.edu/texts/Saint-Denis/SugerAdmin.html;
consulted 3/4/2018.

Cherian, J., 'Influence of Isaac Newton in the Development of Economic Thought', https://
medium.com/@joel.cherian/influence-of-isaac-newton-in-the-development-of-economic-
thought-741683a12185; consulted 12/5/2020.

Clark, K., 'Unicorns aren't profitable, and Wall Street doesn't care', Tech Crunch (26 March 2019),
https://techcrunch.com/2019/03/26/unicorns-arent-profitable-wall-street-doesnt-care/;
consulted 14/05/2010.

Cowen, R., 'Medieval Silver and Gold', http://mygeologypage.ucdavis.edu/cowen/~gel115/115CH7.
html.

Crafts, N.F.R., 'British Economic Growth during the Industrial Revolution Oxford' (1985), www.
ehs.org.uk/dotAsset/15457c19-e7bd-4045-a056-30a3efac2d47.pdf.

Crittall, E. (ed.), 'Textile industries since 1550', in A History of the County of Wiltshire: volume 4
(London, 1959), pp.148–82. British History Online, http://www.british-history.ac.uk/vch/
wilts/vol4/pp148-182; accessed 3 August 2019.

CTV news, 15 September 2017, URL https://www.ctvnews.ca/sci-tech/in-namibia-1533-
portuguese-shipwreck-s-relics-hidden-away-1.3590932; consulted 17/7/2018.

Department of the Arts of Africa, Oceania, and the Americas, 'The Empires of the Western Sudan:
Ghana Empire', in Heilbrunn Timeline of Art History (New York: The Metropolitan Museum of
Art, 2000), http://www.metmuseum.org/toah/hd/ghan/hd_ghan.htm; consulted 05/06/2002.

Ecology Global Network, http://www.ecology.com/population-estimates-year-2050/; consulted 4/4/2018.

Edberg, R., *Runriket Täby-Vallentuna – en handledning* (in Swedish). stockholms.lans.museum (2007), https://www.academia.edu/2252712/Runriket_T%C3%A4by-Vallentuna_--_en_handledning; consulted 31/5/2020.

en.wikipedia.org/wiki/List_of_wars_by_death_toll#Modern_wars_with_greater_than_25,000_deaths_by_death_toll; consulted 3/2/2019.

ETCSL project, Faculty of Oriental Studies, University of Oxford: 'Enmerkar and the lord of Aratta: c.1.8.2.3', URL http://etcsl.orinst.ox.ac.uk/cgi-bin/etcsl.cgi; consulted 1/8/2017.

'Federal Budget Outlays for Defense Functions: 1980 to 2002 Military Personnel U.S. Military Ranks', cited at www.infoplease.com/us/military-personnel/us-military-spending-1946-2009; consulted 25/11/2019.

Frankenfield, J., 'How Much of the World's Money is in Bitcoin?', *Investopedia* (25 June 2019), URL https://www.investopedia.com/tech/how-much-worlds-money-bitcoin/; consulted 13/11/2019.

Georgia Gold History, URL http://dlg.galileo.usg.edu/dahlonega/history.php; consulted 5/11/2021.

Governors' Gallery: Peter Burnett, URL https://governors.library.ca.gov/addresses/s_01-Burnett2.html; consulted 2/11/2021.

Green, Monica H., 'Taking "Pandemic" Seriously: Making the Black Death Global', *The Medieval Globe*, Vol. 1, No. 1, Article 4, https://scholarworks.wmich.edu/tmg/vol1/iss1/4; consulted 29/12/2019.

Greenewalt, C.H. Jr., 'Gold and Silver Refining at Sardis', https://sardisexpedition.org/en/essays/latw-greenewalt-gold-silver-refining; consulted 30/05/2020.

Haider, N., 'Prices and Wages in India (1200–1800); Source Material, Historiography and New Directions', *Towards a Global History of Prices and Wages* (Utrecht 19–21 August 2004), unpublished, URL http://www.iisg.nl/hp.

Halikowski Smith, S., 'Portugal and the European spice trade, 1480–1580', European University Institute (2001), EUI PhD theses, Department of History and Civilization, p.361, retrieved from Cadmus, European University Institute Research Repository, http://hdl.handle.net/1814/5828; consulted 22/4/2020.

Jarus, O., 'Egyptian mummies covered in gold are rare, and we may have just found the oldest', *Livescience* (31 January 2023), URL https://www.livescience.com/oldest-gold-covered-egyptian-mummy; consulted 12/1/2024.

'Key Documents in the History of Gold, V.2, The Heyday of the Gold Standard, 1820–1930', p.117, URL https://www.gold.org/sites/default/files/documents/1900mar14.pdf; consulted 5/11/2019.

LaBorde, L., 'Money – Then and Now: Instalment VII: H.L., Hunt's Boys and the Circle K Cowboys', gold-eagle.com (26 January 2004), www.gold-eagle.com/article/money-then-and-now.

Maddison, A., 'Historical Statistics of the World Economy: 1–2008 AD', www.ggdc.net/maddison/Historical_Statistics/.

Markley, B., 'Custer's Gold', *True West* (April 2018), URL https://truewestmagazine.com/article/custers-gold/; consulted 6/11/2021.

'Mariner's Museum Exploration Through the Ages, Martin Frobisher' (2004), URL ushistoryatlas.com/era1/USHAcom_PS_U01_frobisher_R2.pdf.

Matsukawa, K., 'European Images of India before the Rise of Orientalism in the Late Eighteenth Century', MPhil thesis, London School of Economics (2000), URL http://etheses.lse.ac.uk/1600/1/U148238.pdf; consulted 15/11/2009.

McLaughlin, L., 'The All-Canadian Route to the Klondike', URL http://hougengroup.com/yukon-history/yukon-nuggets/the-all-candian-route-to-the-klondike/; consulted 2/11/2019.

measuringworth.com/calculators/ppowerus/; consulted 18/10/2019.

'Mexica (Aztec) & Tlaxcala accounts of the Spanish Conquest, 1500s', URL https://nationalhumanitiescenter.org/pds/amerbegin/contact/text7/mexica_tlaxcala.pdf; consulted 15/1/2024.

Mikosch, E., 'The Manufacture And Trade Of Luxury Textiles In The Age Of Mercantilism', *Textile Society of America Symposium Proceedings*, Textile Society of America (1990), URL digitalcommons.unl.edu/cgi/viewcontent.cgi?article=1611&context=tsaconf; consulted 10/5/2019.

Millerman, A.J., 'The Spinning of Ur: How Sir Leonard Woolley, James R., Ogden and the British Museum interpreted and represented the past to generate funding for the excavation of Ur in the 1920s and 1930s', PhD Thesis, University of Manchester (Humanities) (2015), https://www.research.manchester.ac.uk/portal/en/theses/the-spinning-of-ur-how-sir-leonard-woolley-james-r-ogden-and-the-british-museum-interpreted-and-represented-the-past-to-generate-funding-for-the-excavation-of-ur-in-the-1920s-and-1930s(d9f0637d-a5a7-41cc-8eda-32646627010d).html; consulted 29/05/2020.

Millman, E., 'The Importance of the Lydian Stater as the World's First Coin', *Ancient History Encyclopedia* (27 March 2015), retrieved from https://www.ancient.eu/article/797/.

Mongiatti, A., 'Analysing and smelting noble metals in sixteenth century Austria: a comparative analytic study', PhD Thesis, Institute of Archaeology, University of London (2010), URL discovery.ucl.ac.uk/18710/1/18710.pdf.

Moore, T.K., 'Credit Finance in the Middle Ages', *Economic History Society Conference 2009*, URL www.ehs.org.uk/dotAsset/2198856a-47ce-475b-8e49-0917b3b1f0d7.pdf; consulted 02/04/2018.

Morys, M., 'The emergence of the Classical Gold Standard, Moneys and Economies During 19th Century (From Europe To Asia)' (January 2012), URL https://www.york.ac.uk/media/economics/documents/cherrydiscussionpapers/1201.pdf; consulted 24/10/2019.

NY Times (27 January 1862), 'WAR FINANCE IN ENGLAND', http://www.nytimes.com/1862/01/27/news/war-finance-england-bank-restriction-act-1797-suspension-specie-payments-for.html?pagewanted=all.

Oberg, J. James, 'Why the Mars Probe went off course', *IEEE Spectrum* (1 December 1999), IEEE, URL https://spectrum.ieee.org/aerospace/robotic-exploration/why-the-mars-probe-went-off-course; consulted 2/1/2020.

O'Brien, P.K., & Palma, N., 'Danger To The Old Lady Of Threadneedle Street? The Bank Restriction Act And The Regime Shift To Paper Money, 1797–1821', *European Review of Economic History* (November 2019), URL https://academic.oup.com/ereh/advance-article-abstract/doi/10.1093/ereh/hez008/5587705?redirectedFrom=fulltext; consulted 18/11/2019.

Palma, N., & Santiago-Caballero, C., 'Patterns of Iberian Economic Growth in the Early Modern Period', in *An Economic History of the Iberian Peninsula, 700–2000*. Cambridge University Press (2004).

Palma, N., Reis, J., & Zhang, M., 'Reconstruction of regional and national population using intermittent census-type data: the case of Portugal, 1527–1864', Historical Methods: A Journal of Quantitative and Interdisciplinary History (2019), URL https://www.tandfonline.com/doi/full/10.1080/01615440.2019.1666762; consulted 18/11/2019.

Palma, P.G.N., 'Harbingers of Modernity: Monetary Injections and European Economic Growth, 1492–1790', PhD thesis, LSE (2015/16), URL https://core.ac.uk/download/pdf/46520038.pdf; consulted 11/07/2019.

Parisi, A.F., *et al.*, 'Can the Late Heavy Bombardment hypothesis be resuscitated?', American Geophysical Union (Fall Meeting 2020), abstract #DI019-0012 (December 2020), URL https://ui.adsabs.harvard.edu/abs/2020AGUFMDI0190012P/abstract; consulted 19/11/2021

Parke, W., *Croesus and Delphi* (1984), URL grbs.library.duke.edu/article/download/5491/5297; consulted 25/8/2017.

Peters, W., 'Der Goldhandel und Goldbergbau im 15. bis 18. Jahrhundert an der Goldkueste (Ghana) und die Aktivitaeten der Brandenburg-Preussen', Zeitschrift der Foerderer des Bergbaus und des Huettenwesens, Nr. 1, 20. Jahrgang (May 1986) trans., URL https://e-docs.geo-leo. de/bitstream/handle/11858/00-1735-0000-0022-C2008/1TRANSLA_%C3%BCberarbeitet_ von_A_Peters.pdf?sequence=1&isAllowed=y.

Pitcairn, I., 'Gold distribution in the Earth's crust', Stockholm University Geological Sciences Project Archive, URL http://www.geo.su.se/index.php/en/project-archive/489-gold-distribution-in-the-earth-s-crust; consulted 4/3/2018.

Porter, J.E., 'Money and Mad Ambition: Economies of Russian Literature 1830–1850', PhD thesis (2011) UC Berkeley, https://escholarship.org/uc/item/9ng5x5qp; consulted 19/05/2020.

Rosevear, A., 'A booklet on the Turnpike Roads around Reading' (Draft) (2004), p.28, http://www.turnpikes.org.uk/Reading%20turnpike%20roads.htm; consulted 5/8/2019.

Rothman, J., '"A Pledge of a Nation": Charting The Economic Aspirations, Political Motivations, and Consequences of Confederate Currency Creation', unpublished MA, American History Department, Brandeis University (May 2009), URL https://bir.brandeis.edu/bitstream/handle/10192/23258/Thesis2.pdf?sequence=1%20Jordan%20Rothman; consulted 22/10/2019.

Sapir-Hen, L., Gadotl, Y., & Finkelstein, I., 'Animal Economy in a Temple City and Its Countryside: Iron Age Jerusalem as a Case Study', Bulletin of the American Schools of Oriental Research, 375, 103 (May 2016).

Schwarz, G.R., 'The History and Development of Caravels', unpublished MA Thesis, University of Texas A&M (2008), https://core.ac.uk/download/pdf/4276764.pdf; consulted 30/05/2020.

Siebold, J., 'Monography on the Portolan World Map, Juan de la Cosa, 1500' (1998), URL http://cartographic-images.net/Cartographic_Images/305_de_la_Cosa.html; consulted 26/7/2018.

Smith, S.A., 'Identifying an Archetype: The Hipponion Tablet and Regional Variations in the Orphic Gold Lamellae', Proceedings from the Document Academy, Vol. 1, Iss. 1, Article 8, https://ideaexchange.uakron.edu/docam/vol1/iss1/8; consulted 10/5/2020.

Southworth, E., 'The Roots of the Dutch Republic's Golden Age Commercial Success', NEH Seminar For School Teachers, 2015, University of Massachusetts Dartmouth, URL http://www1.umassd.edu/euro/2015papers/southworth.pdf; accessed 16/08/2019.

Stewart, H., 'This is how we let the credit crunch happen, Ma'am', Guardian (26 July 2009), https://www.theguardian.com/uk/2009/jul/26/monarchy-credit-crunch; consulted 12/5/2020.

Story of Sinuhe, https://www.ucl.ac.uk/museums-static/digitalegypt//literature/sanehat/text.html; consulted 13/07/2021.

Trundle, M.F., 'The Classical Greek Mercenary and his Relationship to the Greek Polis', McMaster University dissertation, URL http://hdl.handle.net/11375/13924; accessed 8/10/17.

Turek, J., 'Prehistoric Ceremonial Warfare: Beginning of Institutionalized Violence', Archaeologies: Journal of the World Archaeological Congress 13 (2017), pp.535–48.

Tye, R., 'Wang Mang' (2013), https://www.academia.edu/356703/Wang_Mang.

Wise, J., 'Nft Statistics 2022: Market Size, Growth, Sales & Trends', https://earthweb.com/nft-statistics/; consulted 27/12/2021.

Wong, A., 'The Untold Story Behind Saudi Arabia's 41-Year US Debt Secret', https://www.bloomberg.com/news/features/2016-05-30/the-untold-story-behind-saudi-arabia-s-41-year-u-s-debt-secret; consulted 31/5/2020.

World Gold Council, 'How much gold has been mined?', https://www.gold.org/about-gold/gold-supply/gold-mining/how-much-gold; consulted 5/5/2020.

Primary Sources

'Annual Report on the Mineral Production of Canada 1906', Dept. of Mines (1908).
Appianus of Alexandria, tr. H. White, The Roman History (Vero Verlag, 2017).
Aristotle, Politics, tr. B. Jowett (Batoche Books, 1999).

Atkins, J., *A Voyage to Guinea, Brasil and the West-Indies, in His Majesty's Ships, the Swallow and Weymouth* (London, 1735).

Azpilcueta, Martín de, *Comentario Resolutorio de Cambios* (Consejo Superior de Investigaciones Científicas, 1965).

Bacon, F., *The Advancement of Learning* (The Floating Press, 2010).

Bartolomé de las Casas, *History of the Indies* (Harper & Row, 1971).

Bodin, J., *Response to the Paradoxes of Malestroit* (Thoemmes Press, 1997).

Brantome, (Pierre de Bourdeile, Seigneur de), *Mémoires, contenans Les Vies des Dames* (Leiden, 1665).

Buvat, J., *Journal de la Régence* (France, 1865).

Camões, Luís Vaz de, *The Lusiads*, tr. Landeg White (Oxford University Press, 1997).

Camus, A., *The Myth of Sisyphus and Other Essays* (Knopf Doubleday Publishing Group, 2018).

Cantemir, D., tr. N. Tinda, *The History of the Growth and Decay of the Othman Empire* (London, 1734).

Cassius Dio, *Roman History* (Harvard University Press, 2001).

Cellini, Benvenuto, *My Life* (Oxford University Press, 2002).

Cicero, *De Officiis*. (tr. P.G. Walsh, Oxford University Press, 2008)

Cobbett, W., *Rural Rides* (London, 1830; Nelson and Sons, 1935).

Columbus, Christopher, *The Journal of his First Voyage to America* (An abstract of the original journal made by ..., Las Casas), tr. Van Wyck Brooks (Jarrolds, 1925).

Corrêa, G., *The Three Voyages of Vasco Da Gama*, tr. H.E.J. Stanley (Hakluyt Society, 1869).

Cortés, H., M.J. Baynard (ed. and trans.), *Five Letters of Cortés to the Emperor* (Norton, 1969).

Dangeau, Marquis de, *Journal* (Cleremont-Ferrand, 2002).

Diodorus Siculus, *The Persian Wars to the Fall of Athens: Books 11–14.34 (480–401 BCEBCE)*, tr. Peter Green (University of Texas Press, 2010).

Diodorus Siculus, *Library of History* 3, 13.

Douglas, S., Baron Glenbervie, *Reports of Cases Argued and Determined in the Court of King's Bench: In the Nineteenth, Twentieth, and Twenty-first [twenty-second, Twenty-third, Twenty-fourth, and Twenty-fifth] Years of the Reign of George III [1778–1785], Volume 2* (Reed and Hunter, 1813).

Dürer, Albrecht, *Diary of his journey to the Netherlands, 1520–21* (Lund Humphries, 1971).

Einhard, *The Life of Charlemagne* (Ann Arbor, 1960).

Ellis, H., *Original Letters Illustrative of English History* (London, 1827), 4 vols.

Eusebius (Caesariensis), *Vita Constantini* (Brepols, 2007).

Fulcher of Chartres, *Historia Hierosolymitana (1095–1127)*, ed. H. Hagenmeyer (Heidelberg).

Gheyn, Jacob de, *The exercise of armes for calivres, mvskettes, and pikes: after the ordre of his excellence Maurits Prince of Orange* (1608).

'Gold Reserves Of Principal Countries, 1913–1925', Federal Reserve Bulletin (April 1926).

Greenlee, W.B., *The Voyage of Pedro Álvares Cabral to Brazil and India: from Contemporary Documents and Narratives* (Routledge, 2017).

Hakluyt, R., *Principal navigations, voyages, traffiques & discoveries of the English nation* (Edinburgh, 1884–90).

Herodotus, *The Histories* (e-artnow, 28 May 2018).

Historia Augusta (Harvard University Press, 1921).

Hoover, H., *The Memoirs of Herbert Hoover: The Great Depression, 1929–41* (Macmillan, 1952).

Hume, D., 'Of Money', *Political Discourses* (Edinburgh, 1752).

Hunter, R.L., *Apollonius of Rhodes* (Cambridge University Press, 1989).

Ibn Battuta, *The Travels of Ibn Battuta: in the Near East, Asia and Africa, 1325–1354* (Courier Corporation, 2013).

Indicopleustes, Cosmas, *Christian topography* (CUP, 2010).

Josephus, F., tr. W. Wiston, *Jewish Antiquities* (Wordsworth Editions, 2006).

Keynes, J.M., *A Tract on Monetary Reform* (Macmillan, 1923).

Kuhrt, A., *The Persian Empire: A Corpus of Sources from the Achaemenid Period* (Routledge, 2013).

Law, J., 'Oeuvres ... de John Law, contenant les principes sur le numéraire, le commerce, le credit et les banques', E.F de Sénovert (ed.) (Paris, 1790).

Lud, Walter, *Description of the Mirror of the World* (1507).

Luther, M., *Works of Martin Luther* (A.J. Holman Company, 1915).

MacNutt, F.A. (ed. & tr.), *De Orbis Novo: The Eight Decades of Peter Martyr D'Anghera* (G.P. Putnam, 1912), Vol. I.

MacNutt, F.A. (ed. & tr.), *The Five Letters of Relation from Fernando Cortes to the Emperor Charles V* (G.P. Putnam's Sons, 1908).

Mahony, J., 'Sketches in the West of Ireland', *Illustrated London News* (13 February 1847).

Marcellinus, Ammianus (Delphi, 2016).

Marco Polo, *Travels*, 2 vols, tr. H. Yule (Courier Corporation, 1993).

Markham, C. (ed.), *Reports on the Discovery of Peru* (Cambridge Library Collection – Hakluyt First Series) (Cambridge University Press, 2010).

McCulloch, J.R. (ed.), *A Select Collection of Rare and Valuable Tracts on Money* (Augustus M. Kelly, 1966).

O'Sullivan, J. (ed.), 'Annexation', *The United States Magazine and Democratic Review*, Vol. 17 (New York, 1845).

Ogilby, J., *Asia* (London, 1673).

Ovid, *Metamorphoses*, Vol. 1 (Harvard University Press, 1960).

Oviedo y Valdés, G. Fernández de, *Oviedo on Columbus* (Brepols, 2000).

Pausanias, *Description of Greece* (Cambridge University Press, 2012).

Pearce, L.E., & Wunsch, C., *Documents of Judean Exiles and West Semites in Babylonia in the Collection of David Sofer* (CDL Press, 2014).

Pepys, S., *Diary* (Good Press, 2019).

Petronius, *Satyricon* (Oxford World's Classics, 2009).

Pliny the Elder, *Natural History* (Penguin, 2004).

Plutarch, *Lives* (Wyatt North Publishing, LLC, 2020).

Plutarch, *On Superstition* (Loeb Classical Library, 1928).

Polybius, *The Histories* (Oxford World's Classics, 2010).

Procopius, *History of the Wars* (B&R Samizdat Express, 2018).

Procopius, *Of the Buildings of Justinian* (Adegi Graphics, 1999).

Procopius, *The Secret History* (Penguin, 2007).

Pseudo-Dionysius (the Areopagite) (Paulist Press, 1987).

'Report on the High Price of Gold Bullion', Parliamentary Papers (1810), Vol. III, p.5.

Rollins, H.E. (ed.), *A Pepysian Garland: Black-Letter Broadside Ballads of the Years 1595–1639* (Cambridge University Press, 1922).

Sandars, N.K.. *The Epic of Gilgamesh* (Penguin, 2006).

Santa Cruz, Alonso de, *Crónica del Emperador Carlos V* (Fb&C, 2018).

Seneca, L.A. (*c.* 3 BCE–65 CE), *Declamations Vol. I* (Harvard University Press, 1999).

Service, Robert W., *The Spell of the Yukon and other verses* (Dodd, 1907).

Smith, Adam, *Lectures on Jurisprudence* (Clarendon Press, 1978).

Smith, Adam, *Wealth of Nations* (Courier Dover Publications, 2019).

Strabo, *The Geography* (Cambridge University Press, 2014).

Suetonius, *The Lives of the Caesars* (Oxford University Press, 2008).

Tacitus, Publius Cornelius, *The Annals of Imperial Rome* (Penguin, 1977).

Thiers, A., *History of the Consulate and the Empire of France under Napoleon*, Vol. 3, 1812–1814.

Tomé Pires, *The Suma Oriental* (Hakluyt Society, 1944).

Vertot, L'Abbé de, *The History of the Knights of Malta* (London, 1728).

Voltaire, *Œuvres complètes de Voltaire* (Garnier, 1879).

Walker's Hibernian Magazine (January 1796).

Xenophon, *The Education of Cyrus* (Cornell University Press, 2015).

Index